Survey of Computer Information Systems

CIS 105 for Glendale Community College

Beskeen | Cram | Duffy | Friedrichsen | Reding | Wermers

CENGAGE
Learning·

Australia • Brazil • Japan • Korea • Mexico • Singapore • Spain • United Kingdom • United States

CENGAGE
Learning·

Survey of Computer Information Systems, CIS 105 for Glendale Community College

Microsoft Office 2013
Beskeen | Cram | Duffy | Friedrichsen | Reding | Wermers

© 2014 Cengage Learning. All rights reserved.

Senior Project Development Manager:
Linda deStefano

Market Development Manager:
Heather Kramer

Senior Production/Manufacturing Manager:
Donna M. Brown

Production Editorial Manager:
Kim Fry

Sr. Rights Acquisition Account Manager:
Todd Osborne

For product information and technology assistance, contact us at
Cengage Learning Customer & Sales Support, 1-800-354-9706

For permission to use material from this text or product,
submit all requests online at **cengage.com/permissions**
Further permissions questions can be emailed to
permissionrequest@cengage.com

This book contains select works from existing Cengage Learning resources and was produced by Cengage Learning Custom Solutions for collegiate use. As such, those adopting and/or contributing to this work are responsible for editorial content accuracy, continuity and completeness.

Compilation © 2013 Cengage Learning

ISBN-13: 978-1-305-00719-2

ISBN-10: 1-305-00719-0

Cengage Learning
5191 Natorp Boulevard
Mason, Ohio 45040
USA
Cengage Learning is a leading provider of customized learning solutions with office locations around the globe, including Singapore, the United Kingdom, Australia, Mexico, Brazil, and Japan. Locate your local office at:
international.cengage.com/region.

Cengage Learning products are represented in Canada by Nelson Education, Ltd.
For your lifelong learning solutions, visit **www.cengage.com/custom.**
Visit our corporate website at **www.cengage.com.**

Printed in the United States of America

Custom Table of Contents

Creating Documents with Word 2013

CASE ▶ You have been hired to work in the Marketing Department at Quest Specialty Travel (QST), a tour company that specializes in cultural tourism and adventure travel. Shortly after reporting to your new office, Ron Dawson, the vice president of marketing, asks you to use Word to create a memo to the marketing staff and a letter to one of the tour hosts.

Unit Objectives

After completing this unit, you will be able to:

- Understand word processing software
- Explore the Word window
- Start a document
- Save a document

- Select text
- Format text using the Mini toolbar and the Ribbon
- Use a document template
- Navigate a document

Files You Will Need

WD A-1.docx

Understand Word Processing Software

Learning Outcomes
- Identify the features of Word
- State the benefits of using a word processing program

A **word processing program** is a software program that includes tools for entering, editing, and formatting text and graphics. Microsoft Word is a powerful word processing program that allows you to create and enhance a wide range of documents quickly and easily. **FIGURE A-1** shows the first page of a report created using Word and illustrates some of the Word features you can use to enhance your documents. The electronic files you create using Word are called **documents**. One of the benefits of using Word is that document files can be stored on a hard disk, flash drive, sky drive, or other storage device, making them easy to transport, exchange, and revise. **CASE** ➤ *Before beginning your memo to the marketing staff, you explore the editing and formatting features available in Word.*

DETAILS

You can use Word to accomplish the following tasks:

- **Type and edit text**

 The Word editing tools make it simple to insert and delete text in a document. You can add text to the middle of an existing paragraph, replace text with other text, undo an editing change, and correct typing, spelling, and grammatical errors with ease.

- **Copy and move text from one location to another**

 Using the more advanced editing features of Word, you can copy or move text from one location and insert it in a different location in a document. You also can copy and move text between documents. This means you don't have to retype text that is already entered in a document.

- **Format text and paragraphs with fonts, colors, and other elements**

 The sophisticated formatting tools in Word allow you to make the text in your documents come alive. You can change the size, style, and color of text, add lines and shading to paragraphs, and enhance lists with bullets and numbers. Creatively formatting text helps to highlight important ideas in your documents.

- **Format and design pages**

 The page-formatting features in Word give you power to design attractive newsletters, create powerful résumés, and produce documents such as research papers, business cards, brochures, and reports. You can change paper size, organize text in columns, and control the layout of text and graphics on each page of a document. For quick results, Word includes preformatted cover pages, pull quotes, and headers and footers, as well as galleries of coordinated text, table, and graphic styles. If you are writing a research paper, Word makes it easy to manage reference sources and create footnotes, endnotes, and bibliographies.

- **Enhance documents with tables, charts, graphics, screenshots, and videos**

 Using the powerful graphics tools in Word, you can spice up your documents with pictures, videos, photographs, screenshots, lines, shapes, and diagrams. You also can illustrate your documents with tables and charts to help convey your message in a visually interesting way.

- **Use Mail Merge to create form letters and mailing labels**

 The Word Mail Merge feature allows you to send personalized form letters to many different people. You can also use Mail Merge to create mailing labels, directories, e-mail messages, and other types of documents.

- **Share documents securely**

 The security features in Word make it quick and easy to remove comments, tracked changes, and unwanted personal information from your files before you share them with others. You can also add a password or a digital signature to a document and convert a file to a format suitable for publishing on the Web.

FIGURE A-1: A report created using Word

Add headers to every page →

Add lines →

Insert graphics →

Format the size and appearance of text →

Create columns of text →

Create tables →

Add bullets to lists →

Create charts →

Align text in paragraphs evenly →

Add page numbers in footers →

Quest Specialty Travel Marketing Report September 2016

QST Client Survey Results

In an effort to develop an economic profile of Quest Specialty Travel clients, the marketing department hired the market research firm Takeshita Consultants, Inc. to create and administer a survey of the QST client base. A secondary goal of the survey was to identify the areas in which QST can improve its tour offerings in each region. Over 8,600 people completed the survey, which was distributed by e-mail and mailed to everyone who has purchased a QST tour in the past five years. Surveys were also completed by people who visited the QST Web site but have not purchased a QST tour. Forty-two percent of the survey recipients responded to the survey.

Survey Methods

The survey was distributed to purchasing clients via mail and e-mail during May and June 2016. The survey was also available on the QST Web site, and was completed by over 1,800 non-clients. The table below shows the distribution of respondents by delivery mode and by sex.

Survey Delivery Mode	Male	Female
E-mail to clients	6,657	7,801
Mail to clients	1,567	1,238
Web site clients	563	442
Web site non-clients	898	987
Other	365	122
Total	10,050	10,590
	Grand Total	**20,640**

Client Profile

A typical QST client is a 42-year-old professional with an annual household income of $84,000. He or she works in the city, owns a home in an urban or suburban area, and has no children living at home.

- 73% graduated from college.
- 32% have a graduate level degree.
- 60% earn more than $60,000 per year.
- 8% earn more than $200,000 per year.
- 45% are employed as professionals.
- 29% are retired.

Travel Preferences

Respondents report they enjoy independent domestic travel, but they prefer an organized tour when traveling abroad. Most cited guide expertise as the primary reason for selecting a QST tour.

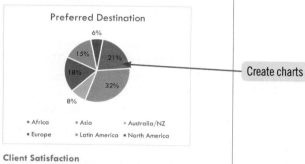

Preferred Destination

Client Satisfaction

On the whole, QST clients gave the quality of QST tours a favorable review. Clients rated the expertise and professionalism of the guides as excellent, the range of tours as very good, and the accommodations and food served as excellent. Equally favorable ratings were given to the sales staff and the attractiveness of QST printed materials. Clients did express interest in a wider selection of tours in South East Asia, particularly Laos, Cambodia, and Vietnam, as well as more European offerings. The response time for tour information ordered from the Web site could also be improved.

► 1

Planning a document

Before you create a new document, it's a good idea to spend time planning it. Identify the message you want to convey, the audience for your document, and the elements, such as tables or charts, you want to include. You should also think about the tone and look of your document—are you writing a business letter, which should be written in a pleasant, but serious tone and have a formal appearance, or are you creating a flyer that must be colorful, eye-catching, and fun to read? The purpose and audience for your document determine the appropriate design. Planning the layout and design of a document involves deciding how to organize the text, selecting the fonts to use, identifying the graphics to include, and selecting the formatting elements that will enhance the message and appeal of the document. For longer documents, such as newsletters, it can be useful to sketch the layout and design of each page before you begin.

Explore the Word Window

When you start Word, the Word start screen opens. It includes a list of recently opened documents and a gallery of templates for creating a new document. **CASE** ▶ *You open a blank document and examine the elements of the Word program window.*

1. **Start Word, then click Blank document**

 A blank document opens in the **Word program window**, as shown in FIGURE A-2. The blinking vertical line in the document window is the **insertion point**. It indicates where text appears as you type.

2. **Move the mouse pointer around the Word program window**

 The mouse pointer changes shape depending on where it is in the Word program window. You use pointers to move the insertion point or to select text to edit. TABLE A-1 describes common pointers in Word.

3. **Place the mouse pointer over a button on the Ribbon**

 When you place the mouse pointer over a button or some other elements of the Word program window, a ScreenTip appears. A **ScreenTip** is a label that identifies the name of the button or feature, briefly describes its function, conveys any keyboard shortcut for the command, and includes a link to associated help topics, if any.

Using FIGURE A-2 **as a guide, find the elements described below in your program window:**

- The **title bar** displays the name of the document and the name of the program. Until you give a new document a different name, its temporary name is Document1. The left side of the title bar contains the **Quick Access toolbar**, which includes buttons for saving a document and for undoing, redoing, and repeating a change. You can modify the Quick Access toolbar to include the commands you use frequently. The right side of the title bar contains the **Microsoft Word Help button**, which you use to access the Word Help system, the **Ribbon Display Options button**, which you use to hide or show the Ribbon and tabs, the resizing buttons, and the program Close button.

- The **FILE tab** provides access to **Backstage view** where you manage files and the information about them. Backstage view includes commands related to working with documents, such as opening, printing, and saving a document. The FILE tab also provides access to your account and to the Word Options dialog box, which is used to customize the way you use Word.

- The **Ribbon** contains the Word tabs. Each **tab** on the Ribbon includes buttons for commands related to editing and formatting documents. The commands are organized in **groups**. For example, the HOME tab includes the Clipboard, Font, Paragraph, Styles, and Editing groups.

- The **document window** displays the current document. You enter text and format your document in the document window.

- The rulers appear in the document window in Print Layout view. The **horizontal ruler** displays left and right document margins as well as the tab settings and paragraph indents, if any, for the paragraph in which the insertion point is located. The **vertical ruler** displays the top and bottom document margins.

- The **vertical** and **horizontal scroll bars** are used to display different parts of the document in the document window. The scroll bars include **scroll boxes** and **scroll arrows**, which you use to scroll.

- The **status bar** displays the page number of the current page, the total number of pages and words in the document, and the status of spelling and grammar checking. It also includes the view buttons, the Zoom slider, and the Zoom level button. You can customize the status bar to display other information.

- The **view buttons** on the status bar allow you to display the document in Read Mode, Print Layout, or Web Layout view.

- The **Zoom slider** and the **Zoom level button** provide quick ways to enlarge and decrease the size of the document in the document window, making it easy to zoom in on a detail of a document or to view the layout of the document as a whole.

Creating Documents with Word 2013

FIGURE A-2: Elements of the Word program window

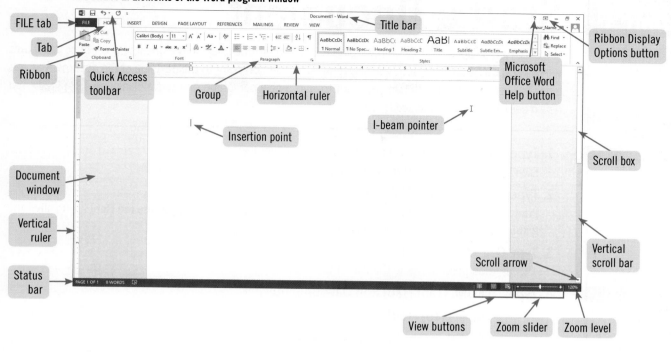

FILE tab

Tab

Ribbon

Quick Access toolbar

Group

Horizontal ruler

Title bar

Microsoft Office Word Help button

Ribbon Display Options button

I-beam pointer

Insertion point

Scroll box

Document window

Vertical ruler

Status bar

Scroll arrow

Vertical scroll bar

View buttons

Zoom slider

Zoom level

TABLE A-1: Common mouse pointers in Word

name	pointer	use to
I-beam pointer	I	Move the insertion point in a document or to select text
Click and Type pointers, including left-align and center-align	I ≡ I	Move the insertion point to a blank area of a document in Print Layout or Web Layout view; double-clicking with a Click and Type pointer automatically applies the paragraph formatting (alignment and indentation) required to position text or a graphic at that location in the document
Selection pointer	⇖	Click a button or other element of the Word program window; appears when you point to elements of the Word program window
Right-pointing arrow pointer	⇗	Select a line or lines of text; appears when you point to the left edge of a line of text in the document window
Hand pointer	🖑	Open a hyperlink; appears when you point to a hyperlink in a task pane or when you press [Ctrl] and point to a hyperlink in a document
Hide white space pointer	⊣⊢	Hide the white space in the top and bottom margins of a document in Print Layout view
Show white space pointer	⊤⊥	Show the white space in the top and bottom margins of a document in Print Layout view

Word 2013

Start a Document

You begin a new document by simply typing text in a blank document in the document window. Word uses **word wrap**, a feature that automatically moves the insertion point to the next line of the document as you type. You only press [Enter] when you want to start a new paragraph or insert a blank line. **CASE** ▶ *You type a quick memo to the marketing staff.*

STEPS

1. **Type Quest Specialty Travel, then press [Enter] twice**

 Each time you press [Enter] the insertion point moves to the start of the next line.

2. **Type TO:, then press [Tab] twice**

 Pressing [Tab] moves the insertion point several spaces to the right. You can use the [Tab] key to align the text in a memo header or to indent the first line of a paragraph.

3. **Type QST Managers, then press [Enter]**

 The insertion point moves to the start of the next line.

4. **Type:** FROM: [Tab] [Tab] Ron Dawson [Enter]

 DATE: [Tab] [Tab] March 13, 2016 [Enter]

 RE: [Tab] [Tab] Marketing Meeting [Enter] [Enter]

 Red or blue wavy lines may appear under the words you typed, indicating a possible spelling or grammar error. Spelling and grammar checking is one of the many automatic features you will encounter as you type. **TABLE A-2** describes several of these automatic features. You can correct any typing errors you make later.

5. **Type The next marketing staff meeting will be held on the 17th of March at 2 p.m. in the conference room on the ground floor., then press [Spacebar]**

 As you type, notice that the insertion point moves automatically to the next line of the document. You also might notice that Word automatically changed "17th" to "17th" in the memo. This feature is called **AutoCorrect**. AutoCorrect automatically makes typographical adjustments and detects and adjusts typing errors, certain misspelled words (such as "taht" for "that"), and incorrect capitalization as you type.

6. **Type Heading the agenda will be the launch of our new Borneo Explorer Trek, a rigorous ten-day tour of the dense jungles, deep caves, and remote villages of Borneo's northern coast, scheduled for September 2017.**

 When you type the first few characters of "September," the Word AutoComplete feature displays the complete word in a ScreenTip. **AutoComplete** suggests text to insert quickly into your documents. You can ignore AutoComplete for now. Your memo should resemble **FIGURE A-3**.

7. **Press [Enter], then type Kai Haketa is in Kuching hammering out the details. A preliminary draft of the tour brochure is attached. Bring your creative ideas for launching this exciting new tour to the meeting.**

 When you press [Enter] and type the new paragraph, notice that Word adds more space between the paragraphs than it does between the lines in each paragraph. This is part of the default style for paragraphs in Word, called the **Normal style**.

8. **Position the I pointer after for (but before the space) in the last sentence of the first paragraph, then click to move the insertion point after "for"**

9. **Press [Backspace] three times, then type to depart in**

 Pressing [Backspace] removes the character before the insertion point.

10. **Move the insertion point before staff in the first sentence, then press [Delete] six times to remove the word "staff" and the space after it**

 Pressing [Delete] removes the character after the insertion point. **FIGURE A-4** shows the revised memo.

FIGURE A-3: Memo text in the document window

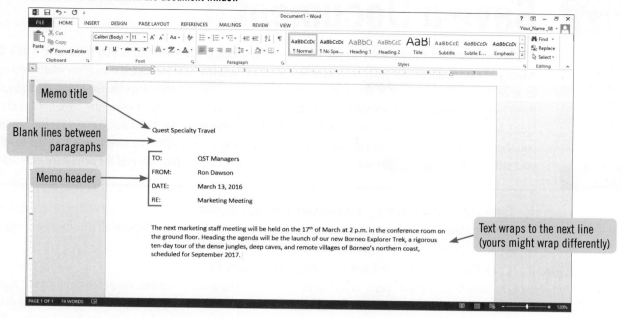

Memo title

Blank lines between paragraphs

Memo header

Quest Specialty Travel

TO:	QST Managers
FROM:	Ron Dawson
DATE:	March 13, 2016
RE:	Marketing Meeting

The next marketing staff meeting will be held on the 17th of March at 2 p.m. in the conference room on the ground floor. Heading the agenda will be the launch of our new Borneo Explorer Trek, a rigorous ten-day tour of the dense jungles, deep caves, and remote villages of Borneo's northern coast, scheduled for September 2017.

Text wraps to the next line (yours might wrap differently)

FIGURE A-4: Edited memo text

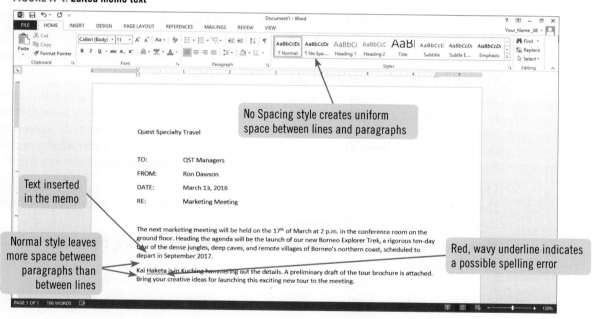

No Spacing style creates uniform space between lines and paragraphs

Quest Specialty Travel

TO:	QST Managers
FROM:	Ron Dawson
DATE:	March 13, 2016
RE:	Marketing Meeting

Text inserted in the memo

The next marketing meeting will be held on the 17th of March at 2 p.m. in the conference room on the ground floor. Heading the agenda will be the launch of our new Borneo Explorer Trek, a rigorous ten-day tour of the dense jungles, deep caves, and remote villages of Borneo's northern coast, scheduled to depart in September 2017.

Kai Haketa is in Kuching hammering out the details. A preliminary draft of the tour brochure is attached. Bring your creative ideas for launching this exciting new tour to the meeting.

Normal style leaves more space between paragraphs than between lines

Red, wavy underline indicates a possible spelling error

TABLE A-2: Automatic features that appear as you type in Word

feature	what appears	to use
AutoComplete	A ScreenTip suggesting text to insert appears as you type	Press [Enter] to insert the text suggested by the ScreenTip; continue typing to reject the suggestion
AutoCorrect	A small blue box appears when you place the pointer over text corrected by AutoCorrect; an AutoCorrect Options button appears when you point to the blue box	Word automatically corrects typos, minor spelling errors, and capitalization, and adds typographical symbols (such as © and ™) as you type; to reverse an AutoCorrect adjustment, click the AutoCorrect Options list arrow, then click the option that will undo the action
Spelling and Grammar	A red wavy line under a word indicates a possible misspelling or a repeated word; a blue wavy line under text indicates a possible grammar error	Right-click red- or blue-underlined text to display a shortcut menu of correction options; click a correction option to accept it and remove the wavy underline

Word 2013

Save a Document

Learning Outcomes
• Save a file using a descriptive filename
• Use the Save As dialog box

To store a document permanently so you can open it and edit it at another time, you must save it as a **file**. When you **save** a document you give it a name, called a **filename**, and indicate the location where you want to store the file. Files created in Word 2013 are automatically assigned the .docx file extension to distinguish them from files created in other software programs. You can save a document using the Save button on the Quick Access toolbar or the Save command on the FILE tab. Once you have saved a document for the first time, you should save it again every few minutes and always before printing so that the saved file is updated to reflect your latest changes. **CASE** ▸ *You save your memo using a descriptive filename and the default file extension.*

1. **Click the Save button 🔲 on the Quick Access toolbar**

 The first time you save a document, the Save As screen opens. The screen displays all the places you can save a file to, including SkyDrive, your computer, or a different location.

TROUBLE

If you don't see the extension .docx as part of the filename, the setting in Windows to display file extensions is not active.

2. **Click Computer in the Save As screen, then click Browse**

 The Save As dialog box opens, as shown in **FIGURE A-5**. The default filename, Quest Specialty Travel, appears in the File name text box. The default filename is based on the first few words of the document. The default file type, Word Document, appears in the Save as type list box. **TABLE A-3** describes the functions of some of the buttons in the Save As dialog box.

3. **Type WD A-Borneo Tour Memo in the File name text box**

 The new filename replaces the default filename. Giving your documents brief descriptive filenames makes it easier to locate and organize them later. You do not need to type .docx when you type a new filename.

4. **Navigate to the location where you store your Data Files**

 You can navigate to a different drive or folder in several ways. For example, you can click a drive or folder in the Address bar or the navigation pane to go directly to that location. Click the double arrow in the Address bar to display a list of drives and folders. You can also double-click a drive or folder in the folder window to change the active location. When you are finished navigating to the drive or folder where you store your Data Files, that location appears in the Address bar. Your Save As dialog box should resemble **FIGURE A-6**.

5. **Click Save**

 The document is saved to the drive and folder you specified in the Save As dialog box, and the title bar displays the new filename, WD A-Borneo Tour Memo.docx.

6. **Place the insertion point before conference in the first sentence, type large, then press [Spacebar]**

 You can continue to work on a document after you have saved it with a new filename.

7. **Click 🔲**

 Your change to the memo is saved. After you save a document for the first time, you must continue to save the changes you make to the document. You also can press [Ctrl][S] to save a document.

Microsoft SkyDrive and Microsoft Office Web Apps

Microsoft SkyDrive is a free file hosting service that allows you to save and sync files to a "cloud" and then access them from any computer that is connected to the Internet. The files you save to Microsoft SkyDrive are available only to the people you grant access, and every file you store on Microsoft SkyDrive is automatically synced so that you can get the most up-to-date version of your files from any computer. When you open a file that is stored on Microsoft SkyDrive, the file opens in its corresponding Office Web App, which is a simplified version of Word, Excel, PowerPoint, or OneNote. Office Web Apps open within the Web browser. Because these programs are online, they take up no computer disk space. Using Office Web Apps, users can upload, create, edit, and share Microsoft Office documents directly within a Web browser. You are connected to SkyDrive when you log into your computer using your Windows account. You can find more information in the "Working in the Cloud" appendix.

FIGURE A-5: Save As dialog box

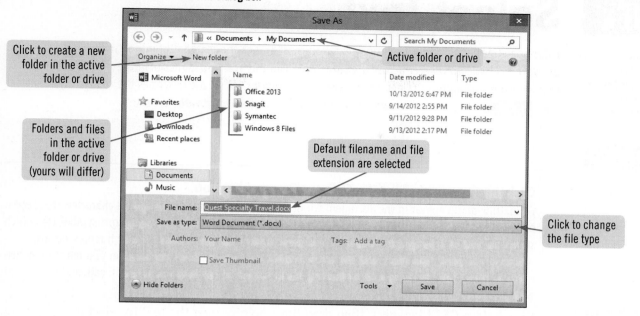

Click to create a new folder in the active folder or drive

Active folder or drive

Folders and files in the active folder or drive (yours will differ)

Default filename and file extension are selected

Click to change the file type

FIGURE A-6: File to be saved to the Unit A folder

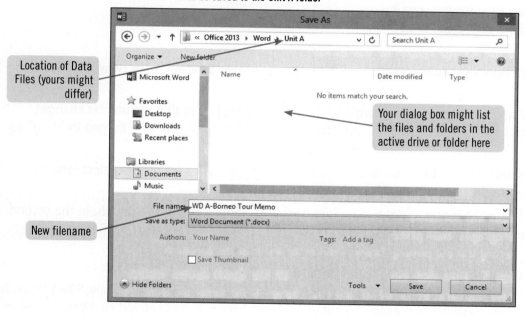

Location of Data Files (yours might differ)

Your dialog box might list the files and folders in the active drive or folder here

New filename

TABLE A-3: Save As dialog box buttons

button	use to
Back	Navigate back to the last location shown in the Address bar
Forward	Navigate to the location that was previously shown in the Address bar
Up to	Navigate to the location above the current location in the folder hierarchy (Windows 8 only)
Organize	Open a menu of commands related to organizing the selected file or folder, including Cut, Copy, Delete, Rename, and Properties
New folder	Create a new folder in the current folder or drive
Change your view	Change the way folder and file information is shown in the folder window in the Save As dialog box; click the Change your view button to toggle between views, or click the list arrow to open a menu of view options

Select Text

Learning Outcomes
• Select text using the mouse
• Use formatting marks

Before deleting, editing, or formatting text, you must **select** the text. Selecting text involves clicking and dragging the I-beam pointer across the text to highlight it. You also can click in the margin to the left of text with the pointer to select whole lines or paragraphs. TABLE A-4 describes the many ways to select text. **CASE** *You revise the memo by selecting text and replacing it with new text.*

STEPS

1. **Click the Show/Hide ¶ button ¶ in the Paragraph group**

 Formatting marks appear in the document window. **Formatting marks** are special characters that appear on your screen but do not print. Common formatting marks include the paragraph symbol (¶), which shows the end of a paragraph—wherever you press [Enter]; the dot symbol (·), which represents a space—wherever you press [Spacebar]; and the arrow symbol (→), which shows the location of a tab stop—wherever you press [Tab]. Working with formatting marks turned on can help you to select, edit, and format text with precision.

2. **Click before QST Managers, then drag the ⌶ pointer over the text to select it**

 The words are selected, as shown in **FIGURE A-7**. For now, you can ignore the faint toolbar that appears over text when you first select it.

3. **Type Marketing Staff**

 The text you type replaces the selected text.

4. **Double-click Ron, type your first name, double-click Dawson, then type your last name**

 Double-clicking a word selects the entire word.

5. **Place the pointer in the margin to the left of the RE: line so that the pointer changes to , click to select the line, then type RE: [Tab] [Tab] Launch of new Borneo trekking tour**

 Clicking to the left of a line of text with the pointer selects the entire line.

6. **Select deep in the third line of the first paragraph, type mysterious, select remote villages, then type sun-kissed beaches**

7. **Select the sentence Kai Haketa is in Kuching hammering out the details. in the second paragraph, then press [Delete]**

 Selecting text and pressing [Delete] removes the text from the document.

8. **Click ¶, then click the Save button ⊟ on the Quick Access toolbar**

 Formatting marks are turned off, and your changes to the memo are saved. The Show/Hide ¶ button is a **toggle button**, which means you can use it to turn formatting marks on and off. The edited memo is shown in **FIGURE A-8**.

FIGURE A-7: Text selected in the memo

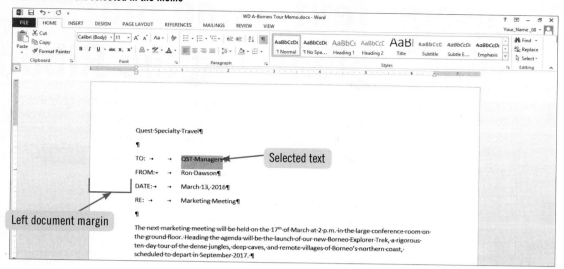

FIGURE A-8: Edited memo with replacement text

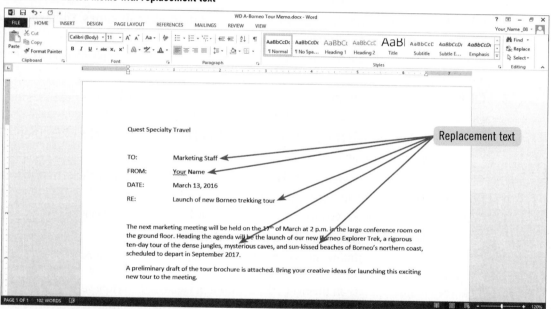

TABLE A-4: Methods for selecting text

to select	use the pointer to
Any amount of text	Drag over the text
A word	Double-click the word
A line of text	Move the pointer to the left of the line, then click
A sentence	Press and hold [Ctrl], then click the sentence
A paragraph	Triple-click the paragraph or double-click with the pointer to the left of the paragraph
A large block of text	Click at the beginning of the selection, press and hold [Shift], then click at the end of the selection
Multiple nonconsecutive selections	Select the first selection, then press and hold [Ctrl] as you select each additional selection
An entire document	Triple-click with the pointer to the left of any text; press [Ctrl][A]; or click the Select button in the Editing group on the HOME tab, and then click Select All

© 2014 Cengage Learning

Creating Documents with Word 2013

Learning
Outcomes
• Apply bold to text
• Increase the font
 size of text
• Print a document

Format Text Using the Mini Toolbar and the Ribbon

Formatting text is a fast and fun way to spruce up the appearance of a document and highlight important information. You can easily change the font, color, size, style, and other attributes of text by selecting the text and clicking a command on the HOME tab. The **Mini toolbar**, which appears above text when you first select it, also includes commonly used text and paragraph formatting commands. **CASE** ▶ *You enhance the appearance of the memo by formatting the text using the Mini toolbar. When you are finished, you preview the memo for errors and then print it.*

STEPS

TROUBLE
If the Mini toolbar disappears, right-click the selection to display it again.

1. **Select** Quest Specialty Travel

 The Mini toolbar appears over the selected text, as shown in **FIGURE A-9**. You click a formatting option on the Mini toolbar to apply it to the selected text. **TABLE A-5** describes the function of the buttons on the Mini toolbar. The buttons on the Mini toolbar are also available on the Ribbon.

QUICK TIP
Click the Decrease Font Size button to decrease the font size.

2. **Click the** Increase Font Size button A˙ **on the Mini toolbar six times, then click the** Bold button B **on the Mini toolbar**

 Each time you click the Grow Font button the selected text is enlarged. Applying bold to the text makes it thicker.

3. **Click the** Center button **in the Paragraph group on the HOME tab**

 The selected text is centered between the left and right margins.

4. **Select** TO:, **click** B, **select** FROM:, **click** B, **select** DATE:, **click** B, **select** RE:, **then click** B

 Bold is applied to the memo header labels.

5. **Click the blank line between the RE: line and the body text, then click the** Bottom Border button ⊞ **in the Paragraph group**

 A single-line border is added between the heading and the body text in the memo.

QUICK TIP
You can customize your Quick Access toolbar to include the Quick Print button, which prints a document using the default print settings.

6. **Save the document, click the** FILE tab, **then click** Print

 Information related to printing the document appears on the Print screen in Backstage view. Options for printing the document appear on the left side of the Print screen and a preview of the document as it will look when printed appears on the right side, as shown in **FIGURE A-10**. Before you print a document, it's a good habit to examine it closely so you can identify and correct any problems.

7. **Click the** Zoom In button ➕ **on the status bar five times, then proofread your document carefully for errors**

 The document is enlarged in print preview. If you notice errors in your document, you need to correct them before you print. To do this, press [Esc] or click the Back button in Backstage view, correct any mistakes, save your changes, click the FILE tab, and then click the Print command again to be ready to print the document.

8. **Click the** Print button **on the Print screen**

 A copy of the memo prints using the default print settings. To change the current printer, change the number of copies to print, select what pages of a document to print, or modify another print setting, you simply change the appropriate setting on the Print screen before clicking the Print button.

9. **Click the** FILE tab, **then click** Close

 The document closes, but the Word program window remains open.

FIGURE A-9: Mini toolbar

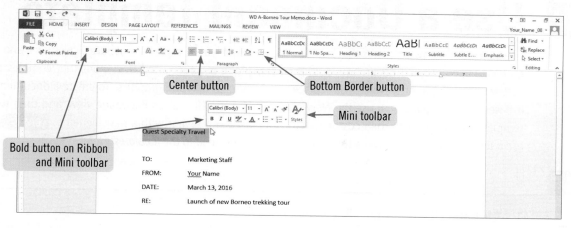

FIGURE A-10: Preview of the completed memo

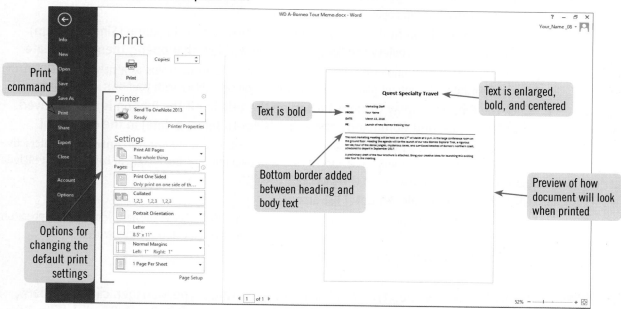

TABLE A-5: Buttons on the Mini toolbar

button	use to	button	use to
Calibri (Body) ▾	Change the font of text	B	Apply bold to text
11 ▾	Change the font size of text	I	Italicize text
A˄	Make text larger	U	Underline text
A˅	Make text smaller	ab ▾	Apply colored highlighting to text
❧	Copy the formats applied to selected text to other text	A ▾	Change the color of text
A Styles	Apply a style to text	☰ ▾	Apply bullets to paragraphs
		1☰ ▾	Apply numbering to paragraphs

© 2014 Cengage Learning

Use a Document Template

Learning Outcomes
- Search for templates
- Customize a template
- Use content controls

Word includes many templates that you can use to create letters, reports, brochures, calendars, and other professionally designed documents quickly. A **template** is a formatted document that contains place-holder text and graphics, which you replace with your own text and graphics. To create a document that is based on a template, you use the New command on the FILE tab in Backstage view, and then select a template to use. You can then customize the document and save it with a new filename. **CASE** *You use a template to create a cover letter for a contract you will send to the Rainforest Hotel in Kuching.*

STEPS

1. **Click the FILE tab, then click New**

 The New screen opens in Backstage view, as shown in **FIGURE A-11**. You can select a template from this window, or search for other templates.

2. **Click Letters in the Suggested Searches section**

 A gallery of letter templates opens in the New screen.

3. **Scroll down until you find the Cover letter for chronological resume (Simple design) thumbnail, click it, preview the template in the window that opens, then click Create**

 The Cover letter for chronological resume (Simple design) template opens as a new document in the document window. It contains placeholder text, which you can replace with your own information.

4. **Click the Ribbon Display Options button on the title bar if the Ribbon is not displayed, click Show Tabs and Commands, then click [Click to select a date] in the document**

 The placeholder text is selected and appears inside a content control. A **content control** is an interactive object that you use to customize a document with your own information. A content control might include placeholder text, a drop-down list of choices, or a calendar.

5. **Click the [Click to select a date] list arrow**

 A calendar opens below the content control. You use the calendar to select the date you want to appear on your document—simply click a date on the calendar to enter that date in the document.

6. **Click the Today button on the calendar**

 The current date replaces the placeholder text.

7. **Click [Recipient Name], type Ms. Yana Roy, click [Title], type Manager, click [Company Name], type Rainforest Hotel, click [Street Address], type P.O. Box 4397, click [City, ST Zip Code], then type Kuching 93100, Malaysia**

 You do not need to drag to select the placeholder text in a content control, you can simply click it. The text you type replaces the placeholder text.

8. **Click [Recipient], type Ms. Roy, click the body text placeholder text, then type Enclosed please find a copy of our contract for the Borneo Explorer Trek tour. We look forward to working with you.**

 The text you type replaces the placeholder text in the greeting line and in the body text of the letter.

9. **If the name in the signature block is not your name, drag to select the text, then type your name, as shown in FIGURE A-12**

 When the document is created, Word automatically enters the user name identified in the Word Options dialog box in the signature block and in the content control in the upper-left corner of the page. This text is not placeholder text, so you have to drag to select it.

10. **Click the FILE tab, click Save As, then save the document as WD A-Rainforest Letter to the location where you store your Data Files**

 The document is saved with the filename WD A-Rainforest Letter.

FIGURE A-11: New screen in Backstage view

FIGURE A-12: Document created using the Cover letter for chronological resume (Simple design) template

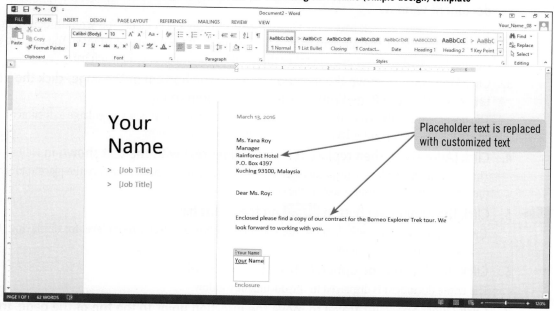

Using the Undo, Redo, and Repeat commands

Word remembers the editing and formatting changes you make so that you can easily reverse or repeat them. You can reverse the last action you took by clicking the Undo button ↶ on the Quick Access toolbar, or you can undo a series of actions by clicking the Undo list arrow ↶ ▾ and selecting the action you want to reverse. When you undo an action using the Undo list arrow, you also undo all the actions above it in the list—that is, all actions that were performed after the action you selected. Similarly, you can keep the change you just reversed by using the Redo button ↷ on the

Quick Access toolbar. The Redo button appears only immediately after clicking the Undo button to undo a change.

If you want to repeat an action you just completed, you can use the Repeat button ↻ on the Quick Access toolbar. For example, if you just typed "thank you," clicking ↻ inserts "thank you" at the location of the insertion point. If you just applied bold, clicking ↻ applies bold to the currently selected text. You also can repeat the last action you took by pressing [F4].

Navigate a Document

Learning Outcomes
• Remove a content control
• Zoom and scroll a document
• Use Word document views

The Word Zoom feature lets you enlarge a document in the document window to get a close-up view of a detail or reduce the size of the document in the document window for an overview of the layout as a whole. You zoom in and out on a document using the tools in the Zoom group on the VIEW tab or you can use the Zoom level buttons and Zoom slider on the status bar. **CASE** ▸ *You find it is helpful to zoom in and out on the document as you finalize the letter.*

STEPS

1. **Click your name in the upper-left corner of the document, right-click the** Your Name **content control, click** Remove Content Control **on the menu that opens, select your name, click the** Decrease Font Size button A˅ **on the Mini toolbar three times, type** Quest Specialty Travel, **click** Job Title, **press** [Backspace] **twice, click** Job Title, **then press** [Backspace] **twice**

 Removing the content control from your name changes the text to static text that you can replace with other text. Pressing [Backspace] removes the Job Title placeholders.

2. **Drag the** vertical scroll box down **until the bottom of the page is visible in your document window**

 The scroll arrows or scroll bars allow you to **scroll** through a document. You scroll through a document when you want to display different parts of the document in the document window. You can also scroll by clicking the scroll arrows above and below the scroll bar, or by clicking the scroll bar.

3. **Click** [Website] **to move the insertion point to the bottom of the page, click the** VIEW **tab, then click the** Page Width button **in the Zoom group**

 The document is enlarged to the width of the document window. When you enlarge a document, the area where the insertion point is located appears in the document window.

4. **Click** [Address 1], **then replace the placeholder text with the text shown in** FIGURE A-13

 The text you type replaces the placeholder text. You do not always need to replace the placeholder text with the type of information suggested in the content control.

5. **Click the** Zoom level button 154% **on the status bar**

 The Zoom dialog box opens. You use the Zoom dialog box to select a zoom level for displaying the document in the document window.

6. **Click the** Whole page option button, **then click** OK

 The entire document is displayed in the document window.

7. **Click** Quest Specialty Travel **to move the insertion point to the top of the page, then move the Zoom slider to the right until the Zoom percentage is 100%**

 Dragging the Zoom slider to the right enlarges the document in the document window. Dragging the zoom slider to the left allows you to see more of the page at a reduced size. You can also move the Zoom slider by clicking a point on the Zoom slide, or by clicking the Zoom Out and Zoom In buttons.

8. **Click the** Read Mode button 📖 **on the status bar**

 The document appears in the document window in Read Mode view. Read Mode view hides the tabs and ribbon to make it easier to read documents on screen. Read Mode view is useful for reading long documents.

9. **Click the** Print Layout view button 🗐 **on the status bar to return to Print Layout view, click the** Zoom In button ➕ **on the status bar twice, then save the document**

 The completed cover letter is shown in FIGURE A-14.

10. **Submit the document to your instructor, close the file, then exit Word**

FIGURE A-13: Zoom slider

FIGURE A-14: Completed letter

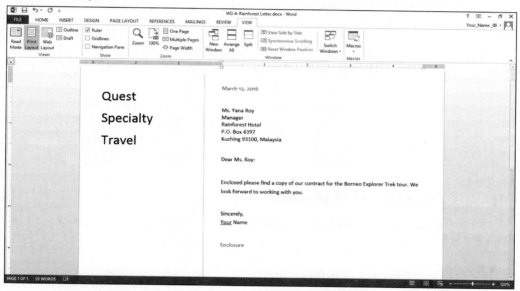

Using Word document views

Document **views** are different ways of displaying a document in the document window. Each Word view provides features that are useful for working on different types of documents. The default view, **Print Layout view**, displays a document as it will look on a printed page. Print Layout view is helpful for formatting text and pages, including adjusting document margins, creating columns of text, inserting graphics, and formatting headers and footers. Also useful is **Read Mode view**, which displays document text so that it is easy to read on screen. Other Word views are helpful for performing specialized tasks. **Web Layout view** allows you to format Web pages or documents that will be viewed on a computer screen. In Web Layout view, a document appears just as it will when viewed with a Web browser. **Outline view** is useful for editing and formatting longer documents that include multiple headings. Outline view allows you to reorganize text by moving the headings. Finally, **Draft view**, shows a simplified layout of a document, without margins, headers and footers, or graphics. When you want to quickly type and edit text, it's often easiest to work in Draft view. You switch between views by clicking the view buttons on the status bar or by using the commands on the VIEW tab. Changing views does not affect how the printed document will appear. It simply changes the way you view the document in the document window.

Practice

Concepts Review

Label the elements of the Word program window shown in FIGURE A-15.

FIGURE A-15

Match each term with the statement that best describes it.

7. Status bar
8. Formatting marks
9. Horizontal ruler
10. Template
11. Ribbon
12. AutoComplete
13. Zoom slider
14. AutoCorrect

a. A formatted document that contains placeholder text
b. Suggests text to insert into a document
c. Fixes certain errors as you type
d. Provides access to Word commands
e. Special characters that appear on screen but do not print
f. Displays tab settings and paragraph indents
g. Enlarges and reduces the document in the document window
h. Displays the number of pages in the current document

Select the best answer from the list of choices.

15. **Which of the following shows the number of words in the document?**
 a. The Ribbon
 b. The title bar
 c. The Mini toolbar
 d. The status bar

16. **Which tab includes buttons for formatting text?**
 a. PAGE LAYOUT
 b. VIEW
 c. HOME
 d. INSERT

17. **Which element of the Word window shows the top and bottom document margins settings?**
 a. Vertical ruler
 b. VIEW tab
 c. Vertical scroll bar
 d. Status bar

18. **What is the default file extension for a document created in Word 2013?**
 a. .dot
 b. .doc
 c. .docx
 d. .dotx

19. **Which of the following is not included in a ScreenTip for a command?**
 a. Alternative location of the command
 b. Link to a help topic on the command
 c. Keyboard shortcut for the command
 d. Description of the function of the command

20. **Which view is best for reading text onscreen?**
 a. Read Mode view
 b. Draft view
 c. Print Layout view
 d. Outline view

Skills Review

1. **Explore the Word program window.**
 a. Start Word and open a new, blank document.
 b. Identify as many elements of the Word program window as you can without referring to the unit material.
 c. Click the FILE tab, then click the Info, New, Save, Save As, Print, Share, and Export commands.
 d. Click the Back button in Backstage view to return to the document window.
 e. Click each tab on the Ribbon, review the groups and buttons on each tab, then return to the HOME tab.
 f. Point to each button on the HOME tab and read the ScreenTips.
 g. Click the view buttons to view the blank document in each view, then return to Print Layout view.
 h. Use the Zoom slider to zoom all the way in and all the way out on the document, then return to 120%.

2. **Start a document.**
 a. In a new blank document, type **Summer in the City Festivals** at the top of the page, then press [Enter] two times.
 b. Type the following, pressing [Tab] as indicated and pressing [Enter] at the end of each line:
 To: [Tab] [Tab] **David Skinner**
 From: [Tab] [Tab] **Your Name**
 Date: [Tab] [Tab] **Today's date**
 Re: [Tab] [Tab] **Reservation confirmation**
 Pages: [Tab] [Tab] **1**
 Fax: [Tab] [Tab] **(802) 555-5478**
 c. Press [Enter] again, then type **Thank you for your interest in our summer festival weekend package, which includes accommodations for three nights in downtown Boston, continental breakfast, and a festival pass. Rooms are still available during the following festivals: International Jazz Festival, Comedy Festival, Boston Fringe Festival, and the Festival of Arts. Please see the attached schedule for festival dates and details.**
 d. Press [Enter], then type **To make a reservation, please call me at (617) 555-7482 or visit our website. Payment must be received in full by the 3rd of June to hold a room. No one knows how to celebrate summer like Bostonians!**
 e. Insert **Grand Prix Festival**, before International Jazz Festival.
 f. Using the [Backspace] key, delete **1** in the Pages: line, then type **2**.
 g. Using the [Delete] key, delete **festival** in the last sentence of the first paragraph.

3. **Save a document.**
 a. Click the Save button on the Quick Access toolbar.
 b. Save the document as **WD A-Skinner Fax** with the default file extension to the location where you store your Data Files.
 c. After your name, type a comma, press [Spacebar], then type **Bookings Manager**
 d. Save the document.

4. **Select text.**
 a. Turn on formatting marks.
 b. Select the **Re:** line, then type **Re:** [Tab] [Tab] **Summer Festival Weekend Package**
 c. Select **three** in the first sentence, then type **two**.
 d. Select **3rd of June** in the second sentence of the last paragraph, type **15th of May**, select **room**, then type **reservation**.
 e. Delete the sentence **No one knows how to celebrate summer like Bostonians!**
 f. Turn off the display of formatting marks, then save the document.

Skills Review (continued)

5. Format text using the Mini toolbar.

a. Select **Summer in the City Festivals**, click the Grow Font button on the Mini toolbar six times, then apply bold.

b. Center **Summer in the City Festivals** on the page.

c. Apply a bottom border under **Summer in the City Festivals**.

d. Apply bold to the following words in the fax heading: **To:**, **From:**, **Date:**, **Re:**, **Pages:**, and **Fax:**.

e. Read the document using the Read Mode view.

f. Return to Print Layout view, zoom in on the document, then proofread the fax.

g. Correct any typing errors in your document, then save the document. Compare your document to FIGURE A-16.

h. Submit the fax to your instructor, then close the document.

6. Create a document using a template.

a. Click the FILE tab, click New, then click Fax.

b. Create a new document using the Fax Coversheet (Professional Design) template.

FIGURE A-16

Summer in the City Festivals

To:	David Skinner
From:	Your Name, Bookings Manager
Date:	April 11, 2016
Re:	Summer Festival Weekend Package
Pages:	2
Fax:	(802) 555-5478

Thank you for your interest in our summer festival weekend package, which includes accommodations for two nights in downtown Boston, continental breakfast, and a festival pass. Rooms are still available during the following festivals: Grand Prix Festival, International Jazz Festival, Comedy Festival, Boston Fringe Festival, and the Festival of Arts. Please see the attached schedule for dates and details.

To make a reservation, please call me at (617) 555-7482 or visit our website. Payment must be received in full by the 15th of May to hold a reservation.

c. Click the "Company Name" placeholder text, type **Summer in the City Festivals**, click the "Company Address" placeholder text, type **Boston, MA**, click the "Phone number" placeholder text, type **Phone (617) 555-7482**, click the "Fax number" placeholder text, type **Fax (617) 555-1176**, click the Web Address placeholder text, then type **www.summerfestboston.com**.

d. Type **Emily Sargent** to replace the "To:" placeholder text; type **555-2119** to replace the "Fax:" placeholder text; click the "Phone:" placeholder text, then press [Delete]; then type **Summer Festivals** to replace the "Re:" placeholder text.

e. If your name is not on the From line, select the text in the From content control, then type your name.

f. Insert today's date using the date content control.

g. Delete the "Pages:" and "CC:" placeholder text.

h. Save the document with the filename **WD A-Sold Out Fax** to the location where you store your Data Files, clicking OK if a warning box opens.

7. View and navigate a document.

a. Scroll down until Comments is near the top of your document window.

b. Replace the Comments placeholder text with the following text: **Packages for the following summer festivals are sold out: First Peoples' Festival, Chamber Music Festival, and Dragon Boat Race Festival. We had expected these packages to be less popular than those for the bigger festivals, but interest has been high. Next year, we will increase our bookings for these festivals by 30%.**

c. Use the Zoom dialog box to view the Whole Page.

d. Use the Zoom slider to set the Zoom percentage at approximately 100%.

e. Read the document using the Read Mode view.

f. Return to Print Layout view, zoom in on the document, then proofread the fax.

Creating Documents with Word 2013

Skills Review (continued)

FIGURE A-17

g. Preview the document, then correct any errors, saving changes if necessary. Compare your document to FIGURE A-17. Submit the document to your instructor, close the file, then exit Word.

Independent Challenge 1

Yesterday you interviewed for a job as marketing director at Chelsea Design Services. You spoke with several people at the company, including Willa Taylor, chief executive officer, whose business card is shown in FIGURE A-18. You need to write a follow-up letter to Ms. Taylor, thanking her for the interview and expressing your interest in the company and the position. She also asked you to send her some samples of your marketing work, which you will enclose with the letter.

Summer in the City Festivals
Boston, MA
Phone (617) 555-7482 | Fax (617) 555-1176 | www.summerfestboston.com

fax

TO:	Emily Sargent		FROM:	Your Name
FAX:	555-2119		PAGES:	
PHONE:			DATE:	4/11/2016
RE:	Summer Festivals		CC:	

☐ Urgent ☐ For Review ☐ Please Comment ☐ Please Reply ☐ Please Recycle

Comments: Packages for the following summer festivals are sold out: First Peoples' Festival, Chamber Music Festival, and Dragon Boat Race Festival. We had expected these packages to be less popular than those for the bigger festivals, but interest has been high. Next year, we will increase our books for these festivals by 30%.

a. Start Word and save a new blank document as **WD A-Taylor Letter** to the location where you store your Data Files.

b. Begin the letter by clicking the No Spacing button in the Styles group. You use this button to apply the No Spacing style to the document so that your document does not include extra space between paragraphs.

c. Type a personal letterhead for the letter that includes your name, address, telephone number, and e-mail address. If Word formats your e-mail address as a hyperlink, right-click your e-mail address, then click Remove Hyperlink. (*Note: Format the letterhead after you finish typing the letter.*)

d. Three lines below the bottom of the letterhead, type today's date.

e. Four lines below the date, type the inside address, referring to FIGURE A-18 for the address information. Be sure to include the recipient's title, company name, and full mailing address in the inside address.

f. Two lines below the inside address, type **Dear Ms. Taylor:** for the salutation.

FIGURE A-18

Willa Taylor
Chief Executive Officer

Chelsea Design Services
www.chelseadesign.com

438 W. 23rd Street, Suite 76
New York, NY 10011
p. 212.555.7028
wtaylor@chelseadesign.co

g. Two lines below the salutation, type the body of the letter according to the following guidelines:
 - In the first paragraph, thank her for the interview. Then restate your interest in the position and express your desire to work for the company. Add any specific details you think will enhance the power of your letter.
 - In the second paragraph, note that you are enclosing three samples of your work, and explain something about the samples you are enclosing.
 - Type a short final paragraph.

h. Two lines below the last body paragraph, type a closing, then four lines below the closing, type the signature block. Be sure to include your name in the signature block.

i. Two lines below the signature block, type an enclosure notation. (*Hint*: An enclosure notation usually includes the word "Enclosures" or the abbreviation "Enc." followed by the number of enclosures in parentheses.)

j. Format the letterhead with bold, centering, and a bottom border.

k. Save your changes.

l. Preview the letter, submit it to your instructor, then close the document and exit Word.

Independent Challenge 2

Your company has recently installed Word 2013 on its company network. As the training manager, it's your responsibility to teach employees how to use the new software productively. Now that they have begun working with Word 2013, several employees have asked you about sharing documents with colleagues using Microsoft SkyDrive. In response, you wrote a memo to all employees explaining Microsoft SkyDrive, some of its features, and how to register for a Windows Live ID. You now need to format the memo before distributing it.

a. Start Word, open the file **WD A-1.docx** from the location where you store your Data Files, then read the memo to get a feel for its contents. Switch to Print Layout view if the document is not already displayed in Print Layout view.

b. Save the file as **WD A-SkyDrive Memo** to the location where you store your Data Files.

c. Replace the information in the memo header with the information shown in FIGURE A-19. Make sure to include your name in the From line and the current date in the Date line.

d. Apply bold to **To:**, **From:**, **Date:**, and **Re:**.

e. Increase the size of **WORD TRAINING MEMORANDUM** to match FIGURE A-19, center the text on the page, add a border below it, then save your changes.

FIGURE A-19

<div style="border:1px solid #000; padding:1em;">

WORD TRAINING MEMORANDUM

To: All employees
From: Your Name, Training Manager
Date: Today's Date
Re: Microsoft SkyDrive

</div>

f. Preview the memo, submit it to your instructor, then close the document and exit Word.

Independent Challenge 3

You are an expert on global warming. The president of the National Parks Association, Elizabeth Pope, has asked you to be the keynote speaker at an upcoming conference on the impact of climate change on the national parks, to be held in Glacier National Park. You use one of the Word letter templates to write a letter to Ms. Pope accepting the invitation and confirming the details. Your letter to Ms. Pope should reference the following information:

- The conference will be held August 4–6, 2016, at the Many Glacier Hotel in the park.
- You have been asked to speak for an hour on Saturday, August 5, followed by one-half hour for questions.
- Ms. Pope suggested the lecture topic "Melting Glaciers, Changing Ecosystems."
- Your talk will include a 45-minute slide presentation.
- The National Parks Association will make your travel arrangements.
- Your preference is to arrive at Glacier Park International Airport in Kalispell on the morning of Friday, August 4, and to depart on Monday, August 7. You would like to rent a car at the airport for the drive to the Many Glacier Hotel.
- You want to fly in and out of the airport closest to your home.

a. Start Word, click the FILE tab, click New, click Letters next to Suggested searches, and then select an appropriate letter template. Save the document as **WD A-Pope Letter** to the location where you store your Data Files.

b. Replace the placeholders in the letterhead with your personal information. Include your name, address, phone number, and e-mail address. Delete any placeholders that do not apply. (*Hints:* Depending on the template you choose, the letterhead might be located at the top or on the side of the document. You can press [Enter] when typing in a placeholder to add an additional line of text. You can also change the format of text typed in a placeholder. If your e-mail address appears as a hyperlink, right-click the e-mail address and click Remove Hyperlink.)

Independent Challenge 3 (continued)

c. Use the [Pick the date] content control to select the current date.

d. Replace the placeholders in the inside address. Be sure to include Ms. Pope's title and the name of the organization. Make up a street address and zip code.

e. Type **Dear Ms. Pope:** for the salutation.

f. Using the information listed previously, type the body of the letter:

- In the first paragraph, accept the invitation to speak.
- In the second paragraph, confirm the important conference details, confirm your lecture topic, and provide any relevant details.
- In the third paragraph, state your travel preferences.
- Type a short final paragraph.

g. Type **Sincerely,** for the closing, then include your name in the signature block.

h. Adjust the formatting of the letter as necessary. For example, remove bold formatting or change the font color of text to a more appropriate color.

i. Proofread your letter, make corrections as needed, then save your changes.

j. Submit the letter to your instructor, close the document, then exit Word.

Independent Challenge 4: Explore

Word includes a wide variety of templates that can help you create professional-looking documents quickly, including business letters, business cards, résumés, calendars, faxes, memos, labels, reports, blog posts, posters, invitations, certificates, newsletters, and holiday and party cards. In this independent challenge, you will explore the variety of Word templates available to you, and use a template to make a document that is helpful to you in your business or personal life. You might create business cards for yourself, a poster for an event, a letter for a job search, a new résumé, or an invitation to a party. Choose a template that allows you to personalize the text.

a. Start Word, click the FILE tab, click New, then click each link after Suggested searches: (Letters, Resume, Fax, Labels, Cards, Calendar, and Blank) to explore the templates available to you.

b. Preview all the templates for the type of document you want to create, and then select one to create a new document.

c. Save the document as **WD A-Template Document** to the location where you store your Data Files.

d. Replace the placeholders in the document with your personal information. Delete any placeholders that do not apply. (*Hints*: You can press [Enter] when typing in a placeholder to add an additional line of text. If an e-mail or web address appears as a hyperlink in your document, right-click the e-mail or web address and then click Remove Hyperlink.)

e. Use the [Pick the date] content control to select a date if your document includes a date placeholder.

f. Experiment with changing the font of the text in your document by using the Font list arrow on the Mini toolbar or in the Font group on the HOME tab. (*Note:* Remember to use the Undo button immediately after you make the change if you do not like the change and want to remove it.)

g. Experiment with changing the font size of the text in your document by using the Font Size list arrow on the Mini toolbar or in the Font group on the HOME tab.

h. Experiment with changing the color of text in your document using the Font Color button on the Mini toolbar or in the Font group on the HOME tab.

i. Make other adjustments to the document as necessary, using the Undo button to remove a change.

j. Save your changes to the document, preview it, submit it to your instructor, then close the document and exit Word.

Visual Workshop

Create the cover letter shown in FIGURE A-20. Before beginning to type, click the No Spacing button in the Styles group on the HOME tab. Add the bottom border to the letterhead after typing the letter. Save the document as **WD A-Johnson Cover Letter** to the location where you store your Data Files, submit the letter to your instructor, then close the document and exit Word.

FIGURE A-20

Your Name

54 Morningside Drive, Iowa City, IA 52242
Tel: 319-555-7283; Fax: 319-555-1445; E-mail: yourname@gmail.com

October 12, 2016

Mr. Silas Johnson
Johnson Associates
712 Burlington Street
Suite 200
Iowa City, IA 52240

Dear Mr. Johnson:

I read of the opening for a public information assistant in the October 11 edition of iowajobs.com, and I would like to be considered for the position. I am a recent graduate of the University of Iowa (UI), and I am interested in pursuing a career in public relations.

My interest in a public relations career springs from my publicly acknowledged writing and journalism abilities. For example, at UI, I was a reporter for the student newspaper and frequently wrote press releases for campus and community events.

I have a wealth of experience using Microsoft Word in professional settings. Last summer, I worked as an office assistant for the architecture firm Coleman & Greenberg, where I used Word to create newsletters, brochures, and financial reports. During the school year, I also worked part-time in the UI Office of Community Relations, where I used the Word mail merge feature to create form letters and mailing labels.

My enclosed resume details my skills and experience. I welcome the opportunity to discuss the position and my qualifications with you. I can be reached at 319-555-7283.

Sincerely,

Your Name

Enc.

Editing Documents

CASE ▶ You have been asked to edit and finalize a press release for a QST promotional lecture series. The press release should provide information about the series so that newspapers, radio stations, and other media outlets can announce it to the public. QST press releases are disseminated by fax and by e-mail. Before distributing the file electronically to your lists of press contacts and local QST clients, you add several hyperlinks and then strip the file of private information.

Unit Objectives

After completing this unit, you will be able to:

- Cut and paste text
- Copy and paste text
- Use the Office Clipboard
- Find and replace text

- Check spelling and grammar
- Research information
- Add hyperlinks
- Work with document properties

Files You Will Need

WD B-1.docx	WD B-5.docx
WD B-2.docx	WD B-6.docx
WD B-3.docx	WD B-7.docx
WD B-4.docx	

Microsoft® product screenshots used with permission from Microsoft® Corporation.

©Tiumanyan/Shutterstock

Cut and Paste Text

The editing features in Word allow you to move text from one location to another in a document. Moving text is often called **cut and paste**. When you **cut** text, it is removed from the document and placed on the **Clipboard**, a temporary storage area for text and graphics that you cut or copy from a document. You can then paste, or insert, text that is stored on the Clipboard in the document at the location of the insertion point. You cut and paste text using the Cut and Paste buttons in the Clipboard group on the HOME tab. You also can move selected text by dragging it to a new location using the mouse. This operation is called **drag and drop**. **CASE** ▸ *You open the press release, save it with a new filename, and then reorganize the information in the press release using the cut-and-paste and drag-and-drop methods.*

STEPS

1. **Start Word, click Blank document, click the FILE tab, click Computer on the Open screen, click Browse to open the Open dialog box, navigate to the location where you store your Data Files, click WD B-1.docx, then click Open**

 The document opens in Print Layout view at 120%. Once you have opened a file, you can edit it and use the Save or the Save As command to save your changes. You use the **Save** command when you want to save the changes you make to a file, overwriting the stored file. You use the **Save As** command when you want to leave the original file intact and create a duplicate file with a different filename, file extension, or location.

2. **Click the FILE tab, click Save As, click Computer, click Browse to open the Save As dialog box, type WD B-Lecture PR in the File name text box, then click Save**

 You can now make changes to the press release file without affecting the original file.

3. **Replace Ron Dawson with your name, scroll down until the headline "Bridget Surette to Speak..." is at the top of your document window, then click the Show/Hide ¶ button ¶ in the Paragraph group on the HOME tab to display formatting marks**

4. **Select Alaskan guide Gilbert Coonan, (including the comma and the space after it) in the third body paragraph, then click the Cut button in the Clipboard group**

 The text is removed from the document and placed on the Clipboard. Word uses two different clipboards: the **system clipboard**, which holds just one item, and the **Office Clipboard** (the Clipboard), which holds up to 24 items. The last item you cut or copy is always added to both clipboards.

5. **Place the insertion point before African (but after the space) in the first line of the third paragraph, then click the Paste button in the Clipboard group**

 The text is pasted at the location of the insertion point, as shown in **FIGURE B-1**. The Paste Options button appears below text when you first paste it in a document. For now you can ignore the Paste Options button.

6. **Press and hold [Ctrl], click the sentence Ticket prices include lunch. in the fourth paragraph, then release [Ctrl]**

 The entire sentence is selected.

7. **Press and hold the mouse button over the selected text until the pointer changes to** ⌖

 The pointer's vertical line is the insertion point. You drag the pointer to position the insertion point where you want the text to be inserted when you release the mouse button.

8. **Drag the pointer's vertical line to the end of the fifth paragraph (between the period and the paragraph mark) as shown in FIGURE B-2, then release the mouse button**

 The selected text is moved to the location of the insertion point. It is convenient to move text using the drag-and-drop method when the locations of origin and destination are both visible on the screen. Text is not placed on the Clipboard when you drag and drop it.

9. **Deselect the text, then click the Save button 🖫 on the Quick Access toolbar**

FIGURE B-1: Moved text with Paste Options button

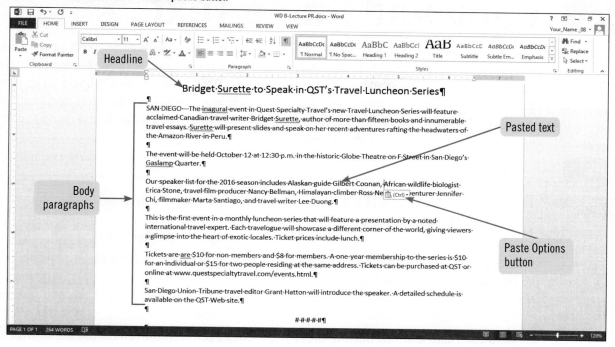

FIGURE B-2: Dragging and dropping text in a new location

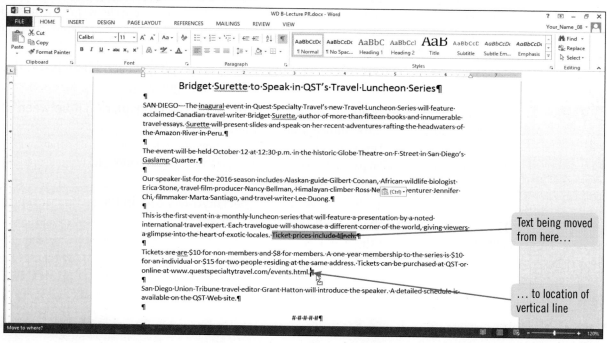

Using keyboard shortcuts

A **shortcut key** is a function key, such as [F1], or a combination of keys, such as [Ctrl][S], that you press to perform a command. For example, instead of using the Cut, Copy, and Paste commands on the Ribbon or the Mini toolbar, you can use the **keyboard shortcuts** [Ctrl][X] to cut text, [Ctrl][C] to copy text, and [Ctrl][V] to paste text. You can also press [Ctrl][S] to save changes to a document instead of clicking the Save button on the Quick Access toolbar or clicking Save on the FILE tab. Becoming skilled at using keyboard shortcuts can help you quickly accomplish many of the tasks you perform in Word. If a keyboard shortcut is available for a command, then it is listed in the ScreenTip for that command.

Copy and Paste Text

Learning Outcomes
• Copy and paste text
• Format pasted text with the Paste Options button

Copying and pasting text is similar to cutting and pasting text, except that the text you **copy** is not removed from the document. Rather, a copy of the text is placed on the Clipboard, leaving the original text in place. You can copy text to the Clipboard using the Copy button in the Clipboard group on the HOME tab, or you can copy text by pressing [Ctrl] as you drag the selected text from one location to another. **CASE** ▶ *You continue to edit the press release by copying text from one location to another using the copy-and-paste and drag-and-drop methods.*

STEPS

QUICK TIP
You can also cut or copy text by right-clicking the selected text, and then clicking the Cut or Copy command on the menu that opens.

1. **Select Travel Luncheon in the headline, then click the Copy button in the Clipboard group on the HOME tab**

 A copy of the selected text is placed on the Clipboard, leaving the original text you copied in place.

2. **Place the insertion point before season in the third paragraph, then click the Paste button in the Clipboard group**

 "Travel Luncheon" is inserted before "season," as shown in FIGURE B-3. Notice that the pasted text is formatted differently than the paragraph in which it was inserted.

3. **Click the Paste Options button, move the mouse over each button on the menu that opens to read its ScreenTip, then click the Keep Text Only (T) button**

 The formatting of "Travel Luncheon" is changed to match the rest of the paragraph. The buttons on the Paste Options menu allow you to change the formatting of pasted text. You can choose to keep the original formatting (Keep Source Formatting), match the destination formatting (Merge Formatting), or paste as unformatted text (Keep Text Only).

4. **Select www.questspecialtytravel.com in the fifth paragraph, press and hold [Ctrl], then press and hold the mouse button until the pointer changes to ▯**

TROUBLE
If you move the text instead of copying it, click the Undo button ↺ on the Quick Access toolbar and repeat Steps 4 and 5.

5. **Drag the pointer's vertical line to the end of the last paragraph, placing it between site and the period, release the mouse button, then release [Ctrl]**

 The text is copied to the last paragraph. Since the formatting of the text you copied is the same as the formatting of the destination paragraph, you can ignore the Paste Options button. Text is not copied to the Clipboard when you copy it using the drag-and-drop method.

6. **Place the insertion point before www.questspecialtytravel.com in the last paragraph, type at followed by a space, then save the document**

 Compare your document with FIGURE B-4.

Splitting the document window to copy and move items in a long document

If you want to copy or move items between parts of a long document, it can be useful to split the document window into two panes. This allows you to display the item you want to copy or move in one pane and the destination for the item in the other pane. To split a window, click the Split button in the Window group on the VIEW tab, and then drag the horizontal split bar that appears to the location you want to split the window. Once the document window is split into two panes, you can use the scroll bars in each pane to display different parts of the document. To copy or move an item from one pane to another, you can use the Cut, Copy, and Paste commands, or you can drag the item between the panes. When you are finished editing the document, double-click the split bar to restore the window to a single pane, or click the Remove Split button in the Window group on the VIEW tab.

FIGURE B-3: Text pasted in document

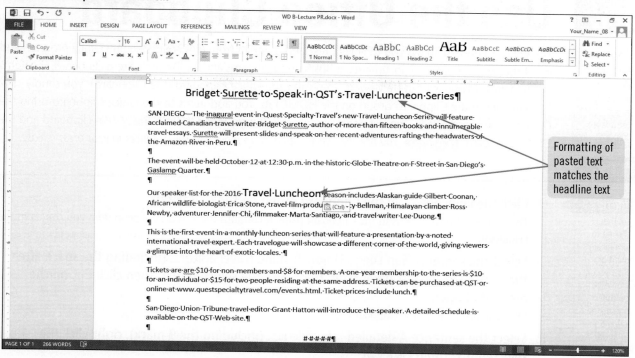

Formatting of pasted text matches the headline text

FIGURE B-4: Copied text in document

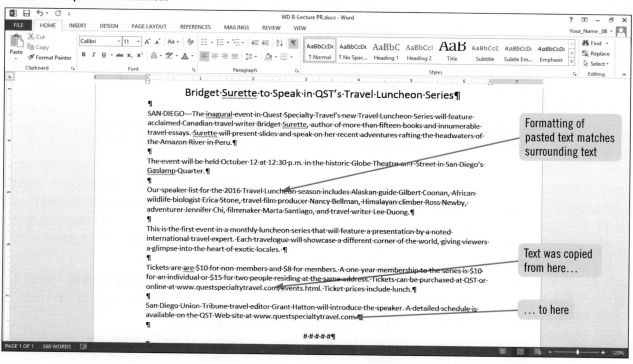

Formatting of pasted text matches surrounding text

Text was copied from here…

… to here

Word 2013

Use the Office Clipboard

Learning Outcomes
- Copy and cut items to the Clipboard
- Paste items from the Clipboard

The Office Clipboard allows you to collect text and graphics from files created in any Office program and insert them into your Word documents. It holds up to 24 items and, unlike the system clipboard, the items on the Office Clipboard can be viewed. To display the Office Clipboard (the Clipboard), you simply click the launcher in the Clipboard group on the HOME tab. You add items to the Office Clipboard using the Cut and Copy commands. The last item you collect is always added to both the system clipboard and the Office Clipboard. **CASE** ▸ *You use the Office Clipboard to move several sentences in your press release.*

STEPS

1. **Click the launcher** ⌐⌐ **in the Clipboard group on the HOME tab**

 The Office Clipboard opens in the Clipboard pane. It contains the Travel Luncheon item you copied in the last lesson.

2. **Select the sentence** San Diego Union-Tribune travel editor... **(including the space after the period) in the last paragraph, right-click the selected text, then click Cut on the menu that opens**

 The sentence is cut to the Clipboard.

3. **Select the sentence** A detailed schedule is... **(including the ¶ mark), right-click the selected text, then click Cut**

 The Clipboard displays the items you cut or copied, as shown in **FIGURE B-5**. The icon next to each item indicates the items are from a Word document. The last item collected is displayed at the top of the Clipboard pane. As new items are collected, the existing items move down the Clipboard.

4. **Place the insertion point at the end of the second paragraph (after "Quarter." but before the ¶ mark), then click the** San Diego Union-Tribune... **item on the Clipboard**

 Clicking an item on the Clipboard pastes the item in the document at the location of the insertion point. Items remain on the Clipboard until you delete them or close all open Office programs.

5. **Place the insertion point at the end of the third paragraph (after "Duong."), then click the** A detailed schedule is... **item on the Clipboard**

 The sentence is pasted into the document.

6. **Select the fourth paragraph, which begins with the sentence** This is the first event... **(including the ¶ mark), right-click the selected text, then click Cut**

 The paragraph is cut to the Clipboard.

7. **Place the insertion point at the beginning of the third paragraph (before "Our..."), click the Paste button in the Clipboard group on the HOME tab, then press [Backspace]**

 The sentences from the "This is the first..." paragraph are pasted at the beginning of the "Our speaker list..." paragraph. You can paste the last item collected using either the Paste command or the Clipboard.

8. **Place the insertion point at the end of the third paragraph (after "www.questspecialtytravel.com." and before the ¶ mark), then press [Delete] twice**

 Two ¶ symbols and the corresponding blank lines between the third and fourth paragraphs are deleted.

9. **Click the Show/Hide ¶ button** ¶ **on in the Paragraph group**

 Compare your press release with **FIGURE B-6**. Note that many Word users prefer to work with formatting marks on at all times. Experiment to see which method you prefer.

10. **Click the Clear All button on the Clipboard pane to remove the items from the Clipboard, click the Close button** ⌧ **on the Clipboard pane, press [Ctrl][Home], then save the document**

 Pressing [Ctrl][Home] moves the insertion point to the top of the document.

FIGURE B-5: Office Clipboard in Clipboard pane

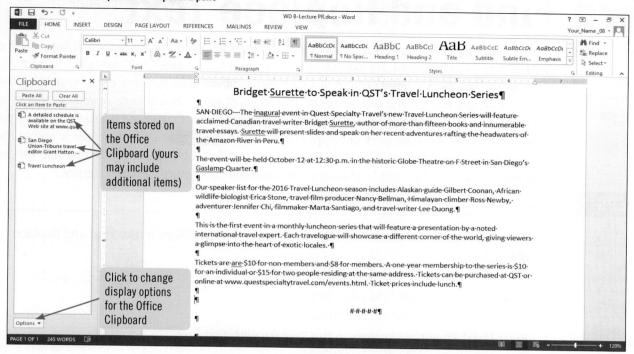

FIGURE B-6: Revised press release

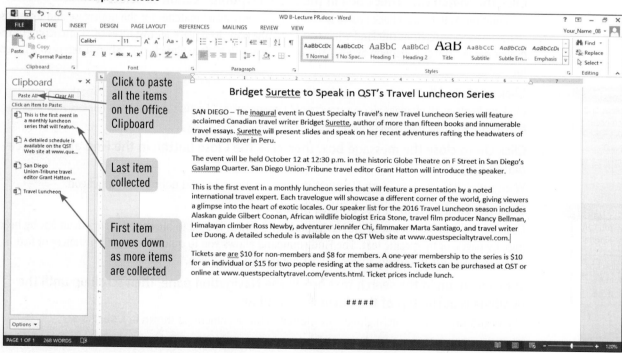

Copying and moving items between documents

You can also use the Clipboard to copy and move items between documents. To do this, open both documents and the Clipboard pane. With multiple documents open, copy or cut an item from one document and then switch to the other document and paste the item. To switch between open documents, point to the Word icon on the taskbar, and then click the document you want to appear in the document window. You can also display more than one document at the same time by clicking the Arrange All button or the View Side by Side button in the Window group on the VIEW tab.

Find and Replace Text

Learning Outcomes
- Replace text
- Find text with the Navigation pane
- Navigate a document

The Find and Replace feature in Word allows you to automatically search for and replace all instances of a word or phrase in a document. For example, you might need to substitute "tour" for "trip." To manually locate and replace each instance of "trip" in a long document would be very time-consuming. Using the Replace command you can find and replace all occurrences of specific text at once, or you can choose to find and review each occurrence individually. You also can use the Find command to locate and highlight every occurrence of a specific word or phrase in a document. **CASE** ▶ *QST has decided to change the name of the lecture series from "Travel Luncheon Series" to "Travel Lecture Series." You use the Replace command to search the document for all instances of "Luncheon" and replace them with "Lecture."*

STEPS

TROUBLE
If any of the Search Options check boxes are selected in your Find and Replace dialog box, deselect them. If Format appears under the Find what or Replace with text box, click in the text box, then click the No Formatting button.

1. **Click the Replace button in the Editing group, then click More in the Find and Replace dialog box**

 The Find and Replace dialog box opens and expands, as shown in **FIGURE B-7**.

2. **Type Luncheon in the Find what text box**

 "Luncheon" is the text that will be replaced.

3. **Press [Tab], then type Lecture in the Replace with text box**

 "Lecture" is the text that will replace "Luncheon."

4. **Click the Match case check box in the Search Options section to select it**

 Selecting the Match case check box tells Word to find only exact matches for the uppercase and lowercase characters you entered in the Find what text box. You want to replace all instances of "Luncheon" in the proper name "Travel Luncheon Series." You do not want to replace "luncheon" when it refers to a lunch-time event.

QUICK TIP
To find, review, and replace each occurrence individually, click Find Next.

5. **Click Replace All**

 Clicking Replace All changes all occurrences of "Luncheon" to "Lecture" in the press release. A message box reports three replacements were made.

6. **Click OK to close the message box, then click the Close button in the Find and Replace dialog box**

 Word replaced "Luncheon" with "Lecture" in three locations, but did not replace "luncheon."

QUICK TIP
Alternately, you can also use the Find tab in the Find and Replace dialog box to find text in a document.

7. **Click the Find button in the Editing group**

 Clicking the Find button opens the Navigation pane, which is used to browse a longer document by headings, by pages, or by specific text. The Find command allows you to quickly locate all instances of text in a document. You use it to verify that Word did not replace "luncheon."

8. **Type luncheon in the search text box in the Navigation pane, then scroll up until the headline is at the top of the document window**

 The word "luncheon" is highlighted and selected in the document, as shown in **FIGURE B-8**.

9. **Click the Close button in the Navigation pane, press [Ctrl][Home], then save the document**

 The highlighting is removed from the text when you close the Navigation pane.

FIGURE B-7: Find and Replace dialog box

Replace only exact matches of upper-case and lowercase characters

Find only complete words

Use wildcards (*) in a search string

Find words that sound like the Find what text

Find and replace all forms of a word

FIGURE B-8: Found text highlighted in document

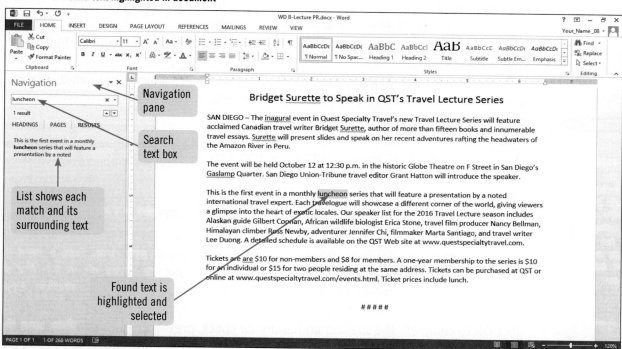

Navigation pane

Search text box

List shows each match and its surrounding text

Found text is highlighted and selected

Word 2013

Navigating a document using the Navigation pane and the Go To command

Rather than scrolling to move to a different place in a longer document, you can use the Navigation pane to quickly move the insertion point to a specific page or a specific heading. To open the Navigation pane, click the Page number button on the status bar, and then click the appropriate link in the Navigation pane for the type of item you want to use to navigate the document.

To move to a specific page, section, line, table, graphic, or other item in a document, you use the Go To tab in the Find and Replace dialog box. On the Go To tab in the Find and Replace dialog box, select the type of item you want to find in the Go to what list box, enter the relevant information about that item, and then click Next to move the insertion point to the item.

Check Spelling and Grammar

Learning Outcomes
• Ignore correctly spelled words
• Correct spelling errors
• Correct grammar errors

When you finish typing and revising a document, you can use the Spelling and Grammar command to search the document for misspelled words and grammar errors. The Spelling and Grammar checker flags possible mistakes, suggests correct spellings, and offers remedies for grammar errors such as subject–verb agreement, repeated words, and punctuation. **CASE** ▶ *You use the Spelling and Grammar checker to search your press release for errors. Before beginning the search, you set the Spelling and Grammar checker to ignore words, such as Surette, that you know are spelled correctly.*

STEPS

TROUBLE
If Word flags your name as misspelled, right-click it, then click Ignore All. If Surette is not flagged as misspelled, skip to Step 3.

1. **Right-click Surette in the headline**

 A menu that includes suggestions for correcting the spelling of "Surette" opens. You can correct individual spelling and grammar errors by right-clicking text that is underlined with a red or blue wavy line and selecting a correction. Although "Surette" is not in the Word dictionary, it is spelled correctly in the document.

2. **Click Ignore All**

 Clicking Ignore All tells Word not to flag "Surette" as misspelled.

3. **Press [Ctrl][Home], click the REVIEW tab, then click the Spelling & Grammar button in the Proofing group**

 The Spelling pane opens, as shown in **FIGURE B-9**. The pane identifies "inagural" as misspelled and suggests a possible correction for the error. The word selected in the suggestions box is the correct spelling.

QUICK TIP
To change the language used by the Word proofing tools, click the Language button in the Language group on the REVIEW tab, click Set Proofing Language, then click the language you prefer in the dialog box that opens.

4. **Click Change**

 Word replaces the misspelled word with the correctly spelled word. Next, the Spelling pane identifies "Gaslmp" as a misspelled word and suggests the correction "Gas lamp." The proper name "Gaslamp Quarter" is spelled correctly in the document.

5. **Click Ignore**

 Word ignores the spelling. Next, the dialog box indicates that "are" is repeated in a sentence.

6. **Click Delete**

 Word deletes the second occurrence of the repeated word, and the Spelling pane closes. Keep in mind that the Spelling and Grammar checker identifies many common errors, but you cannot rely on it to find and correct all spelling and grammar errors in your documents, or to always suggest a valid correction. Always proofread your documents carefully.

QUICK TIP
If Word flags a grammar error, the suggested correction is shown in the Grammar pane.

7. **Click OK to complete the spelling and grammar check, press [Ctrl][Home], then save the document**

FIGURE B-9: Spelling pane

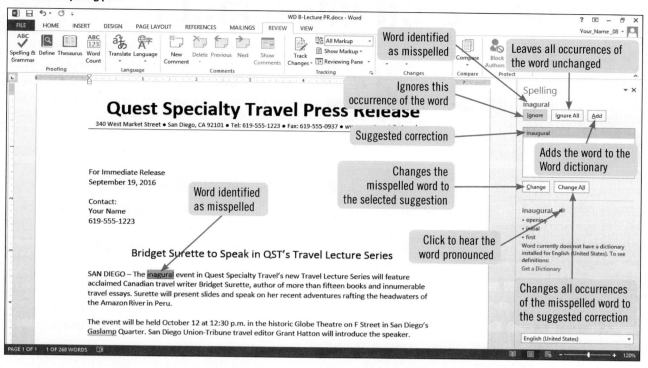

Inserting text with AutoCorrect

As you type, AutoCorrect automatically corrects many commonly misspelled words. By creating your own AutoCorrect entries, you can set Word to insert text that you type often, such as your name or contact information, or to correct words you misspell frequently. For example, you could create an AutoCorrect entry so that the name "Ronald T. Dawson" is automatically inserted whenever you type "rtd" followed by a space. You create AutoCorrect entries and customize other AutoCorrect and AutoFormat options using the AutoCorrect dialog box. To open the AutoCorrect dialog box, click the FILE tab, click Options, click Proofing in the Word Options dialog box that opens, and then click AutoCorrect Options. On the AutoCorrect tab in the AutoCorrect dialog box, type the text you want to be corrected automatically in the Replace text box (such as "rtd"), type the text you want to be inserted in its place automatically in the With text box (such as "Ronald T. Dawson"), and then click Add. The AutoCorrect entry is added to the list. Click OK to close the AutoCorrect dialog box, and then click OK to close the Word Options dialog box. Word inserts an AutoCorrect entry in a document when you press [Spacebar] or a punctuation mark after typing the text you want Word to correct. For example, Word inserts "Ronald T. Dawson" when you type "rtd" followed by a space. If you want to remove an AutoCorrect entry you created, simply open the AutoCorrect dialog box, select the AutoCorrect entry you want to remove in the list, click Delete, click OK, and then click OK to close the Word Options dialog box.

Research Information

Learning Outcomes
- Find synonyms using the Thesaurus
- Check word count

The Word research features allow you to quickly search reference sources and the World Wide Web for information related to a word or phrase. Among the reference sources available are a Thesaurus, which you can use to look up synonyms for awkward or repetitive words, as well as dictionary and translation sources. **CASE** ▶ *After proofreading your document for errors, you decide the press release would read better if several adjectives were more descriptive. You use the Thesaurus to find synonyms.*

STEPS

1. **Scroll down until the headline is displayed at the top of your screen**

2. **Select noted in the first sentence of the third paragraph, then click the Thesaurus button in the Proofing group on the REVIEW tab**

 The Thesaurus pane opens, as shown in **FIGURE B-10**. "Noted" appears in the search text box, and possible synonyms for "noted" are listed under the search text box.

QUICK TIP

To look up synonyms for a different word, type the word in the search text box, then click the search button.

3. **Point to prominent in the list of synonyms**

 A shaded box containing a list arrow appears around the word.

4. **Click the list arrow, click Insert on the menu that opens, then close the Thesaurus pane**

 "Prominent" replaces "noted" in the press release.

5. **Right-click innumerable in the first sentence of the first paragraph, point to Synonyms on the menu that opens, then click numerous**

 "Numerous" replaces "innumerable" in the press release.

6. **Select the four paragraphs of body text, then click the Word Count button in the Proofing group**

 The Word Count dialog box opens, as shown in **FIGURE B-11**. The dialog box lists the number of pages, words, characters, paragraphs, and lines included in the selected text. Notice that the status bar also displays the number of words included in the selected text and the total number of words in the entire document. If you want to view the page, character, paragraph, and line count for the entire document, make sure nothing is selected in your document, and then click Word Count in the Proofing group.

7. **Click Close, press [Ctrl][Home], then save the document**

8. **Click the FILE tab, click Save As, navigate to the location where you store your files, type WD B-Lecture PR Public in the File name text box, then click Save**

 The WD B-Lecture PR file closes, and the WD B-Lecture PR Public file is displayed in the document window. You will modify this file to prepare it for electronic release to the public.

Publishing a blog directly from Word

A **blog**, which is short for weblog, is an informal journal that is created by an individual or a group and available to the public on the Internet. A blog usually conveys the ideas, comments, and opinions of the blogger and is written using a strong personal voice. The person who creates and maintains a blog, the **blogger**, typically updates the blog regularly. If you have or want to start a blog, you can configure Word to link to your blog site so that you can write, format, and publish blog entries directly from Word.

To create a new blog post, click the FILE tab, click New, then double-click Blog post to open a predesigned blog post document that you can customize with your own text, formatting, and images. You can also publish an existing document as a blog post by opening the document, clicking the FILE tab, clicking Share, and then clicking Post to Blog. In either case, Word prompts you to log onto your personal blog account. To blog directly from Word, you must first obtain a blog account with a blog service provider. Resources, such as the Word Help system and online forums, provide detailed information on obtaining and registering your personal blog account with Word.

FIGURE B-10: Thesaurus pane

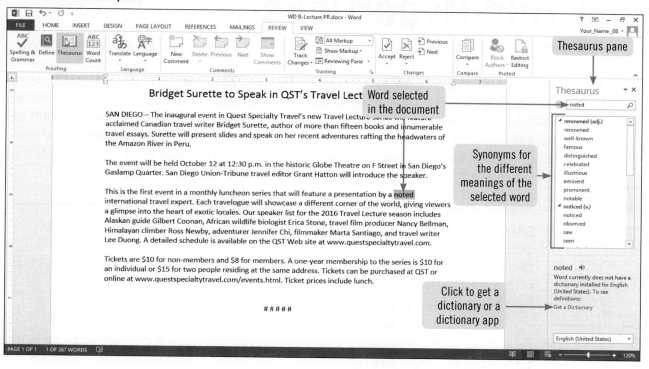

FIGURE B-11: Word Count dialog box

Using a dictionary and other apps for Word

Instead of a built-in dictionary, Word includes the ability to install a free dictionary app from the Office Store that you can use to look up the definitions of words. A dictionary app is just one of many Apps for Office that are available in Word. **Apps for Office** are small programs embedded in Word that allow you to access information on the Web without having to leave Word. For example, you can look up something on Wikipedia, insert an online map in one of your documents, or access dictionaries and other reference sources, all from within Word using an app. To install the free dictionary app from the Office Store for the first time, click the Define button In the Proofing group on the REVIEW tab, decide which dictionary you want, and then click the Download button associated with the dictionary you want in order to install that dictionary. After the dictionary is installed, it will open automatically in the Dictionary pane whenever you click Define. If you want to download other dictionaries or other apps, click the Apps for Office button in the Apps group on the INSERT tab, click More apps, find the app you want, and then click Add or Buy. Some apps are free, and some require purchase. Word allows you to choose one dictionary app for free. To use an app, click the Apps for Office button, click My Apps to see your list of apps, and then double-click the app you want to use.

Add Hyperlinks

**Learning
Outcomes**
• Insert a hyperlink
• Test hyperlinks
• E-mail a document
 from Word

A **hyperlink** is text or a graphic that, when clicked, "jumps" the viewer to a different location or program. When a document is viewed on screen, hyperlinks allow readers to link (or jump) to a Web page, an e-mail address, a file, or a specific location in a document. When you create a hyperlink in a document, you select the text or graphic you want to use as a hyperlink and then you specify the location you want to jump to when the hyperlink is clicked. You create a hyperlink using the Hyperlink button in the Links group on the INSERT tab. Text that is formatted as a hyperlink appears as colored, underlined text. **CASE** ▶ *Hundreds of people on your lists of press and client contacts will receive the press release by e-mail or Internet fax. To make it easier for these people to access additional information about the series, you add several hyperlinks to the press release.*

STEPS

QUICK TIP

By default, Word automatically creates a hyperlink to an e-mail address or URL when you type the address or URL in a document.

1. **Select your name, click the INSERT tab, then click the Hyperlink button in the Links group**

 The Insert Hyperlink dialog box opens, as shown in **FIGURE B-12**. You use this dialog box to specify the location you want to jump to when the hyperlink—in this case, your name—is clicked.

2. **Click E-mail Address in the Link to section**

 The Insert Hyperlink dialog box changes so you can create a hyperlink to your e-mail address.

3. **Type your e-mail address in the E-mail address text box, type Travel Lecture Series in the Subject text box, then click OK**

 As you type, Word automatically adds mailto: in front of your e-mail address. After you close the dialog box, the hyperlink text—your name—is formatted in blue and underlined.

QUICK TIP

To remove a hyperlink, right-click it, then click Remove Hyperlink. Removing a hyperlink removes the link, but the text remains.

4. **Press and hold [Ctrl], then click the your name hyperlink**

 An e-mail message addressed to you with the subject "Travel Lecture Series" opens in the default e-mail program. People can use this hyperlink to send you an e-mail message.

5. **Close the e-mail message window, clicking No if you are prompted to save**

 The hyperlink text changes to purple, indicating the hyperlink has been followed.

6. **Scroll down, select Gaslamp Quarter in the second paragraph, click the Hyperlink button, click Existing File or Web Page in the Link to section, type www.gaslamp.org in the Address text box, then click OK**

 As you type the Web address, Word automatically adds "http://" in front of "www." The text "Gaslamp Quarter" is formatted as a hyperlink to the Gaslamp Quarter Association home page at www.gaslamp.org. When clicked, the hyperlink will open the Web page in the default browser window.

7. **Select detailed schedule in the last sentence of the third paragraph, click the Hyperlink button, type www.questspecialtytravel.com in the Address text box, then click OK**

 The text "detailed schedule" is formatted as a hyperlink to the QST Web site. If you point to a hyperlink in Word, the link to location appears in a ScreenTip. You can edit ScreenTip text to make it more descriptive.

QUICK TIP

You can also edit the hyperlink destination or the hyperlink text.

8. **Right-click Quarter in the Gaslamp Quarter hyperlink, click Edit Hyperlink, click ScreenTip in the Edit Hyperlink dialog box, type Map, parking, and other information about the Gaslamp Quarter in the ScreenTip text box, click OK, click OK, save your changes, then point to the Gaslamp Quarter hyperlink in the document**

 The ScreenTip you created appears above the Gaslamp Quarter hyperlink, as shown in **FIGURE B-13**.

TROUBLE

If you are not working with an active Internet connection, skip this step.

9. **Press [Ctrl], click the Gaslamp Quarter hyperlink, click the Word icon 🔲 on the taskbar, press [Ctrl], click the detailed schedule hyperlink, verify the links opened in your browser, close the tabs, then click 🔲 to return to the press release**

 Before distributing a document, it's important to test each hyperlink to verify it works as you intended.

FIGURE B-12: Insert Hyperlink dialog box

Create a hyperlink to a Web page or file

Create a hyperlink to a location in the current file

Create a hyperlink to a new blank document

Create a hyperlink to an e-mail address

Text selected to be formatted as a hyperlink

Files in the current drive or folder (yours might differ)

FIGURE B-13: Hyperlinks in the document

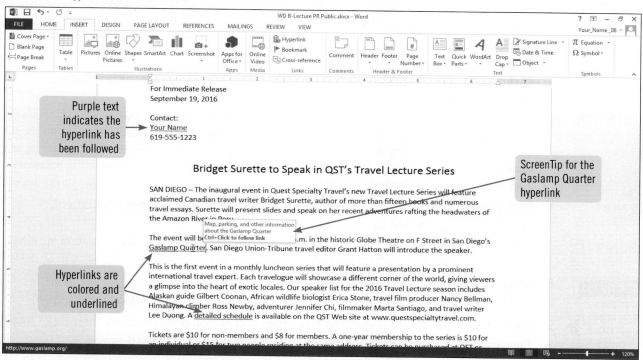

Purple text indicates the hyperlink has been followed

ScreenTip for the Gaslamp Quarter hyperlink

Hyperlinks are colored and underlined

Sharing documents directly from Word, including e-mailing and faxing

Word includes several options for distributing and sharing documents over the Internet directly from within Word, including saving a document to SkyDrive for others to view and edit, e-mailing a document, presenting a document online so others can view it in a Web browser, and posting a document to a blog. To share a document, open the file in Word, click the FILE tab, click Share, and then click one of the Share options. When you e-mail a document from within Word, the document is sent as an attachment to an e-mail message using your default e-mail program. You can choose to attach the document as a Word file, a .pdf file, or an .xps file, or to send it as an Internet fax. When you click an option, a message window opens that includes the filename of the current file as the message subject and the file as an attachment. Type the e-mail address(es) of the recipient(s) in the To and Cc text boxes, any message you want in the message window, and then click Send on the message window toolbar to send the message. The default e-mail program sends a copy of the document to each recipient. Note that faxing a document directly from Word requires registration with a third-party Internet fax service. Fax services generally charge a monthly or per page fee for sending and receiving faxes.

Work with Document Properties

Learning Outcomes
• Edit document properties
• Remove document properties
• Modify advanced document properties

Before you distribute a document electronically to people outside your organization, it's wise to make sure the file does not include embedded private or confidential information. The Info screen in Backstage view includes tools for stripping a document of sensitive information, for securing its authenticity, and for guarding it from unwanted changes once it is distributed to the public. One of these tools, the Document Inspector, detects and removes unwanted private or confidential information from a document. **CASE** ▸ *Before sending the press release to the public, you remove all identifying information from the file.*

STEPS

1. **Press [Ctrl][Home], then click the FILE tab**

 Backstage view opens with the Info screen displayed. The left side of the Info screen includes options related to stripping the file of private information. See **TABLE B-1**. The right side of the Info screen displays basic information about the document. Notice that the file contains document properties. You want to remove these before you distribute the press release to the public.

2. **Click the Properties button on the right side of the Info screen, then click Show Document Panel**

 The Document Properties panel opens above the document window, as shown in **FIGURE B-14**. It shows the standard document properties for the press release. **Document properties** are user-defined details about a file that describe its contents and origin, including the name of the author, the title of the document, and keywords that you can assign to help organize and search your files. You decide to remove this information from the file before you distribute it electronically.

3. **Click the FILE tab, click the Check for Issues button, then click Inspect Document, clicking Yes if prompted to save changes**

 The Document Inspector dialog box opens. You use this dialog box to indicate which private or identifying information you want to search for and remove from the document.

4. **Make sure all the check boxes are selected, then click Inspect**

 After a moment, the Document Inspector dialog box indicates the file contains document properties.

5. **Click Remove All next to Document Properties and Personal Information, then click Close**

 The standard document property information is removed from the press release document.

6. **Click the Properties button on the Info screen, then click Show Document Panel**

 The Document Properties panel opens and shows the document properties have been removed from the file.

7. **Click the Close button in the Document Properties panel, save the document, submit it to your instructor, close the file, then exit Word**

 The completed press release is shown in **FIGURE B-15**.

TABLE B-1: Options on the Info screen

option	use to
Protect Document	Mark a document as final so that it is read-only and cannot be edited; encrypt a document so that a password is required to open it; restrict what kinds of changes can be made to a document and by whom; and add a digital signature to a document to verify its integrity
Check for Issues	Detect and remove unwanted information from a document, including document properties and comments; check for content that people with disabilities might find difficult to read; and check the document for features that are not supported by previous versions of Microsoft Word
Manage versions	Browse and recover draft versions of unsaved files

© 2014 Cengage Learning

FIGURE B-14: Document Properties panel

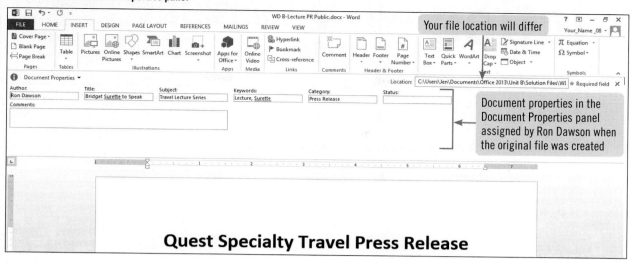

Quest Specialty Travel Press Release

FIGURE B-15: Completed press release for electronic distribution

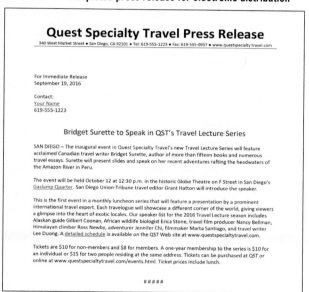

Viewing and modifying advanced document properties

The Document Properties panel includes summary information about the document that you enter to suit your needs. To view more detailed document properties, including those entered automatically by Word when the document is created, click the Document Properties button in the Document Properties panel, and then click Advanced Properties to open the Properties dialog box. You can also click the Properties button on the Info screen and then click Advanced Properties to open the Properties dialog box. The General, Statistics, and Contents tabs of the Properties dialog box display information about the file that is automatically created and updated by Word. The General tab shows the file type, location, size, and date and time the file was created and last modified; the Statistics tab displays information about revisions to the document along with the number of pages, words, lines, paragraphs, and characters in the file; and the Contents tab shows the title of the document.

You can define other document properties using the Properties dialog box Summary and Custom tabs. The Summary tab shows information similar to the information shown in the Document Properties panel. The Custom tab allows you to create new document properties, such as client, project, or date completed. To create a custom property, select a property name in the Name list box on the Custom tab, use the Type list arrow to select the type of data you want for the property, type the identifying detail (such as a project name) in the Value text box, and then click Add. When you are finished viewing or modifying the document properties, click OK to close the Properties dialog box, then click the Close button on the Document Properties panel.

Word 2013

Practice

Put your skills into practice with **SAM Projects!** SAM Projects for this unit can be found online. If you have a SAM account, go to www.cengage.com/sam2013 to download the most recent Project Instruction and Start Files.

Concepts Review

Label the elements of the Word program window shown in FIGURE B-16.

FIGURE B-16

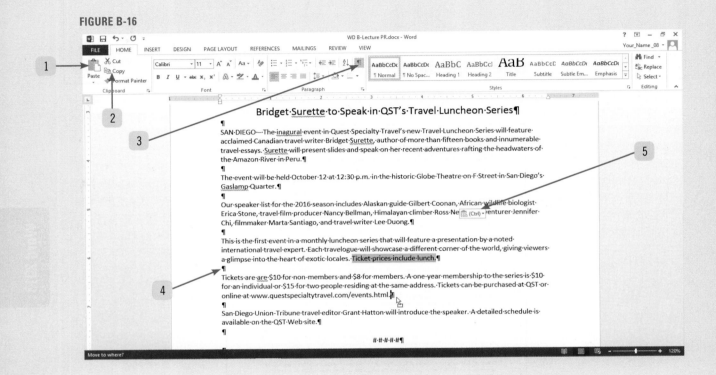

Match each term with the statement that best describes it.

6. System clipboard
7. Cut
8. Shortcut key
9. Document properties
10. Thesaurus
11. App for Office
12. Paste
13. Office Clipboard
14. Hyperlink

a. Command used to insert text stored on the Clipboard into a document

b. Temporary storage area for up to 24 items collected from Office files

c. Temporary storage area for only the last item cut or copied from a document

d. A function key or a combination of keys that perform a command when pressed

e. Text or a graphic that jumps the reader to a different location or program when clicked

f. A program that accesses information on the Web from within Word

g. User-defined details about a file that describe its contents and origin

h. Feature used to suggest synonyms for words

i. Command used to remove text from a document and place it on the Clipboard

Select the best answer from the list of choices.

15. What is the keyboard shortcut for the Paste command?

 a. [Ctrl][V]

 b. [Ctrl][C]

 c. [Ctrl][P]

 d. [Ctrl][X]

16. Which command is used to display a document in two panes in the document window?

 a. New Window

 b. Split

 c. Two Pages

 d. Arrange All

17. Which of the following statements is *not* true?

 a. The last item cut or copied from a document is stored on the system clipboard.

 b. You can view the contents of the Office Clipboard.

 c. When you move text by dragging it, a copy of the text you move is stored on the system clipboard.

 d. The Office Clipboard can hold more than one item.

18. To locate and select all instances of a word in a document, which command do you use?

 a. Find

 b. Search

 c. Highlight

 d. Show/Hide

19. Which of the following is an example of a document property?

 a. Language

 b. Permission

 c. Keyword

 d. URL

20. A hyperlink *cannot* be linked to which of the following?

 a. E-mail address

 b. Document

 c. Web page

 d. ScreenTip

Skills Review

1. Cut and paste text.

 a. Start Word, click the Open Other Documents link, open the file WD B-2.docx from the location where you store your Data File, then save the document with the filename **WD B-PAOS 2016 PR**.

 b. Select **Your Name** and replace it with your name.

 c. Display paragraph and other formatting marks in your document if they are not already displayed.

 d. Use the Cut and Paste buttons to switch the order of the two sentences in the fourth body paragraph (which begins New group shows...).

 e. Use the drag-and-drop method to switch the order of the second and third paragraphs.

 f. Adjust the spacing if necessary so that there is one blank line between paragraphs, then save your changes.

2. Copy and paste text.

 a. Use the Copy and Paste buttons to copy **PAOS 2013** from the headline and paste it before the word **map** in the third paragraph.

 b. Change the formatting of the pasted text to match the formatting of the third paragraph, then insert a space between **2013** and **map** if necessary.

 c. Use the drag-and-drop method to copy **PAOS** from the third paragraph and paste it before the word **group** in the second sentence of the fourth paragraph, then save your changes.

3. Use the Office Clipboard.

 a. Use the launcher in the Clipboard group to open the Clipboard pane.

 b. Scroll so that the first body paragraph is displayed at the top of the document window.

 c. Select the fifth paragraph (which begins Studio location maps...) and cut it to the Clipboard.

 d. Select the third paragraph (which begins Portsmouth is easily accessible...) and cut it to the Clipboard.

 e. Use the Clipboard to paste the Studio location maps... item as the new fourth paragraph.

 f. Use the Clipboard to paste the Portsmouth is easily accessible... item as the new fifth paragraph.

 g. Adjust the spacing if necessary so there is one blank line between each of the six body paragraphs.

 h. Turn off the display of formatting marks, clear and close the Clipboard pane, then save your changes.

Skills Review (continued)

4. Find and replace text.

 a. Using the Replace command, replace all instances of **2013** with **2016**.

 b. Replace all instances of **tenth** with **twelfth**.

 c. Replace all instances of the abbreviation **st** with **street**, taking care to replace whole words only when you perform the replace. (*Hint*: Deselect Match case if it is selected.)

 d. Click the Find tab, deselect the Find whole words only check box, click the Reading Highlight button, click Highlight All, close the dialog box, then view all instances of **st** in the document to make sure no errors occurred when you replaced st with street.

 e. Click the Find button to open the Navigation pane, notice the results and the highlighted text, close the Navigation pane, then save your changes to the press release. (*Note: You can see the highlighted results using either the Reading Highlight button in the Find and Replace dialog box or the Navigation pane.*)

5. Check spelling and grammar and research information.

 a. Switch to the REVIEW tab.

 b. Move the insertion point to the top of the document, then use the Spelling & Grammar command to search for and correct any spelling and grammar errors in the press release. (*Hint*: Riverwalk is not misspelled.)

 c. Use the Thesaurus to replace **thriving** in the second paragraph with a different suitable word, then close the Thesaurus pane.

 d. Check the word count of the press release.

 e. Proofread your press release, correct any errors, then save your changes.

6. Add hyperlinks.

 a. Save the document as **WD B-PAOS 2016 PR Public**, then switch to the INSERT tab.

 b. Select your name, then open the Insert Hyperlink dialog box.

 c. Create a hyperlink to your e-mail address with the subject **PAOS 2016**.

 d. Test the your name hyperlink, then close the message window that opens and click No if a message window opens. (*Hint*: Press [Ctrl], then click the hyperlink.)

 e. Select **NEA** in the last paragraph of the press release, then create a hyperlink to the Web page with the URL **www.nea.gov**.

 f. Right-click the NEA hyperlink, then edit the hyperlink ScreenTip to become **Information on the National Endowment for the Arts**.

 g. Point to the NEA hyperlink to view the new ScreenTip, then save your changes.

 h. If you are working with an active Internet connection, press [Ctrl], click the NEA hyperlink, view the NEA home page in the browser window, then close the browser window and return to Word. The finished press release is shown in **FIGURE B-17**.

FIGURE B-17

PRESS RELEASE

FOR IMMEDIATE RELEASE
September 7, 2016

Contact:
Your Name
910-555-2938

PAOS 2016
Portsmouth Artists Open Their Studios to the Public

PORTSMOUTH, NH -- The fall 2016 Open Studios season kicks off with Portsmouth Artists Open Studios on Saturday and Sunday, October 13 and 14, from 11 a.m. to 6 p.m. More than 60 Portsmouth artists will open their studios and homes to the public for this annual event, now in its twelfth year.

Portsmouth is a historic and diverse city, long home to a flourishing community of artists. Quiet residential streets lined with charming Victorians edge a vibrant commercial and industrial zone, all peppered with the studios of printmakers, sculptors, painters, glass and jewelry makers, illustrators, potters, photographers, watercolorists, and other artists working in a wide range of mediums.

Internationally celebrated sculptor Eva Russo will display her new work in the rotunda of City Hall. New PAOS group shows will open at the Atlantic Gallery and at the Mermaid Café, both on Market Street.

Studio location maps will be available prior to the opening at businesses and public libraries, and on the days of the event at the Riverwalk. Riverwalk is located at the junction of Market Street and Dock Street in downtown Portsmouth.

Portsmouth is easily accessible from all points in New England by car or bus, and from other cities by air. On Saturday, non-Portsmouth residents may park in permit-only areas provided they display a copy of the PAOS 2016 map on the dashboard. There is no parking restrictions on Sundays in Portsmouth.

PAOS 2016 receives funds from participating artists and from the Portsmouth Arts Council, the North Hampshire Cultural Council, and the NEA, with valuable support from local universities and businesses.

#####

Skills Review (continued)

7. Work with document properties.

a. Click the FILE tab, click the Properties button on the Info screen, then open the Document Properties panel to view the document properties for the press release.

b. Click the FILE tab to return to Backstage view with the Info screen displayed, then use the Check for Issues command to run the Document Inspector.

c. Remove the document property and personal information data, close the Document Inspector, return to the HOME tab, close the Document Properties panel, then save your changes.

d. Save the document, submit it to your instructor, close the file, then exit Word.

Independent Challenge 1

Because of your success in revitalizing a historic theatre in Christchurch, New Zealand, you were hired as the director of The Brisbane Town Hall Theatre in Brisbane, Australia, to breathe life into its theatre revitalization efforts. After a year on the job, you are launching your first major fund-raising drive. You'll create a fund-raising letter for the Town Hall Theatre by modifying a letter you wrote for the Lyric Theatre in Christchurch.

a. Start Word, open the file WD B-3.docx from the location where you store your Data Files, then save it as **WD B-Theatre Fundraising Letter**.

b. Replace the theatre name and address, the date, the inside address, and the salutation with the text shown in FIGURE B-18.

FIGURE B-18

c. Use the Replace command to replace all instances of **Christchurch** with **Brisbane**.

d. Use the Replace command to replace all instances of **Lyric** with **Town Hall**.

The Brisbane Town Hall Theatre
738 Petrie Terrace, Brisbane QLD 4000, Australia

April 14, 2016

Ms. Ainslie Richard
46-12 Jacaranda St.
Brisbane QLD 4013

Dear Ms. Richard:

e. Use the Replace command to replace all instances of **New Zealanders** with **Australians**.

f. Use the Find command to locate the word **considerable**, then use the Thesaurus to replace the word with a synonym.

g. Move the fourth body paragraph so that it becomes the second body paragraph.

h. Create an AutoCorrect entry that inserts **Executive Director** whenever you type **exd**.

i. Replace Your Name with your name in the signature block, select Title, then type **exd** followed by a space.

j. Use the Spelling and Grammar command to check for and correct spelling and grammar errors.

k. Delete the AutoCorrect entry you created for exd. (*Hint*: Open the AutoCorrect dialog box, select the AutoCorrect entry you created, then click [Delete].)

l. Open the Document Properties panel, add your name as the author, change the title to **Brisbane Town Hall Theatre**, add the keyword **fund-raising**, then add the comment **Letter for the capital campaign**.

m. Open the Properties dialog box, review the properties on the Summary tab, then review the paragraph, line, word, and character count on the Statistics tab.

n. On the Custom tab, add a property named **Project** with the value **Capital Campaign**, then close the dialog box and the Document Properties panel.

o. Proofread the letter, correct any errors, save your changes, submit a copy to your instructor, close the document, then exit Word.

Independent Challenge 2

An advertisement for job openings in Chicago caught your eye and you have decided to apply. The ad, shown in FIGURE B-19, was printed in last weekend's edition of your local newspaper. Instead of writing a cover letter from scratch, you revise a draft of a cover letter you wrote several years ago for a summer internship position.

FIGURE B-19

World Data Designs

Career Opportunities in Chicago

World Data Designs, an established software development firm with offices in North America, Asia, and Europe, is seeking candidates for the following positions in its Chicago facility:

Instructor
Responsible for delivering software training to our expanding Midwestern customer base. Duties include delivering hands-on training, keeping up-to-date with product development, and working with the Director of Training to ensure the high quality of course materials. Successful candidate will have excellent presentation skills and be proficient in Microsoft PowerPoint and Microsoft Word. Position B12C6

Administrative Assistant
Proficiency with Microsoft Word a must! Administrative office duties include making travel arrangements, scheduling meetings, taking notes and publishing meeting minutes, handling correspondence, and ordering office supplies. Must have superb multitasking abilities, excellent communication, organizational, and interpersonal skills, and be comfortable working with e-mail and the Internet. Position B16F5

Copywriter
The ideal candidate will have marketing or advertising writing experience in a high tech environment, including collateral, newsletters, and direct mail. Experience writing for the Web, broadcast, and multimedia is a plus. Fluency with Microsoft Word required. Position C13D4

Positions offer salary, excellent benefits, and career opportunities.

Send resume and cover letter referencing position code to:

Meredith Lackey
Director of Recruiting
World Data Designs
600 North Michigan Ave.
Chicago, IL 60610

a. Read the ad shown in FIGURE B-19 and decide which position to apply for. Choose the position that most closely matches your qualifications.

b. Start Word, open WD B-4.docx from the location where you store your Data Files, then save it as **WD B-Cover Letter**.

c. Replace the name, address, telephone number, and e-mail address in the letterhead with your own information.

d. Remove the hyperlink from the e-mail address.

e. Replace the date with today's date, then replace the inside address and the salutation with the information shown in FIGURE B-19.

f. Read the draft cover letter to get a feel for its contents.

g. Rework the text in the body of the letter to address your qualifications for the job you have chosen to apply for in the following ways:

- Delete the third paragraph.
- Adjust the first sentence of the first paragraph as follows: specify the job you are applying for, including the position code, and indicate where you saw the position advertised.
- Move the first sentence in the last paragraph, which briefly states your qualifications and interest in the position, to the end of the first paragraph, then rework the sentence to describe your current qualifications.
- Adjust the second paragraph as follows: describe your work experience and skills. Be sure to relate your experience and qualifications to the position requirements listed in the advertisement. Add a third paragraph if your qualifications are extensive.
- Adjust the final paragraph as follows: politely request an interview for the position and provide your phone number and e-mail address.

h. Include your name in the signature block.

i. When you are finished revising the letter, check it for spelling and grammar errors, and correct any mistakes. Make sure to remove any hyperlinks.

j. Save your changes to the letter, submit the file to your instructor, close the document, then exit Word.

Independent Challenge 3

As administrative director of continuing education, you drafted a memo to instructors asking them to help you finalize the course schedule for next semester. Today, you'll examine the draft and make revisions before distributing it as an e-mail attachment.

a. Start Word, open the file WD B-5.docx from the drive and folder where you store your Data Files, then save it as **WD B-Business Courses Memo**.

Independent Challenge 3 (continued)

b. Replace Your Name with your name in the From line, then scroll until the first body paragraph is at the top of the screen.

c. Use the Split command on the VIEW tab to split the window under the first body paragraph, then scroll until the last paragraph of the memo is displayed in the bottom pane.

d. Use the Cut and Paste buttons to move the sentence **If you are planning to teach...** from the first body paragraph to become the first sentence in the last paragraph of the memo.

e. Double-click the split bar to restore the window to a single pane.

f. Use the [Delete] key to merge the first two paragraphs into one paragraph.

g. Use the Clipboard to reorganize the list of twelve-week courses so that the courses are listed in alphabetical order, then clear and close the Clipboard.

h. Use the drag-and-drop method to reorganize the list of one-day seminars so that the seminars are listed in alphabetical order.

i. Select the phrase "Web site" in the first paragraph, then create a hyperlink to the URL **www.course.com** with the ScreenTip **Spring 2017 Business Courses**.

j. Select "e-mail me" in the last paragraph, then create a hyperlink to your e-mail address with the subject **Final Business Course Schedule**.

k. Use the Spelling and Grammar command to check for and correct spelling and grammar errors.

l. Use the Document Inspector to strip the document of document property information, ignore any other content that is flagged by the Document Inspector, then close the Document Inspector.

m. Proofread the memo, correct any errors, save your changes, submit a copy to your instructor, close the document, then exit Word.

Independent Challenge 4: Explore

Reference sources—dictionaries, thesauri, style and grammar guides, and guides to business etiquette and procedure—are essential for day-to-day use in the workplace. Much of this reference information is available on the World Wide Web. In this independent challenge, you will locate reference sources that might be useful to you, including the Apps for Office resource that is available for Word 2013. Your goal is to familiarize yourself with online reference sources and Apps for Word so you can use them later in your work. You will insert a screenshot of the Apps for Word 2013 Web page in your document.

a. Start Word, open the file WD B-6.docx from the location where you store your Data Files, then save it as **WD B-References**. This document contains the questions you will answer about the Web reference sources you find and Apps for Office. You will type your answers to the questions in the document.

b. Replace the placeholder text at the top of the WD B-References document with your name and the date.

c. Use your favorite search engine to search the Web for grammar and style guides, dictionaries, and thesauri. Use the keywords **grammar**, **usage**, **dictionary**, **glossary**, or **thesaurus** to conduct your search.

d. Complete question 1 of the WD B-References document, making sure to format the Web site names as hyperlinks to the Web sites.

e. Read question 2 of the WD B-References document, then move the insertion point under question 2.

f. Click the Apps for Office button in the Apps group on the INSERT tab, then click More apps in the Apps for Office window that opens. (*Note: You may see Office Store instead of More apps.*) Explore the apps available on the Apps for Word 2013 Web page that opens in your browser.

g. Switch to the WD B-References document in Word. Close the Apps for Office window if it is still open.

h. With the insertion point below question 2, click the Screenshot button in the Illustrations group on the INSERT tab. The Available Windows gallery opens.

i. Read the ScreenTip for each thumbnail in the gallery, find the Apps for Word - Office.com window thumbnail in the gallery, click it, then click Yes in the dialog box that opens. A screenshot of the Apps for Word 2013 is inserted in the WD B-References document.

j. Save the document, submit a copy to your instructor, close the document, then exit Word.

Visual Workshop

Open WD B-7.docx from the drive and folder where you store your Data Files, then save the document as **WD B-Visa Letter**. Replace the placeholders for the date, letterhead, inside address, salutation, and closing with the information shown in FIGURE B-20, then use the Office Clipboard to reorganize the sentences to match FIGURE B-20. Correct spelling and grammar errors, remove the document property information from the file, then submit a copy to your instructor.

FIGURE B-20

Your Name
4637 East 12th Street, Apt. 6, New York, NY 20211; Tel: 212-555-2840

1/3/2016

Embassy of Japan
2520 Massachusetts Avenue NW
Washington, DC 20008

Dear Sir or Madam:

I am applying for a long-stay tourist visa to Japan, valid for four years. I am scheduled to depart for Tokyo on March 13, 2016, returning to Chicago on September 8, 2016.

During my stay in Japan, I will be interviewing musicians and recording footage for a film I am making on contemporary Japanese music. I would like a multiple entry visa valid for four years so I can return to Japan after this trip to follow up on my initial research. I will be based in Tokyo, but I will be traveling frequently to record performances and to meet with musicians and producers.

Included with this letter are my completed visa application form, my passport, a passport photo, a copy of my return air ticket, and the visa fee. Please contact me if you need further information.

Sincerely,

Your Name

Enc: 5

Formatting Text and Paragraphs

CASE You have finished drafting the text for a two-page flyer advertising last minute specials for October tours. Now, you need to format the flyer so it is attractive and highlights the significant information.

Unit Objectives

After completing this unit, you will be able to:

- Format with fonts
- Use the Format Painter
- Change line and paragraph spacing
- Align paragraphs
- Work with tabs

- Work with indents
- Add bullets and numbering
- Add borders and shading
- Insert online pictures

Files You Will Need

WD C-1.docx WD C-4.docx

WD C-2.docx WD C-5.docx

WD C-3.docx WD C-6.docx

©Tumanyan/Shutterstock

Format with Fonts

Learning Outcomes
- Change font and font size
- Change font color
- Select an entire document

Formatting text with fonts is a quick and powerful way to enhance the appearance of a document. A **font** is a complete set of characters with the same typeface or design. Arial, Times New Roman, Courier, Tahoma, and Calibri are some of the more common fonts, but there are hundreds of others, each with a specific design and feel. Another way to change the appearance of text is to increase or decrease its **font size**. Font size is measured in points. A **point** is 1/72 of an inch. **CASE** ▶ *You change the font and font size of the body text, title, and headings in the flyer. You select fonts and font sizes that enhance the sales tone of the document and help to structure the flyer visually for readers.*

STEPS

1. **Start Word, open the file WD C-1.docx from the location where you store your Data Files, save it as WD C-Last Minute Deals, then change the zoom level to 120%**
 Notice that the name of the font used in the document, Calibri, is displayed in the Font list box in the Font group. The word "(Body)" in the Font list box indicates Calibri is the font used for body text in the current theme, the default theme. A **theme** is a related set of fonts, colors, styles, and effects that is applied to an entire document to give it a cohesive appearance. The font size, 11, appears in the Font Size list box in the Font group.

 QUICK TIP
 There are two types of fonts: serif fonts have a small stroke, called a serif, at the ends of characters; sans serif fonts do not have a serif. Garamond is a serif font. Trebuchet MS is a sans serif font.

2. **Scroll the document to get a feel for its contents, press [Ctrl][Home], press [Ctrl][A] to select the entire document, then click the Font list arrow in the Font group**
 The Font list, which shows the fonts available on your computer, opens as shown in **FIGURE C-1**. The font names are formatted in the font. Font names can appear in more than one location on the Font list.

3. **Drag the pointer slowly down the font names in the Font list, drag the scroll box to scroll down the Font list, then click Garamond**
 As you drag the pointer over a font name, a preview of the font is applied to the selected text. Clicking a font name applies the font. The font of the flyer changes to Garamond.

 QUICK TIP
 You can also type a font size in the Font Size text box.

4. **Click the Font Size list arrow in the Font group, drag the pointer slowly up and down the Font Size list, then click 12**
 As you drag the pointer over a font size, a preview of the font size is applied to the selected text. Clicking 12 increases the font size of the selected text to 12 points.

 QUICK TIP
 To use a different set of theme colors, click the DESIGN tab, click the Colors button in the Document Formatting group, then select a different color set.

5. **Select the title Quest Specialty Travel Last Minute Travel Deals, click the Font list arrow, scroll to and click Trebuchet MS, click the Font Size list arrow, click 22, then click the Bold button B in the Font group**
 The title is formatted in 22-point Trebuchet MS bold.

6. **Click the Font Color list arrow A in the Font group**
 A gallery of colors opens. It includes the set of theme colors in a range of tints and shades as well as a set of standard colors. You can point to a color in the gallery to preview it applied to the selected text.

7. **Click the Green, Accent 6 color as shown in FIGURE C-2, then deselect the text**
 The color of the title text changes to green. The active color on the Font Color button also changes to green.

 TROUBLE
 If the mini toolbar closes, select the text again.

8. **Scroll down, select the heading Rajasthan Desert Safari, then, using the Mini toolbar, click the Font list arrow, click Trebuchet MS, click the Font Size list arrow, click 14, click B, click A, then deselect the text**
 The heading is formatted in 14-point Trebuchet MS bold with a green color.

9. **Press [Ctrl][Home], then click the Save button on the Quick Access toolbar**
 Compare your document to **FIGURE C-3**.

FIGURE C-1: Font list

FIGURE C-1: **Font list**

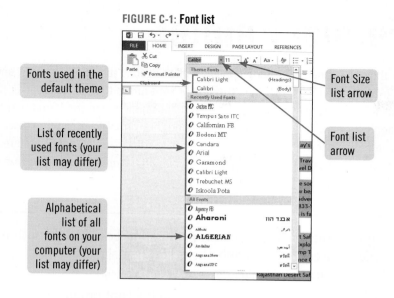

Fonts used in the default theme

List of recently used fonts (your list may differ)

Font Size list arrow

Font list arrow

Alphabetical list of all fonts on your computer (your list may differ)

FIGURE C-2: **Font Color Palette**

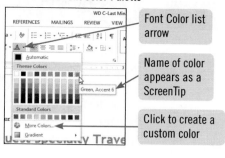

Font Color list arrow

Name of color appears as a ScreenTip

Click to create a custom color

FIGURE C-3: **Document formatted with fonts**

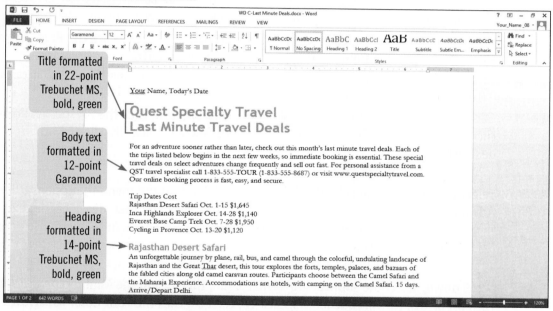

Title formatted in 22-point Trebuchet MS, bold, green

Body text formatted in 12-point Garamond

Heading formatted in 14-point Trebuchet MS, bold, green

Adding a drop cap

A fun way to illustrate a document with fonts is to add a drop cap to a paragraph. A **drop cap** is a large initial capital letter, often used to set off the first paragraph of an article. To create a drop cap, place the insertion point in the paragraph you want to format, click the INSERT tab, and then click the Drop Cap button in the Text group to open a menu of Drop cap options. Preview and select one of the options on the menu, or click Drop Cap Options to open the Drop Cap dialog box, shown in **FIGURE C-4**. In the Drop Cap dialog box, select the position, font, number of lines to drop, and the distance you want the drop cap to be from the paragraph text, and then click OK. The drop cap is added to the paragraph as a graphic object.

Once a drop cap is inserted in a paragraph, you can modify it by selecting it and then changing the settings in the Drop Cap dialog box. For even more interesting effects, you can enhance a drop cap with font color, font styles, or font effects. You can also fill the graphic object with shading or add a border around it. To enhance a drop cap, first select it, and then experiment with the formatting options available in the Font dialog box and in the Borders and Shading dialog box.

FIGURE C-4: **Drop Cap dialog box**

Use the Format Painter

You can dramatically change the appearance of text by applying different font styles, font effects, and character-spacing effects. For example, you can use the buttons in the Font group to make text darker by applying **bold** or to make text slanted by applying *italic*. When you are satisfied with the formatting of certain text, you can quickly apply the same formats to other text using the Format Painter. The **Format Painter** is a powerful Word feature that allows you to copy all the format settings applied to selected text to other text that you want to format the same way. **CASE** ▶ *You spice up the appearance of the text in the document by applying different font styles and text effects.*

STEPS

1. **Select immediate booking is essential in the first body paragraph, click the Bold button B on the Mini toolbar, select the entire paragraph, then click the Italic button I**
 The phrase "immediate booking is essential" is bold, and the entire paragraph is italic.

2. **Select Last Minute Travel Deals, then click the launcher ⌐ in the Font group**
 The Font dialog box opens, as shown in FIGURE C-5. You can use the options on the Font tab to change the font, font style, size, and color of text, and to add an underline and apply font effects to text.

3. **Scroll down the Size list, click 48, click the Font color list arrow, click the Blue, Accent 5 color in the Theme Colors, then click the Text Effects button**
 The Format Text Effects dialog box opens with the Text Fill & Outline options displayed. You can also use this dialog box to apply text effects, such as shadow, reflection, and 3-D effects to selected text.

4. **Click the Text Effects icon in the dialog box, click Shadow, click the Presets list arrow, click Offset Diagonal Bottom Right in the Outer section, click OK, click OK, then deselect the text**
 The text is larger, blue, and has a shadow effect.

5. **Select Last Minute Travel Deals, right-click, click Font on the menu that opens, click the Advanced tab, click the Scale list arrow, click 80%, click OK, then deselect the text**
 You use the Advanced tab in the Font dialog box to change the scale, or width, of the selected characters, to alter the spacing between characters, or to raise or lower the characters. Decreasing the scale of the characters makes them narrower and gives the text a tall, thin appearance, as shown in FIGURE C-6.

6. **Scroll down, select the subheading Camel Safari, then, using the Mini toolbar, click the Font list arrow, click Trebuchet MS, click B, click I, click the Font Color list arrow A ▾, click the Blue, Accent 5 color in the Theme Colors, then deselect the text**
 The subheading is formatted in Trebuchet MS, bold, italic, and blue.

7. **Select Camel Safari, then click the Format Painter button in the Clipboard group**
 The pointer changes to 🖌I.

8. **Scroll down, select Maharaja Experience with the 🖌I pointer, then deselect the text**
 The subheading is formatted in Trebuchet MS, bold, italic, and blue, as shown in FIGURE C-7.

9. **Scroll up, select Rajasthan Desert Safari, then double-click the Format Painter button**
 Double-clicking the Format Painter button allows the Format Painter to remain active until you turn it off. By keeping the Format Painter active, you can apply formatting to multiple items.

10. **Scroll down, select the headings Inca Highlands Explorer, Everest Base Camp Trek, and Cycling in Provence with the pointer, click the Format Painter button to turn off the Format Painter, then save your changes**
 The headings are formatted in 14-point Trebuchet MS bold with a green font color.

FIGURE C-5: Font tab in Font dialog box

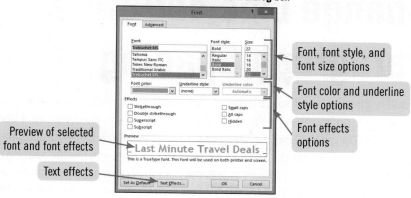

Font, font style, and font size options

Font color and underline style options

Font effects options

Preview of selected font and font effects

Text effects

FIGURE C-6: Font and character spacing effects applied to text

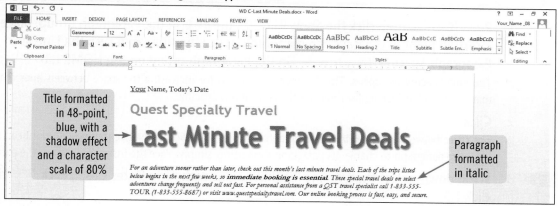

Title formatted in 48-point, blue, with a shadow effect and a character scale of 80%

Paragraph formatted in italic

FIGURE C-7: Formats copied and applied using the Format Painter

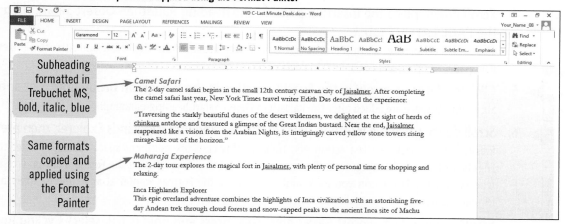

Subheading formatted in Trebuchet MS, bold, italic, blue

Same formats copied and applied using the Format Painter

Underlining text

Another creative way to call attention to text and to jazz up the appearance of a document is to apply an underline style to words you want to highlight. The Underline list arrow in the Font group displays straight, dotted, wavy, dashed, and mixed underline styles, along with a gallery of colors to choose from. To apply an underline to text, simply select it, click the Underline list arrow, and then select an underline style from the list. For a wider variety of underline styles, click More Underlines in the list, and then select an underline style in the Font dialog box. You can change the color of an underline at any time by selecting the underlined text, clicking the Underline list arrow, pointing to Underline Color, and then choosing from the options in the color gallery. If you want to remove an underline from text, select the underlined text, and then click the Underline button.

Learning Outcomes
- Add spacing under paragraphs
- Change line spacing in paragraphs
- Apply styles to text

Change Line and Paragraph Spacing

Increasing the amount of space between lines adds more white space to a document and can make it easier to read. Adding space before and after paragraphs can also open up a document and improve its appearance. You use the Line and Paragraph Spacing list arrow in the Paragraph group on the HOME tab to quickly change line spacing. To change paragraph spacing, you use the Spacing options in the Paragraph group on the PAGE LAYOUT tab. Both line and paragraph spacing are measured in points. **CASE** *You increase the line spacing of several paragraphs and add extra space under each heading to give the flyer a more open feel. You work with formatting marks turned on, so you can see the paragraph marks (¶).*

STEPS

1. **Press [Ctrl][Home], click the Show/Hide ¶ button ¶ in the Paragraph group, place the insertion point in the italicized paragraph under the title, then click the Line and Paragraph Spacing list arrow ⌐ in the Paragraph group on the HOME tab**

 The Line Spacing list opens. This list includes options for increasing the space between lines. The check mark on the Line Spacing list indicates the current line spacing.

2. **Click 1.15**

 The space between the lines in the paragraph increases to 1.15 lines. Notice that you do not need to select an entire paragraph to change its paragraph formatting; simply place the insertion point in the paragraph.

 QUICK TIP
 Word recognizes any string of text that ends with a paragraph mark as a paragraph, including titles, headings, and single lines in a list.

3. **Scroll down, select the five-line list that begins with "Trip Dates Cost", click ⌐, then click 1.5**

 The line spacing between the selected paragraphs changes to 1.5. To change the paragraph-formatting features of more than one paragraph, you must select the paragraphs.

4. **Scroll down, place the insertion point in the heading Rajasthan Desert Safari, then click the PAGE LAYOUT tab**

 The paragraph spacing settings for the active paragraph are shown in the Before and After text boxes in the Paragraph group on the PAGE LAYOUT tab.

 QUICK TIP
 You can also type a number in the Before and After text boxes.

5. **Click the After up arrow in the Spacing section in the Paragraph group until 6 pt appears**

 Six points of space are added after the Rajasthan Desert Safari heading paragraph.

 TROUBLE
 If your [F4] key does not work, use the After up arrow to apply 6 pts of space to the headings listed in Steps 6 and 7, then continue with Step 8.

6. **Scroll down, place the insertion point in the heading Inca Highlands Explorer, then press [F4]**

 Pressing [F4] repeats the last action you took. In this case, six points of space are added after the Inca Highlands Explorer heading. Note that using [F4] is not the same as using the Format Painter. Pressing [F4] repeats only the last action you took, and you can use the Format Painter at any time to apply multiple format settings.

7. **Scroll down, select Everest Base Camp Trek, press and hold [Ctrl], select Cycling in Provence, release [Ctrl], then press [F4]**

 When you press [Ctrl] as you select items, you can select and format multiple items at once. Six points of space are added after each heading.

 QUICK TIP
 Adjusting the space between paragraphs is a more precise way to add white space to a document than inserting blank lines.

8. **Press [Ctrl][Home], place the insertion point in Last Minute Travel Deals, then click the Before up arrow in the Spacing section in the Paragraph group twice so that 12 pt appears**

 The second line of the title has 12 points of space before it, as shown in FIGURE C-8.

9. **Click the HOME tab, click ¶, then save your changes**

FIGURE C-8: Line and paragraph spacing applied to document

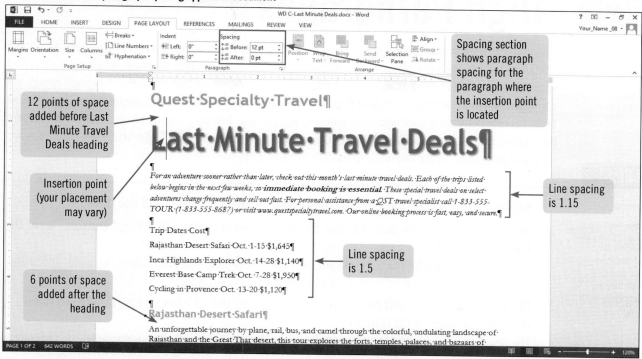

Spacing section shows paragraph spacing for the paragraph where the insertion point is located

12 points of space added before Last Minute Travel Deals heading

Insertion point (your placement may vary)

6 points of space added after the heading

Line spacing is 1.15

Line spacing is 1.5

Formatting with Quick Styles

You can also apply multiple format settings to text in one step by applying a style. A **style** is a set of formats, such as font, font size, and paragraph alignment, that is named and stored together. Formatting a document with styles is a quick and easy way to give it a professional appearance. To make it even easier, Word includes sets of styles, called **Quick Styles**, that are designed to be used together in a document to make it attractive and readable. A Quick Style set includes styles for a title, several heading levels, body text, quotes, and lists. The styles in a Quick Style set use common fonts, colors, and formats so that using the styles together in a document gives the document a cohesive look.

To view the active set of Quick Styles, click the More button ⟱ in the Styles group on the HOME tab to expand the Quick Styles gallery, shown in **FIGURE C-9**. As you move the pointer over each style in the gallery, a preview of the style is applied to the selected text. To apply a style to the selected text, you simply click the style in the Quick Styles gallery. To remove a style from

FIGURE C-9: Quick Styles gallery

AaBbCcDc	AaBbCcDc	AaBbC	AaBbCcl	AaB	AaBbCcD	AaBbCcDc	AaBbCcDc
¶ Normal	No Spacing	Heading 1	Heading 2	Title	Subtitle	Subtle Em…	Emphasis
AaBbCcDc	**AaBbCcDc**	AaBbCcDc	AaBbCcDc	AABBCCDC	AABBCCDC	**AaBbCcDc**	AaBbCcDc
Intense E…	Strong	Quote	Intense Q…	Subtle Ref…	Intense R…	Book Title	¶ List Para…

Create a **S**tyle
Clear Formatting
Apply Styles…

selected text, you click the Clear All Formatting button ⟐ in the Font group or the Clear Formatting command in the Quick Styles gallery.

If you want to change the active set of Quick Styles to a Quick Style set with a different design, click the DESIGN tab, click the More button ⟱ in the Document Formatting group, and then select the Quick Style set that best suits your document's content, tone, and audience. When you change the Quick Style set, a complete set of new fonts and colors is applied to the entire document. You can also change the color scheme or font used in the active Quick Style set by clicking the Colors or Fonts buttons, and then selecting from the available color schemes or font options.

Align Paragraphs

Changing paragraph alignment is another way to enhance a document's appearance. Paragraphs are aligned relative to the left and right margins in a document. By default, text is **left-aligned**, which means it is flush with the left margin and has a ragged right edge. Using the alignment buttons in the Paragraph group, you can **right-align** a paragraph—make it flush with the right margin—or **center** a paragraph so that it is positioned evenly between the left and right margins. You can also **justify** a paragraph so that both the left and right edges of the paragraph are flush with the left and right margins. **CASE** ▶ *You change the alignment of several paragraphs at the beginning of the flyer to make it more visually interesting.*

STEPS

1. **Replace** Your Name, Today's Date **with your name, a comma, and the date**

2. **Select your name, the comma, and the date, then click the** Align Right button ≡ **in the Paragraph group**

 The text is aligned with the right margin. In Page Layout view, the place where the white and shaded sections on the horizontal ruler meet shows the left and right margins.

3. **Place the insertion point between your name and the comma, press** [Delete] **to delete the comma, then press** [Enter]

 The new paragraph containing the date is also right-aligned. Pressing [Enter] in the middle of a paragraph creates a new paragraph with the same text and paragraph formatting as the original paragraph.

4. **Select the** two-line title, **then click the** Center button ≡ **in the Paragraph group**

 The two paragraphs that make up the title are centered between the left and right margins.

5. **Scroll down as needed, place the insertion point in the** Rajasthan Desert Safari **heading, then click** ≡

 The Rajasthan Desert Safari heading is centered.

6. **Place the insertion point in the italicized paragraph under the title, then click the** Justify button ≡ **in the Paragraph group**

 The paragraph is aligned with both the left and right margins, as shown in **FIGURE C-10**. When you justify a paragraph, Word adjusts the spacing between words so that each line in the paragraph is flush with the left and the right margins.

7. **Scroll down, place the insertion point in** Rajasthan Desert Safari, **then click the** launcher ⬓ **in the Paragraph group**

 The Paragraph dialog box opens, as shown in **FIGURE C-11**. The Indents and Spacing tab shows the paragraph format settings for the paragraph where the insertion point is located. You can check or change paragraph format settings using this dialog box.

8. **Click the** Alignment list arrow, **click** Left, **click** OK, **then save your changes**

 The Rajasthan Desert Safari heading is left-aligned.

FIGURE C-10: Modified paragraph alignment

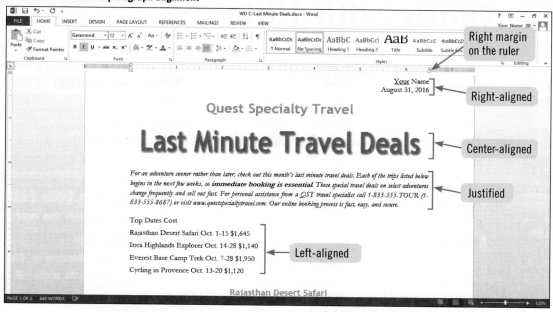

FIGURE C-11: Indents and Spacing tab in the Paragraph dialog box

Formatting a document using themes

Changing the theme applied to a document is another powerful and efficient way to tailor a document's look and feel, particularly when a document is formatted with a Quick Style set. By default, all documents created in Word are formatted with the default Office theme—which uses Calibri as the font for the body text—but you can change the theme at any time to fit the content, tone, and purpose of a document. When you change the theme for a document, a complete set of new theme colors, fonts, and effects is applied to the whole document.

To preview how various themes look when applied to the current document, click the Themes button in the Document Formatting group on the DESIGN tab, and then move the pointer over each theme in the gallery and notice how the document changes. When you click the theme you like, all document content that uses theme colors, all text that is formatted with a style, including default body text, and all table styles and graphic effects change to the colors, fonts, and effects used by the theme. In addition, the gallery of colors changes to display the set of theme colors, and the active Quick Style set changes to employ the theme colors and fonts. Note that changing the theme does not change the non-theme-based font formatting that has already been applied. For example, if you changed the font of text, applied bold to text, or changed the font color of text to a standard or custom color, that formatting remains in place.

If you want to tweak the document design further, you can modify it by applying a different set of theme colors, heading and body text fonts, or graphic effects. To do this, simply click the Colors, Fonts, or Effects button in the Document Formatting group, move the pointer over each option in the gallery to preview it in the document, and then click the option you like best.

Work with Tabs

Learning Outcomes
• Set tab stops and tab leaders
• Modify tabs
• Use tabs to align text

Tabs allow you to align text at a specific location in a document. A **tab stop** is a point on the horizontal ruler that indicates the location at which to align text. By default, tab stops are located every 1/2" from the left margin, but you can also set custom tab stops. Using tabs, you can align text to the left, right, or center of a tab stop, or you can align text at a decimal point or insert a bar character. **TABLE C-1** describes the different types of tab stops. You set tabs using the horizontal ruler or the Tabs dialog box. **CASE** ▶ *You use tabs to format the summary information on last minute tour deals so it is easy to read.*

STEPS

QUICK TIP
To remove a tab stop, drag it off the ruler.

1. **Scroll as needed, then select the** five-line list **beginning with "Trip Dates Cost"**

 Before you set tab stops for existing text, you must select the paragraphs for which you want to set tabs.

2. **Point to the** tab indicator ⌊ **at the left end of the horizontal ruler**

 The icon that appears in the tab indicator indicates the active type of tab; pointing to the tab indicator displays a ScreenTip with the name of the active tab type. By default, left tab is the active tab type. Clicking the tab indicator scrolls through the types of tabs and indents.

3. **Click the** tab indicator **to see each of the available tab and indent types, make** Left Tab ⌊ **the active tab type, click the 1" mark on the horizontal ruler, then click the 3½" mark on the horizontal ruler**

 A left tab stop is inserted at the 1" mark and the 3½" mark on the horizontal ruler. Clicking the horizontal ruler inserts a tab stop of the active type for the selected paragraph or paragraphs.

4. **Click the** tab indicator **twice so the** Right Tab icon ⌟ **is active, then click the 5" mark on the horizontal ruler**

 A right tab stop is inserted at the 5" mark on the horizontal ruler, as shown in **FIGURE C-12**.

5. **Place the insertion point before** Trip **in the first line in the list, press [Tab], place the insertion point before** Dates**, press [Tab], place the insertion point before** Cost**, then press [Tab]**

 Inserting a tab before "Trip" left-aligns the text at the 1" mark, inserting a tab before "Dates" left-aligns the text at the 3½" mark, and inserting a tab before "Cost" right-aligns "Cost" at the 5" mark.

6. **Insert a tab at the beginning of each remaining line in the list**

 The paragraphs left-align at the 1" mark.

QUICK TIP
Place the insertion point in a paragraph to see the tab stops for that paragraph on the horizontal ruler.

7. **Insert a tab before each** Oct. **in the list, then insert a tab before each** $ **in the list**

 The dates left-align at the 3½" mark. The prices right-align at the 5" mark.

8. **Select the** five lines of tabbed text**, drag the right tab stop to the 5½" mark on the horizontal ruler, then deselect the text**

 Dragging the tab stop moves it to a new location. The prices right-align at the 5½" mark.

QUICK TIP
Double-click a tab stop on the ruler to open the Tabs dialog box.

9. **Select the last** four lines of tabbed text**, click the** launcher 🔲 **in the Paragraph group, then click the Tabs button at the bottom of the Paragraph dialog box**

 The Tabs dialog box opens, as shown in **FIGURE C-13**. You can use the Tabs dialog box to set tab stops, change the position or alignment of existing tab stops, clear tab stops, and apply tab leaders to tabs. **Tab leaders** are lines that appear in front of tabbed text.

10. **Click 3.5" in the Tab stop position list box, click the 2 option button in the Leader section, click Set, click 5.5" in the Tab stop position list box, click the 2 option button in the Leader section, click Set, click OK, deselect the text, then save your changes**

 A dotted tab leader is added before each 3.5" and 5.5" tab stop in the last four lines of tabbed text, as shown in **FIGURE C-14**.

Formatting Text and Paragraphs

FIGURE C-12: Left and right tab stops on the horizontal ruler

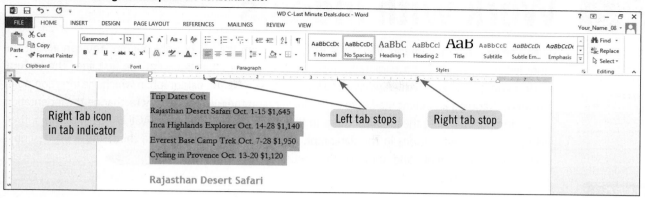

FIGURE C-13: Tabs dialog box

FIGURE C-14: Tab leaders

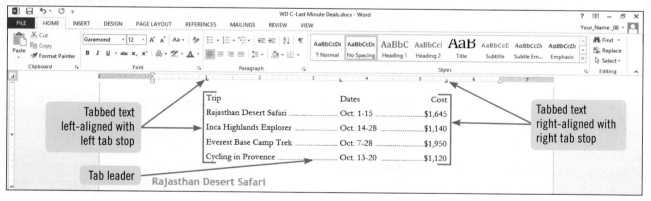

TABLE C-1: Types of tabs

tab	use to
L Left tab	Set the start position of text so that text runs to the right of the tab stop as you type
⊥ Center tab	Set the center align position of text so that text stays centered on the tab stop as you type
⌐ Right tab	Set the right or end position of text so that text moves to the left of the tab stop as you type
⊥ Decimal tab	Set the position of the decimal point so that numbers align around the decimal point as you type
⏐ Bar tab	Insert a vertical bar at the tab position

Work with Indents

Learning Outcomes
- Indent a paragraph
- Indent the first line of a paragraph

When you **indent** a paragraph, you move its edge in from the left or right margin. You can indent the entire left or right edge of a paragraph, just the first line, or all lines except the first line. The **indent markers** on the horizontal ruler indicate the indent settings for the paragraph in which the insertion point is located. Dragging an indent marker to a new location on the ruler is one way to change the indentation of a paragraph; changing the indent settings in the Paragraph group on the PAGE LAYOUT tab is another; and using the indent buttons in the Paragraph group on the HOME tab is a third. **TABLE C-2** describes different types of indents and some of the methods for creating each. **CASE** ▶ *You indent several paragraphs in the flyer.*

STEPS

1. **Press [Ctrl][Home], place the insertion point in the italicized paragraph under the title, then click the Increase Indent button ⬛ in the Paragraph group on the HOME tab**

 The entire paragraph is indented ½" from the left margin, as shown in **FIGURE C-15**. The indent marker also moves to the ½" mark on the horizontal ruler. Each time you click the Increase Indent button, the left edge of a paragraph moves another ½" to the right.

2. **Click the Decrease Indent button ⬛ in the Paragraph group**

 The left edge of the paragraph moves ½" to the left, and the indent marker moves back to the left margin.

3. **Drag the First Line Indent marker ▽ to the ¼" mark on the horizontal ruler**

 FIGURE C-16 shows the First Line Indent marker being dragged. The first line of the paragraph is indented ¼". Dragging the First Line Indent marker indents only the first line of a paragraph.

4. **Scroll to the bottom of page 1, place the insertion point in the quotation, click the PAGE LAYOUT tab, click the Indent Left text box in the Paragraph group, type .5, click the Indent Right text box, type .5, then press [Enter]**

 The left and right edges of the paragraph are indented ½" from the margins, as shown in **FIGURE C-17**.

5. **Press [Ctrl][Home], place the insertion point in the italicized paragraph, then click the launcher ⬛ in the Paragraph group**

 The Paragraph dialog box opens. You can use the Indents and Spacing tab to check or change the alignment, indentation, and paragraph and line spacing settings applied to a paragraph.

6. **Click the Special list arrow, click (none), click OK, then save your changes**

 The first line indent is removed from the paragraph.

Applying text effects and clearing formatting

The Word Text Effects and Typography feature allows you to add visual appeal to your documents by adding special text effects to text, including outlines, shadows, reflections, and glows. The feature also includes a gallery of preformatted combined text effect styles, called **WordArt**, that you can apply to your text to format it quickly and easily. To apply a WordArt style or a text effect to text, simply select the text, click the Text Effects and Typography button in the Font group on the HOME tab, and select a WordArt style from the gallery or point to a type of text effect, such as reflection or shadow, to open a gallery of styles related to that type of text effect. Experiment with combining text effect styles to give your text a striking appearance.

If you are unhappy with the way text is formatted, you can use the Clear All Formatting command to return the text to the default format settings. The default format includes font and paragraph formatting: text is formatted in 11-point Calibri, and paragraphs are left-aligned with 1.15 point line spacing, 10 points of space after, and no indents. To clear formatting from text and return it to the default format, select the text you want to clear, and then click the Clear All Formatting button in the Font group on the HOME tab. If you prefer to return the text to the default font and remove all paragraph formatting, making the text 11-point Calibri, left-aligned, single spaced, with no paragraph spacing or indents, select the text and then simply click the No Spacing button in the Styles group on the HOME tab.

FIGURE C-15: Indented paragraph

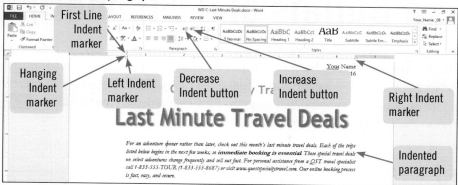

FIGURE C-16: Dragging the First Line Indent marker

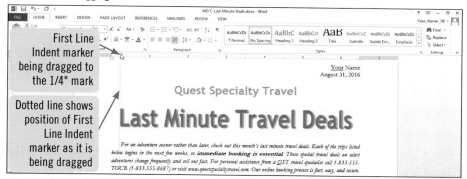

FIGURE C-17: Paragraph indented from the left and right

TABLE C-2: Types of indents

indent type: description	to create
Left indent: The left edge of a paragraph is moved in from the left margin	Drag the Left Indent marker ☐ on the ruler to the right to the position where you want the left edge of the paragraph to align; when you drag the left indent marker, all the indent markers move as one
Right indent: The right edge of a paragraph is moved in from the right margin	Drag the Right Indent marker △ on the ruler to the left to the position where you want the right edge of the paragraph to align
First line indent: The first line of a paragraph is indented more than the subsequent lines	Drag the First Line Indent marker ▽ on the ruler to the right to the position where you want the first line of the paragraph to begin; or activate the First Line Indent marker ▽ in the tab indicator, and then click the ruler at the position where you want the first line of the paragraph to begin
Hanging indent: The subsequent lines of a paragraph are indented more than the first line	Drag the Hanging Indent marker △ on the ruler to the right to the position where you want the hanging indent to begin; or activate the Hanging Indent marker △ in the tab indicator, and then click the ruler at the position where you want the second and remaining lines of the paragraph to begin; when you drag the hanging indent marker, the left indent marker moves with it.
Negative indent (or Outdent): The left edge of a paragraph is moved to the left of the left margin	Drag the Left Indent marker ☐ on the ruler left to the position where you want the negative indent to begin; when you drag the left indent marker, all markers move as one

Add Bullets and Numbering

Formatting a list with bullets or numbering can help to organize the ideas in a document. A **bullet** is a character, often a small circle, that appears before the items in a list to add emphasis. Formatting a list as a numbered list helps illustrate sequences and priorities. You can quickly format a list with bullets or numbering by using the Bullets and Numbering buttons in the Paragraph group on the HOME tab. **CASE** ▶ *You format the lists in your flyer with numbers and bullets.*

STEPS

1. **Scroll until the** Everest Base Camp Trek heading **is at the top of your screen**

2. **Select the** three-line list **of 3-day add-ons, click the** HOME tab, **then click the** Numbering list arrow ⫶≡ ▾ **in the Paragraph group**

 The Numbering Library opens, as shown in **FIGURE C-18**. You use this list to choose or change the numbering style applied to a list. You can drag the pointer over the numbering styles to preview how the selected text will look if the numbering style is applied.

3. **Click the numbering style called out in** FIGURE C-18

 The paragraphs are formatted as a numbered list.

4. **Place the insertion point after** Pokhara — Valley of Lakes, **press [Enter], then type** Temples of Janakpur

 Pressing [Enter] in the middle of the numbered list creates a new numbered paragraph and automatically renumbers the remainder of the list. Similarly, if you delete a paragraph from a numbered list, Word automatically renumbers the remaining paragraphs.

5. **Click** 1 **in the list**

 Clicking a number in a list selects all the numbers, as shown in **FIGURE C-19**.

6. **Click the** Bold button **B in the Font group**

 The numbers are all formatted in bold. Notice that the formatting of the items in the list does not change when you change the formatting of the numbers. You can also use this technique to change the formatting of bullets in a bulleted list.

7. **Select the list of items under "Last minute participants in the Everest Base Camp trek...", then click the** Bullets button ⫶≡ **in the Paragraph group**

 The four paragraphs are formatted as a bulleted list using the most recently used bullet style.

8. **Click a** bullet **in the list to select all the bullets, click the** Bullets list arrow ⫶≡ ▾ **in the Paragraph group, click the** check mark bullet style, **click the** document **to deselect the text, then save your changes**

 The bullet character changes to a check mark, as shown in **FIGURE C-20**.

Creating multilevel lists

You can create lists with hierarchical structures by applying a multilevel list style to a list. To create a **multilevel list**, also called an outline, begin by applying a multilevel list style using the Multilevel List list arrow ⫶≡ ▾ in the Paragraph group on the HOME tab, then type your outline, pressing [Enter] after each item. To demote items to a lower level of importance in the outline, place the insertion point in the item, then click the Increase Indent button ⫶≡ in the Paragraph group on the HOME tab. Each time you indent a paragraph, the item is demoted to a lower level in the outline. Similarly, you can use the Decrease Indent button ⫶≡ to promote an item to a higher level in the outline. You can also create a hierarchical structure in any bulleted or numbered list by using ⫶≡ and ⫶≡ to demote and promote items in the list. To change the multilevel list style applied to a list, select the list, click ⫶≡ ▾ and then select a new style.

FIGURE C-18: Numbering Library

FIGURE C-19: Numbered list

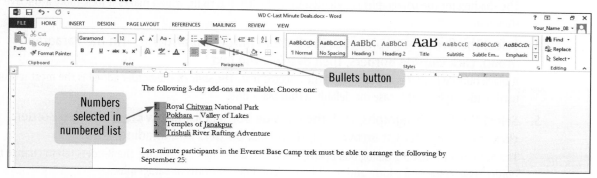

FIGURE C-20: Check mark bullets applied to list

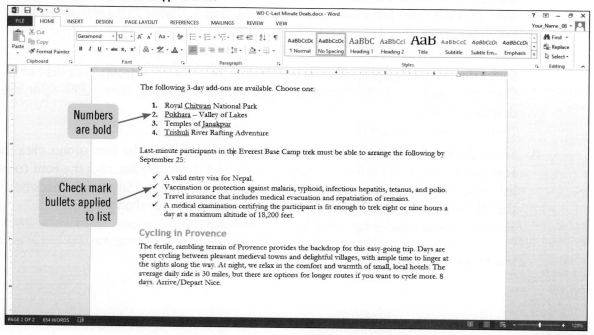

Add Borders and Shading

Learning Outcomes
- Apply shading to text
- Apply borders to text
- Highlight text

Borders and shading can add color and splash to a document. **Borders** are lines you add above, below, to the side, or around words or paragraphs. You can format borders using different line styles, colors, and widths. **Shading** is a color or pattern you apply behind words or paragraphs to make them stand out on a page. You apply borders and shading using the Borders button and the Shading button in the Paragraph group on the HOME tab. **CASE** ▶ *You enhance the tabbed text of the last minute tours schedule by adding shading to it. You also apply a border around the tabbed text to set it off from the rest of the document.*

STEPS

1. **Press [Ctrl][Home], then scroll down until the tabbed text is at the top of your screen**

2. **Select the five paragraphs of tabbed text, click the Shading list arrow in the Paragraph group on the HOME tab, click the Green, Accent 6, Lighter 60% color, then deselect the text**

 Light green shading is applied to the five paragraphs. Notice that the shading is applied to the entire width of the paragraphs, despite the tab settings.

3. **Select the five paragraphs, drag the Left Indent marker ☐ to the ¾" mark on the horizontal ruler, drag the Right Indent marker △ to the 5¾" mark, then deselect the text**

 The shading for the paragraphs is indented from the left and right, which makes it look more attractive, as shown in FIGURE C-21.

4. **Select the five paragraphs, click the Bottom Border list arrow ⊞ ▾ in the Paragraph group, click Outside Borders, then deselect the text**

 A black outside border is added around the selected text. The style of the border added is the most recently used border style, in this case the default, a thin black line.

5. **Select the five paragraphs, click the Outside Borders list arrow ⊞ ▾, click No Border, click the No Border list arrow ⊞ ▾, then click Borders and Shading**

 The Borders and Shading dialog box opens, as shown in FIGURE C-22. You use the Borders tab to change the border style, color, and width, and to add boxes and lines to words or paragraphs.

6. **Click the Box icon in the Setting section, scroll down the Style list, click the double-line style, click the Color list arrow, click the Blue, Accent 5, Darker 25% color, click the Width list arrow, click 1½ pt, click OK, then deselect the text**

 A 1½-point dark blue double-line border is added around the tabbed text.

7. **Select the five paragraphs, click the Bold button B in the Font group, click the Font Color list arrow A ▾ in the Font group, click the Blue, Accent 5, Darker 25% color, then deselect the text**

 The text changes to bold dark blue.

8. **Select the first line in the tabbed text, click the launcher ⌐ in the Font group, click the Font tab if it is not the active tab, scroll and click 14 in the Size list, click the Font color list arrow, click the Green, Accent 6, Darker 25% color, click the Small caps check box in the Effects section, click OK, deselect the text, then save your changes**

 The text in the first line of the tabbed text is enlarged and changed to green small caps, as shown in FIGURE C-23. When you change text to small caps, the lowercase letters are changed to uppercase letters in a smaller font size.

FIGURE C-21: Shading applied to the tabbed text

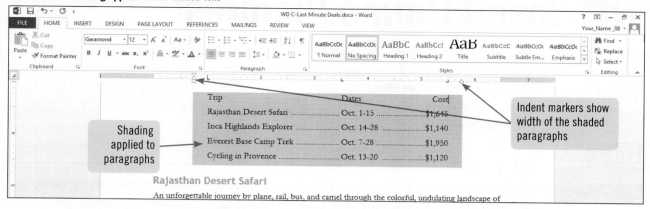

Shading applied to paragraphs

Indent markers show width of the shaded paragraphs

FIGURE C-22: Borders tab in Borders and Shading dialog box

Select border formats before applying them in the Preview area

Click to change the location of the border relative to the text

Choose a line style

Preview of border settings

Click buttons or edges of preview to apply borders

Choose to apply the settings to a paragraph or to selected text

FIGURE C-23: Borders and shading applied to the document

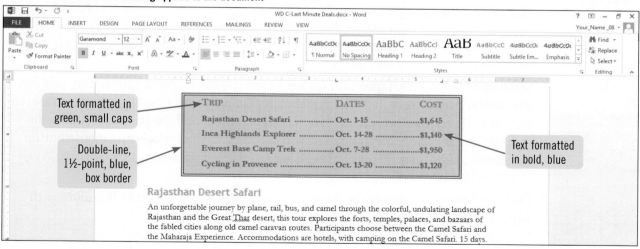

Text formatted in green, small caps

Double-line, 1½-point, blue, box border

Text formatted in bold, blue

Highlighting text in a document

The Highlight tool allows you to mark and find important text in a document. **Highlighting** is transparent color that is applied to text using the Highlight pointer. To highlight text, click the Text Highlight Color list arrow in the Font group on the HOME tab, select a color, then use the I-beam part of the pointer to select the text you want to highlight. Click to turn off the Highlight pointer. To remove highlighting, select the highlighted text, click then click No Color. Highlighting prints, but it is used most effectively when a document is viewed on screen.

Insert Online Pictures

Clip art is a collection of graphic images that you can insert into a document. Office.com Clip art images are royalty-free photos and illustrations that you can add to a document using the Online Pictures command on the INSERT tab. Once you insert a clip art image, you can wrap text around it, resize it, enhance it, and move it to a different location. **CASE** *You illustrate the second page of the document with an online clip art image.*

STEPS

1. **Scroll to the top of page 2, place the insertion point before Inca Highlands Explorer, click the INSERT tab, then click the Online Pictures button in the Illustrations group**
 The Insert Pictures window opens. You can use this to search Office.com for images related to a keyword.

2. **Type Machu Picchu in the Office.com Clip Art search text box, then press [Enter]**
 Images that have the keyword "Machu Picchu" associated with them appear in the Office.com Clip Art window, as shown in FIGURE C-24.

3. **Click the clip called out in FIGURE C-24, then click Insert**
 The clip is inserted at the location of the insertion point. When a graphic is selected, the active tab changes to the PICTURE TOOLS FORMAT tab. This tab contains commands used to adjust, enhance, arrange, and size graphics. The white squares that appear on the square edges of the graphic are the **sizing handles**.

4. **Type 2 in the Shape Height text box in the Size group on the PICTURE TOOLS FORMAT tab, then press [Enter]**
 The size of the graphic is reduced. When you decreased the height of the graphic, the width decreased proportionally. You can also resize a graphic proportionally by dragging a corner sizing handle. Until you apply text wrapping to a graphic, it is part of the line of text in which it was inserted (an **inline graphic**). To move a graphic independently of text, you must make it a **floating graphic**.

5. **Click the Position button in the Arrange group, then click Position in Middle Center with Square Text Wrapping**
 The graphic is moved to the middle of the page and the text wraps around it. Applying text wrapping to the graphic made it a floating graphic. A floating graphic can be moved anywhere on a page. You can also wrap text around a graphic using the Layout Options button.

6. **Scroll up until the Inca Highlands Explorer heading is at the top of your screen, position the pointer over the graphic, when the pointer changes to ⁺⁺ drag the graphic up and to the left so its edges align with the left margin and the top of the paragraph under the Inca Highlands Explorer heading as shown in FIGURE C-25, then release the mouse button**
 The graphic is moved to the upper-left corner of the page. Green alignment guides may appear to help you align the image with the margins.

7. **Click the Position button in the Arrange group, then click Position in Top Right with Square Text Wrapping**
 The graphic is moved to the upper-right corner of the page.

8. **Click the Picture Effects button in the Picture Styles group, point to Soft Edges, point to each style to see a preview of the style applied to the graphic, then click 2.5 point**
 A soft edge effect is applied to the graphic.

9. **Click the VIEW tab, then click the Multiple Pages button in the Zoom group**
 The completed document is shown in FIGURE C-26.

10. **Save your changes, submit the document to your instructor, then close the document and exit Word**

FIGURE C-24: Office.com Clip Art window

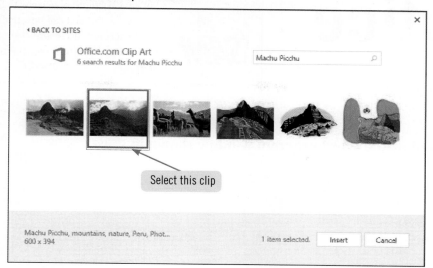

FIGURE C-25: Graphic being moved to a new location

FIGURE C-26: Completed Document

Practice

Concepts Review

Label each element of the Word program window shown in FIGURE C-27.

FIGURE C-27

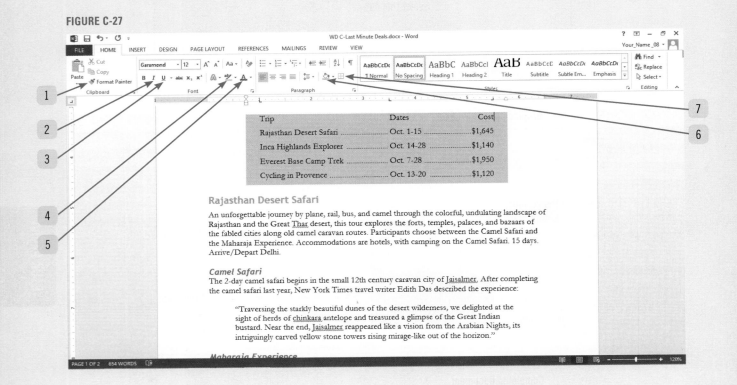

Match each term with the statement that best describes it.

8. **Floating graphic**

9. **Point**

10. **Bullet**

11. **Highlight**

12. **Inline graphic**

13. **Border**

14. **Style**

15. **Shading**

a. A graphic symbol that appears at the beginning of a paragraph in a list

b. Transparent color that is applied to text to mark it in a document

c. A set of format settings

d. An image that text wrapping has been applied to

e. An image that is inserted as part of a line of text

f. A line that can be applied above, below, or to the sides of a paragraph

g. A unit of measurement equal to $\frac{1}{72}$ of an inch

h. Color or pattern that is applied behind text to make it look attractive

Select the best answer from the list of choices.

16. **Which dialog box is used to change the scale of characters?**
 - **a.** Font
 - **b.** Tabs
 - **c.** Paragraph
 - **d.** Borders and Shading

17. **What is Calibri?**
 - **a.** A style
 - **b.** A font
 - **c.** A character format
 - **d.** A text effect

18. **What is the most precise way to increase the amount of white space between two paragraphs?**
 - **a.** Change the before paragraph spacing for the second paragraph
 - **b.** Change the line spacing of the paragraphs
 - **c.** Indent the paragraphs
 - **d.** Change the font size

19. **Which type of indent results in subsequent lines of a paragraph being indented more than the first line?**
 - **a.** First line indent
 - **b.** Right indent
 - **c.** Hanging indent
 - **d.** Negative indent

20. **Which command is used to add a reflection or an outline to text?**
 - **a.** Strikethrough
 - **b.** Underline
 - **c.** Change Case
 - **d.** Text Effects and Typography

Skills Review

1. **Format with fonts.**
 - **a.** Start Word, open the file WD C-2.docx from the location where you store your Data Files, save it as **WD C-Jackson EDA Report**, then scroll through the document to get a feel for its contents.
 - **b.** Press [Ctrl][A], then format the text in 12-point Californian FB. Choose a different serif font if Californian FB is not available to you.
 - **c.** Press [Ctrl][Home], format the report title **Town of Jackson** in 28-point Berlin Sans FB Demi. Choose a different sans serif font if Berlin Sans FB Demi is not available to you.
 - **d.** Change the font color of the report title to Gold, Accent 4, Darker 25%.
 - **e.** Format the subtitle **Economic Development Authority Report Executive Summary** in 16-point Berlin Sans FB Demi, then press [Enter] before Executive in the subtitle.
 - **f.** Format the heading **Mission Statement** in 14-point Berlin Sans FB Demi with the Gold, Accent 4, Darker 25% font color.
 - **g.** Press [Ctrl][Home], then save your changes to the report.

2. **Copy formats using the Format Painter.**
 - **a.** Use the Format Painter to copy the format of the Mission Statement heading to the following headings: **Guiding Principles**, **Issues**, **Proposed Actions**.
 - **b.** Show formatting marks, then format the paragraph under the Mission Statement heading in italic.
 - **c.** Format **Years Population Growth**, the first line in the four-line list under the Issues heading, in bold, small caps, with Gold, Accent 4, Darker 50% font color.
 - **d.** Change the font color of the next two lines under Years Population Growth to Gold, Accent 4, Darker 50%.
 - **e.** Format the line **Source: Office of State Planning** in italic, then save your changes.

3. **Change line and paragraph spacing.**
 - **a.** Change the line spacing of the three-line list under the first body paragraph to 1.5 lines.
 - **b.** Add 6 points of space after the title Town of Jackson. Add 18 points of space before and 6 points of space after the Executive Summary line in the subtitle.
 - **c.** Add 12 points of space after the Mission Statement heading, then add 12 points of space after each additional heading in the report (Guiding Principles, Issues, Proposed Actions).

Skills Review (continued)

d. Add 6 points of space after each paragraph in the list under the Guiding Principles heading.

e. Change the line spacing of the four-line list under the Issues heading that begins with Years Population Growth to 1.15.

f. Add 6 points of space after each paragraph under the Proposed Actions heading.

g. Press [Ctrl][Home], then save your changes to the report.

4. Align paragraphs.

a. Press [Ctrl][A] to select the entire document, then justify all the paragraphs.

b. Center the three-line report title.

c. Press [Ctrl][End], press [Enter], type your name, press [Enter], type the current date, then right-align your name and the date.

d. Save your changes to the report.

5. Work with tabs.

a. Scroll up and select the four-line list of population information under the Issues heading.

b. Set left tab stops at the 2" mark and the 3¾" mark.

c. Insert a tab at the beginning of each line in the list.

d. In the first line, insert a tab before Population. In the second line, insert a tab before 4.5%. In the third line, insert a tab before 53%.

e. Select the first three lines, then drag the second tab stop to the 3" mark on the horizontal ruler.

f. Press [Ctrl][Home], then save your changes to the report.

6. Work with indents.

a. Indent the paragraph under the Mission Statement heading ½" from the left and ½" from the right.

b. Indent the first line of the paragraph under the Guiding Principles heading ½".

c. Indent the first line of the three body paragraphs under the Issues heading ½".

d. Press [Ctrl][Home], then save your changes to the report.

7. Add bullets and numbering.

a. Apply bullets to the three-line list under the first body paragraph. Change the bullet style to small black circles if that is not the current bullet symbol.

b. Change the font color of the bullets to Gold, Accent 4, Darker 25%.

c. Scroll down until the Guiding Principles heading is at the top of your screen.

d. Format the six-paragraph list under Guiding Principles as a numbered list.

e. Format the numbers in 14-point Berlin Sans FB Demi, then change the font color to Gold, Accent 4, Darker 25%.

f. Scroll down until the Proposed Actions heading is at the top of your screen, then format the paragraphs under the heading as a bulleted list using check marks as the bullet style.

g. Change the font color of the bullets to Gold, Accent 4, Darker 25%, press [Ctrl][Home], then save your changes to the report.

8. Add borders and shading.

a. Add a 1-point Gold, Accent 4, Darker 50% border below the Mission Statement heading.

b. Use the Format Painter or the [F4] keys to add the same border to the other headings in the report (Guiding Principles, Issues, Proposed Actions).

c. Under the Issues heading, select the first three lines of tabbed text, which are formatted in gold, then apply Gold, Accent 4, Lighter 60% shading to the paragraphs.

d. Select the first three lines of tabbed text again if necessary, then add a 1½ -point Gold, Accent 4, Darker 50% single line box border around the paragraphs.

e. Indent the shading and border around the paragraphs 1¾" from the left and 1¾" from the right.

f. Turn off formatting marks, then save your changes.

Skills Review (continued)

9. **Insert online pictures.** *(Note: To complete these steps, your computer must be connected to the Internet.)*

 a. Press [Ctrl][Home], then open the Insert Pictures window.

 b. Search using Office.com Clip Art to find images related to the keywords **town council**.

 c. Insert the image shown in **FIGURE C-28**. *(Note: Select a different clip if this one is not available to you. It is best to select a clip that is similar in shape to the clip shown in **FIGURE C-28**.)*

 d. Use the Shape Width text box in the Size group on the PICTURE TOOLS FORMAT tab to change the width of the image to 1.5".

 e. Use the Position command to position the image in the top left with square text wrapping.

 f. Apply a Perspective Diagonal Upper Right shadow style to the image.

 g. Drag the image up so that the bottom edge of the graphic aligns with the Quality of life bullet and the left edge aligns with the left margin. Use the green alignment guides to help you position the image. *(Hint:* All the text in the numbered list should fit on page 1. Adjust the size or position of the image if necessary so that all the text in the numbered list fits on page 1.)

 h. Save your changes to the document, submit it to your instructor, close the file, and then exit Word.

FIGURE C-28

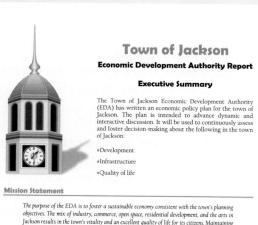

Word 2013

Independent Challenge 1

You are an estimator for Solar Home Design | Build in Springfield, Illinois. You have drafted an estimate for a home renovation job and you need to format it. It's important that your estimate have a clean, striking design, and reflect your company's professionalism.

a. Start Word, open the file WD C-3.docx from the drive and folder where you store your Data Files, save it as **WD C-Solar Home**, then read the document to get a feel for its contents. FIGURE C-29 shows how you will format the letterhead.

FIGURE C-29

SOLARHOME Design | Build

375 West Street, Springfield, IL 62705; Tel: 217-555-3202; www.solarhomedesignbuild.com

b. Select the entire document, change the style to No Spacing, then change the font to 11-point Calibri Light.

c. In the first line of the letterhead, format **Solar Home** in 30-point Arial Black, then apply all caps. Format **SOLAR** with the Blue, Accent 5 font color, format **HOME** with the Blue, Accent 5, Lighter 40% font color, then delete the space between the two words. Format **Design | Build** in 30-point Arial with a Blue, Accent 5, Darker 25% font color. (*Hint*: Type 30 in the Font Size text box, then press [Enter].)

d. Format the next line in 10-point Arial with a Blue, Accent 5, Darker 25% font color.

e. Center the two-line letterhead.

f. Add a 2¼-point dotted Blue, Accent 5, Darker 25% border below the address line paragraph.

g. With the insertion point in the address line, open the Borders and Shading dialog box, click Options to open the Border and Shading Options dialog box, change the Bottom setting to **5** points, then click OK twice to close the dialog boxes and to adjust the location of the border relative to the line of text.

h. Format the title **Proposal of Renovation** in 14-point Arial, then center the title.

i. Format the following headings (including the colons) in 11-point Arial: **Date**, **Work to be performed for and at**, **Scope of work**, **Payment schedule**, and **Agreement**.

j. Select the 14-line list under **Scope of work** that begins with **Demo of all...**, then change the paragraph spacing to add 4 points of space after each paragraph in the list. (*Hint*: Select 0 pt in the After text box, type 4, then press Enter.)

k. With the list selected, set a right tab stop at the 6¼" mark, insert tabs before every price in the list, then apply dotted line tab leaders.

l. Format the list as a numbered list, then apply bold to the numbers.

m. Apply bold and italic to the two lines, **Total estimated job cost...** and **Approximate job time...** below the list.

n. Replace Your Name with your name in the signature block, select the signature block (Respectfully submitted through your name), set a left tab stop at the 3¼" mark, then indent the signature block using tabs.

o. Examine the document carefully for formatting errors, and make any necessary adjustments.

p. Save the document, submit it to your instructor, then close the file and exit Word.

Independent Challenge 2

Your employer, the Silver Center for Contemporary Arts in Halifax, Nova Scotia, is launching a membership drive. Your boss has written the text for a flyer advertising Silver membership, and asks you to format it so that it is eye catching and attractive.

a. Open the file WD C-4.docx from the drive and folder where you store your Data Files, save it as **WD C-Silver 2016**, then read the document. FIGURE C-30 shows how you will format the first several paragraphs of the flyer.

FIGURE C-30

MEMBERSHIP DRIVE

2016

What we do for ARTISTS

Since 1982, the artist residency program at the Silver Center for Contemporary Arts has supported the work of more than 1500 artists from all over Canada and from 40 other nations. The residency awards include studio and living space, a monthly stipend to help artists with their expenses, and use of specialized equipment for all types of visual and performance art. Each artist gives a public lecture or performance at the Silver.

b. Select the entire document, change the style to No Spacing, then change the font to 10-point Candara.

c. Center the first line, **Membership Drive**, and apply shading to the paragraph. Choose a dark custom shading color of your choice for the shading color. (*Hint*: Click More Colors, then select a color from the Standard or Custom tab.) Format the text in 24-point Candara, bold, with a white font color. Expand the character spacing by 10 points. (*Hint*: Use the Advanced tab in the Font dialog box. Set the Spacing to Expanded, and then type **10** in the By text box.)

d. Format the second line, **2016**, in 48-point Candara bold. Apply the Gradient Fill-Gray text effect style to the text. (*Hint*: Use the Text Effects and Typography button.) Expand the character spacing by 10 points, and change the character scale to 250%. Center the line.

e. Format each **What we do for...** heading in 11-point Candara, bold. Change the font color to the same custom color used for shading the title. (*Note*: The color now appears in the Recent Colors section of the Font Color gallery.) Add a single-line ½-point black border under each heading.

f. Format each subheading (**Gallery**, **Lectures**, **Library**, **All members...**, and **Membership Levels**) in 10-point Candara, bold. Add 3 points of spacing before each paragraph. (*Hint*: Select 0 in the Before text box, type 3, then press Enter.)

g. Indent each body paragraph ¼", except for the lines under the **What we do for YOU** heading.

h. Format the four lines under the **All members...** subheading as a bulleted list. Use a bullet symbol of your choice, and format the bullets in the custom font color.

i. Indent the five lines under the **Membership Levels** heading ¼". For these five lines, set left tab stops at the 1¼" mark and the 2¼" mark on the horizontal ruler. Insert tabs before the price and before the word All in each of the five lines.

j. Format the name of each membership level (**Artistic**, **Conceptual**, etc.) in 10-point Candara, bold, italic, with the custom font color.

k. Format the **For more information** heading in 14-point Candara, bold, with the custom font color, then center the heading.

l. Center the last two lines, replace Your Name with your name, then apply bold to your name.

m. Examine the document carefully for formatting errors, and make any necessary adjustments.

n. Save the flyer, submit it to your instructor, then close the file and exit Word.

Independent Challenge 3

One of your responsibilities as program coordinator at Solstice Mountain Sports is to develop a program of winter outdoor learning and adventure workshops. You have drafted a memo to your boss to update her on your progress. You need to format the memo so it is professional looking and easy to read. (*Note*: *To complete these steps, your computer must be connected to the Internet.*)

a. Start Word, open the file WD C-5.docx from the drive and folder where you store your Data Files, then save it as **WD C-Mountain Memo**.

b. Select the **Solstice Mountain Sports Memorandum** heading, apply the Quick Style Title to it, then center the heading. (*Hint*: Open the Quick Style gallery, then click the Title style.)

c. In the memo header, replace Today's Date and Your Name with the current date and your name.

d. Select the four-line memo header, set a left tab stop at the ¾" mark, then insert tabs before the date, the recipient's name, your name, and the subject of the memo.

e. Apply the Quick Style Strong to **Date:**, **To:**, **From:**, and **Re:**.

f. Apply the Quick Style Heading 2 to the headings **Overview**, **Workshops**, **Accommodations**, **Fees**, and **Proposed winter programming**.

g. Under the Fees heading, apply the Quick Style Emphasis to the words **Workshop fees** and **Accommodations fees**.

h. Add a clip art image of a snowflake to the first page, wrap text around the image, then resize it and position it so it fits into the memo header below the title and aligns with the right margin.

i. On the second page of the document, format the list under the **Proposed winter programming** heading as a multilevel list. FIGURE C-31 shows the hierarchical structure of the outline. (*Hint*s: The list is on pages 2 and 3 so be sure to select the entire list before applying the multilevel style. Apply a multilevel list style, then use the Increase Indent and Decrease Indent buttons to change the level of importance of each item.)

j. Change the outline numbering style to the bullet numbering style shown in FIGURE C-31 if a different style is used in your outline.

k. Add a clip art image that relates to snowboarding or skiing to page 2. Select an image that fits the tone of the document. Wrap text around the graphic, then resize it and position it so it aligns with the right margin.

l. Zoom out on the memo so that two pages are displayed in the document window, then, using the Change Case button, change the title Solstice Mountain Sports Memorandum so that only the initial letter of each word is capitalized. Resize and reposition the clip art as needed so that it fits in the memo header.

m. Using the Fonts button on the DESIGN tab, change the fonts to a font set of your choice. Choose fonts that allow the document to fit on two pages. Resize and reposition the clip art as needed so that it fits in the memo header.

n. Using the Colors button on the DESIGN tab, change the colors to a color palette of your choice.

o. Apply different styles and adjust other formatting elements as necessary to make the memo attractive, eye catching, and readable. The finished memo should fit on two pages.

p. Save the document, submit it to your instructor, then close the file and exit Word.

FIGURE C-31

Proposed winter programming

- ❖ Skiing, Snowboarding, and Snowshoeing
 - ➤ Skiing and Snowboarding
 - ▪ Cross-country skiing
 - Cross-country skiing for beginners
 - Intermediate cross-country skiing
 - Inn-to-inn ski touring
 - Moonlight cross-country skiing
 - ▪ Telemarking
 - Basic telemark skiing
 - Introduction to backcountry skiing
 - Exploring on skis
 - ▪ Snowboarding
 - Backcountry snowboarding
 - ➤ Snowshoeing
 - ▪ Beginner
 - Snowshoeing for beginners
 - Snowshoeing and winter ecology
 - ▪ Intermediate and Advanced
 - Intermediate snowshoeing
 - Guided snowshoe trek
 - Above tree line snowshoeing
- ❖ Winter Hiking, Camping, and Survival
 - ➤ Hiking
 - ▪ Beginner
 - Long-distance hiking
 - Winter summits
 - Hiking for women
 - ➤ Winter camping and survival
 - ▪ Beginner
 - Introduction to winter camping
 - Basic winter mountain skills
 - Building snow shelters
 - ▪ Intermediate
 - Basic winter mountain skills II
 - Ice climbing
 - Avalanche awareness and rescue

Independent Challenge 4: Explore

The fonts you choose for a document can have a major effect on the document's tone. Not all fonts are appropriate for use in a business document, and some fonts, especially those with a definite theme, are appropriate only for specific purposes. In this Independent Challenge, you will use font formatting and other formatting features to design a letterhead and a fax coversheet for yourself or your business. The letterhead and coversheet should not only look professional and attract interest, but also say something about the character of your business or your personality. **FIGURE C-32** shows an example of a business letterhead.

a. Start Word, and save a new blank document as **WD C-Personal Letterhead** to the drive and folder where you store your Data Files.

b. Type your name or the name of your business, your address, your phone number, your fax number, and your Web site or e-mail address.

c. Format your name or the name of your business in a font that expresses your personality or says something about the nature of your business. Use fonts, font colors, text effects and typography, borders, shading, paragraph formatting, and other formatting features to design a letterhead that is appealing and professional.

d. Save your changes, submit the document to your instructor, then close the file.

e. Open a new blank document, and save it as **WD C-Personal Fax Coversheet**. Type FAX, your name or the name of your business, your address, your phone number, your fax number, and your Web site or e-mail address at the top of the document.

f. Type a fax header that includes the following: Date:, To:, From:, Re:, Pages:, and Comments.

g. Format the information in the fax coversheet using fonts, font effects, borders, shading, paragraph formatting, and other formatting features. Since a fax coversheet is designed to be faxed, all fonts and other formatting elements should be black.

h. Save your changes, submit the document to your instructor, close the file, then exit Word.

FIGURE C-32

Lilliana Sandoval Graphic Design

443 Sanchez Street, 6th floor, Santa Fe, NM 87501 Tel: 505-555-9767 Fax: 505-555-2992 www.lilsandoval.com

Visual Workshop

Open the file WD C-6.docx from the drive and folder where you store your Data Files. Create the menu shown in FIGURE C-33. (*Hints*: Find the clip art image using the keyword **diner**, then use the sizing handles to resize the graphic to be approximately 1.5" tall and 1.3" wide. Choose a different appropriate image if the image shown in the figure is not available. Use Tempus Sans ITC or a similar font for the text. Add color, bold, and italic as shown in the figure. Change the font size of the café name to 22 points, the font size of Daily Lunch Specials to 14 points, the font size of the menu to 12 points, and the font size of the italicized text at the bottom to 10 points. Format the prices using tabs and leader lines. Use paragraph spacing to adjust the spacing between paragraphs so that all the text fits on one page. Make other adjustments as needed so your menu is similar to the one shown in FIGURE C-33.) Save the menu as **WD C-JP Cafe Menu**, then submit a copy to your instructor. (*Note*: *To complete these steps, your computer must be connected to the Internet*.)

FIGURE C-33

JP's Fish & Farm Café

Daily Lunch Specials

Monday
Wild Mushroom Quiche: Wild shitake and oyster mushrooms and spinach in a light and flakey quiche, served with a meadow side salad. .. $13.00

Tuesday
Potato-Fish Chowder: Thick, rich, New England style fish chowder served with crusty bread and a side of organic greens. ..$14.00

Wednesday
Harvest Vegetarian Chili: Seasonal vegetables and four types of beans, served with homemade tortilla chips and a meadow side salad. .. $14.00

Thursday
Veggie Pot Pie: Local organic seasonal vegetables, kale, and chipotle miso gravy in a light and flakey crust, served with a side of organic greens. ... $13.00

Friday
Wild Turkey Club: Roasted organic turkey, crisp bacon, mixed greens, tomato, and sun-dried tomato mayo on homemade toasted triple seed. ... $14.00

Saturday
Wild Salmon on a Field of Greens: Wild salmon and seasonal vegetables on a bed of organic greens, topped with our house dressing and served with homemade rolls. $16.00

Sunday
Chicken and Shitake Quesadilla: Roasted organic chicken, shitake mushroom, avocado, and cheddar in a homemade tortilla, served with fresh salsa and a meadow side salad. $16.00

We strive to serve local organic produce. Our meat and seafood is sustainably farmed or harvested, and all our meats are naturally fed and antibiotic, hormone, and steroid free. Chef: Your Name

Formatting Documents

CASE You have written and formatted the text for an informational report for QST clients about staying healthy while traveling. You are now ready to format the pages. You plan to organize the text in columns, to illustrate the report with a table, and to add footnotes and a bibliography.

Unit Objectives

After completing this unit, you will be able to:

- Set document margins
- Create sections and columns
- Insert page breaks
- Insert page numbers
- Add headers and footers

- Insert a table
- Add footnotes and endnotes
- Insert citations
- Manage sources and create a bibliography

Files You Will Need

WD D-1.docx	WD D-5.docx
WD D-2.docx	WD D-6.docx
WD D-3.docx	WD D-7.docx
WD D-4.docx	

Set Document Margins

Learning Outcomes
• Set custom margins
• Change paper size
• Change page orientation

Changing a document's margins is one way to change the appearance of a document and control the amount of text that fits on a page. The **margins** of a document are the blank areas between the edge of the text and the edge of the page. When you create a document in Word, the default margins are 1" at the top, bottom, left, and right sides of the page. You can adjust the size of a document's margins using the Margins command on the PAGE LAYOUT tab or using the rulers. **CASE** *The report should be a four-page document when finished. You begin by reducing the size of the document margins so that more text fits on each page.*

STEPS

TROUBLE
Click the Ruler check box in the Show group on the VIEW tab to display the rulers if they are not already displayed.

1. **Start Word, open the file WD D-1.docx from the location where you store your Data Files, then save it as WD D-Healthy Traveler**

 The report opens in Print Layout view.

2. **Scroll through the report to get a feel for its contents, then press [Ctrl][Home]**

 The report is currently five pages long. Notice that the status bar indicates the page where the insertion point is located and the total number of pages in the document.

3. **Click the PAGE LAYOUT tab, then click the Margins button in the Page Setup group**

 The Margins menu opens. You can select predefined margin settings from this menu, or you can click Custom Margins to create different margin settings.

QUICK TIP
You can also click the launcher in the Page Setup group to open the Page Setup dialog box.

4. **Click Custom Margins**

 The Page Setup dialog box opens with the Margins tab displayed, as shown in **FIGURE D-1**. You can use the Margins tab to change the top, bottom, left, or right document margin, to change the orientation of the pages from portrait to landscape, and to alter other page layout settings. **Portrait orientation** means a page is taller than it is wide; **landscape orientation** means a page is wider than it is tall. This report uses portrait orientation. You can also use the Orientation button in the Page Setup group on the PAGE LAYOUT tab to change the orientation of a document.

5. **Click the Top down arrow three times until 0.7" appears, then click the Bottom down arrow until 0.7" appears**

 The top and bottom margins of the report will be .7".

QUICK TIP
The minimum allowable margin settings depend on your printer and the size of the paper you are using. Word displays a warning message if you set margins that are too narrow for your printer.

6. **Press [Tab], type .7 in the Left text box, press [Tab], then type .7 in the Right text box**

 The left and right margins of the report will also be .7". You can change the margin settings by using the arrows or by typing a value in the appropriate text box.

7. **Click OK**

 The document margins change to .7", as shown in **FIGURE D-2**. The location of each margin (right, left, top, and bottom) is shown on the horizontal and vertical rulers at the intersection of the white and shaded areas. You can also change a margin setting by using the pointer to drag the intersection to a new location on the ruler.

8. **Click the VIEW tab, then click the Multiple Pages button in the Zoom group**

 The first three pages of the document appear in the document window.

9. **Scroll down to view all five pages of the report, press [Ctrl][Home], click the 100% button in the Zoom group, then save your changes**

FIGURE D-1: Margins tab in Page Setup dialog box

Default margin settings →
Set gutter margin →
Select page orientation →
Select gutter position
Set mirror margins and other page layout options
Preview of margin settings
Select part of document to apply settings to

FIGURE D-2: Report with smaller margins

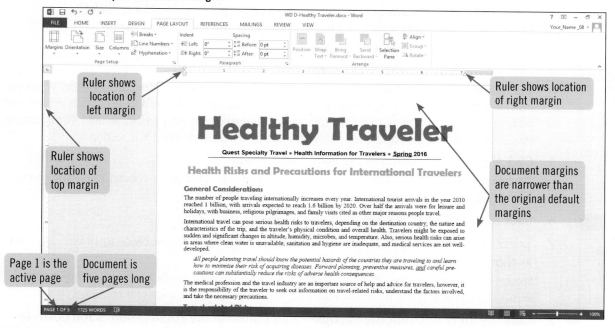

Ruler shows location of left margin
Ruler shows location of top margin
Page 1 is the active page
Document is five pages long
Ruler shows location of right margin
Document margins are narrower than the original default margins

Changing orientation, margin settings, and paper size

By default, the documents you create in Word use an 8½" x 11" paper size in portrait orientation with the default margin settings. You can change the orientation, margin settings, and paper size to common settings using the Orientation, Margins, and Size buttons in the Page Setup group on the PAGE LAYOUT tab. You can also adjust these settings and others in the Page Setup dialog box. For example, to change the layout of multiple pages, use the Multiple pages list arrow on the Margins tab to create pages that use mirror margins, that include two pages per sheet of paper, or that are formatted using a book fold. **Mirror margins** are used in a document with facing pages, such as a magazine, where the margins on the left page of the document are a mirror image of the margins on the right page. Documents with mirror margins have inside and outside margins, rather than right and left margins. Another type of margin is a gutter margin, which is used in documents that are bound, such as books. A **gutter** adds extra space to the left, top, or inside margin to allow for the binding. Add a gutter to a document by adjusting the setting in the Gutter position text box on the Margins tab. To change the size of the paper used, use the Paper size list arrow on the Paper tab to select a standard paper size, or enter custom measurements in the Width and Height text boxes.

Create Sections and Columns

Learning Outcomes
- Customize the status bar
- Insert section breaks
- Format text in columns

Dividing a document into sections allows you to format each section of the document with different page layout settings. A **section** is a portion of a document that is separated from the rest of the document by section breaks. **Section breaks** are formatting marks that you insert in a document to show the end of a section. Once you have divided a document into sections, you can format each section with different column, margin, page orientation, header and footer, and other page layout settings. By default, a document is formatted as a single section, but you can divide a document into as many sections as you like. **CASE** *You insert a section break to divide the document into two sections, and then format the text in the second section in two columns. First, you customize the status bar to display section information.*

STEPS

QUICK TIP
Use the Customize Status Bar menu to turn on and off the display of information in the status bar.

1. **Right-click the status bar, click Section on the Customize Status Bar menu that opens (if it is not already checked), then click the document to close the menu**
 The status bar indicates the insertion point is located in section 1 of the document.

2. **Click the HOME tab, then click the Show/Hide ¶ button ¶ in the Paragraph group**
 Turning on formatting marks allows you to see the section breaks you insert in a document.

3. **Place the insertion point before the heading General Considerations, click the PAGE LAYOUT tab, then click the Breaks button in the Page Setup group**
 The Breaks menu opens. You use this menu to insert different types of section breaks. See TABLE D-1.

QUICK TIP
A section break stores the formatting information for the preceding section.

4. **Click Continuous**
 Word inserts a continuous section break, shown as a dotted double line, above the heading. When you insert a section break at the beginning of a paragraph, Word inserts the break at the end of the previous paragraph. The section break stores the formatting information for the previous section. The document now has two sections. Notice that the status bar indicates the insertion point is in section 2.

5. **Click the Columns button in the Page Setup group**
 The columns menu opens. You use this menu to format text using preset column formats or to create custom columns.

QUICK TIP
When you delete a section break, you delete the section formatting of the text before the break. That text becomes part of the following section, and it assumes the formatting of that section.

6. **Click More Columns to open the Columns dialog box**

7. **Select Two in the Presets section, click the Spacing down arrow twice until 0.3" appears as shown in FIGURE D-3, then click OK**
 Section 2 is formatted in two columns of equal width with .3" of spacing between, as shown in FIGURE D-4. Formatting text in columns is another way to increase the amount of text that fits on a page.

8. **Click the VIEW tab, click the Multiple Pages button in the Zoom group, scroll down to examine all four pages of the document, press [Ctrl][Home], then save the document**
 The text in section 2—all the text below the continuous section break—is formatted in two columns. Text in columns flows automatically from the bottom of one column to the top of the next column.

TABLE D-1: Types of section breaks

section	function
Next page	Begins a new section and moves the text following the break to the top of the next page
Continuous	Begins a new section on the same page
Even page	Begins a new section and moves the text following the break to the top of the next even-numbered page
Odd page	Begins a new section and moves the text following the break to the top of the next odd-numbered page

© 2014 Cengage Learning

FIGURE D-3: Columns dialog box

Select a preset format for columns

Change the number of columns

Select to add a line between columns

Set custom widths and spacing for columns

Set space between columns

Preview of current settings

Select to create columns of equal width

Select part of document to apply format to

FIGURE D-4: Continuous section break and columns

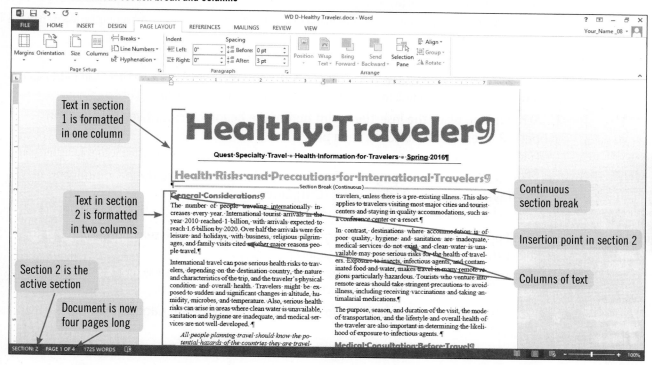

Text in section 1 is formatted in one column

Text in section 2 is formatted in two columns

Section 2 is the active section

Document is now four pages long

Continuous section break

Insertion point in section 2

Columns of text

Changing page layout settings for a section

Dividing a document into sections allows you to vary the layout of a document. In addition to applying different column settings to sections, you can apply different margins, page orientation, paper size, vertical alignment, header and footer, page numbering, footnotes, endnotes, and other page layout settings. For example, if you are formatting a report that includes a table with many columns, you might want to change the table's page orientation to landscape so that it is easier to read. To do this, you would insert a section break before and after the table to create a section that contains only the table, and then you would change the page orientation of the section that contains the table to landscape. If the table does not fill the page, you could also change the vertical alignment of the table so that it is centered vertically on the page. To do this, use the Vertical alignment list arrow on the Layout tab of the Page Setup dialog box.

To check or change the page layout settings for an individual section, place the insertion point in the section, then open the Page Setup dialog box. Select any options you want to change, click the Apply to list arrow, click This section, then click OK. When you select This section in the Apply to list box, the settings are applied to the current section only. When you select This point forward, the settings are applied to the current section and all sections that follow it. If you select Whole document in the Apply to list box, the settings are applied to all the sections in the document. Use the Apply to list arrow in the Columns dialog box or the Footnote and Endnote dialog box to change those settings for a section.

Insert Page Breaks

Learning Outcomes
- Insert and delete page breaks
- Insert a column break
- Balance columns

As you type text in a document, Word inserts an **automatic page break** (also called a soft page break) when you reach the bottom of a page, allowing you to continue typing on the next page. You can also force text onto the next page of a document by using the Breaks command to insert a **manual page break** (also called a hard page break). Another way to control the flow of text is to apply pagination settings using the Line and Page breaks tab in the Paragraph dialog box. **CASE** ▶ *You insert manual page breaks where you know you want to begin each new page of the report.*

STEPS

1. **Click the 100% button, scroll to the bottom of page 1, place the insertion point before the heading** Malaria: A Serious..., **click the PAGE LAYOUT tab, then click the Breaks button in the Page Setup group**

 The Breaks menu opens. You also use this menu to insert page, column, and text-wrapping breaks. TABLE D-2 describes these types of breaks.

QUICK TIP
To control the flow of text between columns, insert a column break to force the text after the break to the top of the next column.

2. **Click** Page

 Word inserts a manual page break before "Malaria: A Serious Health Risk for Travelers" and moves all the text following the page break to the beginning of the next page, as shown in FIGURE D-5.

3. **Scroll down, place the insertion point before the heading** Preventive Options... **on page 2, press and hold [Ctrl], then press [Enter]**

 Pressing [Ctrl][Enter] is a fast way to insert a manual page break. The heading is forced to the top of the third page.

4. **Scroll to the bottom of page 3, place the insertion point before the heading** Insurance for Travelers **on page 3, then press [Ctrl][Enter]**

 The heading is forced to the top of the fourth page.

QUICK TIP
You can also double-click a page break to select it, and then press [Delete] to delete it.

5. **Scroll up, click to the left of the page break on page 2 with the selection pointer ⤢ to select the page break, then press [Delete]**

 The manual page break is deleted and the text from pages 2 and 3 flows together. You can also use the selection pointer to click to the left of a section or a column break to select it.

QUICK TIP
You can balance columns of unequal length on a page by inserting a continuous section break at the end of the last column on the page.

6. **Place the insertion point before the heading** Medical Kit... **on page 2, then press [Ctrl][Enter]**

 The heading is forced to the top of the third page.

7. **Click the VIEW tab, click the Multiple Pages button in the Zoom group, scroll to view all four pages of the document, then save your changes**

 Pages 1, 2, and 3 are shown in FIGURE D-6.

Controlling automatic pagination

Another way to control the flow of text between pages (or between columns) is to apply pagination settings to specify where Word positions automatic page breaks. To apply automatic pagination settings, simply select the paragraphs(s) or line(s) you want to control, click the launcher in the Paragraph group on the HOME or PAGE LAYOUT tab, click the Line and Page Breaks tab in the Paragraph dialog box, and then select one or more of the following settings in the Pagination section before clicking OK.

- Keep with next: Apply to any paragraph you want to appear together with the next paragraph in order to prevent the page or column from breaking between the paragraphs.

- Keep lines together: Apply to selected paragraph or lines to prevent a page or column from breaking in the middle of a paragraph or between certain lines.
- Page break before: Apply to add an automatic page break before a specific paragraph.
- Widow/Orphan control: Turned on by default; ensures at least two lines of a paragraph appear at the top and bottom of every page or column by preventing a page or column from beginning with only the last line of a paragraph (a **widow**), or ending with only the first line of a new paragraph (an **orphan**).

FIGURE D-5: Manual page break in document

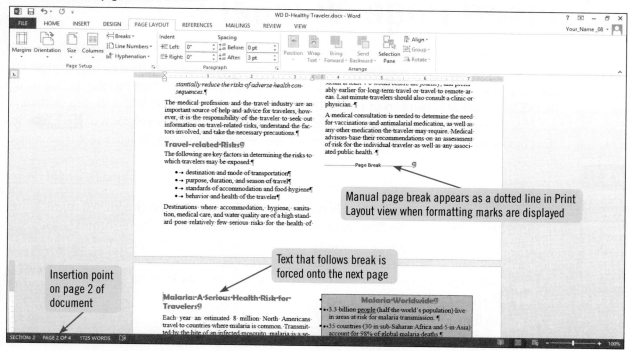

Manual page break appears as a dotted line in Print Layout view when formatting marks are displayed

Text that follows break is forced onto the next page

Insertion point on page 2 of document

FIGURE D-6: Pages 1, 2, and 3

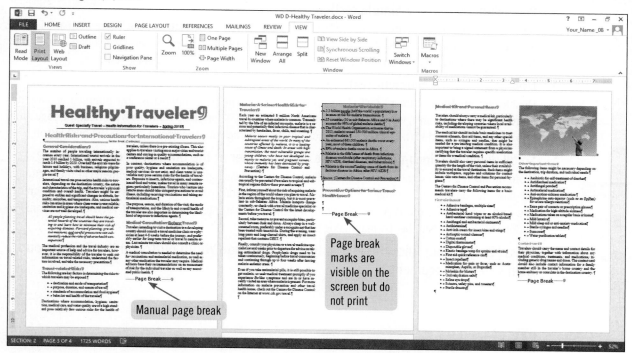

Manual page break

Page break marks are visible on the screen but do not print

TABLE D-2: Types of breaks

break	function
Page	Forces the text following the break to begin at the top of the next page
Column	Forces the text following the break to begin at the top of the next column
Text Wrapping	Forces the text following the break to begin at the beginning of the next line

Formatting Documents

Insert Page Numbers

If you want to number the pages of a multiple-page document, you can insert a page number field to add a page number to each page. A **field** is a code that serves as a placeholder for data that changes in a document, such as a page number or the current date. When you use the Page Number button on the INSERT tab to add page numbers to a document, you insert the page number field at the top, bottom, or side of any page, and Word automatically numbers all the pages in the document for you. **CASE** ➤ *You insert a page number field so that page numbers will appear centered between the margins at the bottom of each page in the document.*

STEPS

QUICK TIP
Point to Current Position to insert a page number field at the location of the insertion point.

1. **Press [Ctrl][Home], click the 100% button in the Zoom group on the VIEW tab, click the Insert tab, then click the Page Number button in the Header & Footer group**

 The Page Number menu opens. You use this menu to select the position for the page numbers. If you choose to add a page number field to the top, bottom, or side of a document, a page number will appear on every page in the document. If you choose to insert it in the document at the location of the insertion point, the field will appear on that page only.

2. **Point to Bottom of Page**

 A gallery of formatting and alignment options for page numbers to be inserted at the bottom of a page opens, as shown in **FIGURE D-7**.

QUICK TIP
To change the location or formatting of page numbers, click the Page Number button, point to a page number location, then select a format from the gallery.

3. **Scroll down the gallery to view the options, scroll to the top of the gallery, then click Plain Number 2 in the Simple section**

 A page number field containing the number 1 is centered in the Footer area at the bottom of page 1 of the document, as shown in **FIGURE D-8**. The document text is gray, or dimmed, because the Footer area is open. Text that is inserted in a Footer area appears at the bottom of every page in a document.

4. **Double-click the document text**

 Double-clicking the document text closes the Footer area. The page number is now dimmed because it is located in the Footer area, which is no longer the active area. When the document is printed, the page numbers appear as normal text. You will learn more about working with the Footer area in the next lesson.

5. **Scroll down the document to see the page number at the bottom of each page**

 Word numbered each page of the report automatically, and each page number is centered at the bottom of the page. If you want to change the numbering format or start page numbering with a different number, you can simply click the Page Number button, click Format Page Numbers, and then choose from the options in the Page Number Format dialog box.

QUICK TIP
To remove page numbers from a document, click the Page Number button, then click Remove Page Numbers.

6. **Press [Ctrl][Home], click the VIEW tab, click the Page Width button in the Zoom group, then save the document**

Moving around in a long document

Rather than scrolling to move to a different place in a long document, you can use the Navigation pane to move the insertion point to the top of a specific page. To open the Navigation pane, click the Find button in the Editing group on the HOME tab, and then click Pages to display a thumbnail of each page in the document in the Navigation pane. Use the scroll box in the Navigation pane to scroll through the thumbnails. Click a thumbnail in the Navigation pane to move the insertion point to the top of that page in the document window.

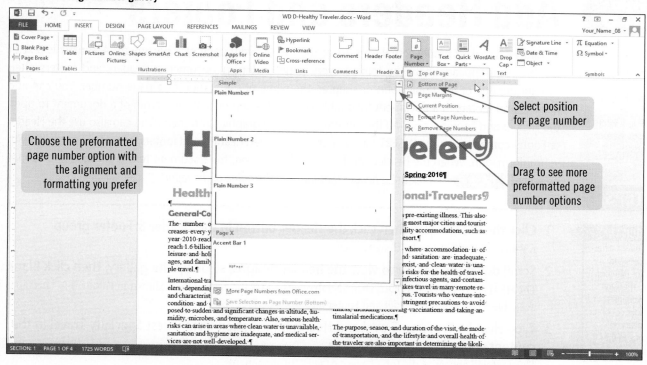

Choose the preformatted page number option with the alignment and formatting you prefer

Select position for page number

Drag to see more preformatted page number options

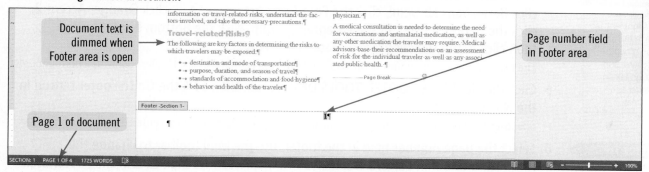

Document text is dimmed when Footer area is open

Page number field in Footer area

Page 1 of document

Inserting Quick Parts

The Word Quick Parts feature makes it easy to insert reusable pieces of content into a document quickly. The **Quick Parts** items you can insert include fields, such as for the current date or the total number of pages in a document; document property information, such as the author and title of a document; and building blocks, which are customized content that you create, format, and save for future use.

To insert a Quick Part into a document at the location of the insertion point, click the Quick Parts button in the Text group on the INSERT tab (or, if headers and footers are open, click the Quick Parts button in the Insert group on the HEADER & FOOTER TOOLS DESIGN tab), and then select the type of Quick Part you want to insert. To insert a field into a document, click Field on the Quick Parts menu that opens, click the name of the field you want to insert in the Field dialog box, and then click OK. Field information is updated automatically each time the document is opened or saved.

To insert a document property, point to Document Property on the Quick Parts menu, and then click the property you want to insert. The property is added to the document as a content control and contains the document property information you entered in the Document Properties panel. If you did not assign a document property, the content control contains a place-holder, which you can replace with your own text. Once you replace the placeholder text—or edit the document property information that appears in the content control—this text replaces the document property information in the Document Properties panel.

To insert a building block, click Building Blocks Organizer on the Quick Parts menu, select the building block you want, and then click Insert. You will learn more about working with building blocks in later lessons.

Word 2013

Add Headers and Footers

Learning Outcomes
- Create and format headers and footers
- Create a different first page header or footer

A **header** is text or graphics that appears at the top of every page of a document. A **footer** is text or graphics that appears at the bottom of every page. In longer documents, headers and footers often contain the title of the publication or chapter, the name of the author, or a page number. You can add headers and footers to a document by double-clicking the top or bottom margin of a document to open the Header and Footer areas, and then inserting text and graphics into them. You can also use the Header or Footer command on the INSERT tab to insert predesigned headers and footers that you can modify with your information. When the header and footer areas are open, the document text is dimmed and cannot be edited. **CASE** *You create a header that includes the name of the report.*

STEPS

QUICK TIP
Unless you set different headers and footers for different sections, the information you insert in any Header or Footer area appears on every page in the document.

1. **Click the INSERT tab, then click the Header button in the Header & Footer group**
 A gallery of built-in header designs opens.

2. **Scroll down the gallery to view the header designs, scroll up the gallery, then click Blank**
 The HEADER & FOOTER TOOLS DESIGN tab opens and is the active tab, as shown in **FIGURE D-9**. This tab is available whenever the Header and Footer areas are open.

3. **Type Healthy Traveler: Travel and Health Information from Quest Specialty Travel in the content control in the Header area**
 This text will appear at the top of every page in the document.

QUICK TIP
You can also use the Insert Alignment Tab button in the Position group to left-, center-, and right-align text in the Header and Footer areas.

4. **Select the header text, click the HOME tab, click the Font list arrow in the Font group, click Berlin Sans FB Demi, click the Font Color list arrow A ·, click Orange, Accent 2, click the Center button in the Paragraph group, click the Bottom Border button ,, then click in the Header area to deselect the text**
 The text is formatted in orange Berlin Sans FB Demi and centered in the Header area with a bottom border.

5. **Click the HEADER & FOOTER TOOLS DESIGN tab, then click the Go to Footer button in the Navigation group**
 The insertion point moves to the Footer area, where a page number field is centered in the Footer area.

QUICK TIP
To change the distance between the header and footer and the edge of the page, change the Header from Top and Footer from Bottom settings in the Position group.

6. **Select the page number field in the footer, use the Mini toolbar to change the formatting to Berlin Sans FB Demi and Orange, Accent 2, then click in the Footer area to deselect the text and field**
 The footer text is formatted in orange Berlin Sans FB Demi.

7. **Click the Close Header and Footer button in the Close group, then scroll down until the bottom of page 1 and the top of page 2 appear in the document window**
 The Header and Footer areas close, and the header and footer text is dimmed, as shown in **FIGURE D-10**.

8. **Press [Ctrl][Home]**
 The report already includes the name of the document at the top of the first page, making the header information redundant. You can modify headers and footers so that the header and footer text does not appear on the first page of a document.

9. **Position the pointer over the header text at the top of page 1, then double-click**
 The Header and Footer areas open. The Options group on the HEADER & FOOTER TOOLS DESIGN tab includes options for creating a different header and footer for the first page of a document, and for creating different headers and footers for odd- and even-numbered pages.

QUICK TIP
To remove headers or footers from a document, click the Header or Footer button, and then click Remove Header or Remove Footer.

10. **Click the Different First Page check box to select it, click the Close Header and Footer button, scroll to see the header and footer on pages 2, 3, and 4, then save the document**
 The header and footer text is removed from the Header and Footer areas on the first page.

Formatting Documents

FIGURE D-9: Header area

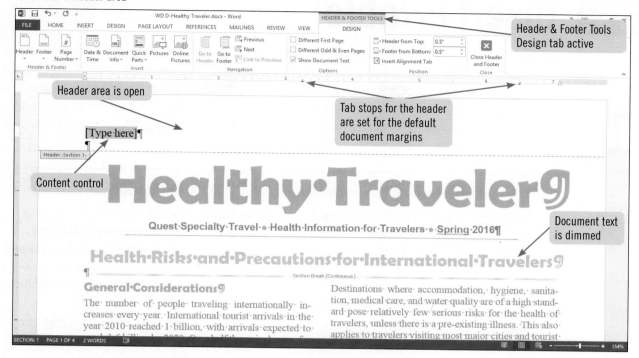

FIGURE D-10: Header and footer in document

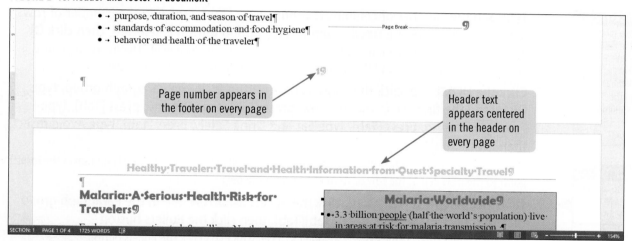

Adding a custom header or footer to the gallery

When you design a header that you want to use again in other documents, you can add it to the Header gallery by saving it as a building block. **Building blocks** are reusable pieces of formatted content or document parts, including headers and footers, page numbers, and text boxes, that are stored in galleries. Building blocks include predesigned content that comes with Word, as well as content that you create and save for future use. For example, you might create a custom header that contains your company name and logo and is formatted using the fonts, border, and colors you use in all company documents.

To add a custom header to the Header gallery, select all the text in the header, including the last paragraph mark, click the Header button, and then click Save Selection to Header Gallery.

In the Create New Building Block dialog box that opens, type a unique name for the header in the Name text box, click the Gallery list arrow and select the appropriate gallery, verify that the Category is General, and then type a brief description of the new header design in the Description text box. This description appears in a ScreenTip when you point to the custom header in the gallery. When you are finished, click OK. The new header appears in the Header gallery under the General category.

To remove a custom header from the Header gallery, right-click it, click Organize and Delete, make sure the appropriate building block is selected in the Building Blocks Organizer that opens, click Delete, click Yes, and then click Close. You can follow the same process to add or remove a custom footer to the Footer gallery.

Word 2013

Insert a Table

Learning Outcomes
- Create a table
- Delete a table
- Apply a table style

Adding a table to a document is a useful way to illustrate information that is intended for quick reference and analysis. A **table** is a grid of columns and rows that you can fill with text and graphics. A **cell** is the box formed by the intersection of a column and a row. The lines that divide the columns and rows of a table and help you see the grid-like structure of the table are called **borders**. A simple way to insert a table into a document is to use the Insert Table command on the INSERT tab. **CASE** ▸ *You add a table to page 2 showing the preventive options for serious travel health diseases.*

STEPS

1. **Scroll until the heading** Preventive Options... **is at the top of your document window**

2. **Select the heading** Preventive Options... **and the two paragraph marks below it, click the** PAGE LAYOUT **tab, click the** Columns button **in the Page Setup group, click** One, **click the** heading **to deselect the text, then scroll down to see the bottom half of page 2**

 A continuous section break is inserted before the heading and after the second paragraph mark, creating a new section, section 3, as shown in FIGURE D-11. The document now includes four sections, with the heading Preventive Options... in Section 3. Section 3 is formatted as a single column.

3. **Place the insertion point before the first paragraph mark below the heading, click the** INSERT **tab, click the** Table button **in the Tables group, then click** Insert Table

 The Insert Table dialog box opens. You use this dialog box to create a blank table.

 > **QUICK TIP**
 > To delete a table, click in the table, click the TABLE TOOLS LAYOUT tab, click the Delete button in the Rows & Columns group, then click Delete Table.

4. **Type** 5 **in the Number of columns text box, press [Tab], type** 6 **in the Number of rows text box, make sure the** Fixed column width option button **is selected, then click** OK

 A blank table with five columns and six rows is inserted in the document. The insertion point is in the upper-left cell of the table, and the TABLE TOOLS DESIGN tab becomes the active tab.

5. **Click the** HOME **tab, click the** Show/Hide ¶ button ¶ **in the Paragraph group, type** Disease **in the first cell in the first row, press [Tab], type** Vaccine, **press [Tab], type** Prophylaxis Drug, **press [Tab], type** Eat and Drink Safely, **press [Tab], type** Avoid Insects, **then press [Tab]**

 Don't be concerned if the text wraps to the next line in a cell as you type. Pressing [Tab] moves the insertion point to the next cell in the row or to the first cell in the next row.

 > **QUICK TIP**
 > You can also click in a cell to move the insertion point to it.

6. **Type** Malaria, **press [Tab][Tab], click the** Bullets list arrow ≔▾ **in the Paragraph group, click the** check mark style, **press [Tab][Tab], then click the** Bullets button ≔

 The active bullet style, a check mark, is added to a cell when you click the Bullets button.

 > **TROUBLE**
 > If you pressed [Tab] after the last row, click the Undo button ↺ on the Quick Access toolbar to remove the blank row.

7. **Type the text shown in** FIGURE D-12 **in the table cells**

8. **Click the** TABLE TOOLS LAYOUT **tab, click the** AutoFit button **in the Cell Size group, click** AutoFit Contents, **click the** AutoFit button **again, then click** AutoFit Window

 The width of the table columns is adjusted to fit the text and then the window.

 > **QUICK TIP**
 > You can also format table text using the buttons on the Mini toolbar or the HOME tab.

9. **Click the** Select button **in the Table group, click** Select Table, **click the** Align Center button ≡ **in the Alignment group, click** Disease **in the table, click the** Select button, **click** Select Column, **click the** Align Center Left button ≡, **then click in the table to deselect the column**

 The text in the table is centered in each cell, and then the text in the first column is left-aligned.

10. **Click the** TABLE TOOLS DESIGN **tab, click the** More button ▾ **in the Table Styles group, scroll down, click the** List Table 3 – Accent 2 style, **then save your changes**

 The List Table 3 - Accent 2 table style is applied to the table, as shown in FIGURE D-13. A **table style** includes format settings for the text, borders, and shading in a table.

FIGURE D-11: New section

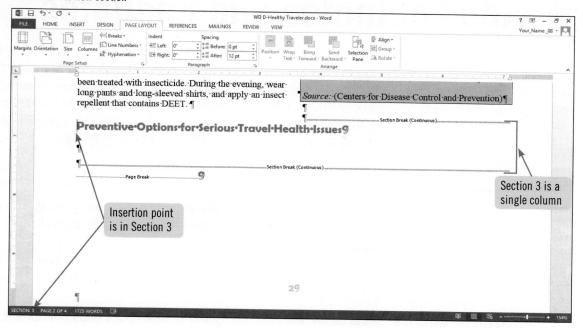

FIGURE D-12: Text in table

FIGURE D-13: Completed table

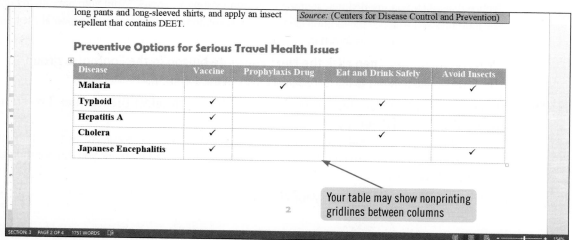

Add Footnotes and Endnotes

Learning Outcomes
- Insert and delete a footnote
- Modify note reference marks
- Convert footnotes to endnotes

Footnotes and endnotes are used in documents to provide further information, explanatory text, or references for text in a document. A **footnote** or **endnote** is an explanatory note that consists of two linked parts: the note reference mark that appears next to text to indicate that additional information is offered in a footnote or endnote, and the corresponding footnote or endnote text. Word places footnotes at the end of each page and endnotes at the end of the document. You insert and manage footnotes and endnotes using the tools in the Footnotes group on the REFERENCES tab. **CASE** *You add several footnotes to the report.*

STEPS

1. **Press [Ctrl][Home], place the insertion point at the end of the first body paragraph in the second column of text (after "resort."), click the REFERENCES tab, then click the Insert Footnote button in the Footnotes group**

 A note reference mark, in this case a superscript 1, appears after "resort.", and the insertion point moves below a separator line at the bottom of the page. A note reference mark can be a number, a symbol, a character, or a combination of characters.

2. **Type Behavior is a critical factor. For example, going outdoors in a malaria-endemic area could result in becoming infected., place the insertion point at the end of the second column of text (after "health"), click the Insert Footnote button, then type It is best to consult a travel medicine specialist.**

 The footnote text appears below the separator line at the bottom of page 1, as shown in FIGURE D-14.

3. **Scroll down until the bottom half of page 3 appears in the document window, place the insertion point at the end of "Medications taken on a regular basis at home" in the second column, click the Insert Footnote button, then type All medications should be stored in carry-on luggage, in their original containers and labeled clearly.**

 The footnote text for the third footnote appears at the bottom of the first column on page 3.

4. **Place the insertion point at the end of "Sunscreen" in the bulleted list in the second column, click the Insert Footnote button, then type SPF 15 or greater.**

 The footnote text for the fourth footnote appears at the bottom of page 3.

5. **Place the insertion point after "Disposable gloves" in the first column, click the Insert Footnote button, type At least two pairs., place the insertion point after "Scissors, safety pins, and tweezers" in the first column, click the Insert Footnote button, then type Pack these items in checked luggage.**

 Notice that when you inserted new footnotes between existing footnotes, Word automatically renumbered the footnotes and wrapped the footnote text to the next column. The new footnotes appear at the bottom of the first column on page 3, as shown in FIGURE D-15.

6. **Press [Ctrl][Home], then click the Next Footnote button in the Footnotes group**

 The insertion point moves to the first reference mark in the document.

7. **Click the Next Footnote button twice, press [Delete] to select the number 3 reference mark, then press [Delete] again**

 The third reference mark and associated footnote are deleted from the document and the footnotes are renumbered automatically. You must select a reference mark to delete a footnote; you can not simply delete the footnote text itself.

8. **Press [Ctrl][Home], then save your changes**

FIGURE D-14: Footnotes in the document

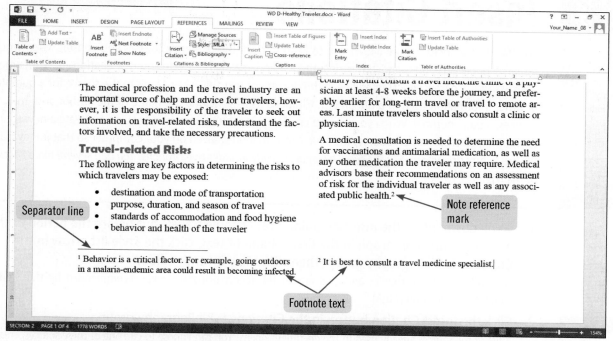

FIGURE D-15: Renumbered footnotes in the document

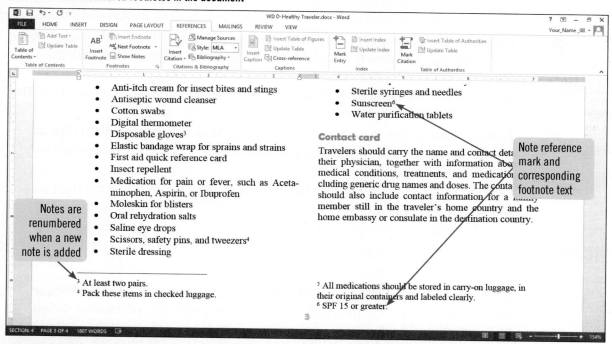

Customizing the layout and formatting of footnotes and endnotes

You can change the location, formatting, and numbering options for footnotes and endnotes in a document using the Footnote and Endnote dialog box. To open the dialog box, click the launcher in the Footnotes group on the REFERENCES tab. Use the list arrows in the Location section of the dialog box to locate footnotes at the bottom of the page (the default) or directly below the text on a page, and to locate endnotes at the end of a document or at the end of a section. Use the Columns list arrow in the Footnote layout section to format footnote text in one or more columns, or to match section layout (the default). Use the options in the Format section of the dialog box to change the number format of the note reference marks, to use a symbol instead of a character, and to change the numbering of footnotes and endnotes. You can choose to apply the settings to a section or to the document as a whole. When you are finished, click Apply.

Insert Citations

The Word References feature allows you to keep track of the reference sources you consult when writing research papers, reports, and other documents, and makes it easy to insert a citation in a document. A **citation** is a parenthetical reference in the document text that gives credit to the source for a quotation or other information used in a document. Citations usually include the name of the author and, for print sources, a page number. When you insert a citation you can use an existing source or create a new source. Each time you create a new source, the source information is saved on your computer so that it is available for use in any document. **CASE** ▸ *The report already includes two citations. You add several more citations to the report.*

STEPS

1. **Scroll down, place the insertion point after "people travel" but before the period at the end of the first paragraph in the first column of text, click the Style list arrow in the Citations & Bibliography group, then click MLA Seventh Edition**

 You will format the sources and citations in the report using the style recommended by the Modern Language Association (MLA).

2. **Click the Insert Citation button in the Citations & Bibliography group**

 A list of the sources already used in the document opens. You can choose to cite one of these sources, create a new source, or add a placeholder for a source. When you add a new citation to a document, the source is added to the list of master sources that is stored on the computer. The new source is also associated with the document.

3. ▸ **Click Add New Source, click the Type of Source list arrow in the Create Source dialog box, scroll down to view the available source types, click Report, then click the Corporate Author check box**

 You select the type of source and enter the source information in the Create Source dialog box. The fields available in the dialog box change, depending on the type of source selected.

4. **Enter the data shown in FIGURE D-16 in the Create Source dialog box, then click OK**

 The citation (World Tourism Organization) appears at the end of the paragraph. Because the source is a print publication, it needs to include a page number.

5. **Click the citation to select it, click the Citation Options list arrow on the right side of the citation, then click Edit Citation**

 The Edit Citation dialog box opens, as shown in FIGURE D-17.

6. ▸ **Type 19 in the Pages text box, then click OK**

 The page number 19 is added to the citation.

7. **Scroll down, place the insertion point at the end of the quotation (after ...consequences.), click the Insert Citation button, click Add New Source, enter the information shown in FIGURE D-18, then click OK**

 A citation for the Web publication that the quotation was taken from is added to the report. No page number is used in this citation because the source is a Web site.

8. **Scroll to the bottom of page 2, click under the table, type Source:, italicize Source:, click after Source:, click the Insert Citation button, then click Johnson, Margaret in the list of sources**

 The citation (Johnson) appears under the table.

9. **Click the citation, click the Citation Options list arrow, click Edit Citation, type 55 in the Pages text box, click OK, then save your changes**

 The page number 55 is added to the citation.

FIGURE D-16: Adding a Report source

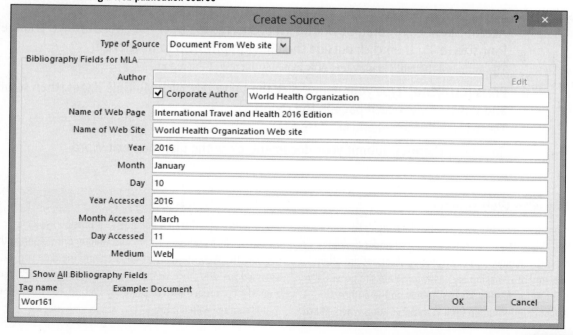

FIGURE D-17: Edit Citation dialog box

FIGURE D-18: Adding a Web publication source

Manage Sources and Create a Bibliography

Learning Outcomes
- Add and delete sources
- Edit a source
- Insert a bibliography field

Many documents require a **bibliography**, a list of sources that you used in creating the document. The list of sources can include only the works cited in your document (a **works cited** list) or both the works cited and the works consulted (a bibliography). The Bibliography feature in Word allows you to generate a works cited list or a bibliography automatically based on the source information you provide for the document. The Source Manager dialog box helps you to organize your sources. **CASE** ▶ *You add a bibliography to the report. The bibliography is inserted as a field and it can be formatted any way you choose.*

STEPS

1. **Press [Ctrl][End] to move the insertion point to the end of the document, then click the Manage Sources button in the Citations & Bibliography group**

 The Source Manager dialog box opens, as shown in **FIGURE D-19**. The Master List shows the two sources you added and any other sources available on your computer. The Current List shows the sources available in the current document. A check mark next to a source indicates the source is cited in the document. You use the tools in the Source Manager dialog box to add, edit, and delete sources from the lists, and to copy sources between the Master and Current Lists. The sources that appear in the Current List will appear in the bibliography.

2. **Click the Baker, Mary source in the Current List**

 A preview of the citation and bibliographical entry for the source in MLA style appears in the Preview box. You do not want this source to be included in your bibliography for the report.

3. **Click Delete**

 The source is removed from the Current List.

4. **Click Close, click the Bibliography button in the Citations & Bibliography group, click References, then scroll up to see the heading References at the top of the field**

 A Bibliography field labeled "References" is added at the location of the insertion point. The bibliography includes all the sources associated with the document, formatted in the MLA style for bibliographies. The text in the Bibliography field is formatted with the default styles.

5. **Select References; apply the following formats: Berlin Sans FB Demi and the Blue, Accent 5 font color; drag down the list of sources to select the entire list and change the font size to 11; then click outside the bibliography field to deselect it**

 The format of the bibliography text now matches the rest of the report.

6. **Press [Ctrl][End], type your name, click the VIEW tab, click Multiple Pages, then scroll up and down to view each page in the report**

 The completed report is shown in **FIGURE D-20**.

7. **Save your changes, submit your document, close the file, then exit Word**

Working with Web sources

Publications found on the Web can be challenging to document. Many Web sites can be accessed under multiple domains, URLs change, and electronic publications are often updated frequently, making each visit to a Web site potentially unique. For these reasons, it's best to rely on the author, title, and publication information for a Web publication when citing it as a source in a research document. If possible, you can include a URL as supplementary information only, along with the date the Web site was last updated and the date you accessed the site. Since Web sites are often removed, it's also a good idea to download or print any Web source you use so that it can be verified later.

FIGURE D-19: Source Manager dialog box

Your Master List will contain the two sources you added and either no additional sources or different additional sources

Preview of the citation and bibliography entry for the selected source in MLA style (as defined by Word)

List of sources associated with the document

Sources with a check mark have a citation in the document

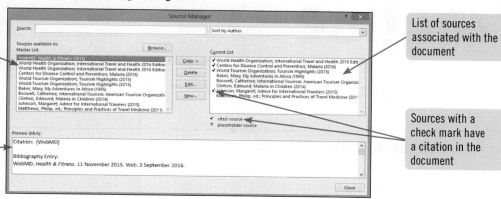

FIGURE D-20: Completed report

Practice

Concepts Review

Label each element shown in FIGURE D-21.

FIGURE D-21

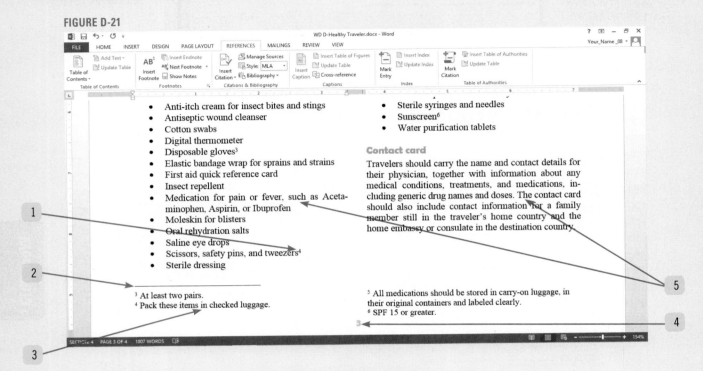

Match each term with the statement that best describes it.

6. Field
7. Table
8. Section break
9. Header
10. Manual page break
11. Footer
12. Bibliography
13. Citation
14. Margin

a. A grid of columns and rows that you can fill with text and graphics
b. A list of the sources used to create a document
c. Text or graphics that appear at the top of every page in a document
d. A formatting mark that forces the text following the mark to begin at the top of the next page
e. Text or graphics that appear at the bottom of every page in a document
f. A placeholder for information that changes
g. A formatting mark that divides a document into parts that can be formatted differently
h. The blank area between the edge of the text and the edge of the page
i. A parenthetical reference in the document text that gives credit to a source

Formatting Documents

Select the best answer from the list of choices.

15. **Which type of break can you insert if you want to force text to begin on the next page?**
 a. Next page section break
 b. Text wrapping break
 c. Column break
 d. Continuous section break

16. **Which type of break do you insert if you want to balance the columns in a section?**
 a. Column break
 b. Text wrapping break
 c. Continuous section break
 d. Manual page break

17. **Which of the following do documents with mirror margins always have?**
 a. Different first page headers and footers
 b. Gutters
 c. Inside and outside margins
 d. Landscape orientation

18. **Which of the following cannot be inserted using the Quick Parts command?**
 a. AutoText building block
 b. Page break
 c. Page number field
 d. Document property

19. **Which appears at the end of a document?**
 a. Footnote
 b. Page break
 c. Citation
 d. Endnote

20. **What name describes formatted pieces of content that are stored in galleries?**
 a. Property
 b. Building Block
 c. Field
 d. Header

Skills Review

1. **Set document margins.**
 a. Start Word, open the file WD D-2.docx from the location where you store your Data Files, then save it as **WD D-Liberty Fitness**.
 b. Change the top and bottom margin settings to Moderate: 1" top and bottom, and .75" left and right.
 c. Save your changes to the document.

2. **Create sections and columns.**
 a. Turn on the display of formatting marks, then customize the status bar to display sections if they are not displayed already.
 b. Insert a continuous section break before the **Welcome to the Liberty Fitness Center** heading.
 c. Format the text in section 2 in two columns, then save your changes to the document.

3. **Insert page breaks.**
 a. Scroll to page 3, then insert a manual page break before the heading **Facilities and Services**. (*Hint:* The page break will appear at the bottom of page 2.)
 b. Scroll down and insert a manual page break before the heading **Membership**, then press [Ctrl][Home].
 c. On page 1, select the heading **Welcome to the Liberty Fitness Center** and the paragraph mark below it, use the Columns button to format the selected text as one column, then center the heading on the page.
 d. Follow the direction in step c to format the heading **Facilities and Services** and the paragraph mark below it on page 3, and the heading **Membership** and the paragraph mark below it on page 4, as one column, with centered text, then save your changes to the document.

4. **Insert page numbers.**
 a. Insert page numbers in the document at the bottom of the page. Select the Plain Number 2 page number style from the gallery.
 b. Close the Footer area, scroll through the document to view the page number on each page, then save your changes to the document.

Skills Review (continued)

5. **Add headers and footers.**

 a. Double-click the margin at the top of a page to open the Header and Footer areas.

 b. With the insertion point in the Header area, click the Quick Parts button in the Insert Group on the HEADER & FOOTER TOOLS DESIGN tab, point to Document Property, then click Author.

 c. Replace the text in the Author content control with your name, press [End] to move the insertion point out of the content control, then press [Spacebar]. (*Note*: If your name does not appear in the header, right-click the Author content control, click Remove Content Control, then type your name in the header.)

 d. Click the Insert Alignment Tab button in the Position group, select the Right option button and keep the alignment relative to the margin, then click OK in the dialog box to close the dialog box and move the insertion point to the right margin.

 e. Use the Insert Date and Time command in the Insert group to insert the current date using a format of your choice as static text. (*Hint*: Be sure the Update automatically check box is not checked.)

 f. Apply italic to the text in the header.

 g. Move the insertion point to the Footer area.

 h. Double-click the page number to select it, then format the page number in bold and italic.

 i. Move the insertion point to the header on page 1, use the HEADER & FOOTER TOOLS DESIGN tab to create a different header and footer for the first page of the document, type your name in the First Page Header area, then apply italic to your name.

 j. Close headers and footers, scroll to view the header and footer on each page, then save your changes to the document.

6. **Insert a table.**

 a. On page 4, double-click the word **Table** at the end of the Membership Rates section to select it, press [Delete], open the Insert Table dialog box, then create a table with two columns and five rows.

 b. Apply the yellow List Table 2- Accent 4 table style to the table.

 c. Press [Tab] to leave the first cell in the header row blank, then type **Rate**.

 d. Press [Tab], then type the following text in the table, pressing [Tab] to move from cell to cell.

Enrollment/Individual	**$100**
Enrollment/Couple	**$150**
Monthly membership/Individual	**$35**
Monthly membership/Couple	**$60**

 e. Select the table, use the AutoFit command on the TABLE TOOLS LAYOUT tab to select the AutoFit to Contents option, and then select the AutoFit to Window option. (*Note*: In this case, AutoFit to Window fits the table to the width of the column of text.)

 f. Save your changes to the document.

7. **Add footnotes and endnotes.**

 a. Press [Ctrl][Home], scroll down, place the insertion point at the end of the first body paragraph, insert a footnote, then type **People who are active live longer and feel better**.

 b. Place the insertion point at the end of the first paragraph under the Benefits of Exercise heading, insert a footnote, then type **There are 1,440 minutes in every day. Schedule 30 of them for physical activity**.

 c. Place the insertion point at the end of the first paragraph under the Tips for Staying Motivated heading, insert a footnote, type **Always consult your physician before beginning an exercise program.**, then save your changes.

8. **Insert citations.**

 a. Place the insertion point at the end of the second paragraph under the Benefits of Exercise heading (after "down from 52% in 2013" but before the period), then be sure the style for citations and bibliography is set to MLA Seventh Edition.

b. Insert a citation, add a new source, enter the source information shown in the Create Source dialog box in **FIGURE D-22**, then click OK.

c. Place the insertion point at the end of the italicized quotation in the second column of text, insert a citation, then select Jason, Laura from the list of sources.

d. Edit the citation to include the page number **25**.

e. Scroll to page 2, place the insertion point at the end of the "Be a morning exerciser" paragraph but before the ending period, insert a citation for WebMD, then save your changes.

FIGURE D-22

9. **Manage sources and create a bibliography.**

a. Press [Ctrl][End], then open the Source Manager dialog box.

b. Select the source Health, National Institute of: ...in the Current List, click Edit, click the Corporate Author check box, edit the entry so it reads **National Institute of Health**, click OK, then click Close.

c. Insert a bibliography labeled References.

d. Select References, then change the font to 14-point Tahoma with a black font color. Pages 1 and 4 of the formatted document are shown in **FIGURE D-23**.

e. Save your changes to the document, submit it to your instructor, then close the document and exit Word.

FIGURE D-23

Independent Challenge 1

You are the owner of a small business called Village Catering. You have begun work on the text for a brochure advertising your business and are now ready to lay out the pages and prepare the final copy. The brochure will be printed on both sides of an 8½" x 11" sheet of paper, and folded in thirds.

a. Start Word, open the file WD D-3.docx from the location where you store your Data Files, then save it as **WD D-Village Catering**. Read the document to get a feel for its contents.

b. Change the page orientation to landscape, and change all four margins to .6".

c. Format the document in three columns of equal width.

d. Insert a next page section break before the heading **Catering Services**.

e. On page 1, insert column breaks before the headings **Sample Tuscan Banquet Menu** and **Sample Indian Banquet Menu**.

f. Change the column spacing in section 1 (which is the first page) to .4", add lines between the columns on the first page, then select the text in the columns in section 1 and center it.

g. Double-click the bottom margin to open the footer area, create a different header and footer for the first page, then type **Call for custom menus designed to your taste and budget.** in the First Page Footer -Section 1- area.

h. Center the text in the footer area, format it in 20-point Papyrus, bold, with a Green, Accent 6 font color, then close headers and footers.

i. On page 2, insert a column break before Your Name, then press [Enter] 22 times to move the contact information to the bottom of the second column.

j. Replace Your Name with your name, then center the contact information in the column.

k. Press [Ctrl][End], insert a column break at the bottom of the second column. Type the text shown in FIGURE D-24 in the third column, then apply the No Spacing style to the text. Refer to the figure as you follow the instructions for formatting the text in the third column.

l. Format Harvest Catering in 28-point Papyrus, bold.

m. Format the remaining text in 12-point Papyrus. Center the text in the third column.

n. Insert the online picture shown in FIGURE D-24 or another appropriate online picture. Do not wrap text around the graphic. (*Hint*: Use the search terms fruits, flowers, and food.)

o. Resize the graphic and add or remove blank paragraphs in the third column of your brochure so that the spacing between elements roughly matches the spacing shown in FIGURE D-24.

p. Apply a 2.5 point soft edge picture effect to the image.

q. Save your changes, then submit a copy to your instructor. If possible, you can print the brochure with the two pages back to back so that the brochure can be folded in thirds.

r. Close the document and exit Word.

FIGURE D-24

Village Catering

Complete catering services available for all types of events. Menus and estimates provided upon request.

Independent Challenge 2

You work in the Campus Safety Department at Mountain State College. You have written the text for an informational flyer about parking regulations on campus, and now you need to format the flyer so it is attractive and readable.

a. Start Word, open the file WD D-4.docx from the drive and folder where you store your Data Files, then save it as **WD D-Parking FAQ**. Read the document to get a feel for its contents.

b. Change all four margins to .7".

c. Insert a continuous section break before **1. May I bring a car to school?** (*Hint*: Place the insertion point before May.)

d. Scroll down and insert a next page section break before **Sample Parking Permit**.

e. Format the text in section 2 in three columns of equal width with .3" of space between the columns.

f. Hyphenate the document using the automatic hyphenation feature. (*Hint*: Use the Hyphenation button in the Page Setup group on the PAGE LAYOUT tab.)

g. Add a 3-point dotted-line bottom border to the blank paragraph under Mountain State College Department of Campus Safety. (*Hint*: Place the insertion point before the paragraph mark under Mountain State College...)

h. Open the Header area, and type your name in the header. Right-align your name, and format it in 10-point Arial.

i. Add the following text to the footer, inserting symbols between words as indicated: **Parking and Shuttle Service Office • 54 Buckley Street • Mountain State College • 942-555-2227**. (*Hint*: Click the Symbol command in the Symbols group on the INSERT tab to insert a symbol. To find a small circle symbol, be sure the font is set to (normal text) and the subset is set to General Punctuation.)

j. Format the footer text in 9-point Arial Black, and center it in the footer.

k. Apply a 3-point dotted-line border above the footer text. Make sure to apply the border to the paragraph.

l. Add a continuous section break at the end of section 2 to balance the columns in section 2.

m. Place the insertion point on page 2 (which is section 4). Change the left and right margins in section 4 to 1". Also change the page orientation of section 4 to landscape.

n. Change the vertical alignment of section 4 to center. (*Hint*: Use the Vertical Alignment list arrow on the Layout tab in the Page Setup dialog box.)

o. Apply an appropriate table style to the table, such as the style shown in FIGURE D-25. (*Hint*: Check and uncheck the options in the Table Style Options group on the TABLE TOOLS DESIGN tab to customize the style so it enhances the table data.)

p. Save your changes, submit your work, close the document, then exit Word.

FIGURE D-25

Sample Parking Permit

Mountain State College
Office of Parking and Shuttle Service

2015-16 Student Parking Permit

License number:	VA 498 359
Make:	Subaru
Model:	Forester
Year:	2007
Color:	Red
Permit Issue Date:	September 8, 2016
Permit Expiration Date:	June 4, 2017

Restrictions:
Parking is permitted in the Mountain State College Greene Street lot 24 hours a day, 7 days a week. Shuttle service is available from the Greene Street lot to campus from 7 a.m. to 7 p.m. Monday through Friday. Parking is also permitted in any on-campus lot from 4:30 p.m. Friday to midnight Sunday.

Independent Challenge 3

A book publisher would like to publish an article you wrote on stormwater pollution in Australia as a chapter in a forthcoming book called *Environmental Issues for the New Millennium*. The publisher has requested that you format your article like a book chapter before submitting it for publication, and has provided you with a style sheet. According to the style sheet, the citations and bibliography should be formatted in Chicago style. You have already created the sources for the chapter, but you need to insert the citations.

a. Start Word, open the file WD D-5.docx from the location where you store your Data Files, then save it as **WD D-Chapter 5**. You will format the first page as shown in FIGURE D-26.

b. Change the font of the entire document to 10-point Book Antigua. If this font is not available to you, select a different font suitable for the pages of a book. Change the alignment to justified.

c. Change the paper size to a custom setting of 6" x 9".

d. Create mirror margins. (*Hint*: Use the Multiple pages list arrow.) Change the top and bottom margins to .8", change the inside margin to .4", change the outside margin to .6", and create a .3" gutter to allow room for the book's binding.

e. Change the Zoom level to Page Width, open the Header and Footer areas, then apply the setting to create different headers and footers for odd- and even-numbered pages.

f. In the odd-page header, type **Chapter 5**, insert a symbol of your choice, type **The Fairy Creek Catchment and Stormwater Pollution**, then format the header text in 9-point Book Antigua italic and right-align the text.

g. In the even-page header, type your name, then format the header text in 9-point Book Antigua italic. (*Note*: The even-page header should be left-aligned.)

h. Insert a left-aligned page number field in the even-page footer area, format it in 10-point Book Antigua, insert a right-aligned page number field in the odd-page footer area, then format it in 10-point Book Antigua.

i. Format the page numbers so that the first page of your chapter, which is Chapter 5 in the book, begins on page 101. (*Hint*: Select a page number field, click the Page Number button, then click Format Page Numbers.)

j. Go to the beginning of the document, press [Enter] 10 times, type **Chapter 5: The Fairy Creek Catchment and Stormwater Pollution**, press [Enter] twice, type your name, then press [Enter] twice.

k. Format the chapter title in 16-point Book Antigua bold, format your name in 14-point Book Antigua, then left-align the title text and your name.

l. Click the REFERENCES tab, make sure the citations and bibliography style is set to Chicago Fifteenth Edition, place the insertion point at the end of the first body paragraph on page 1 but before the ending period, insert a citation for Alice Burke, et. al., then add the page number 40 to the citation.

m. Add the citations listed in TABLE D-3 to the document using the sources already associated with the document.

FIGURE D-26

TABLE D-3

page	location for citation	source	page number
2	End of the first complete paragraph (after ...WCSMP, but before the period)	City of Weston	3
3	End of the first complete paragraph (after ...pollution, but before the colon)	Jensen	135
4	End of first paragraph (after ...health effects, but before the period)	City of Weston	5
4	End of fourth bulleted list (after 1 month.)	Seawatch	None
5	End of second paragraph (after ...problem arises, but before the period)	Burke, et. al.	55
5	End of first sentence (after ...stormwater system, but before the period)	City of Weston	7
6	End of first paragraph under Conclusion (after ...include, but before the colon)	Jensen	142

© 2014 Cengage Learning

Independent Challenge 3 (continued)

n. Press [Ctrl][End], insert a Works Cited list, format the Works Cited heading in 11-point Book Antigua, black font color, bold, then format the list of works cited in Book Antigua.

o. Scroll to page 4 in the document, place the insertion point at the end of the paragraph above the Potential health effects... heading, press [Enter] twice, type **Table 1: Total annual pollutant loads per year in the Fairy Creek Catchment**, press [Enter] twice, then format the text you just typed as bold if it is not bold.

p. Insert a table with four columns and four rows.

q. Type the text shown in FIGURE D-27 in the table. Do not be concerned when the text wraps to the next line in a cell.

FIGURE D-27

Area	Nitrogen	Phosphorus	Suspended solids
Fairy Creek	9.3 tonnes	1.2 tonnes	756.4 tonnes
Durras Arm	6.2 tonnes	.9 tonnes	348.2 tonnes
Cabbage Tree Creek	9.8 tonnes	2.3 tonnes	485.7 tonnes

r. Apply the Grid Table 1 Light table style. Make sure the text in the header row is bold, then remove any bold formatting from the text in the remaining rows.

s. Use AutoFit to make the table fit the contents, then use AutoFit to make the table fit the window.

t. Save your changes, submit your work, then close the document and exit Word.

Independent Challenge 4: Explore

One of the most common opportunities to use the page layout features of Word is when formatting a research paper. The format recommended by the *MLA Handbook for Writers of Research Papers*, a style guide that includes information on preparing, writing, and formatting research papers, is the standard format used by many schools, colleges, and universities. In this independent challenge, you will research the MLA guidelines for formatting a research paper and use the guidelines you find to format the pages of a sample research report.

a. Use your favorite search engine to search the Web for information on the MLA guidelines for formatting a research report. Use the keywords **MLA Style** and **research paper format** to conduct your search.

b. Look for information on the proper formatting for the following aspects of a research paper: paper size, margins, title page or first page of the report, line spacing, paragraph indentation, and page numbers. Also find information on proper formatting for citations and a works cited page. Print the information you find.

c. Start Word, open the file WD D-6.docx from the drive and folder where you store your Data Files, then save it as **WD D-Research Paper**. Using the information you learned, format this document as a research report.

d. Adjust the margins, set the line spacing, and add page numbers to the document in the format recommended by the MLA. Use **The Maori History of New Zealand** as the title for your sample report, use your name as the author name, and use the name of the course you are enrolled in currently as well as the instructor's name for that course. Make sure to format the title page exactly as the MLA style dictates.

e. Format the remaining text as the body of the research report. Indent the first line of each paragraph rather than use quadruple spacing between paragraphs.

f. Create three sources, insert three citations in the document—a book, a journal article, and a Web site—and create a works cited page, following MLA style. If necessary, edit the format of the citations and works cited page to conform to MLA format. (*Note*: For this practice document, you are allowed to make up sources. Never make up sources for real research papers.)

g. Save the document, submit a copy to your instructor, close the document, then exit Word.

Visual Workshop

Open the file WD D-7.docx from the location where you store your Data Files, then modify it to create the article shown in **FIGURE D-28**. (*Hint*: Change all four margins to .6". Add the footnotes as shown in the figure. To locate the graphic image, search using the keywords **oak leaves**. Select a different graphic if the graphic shown in the figure is not available to you.) Save the document with the filename **WD D-Perennial**, then print a copy.

FIGURE D-28

GARDENER'S CORNER

Putting a Perennial Garden to Bed

By Your Name

A sense of peace descends when a perennial garden is put to bed for the season. The plants are safely tucked in against the elements, and the garden is ready to welcome the winter. When the work is done, you can sit back and anticipate the bright blooms of spring. Many gardeners are uncertain about how to close a perennial garden. This week's column demystifies the process.

Clean up

Garden clean up can be a gradual process—plants will deteriorate at different rates, allowing you to do a little bit each week.

- Edge beds and borders and remove stakes, trellises, and other plant supports.
- Dig and divide irises, daylilies, and other early bloomers.
- Cut back plants when foliage starts to deteriorate, then rake all debris out of the garden and pull any weeds that remain.

Plant perennials

Fall is the perfect time to plant perennials.[1] The warm, sunny days and cool nights provide optimal conditions for new root growth, without the stress of summer heat.

- Dig deeply and enhance soil with organic matter.
- Use a good starter fertilizer to speed up new root growth and establish a healthy base.
- Untangle the roots of new plants before planting.

- Water after planting as the weather dictates, and keep plants moist for several days.

Add compost

Organic matter is the key ingredient to healthy garden soil. Composting adds nutrients to the soil, helps the soil retain water and nutrients, and keeps the soil well aerated. If you take care of the soil, your plants will become strong and disease resistant.[2]

Before adding compost, use an iron rake to loosen the top few inches of soil. Spread a one to two inch layer of compost over the entire garden—the best compost is made up of yard waste and kitchen scraps—and then refrain from stepping on the area and compacting the soil.

Winter mulch

Winter protection for perennial beds can only help plants survive the winter. Winter mulch prevents the freezing and thawing cycles, which cause plants to heave and eventually die. Here's what works and what doesn't:

- Always apply mulch after the ground is frozen.
- Never apply generic hay because it contains billions of weed seeds. Also, whole leaves and bark mulch hold too much moisture.[3]
- Use a loose material to allow air filtration. Straw and salt marsh hay are excellent choices for mulch.
- Remove the winter mulch in the spring as soon as new growth begins.

[1] Fall is also an excellent time to plant shrubs and trees.
[2] You can buy good compost, but it is easy and useful to make it at home. Composting kitchen scraps reduces household garbage by about one-third.

[3] If using leaves, use only stiff leaves, such as Oak or Beech. Soft leaves, such as Maple, make it difficult for air and water to filtrate.

Develop Multipage Documents

CASE As a marketing assistant at the head office of Quest Specialty Travel in San Diego, you have been asked to edit and format a set of guidelines to help QST managers sponsor tour presentations, tour information sessions, and travel clubs. You start by working in Outline view to revise the structure for the guidelines, and then you use several advanced Word features to format the document for publication.

Unit Objectives

After completing this unit, you will be able to:

- Build a document in Outline view
- Work in Outline view
- Navigate a document
- Insert a table of contents
- Mark text for an index

- Generate an index
- Insert footers in multiple sections
- Insert headers in multiple sections
- Finalize a multipage document

Files You Will Need

WD I-1.docx	WD I-6.docx
WD I-2.docx	WD I-7.docx
WD I-3.docx	WD I-8.docx
WD I-4.docx	WD I-9.docx
WD I-5.docx	WD I-10.docx

Build a Document in Outline View

Learning Outcomes
• Open Outline view
• Demote and promote headings

You work in Outline view to organize the headings and subheadings that identify topics and subtopics in multipage documents. In Outline view, each heading is assigned a level from 1 to 9, with Level 1 being the highest level and Level 9 being the lowest level. In addition, you can assign the Body Text level to each paragraph of text that appears below a document heading. Each level is formatted with one of Word's predefined styles. For example, Level 1 is formatted with the Heading 1 style, and the Body Text level is formatted with the Normal style. **CASE** *You work in Outline view to develop the structure of the Tour Presentation Guidelines.*

STEPS

1. **Start Word, create a new blank document, click the** VIEW **tab, then click the** Outline **button in the Views group**

 The document appears in Outline view. Notice that the OUTLINING tab is now active. TABLE I-1 describes the buttons on the OUTLINING tab.

TROUBLE
If the headings do not appear blue and bold, click the Show Text Formatting check box in the Outline Tools group to select it.

2. **Type** Tour Presentation

 FIGURE I-1 shows the text in Outline view. By default, the text appears at the left margin and is designated as Level 1. By default, Level 1 text is formatted with the Heading 1 style. You will work more with styles in the next unit.

3. **Press [Enter], click the** Demote **button** ⇥ **in the Outline Tools group to move to Level 2, then type** Presentation Structure

 The text is indented, designated as Level 2, and formatted with the Heading 2 style.

4. **Press [Enter], then click the** Demote to Body Text **button** ⇨ **in the Outline Tools group**

5. **Type the following text:** Three activities relate to the organization of a QST Tour Presentation: gather personnel, advertise the event, and arrange the physical space.

 The text is indented, designated as Body Text level, and formatted with the Normal style. Notice that both the Level 1 and Level 2 text are preceded by a plus symbol ⊕. This symbol indicates that the heading includes subtext, which could be another subheading or a paragraph of body text.

6. **Press [Enter], then click the** Promote to Heading 1 **button** ⇤ **in the Outline Tools group**

 The insertion point returns to the left margin and the Level 1 position.

7. **Type** Personnel, **press [Enter], then save the document as** WD I-Tour Presentation Outline **to the location where you store your Data Files**

 When you create a long document, you often enter all the headings and subheadings first to establish the overall structure of your document.

QUICK TIP
You can press [Tab] to move from a higher level to a lower level, and you can press [Shift][Tab] to move from a lower level to a higher level.

8. **Use the** Promote ⇤**,** Demote ⇥**, and** Promote to Heading 1 ⇤ **buttons to complete the outline shown in** FIGURE I-2

9. **Place the insertion point after Tour Presentation at the top of the page, press [Enter], click** ⇨**, type** Prepared by **followed by your name, save the document, submit it to your instructor, then close it**

FIGURE I-1: Text in Outline view

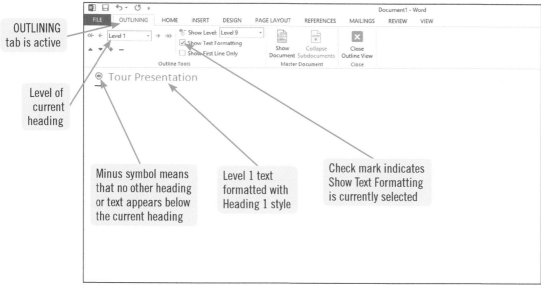

OUTLINING tab is active

Level of current heading

Minus symbol means that no other heading or text appears below the current heading

Level 1 text formatted with Heading 1 style

Check mark indicates Show Text Formatting is currently selected

FIGURE I-2: Completed outline

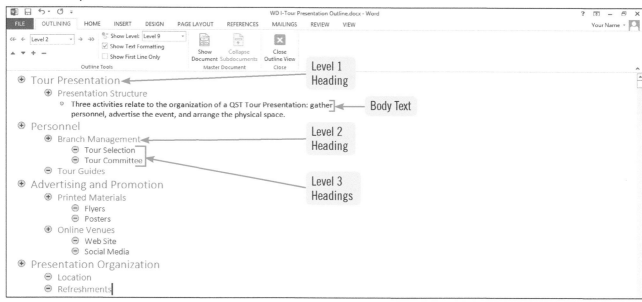

Level 1 Heading

Body Text

Level 2 Heading

Level 3 Headings

TABLE I-1: Frequently used outlining buttons in the Outline Tools group on the OUTLINING tab

button	use to	button	use to
⇐	Promote text to Heading 1	▲	Move a heading and its text up one line
←	Promote text one level	▼	Move a heading and its text down one line
→	Demote text one level	＋	Expand text
⇒	Demote to body text	—	Collapse text

Work in Outline View

Learning Outcomes
• Collapse/expand headings: Outline view
• Move headings
• Show levels

In Outline view, you can promote and demote headings and subheadings and move or delete whole blocks of text. When you move a heading in Outline view, all of the text and subheadings under that heading move with the heading. You also can use the Collapse, Expand, and Show Level commands on the OUTLINING tab to view all or just some of the headings and subheadings. For example, you can choose to view just the headings assigned to Level 1 so that you can quickly evaluate the main topics of your document. **CASE** ▶ *You work in Outline view to develop a draft of the guidelines for running a tour presentation. In Outline view, each heading is formatted with a heading style based on its corresponding level.*

STEPS

1. **Open the file WD I-1.docx from the location where you store your Data Files, save the document as WD I-Tour Presentation Guidelines, scroll through the document to get a sense of its content, click the VIEW tab, then click Outline in the Views group**

 The document changes to Outline view, and the OUTLINING tab opens. The chart at the end of the document is not visible in Outline view.

2. **Click the Show Level list arrow in the Outline Tools group, then click Level 1**

 Only the headings assigned to Level 1 appear. All the headings assigned to Level 1 are formatted with the Heading 1 style. Notice that the title of the document Tour Presentation Guidelines does not appear because the title text is not formatted as Level 1.

3. **Click the plus sign ⊕ to the left of Printed Materials**

 The heading and all its subtext (which is hidden because the topic is collapsed) are selected.

QUICK TIP
You can use [Ctrl] to select multiple non-adjacent headings.

4. **Press and hold [Shift], click the heading Online Venues, release [Shift], then click the Demote button → in the Outline Tools group**

 You use [Shift] to select several adjacent headings at once. The headings are demoted one level to Level 2, as shown in **FIGURE I-3**.

5. **Press [Ctrl][A] to select all the headings, then click the Expand button ➕ in the Outline Tools group**

 The outline expands to show all the subheadings and body text associated with each of the selected headings along with the document title. You can also expand a single heading by selecting only that heading and then clicking the Expand button.

6. **Click the plus sign ⊕ next to Advertising and Promotion, click the Collapse button ➖ in the Outline Tools group two times to collapse all the subheadings and text associated with the heading, then double-click ⊕ next to Personnel to collapse it**

 You can double-click headings to expand or collapse them, or you can use the Expand or Collapse buttons.

QUICK TIP
You can also use the mouse pointer to drag a heading up or down to a new location in the outline. A horizontal line appears as you drag to indicate the placement.

7. **Click the Move Up button ▲ in the Outline Tools group once, then double-click ⊕ next to Personnel**

 When you move a heading in Outline view, all subtext and text associated with the heading also move.

8. **Click the Show Level list arrow, select Level 3, double-click ⊕ next to Printed Materials under the Advertising and Promotion heading, click ⊕ next to Counter Items, then press [Delete]**

 The Counter Items heading and its associated subtext are deleted from the document. The revised outline is shown in **FIGURE I-4**.

9. **Click the Show Level list arrow, click All Levels, click the Close Outline View button in the Close group, then save the document**

FIGURE I-3: **Headings demoted to Level 2**

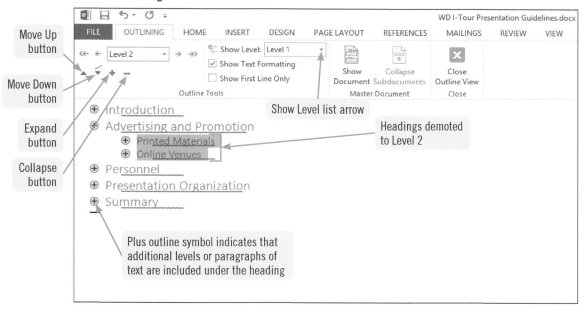

Move Up button

Move Down button

Expand button

Collapse button

Show Level list arrow

Headings demoted to Level 2

Plus outline symbol indicates that additional levels or paragraphs of text are included under the heading

FIGURE I-4: **Revised outline**

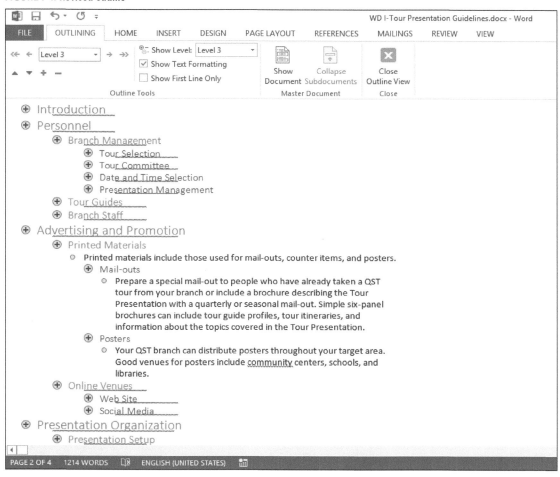

Navigate a Document

After you develop the headings and subheadings that make up the structure of your document in Outline view, you work in Print Layout view to add more text. You can expand and collapse headings and subheadings in Print Layout view so you can quickly see the structure of your document. Finally, you can make adjustments to the document structure in the Navigation pane, which you open from Print Layout view. The **Navigation pane** opens along the left side of the document window and shows all the headings and subheadings in the document. You can click a heading in the Navigation pane to move directly to it, and you can drag and drop headings to change their order just like you do in Outline view. You can also view thumbnails of the document pages in the Navigation pane. In addition to using the Navigation pane to navigate a document, you can create cross-references in your document. A **cross-reference** is text that electronically refers the reader to another part of the document, such as a numbered paragraph, a heading, or a figure. **CASE** ▶ *You expand and collapse headings in Print Layout view, work in the Navigation pane to make further changes to the document and then add a cross-reference to a heading.*

STEPS

1. **Press [Ctrl][Home], click Introduction, move the mouse slightly to the left to show the ◢, then click ◢**

 The paragraph under the Introduction heading is hidden. You can click ▷ to expand the heading again so you read the text associated with it.

2. **Right-click Introduction, point to Expand/Collapse, then click Collapse All Headings**

 Only Level 1 headings are visible.

3. **Right-click Introduction, point to Expand/Collapse, then click Expand All Headings**

 All headings and their associated text are visible again.

4. **Click the VIEW tab, click the Navigation Pane check box in the Show group, then click Branch Staff in the Navigation pane**

 The Branch Staff subheading is selected in the Navigation pane, and the insertion point moves to the Branch Staff subheading in the document.

5. **Drag Branch Staff up so that it appears above Tour Guides as shown in FIGURE I-5**

 The order of the headings in the Navigation pane and in the document change.

6. **Click PAGES at the top of the Navigation pane, scroll up and click the page 1 thumbnail, then double-click summary in paragraph 2 of the Introduction to select it**

7. **Click the INSERT tab, click Cross-reference in the Links group, click the Reference type list arrow, then click Heading**

 The Cross-reference dialog box opens and all the headings and subheadings in the document are listed.

8. **Scroll to and click Summary as shown in FIGURE I-6**

 In the Cross-reference dialog box you can also create a cross-reference to a numbered item, a bookmark, a footnote or an endnote, an equation that has been created with the Equation Editor, a figure such as a chart, a picture, or a diagram, and a table.

9. **Click Insert, click Close, then insert a space after Summary**

 The word "Summary" is now a hyperlink to the Summary heading at the end of the document.

10. **Move the pointer over Summary to show the Click message, press and hold [Ctrl] to show 🖑, click Summary to move directly to the Summary heading, click ✖ to close the Navigation pane, then save the document**

FIGURE I-5: **Changing the order of a subheading in the Navigation pane**

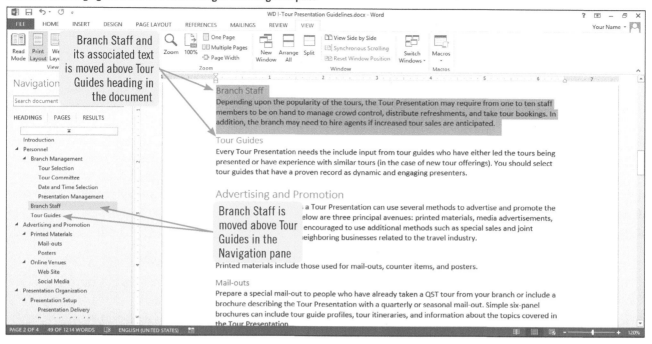

FIGURE I-6: **Cross-reference dialog box**

Using bookmarks

A **bookmark** identifies a location or a selection of text in a document. To create a bookmark, you first move the insertion point to the location in the text that you want to reference. This location can be a word, the beginning of a paragraph, or a heading. Click the INSERT tab, then click Bookmark in the Links group to open the Bookmark dialog box. In this dialog box, you type a name (which cannot contain spaces) for the bookmark, then click Add. To find a bookmark, press [Ctrl][G] to open the Find and Replace dialog box with the Go To tab active, click Bookmark in the Go to what list box, click the Enter bookmark name list arrow to see the list of bookmarks in the document, select the bookmark you require, click Go To, then close the Find and Replace dialog box. To delete a bookmark you no longer need, click Bookmark in the Links group, click the bookmark you want to remove, then click Delete in the Bookmark dialog box.

Insert a Table of Contents

Learning Outcomes
• Insert a table of contents
• Update a table of contents

Readers refer to a table of contents to obtain an overview of the topics and subtopics covered in a multipage document. When you generate a table of contents, Word searches for headings, sorts them by heading levels, and then displays the completed table of contents in the document. By default, a table of contents lists the top three heading levels in a document. Consequently, before you create a table of contents, you must ensure that all headings and subheadings are formatted with heading styles such as Heading 1, Heading 2, and Heading 3. When you work in Outline view, the correct heading styles are assigned automatically to text based on the outline level of the text. For example, the Heading 1 style is applied to Level 1 text, the Heading 2 style to Level 2 text, and so on. **CASE** *You are pleased with the content of the document and are now ready to create a new page that includes a table of contents. You use commands on the REFERENCES tab to generate a table of contents.*

STEPS

1. **Press [Ctrl][Home], click the** INSERT **tab, then click** Blank Page **in the Pages group**

2. **Press [Ctrl][Home], click the** HOME **tab, then click the** Clear All Formatting button 🖌️ **in the Font group**
 The insertion point is positioned at the left margin where the table of contents will begin.

3. **Click the** REFERENCES **tab, then click the** Table of Contents button **in the Table of Contents group**
 A gallery of predefined styles for a table of contents opens.

4. **Click** Automatic Table 2 **as shown in** FIGURE 1-7, **then scroll up to see the table of contents**
 A table of contents that includes all the Level 1, 2, and 3 headings is inserted on page 1.

5. **Click the** Table of Contents button **in the Table of Contents group, click** Custom Table of Contents **to open the Table of Contents dialog box, click the** Formats list arrow, **then click** Formal
 The Table of Contents dialog box opens, as shown in FIGURE I-8.

6. **Click** OK, **click** Yes, **click the** VIEW **tab, click the** Navigation Pane check box **in the Show group to open the Navigation pane, then click** HEADINGS **at the top of the Navigation pane**
 In the Navigation pane, you can move quickly to a section of the document and delete it.

7. **Right-click the** Presentation Management subheading **below the Branch Management subheading in the Personnel section, then click** Delete
 The Presentation Management subheading and its related subtext are deleted from the document but the heading is not yet deleted from the table of contents.

8. **Scroll to the top of the table of contents, then click** Update Table
 The table of contents is updated. The Presentation Management subheading is no longer listed in the table of contents.

9. **Move the pointer over the heading** Online Venues, **press [Ctrl], click** Online Venues, **then save the document**
 The insertion point moves to the Online Venues heading in the document. The Navigation pane remains open.

FIGURE I-7: **Inserting an automatic table of contents**

FIGURE I-8: **Table of Contents dialog box**

Word 2013

Mark Text for an Index

Learning
Outcomes
• Mark index entries
• Search for text

An **index** lists many of the terms and topics included in a document, along with the pages on which they appear. An index can include main entries, subentries, and cross-references. **CASE** ▶ *To help readers quickly find main concepts in the document, you decide to generate an index. You get started by marking the terms that you want to include as main entries in the index.*

STEPS

1. **Press [Ctrl][Home], press [Ctrl], then click Introduction in the table of contents**
 The insertion point moves to the Introduction heading in the document.

2. **Click Personnel in the Navigation pane, select branch staff in the second line under the Personnel heading in the document, click the REFERENCES tab, then click the Mark Entry button in the Index group**
 The Mark Index Entry dialog box opens. By default, the selected text is entered in the Main entry text box and is treated as a main entry in the index.

3. **Click Mark All, click the Mark Index Entry dialog box title bar, then use your mouse to drag the dialog box down so you can see "branch staff" as shown in** FIGURE I-9**.**
 Notice the term "branch staff" is marked with the XE field code. **XE** stands for **Index Entry**. When you mark an entry for the index, the paragraph marks are turned on automatically so that you can see hidden codes such as paragraph marks, field codes, page breaks, and section breaks. These codes do not appear in the printed document. The Mark Index Entry dialog box remains open so that you can continue to mark text for inclusion in the index.

4. **Click anywhere in the document to deselect the current index entry, click RESULTS at the top of the Navigation pane, then type branch manager in the Search Document text box in the Navigation pane**
 Each occurrence of the term "branch manager" is shown in context and in bold in the Navigation pane, and each occurrence is highlighted in the document.

5. **Click the first instance of branch manager in the Navigation pane, then click the title bar of the Mark Index Entry dialog box**
 The text "branch manager" appears in the Main entry text box in the Mark Index Entry dialog box.

6. **Click Mark All**
 All instances of "branch manager" in the document are marked for inclusion in the index.

7. **Click anywhere in the document, type theme in the Search Document text box, click the result in the Navigation pane, click the title bar of the Mark Index Entry dialog box, then click Mark All**

QUICK TIP
Make sure you click in the document to deselect the currently selected text before you enter another search term.

8. **Follow the procedure in Step 7 to find and mark all instances of the following main entries: brochures, target market, Ron Dawson, and shopping cart**

9. **Click** �x **to close the Mark Index Entry dialog box, then scroll up until you see the document title (Tour Presentation Guidelines)**
 You see two entries marked for the index, as shown in FIGURE I-10. The other entries you marked are further down the document.

FIGURE I-9: **Selected text in the Mark Index Entry dialog box**

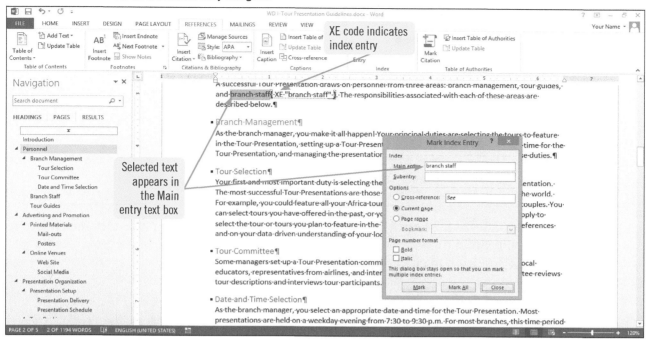

FIGURE I-10: **Index entries on the first page of the document**

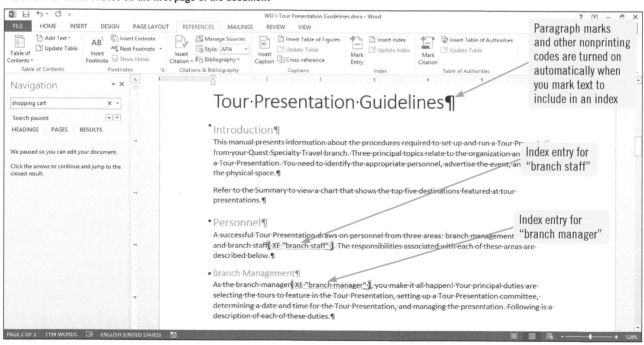

Word 2013

Generate an Index

Learning Outcomes
• Mark index subentries
• Insert a cross-reference in an index
• Generate an index

In addition to main entries, an index often includes subentries and cross-references. A **subentry** is text included under a main entry. For example, you could mark the text "shopping cart" as a subentry to appear under the main entry "Web site." A **cross-reference** in an index refers the reader to another entry in the index. For example, a cross-reference in an index might read, "lecture. *See* events." Once you have marked all the index entries, you select a design for the index, and then you generate it. If you make changes to the document, you can update the index just like you update a table of contents. **CASE** ▶ *You mark one subentry and one cross-reference for the index, create a new last page in the document, and then generate the index. You add one new main entry, and then update the index to reflect this change.*

STEPS

1. **Type airlines in the Search Document text box in the Navigation pane, click the entry that appears in the Navigation pane, then click Mark Entry in the Index group on the REFERENCES tab to open the Mark Index Entry dialog box**
 The search term "airlines" is already entered into the Mark Index Entry dialog box.

2. **Type Tour Committee in the Main entry text box, click in the Subentry text box, type airline representatives in the Subentry text box as shown in FIGURE I-11, then click Mark**
 The first and only instance of the text "airlines" is marked as a subentry renamed "airline representatives" that will appear following the Main entry, Tour Committee.

3. **Click anywhere in the document, type laptops in the Search Document text box, click the Cross-reference option button in the Mark Index Entry dialog box, click after See, type bookings as shown in FIGURE I-12, then click Mark**
 You need to also mark "bookings" so the Index lists the page number for "bookings."

TROUBLE
Drag the Mark Index Entry dialog box out of the way as needed to see the selected phrase.

4. **Click anywhere in the document, type bookings in the Search Document text box, click the entry in the Navigation pane that contains the phrase "bookings on the spot" (the fourth entry), double-click bookings in the phrase "bookings on the spot" in the document, click the Mark Index Entry dialog box, click Mark, then click Close**
 The term "laptops" is cross-referenced to the term "bookings" in the same paragraph. Now that you have marked entries for the index, you can generate the index at the end of the document.

5. **Press [Ctrl][End], press [Ctrl][Enter], type Index, press [Enter], select Index, click the HOME tab, apply 18 pt, bold, and center alignment formatting, then click at the left margin below Index**

6. **Click the REFERENCES tab, click Insert Index in the Index group, click the Formats list arrow in the Index dialog box, scroll down the list, click Formal, then click OK**
 Word has collected all the index entries, sorted them alphabetically, included the appropriate page numbers, and removed duplicate entries.

QUICK TIP
The refreshments entry that appears in the table of contents is not included because it appears before the entry you selected.

7. **Search for refreshments, click the second instance of "refreshments" (below Refreshments 4) in the search results in the Navigation pane, click the Mark Entry button in the Index Group, then click Mark All**
 The index now includes each instance of refreshments from the selected text to the end of the document.

8. **Close the dialog box and Navigation pane, scroll to the end of the document, right-click the index, click Update Field, click Index to deselect the index, then save the document**
 The updated index is shown in FIGURE I-13.

FIGURE I-11: **Subentry in the Mark Index Entry dialog box**

FIGURE I-12: **Cross-reference in the Mark Index Entry dialog box**

FIGURE I-13: **Completed index**

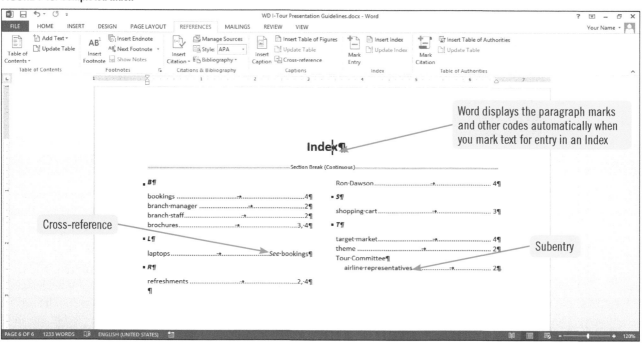

Insert Footers in Multiple Sections

Multipage documents often consist of two or more sections that you can format differently. For example, you can include different text in the footer for each section, and you can change how page numbers are formatted from section to section. **CASE** ▶ *You want to divide the report into two sections, and then format the headers and footers differently in each section. The diagram in* FIGURE I-14 *explains how the footer should appear on each of the first three pages in the document.*

STEPS

1. **Press [Ctrl][Home] to move to the top of the document, right-click the status bar, click Section if it does not have a check mark next to it, scroll to the page break, click to the left of it, click the PAGE LAYOUT tab, then click Breaks in the Page Setup group**

 You can see the page break because the paragraph marks were turned on when you marked entries for inclusion in the index. When you work with sections, you should leave paragraph marks showing so you can see the codes that Word inserts for section breaks and page breaks.

2. **Click Next Page under Section Breaks, press [Delete] to remove the original page break, then press [Delete] to remove the extra blank line**

 The document is divided into two sections. Section 1 contains the Table of Contents and section 2 contains the rest of the document.

3. **Press [Ctrl][Home], click the INSERT tab, click the Footer button in the Header & Footer group, then click Blank (Three Columns)**

 The footer area opens showing the Blank (Three Columns) format.

4. **Click to the left of the placeholder text to select all three items, press [Delete], press [Tab] once, type Page, press [Spacebar], click the Page Number button in the Header & Footer group, point to Current Position, then click Plain Number (the top selection)**

 The current footer for the entire document contains the word Page and a page number.

5. **Click the Page Number button, click Format Page Numbers, click the Number format list arrow, click i, ii, iii, then click OK**

 The page number in the footer area of the table of contents page is formatted as i.

QUICK TIP
Clicking Next
moved the insertion
point to the next
footer, which in this
case is also the next
section, as indicated
by the section
number in the
status bar and on
the Footer tab.

6. **Click Next in the Navigation group, then click the Link to Previous button in the Navigation group to deselect it**

 You deselect the Link to Previous button to make sure that the text you type into the footer appears only in the footer in section 2. You must deselect the Link to Previous button each time you want the header or footer in a section to be unique.

7. **Type your name, then press [Tab] once to move Page 2 to the right margin**

 By default, Word continues numbering the pages in section 2 based on the page numbers in section 1. The footer in section 2 starts with Page 2 because section 1 contains just one page. You want section 2 to start with Page 1 because the first page in section 2 is the first page of the report. Note also that the i, ii, iii format is not applied to the page number in section 2. Changes to page number formatting apply only to the section in which the change is made originally (in this case, section 1).

8. **Click the Page Number button, click Format Page Numbers, click the Start at option button, verify that 1 appears, click OK, then compare the footer to** FIGURE I-15

9. **Click the Close Header and Footer button, then save the document**

FIGURE I-14: **Diagram of section formatting for footers**

FIGURE I-15: **Completed footer**

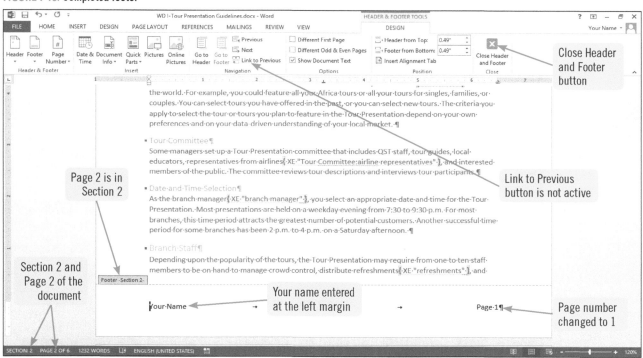

Using text flow options

You adjust text flow options to control how text in a multipage document breaks across pages. To change text flow options, you use the Paragraph dialog box. To open the Paragraph dialog box, click the launcher in the Paragraph group on the HOME tab, and then select the Line and Page Breaks tab. In the Pagination section, you can choose to select or deselect four text flow options.

For example, you select the Widow/Orphan control option to prevent the last line of a paragraph from printing at the top of a page (a widow) or the first line of a paragraph from printing at the bottom of a page (an orphan). By default, Widow/Orphan control is active. You can also select the Keep lines together check box to keep a paragraph from breaking across two pages.

Insert Headers in Multiple Sections

Learning
Outcomes
• Insert headers in sections
• Add a cover page

When you divide your document into sections, you can modify the header to be different in each section. As you learned in the previous lesson, you must deselect the Link to Previous button when you want the text of a header (or footer) in a new section to be different from the header (or footer) in the previous section. **CASE** ▶ *The diagram in* FIGURE I-16 *shows that text will appear in the header on every page in section 2. You do not want any text to appear in the header on the table of contents page (section 1). You modify the headers in the two sections of the document and then add a cover page.*

STEPS

1. **Press [Ctrl][Home] to move to the top of the document, then double-click in the blank area above Table of Contents**
 The header area opens. The Header -Section 1- identifier appears along with the HEADER & FOOTER TOOLS DESIGN tab. Refer to FIGURE I-16. Notice that you do not want text in the header in section 1.

2. **Click Next in the Navigation group, then click the Link to Previous button to deselect it**
 The identifier Header -Section 2- appears. You want text to appear on all the pages of section 2. You deselect the Link to Previous button so that the text you type appears only on this page and on subsequent pages.

3. **Type Quest Specialty Travel, select the text, then use the Mini toolbar to increase the font size to 14 pt, apply bold, and apply italic**

4. **Click the Close Header and Footer button, notice that the page number for the Introduction in the table of contents is page 2, scroll up to see the Table of Contents head, click the Table of Contents head, click Update Table, then click OK**
 The page numbers in the table of contents are updated.

5. **Press [Ctrl][End] to move to the Index page, right-click the index, then click Update Field**
 The page numbers in the index are updated.

6. **Press [Ctrl][Home], click the INSERT tab, click Cover Page in the Pages group, scroll to view the selections, then select the Semaphore style**
 Several placeholders called content controls are included on the cover page. Before you add text to the content controls you want to keep, you delete the ones you don't need.

7. **Click DATE at the top of the page to show the Publish Date content control handle, click the content control handle to select it (the handle turns blue gray and the text in the control is shaded with light blue), press [Delete], click the frame of the text box that remains, press [Delete], then scroll to and delete the Company Address content control but not the text box surrounding it**

8. **Enter text as shown in** FIGURE I-17

9. **Save the document**

FIGURE I-16: **Diagram of section formatting for headers**

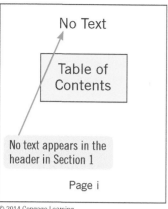

© 2014 Cengage Learning

FIGURE I-17: **Text to type in cover page**

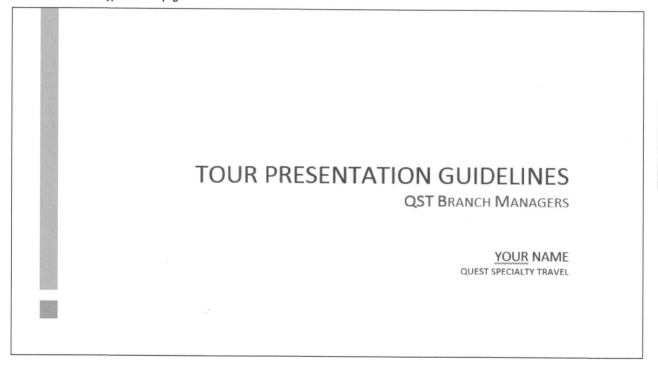

Understanding headers, footers, and sections

One reason you divide a document into sections is so that you can modify the page layout and the headers and footers differently in different sections. You can even modify the header and footer within a section because each section consists of two parts. The first part of a section is the first page, and the second part of the section is the remaining pages in the section. This section structure allows you to omit the header and footer on the first page of section 2, and then include the header and footer on all subsequent pages in section 2. To do this, place the insertion point in the section you want to modify, then click the Different First Page check box in the Options group to specify that you wish to include a different header and/or footer (or no header and footer at all) on the first page of a section. In addition, you can also choose to format odd and even pages in a document in different ways by clicking the Different Odd & Even Pages check box in the Options group. For example, you can choose to right-align the document title on odd-numbered pages and left-align the chapter indicator on even-numbered pages.

Finalize a Multipage Document

The Resume Reading feature takes you to the last location you were working on before you saved and closed a document. You can customize the table of contents so that readers can identify the document structure. By default, a table of contents shows only headings formatted with the Heading 1, Heading 2, or Heading 3 styles (Levels 1, 2, and 3 in Outline view). You can also include headings formatted with other styles, such as the Title style or a style you create. **CASE** *You use the Resume Reading feature, modify the headers and footers, and then customize the table of contents.*

STEPS

1. **Make sure you've saved the document, press [Ctrl][G], be sure Page in the Go to what area is selected, type 5, click Go To, click Close, close the document, open the document, then click the Welcome back! notice**

 The Resume Reading feature returns you to where you were working before saving and closing the document.

2. **Scroll up to view the page break below the chart, select the page break, click the PAGE LAYOUT tab, click Breaks, then click Next Page in the Section Breaks area**

3. **Open WD I-2.docx, press [Ctrl][A] to select all the text, press [Ctrl][C] to copy all the text, switch to the WD I-Tour Presentation Guidelines document, press [Ctrl][V], click the FILE tab, click Save As, then save the document as WD I-Tour Guidelines**

 The three pages of the Information Session Guidelines document appear in their own section.

4. **Scroll up to the Table of Contents page, double-click in the header area for section 1, click Next, select Quest Specialty Travel, type Tour Presentation Guidelines, click Next, click the Link to Previous button in the Navigation group to deselect it, change the header text to Information Session Guidelines, then close the header**

5. **Scroll to the Index page, insert a Next Page section break to the left of Index, double-click in the header area, click the Link to Previous button, delete the header text, then close the header**

 The document now contains four sections, and you have modified the header text in sections 2, 3, and 4.

6. **Scroll up to the table of contents page and click the table of contents, click Update Table, click the Update entire table option button, then click OK**

7. **Click the REFERENCES tab, click the Table of Contents button, click Custom Table of Contents, click Options, select 1 next to Heading 1, type 2, type 3 next to Heading 2, type 4 next to Heading 3 as shown in FIGURE I-18, scroll down to Title, type 1 in the TOC level text box, then click OK until you are returned to the document**

 The Information Session document starts at page 1 and you want page numbering to be consecutive.

8. **Press [Ctrl], click Information Session Guidelines in the table of contents, scroll to the footer (you'll see Page 1), double-click in the footer, click the Page Number button in the Header & Footer group, click Format Page Numbers, click the Continue from previous section option button, then click OK**

9. **Click Next in the Navigation group, click the Page Number button in the Header & Footer group, click Format Page Numbers, click the Continue from previous section option button, click OK, exit the footer area, update the table of contents for page numbers only, reduce the zoom to 90% and compare the revised table of contents to FIGURE I-19, then save and close all documents and exit Word**

FIGURE I-18: **Table of Contents Options dialog box**

Scroll to see other TOC levels, including Title

FIGURE I-19: **Revised table of contents**

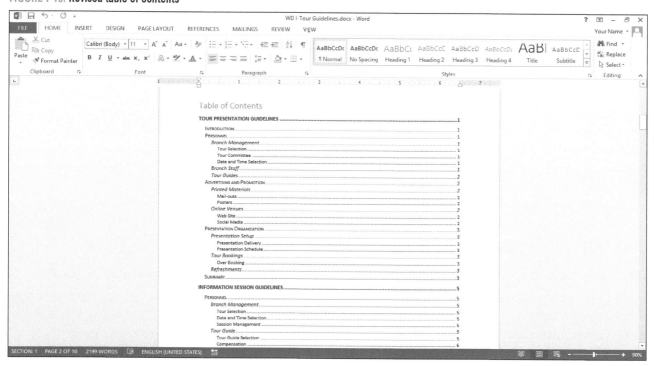

Using Advanced Print Options

With Word 2013, you can scale a document to fit a different paper size and you can choose to print pages from specific sections or a series of sections, even when the page numbering restarts in each section. To scale a document, click the FILE tab, click Print, click the 1 Page Per Sheet list arrow, then click Scale to Paper Size and view the list of paper sizes available. You can also choose to print a multiple-page document on fewer sheets; for example, you can print the document on two pages per sheet up to 16 pages per sheet. In the Print dialog box, you can also specify how to print the pages of a multiple-section document that uses different page numbering in each section. You need to enter both the page number and the section number for the range of pages you wish to print. The syntax required is: PageNumberSectionNumber-PageNumberSectionNumber which is shortened to p#s#-p#s#. For example, if you want to print from page 1 of section one to page 4 of section three, you enter p1s1-p4s3 in the Pages text box in the Settings area, and then click Print.

Practice

Concepts Review

Label the numbered items on the OUTLINING tab shown in FIGURE I-20.

FIGURE I-20

1 2 3 4 5

Match each term with the statement that best describes it.

6. **Demote button**
7. **Table of Contents**
8. **Resume Reading**
9. **Footer**
10. **Cross-reference**
11. **Link to Previous button**
12. **Mark All**

a. Used to enter a lower-level heading in Outline view
b. Text that appears at the bottom of every page in a document or section
c. Text that electronically refers the reader to another part of the document
d. Click to designate each instance of a specific term for inclusion in an index
e. List of topics and subtopics usually with page numbers, and shown at the beginning of a document
f. Deselect to create a header or footer in one section that is different from the header or footer in a previous section
g. Feature that allows you to return to the last place you were working in a document before you saved and closed it

Select the best answer from the list of choices.

13. **On the OUTLINING tab, which button do you click to move directly to Level 1 from any other level?**
 a. ←
 b. →
 c. ←←
 d. ✚

14. **Which symbol in Outline view indicates that a heading includes subtext such as subheadings or paragraphs of text?**
 a. ━
 b. ⊕
 c. ▲
 d. ✚

15. **Which of the following options do you select when you want to search for text from the Navigation pane?**
 a. HEADINGS
 b. RESULTS
 c. SEARCH
 d. FIND TEXT

16. **Which index entry appears subordinate to a main entry?**
 a. Cross-reference
 b. Next entry
 c. Mark place
 d. Subentry

17. **Which tab contains the commands used to create an index?**
 a. PAGE LAYOUT
 b. INSERT
 c. REVIEW
 d. REFERENCES

Skills Review

1. Build a document in Outline view.

 a. Start Word, create a new blank document, then switch to Outline view from the VIEW tab.

 b. Type **Introduction** followed by your name as a Level 1 heading, press [Enter], type **Partnership Conditions** as another Level 1 heading, then press [Enter].

FIGURE I-21

⊖ Introduction by Your Name
⊕ Partnership Conditions
 ○ This section provides background information about Arcadia Training and discusses how the partnership could benefit both Markham Communications and Arcadia Training.
 ⊖ Background
 ⊖ Benefits
 ⊖ Partnership Need
⊕ Products and Services
 ⊖ Arcadia Training Services
 ⊖ Markham Communications
 ⊖ Package Opportunities
⊕ Financial Considerations
 ⊖ Projected Revenues
 ⊖ Financing Required
⊖ Conclusion

 c. Type the text shown in FIGURE I-21 as body text under the Partnership Conditions heading.

 d. Type **Background**, then use the Demote button to demote it to a Level 2 heading.

 e. Use the Promote button to type the heading **Benefits** as a Level 2 heading, then complete the outline, as shown in FIGURE I-21.

 f. Save the document as **WD I-Partnership Outline** to the location where you store your Data Files, then close the document.

2. Work in Outline view.

 a. Open the file WD I-3.docx from the location where you store your Data Files, save it as **WD I-Partnership Proposal**, switch to Outline view, then show all Level 1 headings.

 b. Move the heading Products and Services above Financial Considerations.

 c. Select the Partnership Conditions heading, expand the heading, collapse Benefits, collapse Partnership Need, then move Benefits and its subtext below Partnership Need and its subtext.

 d. Collapse the Partnership Conditions section to show only the Level 1 heading.

 e. Show all levels of the outline, close Outline view, then save the document.

3. Navigate a document.

 a. In Print Layout view, collapse all the headings in the document.

 b. Open the Navigation pane, navigate to Financing Required, expand the heading, then change "six months" to **year** in the last line of the paragraph below the Financing Required heading.

 c. Expand all headings in Print Layout view.

 d. Click the Package Opportunities heading in the Navigation pane, then use the Navigation pane to delete the heading and its subtext.

 e. View the thumbnails of the document pages in the Navigation pane, click the first page, close the Navigation pane, scroll to the Benefits heading, then select the text "Projected Revenues" at the end of the paragraph.

 f. Create a cross-reference from the text Projected Revenues to the Projected Revenues heading.

 g. Test the cross-reference, then save the document.

4. Insert a table of contents.

 a. Go to the top of the document.

 b. Insert a page break, then return to the top of the document.

 c. Insert the Automatic Table 2 predefined table of contents style.

 d. Replace it with a custom table of contents using the Fancy format.

 e. Use [Ctrl][click] to navigate to Partnership Need in the document, open the Navigation pane, view the document headings, then right-click and delete the Partnership Need heading from the Navigation pane.

 f. Update the table of contents, then save the document.

Skills Review (continued)

5. **Mark entries for an index.**

 a. Show the RESULTS section of the Navigation pane, find the words **computer labs**, and mark all occurrences for inclusion in the index.

 b. Find and mark only the first instance of each of the following main entries: **Web page design, Networking, software training**, and **PowerPoint**. (*Hint:* Click Mark instead of Mark All.)

 c. Save the document.

6. **Generate an index.**

 a. Find **online publishing**, click in the Mark Index Entry dialog box, select online publishing in the Main entry text box, type **Markham Communications Products** as the Main entry and **online publishing** as the Subentry, then click Mark All.

 b. Repeat the process to insert **business writing seminars** as a subentry of Arcadia Training.

 c. Find the text **courses**, then create a cross-reference in the Mark Index Entry dialog box to **software training**. Note that you already have an index entry for software training.

 d. Close the Mark Index Entry dialog box and the Navigation pane.

 e. Insert a new page at the end of the document, type **Index** at the top of the page, and format it with bold and 18 pt and center alignment.

 f. Double-click below the index, clear any formatting so the insertion point appears at the left margin, then insert an index in the Fancy format.

 g. Find and mark all instances of **Seattle**, scroll to the index page, update the index so it includes the new entry, close the Mark Index Entry dialog box and the Navigation pane, then save the document.

7. **Insert footers in multiple sections.**

 a. At the top of the document, select the page break below the Table of Contents, replace it with a Next Page section break, then remove the page break and the extra blank line.

 b. On the table of contents page, insert a footer using the Blank (Three Columns) format.

 c. Delete the placeholders, type your name, press [Tab] twice, type **Page**, press [Spacebar], then insert a page number at the current position using the Plain Number format.

 d. Change the format of the page number to i, ii, iii.

 e. Go to the next section, then deselect the Link to Previous button.

 f. Format the page number to start at 1.

 g. Exit the footer area, scroll through the document to verify that the pages are numbered correctly, scroll to and update the page numbers in the table of contents, then save the document.

8. **Insert headers in multiple sections.**

 a. Move to the top of the document, then double-click to position the insertion point in the header area.

 b. Go to the next section, then deselect the Link to Previous button.

 c. Type **Markham Communications**, then apply bold and italic.

 d. Exit the header area, then scroll through the document to verify that the header text does not appear on the table of contents and that it does appear on all subsequent pages.

 e. Insert a cover page using the Whisp style, then delete the Date content control.

 f. Enter **Partnership Agreement Proposal** as the Document title, **Markham Communications** as the Document subtitle, and your name where indicated.

 g. Delete the Company Name content control.

 h. Save the document.

9. **Finalize a multipage document.**

 a. Go to the Index page, then save and close the document.

 b. Open the document, then use the Resume Reading feature to return to the last page of the document.

 c. Scroll up to the Page Break after the Conclusion, then replace the page break with a Next Page section break.

Skills Review (continued)

d. Open the file WD I-4.docx from the drive and folder where you store your Data Files, copy all the text, paste it into the Partnership Agreement Proposal document, then save the document as **WD I-Partnership Agreements**.

e. From the table of contents page, access the Header area, move to section 2, replace Markham Communications with **Arcadia Training**, move to section 3, click the Link to Previous button, then replace Arcadia Training with **Parallel Presenters**.

f. Exit the header, insert a Next Page section break before the index, and delete the page break and the extra blank line, open the header area in section 4 (the index page), then deselect the Link to Previous button and remove the header from the index page.

g. Check that the correct headers appear in each of the four sections, then update the table of contents page (select the Update entire table option).

h. Modify the table of contents options so that Heading 1 corresponds to TOC level 2 text, Heading 2 corresponds to TOC level 3 text, Heading 3 corresponds to TOC level 4 text, and Title text corresponds to TOC level 1 text.

i. Modify the footers in sections 3 and 4 so that the page numbering is continuous. You should see page 6 on the index page.

j. Update the index and table of contents pages, compare your document to the pages from the completed document shown in FIGURE I-22, save the document, submit all files to your instructor, close it, then exit Word.

FIGURE I-22

Independent Challenge 1

You work in the Finance Department of Holistic Fitness. Recently, the owners began selling franchises. Your supervisor asks you to format a report that details the development of these franchise operations.

a. Start Word, open the file WD I-5.docx from the drive and folder where you store your Data Files, then save it as **WD I-Holistic Fitness Franchises**.

b. In Outline view, organize the document as shown in the following table, starting with Introduction, followed by Scope of the Report, and then moving column by column. Text that you designate as headings will be formatted with the blue font color.

heading	level	heading	level	heading	level
Introduction	1	Maureen Knowles	2	Philadelphia Clientele	3
Scope of the Report	2	Franchise Locations	1	New York	2
Owner Information	1	Boston	2	New York Clientele	3
Don Green	2	Boston Clientele	3	Opening Schedules	2
Jorge Morales	2	Philadelphia	2		

© 2014 Cengage Learning

c. Show level 3, then switch the order of New York and its subtext so it follows Boston and its subtext.

d. In Print Layout view, collapse all the headings to show only Level 1 headings, then expand the headings again.

e. Show the Navigation pane, then move the Opening Schedules heading so it appears just below Franchise Locations.

f. Starting from the top of the document, find the text listed in column 1, and mark all instances of that text as Main entry or subentry for an index, based on the information in columns 2 and 3.

find this text	main entry	subentry
Boston	Location	Boston
New York	Location	New York
Philadelphia	Location	Philadelphia
Don Green	Owner	Don Green
Jorge Morales	Owner	Jorge Morales
Maureen Knowles	Owner	Maureen Knowles
marketing vice president	marketing vice president	
mall	mall	

© 2014 Cengage Learning

g. Find Best Fitness, then make it a main entry with a cross-reference to **Don Green**.

h. Insert a new page at the end of the document, type **Index** as the page title, format it with bold, a larger font size, and center alignment, then generate an index in the Modern format.

i. At the top of the document, insert a Next Page section break, then on the new first page, insert an automatic table of contents using the Automatic Table 1 style.

j. Add and format a header and footer so that the completed document appears as follows:

location	contents
Table of Contents page (section 1)	Footer containing your name at the left margin and Page i at the right margin
Page 1 and the following pages of the report (section 2)	Footer containing your name at the left margin and Page 1 at the right margin
Page 1 and the following pages of the report (section 2)	Header containing the text Holistic Fitness Franchises, centered, and bold

© 2014 Cengage Learning

k. Scroll through the document to ensure the headers and footers are correct, click the Index heading when you get to the Index page, then save and close the document.

l. Open the document and click the Resume Reading message to return to the Index page, update the index page, then scroll up and update the table of contents page.

m. Save the document, submit your file to your instructor, then close the document.

Independent Challenge 2

As the program assistant at Lakeview College in Minnesota, you are responsible for creating and formatting reports about programs at the college. You work in Outline view to create a report for a college program of your choice.

a. Start Word, create a new blank document, then save it as **WD I-Program Information Report**.

b. In Outline view, enter the headings and subheadings for the report as shown in the table starting with **Program Overview**, followed by **Career Opportunities**. You need to substitute appropriate course names for Course 1, Course 2, and so on. For example, courses in the first

heading	level	heading	level
Program Overview	1	[Enter name for Course 1]	3
Career Opportunities	2	[Enter name for Course 2]	3
Admission Requirements	2	Second Term	2
Program Content	1	[Enter name for Course 1]	3
First Term	2	[Enter name for Course 2]	3

© 2014 Cengage Learning

term of a business studies program could be **Introduction to Business, Marketing Basics**, and so on. You choose the program and courses you want to include in the report.

c. Enter one paragraph of appropriate body text for the following headings: Program Overview, Career Opportunities, and Admission Requirements, then enter short course descriptions for each of the four courses included in the document. For ideas, refer to college Web sites and catalogs. Collapse all the headings to Level 1.

d. In Print Layout view, add a cover page using the style of your choice. Include the name of the program as the title (for example, **Business Program**), the name of the college (**Lakeview College, Minnesota**) as the subtitle, and your name where indicated. Remove all other content controls. If the cover page style you choose does not include a content control for a subtitle, enter the information as text and format it attractively.

e. Insert a Next Page section break following the cover page, then insert a page break in the body of the report to spread the report over two pages if it does not already flow to two pages.

f. Format the cover page (section 1) with no header and no footer.

g. Go to the section 2 header and deselect the Different First Page check box in the Options group so that you see Header - Section 2 in the tab below the header area, not First Page Header - Section 2. Format the section 2 header with a right-aligned page number starting with Page 1 using the 1, 2, 3 format. Make sure you deselect Link to Previous.

h. Format the section 2 footer with the name of the program left-aligned in the footer and your name right-aligned. Make sure you deselect Link to Previous.

i. Insert a next page section break above the Program Overview heading.

j. Scroll up to the new blank page, then insert an automatic table of contents in either the Automatic Table 1 or Automatic Table 2 formats. Replace the table of contents with a custom table of contents that uses the format of your choice (for example, Classic, Fancy, etc.).

k. Customize the table of contents so that it includes only Heading 1 at TOC level 1 and Heading 3 at TOC level 2. None of the Heading 2 headings should appear in the revised table of contents.

l. Double click in the header area on the table of contents page, then delete Page 1.

m. Go to the next section (Section 3), click the Link to Previous button to deselect it, then insert Page 1 right-aligned. Be sure the page number starts at 1. Verify that the header appears on both pages of the section 3 header and that the footer appears on all pages except the cover page.

n. Update the table of contents, save the document, close it, then submit your file to your instructor.

Independent Challenge 3

Many businesses post job opportunities on their Web sites. You can learn a great deal about opportunities in a wide range of fields just by checking out the job postings on these Web sites. You decide to create a document that describes a selection of jobs available on an employment Web site of your choice.

a. Use your favorite search engine and the search phrase **job search** to find Web sites that post jobs online. Popular sites include jobs.com, workopolis.com, and monster.com.

b. On the Web site you chose, identify two job categories (e.g., Marketing and Web Page Development, or Accounting and Administration) and then find two jobs that appeal to you and that you may even wish to apply for. You can choose to search for jobs in your home town or in another location.

c. Create a new document in Word, then save it as **WD I-Online Job Opportunities**.

d. In Outline view, set up the document starting with the name of the employment Web site (e.g., monster.com), and followed by Job Category 1 as shown in the table. (*Note*: You need to enter specific text for headings such as **Marketing** for Job Category 1 and **Marketing Assistant** for Job Posting.)

heading	level
Name of Web Site	1
Job Category 1	2
Job Name	3
Summary of Job Posting	Body Text
Job Category 2	2
Job Name	3
Summary of Job Posting	Body Text

© 2014 Cengage Learning

e. Complete the Word document with information you find on the Web site. Include a short description of each job you select, and list some of the job duties. You do not need to include the entire job posting. If you copy selected text from a Web site, make sure you clear the formatting so that the text in the document is formatted only with the Normal style. Edit any copied text so that only the most important information is included.

f. Divide the document into two pages so that each job posting appears on one page.

g. Above the first job posting, enter the following text: **Following is a description of two jobs that interest me. The first job is a[n] [name of job] and the second job is a[n] [name of job]. Information in this report was copied from the [Web site name or URL] Web site on [date].** Make sure you substitute the job titles you've identified for [name of job], the name of the Web site name or its URL for the [Web site name or URL], and the date you created the report for [date].

h. Make each job title a cross-reference to the appropriate heading in your outline, then test the cross-references.

i. Insert a header that starts on page 1 and includes the text **Online Job Opportunities for** followed by your name, then include a page number on each page of the document in the footer.

j. Save the document and submit the file to your instructor, then close the document.

Independent Challenge 4: Explore

You work for an author who has just written a series of vignettes about her travels in France and Italy. The author hopes to publish the vignettes and accompanying illustrations in a book called *Lyric Journals*. She has written a short proposal that she plans to present to publishers. As her assistant, your job is to create a proposal that includes three of the vignettes, each with a unique header. You will further explore the features available in Outline view by using some of the tools available in the Master Document group.

a. Start Word, open WD I-6.docx, then save it as **WD I-Lyric Journals Proposal**. Keep the document open.

b. Open WD I-7.docx, save it as **WD I-Lyric Journals Lavender**, then close it.

c. Open WD I-8.docx, save it as **WD I-Lyric Journals Ocher**, then close it.

d. Open WD I-9.docx, save it as **WD I-Lyric Journals Roman Rain**, then close it.

e. From the WD I-Lyric Journals Proposal document, switch to Outline view, then promote the Lyric Journals Overview heading to Level 1.

f. Click at the end of the outline on the first blank line after the last sentence.

g. Click the Show Document button in the Master Document group.

h. Click the Insert button in the Master Document group, navigate to the location where you saved the files for this challenge, double-click WD I-Lyric Journals Lavender.

i. Repeat step h to insert WD I-Lyric Journals Ocher as a subdocument, then repeat step h once more to insert WD I-Lyric Journals Roman Rain as a subdocument. The master document now consists of introductory text and three subdocuments.

j. Click the Collapse Subdocuments button in the Master Document group, then click OK in response to the message. Scroll down as needed to see that each document is now a hyperlink.

k. Press the [Ctrl] key and click the hyperlink to the Lyric Journals Lavender document. View the document, then close it.

l. Click the Expand Subdocuments button, then close Outline view.

m. At the top of the document, add a next page section break, then at the top of the new blank page, insert one of the automatic table of contents.

n. Replace the table of contents with a custom table of contents that uses the Formal format.

o. Insert a footer at the bottom of the table of contents page that includes your name at the left margin and the page number formatted in lower case Roman numerals (i) at the right margin.

p. Go to section 2, deselect Link to Previous, then format the page numbers so they start at 1.

q. Create a header for each section as shown in the table below. Make sure you deselect Link to Previous each time you go to a new section. Enter the text for each header at the left margin and format it with italics. The document contains a total of seven sections and five pages. Note that extra sections are inserted when you insert subdocuments.

section	contains	header text
1	Table of Contents	no header
2	Overview	Lyric Journals Overview
3	Lavender	Lavender
5	Ocher	Ocher
7	Roman Rain	Roman Rain

© 2014 Cengage Learning

r. Update the table of contents, save the document, submit a copy of all four documents to your instructor, then close the document. Note that when you open the document again, the three subdocuments will appear as hyperlinks.

Visual Workshop

Open the file WD I-10.docx from the drive and folder where you store your Data Files, then save it as **WD I-Term Paper Outline**. Modify the outline so that it appears as shown in FIGURE I-23. You need to change the order of some sections. In Print Layout view, insert a next page section break at the beginning of the document, then generate a table of contents using the Automatic Table 2 format and the custom Distinctive format. Insert a page break before Social Networking Development in the text, create a footer in section 2 (remember to deselect Link to Previous) with your name at the left margin and a page number that starts with 1 at 0 right margin. Make sure no text appears in the footer in section 1. Update the table of contents so that it appears as shown in FIGURE I-24. Save and close the document, then submit the file to your instructor.

FIGURE I-23

⊕ Introduction
 ⊖ Social Media Definition
 ⊖ Social Media Challenges
⊕ Marketing Implications
 ⊕ Global Developments
 ⊖ Europe
 ⊖ Asia
 ⊕ Emerging Markets
 ⊖ South America
 ⊖ India
 ⊖ Product Placement
⊕ Social Networking Development
 ⊖ Personalization
 ⊖ Customization
⊕ Privacy Issues
 ⊖ Consent
 ⊖ Sharing
⊕ Conclusion
 ⊙

FIGURE I-24

Table of Contents

Working with Styles and Templates

CASE As a special projects assistant at Quest Specialty Travel (QST) in San Diego, you've been asked to produce profiles of the top QST tour guides for distribution at the company's annual meeting. To save time, you modify styles in an existing profile, create new styles, and then develop a template on which to base each tour guide profile. This template includes a custom Style Set.

Unit Objectives

After completing this unit, you will be able to:

- Explore styles and templates
- Modify built-in styles
- Create paragraph styles
- Create character and linked styles
- Create list and table styles
- Create a Style Set
- Manage styles
- Create a template
- Modify and attach a template

Files You Will Need

WD J-1.docx	WD J-8.docx
WD J-2.docx	WD J-9.docx
WD J-3.docx	WD J-10.docx
WD J-4.docx	WD J-11.docx
WD J-5.docx	WD J-12.docx
WD J-6.docx	WD J-13.docx
WD J-7.docx	

©Tumanyan/Shutterstock

Explore Styles and Templates

Learning Outcomes
- Define why to use styles
- Identify style types
- Define why to use templates

You use styles and templates to automate document-formatting tasks and to ensure consistency among related documents. A **style** consists of formats such as font, font size, and alignment that you name and then save as one set. For example, the settings for a style called Main Head could be Arial font, 14-pt font size, bold, and a bottom border. Each time you apply the Main Head style to selected text, all format settings included in the style are applied. A **template** is a file that contains the basic structure of a document, such as the page layout, headers and footers, styles, graphic elements, and boilerplate text. **CASE** ▸ *You plan to use styles to format a tour guide profile and then create a template for a series of tour guide profiles. You start by familiarizing yourself with styles and templates.*

DETAILS

Information about how you can use styles and templates to help you format documents quickly and efficiently follows:

- You apply styles to selected text from the Styles gallery on the HOME tab. Using styles helps you save time in two ways. First, when you apply a style, you apply a set of formats all at once. Second, if you modify a style by changing one or more of the formats associated with that style, all text formatted with that style is updated automatically. For example, suppose you apply a style named "Section Head" to each section head in a document. If you then modify the formatting associated with the Section Head style, Word automatically updates all the text formatted with the Section Head style. As discussed in Unit I, default heading styles are applied automatically to headings and subheadings when you work in Outline view to create the structure of a document. For example, the Heading 1 style is applied to text associated with Level 1, the Heading 2 style is applied to text associated with Level 2, and so on. You can modify a default heading style or you can create a new heading style.

- In Word, you can choose from 17 built-in Style Sets on the DESIGN tab or you can create your own Style Set. Each **Style Set** contains **styles** for text elements such as headings, titles, subtitles, and lists. All of the styles associated with a Style Set are stored in the **Styles gallery.**

- Word includes five major style categories. A **paragraph style** includes font formats, such as font and font size, and paragraph formats, such as line spacing or tabs. You use a paragraph style when you want to format all of the text in a paragraph at once. A **character style** includes character formats only, such as font, font size, and font color. You use a character style to apply character format settings only to selected text within a paragraph. A **linked style** contains both a character style and a paragraph style. Either the character style or the paragraph style is applied depending on whether you click in a paragraph to select the entire paragraph or you select specific text. A **table style** specifies how you want both the table grid and the text in a table to appear. A **list style** allows you to format a series of lines with numbers or bullets and with selected font and paragraph formats. FIGURE J-1 shows a document formatted with the five style types. These styles have been saved in a new Style Set called QST Profiles.

- Every document you create in Word is based on a template. Most of the time, this template is the **Normal template** because the Normal template is loaded automatically when you start a new document. The styles assigned to the Normal template, such as Normal, Title, Heading 1, Heading 2, and so on, are the styles you see in the Styles gallery on the HOME tab when you open a new document.

- Word includes a number of built-in templates. In addition, you can access a variety of templates online. You can also create a template that includes a custom Style Set. Finally, you can attach a template to an existing document and then apply the styles included with the template to text in the document.

Paragraph styles apply formatting to a paragraph, which might be one or more lines of text

Len Barclay

Early Life

Len Barclay was born in 1975 in Portland, Oregon. His father, a schoolteacher from Japan, taught Len to speak fluent Japanese and to appreciate all aspects of the Japanese culture.

Tour Guide Career

After graduating with honors from the University of Oregon, Len spent several years traveling through Europe and Asia before settling in Seattle, where got a job with QST Seattle. Len quickly put his unique gifts to work developing tours to Asia. Within three years, Len's tours to China, Vietnam, and Japan have attracted hundreds of repeat customers.

A **Linked** style applies formatting to text within a paragraph or to an entire paragraph depending on how text is selected

Tours with QST

Len is the resident expert on Japan at QST Seattle. Following is information about the two most popular Japan tours that he hosts and the schedule for those tours.

Top Tours

→ *Old Japan*: Travel back in time and live like the shoguns! Sleep in quaint ryokans (Japanese country inns), chant with the monks in the monasteries of sacred Mount Koya, then stroll around the ancient temples of Kyoto.

→ *Natural Japan*: Follow in the footsteps of millions of pilgrims as you climb Mount Fuji to greet the rising sun, wander the charming streets of old-world Takayama, then slip into the steaming waters of a natural onsen (hot springs) deep in the green valleys of the Japan Alps.

A **List** style adds bullets or numbers to a series of paragraphs

A **Character** style applies formatting to text within a paragraph; this character style includes orange and italic

Tour Schedule

Tour Name	Duration	Start Dates
Natural Japan	10 days	February 25, March 25, April 25
Old Japan	8 days	April 15, May 15, June 15

Your Name, **QST San Diego**, 340 West Market Street, San Diego, CA 92101
www.questspecialtytravel.com

A **Table** style applies formatting to a table grid and table text

Understanding Themes, Style Sets, and the Normal style

Style Sets are not the same as themes but they work with themes to provide you with an almost unlimited range of formatting options. A theme is a set of unified design elements including theme colors, theme fonts for body text and headings, and theme effects for graphics. When you apply a theme to a document, you can further modify the appearance of the text, colors, and graphics in the document by applying one of the 17 built-in Style Sets. You can then modify the appearance even further by changing the settings of the styles associated with the Style Set.

Text that you type into a blank document is formatted with the Normal style from the default Style Set associated with the Office 2013 theme until you specify otherwise. By default, text formatted with the Normal style uses the 11-point Calibri font and is left-aligned, with a line spacing of 1.08 within a paragraph and 8 pt After Paragraph spacing. When you select a new Style Set, the styles associated with that Style Set are applied to the document.

Modify Built-in Styles

Learning Outcomes
• Modify a style
• Update a style

Word includes built-in styles, such as the Normal, Title, Heading 1, and Heading 2 styles, for each built-in Style Set. The styles associated with the active Style Set are displayed in the Styles gallery on the HOME tab. These styles along with other, less frequently used styles, can also be accessed from the Styles task pane. You can personalize documents by modifying any style. **CASE** ▸ *You modify the Normal style currently applied to all body text in a profile of Len Barclay, a tour guide from QST Seattle. You also modify the Heading 1 style and the Title style.*

STEPS

1. **Start Word, open the file** WD J-1.docx **from the location where you store your Data Files, save the file as** WD J-Profile of Len Barclay, **click in the paragraph below "Early Life," right-click** Normal **in the Styles gallery on the HOME tab, then click** Modify
 The Modify Style dialog box opens, as shown in FIGURE J-2.

2. **Click the** Font list arrow **in the Formatting area, scroll to and select** Bookman Old Style, **click the** Font Size list arrow, **click** 12, **then click** OK
 The Modify Style dialog box closes, and all body text in the document is modified automatically to match the new settings for the Normal style.

3. **Select the** Early Life **heading, then use the commands in the Font group to change the font to** Bookman Old Style **and the font color to** Green, Accent 6, Darker 50%
 You made changes to the character formatting for the selected text.

4. **Be sure the Early Life heading is still selected, click the** Borders list arrow ▦ ▾ **in the Paragraph group, click the** Bottom Border button, **click the** PAGE LAYOUT **tab, click the** Spacing Before text box **in the Paragraph group, type** 10, **click the** Spacing After text box, **type** 6, **then press** [Enter]
 You made changes to the paragraph formatting for the selected text.

5. **Click the** HOME **tab, right-click** Heading 1 **in the Styles gallery to open the menu shown in** FIGURE J-3, **then click** Update Heading 1 to Match Selection
 The Heading 1 style is updated to match the formatting options you applied to the Early Life heading. All headings in the text that are formatted with the Heading 1 style are updated to match the new Heading 1 style. Notice that the Heading 1 style in the Styles gallery shows a preview of the formatting associated with the Heading 1 style.

6. **Click the launcher** ⬚ **in the Styles group to open the Styles task pane**
 By default, the **Styles task pane** lists a selection of the styles available in the active Style Set. The Styles task pane also includes options for creating new styles, using the Style Inspector, and managing styles.

7. **Select** Len Barclay **at the top of the page, point to** Title **in the Styles task pane, click the list arrow that appears, then click** Modify

8. **Change the font to** Bookman Old Style, **click the** Automatic list arrow, **select the** Green, Accent 6, Darker 50% **color box, then click** OK
 The selected text in the document and the preview of the Title style in the Styles gallery changes to show the new settings.

9. **Save the document**
 You have used three methods to modify the formatting attached to a style. You can modify the style using the Modify Styles dialog box, you can make changes to text associated with a style and then update the style to match the selected text, or you can modify a style from the Styles task pane. You generally use this last method when you need to modify a style that does not appear in the Styles gallery.

Name of selected style; changes made in this dialog box will be applied to this style in the active Style Set

Modifications you make to the Normal style apply to text formatted with the Normal style in this document only

Formats currently associated with the Normal style

Options for applying modifications made to this style

FIGURE J-3: Updating the Heading 1 style with new formats

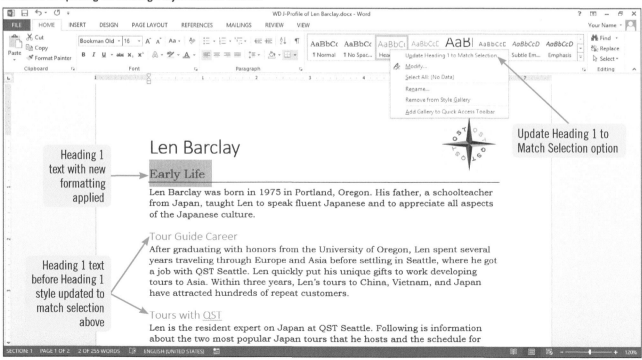

Heading 1 text with new formatting applied

Update Heading 1 to Match Selection option

Heading 1 text before Heading 1 style updated to match selection above

Create Paragraph Styles

Learning Outcomes
• Create a paragraph style
• Apply a paragraph style

Instead of using the built-in styles, you can create your own styles. You can base a new style on an existing style or you can base it on no style. When you base a style on an existing style, both the formatting associated with the existing style and any new formatting you apply are associated with the new style. One type of style you can create is a paragraph style. A paragraph style is a combination of character and paragraph formats that you name and store as a set. You can create a paragraph style and then apply it to any paragraph. Any line of text followed by a hard return is considered a paragraph, even if the line consists of only one or two words. **CASE** *You create a new paragraph style called Guide Subtitle and apply it to two headings in the document.*

STEPS

1. **Scroll to and select the heading** Top Tours, **then click the** New Style button ⊞ **at the bottom of the Styles task pane**

 The Create New Style from Formatting dialog box opens. You use this dialog box to enter a name for the new style, select a style type, and select the formatting options you want associated with the new style.

2. **Type** Guide Subtitle **in the Name text box**

 The Guide Subtitle style is based on the Normal style because the selected text is formatted with the Normal style. When you create a new style, you can base it on the style applied to the selected text if a style has been applied to that text, another style by selecting a style in the Style based on list box, or no preset style. You want the new style to also include the formatting associated with the Normal style so you leave Normal as the Style based on setting.

3. **Click** 12 **in the font size text box, type** 13, **click the** Italic button I, **click the** Automatic **list arrow, click the** Green, Accent 6, Darker 25% **color box, then click** OK

4. **Select the heading** Tour Schedule **(you may need to scroll down), then click** Guide Subtitle **in the Styles task pane**

 The new Guide Subtitle style is applied to two headings in the document.

5. **Click the** Show Preview **check box at the bottom of the Styles task pane to select it if it is not already selected**

 With the Show Preview option active, you can quickly see the formatting associated with each of the predefined styles and the new style you created.

6. **Move your mouse over** Guide Subtitle **in the Styles task pane to show the settings associated with the Guide Subtitle style**

 The Styles task pane and the document are shown in FIGURE J-4.

7. **Click** Options **at the bottom of the Styles task pane, then click the** Select styles to show **list arrow**

 The Style Pane Options dialog box appears as shown in FIGURE J-5. You can choose to show recommended styles (the default setting), all the styles associated with the Style Set, or just the styles currently in use.

8. **Click** In use, **then click** OK

 Only the styles currently applied to the document are displayed in the Styles task pane.

9. **Save the document**

FIGURE J-4: Formatting associated with Guide Subtitle style

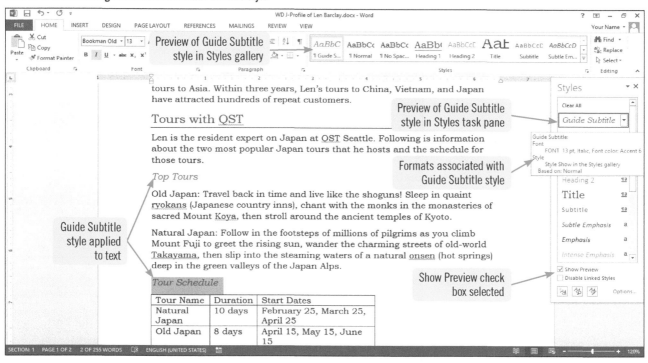

FIGURE J-5: Style Pane Options dialog box

Revealing style formatting

Word includes two ways to quickly determine exactly what styles and formatting are applied to selected text. These methods are useful when you apply a style to text and not all the formatting changes you expect to be made are made. To find out why, use the Style Inspector to open the Reveal Formatting task pane. To open the Style Inspector, click the text formatted with the style, then click the Style Inspector button at the bottom of the Styles task pane. The **Style Inspector** lists the styles applied to the selected text and indicates if any extra formats were applied that are not included in

the style. For example, another user could apply formatting such as bold and italic that is not included in the style. You can clear these formats by clicking one of the four buttons along the right side of the Style Inspector or by clicking Clear All to remove all extra formats. If you need to investigate even further, you can click the Reveal Formatting button at the bottom of the Style Inspector to open the Reveal Formatting task pane. The **Reveal Formatting task pane** lists exactly which formats are applied to the character, paragraph, and section of the selected text.

Create Character and Linked Styles

A character style includes character format settings—such as font, font size, bold, and italic—that you name and save as a style. You apply a character style to selected text within a paragraph. Any text in the paragraph that is not formatted with the character style is formatted with the currently applied paragraph style. A linked style includes both character formats and paragraph formats, just like a paragraph style. The difference is that you can apply the paragraph style associated with a linked style to an entire paragraph or you can apply the character style associated with the linked style to selected text within a paragraph. Linked styles are therefore very versatile. **CASE** ▸ *You create a character style called Tours to apply to each tour name and a linked style called QST to apply to each instance of QST Seattle.*

STEPS

1. **Select the text** Old Japan **in the section below Top Tours, press and hold [Ctrl], then select the text** Natural Japan **at the beginning of the next paragraph**

2. **Click the** New Style button 🖎 **at the bottom of the Styles task pane, type** Tours **in the Name text box, click the** Style type list arrow, **then click** Character

3. **Select these character formatting settings: the** Bookman Old Style font, 12 pt, Italic, **and the** Green, Accent 6, Darker 25% font color, **click OK, then click away from the text to deselect it**
 The text you selected is formatted with the Tours character style.

4. **Select** Old Japan, **change the font color to** Orange, Accent 2, Darker 25%, **right-click** Tours **in the Styles task pane to open the menu shown in** FIGURE J-6, **then click** Update Tours to Match Selection
 Both of the phrases formatted with the Tours character style are updated.

5. **Scroll up and select** QST Seattle **in the paragraph below Tour Guide Career, click the** Text Effects and Typography list arrow 🅰 ▾ **in the Font group, then select the** Fill – Blue, Accent 1, Shadow **(first row, second column)**

6. **Right-click the selected text, click** Styles **on the Mini toolbar, then click** Create a Style
 The Create New Style from Formatting dialog box opens.

7. **Type** QST **as the style name, click** Modify, **then click the** Center button ≡
 In the Create New Style from Formatting dialog box, you see that the Linked (paragraph and character) style type is automatically assigned when you create a new style from selected text. The style you created includes character formatting (the text effect format) and paragraph formatting (center alignment).

8. **Click OK, click anywhere in the paragraph under Early Life, then click** QST **in the Styles task pane**
 The entire paragraph is formatted with the QST style, as shown in FIGURE J-7. Both the character formatting and the paragraph formatting associated with the QST linked style are applied to the paragraph, but only the character formatting associated with the QST linked style is applied to the QST Seattle text in the next paragraph.

9. **Click the** Undo button ↺ **on the Quick Access toolbar, scroll to the paragraph below the Tours with QST heading, select** QST Seattle **in the paragraph, click** QST **in the Styles task pane, then save the document**

FIGURE J-6: Updating the Tours character style

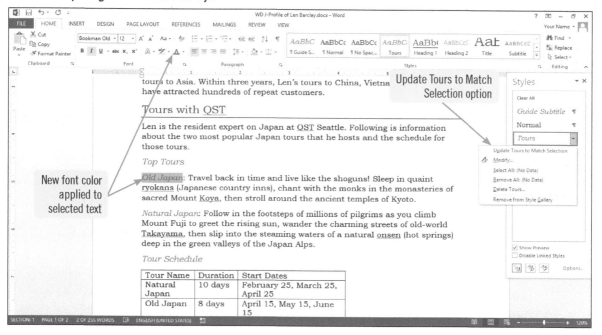

FIGURE J-7: QST linked style applied to a paragraph and to selected text

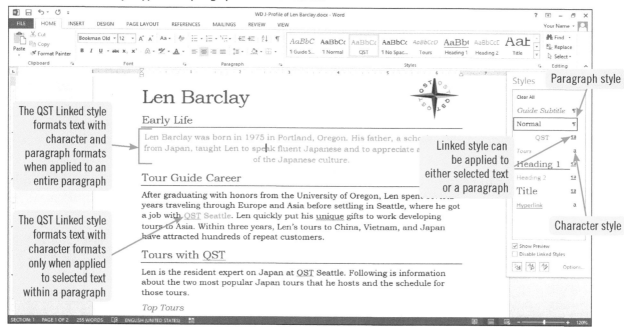

Identifying paragraph, character, and linked styles

Style types are identified in the Styles task pane by different symbols. Each paragraph style is marked with a paragraph symbol: ¶. You can apply a paragraph style just by clicking in any paragraph or line of text and selecting the style. The most commonly used predefined paragraph style is the Normal style. Each character style is marked with a character symbol: a. You apply a character style by clicking anywhere in a word or by selecting a phrase within a paragraph. Built-in character styles include Emphasis, Strong, and Book Title. Each linked style is marked with both a paragraph symbol and a character symbol: ¶a. You can click anywhere in a paragraph to apply the linked style to the entire paragraph, or you can select text and then apply only the character formats associated with the linked style to the selected text. Predefined linked styles include Heading 1, Title, and Quote.

Create List and Table Styles

**Learning
Outcomes**
• Create a list style
• Create a table
 style

A list style includes settings that format a series of paragraphs so they appear related in some way. For example, you can create a list style that adds bullet characters to paragraphs or sequential numbers to a list of items. A table style includes formatting settings for the table grid and the table text. **CASE** ➤ *You create a list style called Tour List with a special bullet character and a table style called Tour Schedule.*

STEPS

1. **Click to the left of** Old Japan **in the Top Tours section, click the** New Style button ⊞ **at the bottom of the Styles task pane, type** Tour List **as the style name, click the** Style type list arrow, **then click** List

 You can also click the Multilevel List button in the Paragraph group on the HOME tab, and then click Define New List Style to open the Define New List Style dialog box and create a new style.

2. **Click the** Bullets button ⊟, **click the** Symbol button ⊠, **click the** Font list arrow, **scroll down and click** Wingdings, **double-click the number in the** Character code text box, **type** 81, **click** OK, **click the** Font Color list arrow, **then click** Blue, Accent 5

 The Create New Style from Formatting dialog box appears as shown in FIGURE J-8.

QUICK TIP
List styles are stored in the List Styles area of the Multilevel List gallery in the document, not in the Styles task pane.

3. **Click** OK, **click** Natural **in the phrase "Natural Japan", click the** Multilevel List button ⊞▾ **in the Paragraph group, move the mouse pointer over the style in the List Styles area and notice the ScreenTip reads** Tour List, **then click the** Tour List **style**

 The bullet character of a blue plane is added, the text is indented, and the spacing above the paragraph is removed. By default, Word removes spacing between paragraphs formatted with a list style, which is part of the List Paragraph style. When you create a list style, the List style type is based on the List Paragraph style.

4. **Scroll down and click in the table, click the** table move handle ⊞ **at the upper-left corner of the table to select the table, click the** New Style button ⊞, **type** Tour Schedule **in the Name text box, click the** Style type list arrow, **then click** Table

 The Create New Style from Formatting dialog box changes to show formatting options for a table.

QUICK TIP
Table styles are stored in the Table Styles gallery on the TABLE TOOLS DESIGN tab, not in the Styles task pane.

5. **Refer to** FIGURE J-9: **select the** Bookman Old Style **font,** 12 pt font size, **a** 1 pt border width, **black (Automatic) border color,** and **Green, Accent 6, Lighter 60% fill color, then click the** All Borders button

6. **Click the** Apply formatting to list arrow, **click** Header row, **change the font color to** white **and the fill color to** Green, Accent 6, Darker 50%, **click the** Align list arrow, **click the** Align Center button, **then click** OK

 The table is formatted with the new Tour Schedule table style, which includes a modified header row.

TROUBLE
If the table columns do not resize, resize each column manually.

7. **Double-click the** right edge **of the table so all text in each row fits on one line**

8. **Click the** TABLE TOOLS DESIGN **tab, right-click the currently selected table style (far-left selection), click** Modify Table Style, **click** Format **in the lower-left corner of the dialog box, click** Table Properties, **click the** Center button **in the Alignment area, click** OK, **then click** OK

 The table is centered as shown in FIGURE J-10 and the center format is part of the table style.

9. **Click below the table to deselect it, then save the document**

FIGURE J-8: Create New Style from Formatting dialog box

Wingdings font selected

Bullets button

List formatting applied to 1st level only; symbol used for bullet

Description of formats applied to Tour List style

Color list arrow

Symbol button

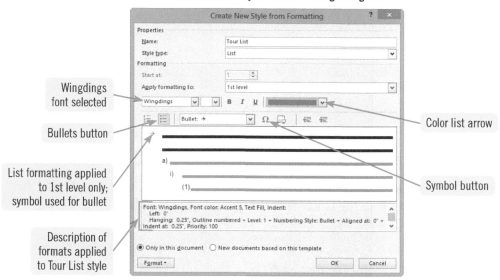

FIGURE J-9: Table formatting selections

Table text font size

Table text font

Border style

Border weight

Border color

All Borders button

Apply formatting to list arrow

Fill Color

Alignment list arrow

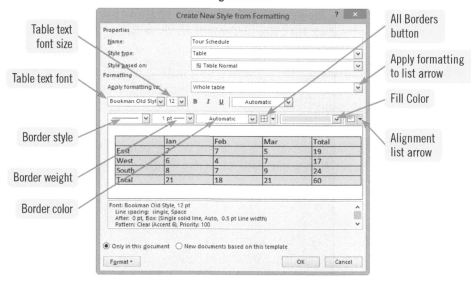

FIGURE J-10: Tour List and Tour Schedule styles applied

Tour Schedule table style in the Table Styles gallery on the TABLE TOOLS DESIGN tab

Styles task pane includes all character, paragraph, and linked styles but not list or table styles

Tour List list style

Tour Schedule table style

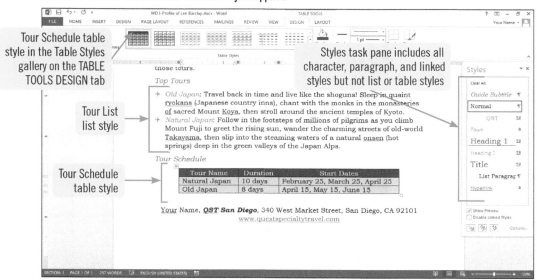

Create a Style Set

**Learning
Outcomes**
• Create a Style Set
• Apply a color
 scheme

Once you have formatted a document with a selection of styles that includes both new and existing styles, you can save all the styles as a new Style Set. You can then apply the Style Set to format other documents. **CASE** ▸ *You create a new Style Set called QST Profiles, and then apply it to another profile.*

STEPS

1. **Press [Ctrl][Home] to move to the top of the document, click the DESIGN tab, then click the More button ⏷ in the Document Formatting group to open the gallery of Style Sets**

2. **Click Save as a New Style Set**
 The Save as a New Style Set dialog box opens to the default location where Style Sets are saved.

3. **Type QST Profiles in the File name text box, then click Save**

4. **Click the More button ⏷ to expand the gallery of Style Sets, move your mouse over the Style Set thumbnail that appears under Custom to show the name of the Style Set as shown in FIGURE J-11, then click the document to close the gallery**
 The QST Profiles Style Set is now one of the Style Sets you can use to format other documents.

5. **Click the Colors button in the Document Formatting group, move the mouse over the various color schemes to see how the document changes, scroll to and click Red Orange, then save the document**
 The color scheme for the document has changed.

6. **Open the file WD J-2.docx from the location where you store your Data Files, save it as WD J-Profile of Kayla Wong, click the DESIGN tab, then show the gallery of Style Sets**
 Kayla Wong's profile is currently formatted with one of the 17 built-in Style Sets. The Title style is applied to "Kayla Wong", and the Heading 1 style is applied to the "Early Life", "Tour Guide Career", and "Tours with QST" headings.

7. **Click the QST Profiles Style Set thumbnail under Custom**
 The QST Profiles Style Set is applied to the text in Kayla Wong's profile, and all the new styles you created in previous lessons, except the Tour List list style and the Tour Schedule table style, are available in the Styles gallery and the Styles task pane. Notice that the Red Orange color scheme you applied to Len Barclay's profile is not applied. Color schemes are not saved with a Style Set. You must reapply the color scheme.

8. **Click the Colors button in the Document Formatting group, then click Red Orange**

9. **Click the HOME tab, apply the Guide Subtitle and Tours styles from the Styles Gallery to the text as shown in FIGURE J-12, then save the document**
 You applied styles associated with the QST Profiles Style Set to document text. You will learn more about managing styles and applying the QST style, the Tour List style, and the Tour Schedule style in the next lesson.

FIGURE J-11: QST Profiles Style Set

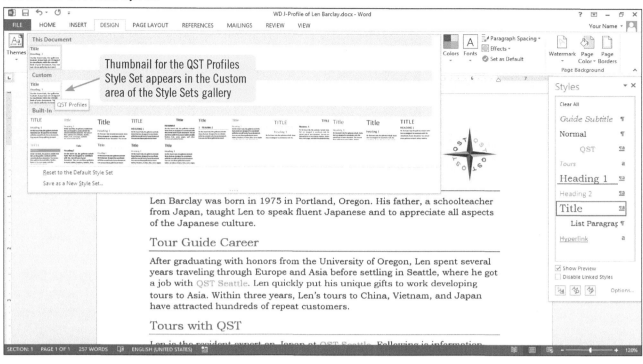

FIGURE J-12: Applying styles from the QST Profiles Style Set

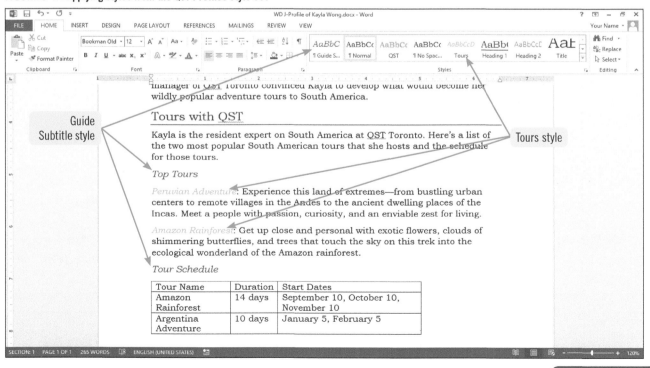

Manage Styles

You can manage styles in many ways. For example, you can rename and delete styles, find and replace styles, and copy styles from one document to another document. After you create list and table styles, you must copy them from the source file (the document where you created the styles) to the target file (the document where you want to use the styles). **CASE** ▶ *You use Find and Replace to find each instance of QST Toronto and replace it with the same text formatted with the QST style, then copy the Tour List and the Tour Schedule styles from Len Barclay's profile (source file) to Kayla Wong's profile (target file).*

STEPS

1. **Press [Ctrl][Home], click** Replace **in the Editing group on the HOME tab, type** QST Toronto **in the Find what text box, press [Tab], then type** QST Toronto **in the Replace with text box**

2. **Click** More, **click** Format, **click** Style, **click** QST Char, **click** OK, **click** Replace All, **click** OK, **then click** Close

 QST Toronto is formatted with the QST Char version of the QST linked style. Notice that only the character formats associated with the QST style were applied to QST Toronto.

3. **Click the launcher** 🔲 **in the Styles group to open the Styles task pane, click the** Manage Styles button 🖉 **at the bottom of the Styles task pane, then click** Import/Export **to open the Organizer dialog box**

 You copy styles from the document shown in the left side of the Organizer dialog box (the source file) to a new document that you open in the right side of the Organizer dialog box (the target file). By default, the target file is the Normal template.

4. **Click** Close File **under the list box on the left, click** Open File, **then navigate to the location where you store your files**

5. **Click the** All Word Templates **list arrow, select** All Word Documents **as shown in** FIGURE J-13, **click** WD J-Profile of Len Barclay.docx, **then click** Open

 The styles assigned to Len Barclay's profile appear in the list box on the left side. This document contains the Tour List and Tour Schedule styles.

6. **Click** Close File **under the list box on the right, click** Open File, **navigate to the location where you store your files, show all Word documents, click** WD J-Profile of Kayla Wong.docx, **then click** Open

7. **Scroll the list of styles on the left side of the Organizer dialog box, click** Tour List, **press and hold [Ctrl], click** Tour Schedule **to select both styles (see** FIGURE J-14), **click** Copy, **then click** Close

8. **Select the** two tour descriptions **(from the heading Peruvian Adventure to the heading Amazon Rainforest), click the** Multilevel List button 📋 **in the Paragraph group, then click the** Tour List style **shown under List Styles**

9. **Select the** table, **click the** TABLE TOOLS DESIGN tab, **click the** Tour Schedule table style, **adjust column widths as needed so no lines wrap, enter your name where indicated, then save and close the document**

 The file WD J-Profile of Len Barclay is again the active document.

FIGURE J-13: **Selecting Word Documents in the Open dialog box**

FIGURE J-13: **Selecting Word Documents in the Open dialog box**

All Word
Documents
selected

All Word Templates
current file type

FIGURE J-14: **Managing styles using the Organizer dialog box**

Tour List and Tour
Schedule selected

Copy button

Source file

Target file

After clicking
Copy, scroll
down to verify
styles have
been copied
from the
source file to
the target file

More ways to manage styles

To rename a style, right-click it in the Styles task pane, click Modify, type a new name, then press [Enter]. To delete a style, right-click the style, then click Delete [Style name]. The style is deleted from the Styles task pane, but it is not deleted from your computer. Click the Manage Styles button at the bottom of the Styles task pane, select the style to delete, click Delete, then click OK to close the Manage Styles dialog box.

Using Find and Replace to Format Text

You work in the Find and Replace dialog box to replace text formatted with one set of character formats such as bold and italic and replace it with the same or different text formatted with different formatting. Click More, enter the text to find, click Format and specify the formats attached to the text (for example, Font, Bold), click the Replace tab, enter the text to replace and click Format to specify the new formats, then click Replace All.

Create a Template

Learning Outcomes
- Create a template
- Create a document based on a template

A quick way to use all the styles contained in a document, including list and table styles, is to create a template. A template contains the basic structure of a document, including all the paragraph, character, linked, list, and table styles. You can create a template from an existing document, or you can create a template from scratch. Templates that you create are stored in the Custom Office Templates folder in your My Documents folder. **CASE** ▸ *You save the Len Barclay profile as a template, modify the template, and then open the template as a new document.*

STEPS

1. **Click the FILE tab, click Save As, click Computer in the list of Save As locations, then click Browse**

2. **Click the Save as type list arrow, then click Word Template (*.dotx)**

 When you select Word Template, the save location automatically changes to the Custom Office Templates folder in the My Documents folder on your computer.

3. **Select the filename in the File name text box, type WD J-Profile Template, then click Save**

 The file is saved as WD J-Profile Template.dotx to the Custom Office Templates folder in the My Documents folder on your computer. The .dotx filename extension identifies this file as a template file.

4. **Select Len Barclay at the top of the document, then type [Enter Guide Name Here]**

TROUBLE
If the plane bullet symbol appears when you delete text under Top Tours, click the HOME tab, then click the Clear All Formatting button in the Font group.

5. **As shown in FIGURE J-15, enter the placeholder text, be sure to leave the contact information at the bottom of the document as part of the template, click FILE, click Close, then click Save**

 Now that you have created a template, you can use it to create a new document that contains all the styles and formatting you want.

6. **Click the FILE tab, click New, then click PERSONAL**

 A document icon named WD-J Profile Template appears.

7. **Click the WD J-Profile Template icon**

 The template opens as a new document. You can enter text into this document and then save the document just as you would any document.

8. **Select the text [Enter Guide Name Here], type Mark Lalonde, then type text in the table and resize the column widths as shown in FIGURE J-16**

9. **Type your name where indicated, click the FILE tab, click Save As, navigate to the location where you store your files, save the document as WD J-Profile of Mark Lalonde, then close the document**

[Enter Guide Name Here]

Early Life

[Describe early life]

Tour Guide Career

[Describe tour guide's career]

Tours with QST

[Introduce two top tours and schedule]

Top Tours

[Describe top tours; format each tour name with the Tours style and format the list with the Tour List style]

Tour Schedule

Tour Name	Duration	Start Dates

Your Name, **QST San Diego**, 340 West Market Street, San Diego, CA 92101
www.questspecialtytravel.com

Tour Schedule

Tour Name	Duration	Start Dates
Dreams of Provence	10 days	May 15, June 15
Barging through Burgundy	7 days	July 1, August 1

Modify and Attach a Template

Learning Outcomes
• Modify a template
• Attach a template

You can modify a template just as you would any Word document. All new documents you create from the modified template will use the new settings. All documents that you created before you modified the template are not changed unless you open the Templates and Add-ins dialog box and direct Word to update styles automatically. **CASE** *You modify the Guide Subtitle style in the Profile Template and then attach the revised template to a profile for Ally Stein. You then delete the QST Profiles Style Set.*

STEPS

1. Click the FILE tab, click Open, navigate to and open the Custom Office Templates folder in the Documents folder, click WD J-Profile Template.dotx, then click Open

2. Show the Styles task pane if it is not open, right-click Guide Subtitle in the Styles task pane, click Modify, apply Bold, change the font size to 14 pt, click OK, select Early Life, apply Bold, right-click Heading 1 in the Styles task pane, then click Update Heading 1 to Match Selection
 You need to resave the QST Profiles Style Set so that the new settings are available to new documents.

3. Click the DESIGN tab, click the More button ⬇ in the Document Formatting group, right-click the thumbnail under This Document, click Save, click QST Profiles.dotx, click Save, click Yes, then save and close the template

4. Open the file WD J-3.docx from the location where you store your Data Files, save the file as WD J-Profile of Ally Stein, click the DESIGN tab, apply the QST Profiles Style Set (under Custom in the Style Set gallery), then change the color scheme to Red Orange

5. Click the FILE tab, click Options, click Customize Ribbon, click the Developer check box in the list of Main Tabs as shown in FIGURE J-17 then click OK
 You use the DEVELOPER tab to work with advanced features such as attaching the Profile Template to Ally's profile and applying all the new styles you created to the document.

6. Click the DEVELOPER tab on the Ribbon, click Document Template in the Templates group, click Attach, navigate to the Custom Office Templates folder in the Documents folder, click WD J-Profile Template.dotx, click Open, click the Automatically update document styles check box, then click OK
 Now you can apply the styles associated with the WD J-Profile Template to Ally's profile.

7. Click the HOME tab, apply styles as shown in FIGURE J-18, be sure your name is on the document, then save and close the document

8. Create a new blank document, click the DESIGN tab, click the More button in the ⬇ Document Formatting group, right-click the thumbnail under Custom, click Delete, then click Yes
 You delete the QST Profiles Style Set from the list of Style Sets so only the default Style Sets appear for the next user of your computer system.

9. Click the FILE tab, click Options, click Customize Ribbon, click the Developer check box to deselect it, click OK, close the Styles task pane, exit Word, then submit all your files to your instructor

Working with Styles and Templates

FIGURE J-17: Adding the DEVELOPER tab to the Ribbon

Customize Ribbon option selected

Developer check box selected

FIGURE J-18: Ally Stein's profile formatted with styles

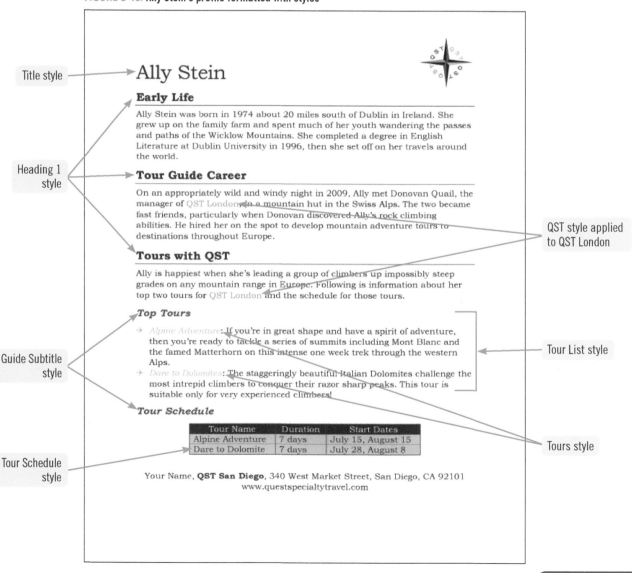

Title style

Heading 1 style

Guide Subtitle style

Tour Schedule style

QST style applied to QST London

Tour List style

Tours style

Practice

Put your skills into Practice with **SAM!** If you have a SAM account, go to www.cengage.com/sam2013 to access SAM assignments for this unit.

Concepts Review

Identify each of the items in FIGURE J-19.

FIGURE J-19

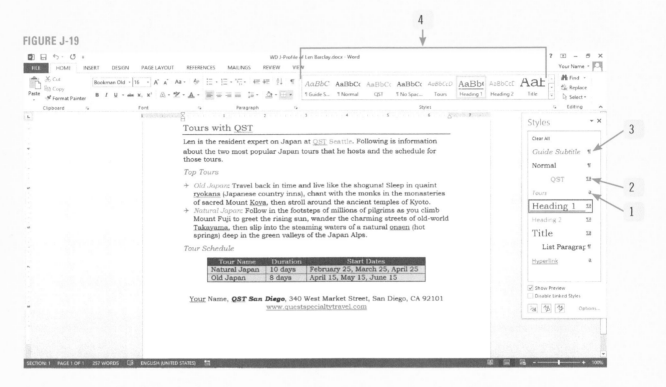

Match each term with the statement that best describes it.

5. **Style Set**

6. **Organizer dialog box**

7. **Template**

8. **Style**

9. **Character style**

a. Character formats that you name and store as a set

b. A file that contains the basic structure of a document in addition to selected styles; can be custom made

c. A collection of character, paragraph, and linked styles that is named and available to all documents

d. Used to copy styles from a source document to a target document

e. A collection of saved formats that is used to provide consistent formatting to related items, such as all Heading 1 text

Select the best answer from the list of choices.

10. What is available in the Style Set gallery?

 a. Themes associated with the current Style Set **c.** Colors associated with the current Style Set

 b. The DEVELOPER tab **d.** Styles associated with the current Style Set

11. How do you modify a style?

 a. Double-click the style in the Styles task pane.

 b. Right-click the style in the Styles gallery, then click Revise.

 c. Right-click the style in the Styles gallery, then click Modify.

 d. Click the style in the Styles task pane, then click New Style.

12. Which of the following definitions best describes a paragraph style?

 a. Format settings applied only to selected text within a paragraph

 b. Format settings applied to a table grid

 c. Format settings applied to all text in a paragraph

 d. Format settings applied to the structure of a document

13. Which of the following style types is not saved with a Style Set?

 a. Table style **c.** Linked style

 b. Paragraph style **d.** Character style

14. Which dialog box do you use to copy styles from one document to another?

 a. Reveal Formatting dialog box **c.** Styles dialog box

 b. Organizer dialog box **d.** Modify Styles dialog box

15. What is the filename extension for a template?

 a. .docx **c.** .dotx

 b. .RTF **d.** .dotm

16. Which tab do you use to attach a template to an existing document?

 a. INSERT **c.** DEVELOPER

 b. REFERENCES **d.** PAGE

Skills Review

1. Modify built-in styles.

 a. Start Word, open the file WD J-4.docx from the location where you store your Data Files, save it as **WD J-Jigsaws_Shaped**, then open the Styles task pane.

 b. Modify the Normal style by changing the font to Times New Roman and the font size to 12 pt.

 c. Select the Map Jigsaws heading, then change the font to Arial, the font size to 18 pt, and the font color to Orange, Accent 2, Darker 25%.

 d. Add a border line below the text.

 e. From the PAGE LAYOUT tab, change the Before spacing to 6 pt and the After spacing to 6 pt.

 f. Update the Heading 1 style so that it uses the new formats.

 g. Modify the Title style by changing the font to Arial and the color to Orange, Accent 2, Darker 50%, then save the document.

2. Create paragraph styles.

 a. Scroll to and select the heading "Marketing Plan," then create a new paragraph style called **Operations** that uses the Arial font, 14 pt, bold, and italic, and changes the font color to Gold, Accent 4, Darker 25%.

 b. Apply the Operations style to "Summary of New Products."

 c. From the Styles task pane, show only the styles currently in use in the document and make sure the Show Preview check box is selected.

 d. Save the document.

Skills Review (continued)

3. Create character and linked styles.

a. Select "France" under Map Jigsaws, then create a new character style named **Jigsaw Theme** that uses the Arial font, 12 pt, Italic, and the Orange, Accent 2, Darker 50% font color.

b. Apply the Jigsaw Theme style to "United States," "Grizzly Bear," and "Dolphin."

c. Select "Bit Part Puzzles" in the first paragraph, apply the Fill - Gold, Accent 4, Soft Bevel text effect, open the Create New Style from Formatting dialog box, name the style **Company**, and select the Linked style type, then select the option to right-align the paragraph.

d. Apply the Company style to the France paragraph, undo the application, then apply the Company style just to the text "Bit Part Puzzles" in the paragraph above the table.

e. Save the document.

4. Create list and table styles.

a. Click to the left of "France" under Map Jigsaws, then define a new list style called **Jigsaw List**. (*Hint:* Click the Multilevel List button in the Paragraph group on the HOME tab, then click Define New List Style.)

b. Change the list style to Bullet, open the Symbol dialog box, verify the Wingdings character set is active, type **216** in the Character code text box, then change the symbol color to Purple in the Standard Colors area.

c. Apply the Jigsaw List style to each paragraph that describes a jigsaw: United States, Grizzly Bear, and Dolphin. (*Hint:* You access the Jigsaw List style by clicking the Multilevel List button.)

d. Select the table at the bottom of the document, then create a new table style called **Jigsaw Table**.

e. Select Gold, Accent 4, Lighter 80% for the fill color, change the border style to 3/4 pt and the border color to Automatic, then apply All Borders to the table.

f. Format the header row with bold, the White font color, the Gold, Accent 4, Darker 50% fill color, and Center alignment, then apply the new table style to your table.

g. With the table selected, double-click between columns to reduce the column sizes.

h. From the TABLE TOOLS DESIGN tab, modify the style by changing the table properties so the table is centered between the left and right margins of the page, then save the document.

5. Create a Style Set.

a. From the DESIGN tab, save the current Style Set as **Jigsaws**, then view the Jigsaws Style Set in the Custom section of the Style Sets gallery.

b. Change the color scheme to Blue, then save the document.

c. Open the file WD J-5.docx from the location where you store your Data Files, then save it as **WD J-Jigsaws_3D**.

d. Apply the Jigsaws Style Set to the document, then apply the Blue color scheme.

e. Apply the Jigsaw Theme style to the four jigsaw titles (e.g., "Eiffel Tower, "Log Cabin," etc.).

f. Apply the Operations style to "Marketing Plan," and "Summary of New Products," then save the document.

6. Manage styles.

a. Position the insertion point at the beginning of the document, open the Replace dialog box, enter **Bit Part Puzzles** in the Find what text box, then enter **Bit Part Puzzles** in the Replace with text box.

b. Open the More options area, select the Style option on the Format menu, select the Company Char style, then replace both instances of Bit Part Puzzles with Bit Part Puzzles formatted with the Company Char style.

c. Open the Manage Styles dialog box from the Styles task pane, then click Import/Export to open the Organizer dialog box.

d. Close the file in the left pane of the Organizer dialog box, then open the file WD J-Jigsaws_Shaped.docx. Remember to navigate to the location where you save files and to change the Files of type to Word documents.

e. Close the file in the right pane of the Organizer dialog box, then open the file WD J-Jigsaws_3D.docx.

f. Copy the Jigsaw List and Jigsaw Table styles from the WD J-Jigsaws_Shaped document to the WD J-Jigsaws_3D document, then close the Organizer dialog box and return to the document.

g. In the file WD J-Jigsaws_3D.docx, apply the Jigsaw List style to each of the four jigsaw descriptions.

h. Select the table, use the TABLE TOOLS DESIGN tab to apply the Jigsaw Table style to the table, reduce the column widths, type your name where indicated at the end of the document, save the document, then close it.

Skills Review (continued)

7. Create a template.

 a. Save the current document (which should be WD J-Jigsaws_Shaped) as a template called **WD J-Jigsaw Descriptions.dotx** in the Custom Office Templates folder in the My Documents folder on your computer.

 b. Select "Shaped Jigsaws" at the top of the page, type **[Enter Category Here]**, then delete text and enter directions so the document appears as shown in FIGURE J-20. (*Hint:* If new text is formatted with a style you don't want associated with that text, such as the Company style, the Heading 1 style, or the Jigsaw Theme, select the formatted text and click the Clear All Formatting button in the Font group on the HOME tab.)

 c. Save and close the template.

 d. Create a new document based on the WD J-Jigsaw Descriptions template. Remember to show the list of PERSONAL templates.

 e. Replace the title of the document with the text **Brain Teaser Jigsaws**, save the document as **WD J-Jigsaws_Brain Teaser** to the location where you store your files, then close it.

FIGURE J-20

[Enter Category Here]
[Describe new products]

[New Jigsaw Type]
[List jigsaws, format types with the Jigsaw Theme style and the list with the Jigsaw List style]

[New Jigsaw Type]
[List jigsaws, format types with the Jigsaw Theme style and the list with the Jigsaw List style]

Marketing Plan

These new products will be marketed exclusively online to consumers through our corporate Web site. At present, there are no plans to make the products available in retail stores.

Summary of New Products

The table shown below includes a brief description of all three of the new lines carried by Bit Part Puzzles.

[Type 1]	[Type 2]	[Type 3]

Prepared by Your Name

8. Modify and attach a template.

 a. Open the template file WD J-Jigsaw Descriptions.dotx, then modify the Title style so that the font is Century Gothic. (*Note:* Be sure to open the template using the FILE and Open commands so you can work on the template document itself.)

 b. Modify the Jigsaw Theme style by changing the font to Georgia.

 c. Resave the Jigsaws Style Set, then save and close the template.

 d. Open the file WD J-6.docx from the location where your Data Files are located, save the file as **WD J-Jigsaws_Landscape**, then from the DESIGN tab, apply the Jigsaws Style Set and select the Blue color scheme.

 e. Show the DEVELOPER tab on the Ribbon, open the Templates and Add-ins dialog box, attach the WD J-Jigsaw Descriptions.dotx template from the Custom Office Templates folder, click the Automatically update document styles check box, then click OK.

 f. Apply styles from the Jigsaws Style Set that are associated with the WD J-Puzzle Descriptions template so that the WD J-Jigsaws_Landscape document resembles the other documents you have formatted for this Skills Review (*Hint:* Remember to apply the Title, Jigsaw Theme, Operations, Jigsaw List, and Jigsaw Table styles, and to apply the Company style to all three instances of "Bit Part Puzzles.")

 g. Enter your name where indicated, then save and close the document.

 h. In a new blank document in Word, from the DESIGN tab, delete the Jigsaws Style Set, then remove the DEVELOPER tab from the Ribbon and exit Word.

 i. Submit your files to your instructor.

Independent Challenge 1

You are the office manager of Green Solutions, a company that creates educational materials for courses and workshops in environmental studies. The annual company fitness day is coming soon, and you need to inform the employees about the date and time. You have already typed the text of the staff notice and included some formatting. Now you need to modify some of the styles, create new styles, create a new Style Set and copy a style to a new document, and then use the Style Set to format another staff notice about a different event.

 a. Start Word, open the file WD J-7.docx from the location where you store your Data Files, then save it as **WD J-Staff Notice of Fitness Day**.

Independent Challenge 1 (continued)

b. Modify and update styles as shown in TABLE J-1.

c. Apply the Heading 1 style to the three headings shown in ALL CAPS in the document.

TABLE J-1

style name	changes
Title	Arial Black font; 22-pt font size; Green, Accent 6, Darker 50%
Heading 1	Arial Black font; 14-pt font size; Green, Accent 6, Darker 25%

© 2014 Cengage Learning

d. Create a new paragraph style called **Event** that uses the Arial font, 20-pt font size, italic, and Blue, Accent 5, Darker 25%, then apply it to "Company Fitness Day."

e. Create a new character style called **Green** that uses the Arial font, 14-pt font size, italic, and Green, Accent 6, Darker 25%.

f. Find every instance of "Green Solutions" and replace it with Green Solutions formatted with the Green style.

g. Modify the Green style by changing the font size to 12 pt.

h. Create a table style called **Activities** using formats as shown in TABLE J-2, then apply the table style to the table in the document.

TABLE J-2

table area	changes
whole table	Fill - Green, Accent 6, Lighter 80%; 1 pt border lines
header row	Fill - Green, Accent 6, Darker 50%; White font color and bold

© 2014 Cengage Learning

i. Save the Style Set as **Staff Events**, change the color scheme to Red Violet, type your name where indicated, then save the document (and keep it open).

j. Open the file WD J-8.docx, save the document as **WD J-Staff Notice of Holiday Party**, apply the Staff Events Style Set, then change the color scheme to Red Violet.

k. Save the file, then open the Organizer dialog box from the Manage Styles dialog box. (*Hint:* Click Import/Export.)

l. In the Organizer dialog box, make WD J-Staff Notice of Fitness Day the source file and WD J-Staff Notice of Holiday Party the target file. Remember to select All Word Documents as the file type when opening the files.

m. Copy the Activities table style from the file WD J-Staff Notice of Fitness Day file to the WD J-Staff Notice of Holiday Party file, then close the Organizer dialog box.

n. Apply styles to selected headings and text in WD J-Staff Notice of Holiday Party to match the Staff Notice of Fitness Day document. (*Hint:* You need to apply the Event, Heading 1, and Green styles, as well as the Activities table style. Note that you can use Find and Replace to find every instance of "Green Solutions" and replace it with Green Solutions formatted with the Green character style.)

o. Type your name where indicated, then save the document.

p. Remove the Staff Events Style Set from the list of Style Sets, then submit the files to your instructor.

Independent Challenge 2

As the owner of the Sunrise Bistro, a vegetarian café in Sante Fe, you need to create two menus—one for spring and one for fall. You have already created an unformatted version of the spring menu and of the fall menu. Now you need to format text in the spring menu with styles, save the styles in a new Style Set called Menus, then use the Menus Style Set to format text in the fall version of the menu. You also need to work in the Organizer dialog box to copy the list and table styles you created for the spring menu to the fall version of the menu.

a. Start Word, open the file WD J-9.docx from the location where you store your Data Files, then save it as **WD J-Sunrise Bistro Spring Menu**. Apply the Slipstream color scheme.

b. Select the title (Sunrise Bistro Spring Menu), apply these formats: Bauhaus 93, 18 pt, a font color of Green, Accent 4, Darker 50%, and Center alignment, then create a new linked style called **Menu Title** based on these formats. (*Hint:* Right-click the formatted text, click the Styles button on the Mini toolbar, click Create a Style, type Menu Title, then click OK. You can verify that the style is a linked style by clicking Modify in the Create New Style from Formatting dialog box.)

Independent Challenge 2 (continued)

c. Select Appetizers, apply the formats Bauhaus 93, 14 pt, italic, a font color of Green, Accent 4, Darker 25%, then create a new linked style from the selection called **Menu Category**.

d. Apply the Menu Category style to each of the remaining main headings: Soups and Salads, Entrees, Desserts, and Opening Times.

e. Click to the left of Feta cheese (the first appetizer), then create a new list style called **Bistro Menu Item** that includes a bullet character from Wingdings symbol 123 (a stylized flower) that is colored Green, Accent 4, Darker 50%.

f. Click the Multilevel List button, right-click the new Bistro Menu Item style in the List Styles area, click Modify, then in the Modify Style dialog box, click Format (bottom left), click Numbering, click More (bottom left), click the Add tab stop at: check box, select the contents of the text box, type **5.5**, click OK, then click OK.

g. Apply the Bistro Menu Item list style (remember to click the Multilevel List button) to all the menu items in each category.

h. Save the styles in a Style Set called **Menus**.

i. Click anywhere in the table, then create a new table style called **Bistro Times** that fills the table cells with a light fill color of your choice and includes border lines, and then format the header row with the corresponding dark fill color of your choice and the white font color, bold, and centering.

j. Modify the Bistro Times table style so that the table is centered between the left and right margins of the page.

k. Type your name where indicated at the bottom of the document, then save the document and keep it open.

l. Open the file WD J-10.docx, save it as **WD J-Sunrise Bistro Fall Menu**, then apply the Menus Style Set.

m. Format the appropriate headings with the Menu Title and Menu Category styles. Note that the Bistro Menu Items list style and the Bistro Times table styles are not saved with the Menus Style Set. You need to copy them separately.

n. Change the color scheme to the color scheme of your choice. You do not need to select the same color scheme you applied to the summer menu.

o. Save the file, then open the Organizer dialog box from the Manage Styles dialog box.

p. In the Organizer dialog box, make WD J-Sunrise Bistro Spring Menu the source file and WD J-Sunrise Bistro Fall Menu the target file. Remember to select All Word Documents as the file type when opening the files.

q. Copy the Bistro Menu Item list style and the Bistro Times table style from the file WD J-Sunrise Bistro Spring Menu file to the WD J-Sunrise Bistro Fall Menu file, then close the Organizer dialog box.

r. In the Fall menu document, apply the Bistro Menu Item list style to the first appetizer (Harvest cheddar cheeses).

s. Click the Multilevel List button, right-click the Bistro Menu Item style, click Modify, then change the bullet symbol for the Menu Item style to Wingdings 124 (a dark flower symbol).

t. Apply the updated Bistro Menu Item list style to all the menu items, apply the Bistro Times table style to the table, type your name where indicated, then remove the Menus style from the list of Style Sets. (*Note:* You may need to modify the colors associated with the table style in order to match the color scheme you selected for this document.)

u. Save the documents, submit all files to your instructor, then close all files.

Independent Challenge 3

As a student in the business program at your local community college, you have volunteered to create a design for a bi-monthly class newsletter and another classmate has volunteered to write text for the first newsletter, which is to be distributed in November. First, you create a template for the newsletter, then you apply the template to the document containing the newsletter text.

a. Open the file WD J-11.docx, then save it as a template called **WD J-Newsletter Template.dotx** to the Custom Office Templates folder in the My Documents folder on your computer.

Independent Challenge 3 (continued)

b. Enter text and create styles as shown in FIGURE J-21. (*Hint:* Use the text in bold for the style names.)

FIGURE J-21

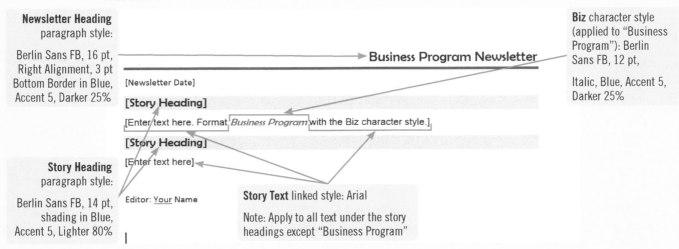

Newsletter Heading paragraph style:

Berlin Sans FB, 16 pt, Right Alignment, 3 pt Bottom Border in Blue, Accent 5, Darker 25%

Biz character style (applied to "Business Program"): Berlin Sans FB, 12 pt,

Italic, Blue, Accent 5, Darker 25%

Business Program Newsletter

[Newsletter Date]

[Story Heading]

[Enter text here. Format *Business Program* with the Biz character style.]

[Story Heading]

[Enter text here]

Story Heading paragraph style:

Berlin Sans FB, 14 pt, shading in Blue, Accent 5, Lighter 80%

Editor: Your Name

Story Text linked style: Arial

Note: Apply to all text under the story headings except "Business Program"

c. Save the Style Set as **Biz Program**.

d. Click to the left of the first [Story Heading], then create two columns from this point forward. (*Hint:* Click the PAGE LAYOUT tab, click the Columns button in the Page Setup group, click More Columns, then in the Columns dialog box, click Two in the Presets section, click the Apply to list arrow, select This point forward, then click OK.)

e. Type your name where indicated, then save and close the template.

f. Start a new document based on the WD J-Newsletter Template, type **November 2016** in place of [Newsletter Date], then type **Class Projects** in place of the first [Story Heading] and **Upcoming Events** in place of the next [Story Heading]. Make sure both headings are formatted with the Story Heading style and that the date is formatted with the Normal style.

g. Save the document as **WD J-Newsletter_November** to the location where you store your files, then close the document.

h. Open the file WD J-12.docx, save it as **WD J-Newsletter_December**, show the DEVELOPER tab on the Ribbon, attach the WD J-Newsletter Template.dotx to the document, apply the Biz Program Style Set via the DESIGN tab, then apply styles and formatting as follows: apply the Newsletter Heading style to the newsletter title, the Story Heading style to all four headings, the Story Text style to all paragraphs of text that are not headings (excluding the date and Editor: Your Name), and the Biz style to Business Program (*Hint:* Use the Find Next, not Replace All, Replace feature to replace three instances of Business Program in the story text (but not to Business Program in the Newsletter Heading.)

i. Apply the two-column format starting at the Class Projects heading. (*Note:* You need to apply the two-column format because options related to the structure of a document saved with a template are lost when you attach the template to an existing document.)

j. Modify the Story Text style so that the font size is 10 pt, then resave the Biz Program Style Set.

k. Click at the end of the document (following your name), click the PAGE LAYOUT tab, click Breaks, then click Continuous to balance the columns in the newsletter.

l. Save and close the document.

m. Open the file WD J-Newsletter Template.dotx (*Hint:* Be sure to open the template using the FILE menu. Do not double-click it.)

n. Apply the Biz Program Style Set again, modify the Newsletter Heading style so the font size is 20 pt. (*Hint:* Make sure you modify the style, not just the heading text.)

o. Resave the Biz Program Style Set.

p. Save and close the template.

Independent Challenge 3 (continued)

q. Open the file WD J-Newsletter_November.docx, attach the updated template and make sure styles automatically update, verify that Newsletter heading text is 20 pt and the story text is 10 pt, then save and close the document.

r. Open the file WD J-Newsletter_December.docx, then verify that the document is updated with the new styles.

s. Save the document, delete the Biz Program Style Set, remove the DEVELOPER tab from the Ribbon, close the document and exit Word, then submit all files to your instructor.

Independent Challenge 4: Explore

From the Microsoft Office Web site, you can access templates that you can use to create and then customize hundreds of different types of documents from calendars to business proposals to trip itineraries. You use keywords to search for a template, select and create it in Word and then modify it for your own purposes. You also explore more options in the Styles task pane. *(Note: To complete these steps your computer must be connected to the Internet.)*

a. Start Word, open a new blank document, click the FILE tab, click New, click in the Search text box, type **itinerary**, then click the Start searching button.

b. Select the template Business trip itinerary, click Create, then save the document as **WD J-Business Trip Itinerary.docx.**

c. Enter your name where indicated above the itinerary table.

d. Select and then delete the Phone number and Travel time columns in the itinerary table, then widen the Comments column so its right edge is even with the border line above the itinerary title.

e. Complete the itinerary table with the information shown in FIGURE J-22.

FIGURE J-22

Business Trip Itinerary \| [Name]						
Date	**Depart from**	**Depart time**	**Destination**	**Arrival time**	**Destination address**	**Comments**
May 2	Vancouver, BC	20:00	London, UK	13:00 (May 3)	Park Place Hotel	Meet with Paul M. for dinner
May 6	London, UK	10:00	Paris, France	14:35	Eiffel Tower Hotel	Train arrives at the Gare du Nord
May 12	Paris, France	9:00	Berlin, Germany	10:30	Aparthotel	Fly from Orly

f. Open the Styles task pane, then click the Style Inspector button at the bottom of the task pane.

g. Click to the left of Business Trip Itinerary and notice that the Style Inspector lists the Title style as the current paragraph formatting.

h. Click Date and notice that the Style Inspector lists the Normal style with the addition of Bold and the Background 1 color. You can use the Style Inspector to determine exactly what formatting is applied to selected text and then clear the formatting if you wish.

i. Click the Reveal Formatting button at the bottom of the Style Inspector and if necessary, move the Styles task pane so you can see the Reveal Formatting task pane that opens to the right of your screen. The Reveal Formatting task pane lists all the formatting applied to the document.

j. Scroll down the Reveal Formatting task pane to view all the settings. You can click the arrow to the right of any heading to see additional settings.

k. Click TABLE STYLE once under the Table heading to open the Table AutoFormat dialog box. In this dialog box you can quickly select a new built-in table style for the table.

l. Click List Table 4 - Accent 6 (green), then click OK to use the Reveal Formatting, Styles, and Style Inspector task panes to make two more modifications of your choice to the document.

m. Close the Reveal Formatting, Styles, and Style Inspector task panes.

n. Select a new color scheme of your choice, save and close the document, exit Word, then submit the file to your instructor.

Visual Workshop

Create a new document, then type the text and create the tables shown in FIGURE J-23. Save the file as **WD J-Price List_ Still Waters Spa**. Do not include any formatting. Select the Violet II color scheme, apply the Title style to the title, then modify the Title style so that it appears as shown in FIGURE J-23. Note that all the colors are variations of the Violet II color scheme, Plum, Accent 1, and the font style for the title and headings is Comic Sans MS font (or a similar font). Apply the Heading 1 style to the names of the price lists, then modify the Heading 1 style so that it appears as shown in FIGURE J-23. Create a new Style Set called **Prices**. Create a table style called **Price List** that formats each table as shown in FIGURE J-23, then modify the column widths as shown. (*Note:* You will not see the center alignment applied until after the column widths are adjusted.) Save the document. Open WD J-13.docx, save it as **WD J-Price List_Ultimate Spa**, apply the Prices Style Set, copy the Price List table style from WD J-Price List_Still Waters Spa to WD J-Price List_Ultimate Spa, then apply styles and modify column widths so the document resembles the document shown in FIGURE J-23. Apply the Green color scheme. Save and close the documents, then submit both files to your instructor.

FIGURE J-23

Still Waters Spa

Essential Oils Price List

Product #	Essential Oil	Price
3300	Basil	$6.50
3500	Clove	$8.00
4000	Ginger	$7.50
4500	Lavender	$6.00

Fragrance Oils Price List

Product #	Fragrance Oil	Price
5000	Blackberry	$7.00
7780	Green Tea	$7.50
7790	Magnolia	$7.00
7792	Plum	$8.00
7795	Vanilla	$7.50

Prepared by Your Name

Creating a Presentation in PowerPoint 2013

CASE ▶ Quest Specialty Travel (QST) is an adventure tour company that provides exclusive travel experiences for its clients. As a tour consultant for QST, one of your responsibilities is to research new vacation tours that QST can sell using the company Web site. You just finished investigating Canadian transcontinental train travel, and now you need to create a presentation using PowerPoint 2013 that describes the results of your research.

Unit Objectives

After completing this unit, you will be able to:

- Define presentation software
- Plan an effective presentation
- Examine the PowerPoint window
- Enter slide text

- Add a new slide
- Apply a design theme
- Compare presentation views
- Print a PowerPoint presentation

Files You Will Need

No files needed.

Define Presentation Software

Presentation software (also called presentation graphics software) is a computer program you use to organize and present information to others. Presentations are typically in the form of a slide show. Whether you are explaining a new product or moderating a meeting, presentation software can help you effectively communicate your ideas. You can use PowerPoint to create informational slides that you display, speaker notes for the presenter, and handouts for the audience. **CASE** *You need to start working on the Canadian train tours presentation. Because you are only somewhat familiar with PowerPoint, you get to work exploring its capabilities.* FIGURE A-1 *shows how a presentation looks printed as handouts.* FIGURE A-2 *shows how the same presentation might look printed as notes for a speaker.*

DETAILS

You can easily complete the following tasks using PowerPoint:

• **Enter and edit text easily**

Text editing and formatting commands in PowerPoint are organized by the task you are performing at the time, so you can enter, edit, and format text information simply and efficiently to produce the best results in the least amount of time.

• **Change the appearance of information**

PowerPoint has many effects that can transform the way text, graphics, and slides appear. By exploring some of these capabilities, you discover how easy it is to change the appearance of your presentation.

• **Organize and arrange information**

Once you start using PowerPoint, you won't have to spend much time making sure your information is correct and in the right order. With PowerPoint, you can quickly and easily rearrange and modify text, graphics, and slides in your presentation.

• **Include information from other sources**

Often, when you create presentations, you use information from a variety of sources. With PowerPoint, you can import text, photographs, numerical data, and facts from files created in programs such as Adobe Photoshop, Microsoft Word, Microsoft Excel, and Microsoft Access. You can also import information from other PowerPoint presentations as well as graphic images from a variety of sources such as the Internet, other computers, a digital camera, or other graphics programs. Always be sure you have permission to use any work that you did not create yourself.

• **Present information in a variety of ways**

With PowerPoint, you can present information using a variety of methods. For example, you can print handout pages or an outline of your presentation for audience members. You can display your presentation as an on-screen slide show using your computer, or if you are presenting to a large group, you can use a video projector and a large screen. If you want to reach an even wider audience, you can broadcast the presentation over the Internet so people anywhere in the world can use a Web browser to view your presentation.

• **Collaborate with others on a presentation**

PowerPoint makes it easy to collaborate or share a presentation with colleagues and coworkers using the Internet. You can use your email program to send a presentation as an attachment to a colleague for feedback. If you have a number of people that need to work together on a presentation, you can save the presentation to a shared workspace such as a network drive or SkyDrive so authorized users in your group with an Internet connection can access the presentation.

Using PowerPoint on a touch screen

You can use PowerPoint 2013 on a Windows 8 computer with a touch-enabled monitor or any other compatible touch screen, such as a tablet computer. Using your fingers, you can use typical touch gestures to create, modify and navigate presentations. To enable touch mode capabilities in PowerPoint, you need to add the Touch Mode button to the Quick Access toolbar. Click the Customize Quick Access Toolbar button, click Touch/Mouse Mode, click the Touch/Mouse Mode button on the Quick Access toolbar then click Touch. In Touch mode, additional space is added around all of the buttons and icons in the Ribbon and the status bar to make them easier to touch. Common gestures that you can use in PowerPoint include double-tapping text to edit it and tapping a slide then dragging it to rearrange it in the presentation.

Plan an Effective Presentation

Before you create a presentation, you need to have a general idea of the information you want to com-
municate. PowerPoint is a powerful and flexible program that gives you the ability to start a presentation
simply by entering the text of your message. If you have a specific design in mind that you want to use,
you can start the presentation by working on the design. In most cases you'll probably enter the text of
your presentation into PowerPoint first and then tailor the design to the message and audience. When
preparing your presentation, you need to keep in mind not only who you are giving it to, but also how
you are presenting it. For example, if you are giving a presentation using a projector, you need to know
what other equipment you will need, such as a sound system and a projector. **CASE** ▶ *Use the plan-
ning guidelines below to help plan an effective presentation.* FIGURE A-3 *illustrates a storyboard for a well-
planned presentation.*

DETAILS

In planning a presentation, it is important to:

- **Determine and outline the message you want to communicate**
 The more time you take developing the message and outline of your presentation, the better your
 presentation will be in the end. A presentation with a clear message that reads like a story and is
 illustrated with appropriate visual aids will have the greatest impact on your audience. Start the
 presentation by giving a general description of Canadian train travel and the types of tours offered by
 Quest Specialty Travel. See FIGURE A-3.

- **Identify your audience and where and how you are giving the presentation**
 Audience and delivery location are major factors in the type of presentation you create. For example, a pre-
 sentation you develop for a staff meeting that is held in a conference room would not necessarily need to be
 as sophisticated or detailed as a presentation that you develop for a large audience held in an auditorium.
 Room lighting, natural light, screen position, and room layout all affect how the audience responds to your
 presentation. You might also broadcast your presentation over the Internet to several people who view the
 presentation on their computers in real time. This presentation will be delivered in a small auditorium to
 QST's management and sales team.

- **Determine the type of output**
 Output choices for a presentation include black-and-white or color handouts, on-screen slide show, or an
 online broadcast. Consider the time demands and computer equipment availability as you decide which
 output types to produce. Because you are speaking in a small auditorium to a large group and have access to
 a computer and projection equipment, you decide that an on-screen slide show is the best output choice for
 your presentation.

- **Determine the design**
 Visual appeal, graphics, and presentation design work to communicate your message. You can choose one of
 the professionally designed themes that come with PowerPoint, modify one of these themes, or create one
 of your own. You decide to choose one of PowerPoint's design themes to convey the new tour information.

- **Decide what additional materials will be useful in the presentation**
 You need to prepare not only the slides themselves but also supplementary materials, including speaker
 notes and handouts for the audience. You use speaker notes to help remember key details, and you pass out
 handouts for the audience to use as a reference during the presentation.

FIGURE A-3: Storyboard of the presentation

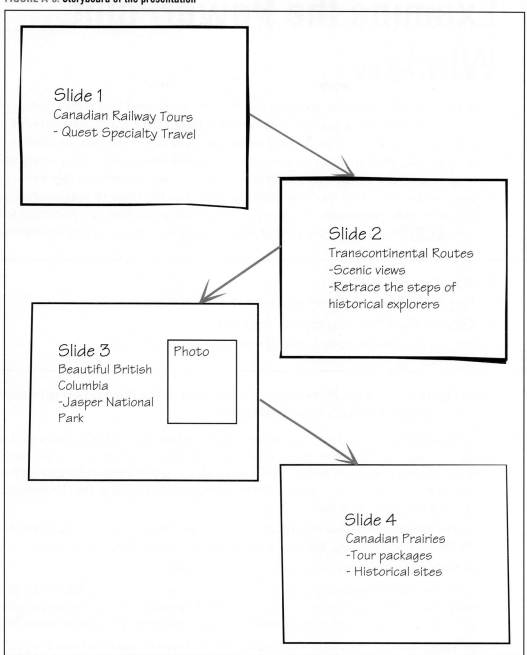

Understanding copyright

Intellectual property is any idea or creation of the human mind. Copyright law is a type of intellectual property law that protects works of authorship, including books, Web pages, computer games, music, artwork, and photographs. Copyright protects the expression of an idea, but not the underlying facts or concepts. In other words, the general subject matter is not protected, but how you express it is, such as when several people photograph the same sunset. Copyright attaches to any original work of authorship as soon as it is created, you do not have to register it with the Copyright Office or display the copyright symbol, ©. Fair use is an exception to copyright and permits the public to use copyrighted material for certain purposes without obtaining prior consent from the owner. Determining whether fair use applies to a work depends on its purpose, the nature of the work, how much of the work you want to copy, and the effect on the work's value. Unauthorized use of protected work (such as downloading a photo or a song from the Web) is known as copyright infringement and can lead to legal action.

Examine the PowerPoint Window

When you first start PowerPoint, you have the ability to choose what kind of presentation you want to use to start—a blank one, or one with a preformatted design. You can also open and work on an existing presentation. PowerPoint has different **views** that allow you to see your presentation in different forms. By default, the PowerPoint window opens in **Normal view**, which is the primary view that you use to write, edit, and design your presentation. Normal view is divided into two areas called **panes**: the pane on the left, called the Thumbnails pane, displays the slides of your presentation as small images, called **slide thumbnails**. The large pane is the Slide pane where you do most of your work on the slide. **CASE** ▶ *The PowerPoint window and the specific parts of Normal view are described below.*

STEPS

1. **Start** PowerPoint 2013
 PowerPoint starts and the PowerPoint start screen opens, as shown in **FIGURE A-4**.

2. **Click the** Blank Presentation slide thumbnail
 The PowerPoint window opens in Normal view as shown in **FIGURE A-5**.

DETAILS

Using Figure A-5 as a guide, examine the elements of the PowerPoint window, then find and compare the elements described below:

• The **Ribbon** is a wide band spanning the top of the PowerPoint window that organizes all of PowerPoint's primary commands. Each set of primary commands is identified by a **tab**; for example, the HOME tab is selected by default, as shown in **FIGURE A-5**. Commands are further arranged into **groups** on the Ribbon based on their function. So, for example, text formatting commands such as Bold, Underline, and Italic are located on the HOME tab, in the Font group.

• The **Thumbnails pane**. You can quickly navigate through the slides in your presentation by clicking the slide thumbnails on this pane. You can also add, delete, or rearrange slides using this pane.

• The **Slide pane** displays the current slide in your presentation.

• The **Quick Access toolbar** provides access to common commands such as Save, Undo, Redo, and Start From Beginning. The Quick Access toolbar is always visible no matter which Ribbon tab you select. This toolbar is fully customizable. Click the Customize Quick Access Toolbar button to add or remove buttons.

• The **View Shortcuts** buttons on the status bar allow you to switch quickly between PowerPoint views.

• The **Notes button** on the status bar allows you to open the Notes pane. The Notes pane is used to type text that references a slide's content. You can print these notes and refer to them when you make a presentation or print them as handouts and give them to your audience. The Notes pane is not visible to the audience when you show a slide presentation in Slide Show view.

• The **Comments button** on the status bar allows you to open the Comments pane. In the Comments pane you can create, edit, select, and delete comments.

• The **status bar**, located at the bottom of the PowerPoint window, shows messages about what you are doing and seeing in PowerPoint, including which slide you are viewing and the total number of slides. In addition, the status bar displays the Zoom slider controls, the Fit slide to current window button 🔲, and information on other functionality such as the presentation theme name, signatures and permissions.

• The **Zoom slider** is in the lower-right corner of the status bar and is used to zoom the slide in and out quickly.

FIGURE A-4: PowerPoint start screen

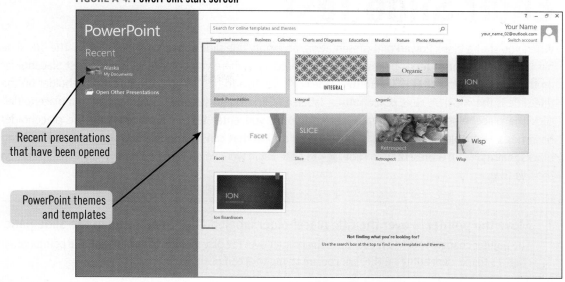

FIGURE A-5: PowerPoint window in Normal view

Viewing your presentation in gray scale or black and white

Viewing your presentation in gray scale (using shades of gray) or pure black and white is very useful when you are printing a presentation on a black-and-white printer and you want to make sure your presentation prints correctly. To see how your color presentation looks in gray scale or black and white, click the VIEW tab, then click either the Grayscale or Black and White button in the Color/Grayscale group. Depending on which button you select, the Grayscale or the Black and White tab appears, and the Ribbon displays different settings that you can customize. If you don't like the way an individual object looks in black and white or gray scale, you can change its color. Click the object while still in Grayscale or Black and White view, then choose an option in the Change Selected Object group on the Ribbon.

Creating a Presentation in PowerPoint 2013

Enter Slide Text

Learning Outcomes
• Enter slide text
• Change slide text

When you start a blank PowerPoint presentation, an empty title slide appears in Normal view. The title slide has two **text placeholders**—boxes with dotted borders—where you enter text. The top text placeholder on the title slide is the **title placeholder**, labeled "Click to add title". The bottom text placeholder on the title slide is the **subtitle text placeholder**, labeled "Click to add subtitle". To enter text in a placeholder, click the placeholder and then type your text. After you enter text in a placeholder, the placeholder becomes a text object. An **object** is any item on a slide that can be modified. Objects are the building blocks that make up a presentation slide. **CASE** ▶ *Begin working on your presentation by entering text on the title slide.*

STEPS

1. **Move the pointer ↳ over the title placeholder labeled Click to add title in the Slide pane**
 The pointer changes to ⇂ when you move the pointer over the placeholder. In PowerPoint, the pointer often changes shape, depending on the task you are trying to accomplish.

2. **Click the title placeholder in the Slide pane**
 The **insertion point**, a blinking vertical line, indicates where your text appears when you type in the placeholder. A **selection box** with a dashed line border and **sizing handles** appears around the placeholder, indicating that it is selected and ready to accept text. When a placeholder or object is selected, you can change its shape or size by dragging one of the sizing handles. See **FIGURE A-6**.

TROUBLE
If you press a wrong key, press [Backspace] to erase the character.

3. **Type Canadian Railway Exploration Tour Series**
 PowerPoint wraps the text to a second line and then center-aligns the title text within the title placeholder, which is now a text object. Notice the text also appears on the slide thumbnail on the Thumbnails pane.

4. **Click the subtitle text placeholder in the Slide pane**
 The subtitle text placeholder is ready to accept text.

5. **Type Presented by, then press [Enter]**
 The insertion point moves to the next line in the text object.

QUICK TIP
To copy text, select the text, click the HOME tab, click the Copy button in the Clipboard group, place the insertion point, then click the Paste button in the Clipboard group.

6. **Type Quest Specialty Tours, press [Enter], type Adventure Tour Series, press [Enter], type your name, press [Enter], then type Tour Consultant**
 Notice the AutoFit Options button ⬌ appears near the text object. The AutoFit Options button on your screen indicates that PowerPoint has automatically decreased the font size of all the text in the text object so it fits inside the text object.

7. **Click the AutoFit Options button ⬌, then click Stop Fitting Text to This Placeholder on the shortcut menu**
 The text in the text object changes back to its original size and no longer fits inside the text object.

8. **In the subtitle text object, position ⇂ to the right of Series, drag left to select the entire line of text, press [Backspace], then click outside the text object in a blank area of the slide**
 The Adventure Tour Series line of text is deleted and the AutoFit Options button menu closes, as shown in **FIGURE A-7**. Clicking a blank area of the slide deselects all selected objects on the slide.

9. **Click the Save button 🖫 on the Quick Access toolbar to open Backstage view, then save the presentation as PPT A-QST in the location where you store your Data Files**
 In Backstage view, you have the option of saving your presentation to your computer or SkyDrive. Notice that PowerPoint automatically entered the title of the presentation as the filename in the Save As dialog box.

FIGURE A-6: Title text placeholder ready to accept text

FIGURE A-7: Text on title slide

Saving fonts with your presentation

When you create a presentation, it uses the fonts that are installed on your computer. If you need to open the presentation on another computer, the fonts might look different if that computer has a different set of fonts. To preserve the look of your presentation on any computer, you can save, or embed, the fonts in your presentation. Click the FILE tab, then click Options. The PowerPoint Options dialog box opens. Click Save in the left pane, then click the Embed fonts in the file check box. Click the Embed all characters option button, then click OK to close the dialog box. Click Save on the Quick Access toolbar. Now the presentation looks the same on any computer that opens it. Using this option, however, significantly increases the size of your presentation, so only use it when necessary. You can freely embed any TrueType or OpenType font that comes with Windows. You can embed other TrueType fonts only if they have no license restrictions.

Add a New Slide

Learning Outcomes
• Add a new slide
• Indent text levels
• Modify slide layout

Usually when you add a new slide to a presentation, you have a pretty good idea of what you want the slide to look like. For example, you may want to add a slide that has a title over bulleted text and a picture. To help you add a slide like this quickly and easily, PowerPoint provides nine standard slide layouts. A **slide layout** contains text and object placeholders that are arranged in a specific way on the slide. You have already worked with the Title Slide layout in the previous lesson. In the event that a standard slide layout does not meet your needs, you can modify an existing slide layout or create a new, custom slide layout. **CASE** ▶ *To continue developing the presentation, you create a slide that defines the new tour series.*

STEPS

1. **Click the New Slide button in the Slides group on the HOME tab on the Ribbon**

 A new blank slide (now the current slide) appears as the second slide in your presentation, as shown in **FIGURE A-8**. The new slide contains a title placeholder and a content placeholder. A **content placeholder** can be used to insert text or objects such as tables, charts, or pictures. Notice the status bar indicates Slide 2 of 2 and the Thumbnails pane now contains two slide thumbnails.

2. **Type Canadian Rail Travel, then click the bottom content placeholder**

 The text you typed appears in the title placeholder, and the insertion point is now at the top of the bottom content placeholder.

3. **Type Dramatic scenery, then press [Enter]**

 The insertion point appears directly below the text when you press [Enter], and a new first-level bullet automatically appears.

4. **Press [Tab]**

 The new first-level bullet is indented and becomes a second-level bullet.

5. **Type Beautiful Canadian prairies, press [Enter], then click the Decrease List Level button** [icon] **in the Paragraph group**

 The Decrease List Level button changes the second-level bullet into a first-level bullet.

6. **Type Retrace the steps of historical explorers, then click the New Slide list arrow in the Slides group**

 The Office Theme layout gallery opens. Each slide layout is identified by a descriptive name.

7. **Click the Content with Caption slide layout, then type Magnificent Canadian Rockies**

 A new slide with three content placeholders appears as the third slide. The text you typed is the title text for the slide.

8. **Click the lower-left placeholder, type Jasper National Park, press [Enter], click the Increase List Level button** [icon], **type Visit the Maligne Valley, press [Enter], then type Spectacular wildlife scenes**

 The Increase List Level button moves the insertion point one level to the right. Notice this text placeholder does not use text bullets to identify separate lines of text.

9. **Click a blank area of the slide, then click the Save button** [icon] **on the Quick Access toolbar**

 The Save button saves all of the changes to the file. Compare your screen with **FIGURE A-9**.

FIGURE A-8: New blank slide in Normal view

New Slide button

New slide thumbnail added to Slides tab

New Slide button list arrow

Title text placeholder

Content placeholder

Current slide number

Total number of slides

FIGURE A-9: New slide with Content with Caption slide layout

Decrease List Level button

Increase List Level button

First-level bullet

Second-level bullet

Three content placeholders based on the slide layout

Entering and printing notes

You can add notes to your slides when there are certain facts you want to remember during a presentation or when there is additional information you want to hand out to your audience. Notes do not appear on the slides when you run a slide show. Use the Notes pane in Normal view or Notes Page view to enter notes for your slides. To open or close the Notes pane, click the Notes button on the status bar. To enter text notes on a slide, click in the Notes pane, then type. If you want to insert graphics as notes, you must use Notes Page view. To open Notes Page view, click the VIEW tab on the Ribbon, then click the Notes

Page button in the Presentation Views group. You can print your notes by clicking the FILE tab on the Ribbon to open Backstage view, then clicking Print. Click the Full Page Slides list arrow in the Settings group (this button retains the last setting for what was printed previously so it might differ) to open the gallery, and then click Notes Pages. Once you verify your print settings, click the Print button. If you don't enter any notes in the Notes pane, and print the notes pages, the slides print as large thumbnails with blank space below the thumbnails to hand write notes.

Apply a Design Theme

PowerPoint provides many design themes to help you quickly create a professional and contemporary looking presentation. A **theme** includes a set of 12 coordinated colors for text, fill, line, and shadow, called **theme colors**; a set of fonts for titles and other text, called **theme fonts**; and a set of effects for lines and fills, called **theme effects** to create a cohesive look. Each theme has at least four custom coordinated variants that provides you with additional color options. In most cases, you would apply one theme to an entire presentation; you can, however, apply multiple themes to the same presentation or even a different theme on each presentation slide. You can use a design theme as is, or you can alter individual elements of the theme as needed. Unless you need to use a specific design theme, such as a company theme or product design theme, it is faser and easier to use one of the themes supplied with PowerPoint. If you design a custom theme, you can save it to use in the future. **CASE** ➤ *You decide to change the default design theme in the presentation to a new one.*

STEPS

1. **Click the Slide 1 thumbnail on the Thumbnails pane**

 Slide 1, the title slide, appears in the Slide pane.

2. **Click the DESIGN tab on the Ribbon, then point to the Facet theme in the Themes group as shown in FIGURE A-10**

 The DESIGN tab appears, and a Live Preview of the Facet theme is displayed on the selected slide. A **Live Preview** allows you to see how your changes affect the slides before actually making the change. The Live Preview lasts about 1 minute, and then your slide reverts back to its original state. The first (far left) theme thumbnail identifies the current theme applied to the presentation, in this case, the default design theme called the Office Theme. Depending on your monitor resolution and screen size, you can see between four and 21 design themes in the Themes group.

3. **Slowly move your pointer ⬐ over the other design themes, then click the Themes group down scroll arrow**

 A Live Preview of the theme appears on the slide each time you pass your pointer over the theme thumbnails, and a ScreenTip identifies the theme names.

4. **Move ⬐ over the design themes, then click the Wisp theme**

 The Wisp design theme is applied to all the slides in the presentation. Notice the new slide background color, graphic elements, fonts, and text color. You decide this theme isn't right for this presentation.

5. **Click the More button ⬇ in the Themes group**

 The Themes gallery window opens. At the top of the gallery window in the This Presentation section is the current theme applied to the presentation. Notice that just the Wisp theme is listed here because when you changed the theme in the last step, you replaced the default theme with the Wisp theme. The Office section identifies all 21 of the standard themes that come with PowerPoint.

6. **Right-click the Organic theme in the Office section, then click Apply to Selected Slides**

 The Organic theme is applied only to Slide 1. You like the Organic theme better, and decide to apply it to all slides.

7. **Right-click the Organic theme in the Themes group, then click Apply to All Slides**

 The Organic theme is applied to all three slides. Preview the next slides in the presentation to see how it looks.

8. **Click the Next Slide button ⬇ at the bottom of the vertical scroll bar**

 Compare your screen to FIGURE A-11.

9. **Click the Previous Slide button ⬆ at the bottom of the vertical scroll bar, then save your changes**

FIGURE A-10: Slide showing a different design theme

FIGURE A-11: Presentation with Organic theme applied

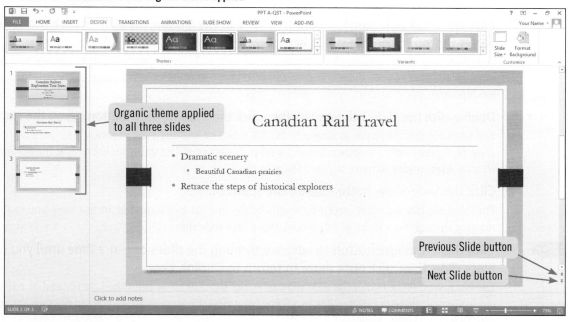

Customizing themes

You are not limited to using the standard themes PowerPoint provides; you can also modify a theme to create your own custom theme. For example, you might want to incorporate your school's or company's colors on the slide background of the presentation or be able to type using fonts your company uses for brand recognition. To change an existing theme, click the VIEW tab on the Ribbon, then click one of the Master buttons in the Master Views group. Click the Theme Colors button, the Theme Fonts button, or the Theme Effects button in the

Background group to make changes to the theme, then save this new theme for future use by clicking the Themes button in the Edit Themes group, then click Save Current Theme. You also have the ability to create a new font theme or color theme from scratch by clicking the Theme Fonts button or the Theme Colors button and then clicking Customize Fonts or Customize Colors. You work in the Create New Theme Fonts or Create New Theme Colors dialog box to define the custom theme fonts or colors.

Compare Presentation Views

PowerPoint has six primary views: Normal view, Outline view, Slide Sorter view, Notes Page view, Slide Show view, and Reading view. Each PowerPoint view displays your presentation in a different way and is used for different purposes. Normal view is the primary editing view where you add text, graphics, and other elements to the slides. Outline view is the view you use to focus on the text of your presentation. Slide Sorter view is primarily used to rearrange slides; however, you can also add slide effects and design themes in this view. You use Notes Page view to type notes that are important for each slide. Slide Show view displays your presentation over the whole computer screen and is designed to show your presentation to an audience. Similar to Slide Show view, Reading view is designed to view your presentation on a computer screen. To move easily among the PowerPoint views, use the View Shortcuts buttons located on the status bar and the VIEW tab on the Ribbon. **TABLE A-1** provides a brief description of the PowerPoint views. **CASE** ▶ *Examine each of the PowerPoint views, starting with Normal view.*

STEPS

1. **Click the VIEW tab on the Ribbon, then click the Outline View button in the Presentation Views group**

 The presentation text is in the Outline pane on the left side of the window as shown in **FIGURE A-12**. Notice the status bar identifies the number of the slide you are viewing and the total number of slides in the presentation.

2. **Click the small slide icon ☐ next to Slide 2 in the Outline pane, then click the Slide Sorter button ⊞ on the status bar**

 Slide Sorter View opens to display a thumbnail of each slide in the presentation in the window. You can examine the flow of your slides and drag any slide or group of slides to rearrange the order of the slides in the presentation.

3. **Double-click the Slide 1 thumbnail, then click the Reading View button ▥ on the status bar**

 The first slide fills the screen as shown in **FIGURE A-13**. Use Reading view to review your presentation or to show your presentation to someone directly on your computer. The status bar controls at the bottom of the window make it easy to move between slides in this view.

4. **Click the Slide Show button ⬒ on the status bar**

 The first slide fills the entire screen now without the title bar and status bar. In this view, you can practice running through your slides as they would appear in a slide show.

5. **Click the left mouse button to advance through the slides one at a time until you see a black slide, then click once more to return to Outline view**

 The black slide at the end of the slide show indicates the slide show is finished. At the end of a slide show you automatically return to the slide and PowerPoint view you were in before you ran the slide show, in this case Slide 1 in Outline view.

6. **Click the Notes Page button in the Presentation Views group**

 Notes Page view appears, showing a reduced image of the current slide above a large text placeholder. You can enter text in this placeholder and then print the notes page for your own use.

7. **Click the Normal button in the Presentation Views group, then click the HOME tab on the Ribbon**

FIGURE A-12: Outline view

FIGURE A-13: Reading view

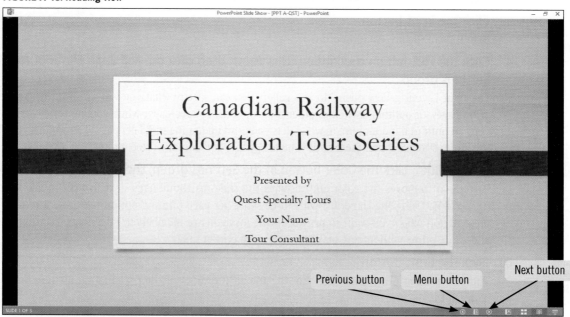

TABLE A-1: PowerPoint views

view name	button	button name	displays
Normal		Normal	The Slide pane and the thumbnails pane at the same time
Outline View	(no View Shortcuts button)		An outline of the presentation and the Slide pane at the same time
Slide Sorter		Slide Sorter	Thumbnails of all slides
Slide Show		Slide Show	Your presentation on the whole computer screen
Reading View		Reading View	Your presentation in a large window on your computer screen
Notes Page	(no View Shortcuts button)		A reduced image of the current slide above a large text box

PowerPoint 2013

Print a PowerPoint Presentation

Learning Outcomes
• Print a presentation
• Set print settings
• Modify color settings

You print your presentation when you want to review your work or when you have completed it and want a hard copy. Reviewing your presentation at different stages of development gives you a better perspective of the overall flow and feel of the presentation. You can also preview your presentation to see exactly how each slide looks before you print the presentation. When you are finished working on your presentation, even if it is not yet complete, you can close the presentation file and exit PowerPoint. **CASE** *You are done working on the tour presentation for now. You save and preview the presentation, then you print the slides and notes pages of the presentation so you can review them later. Before leaving for the day, you close the file and exit PowerPoint.*

STEPS

1. **Click the Save button 🖫 on the Quick Access toolbar, click the FILE tab on the Ribbon, then click Print**

 The Print window opens as shown in FIGURE A-14. Notice the preview pane on the right side of the window displays the first slide of the presentation. If you do not have a color printer, you will see a grayscale image of the slide.

2. **Click the Next Page button ▶ at the bottom of the Preview pane, then click ▶ again**

 Each slide in the presentation appears in the preview pane.

3. **Click the Print button**

 Each slide in the presentation prints.

4. **Click the FILE tab on the Ribbon, click Print, then click the Full Page Slides button in the Settings group**

 The Print Layout gallery opens. In this gallery you can specify what you want to print (slides, handouts, notes pages, or outline), as well as other print options. To save paper when you are reviewing your slides, you can print in handout format, which lets you print up to nine slides per page. The options you choose in the Print window remain there until you change them or close the presentation.

5. **Click 3 Slides, click the Color button in the Settings group, then click Pure Black and White**

 PowerPoint removes the color and displays the slides as thumbnails next to blank lines as shown in FIGURE A-15. Using the Handouts with three slides per page printing option is a great way to print your presentation when you want to provide a way for audience members to take notes. Printing pure black-and-white prints without any gray tones can save printer toner.

6. **Click the Print button**

 The presentation prints one page showing the all the slides of the presentation as thumbnails next to blank lines.

7. **Click the FILE tab on the Ribbon, then click Close**

 If you have made changes to your presentation, a Microsoft PowerPoint alert box opens asking you if you want to save changes you have made to your presentation file.

8. **Click Save, if necessary, to close the alert box**

 Your presentation closes.

9. **Click the Close button ✕ in the Title bar**

 The PowerPoint program closes, and you return to the Windows desktop.

Microsoft Office Web Apps

All Office programs include the capability to incorporate feedback—called online collaboration—across the Internet or a company network. Using **cloud computing** (work done in a virtual environment), you can take advantage of Web programs called Microsoft Office Web Apps, which are simplified versions of the programs found in the Microsoft Office 2013 suite. Because these programs are online, they take up no computer disk space and are accessed using Microsoft SkyDrive, a free service from Microsoft. Using Microsoft SkyDrive, you and your colleagues can create and store documents in the "cloud" and make the documents available to whomever you grant access. To use Microsoft SkyDrive, you need to create a free Microsoft account and establish a Windows Live ID, which you obtain at the Microsoft web site. You can find more information in the "Working in the Cloud" appendix.

Practice

Concepts Review

Label each element of the PowerPoint window shown in FIGURE A-16.

FIGURE A-16

Match each term with the statement that best describes it.

11. **Sizing handle**
12. **Slide Show view**
13. **Theme**
14. **Zoom slider**
15. **Reading view**
16. **Slide Layout**

a. Placeholders arranged in a specific way on the slide
b. Used to change the size of an object
c. A view that is used to review a presentation or to show someone a presentation directly on a computer screen
d. A view that displays a presentation to show to an audience
e. Set of coordinated colors, fonts, and effects
f. Allows you to change the size of the slide in the window

Select the best answer from the list of choices.

17. Which statement about PowerPoint is *not* correct?
 a. Graphic images from a digital camera can be inserted into PowerPoint.
 b. A presentation can be broadcast over the Internet.
 c. You can use PowerPoint to create a database of information.
 d. You can import text and numerical data into PowerPoint.

18. Which feature on the status bar allows you to quickly switch between views?
 a. Fit slide to current window button
 b. Switch view button
 c. Zoom Slider
 d. View Shortcuts

19. Finish the following sentence: "Copyright attaches to any original work of authorship,...":
 a. After you register it with the Copyright Office.
 b. As soon as it is created.
 c. Under the Fair Use policy.
 d. Only when it displays the copyright symbol ©.

20. Other than the Slide pane, where else can you enter slide text?
 a. Outline view
 b. Slides tab
 c. Reading pane
 d. Notes Page view

21. According to this unit, what are the building blocks of a presentation?
 a. Slides
 b. Graphics
 c. Placeholders
 d. Objects

22. The view that fills the entire screen with each slide in the presentation including the title bar is called:
 a. Slide Show view.
 b. Fit to window view.
 c. Reading view.
 d. Normal view.

23. Which of the following is not included in a design theme?
 a. Fonts
 b. Colors
 c. Pictures
 d. Normal view

24. What is the function of the slide layout?
 a. Puts all your slides in order.
 b. Shows you which themes you can apply.
 c. Defines how all the elements on a slide are arranged.
 d. Enables you to apply a template to the presentation.

Skills Review

1. **Examine the PowerPoint window.**
 a. Start PowerPoint, if necessary then open a new blank presentation.
 b. Identify as many elements of the PowerPoint window as you can without referring to the unit material.
 c. Be able to describe the purpose or function of each element.
 d. For any elements you cannot identify, refer to the unit.

2. **Enter slide text.**
 a. In the Slide pane in Normal view, enter the text **Historic Hendra Stamp Mill & Hotel** in the title placeholder.
 b. In the subtitle text placeholder, enter **Nevada Ghost Town Preservation Society**.
 c. On the next line of the placeholder, enter your name.
 d. Deselect the text object.
 e. Save the presentation using the filename **PPT A-Dun Glen** to location where you store your Data Files.

Skills Review (continued)

3. Add a new slide.

 a. Create a new slide.

 b. Using FIGURE A-17, enter text on the slide.

 c. Create another new slide.

 d. Using FIGURE A-18, enter text on the slide.

 e. Save your changes.

4. Apply a design theme.

 a. Click the DESIGN tab.

 b. Click the Themes group More button, then point to all of the themes.

 c. Locate the Slice theme, then apply it to the selected slide.

 d. Select Slide 1.

 e. Locate the Integral theme, then apply it to Slide 1.

 f. Apply the Integral theme to all of the slides in the presentation.

 g. Use the Next Slide button to move to Slide 3, then save your changes.

5. Compare presentation views.

 a. Click the VIEW tab, then click the Outline View button in the Presentation Views group.

 b. Click the Slide Sorter button in the Presentation Views group.

 c. Click the Notes Page button in the Presentation Views group, then click the Previous Slide button twice.

 d. Click the Reading View button in the Presentation Views group, then click the Next button on the status bar.

 e. Click the Normal button on the status bar, then click the Slide Show button.

 f. Advance the slides until a black screen appears, then click to end the presentation.

 g. Save your changes.

6. Print a PowerPoint presentation.

 a. Print all the slides as handouts, 4 Slides Horizontal, in color.

 b. Print the presentation outline.

 c. Close the file, saving your changes.

 d. Exit PowerPoint.

FIGURE A-17

HISTORIC HENDRA STAMP MILL

Located in Dun Glen, NV

Built in 1866 by James Hendra
- Gold miner and explorer
- Dun Glen NV founding father

Operated from 1866 to 1904

Processed over 1200 tons of material

Removed over $6 million in gold ($143 million today)

FIGURE A-18

HENDRA HOTEL HISTORY

James Hendra purchased the Dun Glen Hotel in 1873
- Originally built by William Chaffee in 1859
- Interior finished with custom milled knotty sugar pine from the Sierra Nevada
- Partially burned down in 1886 due to oil lamp fire in lobby

12 Hotel rooms
- Rooms rented for 25 cents a day or 2 dollars a week in 1873

Hendra died in 1910
- Hotel closed in 1911

Independent Challenge 1

You work for GTO Broadband Industries, a business that offers rural broadband Internet service and network server management. One of your jobs at the company is to present the company's services to local government and community meetings. Your boss has asked you to create a company profile presentation that describes the services GTO offers.

a. Start PowerPoint then open a new blank presentation.

b. In the title placeholder on Slide 1, type **GTO Broadband Industries**.

c. In the subtitle placeholder, type your name, press [Enter], then type today's date.

d. Apply the Slice design theme to the presentation.

e. Save your presentation with the filename **PPT A-Broadband** to the location where you store your Data Files.

f. Use FIGURE A-19 and FIGURE A-20 to add two more slides to your presentation. (*Hint*: Slide 2 uses the Comparison layout.)

g. Use the buttons on the VIEW tab to switch between all of PowerPoint's views.

h. Print the presentation using handouts, 3 Slides, in black and white.

i. Save and close the file, then exit PowerPoint.

FIGURE A-19

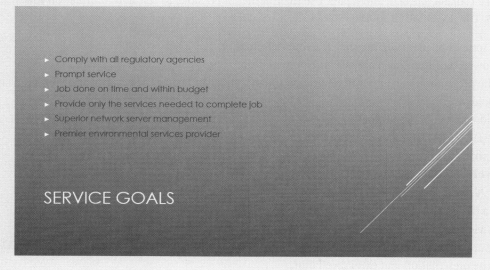

FIGURE A-20

Independent Challenge 2

You have recently been promoted to sales manager at Goodrich Hardwood Industries, which sells and distributes specialty hardwood products used in flooring, cabinets, and furniture. Part of your job is to present company sales figures at a yearly sales meeting. Use the following information as the basis for units of wood sold nationally in your presentation: 425 units cherry, 260 units birch, 146 units hickory, 580 units mahogany, 345 units Brazilian walnut, 230 units American walnut, and 120 units pine. Assume that Goodrich Hardwood has five sales regions throughout the country: West, South, Midwest, Mid Atlantic, and Northeast. Also, assume the sales in each region rose between 1.5% and 4% over last year, and gross sales reached $67 million. The presentation should have at least five slides.

a. Spend some time planning the slides of your presentation. What is the best way to show the information provided? What other information could you add that might be useful for this presentation?

b. Start PowerPoint.

c. Give the presentation an appropriate title on the title slide, and enter today's date and your name in the subtitle placeholder.

d. Add slides and enter appropriate slide text.

e. On the last slide of the presentation, include the following information:
Goodrich Hardwood Industries
"Your specialty hardwood store"

f. Apply a design theme. A typical slide might look like the one shown in **FIGURE A-21**.

g. Switch views. Run through the slide show at least once.

h. Save your presentation with the filename **PPT A-Goodrich** where you store your Data Files.

i. Close the presentation and exit PowerPoint.

FIGURE A-21

TOTAL SALES BY UNIT

580 units – Mahogany
425 units – Cherry
345 units – Brazilian walnut
260 units – Birch
230 units – American walnut
146 units – Hickory
120 units – Pine

Independent Challenge 3

You work for Jamison Corporation, a company in Council Bluffs, Iowa, that is the primary international distributor of products made in Iowa. The marketing manager has asked you to plan and create a PowerPoint presentation that describes the products Iowa exports and the countries that import products made in Iowa. Describe Iowa's top exports, which include tractors, fresh and frozen pork meat, soybeans, corn, and aircraft engine parts. Also include information on top importers of Iowan products: Canada, Mexico, and Japan. Use the Internet, if possible, to research information that will help you formulate your ideas. The presentation should have at least five slides.

a. Spend some time planning the slides of your presentation.

b. Start PowerPoint then open a new blank presentation.

c. Give the presentation an appropriate title on the title slide, and enter today's date and your name in the subtitle placeholder.

d. Add slides and enter appropriate slide text.

e. On the last slide of the presentation, type the following information:
Jamison Corp.
Council Bluffs, Iowa
Your Name

f. Apply a design theme.

g. Switch views. Run through the slide show at least once.

h. Save your presentation with the filename **PPT A-Jamison** to the location where you store your Data Files.

i. Close the presentation and exit PowerPoint.

Independent Challenge 4: Explore

You are a member of the Local Charity Society (LCS), a non-profit organization in Bellingham, Washington. It raises money throughout the year to support community needs such as schools, youth organizations, and other worthy causes. This year LCS has decided to support the Simpson Youth Center by hosting a regional barbeque cook-off, called the Master Pit-master Competition. The competition includes over 20 cooking teams from a five-state region. Create a presentation that describes the event.

a. Spend some time planning the slides of your presentation. Assume the following: the competition is a 2-day event; event advertising will be multistate wide; musical groups will be invited; there will events and games for kids; the event will be held at the county fairgrounds. Use the Internet, if possible, to research information that will help you formulate your ideas.

b. Start PowerPoint then open a new blank presentation.

c. Give the presentation an appropriate title on the title slide, and enter your name and today's date in the subtitle placeholder.

d. Add slides and enter appropriate slide text. You must create at least three slides.

e. Apply a Design Theme. Typical slides might look like the ones shown in FIGURE A-22 and FIGURE A-23.

f. View the presentation.

g. Save your presentation with the filename **PPT A-Pitmaster** to the location where you store your Data Files.

h. Close the presentation and exit PowerPoint.

FIGURE A-22

JUDGING CATEGORIES

- Saturday – Prelims
 - 12:00pm – Brisket
 - 1:15pm – Chicken
 - 2:00pm - Sauces
 - 3:30pm – Pork
 - 4:15pm – Ribs
- Sunday – Finals
 - 12:00 am – Chicken
 - 12:30am – Sauces
 - 2:30pm – Brisket
 - 3:30pm – Ribs
 - 4:00pm - Pork
 - 4:45pm – Winner's Cook-off Round

FIGURE A-23

SIMPSON YOUTH CENTER

- Youth organization for over 450 local boys and girls
 - After-school programs
 - Education tutoring
 - Work-skills training
 - Counseling
 - Summer camps
 - Winter camps

Visual Workshop

Create the presentation shown in FIGURE A-24 and FIGURE A-25. Make sure you include your name on the title slide. Save the presentation as **PPT A-LGS** to the location where you store your Data Files. Print the slides.

FIGURE A-24

FIGURE A-25

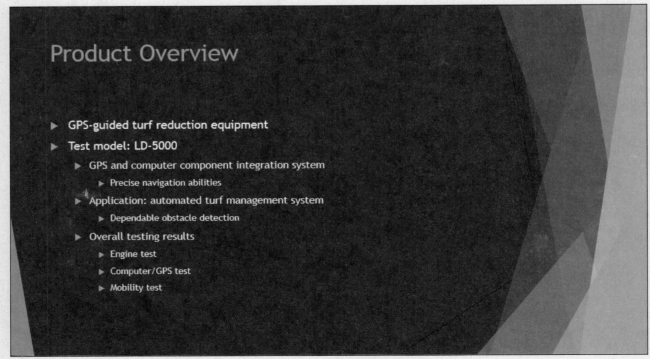

Modifying a Presentation

CASE ▶ You continue working on your Canadian Train tour presentation. In this unit, you'll enter text using Outline view, then you'll format text, create a SmartArt graphic, draw and modify objects, and add slide footer information in the presentation.

Unit Objectives

After completing this unit, you will be able to:

- Enter text in Outline view
- Format text
- Convert text to SmartArt
- Insert and modify shapes

- Rearrange and merge shapes
- Edit and duplicate shapes
- Align and group objects
- Add slide footers

Files You Will Need

PPT B-1.pptx PPT B-4.pptx
PPT B-2.pptx PPT B-5.pptx
PPT B-3.pptx

Enter Text in Outline View

Learning Outcomes
- Enter text in Outline view
- Create a new slide

You can enter presentation text by typing directly on the slide in the Slide pane, or, if you need to focus on the text of the presentation, you can enter text in Outline view. Text in Outline view is organized so the headings, or slide titles, appear at the top of the outline. Each subpoint, or each line of bulleted text, appears as one or more indented lines under the title. Each indent in the outline creates another level of bulleted text on the slide. **CASE** ➤ *You switch to Outline view to enter text for two more slides for your presentation.*

STEPS

QUICK TIP

To open a PowerPoint 97-2007 presentation in PowerPoint 2013, open the presentation, click the FILE tab, click the Convert button, name the file in the Save As dialog box, then click Save.

1. **Start PowerPoint, open the presentation PPT B-1.pptx from the location where you store your Data Files, then save it as PPT B-QST.pptx**

 A presentation with the new name appears in the PowerPoint window.

2. **Click the Slide 2 thumbnail in the Thumbnails pane, click the New Slide button list arrow in the Slides group, then click Title and Content**

 A new slide, Slide 3, with the Title and Content layout appears as the current slide below Slide 2.

3. **Click the VIEW tab on the Ribbon, then click the Outline View button in the Presentation Views group**

 The text of the presentation appears in the Outline pane next to the Slide pane. The slide icon and the insertion point for Slide 3 are highlighted, indicating it is selected and ready to accept text. Text that you enter next to a slide icon becomes the title for that slide.

4. **Type Atlantic Region Stations, press [Enter], then press [Tab]**

 When you pressed [Enter] after typing the title, you created a new slide. However, because you want to enter bulleted text on Slide 3, you then pressed [Tab] so the text you type will be entered as bullet text on Slide 3. See **FIGURE B-1**.

5. **Type Halifax, press [Enter], type Moncton, press [Enter], type Gaspe, press [Enter], type Sussex, press [Enter], type Amherst, then press [Enter]**

 Each time you press [Enter], the insertion point moves down one line.

6. **Press [Shift][Tab]**

 Because you are working in Outline view, a new slide with the same layout, Slide 4, is created when you press [Shift][Tab].

QUICK TIP

Press [Ctrl][Enter] while the cursor is in the text object to create a new slide with the same layout as the previous slide.

7. **Type Atlantic Region Tour Packages, press [Ctrl][Enter], type Adventure, press [Enter], type Cultural, press [Enter], type Shopping, press [Enter], then type Wildlife**

 Pressing [Ctrl][Enter] while the insertion point is in the title text object moves the cursor into the content placeholder.

8. **Position the pointer on the Slide 3 icon ▭ in the Outline pane**

 The pointer changes to ✥. The Atlantic Region Stations slide, Slide 3, is out of order.

9. **Drag ▭ down until a horizontal indicator line appears above the Slide 5 icon, then release the mouse button**

 The third slide moves down and switches places with the fourth slide as shown in **FIGURE B-2**.

10. **Click the Normal button ▣ on the status bar, then save your work**

 The Outline pane closes, and the Thumbnails pane is now visible in the window.

FIGURE B-1: Outline view showing new slide

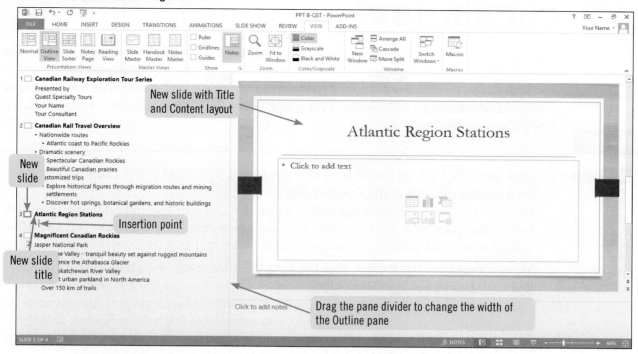

FIGURE B-2: Outline view showing moved slide

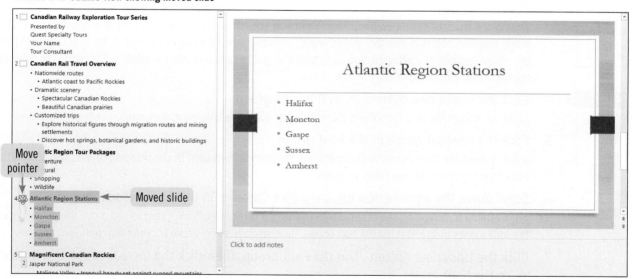

Using proofing tools for other languages

If you have a presentation in another language, how would you check the spelling and grammar of that presentation? Every version of PowerPoint contains a language pack with a primary language, such as English, Italian, or Arabic. Each language pack includes additional languages other than the primary language. For example, the English language pack also includes French and Spanish. So, let's say you have an English version of PowerPoint and you want to check the spelling of a presentation that is written in French. To check the spelling of a French presentation, click a text object on a slide, click the REVIEW tab on the Ribbon, click the Language button in the Language group, then click Set Proofing Language to open the Language dialog box. Click one of the French options from the list, then click OK. Only languages in the list with a spelling symbol are available to use for checking spelling and grammar. Now when you check the spelling, PowerPoint will do so in French. If your version of PowerPoint does not have the language you want to use, you can purchase additional language packs from Microsoft.

Format Text

Learning
Outcomes
• Modify text
 characteristics

Once you have entered and edited the text in your presentation, you can modify the way the text looks to emphasize your message. Important text should be highlighted in some way to distinguish it from other text or objects on the slide. For example, if you have two text objects on the same slide, you could draw attention to one text object by changing its color, font, or size. **CASE** > *You decide to format the text on Slide 2 of the presentation.*

STEPS

QUICK TIP
To show or hide the Mini toolbar, click the FILE tab on the Ribbon, click Options, then click the Show Mini Toolbar on selection check box.

1. **Click the HOME tab on the Ribbon, click the Slide 2 thumbnail in the Thumbnails pane, then double-click Rail in the title text object**

 The word "Rail" is selected, and a Mini toolbar appears above the text. The **Mini toolbar** contains basic text-formatting commands, such as bold and italic, and appears when you select text using the mouse. This toolbar makes it quick and easy to format text, especially when the HOME tab is closed.

2. **Move ⌕ over the Mini toolbar, click the Font Color list arrow** ⏺⏷ **, then click the Dark Red color box under Standard Colors**

 The text changes color to dark red as shown in FIGURE B-3. When you click the Font Color list arrow, the Font Color gallery appears showing the Theme Colors and Standard Colors. ScreenTips help identify font colors. Notice that the Font Color button on the Mini toolbar and the Font Color button in the Font group on the HOME tab change color to reflect the new color choice, which is now the active color.

QUICK TIP
To select an unselected text object, press [Shift], click the text object, then release [Shift].

3. **Move the pointer over the title text object border until the pointer changes to ⌖, then click the border**

 The border changes from a dashed to a solid line as you move the pointer over the text object border. The entire title text object is selected, and changes you make now affect all of the text in the text object. When the whole text object is selected, you can change its size, shape, and other attributes. Changing the color of the text helps emphasize it.

QUICK TIP
For more text formatting options, right-click a text object, then click Format Text Effects to open the Format Shape - Text Options pane.

4. **Click the Font Color button** ⏺ **in the Font group**

 All of the text in the title text object changes to the current active color, dark red.

5. **Click the Font list arrow in the Font group**

 A list of available fonts opens with Garamond, the current font used in the title text object, selected at the top of the list in the Theme Fonts section.

6. **Scroll down the alphabetical list, then click Castellar in the All Fonts section**

 The Castellar font replaces the original font in the title text object. Notice that as you move the pointer over the font names in the font list the text on the slide displays a Live Preview of the different font choices.

7. **Click the Underline button** ⎁ **in the Font group, then click the Increase Font Size button** ⏶ **in the Font group**

 All of the text now displays an underline and increases in size to 44.

8. **Click the Character Spacing button** ⏷ **in the Font group, then click Very Loose**

 The spacing between the letters in the title increases. Compare your screen to FIGURE B-4.

9. **Click a blank area of the slide outside the text object to deselect it, then save your work**

 Clicking a blank area of the slide deselects all objects that are selected.

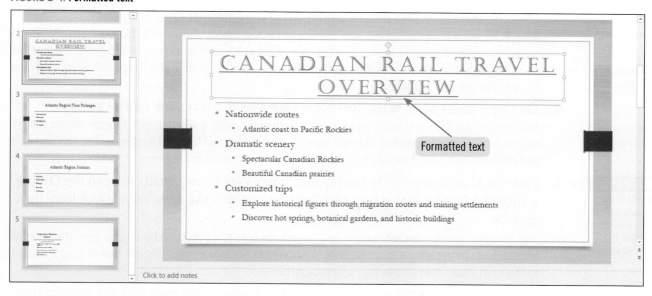

Replacing text and fonts

As you review your presentation, you may decide to replace certain text or fonts throughout the entire presentation using the Replace command. Text can be a word, phrase, or sentence. To replace specific text, click the HOME tab on the Ribbon, then click the Replace button in the Editing group. In the Replace dialog box, enter the text you want to replace, then enter the text you want to use as its replacement. You can also use the Replace command to replace one font for another. Simply click the Replace button list arrow in the Editing group, then click Replace Fonts to open the Replace Font dialog box.

Convert Text to SmartArt

Learning Outcomes
• Create a SmartArt graphic
• Modify the SmartArt design

Sometimes when you are working with text it just doesn't capture your attention, no matter how you dress it up with color or other formatting attributes. The ability to convert text to a SmartArt graphic increases your ability to create dynamic-looking text. A **SmartArt** graphic is a professional-quality diagram that visually illustrates text. There are eight categories, or types, of SmartArt graphics that incorporate graphics to illustrate text differently. For example, you can show steps in a process or timeline, show proportional relationships, or show how parts relate to a whole. You can create a SmartArt graphic from scratch or create one by converting existing text you have entered on a slide with a few simple clicks of the mouse. **CASE** *You want the presentation to appear visually dynamic so you convert the text on Slide 3 to a SmartArt graphic.*

STEPS

1. **Click the Slide 3 thumbnail in the Thumbnails pane, click Adventure in the text object, then click the Convert to SmartArt Graphic button in the Paragraph group**

 A gallery of SmartArt graphic layouts opens. As with many features in PowerPoint, you can preview how your text will look prior to applying the SmartArt graphic layout by using PowerPoint's Live Preview feature. You can review each SmartArt graphic layout and see how it changes the appearance of the text.

2. **Move ▷ over the SmartArt graphic layouts in the gallery**

 Notice how the text becomes part of the graphic and the color and font changes each time you move the pointer over a different graphic layout. SmartArt graphic names appear in ScreenTips.

3. **Click the Vertical Picture Accent List layout in the SmartArt graphics gallery**

 A SmartArt graphic appears on the slide in place of the text object, and a new SMARTART TOOLS DESIGN tab opens on the Ribbon as shown in **FIGURE B-5**. A SmartArt graphic consists of two parts: the SmartArt graphic itself and a Text pane where you type and edit text. This graphic also has placeholders where you can add pictures to the SmartArt graphic.

4. **Click each bullet point in the Text pane, then click the Text pane control button 🔲**

 Notice that each time you select a bullet point in the text pane, a selection box appears around the text objects in the SmartArt graphic. The Text pane control opens and closes the Text pane. You can also open and close the Text pane using the Text Pane button in the Create Graphic group.

5. **Click the More button 🔻 in the Layouts group, click More Layouts to open the Choose a SmartArt Graphic dialog box, click Relationship, click the Basic Venn layout icon, then click OK**

 The SmartArt graphic changes to the new graphic layout. You can radically change how the SmartArt graphic looks by applying a SmartArt Style. A **SmartArt Style** is a preset combination of simple and 3-D formatting options that follows the presentation theme.

6. **Move ▷ slowly over the styles in the SmartArt Styles group, then click the More button 🔻 in the SmartArt Styles group**

 A Live Preview of each style is displayed on the SmartArt graphic. The SmartArt styles are organized into sections; the top group offers suggestions for the best match for the document, and the bottom group shows you all of the possible 3-D styles that are available.

7. **Move ▷ over the styles in the gallery, then click Cartoon in the 3-D section**

 Notice how this new style adds a black outline and shading to each object to achieve the 3-D effect.

8. **Click a blank area of the slide outside the SmartArt graphic object to deselect it, then save your work**

 Compare your screen to **FIGURE B-6**.

FIGURE B-5: Text converted to a SmartArt graphic

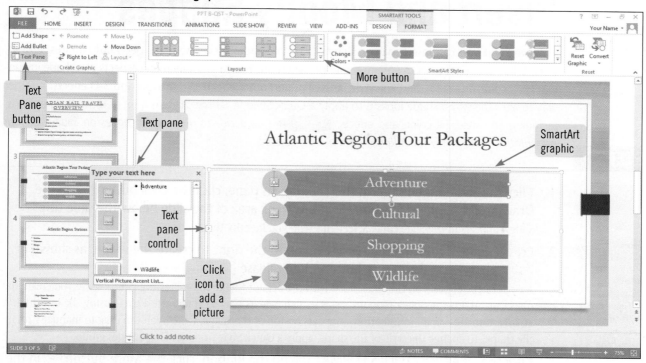

FIGURE B-6: Final SmartArt graphic

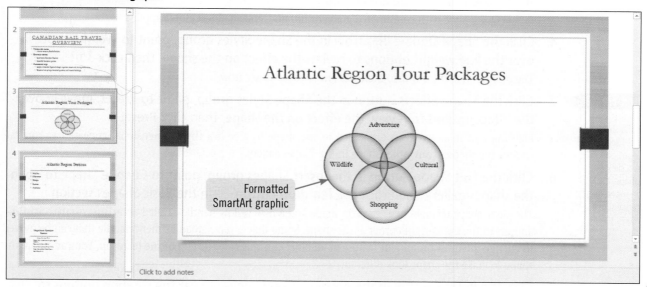

Choosing SmartArt graphics

When choosing a SmartArt graphic to use on your slide, remember that you want the SmartArt graphic to communicate the message of the text effectively; not every SmartArt graphic layout achieves that goal. You must consider the type of text you want to illustrate. For example, does the text show steps in a process, does it show a continual process, or does it show nonsequential information? The answer to this question will dictate the type of SmartArt graphic layout you should choose. Also, the amount of text you want to illustrate will have an effect on the SmartArt graphic layout you choose. Most of the time key points will be the text you use in a SmartArt graphic. Finally, some SmartArt graphic layouts are limited by the number of shapes they can accommodate, so be sure to choose a graphic layout that can illustrate your text appropriately. Experiment with the SmartArt graphic layouts until you find the right one, and have fun in the process!

Insert and Modify Shapes

Learning
Outcomes
• Create a shape
• Modify a shape's
 style

In PowerPoint you can insert many different types of shapes including lines, geometric figures, arrows, stars, callouts, and banners to enhance your presentation. You can modify many aspects of a shape including its fill color, line color, and line style, as well as add other effects like shadow and 3-D effects. Another way to alter the way a shape looks is to apply a Quick Style. A **Quick Style** is a set of formatting options, including line style, fill color, and effects. **CASE** ▶ *You decide to draw some shapes on Slide 4 of your presentation that identify the Atlantic regional train stations.*

STEPS

1. **Click the Slide 4 thumbnail in the Thumbnails pane, click the Oval button ⬭ in the Drawing group, then position ✛ in the blank area of the slide below the slide title**
 Slide 4 appears in the Slide pane. ScreenTips help you identify the shapes.

2. **Press and hold [Shift], drag ✛ down and to the right to create the shape, as shown in FIGURE B-7, release the mouse button, then release [Shift]**
 A circle shape appears on the slide, filled with the default theme color. Pressing [Shift] while you create the object maintains the object proportions as you change its size, so you create a circle using the oval tool. A **rotate handle**—small round arrow—appears on top of the shape, which you can drag to manually rotate the shape. To change the style of the shape, apply a Quick Style from the Shape Styles group.

3. **Click the DRAWING TOOLS FORMAT tab on the Ribbon, click the More button ⯆ in the Shape Styles group, move ⯈ over the styles in the gallery to review the effects on the shape, then click Subtle Effect - Blue-Grey, Accent 3**
 A blue Quick Style with coordinated gradient fill, line, and shadow color is applied to the shape.

4. **Click the Shape Outline list arrow in the Shape Styles group, point to Weight, move ⯈ over the line weight options to review the effect on the shape, then click 3 pt**
 The outline weight (or width) increases and is easier to see now.

5. **Click the Shape Effects button in the Shape Styles group, point to Preset, move ⯈ over the effect options to review the effect on the shape, then click Preset 3**
 Lighting and shadow effects are added to the shape to give it a three-dimensional appearance. You can change the shape to any other shape in the shapes gallery.

6. **Click the Edit Shape button in the Insert Shapes group, point to Change Shape to open the shapes gallery, then click the Teardrop button ⬭ in the Basic Shapes section**
 The circle shape changes to a teardrop shape and a new yellow handle—called an **adjustment handle**—appears in the upper-right corner of the shape. Some shapes have an adjustment handle that can be moved to change the most prominent feature of an object, in this case the end of the teardrop. You can rotate the shape to make the shape look different.

7. **Click the Rotate button in the Arrange group, move ⯈ over the rotation options to review the effect on the shape, then click Flip Vertical**
 Notice that the rotate handle is now on the bottom of the shape indicating that the shape has flipped vertically, or rotated 180 degrees, as shown in **FIGURE B-8**. You prefer the circle shape, and you decide the shape looks better rotated back the way it was before.

8. **Click the Undo button list arrow �beff
 ⤺ ▾ in the Quick Access Toolbar, click Change Shape, click a blank area of the slide, then save your work**
 The last two commands you performed are undone, and the shape changes back to a circle and is flipped back to its original position. Clicking a blank area of the slide deselects all objects that are selected.

FIGURE B-7: Oval shape added to slide

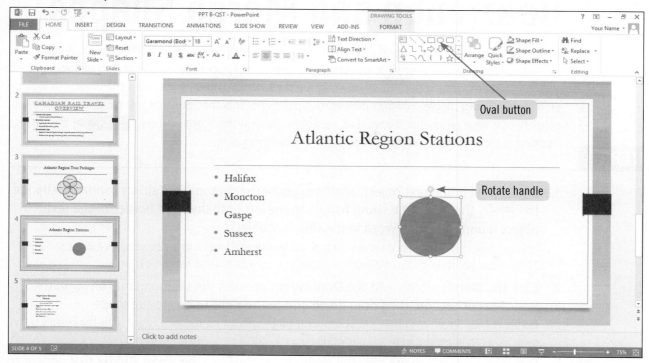

FIGURE B-8: Rotated teardrop shape

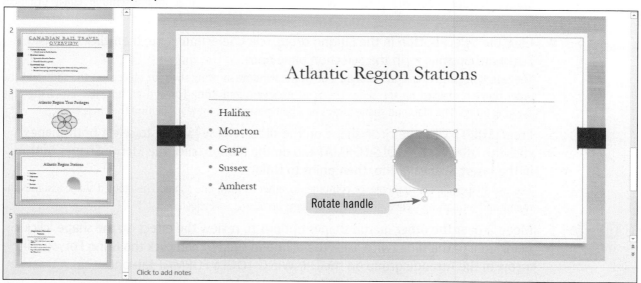

Use the Eyedropper to match colors

As you develop your presentation and work with different shapes and pictures, sometimes from other sources, there may be a certain color that is not in the theme colors of the presentation that you want to capture and apply to objects in your presentation. To capture a color on a specific slide, select any object on the slide, click any button list arrow with a color feature, such as the Shape Fill button or the Shape Outline button on the DRAWING TOOLS FORMAT tab, then click Eyedropper. Move the over the color you want to capture and pause, or hover. As you hover over a color, a Live Preview of the color appears and the RGB (Red Green Blue) values, called coordinates, appear in a ScreenTip. Click when you see the color you want to capture. The new color now appears in any color gallery under Recent Colors. If you decide not to capture a new color, press [Esc] to close the Eyedropper without making any change.

PowerPoint 2013

Rearrange and Merge Shapes

Learning Outcomes
- Reorder shapes
- Combine shapes together

Every object on a slide, whether it is a shape, a picture, a text object, or any other object, is placed, or stacked, on the slide in the order it was created, like pieces of paper placed one on top of another. Each object on a slide can be moved up or down in the stack depending how you want the objects to look on the slide. **Merging** shapes, which combines multiple shapes together, provides you the potential to create a variety of unique geometric shapes that are not available in the Shapes gallery. **CASE** ▶ *You create a diamond shape on Slide 4 and then merge it with the circle shape.*

STEPS

1. **Click Gaspe in the text object, position ▷ over the right-middle sizing handle, ▷ changes to ◁▭▷, then drag the sizing handle to the left until the right border of the text object is under the first word in the title text object**

 The width of the text object decreases. When you position ▷ over a sizing handle, it changes to ◁▭▷. This pointer points in different directions depending on which sizing handle it is over.

2. **Click the More button ▼ in the Drawing group, click the Diamond button ◇ in the Basic Shapes section, then drag down and to the right to create the shape**

 Compare your screen to **FIGURE B-9**. A diamond shape appears on the slide, filled with the default theme color. You can move shapes by dragging them on the slide.

TROUBLE
If Smart Guides do not appear, right-click a blank area of the slide, point to Grid and Guides, then click Smart Guides.

3. **Drag the diamond shape over the circle shape, then use the Smart Guides that appear to position the diamond shape in the center of the circle shape where the guides intersect**

 Smart Guides, help you position objects relative to each other and determine equal distances between objects.

4. **Click the Select button in the Editing group, click Selection Pane, then click the Send Backward button ▼ in the Selection pane once**

 The Selection pane opens on the right side of the window showing the four objects on the slide and the order they are stacked on the slide. The Send Backward and Bring Forward buttons let you change the stacking order. The diamond shape moves back one position in the stack behind the circle shape.

5. **Press [SHIFT], click the circle shape on the slide, release [SHIFT] to select both shapes, click the DRAWING TOOLS FORMAT tab on the Ribbon, click the Merge Shapes button in the Insert Shapes group, then point to Union**

 The two shapes appear to merge, or combine, together to form one shape. The merged shape assumes the theme and formatting style of the diamond shape because it was selected first.

QUICK TIP
To move an object to the top of the stack, click the Bring Forward arrow, then click Bring to Front. To move an object to the bottom of the stack, click the Send Backward arrow, then click Send to Back.

6. **Move ▷ over the other merge shapes options to review the effect on the shape, click a blank area of the slide twice, click the diamond shape, then click the Bring Forward list arrow in the Arrange group on the DRAWING TOOLS FORMAT tab once**

 Each merge option produces a different result. The diamond shape moves back to the top of the stack. Now, you want to see what happens when you select the circle shape first before you merge the two shapes together.

7. **Click the circle shape, press [SHIFT], click the diamond shape, click the Merge Shapes button in the Insert Shapes group, then point to Union**

 The merged shape adopts the theme and formatting style of the circle shape.

8. **Point to each of the merge shapes options, then click Subtract**

 The two shapes merge into one shape. This merge option deletes the area of all shapes from the first shape you selected, so in this case the area of the diamond shape is deleted from the circle shape. The merged shape is identified as Freeform 6 in the Selection pane. See **FIGURE B-10**.

9. **Click the Selection Pane button in the Arrange group, click a blank area of the slide, then save your work**

FIGURE B-9: Diamond shape added to slide

FIGURE B-9: Diamond shape added to slide

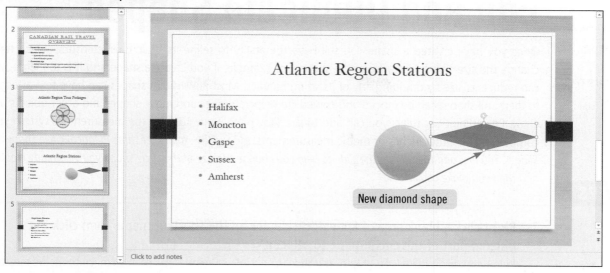

FIGURE B-10: New Merged shape

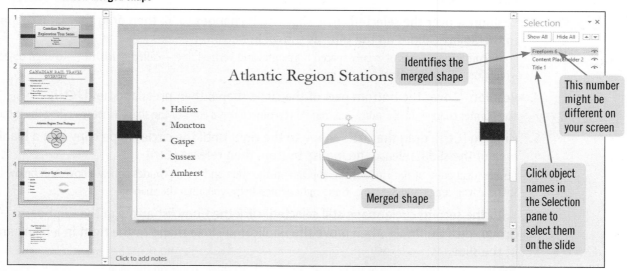

Changing the size and position of shapes

Usually when you resize a shape you can simply drag one of the sizing handles around the outside of the shape, but sometimes you may need to resize a shape more precisely. When you select a shape, the DRAWING TOOLS FORMAT tab appears on the Ribbon, offering you many different formatting options including some sizing commands located in the Size group.

The Width and Height commands in the Size group allow you to change the width and height of a shape. You also have the option to open the Format Shape pane, which allows you to change the size of a shape, as well as the rotation, scale, and position of a shape on the slide.

Edit and Duplicate Shapes

Once you have created a shape you still have the ability to refine its basic characteristics, which helps change the size and appearance of the shape. For example, if you create a shape and it is too large, you can reduce its size by dragging any of its sizing handles. Most PowerPoint shapes can have text attached to them. All shapes can be moved and copied. To help you resize and move shapes and other objects precisely, PowerPoint has rulers you can add to the Slide pane. Rulers display the measurement system your computer uses, either inches or metric measurements. **CASE** *You want three identical circle shapes on Slide 4. You first add the ruler to the slide to help you change the size of the circle shape you've already created, and then you make copies of it.*

STEPS

1. **Right-click a blank area of Slide 4, click Ruler on the shortcut menu, then click the bottom part of the circle shape to select it**

 Rulers appear on the left and top of the Slide pane. Unless the ruler has been changed to metric measurements, it is divided into inches and half-inch and eighth-inch marks. Notice the current location of the ⌖ is identified on both rulers by a small dotted red line in the ruler.

2. **Press [Shift], drag the lower-right sizing handle on the circle shape up and to the left approximately 1/4", release the mouse button, then release [Shift]**

 The distance of a quarter-inch on the ruler is the distance between two lines. The circle shape is now slightly smaller in diameter.

3. **Position ⌖ over the selected circle shape so it changes to ⬩, then drag the circle shape to the Smart Guides on the slide as shown in FIGURE B-11**

 PowerPoint uses a series of evenly spaced horizontal and vertical lines—called **gridlines**—to align objects, which force objects to "snap" to the grid.

4. **Position ⬩ over the bottom part of the circle shape, then press and hold [Ctrl]**

 The pointer changes to ⬩, indicating that PowerPoint makes a copy of the shape when you drag the mouse.

5. **Holding [Ctrl], drag the circle shape to the right until the circle shape copy is in a blank area of the slide, release the mouse button, then release [Ctrl]**

 An identical copy of the circle shape appears on the slide and Smart Guides appear above and below the shape as you drag the new shape to the right, which helps you align the shapes.

6. **With the second circle shape still selected, click the Copy list arrow in the Clipboard group, click Duplicate, then move the duplicated circle shape to the right in a blank area of the slide**

 You have duplicated the circle shape twice and now have three shapes on the slide.

7. **Click the VIEW tab on the Ribbon, click the Ruler check box in the Show group, click the HOME tab, then type Excursions**

 The ruler closes, and the text you type appears in the selected circle shape and becomes a part of the shape. Now if you move or rotate the shape, the text moves with it. Compare your screen with FIGURE B-12.

8. **Click the middle circle shape, type Getaways, click the left circle shape, type Holidays, click in a blank area of the slide, then save your work**

 All three circle shapes include text.

FIGURE B-11: Merged shape moved on slide

FIGURE B-12: Duplicated shapes

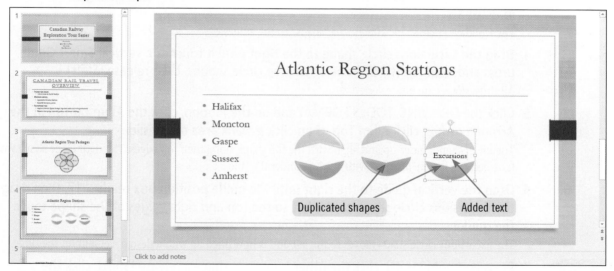

Editing points of a shape

If you want to customize the form (or outline) of any shape in the shapes gallery, you can modify its edit points. To display a shape's edit points, select the shape you want to modify, click the DRAWING TOOLS FORMAT tab on the Ribbon, click the Edit Shape button in the Insert Shapes group, then click Edit Points. Black edit points appear on the shape. To change the form of a shape, drag a black edit point. When you click a black edit point white square edit points appear on either side of the black edit point, which allow you to change the curvature of a line between two black edit points. When you are finished with your custom shape, you can save it as picture and reuse it in other presentations or other files. To save the shape as a picture, right-click the shape, then click Save as Picture.

Align and Group Objects

Learning Outcomes
- Move shapes using guides
- Align and group shapes
- Distribute shapes

After you are finished creating and modifying your objects, you can position them accurately on the slide to achieve the look you want. Using the Align commands in the Arrange group, you can align objects relative to each other by snapping them to the gridlines on a slide or to guides that you manually position on the slide. The Group command groups two or more objects into one object, which secures their relative position to each other and makes it easy to edit and move them. The Distribute commands on the Align list evenly space objects horizontally or vertically relative to each other or the slide. **CASE** ▶ *You are ready to position and group the circle shapes on Slide 4 to finish the slide.*

STEPS

1. **Right-click a blank area of the slide, point to Grid and Guides on the shortcut menu, then click Guides**

 The PowerPoint guides appear as dotted lines on the slide and usually intersect at the center of the slide. Guides help you position objects precisely on the slide.

2. **Position ⃗ over the horizontal guide in a blank area of the slide, notice the pointer change to ÷, press and hold the mouse button until the pointer changes to a measurement guide box, then drag the guide up until the guide position box reads .42**

3. **Drag the vertical guide to the left until the guide position box reads 2.92, then drag the Holidays circle shape so the top and left edges of the shape touch the guides as shown in FIGURE B-13**

 The Holidays circle shape attaches or "snaps" to the guides.

4. **Drag the Excursions circle shape to the right until it touches a vertical Smart Guide, press and hold [Shift], click the other two circle shapes, then release [Shift]**

 All three shapes are now selected.

5. **Click the DRAWING TOOLS FORMAT tab on the Ribbon, click the Align button in the Arrange group, click Align Top, then click a blank area of the slide**

 The lower shapes move up and align with the top shape along their top edges. The right circle shape would look better if it were lined up with the line under the title.

6. **Drag the vertical guide to the right until the guide position box reads 5.17, then drag the Excursions circle shape to the left so the top and right edges of the shape touch the guides**

 The Excursions circle shape moves to the left and is now lined up with a design element on the slide.

7. **Press and hold [Shift], click the other two circle shapes, release [Shift], click the DRAWING TOOLS FORMAT tab, then click the Align button in the Arrange group**

8. **Click Distribute Horizontally, click the Group button in the Arrange group, then click Group**

 The shapes are now distributed equally between themselves and grouped together to form one object without losing their individual attributes, as shown in FIGURE B-14. Notice that the sizing handles and rotate handle now appear on the outer edge of the grouped object, not around each individual object.

9. **Drag the horizontal guide to the middle of the slide until its guide position box reads 0.00, then drag the vertical guide to the middle of the slide until its guide position box reads 0.00**

10. **Click the VIEW tab on the Ribbon, click the Guides check box in the Show group, click a blank area of the slide, then save your work**

 The guides are no longer displayed on the slide

FIGURE B-13: Repositioned shape

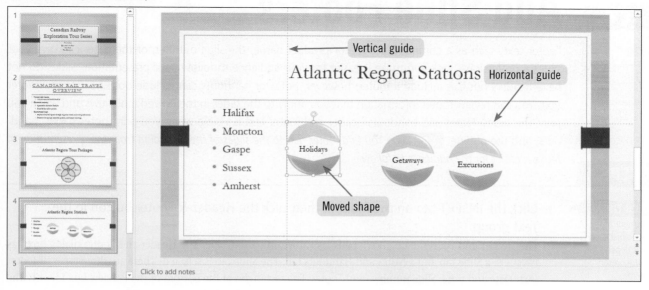

FIGURE B-14: Aligned and grouped shapes

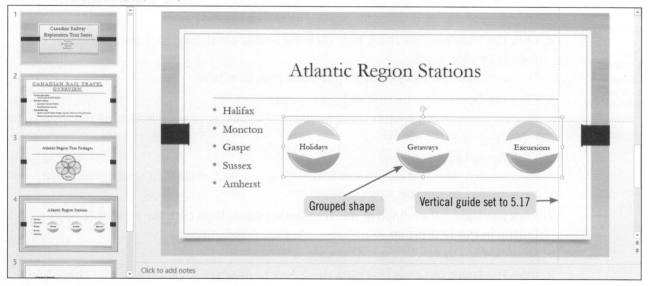

Distributing objects

There are two ways to distribute objects in PowerPoint: relative to each other and relative to the slide edge. If you choose to distribute objects relative to each other, PowerPoint evenly divides the empty space between all of the selected objects. When distributing objects in relation to the slide, PowerPoint evenly splits the empty space from slide edge to slide edge between the selected objects. To distribute objects relative to each other, click the Align button in the Arrange group on the DRAWING TOOLS FORMAT tab, then click Align Selected Objects. To distribute objects relative to the slide, click the Align button in the Arrange group on the DRAWING TOOLS FORMAT tab, then click Align to Slide.

PowerPoint 2013

Add Slide Footers

Learning
Outcomes
• Add footer text to
 slides

Footer text, such as a company, school, or product name, the slide number, or the date, can give your slides a professional look and make it easier for your audience to follow your presentation. Slides do not have headers but can include a footer; however, notes or handouts can include both header and footer text. You can review footer information that you apply to the slides in the PowerPoint views and when you print the slides. Notes and handouts header and footer text is visible when you print notes pages, handouts, and the outline. **CASE** ➤ *You add footer text to the slides of the Canadian train tour presentation to make it easier for the audience to follow.*

STEPS

QUICK TIP
The placement of the footer text objects on the slide is dependent on the presentation theme.

1. **Click the INSERT tab on the Ribbon, then click the Header & Footer button in the Text group**

 The Header and Footer dialog box opens, as shown in FIGURE B-15. The Header and Footer dialog box has two tabs: a Slide tab and a Notes and Handouts tab. The Slide tab is selected. There are three types of footer text, Date and time, Slide number, and Footer. The rectangles at the bottom of the Preview box identify the default position and status of the three types of footer text placeholders on the slides.

2. **Click the Date and time check box to select it**

 The date and time options are now available to select. The Update automatically date and time option button is selected by default. This option updates the date and time every time you open or print the file.

QUICK TIP
If you want a specific date to appear every time you view or print the presentation, click the Fixed date option button, then type the date in the Fixed text box.

3. **Click the Update automatically list arrow, then click the second option in the list**

 The day is added to the date, and the month is spelled out.

4. **Click the Slide number check box, click the Footer check box, click the Footer text box, then type your name**

 The Preview box now shows all three footer placeholders are selected.

5. **Click the Don't show on title slide check box**

 Selecting this check box prevents the footer information you entered in the Header and Footer dialog box from appearing on the title slide.

6. **Click Apply to All**

 The dialog box closes, and the footer information is applied to all of the slides in your presentation except the title slide. Compare your screen to FIGURE B-16.

7. **Click the Slide 1 thumbnail in the Thumbnails pane, then click the Header & Footer button in the Text group**

 The Header and Footer dialog box opens again.

8. **Click the Don't show on title slide check box to deselect it, click the Footer check box, then select the text in the Footer text box**

TROUBLE
If you click Apply to All in Step 9, click the Undo button on the Quick Access toolbar and repeat Steps 7, 8, and 9.

9. **Type Once in a lifetime travel experiences, click Apply, then save your work**

 Only the text in the Footer text box appears on the title slide. Clicking Apply applies the footer information to just the current slide.

10. **Submit your presentation to your instructor, then exit PowerPoint**

FIGURE B-15: Header and Footer dialog box

Shows where footer text appears on the slide

FIGURE B-16: Footer information added to presentation

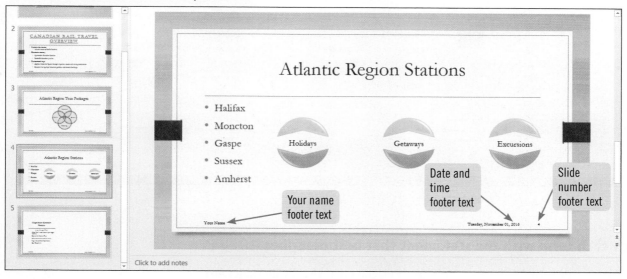

Your name footer text

Date and time footer text

Slide number footer text

Creating superscript and subscript text

Superscript or subscript text is a number, figure, symbol, or letters that appears smaller than other text and is positioned above or below the normal line of text. A common superscript in the English language is the sign indicator next to number, such as, 1^{st} or 3^{rd}. Other examples of superscripts are the trademark symbol™ and the copyright symbol©. To create superscript text in PowerPoint, select the text, number, or symbol, then press [CTRL] [SHIFT] [+] at the same time. Probably the most familiar subscript text are the numerals in chemical compounds and formulas, for example, H_2O and CO_2. To create subscript text, select the text, number, or symbol, then press [CTRL] [=] at the same time. To change superscript or subscript text back to normal text, select the text, then press [CTRL] [Spacebar].

Practice

Put your skills into practice with **SAM Projects**! SAM Projects for this unit can be found online. If you have a SAM account, go to www.cengage.com/sam2013 to download the most recent Project Instruction and Start Files.

Concepts Review

Label each element of the PowerPoint window shown in FIGURE B-17.

FIGURE B-17

Match each term with the statement that best describes it.

9. **SmartArt graphic**	**a.** A diagram that visually illustrates text
10. **Merge**	**b.** A preset combination of formatting options you apply to an object
11. **Adjustment handle**	**c.** Combines multiple shapes together into one shape
12. **Smart Guides**	**d.** Yellow handle that changes the most prominent feature of an object
13. **Quick Style**	**e.** Short red dashed lines that appear on the slide
14. **Rotate handle**	**f.** Use to drag to turn an object

Select the best answer from the list of choices.

15. What appears just above text when it is selected?

 a. AutoFit Options button **c.** QuickStyles

 b. Mini toolbar **d.** Option button

16. Which of the following statements is *not* true about Outline view?

 a. It is organized using headings and subpoints.

 b. Pressing [Enter] moves the insertion point down one line.

 c. Each line of indented text creates a new slide title.

 d. Headings are the same as slide titles.

17. Why would you use the Eyedropper tool?

 a. To save a 3-D effect for future use **c.** To soften the edges of a shape

 b. To pick up font styles from a text object **d.** To add a new color to the color gallery

18. Which of the following statements about merged shapes is *not* true?

 a. A merged shape is a combination of multiple shapes.

 b. Merged shapes are unique geometric shapes found in the shapes gallery.

 c. A merged shape assumes the theme of the shape that is selected first.

 d. The stacking order of shapes changes the way a merged shape looks.

19. A professional-quality diagram that visually illustrates text best describes which of the following?

 a. A SmartArt graphic **c.** A merged shape

 b. A SmartArt Style **d.** A subscript

20. What do objects snap to when you move them?

 a. Shape edges **c.** Gridlines

 b. Anchor points **d.** Slide edges

21. What is *not* true about grouped objects?

 a. Each object is distributed relative to the slide edges.

 b. Grouped objects have one rotate handle.

 c. Grouped objects act as one object but maintain their individual attributes.

 d. Sizing handles appear around the grouped object.

Skills Review

1. Enter text in Outline view.

 a. Open the presentation PPT B-2. pptx from the location where you store your Data Files, then save it as **PPT B-ProPool**. The completed presentation is shown in FIGURE B-18.

 b. Create a new slide after Slide 2 with the Title and Content layout.

 c. Open Outline view, then type **Use and Application**.

 d. Press [Enter], press [Tab], type **City water utilities**, press [Enter], type **State water districts**, press [Enter], type **Private water sources**, press [Enter], then type **Commercial pools**.

FIGURE B-18

Skills Review (continued)

 e. Move Slide 3 below Slide 4, then, switch back to Normal view.

 f. Click the HOME tab, then save your changes.

2. Format text.

 a. Go to Slide 1.

 b. Select the name R.J. Palmer, then move the pointer over the Mini toolbar.

 c. Click the Font Color list arrow, then click Red under Standard Colors.

 d. Select the text object, then change all of the text to the color Red.

 e. Click the Font Size list arrow, then click 24.

 f. Click the Italic button.

 g. Click the Character Spacing button, then click Very Tight.

 h. Save your changes.

3. Convert text to SmartArt.

 a. Click the text object on Slide 4.

 b. Click the Convert to SmartArt Graphic button, then apply the Basic Cycle graphic layout to the text object.

 c. Click the More button in the Layouts group, click More Layouts, click Matrix in the Choose a SmartArt Graphic dialog box, click Grid Matrix, then click OK.

 d. Click the More button in the SmartArt Styles group, then apply the Moderate Effect style from the Best Match for Document group to the graphic.

 e. Close the text pane if necessary, then click outside the SmartArt graphic in a blank part of the slide.

 f. Save your changes.

4. Insert and modify shapes.

 a. Go to Slide 3, then add rulers to the Slide pane.

 b. Click the More button in the Drawing group to open the Shapes gallery, click the Plus button in the Equation Shapes section, press [Shift], then draw a two inch shape in a blank area of the slide.

 c. On the DRAWING TOOLS FORMAT tab, click the More button in the Shape Styles group, then click Colored Fill – Green, Accent 6.

 d. Click the Shape Effects button, point to Shadow, then click Offset Diagonal Bottom Right.

 e. Click the Shape Outline list arrow, then click Black, Text 1, Lighter 50% in the Theme Colors section.

FIGURE B-19

 f. Drag the Plus shape to the small open area in the middle of the diagram, adjust the shape if needed to make it fit in the space as shown in FIGURE B-19, then save your changes.

5. Rearrange and merge shapes.

 a. Click the title text object on Slide 3, then drag the bottom-middle sizing handle up to fit the text in the text object.

 b. Click the More button in the Insert Shapes group, click the Hexagon button in the Basic Shapes section, press and hold [Shift], then draw a 1-inch shape.

 c. Drag the hexagon shape over top of the plus shape and center it, then open the Selection pane.

 d. Send the hexagon shape back one level, press [Shift], click the plus shape, then click the Merge Shapes button in the Insert Shapes group on the DRAWING TOOLS FORMAT tab.

e. Point to each of the merge shapes options, click a blank area of the slide twice, then click the plus shape.

f. Send the plus shape back one level, press [Shift], click the hexagon shape, click the Merge Shapes button, then click Combine.

g. Close the Selection pane, then save your work.

6. Edit and duplicate shapes.

a. Select the up-angled shape to the right of the merged shape, then using [Ctrl] make one copy of the shape.

b. Use Smart Guides to align the new up-angled shape just to the right of the original shape.

c. Click the Rotate button in the Arrange group, click Flip Vertical, click the Undo button, click the Rotate button, then click Flip Horizontal.

d. Type **Bypass**, click the up-angled shape to the right of the merged shape, type **Flow In**, click the down-angled shape to the left of the merged shape, then type **Flow Out**.

e. Click the arrow shape above the merged shape, then drag the top-middle sizing handle down 1/2 inch.

f. Click a blank area of the slide, add the guides to the Slide pane, then save your changes.

7. Align and group objects.

a. Move the vertical guide to the left until 3.83 appears, drag a selection box to select the five small green triangle shapes at the bottom of the slide, then click the DRAWING TOOLS FORMAT tab.

b. Click the Align button in the Arrange group, click Align Middle, click the Align button, then click Distribute Horizontally.

c. Click the Rotate button in the Arrange group, click Rotate Left 90º, click the Group button in the Arrange group, then click Group.

d. Move the grouped triangle shape object to the guide in the blank space on the down-angled shape to the left of the merged shape.

e. Duplicate the grouped triangle shape object, then rotate the new object to the left 90º.

f. Duplicate the rotated grouped triangle shape object, then move the two new triangle shape objects on the slide as shown in FIGURE B-20.

g. Set the guides back to 0.00, remove the guides from your screen, remove the rulers, then save your work.

FIGURE B-20

8. Add slide footers.

a. Open the Header and Footer dialog box.

b. On the Slide tab, click the Date and time check box to select it, then click the Fixed option button.

c. Add the slide number to the footer.

d. Type your name in the Footer text box.

e. Apply the footer to all of the slides except the title slide.

f. Open the Header and Footer dialog box again, then click the Notes and Handouts tab.

g. Click the Date and time check box, then type today's date in the Fixed text box.

h. Type the name of your class in the Header text box, then click the Page number check box.

i. Type your name in the Footer text box.

j. Apply the header and footer information to all the notes and handouts, then save your changes.

k. Submit your presentation to your instructor, close the presentation, then exit PowerPoint.

Independent Challenge 1

You are the director of the Performing Arts Center in Baton Rouge, Louisiana, and one of your many duties is to raise funds to cover operation costs. One of the primary ways you do this is by speaking to businesses, community clubs, and other organizations throughout the region. Every year you speak to many organizations, where you give a short presentation detailing what the theater center plans to do for the coming season. You need to continue working on the presentation you started already.

 a. Start PowerPoint, open the presentation PPT B-3.pptx from the location where you store your Data Files, and save it as **PPT B-Center**.

 b. Use Outline view to enter the following as bulleted text on the Commitment to Excellence slide:
 Excellence
 Testing
 Study
 Diligence

 c. Apply the Ion Boardroom design theme to the presentation.

 d. Change the font color of each play name on Slide 3 to Orange, Accent 4.

 e. Change the bulleted text on Slide 5 to the Vertical Box List SmartArt Graphic, then apply the Inset SmartArt style.

 f. Add your name and slide number as a footer on the slides, then save your changes.

 g. Submit your presentation to your instructor, close your presentation, then exit PowerPoint.

Independent Challenge 2

You are a manager for RC Investments Inc., a financial services company. You have been asked by your boss to develop a presentation outlining important details and aspects of the mortgage process to be used at a financial seminar.

 a. Start PowerPoint, open the presentation PPT B-4.pptx from the location where you store your Data Files, and save it as **PPT B-RC Investments**.

 b. Apply an Office Theme Dark design theme to the presentation.

 c. On Slide 4 select the three shapes, Banks, Mortgage Bankers, and Private Investors, release [Shift], then using the Align command distribute them vertically and align them to their left edges.

 d. Select the blank shape, type **Borrower**, press [Shift], select the Mortgage Broker and Mortgage Bankers shapes, release [Shift], then using the Align command distribute them horizontally and align them to the middle.

 e. Select all of the shapes, then apply Moderate Effect – Orange, Accent 2 from the Shape Styles group.

 f. Create a diamond shape, then merge it with the Borrower shape as shown in FIGURE B-21.

 g. Using the Arrow shape from the Shapes gallery, draw a 4 1/2-pt arrow between all of the shapes. (*Hint*: Draw one arrow shape, change the line weight using the Shape Outline list arrow, then duplicate the shape.)

 h. Group all the shapes together.

 i. Add the page number and your name as a footer on the notes and handouts, then save your changes.

 j. Submit your presentation to your instructor, close your presentation, then exit PowerPoint.

FIGURE B-21

Independent Challenge 3

You are an independent distributor of natural foods in Eugene, Oregon. Your business, Coast Natural Foods, has grown progressively since its inception 10 years ago, but sales have leveled off over the last 12 months. In an effort to stimulate growth, you decide to purchase Gemco Foods Inc., a natural food dealer in Idaho and Washington, which would allow your company to begin expanding into surrounding states. Use PowerPoint to develop a presentation you can use to gain a financial backer for the acquisition. Create your own information for the presentation.

a. Start PowerPoint, create a new presentation, then apply the Wisp design theme to the presentation.
b. Type **A Plan for Growth** as the main title on the title slide, and **Coast Natural Foods** as the subtitle.
c. Save the presentation as **PPT B-Natural Foods** to the location where you store your Data Files.
d. Add five more slides with the following titles: Slide 2, **History**; Slide 3, **Trends**; Slide 4, **Growth**; Slide 5, **Funding**; Slide 6, **Management Team**.
e. Enter appropriate text into the text placeholders of the slides. Use both the Slide pane and Outline view to enter text.
f. Convert text on one slide to a SmartArt graphic, then apply the SmartArt graphic style Inset Effect.
g. Create two shapes, format the shapes, then merge the shapes together.
h. View the presentation as a slide show, then view the slides in Slide Sorter view.
i. Add the slide number and your name as a footer on the slides, then save your changes.
j. Submit your presentation to your instructor, close your presentation, then exit PowerPoint.

Independent Challenge 4: Explore

Your computer instructor at Tri-Cities College has been asked by the department head to convert her Computer Basics 101 course into an accelerated night course designed for adult students. Your instructor has asked you to help her create a presentation for the class that she can post on the Internet. Most of the basic text information is already on the slides, you primarily need to add a theme and other object formatting.

a. Start PowerPoint, open the presentation PPT B-5.pptx from the location where you store your Data Files, and save it as **PPT B-Computer 101**.
b. Add a new slide after the Course Facts slide with the same layout, type **Course Details** in the title text placeholder, then enter the following as bulleted text in Outline view:
 Information systems
 Networking
 Applied methods
 Technology solutions
 Software design
 Applications
c. Apply the Savon design theme to the presentation.
d. Select the title text object on Slide 1 (*Hint*: Press [Shift] to select the whole object), then change the text color to Orange.
e. Change the font of the title text object to FELIX TITLING, then decrease the font size to 40.
f. Click the subtitle text object on Slide 1, then change the character spacing to Loose.
g. Change the text on Slide 4 to a SmartArt graphic. Use an appropriate diagram type for a list.
h. Change the style of the SmartArt diagram using one of the SmartArt Styles, then view the presentation in Slide Show view.
i. Add the slide number and your name as a footer on the notes and handouts, then save your changes.
j. Submit your presentation to your instructor, close your presentation, then exit PowerPoint.

Visual Workshop

Create the presentation shown in FIGURE B-22 and FIGURE B-23. Add today's date as the date on the title slide. Save the presentation as **PPT B-Ohio Trade** to the location where you store your Data Files. (*Hint*: The SmartArt style used for the SmartArt is a 3D style.) Review your slides in Slide Show view, then add your name as a footer to the notes and handouts. Submit your presentation to your instructor, save your changes, close the presentation, then exit PowerPoint.

FIGURE B-22

FIGURE B-23

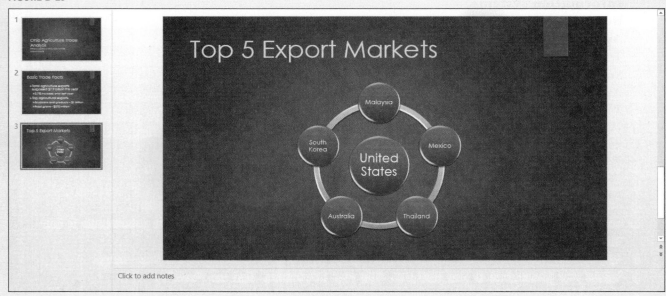

Inserting Objects into a Presentation

CASE In this unit, you continue working on the presentation by inserting text from Microsoft Word and visual elements, including a photograph, table, and a chart, into the presentation. You format these objects using PowerPoint's powerful object-editing features.

Unit Objectives

After completing this unit, you will be able to:

- Insert text from Microsoft Word
- Insert and style a picture
- Insert a text box
- Insert a chart

- Enter and edit chart data
- Insert slides from other presentations
- Insert a table
- Insert and format WordArt

Files You Will Need

PPT C-1.pptx	PPT C-10.pptx
PPT C-2.docx	PPT C-11.pptx
PPT C-3.jpg	PPT C-12.jpg
PPT C-4.pptx	PPT C-13.pptx
PPT C-5.pptx	PPT C-14.docx
PPT C-6.docx	PPT C-15.jpg
PPT C-7.jpg	PPT C-16.jpg
PPT C-8.pptx	PPT C-17.jpg
PPT C-9.pptx	PPT C-18.jpg

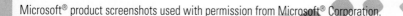

Insert Text from Microsoft Word

Learning Outcomes
- Create slides using Outline view
- Move and delete slides

It is easy to insert documents saved in Microsoft Word format (.docx), Rich Text Format (.rtf), plain text format (.txt), and HTML format (.htm) into a PowerPoint presentation. If you have an outline saved in a document file, you can import it into PowerPoint to create a new presentation or create additional slides in an existing presentation. When you import a document into a presentation, PowerPoint creates an outline structure based on the styles in the document. For example, a Heading 1 style in the Word document becomes a slide title and a Heading 2 style becomes the first level of text in a bulleted list. If you insert a plain text format document into a presentation, PowerPoint creates an outline based on the tabs at the beginning of the document's paragraphs. Paragraphs without tabs become slide titles, and paragraphs with one tab indent become first-level text in bulleted lists. **CASE** *You have a Microsoft Word document with information about intercontinental Canadian train routes that you want to insert into your presentation to create several new slides.*

STEPS

QUICK TIP
While in Normal view you can click the Normal button in the status bar to go to Outline view.

1. **Start PowerPoint, open the presentation PPT C-1.pptx from the location where you store your Data Files, save it as PPT C-QST, click the VIEW tab on the Ribbon, then click the Outline View button in the Presentation Views group**

2. **Click the Slide 4 icon ⬜ in the Outline pane, click the HOME tab on the Ribbon, click the New Slide button list arrow in the Slides group, then click Slides from Outline**

 Slide 4 appears in the Slide pane. The Insert Outline dialog box opens. Before you insert an outline into a presentation, you need to determine where you want the new slides to be placed. You want the text from the Word document inserted as new slides after Slide 4.

3. **Navigate to the location where you store your Data Files, click the Word document file PPT C-2.docx, then click Insert**

 Six new slides (5, 6, 7, 8, 9 and 10) are added to the presentation, and the new Slide 5 appears in the Slide pane. See **FIGURE C-1**.

4. **Click the down scroll arrow ▾ in the Outline pane and read the text for all the new slides, then click the Normal button 🔲 on the status bar**

 The information on Slides 5 and 6 refer to obsolete train routes and are not needed for this presentation.

5. **Press [Shift], click the Slide 6 thumbnail in the Thumbnails pane, then click the Cut button in the Clipboard group**

 Slides 5 and 6 are deleted, and the next slide down (Explorer's Trail West) becomes the new Slide 5 and appears in the Slide pane.

6. **Click the Slide 6 thumbnail in the Thumbnails pane, then drag it above Slide 5**

 Slide 6 and Slide 5 change places. All of the new slides in the presentation now follow the same theme. You want the text of the inserted outline to adopt the theme fonts of the presentation.

QUICK TIP
You can also use Slide Sorter view to move slides around in the presentation.

7. **Press [Shift], click the Slide 8 thumbnail in the Thumbnails pane, release [Shift], click the Reset button in the Slides group, then click the Save button 🖫 on the Quick Access toolbar**

 Notice the font type and formatting attributes of the slide text changes to reflect the current theme fonts for the presentation. The Reset button resets the slide placeholders to their default position, size, and text formatting based on the Organic presentation design theme. Compare your screen to **FIGURE C-2**.

FIGURE C-1: Outline pane showing imported text

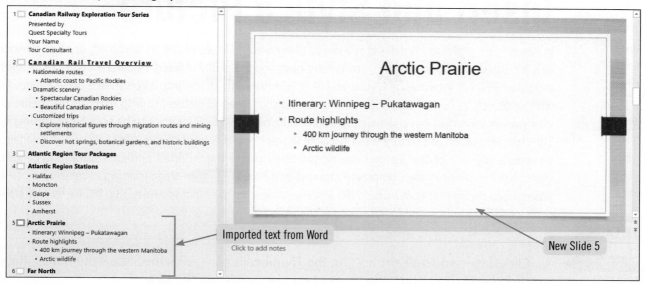

FIGURE C-2: Slides reset to Organic theme default settings

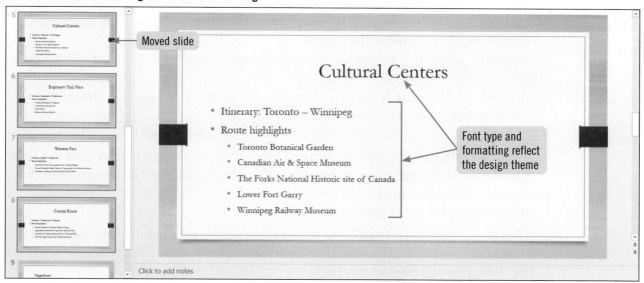

Sending a presentation using email

You can send a copy of a presentation over the Internet to a reviewer to edit and add comments. You can use Microsoft Outlook to send your presentation. Although your email program allows you to attach files, you can send a presentation using Outlook from within PowerPoint. Click the FILE tab, click Share, click Email in the center pane, then click Send as Attachment. Outlook opens and automatically creates an email with a copy of the presentation attached to it. You can also attach and send a PDF copy or an XPS copy of the presentation using your email program. Both of these file formats preserve document formatting, enable file sharing, and can be viewed online and printed.

Insert and Style a Picture

In PowerPoint, a **picture** is defined as a digital photograph, a piece of line art or clip art, or other artwork that is created in another program. PowerPoint gives you the ability to insert 14 different types of pictures including JPEG File Interchange Format and BMP Windows Bitmap files into a PowerPoint presentation. As with all objects in PowerPoint, you can format and style inserted pictures to help them fit the theme of your presentation. You can also hide a portion of the picture you don't want to be seen by **cropping** it. The cropped portion of a picture is still available to you if you ever want to show that part of picture again. To reduce the size of the file you can permanently delete the cropped portion by applying picture compression settings in the Compress Pictures dialog box. **CASE** *Using your digital camera, you took photographs during your train tours. In this lesson you insert a picture that you saved as a JPG file on your computer, and then you crop and style it to best fit the slide.*

STEPS

1. **Click the down scroll arrow ▼ in the Thumbnails pane, click the Slide 9 thumbnail, then click the Pictures icon in the content placeholder on the slide**

 The Insert Picture dialog box opens displaying the pictures available in the default Pictures library.

2. **Navigate to location where you store your Data Files, select the picture file PPT C-3.jpg, then click Insert**

 The picture fills the content placeholder on the slide, and the PICTURE TOOLS FORMAT tab opens on the Ribbon. The picture would look better if you cropped some of the image.

3. **Click the Crop button in the Size group, then place the pointer over the lower-right corner cropping handle of the picture**

 The pointer changes to ⌐. When the Crop button is active, cropping handles appear next to the sizing handles on the selected object.

4. **Drag the corner of the picture up and to the left as shown in FIGURE C-3, release the mouse button, then press [Esc]**

 PowerPoint has a number of picture formatting options, and you decide to experiment with some of them.

5. **Click the More button ▼ in the Picture Styles group, move your pointer over the style thumbnails in the gallery to see how the different styles change the picture, then click Rotated, White (3rd row)**

 The picture now has a white frame and is rotated slightly to the left.

6. **Click the Corrections button in the Adjust group, move your pointer over the thumbnails to see how the picture changes, then click Sharpen: 50% in the Sharpen/Soften section**

 The picture clarity is better.

7. **Click the Artistic Effects button in the Adjust group, move your pointer over the thumbnails to see how the picture changes, then click a blank area of the slide**

 The artistic effects are all interesting, but none of them will work well for this picture.

8. **Drag the picture to the center of the blank area of the slide, click a blank area on the slide, then save your changes**

 Compare your screen to FIGURE C-4.

FIGURE C-3: Using the cropping pointer to crop a picture

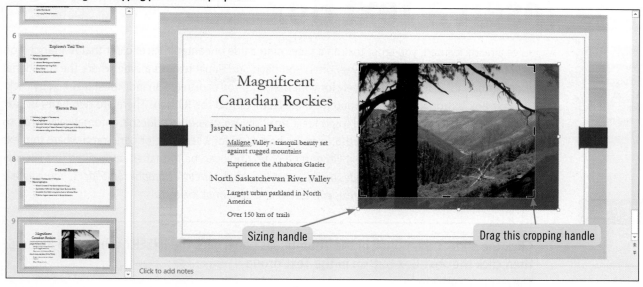

FIGURE C-4: Cropped and styled picture

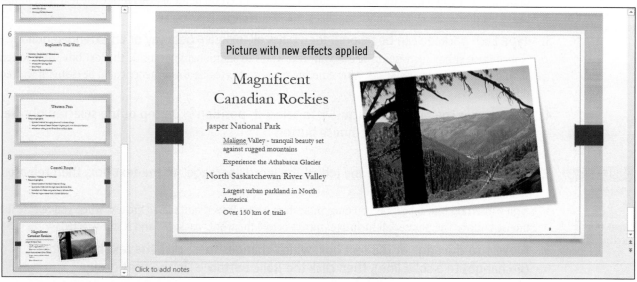

Saving slides as graphics

You can save PowerPoint slides as graphics and later use them in other presentations, in graphics programs, and on Web pages. Display the slide you want to save, click the FILE tab, then click Save As. Select the location where you want to save the file. In the Save As dialog box, click the Save as type list arrow, select the desired graphics format, then name the file. Graphics format choices include GIF Graphics Interchange Format (*.gif), JPEG File Interchange Format (*.jpg), PNG Portable Network Graphics Format (*.png), TIFF Tag Image File Format (*.tif), and Device Independent Bitmap (*.bmp). Click Save, then click the desired option when the alert box appears asking if you want to save all the slides or only the current slide.

Insert a Text Box

**Learning
Outcomes**
• Insert a text box
• Format text in a
 text box
• Resize and move a
 text box

As you've already learned, you enter text on a slide using a title or content placeholder that is arranged on the slide based on a slide layout. Every so often you need additional text on a slide where the traditional placeholder does not place text effectively for your message. You can create an individual text box by clicking the Text Box button in the Text group on the INSERT tab on the Ribbon. There are two types of text boxes that you can create: a text label, used for a small phrase where text doesn't automatically wrap to the next line inside the box, and a word-processing box, used for a sentence or paragraph where the text wraps inside the boundaries of the box. Either type of text box can be formatted and edited just like any other text object. **CASE** ▶ *You decide to add a text box to the SmartArt graphic on Slide 3. You create a word-processing box on the slide, enter text, edit text, and then format the text.*

STEPS

1. **Click the Slide 3 thumbnail in the Thumbnails pane, click the INSERT tab on the Ribbon, then click the Text Box button in the Text group**
 The pointer changes to ↓.

QUICK TIP
To create a text
label, click the Text
Box button, position
the pointer on the
slide, click once,
then enter your text.

2. **Move ↓ to the blank area of the slide to the left of the SmartArt graphic, then drag the pointer ⊢ down and toward the right about 3" to create a text box**
 When you begin dragging, an outline of the text box appears, indicating the size of the text box you are drawing. After you release the mouse button, a blinking insertion point appears inside the text box, in this case a word-processing box, indicating that you can enter text.

3. **Type Each package can be tailored for a quick all-inclusive getaway or an extended holiday**
 Notice the text box increases in size as your text wraps to additional lines inside the text box. Your screen should look similar to FIGURE C-5. After entering the text, you realize the sentence could be clearer if written differently.

4. **Drag ⊺ over the phrase all-inclusive to select it, position ⇗ on top of the selected phrase, then press and hold the left mouse button**
 The pointer changes to ⇖.

TROUBLE
If there is no space
after the word
"inclusive," click
after the word, then
press [Spacebar].

5. **Drag the selected words to the left of the word "package" in the text box, then release the mouse button**
 A grey insertion line appears as you drag, indicating where PowerPoint places the text when you release the mouse button. The phrase "all-inclusive" moves before the word "package" and is still selected.

6. **Move ⊺ to the edge of the text box, which changes to ⇖, click the text box border (it changes to a solid line), then click the Italic button *I* in the Font group**
 All of the text in the text box is italicized.

QUICK TIP
Click the Shape
Outline list arrow in
the Drawing group,
then click Weight or
Dashes to change
the outline width or
style of a text object.

7. **Click the Shape Fill list arrow in the Drawing group, click the Blue-Gray, Accent 3, Lighter 60% color box, click the Shape Outline list arrow in the Drawing group, then click the Orange, Accent 5 color box**
 The text object is now filled with a light blue color and has a light orange outline.

8. **Drag the right-middle sizing handle of the text box to the right until all the text fits on two lines, position ⇖ over the text box edge, then drag the text box to the Smart Guide on the slide as shown in FIGURE C-6**

9. **Click the Reading View button 📖 on the status bar, review the slide, press [Esc], then save your changes**

FIGURE C-5: New text object

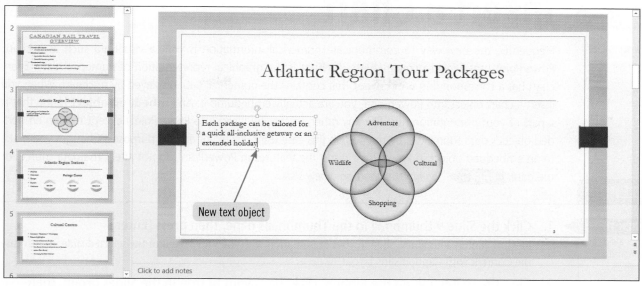

FIGURE C-6: Formatted text object

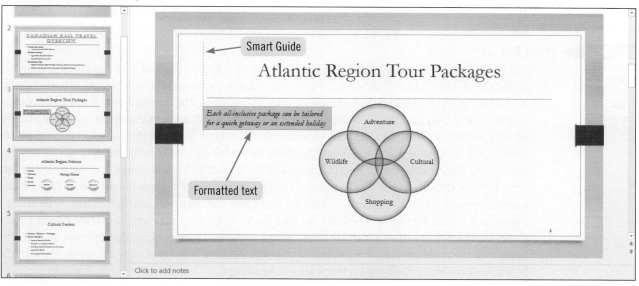

Changing text box defaults

You can change the default formatting characteristics of text boxes you create using the Text Box button on the INSERT tab. To change the formatting defaults for text boxes, select an existing formatted text box, or create a new one and format it using any of PowerPoint's formatting commands. When you are ready to change the text box defaults, press [Shift], right-click the formatted text box, release [Shift], then click Set as Default Text Box on the shortcut menu. Any new text boxes you create now will display the formatting characteristics of this formatted text box.

Insert a Chart

Learning
Outcomes
• Insert a new chart
 on a slide

Frequently, the best way to communicate numerical information is with a visual aid such as a chart. PowerPoint uses Excel to create charts. A **chart** is the graphical representation of numerical data. Every chart has a corresponding **worksheet** that contains the numerical data displayed by the chart. When you insert a chart object into PowerPoint, you are actually embedding it. An **embedded object** is one that is a part of your presentation (just like any other object you insert into PowerPoint) except that an embedded object's data source can be opened, in this case using Excel, for editing purposes. Changes you make to an embedded object in PowerPoint using the features in PowerPoint do not affect the data source for the data. **CASE** ▶ *You insert a chart on a new slide.*

STEPS

1. **Click the** Slide 9 thumbnail **in the Thumbnails pane, then press** [Enter]

 Pressing [Enter] adds a new slide to your presentation with the slide layout of the selected slide, in this case the Content with Caption slide layout.

2. **Click the** HOME tab **on the Ribbon, click the** Layout button **in the Slides group, then click** Title and Content

 The slide layout changes to the Title and Content layout.

3. **Click the** Title placeholder, **type** Customer Survey, **then click the** Insert Chart icon 📊 **in the Content placeholder**

 The Insert Chart dialog box opens as shown in FIGURE C-7. Each chart type includes a number of 2D and 3D styles. The Clustered Column chart is the default 2D chart style. For a brief explanation of chart types, refer to TABLE C-1.

4. **Click** OK

 The PowerPoint window displays a clustered column chart below a worksheet with sample data, as shown in FIGURE C-8. The CHART TOOLS DESIGN tab on the Ribbon contains commands you use in PowerPoint to work with the chart. The worksheet consists of rows and columns. The intersection of a row and a column is called a **cell**. Cells are referred to by their row and column location; for example, the cell at the intersection of column A and row 1 is called cell A1. Each column and row of data in the worksheet is called a **data series**. Cells in column A and row 1 contain **data series labels** that identify the data or values in the column and row. "Category 1" is the data series label for the data in the second row, and "Series 1" is a data series label for the data in the second column. Cells below and to the right of the data series labels, in the shaded blue portion of the worksheet, contain the data values that are represented in the chart. Cells in row 1 appear in the chart **legend** and describe the data in the series. Each data series has corresponding **data series markers** in the chart, which are graphical representations such as bars, columns, or pie wedges. The boxes with the numbers along the left side of the worksheet are **row headings**, and the boxes with the letters along the top of the worksheet are **column headings**.

5. **Move the pointer over the worksheet, then click cell** C4

 The pointer changes to ✛. Cell C4, containing the value 1.8, is the selected cell, which means it is now the **active cell**. The active cell has a thick green border around it.

6. **Click the** Close button ✖ **on the worksheet title bar, then click the** Quick Layout button **in the Chart Layouts group**

 The worksheet window closes, and the Quick Layout gallery opens.

7. **Move** ⌖ **over all the layouts in the gallery, then click** Layout 1

 This new layout moves the legend to the right side of the chart and increases the size of the data series markers.

8. **Click in a blank area of the slide to deselect the chart, then save your changes**

 The CHART TOOLS DESIGN tab is no longer active.

FIGURE C-7: Insert Chart dialog box

FIGURE C-8: Worksheet open with data for the chart

TABLE C-1: Chart types

chart type	icon looks like	use to
Column		Track values over time or across categories
Line		Track values over time
Pie		Compare individual values to the whole
Bar		Compare values in categories or over time
Area		Show contribution of each data series to the total over time
X Y (Scatter)		Compare pairs of values
Stock		Show stock market information or scientific data
Surface		Show value trends across two dimensions
Radar		Show changes in values in relation to a center point
Combo		Use multiple types of data markers to compare values

PowerPoint 2013

Enter and Edit Chart Data

Learning Outcomes
• Change chart data values
• Format a chart

After you insert a chart into your presentation, you need to replace the sample information with the correct data. If you have data in an Excel worksheet, you can import it from Excel; otherwise, you can type your own data into the worksheet. As you enter data and make other changes in the worksheet, the chart on the slide automatically reflects the new changes. **CASE** *You enter and format survey data you collected that asked people to positively rate four train tours with respect to three factors: suite accommodations, food quality, and overall trip satisfaction.*

STEPS

1. **Click the chart on Slide 10, then click the Edit Data button in the Data group on the CHART TOOLS DESIGN tab on the Ribbon**
 The chart is selected and the worksheet opens in a separate window. The information in the worksheet needs to be replaced with the correct data.

QUICK TIP
Click the chart in the PowerPoint window, then move your pointer over each bar in the chart to see the data source values.

2. **Click the Series 1 cell, type Suite, press [Tab], type Food, press [Tab], then type Overall**
 The data series labels, describing three survey factors, are entered in the worksheet and display in the legend on the chart. Pressing [Tab] moves the active cell from left to right one cell at a time in a row. Pressing [Enter] in the worksheet moves the active cell down one cell at a time in a column.

3. **Click the Category 1 cell, type Atlantic, press [Enter], type Prairie, press [Enter], type Rockies, press [Enter], type Pacific, then press [Enter]**
 The data series labels, describing the tour regions, are entered in the worksheet and appear along the bottom of the chart on the x-axis. The x-axis is the horizontal axis also referred to as the **category axis**, and the y-axis is the vertical axis also referred to as the **value axis**.

4. **Enter the data shown in FIGURE C-9 to complete the worksheet, then press [Enter]**
 Notice that the height of each column in the chart, as well as the values along the y-axis, adjust to reflect the numbers you typed. You have finished entering the data in the Excel worksheet.

5. **Click the Switch Row/Column button in the Data group**
 The data charted on the x-axis switches with the y-axis. Notice the legend now displays the row data series labels for each tour region.

6. **Click the Close button ✖ on the worksheet title bar, then click the Chart Title text box object in the chart**
 The worksheet window closes.

QUICK TIP
You can also change the chart style by clicking a style option in the Chart Styles group on the CHART TOOLS DESIGN tab.

7. **Type Guest Satisfaction, click a blank area of the chart, then click the Chart Styles button to the right of the chart to open the Chart Styles gallery**
 The Chart Styles gallery opens on the left side of the chart with STYLE selected.

8. **Scroll down the gallery, click Style 6, click COLOR at the top of the Chart Styles gallery, then click Color 2 in the Colorful section**
 The new chart style and color gives the column data markers a professional look as shown in FIGURE C-10.

9. **Click a blank area on the slide, then save the presentation**
 The Chart Styles gallery closes.

FIGURE C-9: Worksheet data for the chart

FIGURE C-10: Formatted chart

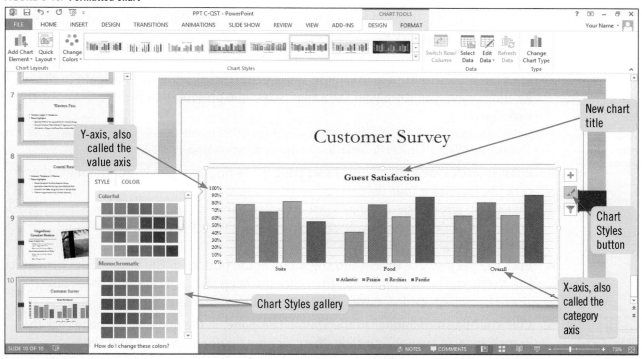

Adding a hyperlink to a chart

You can add a hyperlink to any object in PowerPoint, including a chart. Select that chart, click the INSERT tab on the Ribbon, then click the Hyperlink button in the Links group. If you are linking to another file, click the Existing File or Web Page button, locate the file you want to link to the chart, then click OK. Or, if you want to link to another slide in the presentation, click the Place in This Document button, click the slide in the list, then click OK. Now, during a slide show you can click the chart to open the linked object. To remove the link, click the chart, click the Hyperlink button in the Links group, then click Remove Link.

Insert Slides from Other Presentations

To save time and energy, you can insert one or more slides you already created in other presentations into an existing presentation or one you are currently working on. One way to share slides between presentations is to open an existing presentation, copy the slides you want to the Clipboard, and then paste them into your open presentation. However, PowerPoint offers a simpler way to transfer slides directly between presentations. By using the Reuse Slides pane, you can insert slides from another presentation or a network location called a Slide Library. A **Slide Library** is folder that you and others can access to open, modify, and review presentation slides. Newly inserted slides automatically take on the theme of the open presentation, unless you decide to use slide formatting from the original source presentation. **CASE** *You decide to insert slides you created for another presentation into the Canadian train tour presentation.*

STEPS

QUICK TIP
You can also open a second presentation window and work on the same presentation in different places at the same time. Click the VIEW tab, then click the New Window button in the Window group.

1. **Click the Slide 4 thumbnail in the Thumbnails pane, click the New Slide list arrow in the Slides group, then click Reuse Slides**
 The Reuse Slides pane opens on the right side of the presentation window.

2. **Click the Browse button in the Reuse Slides pane, click Browse File, navigate to the location where you store your Data Files, select the presentation file PPT C-4.pptx, then click Open**
 Six slide thumbnails are displayed in the pane with the first slide thumbnail selected as shown in FIGURE C-11. The slide thumbnails identify the slides in the **source presentation**, PPT C-4.pptx.

3. **Point to each slide in the Reuse Slides pane list to display a preview of the slide, then click the Manitoba Tour slide**
 The new slide appears in the Thumbnails pane and Slide pane in your current presentation as the new Slide 5. Notice the new slide assumes the design style and formatting of your presentation, which is called the **destination presentation**.

4. **Click the Keep source formatting check box at the bottom of the Reuse Slides pane, click the Northern Quebec Tour slide, then click the Keep source formatting check box**
 This new slide keeps the design style and formatting of the source presentation.

QUICK TIP
To copy noncontiguous slides, open Slide Sorter view, click the first slide thumbnail, press and hold [Ctrl], click each additional slide thumbnail, release [Ctrl], then click the Copy button.

5. **Click the Slide 4 thumbnail in the Thumbnails pane, in the Reuse Slides pane click the Trans Canadian Luxury Tour slide, then click the Southern Ontario Tour slide**
 Two more slides are inserted into the presentation with the design style and formatting of the destination presentation. You realize that slides 6 and 8 are not needed for this presentation.

6. **With the Slide 6 thumbnail still selected in the Thumbnails pane, press [Ctrl], click the Slide 8 thumbnail, release [Ctrl], right-click the Slide 8 thumbnail, then click Delete Slide in the shortcut menu**
 Slides 6 and 8 are deleted. Objects on the inserted slides may not be in the correct position on the slide. To ensure objects are positioned correctly on the slide, you can reset the slide defaults.

7. **Click the Slide 6 thumbnail in the Thumbnails pane, press [Shift], click the Slide 5 thumbnail, release [Shift], then click the Reset button in the Slides group**
 The selected slides are set back to the original default settings for this design theme.

8. **Click the Reuse Slides pane Close button ⊠, then save the presentation**
 The Reuse Slides pane closes. Compare your screen to FIGURE C-12.

FIGURE C-11: Presentation window with Reuse Slides pane open

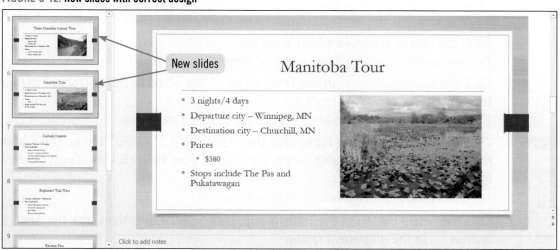

FIGURE C-12: New slides with correct design

Working with multiple windows

Another way to work with information in multiple presentations is to arrange the presentation windows on your monitor so you see each window side by side. Open each presentation, click the VIEW tab on the Ribbon in any presentation window, then click the Arrange All button in the Window group. Each presentation you have open is placed next to each other so you can easily drag, or transfer, information between the presentations. If you are working with more than two open presentations, you can overlap the presentation windows on top of one another. Open all the presentations you want, then click the Cascade Windows button in the Window group. Now you can to easily jump from one presentation to another by clicking on the presentation title bar or any part of the presentation window.

Insert a Table

As you create your presentation, you may have some information that would look best organized in rows and columns. For example, if you want to compare the basic details of different train accommodations side by side, a table is ideal for this type of information. Once you have created a table, two new tabs, the TABLE TOOLS DESIGN tab and the TABLE TOOLS LAYOUT tab, appear on the Ribbon. You can use the commands on the table tabs to apply color styles, change cell borders, add cell effects, add rows and columns to your table, adjust the size of cells, and align text in the cells. **CASE** *You decide a table best illustrates the different levels of accommodation services offered by the train tour company.*

STEPS

1. **Right-click** Slide 4 **in the Slides Thumbnails pane, click** New Slide **on the shortcut menu, click the** title placeholder, **then type** Accommodations
 A new slide with the Title and Content layout appears.

2. **Click the** Insert Table icon ▦, **click the** Number of columns down arrow **once until** 4 **appears, click the** Number of rows up arrow **twice until** 4 **appears, then click** OK
 A formatted table with four columns and four rows appears on the slide, and the TABLE TOOLS DESIGN tab opens on the Ribbon. The table has 16 cells. The insertion point is in the first cell of the table and is ready to accept text.

3. **Type** Classic, **press** [Tab], **type** Deluxe, **press** [Tab], **type** Luxury, **press** [Tab], **type** Business, **then press** [Tab]
 The text you typed appears in the top four cells of the table. Pressing [Tab] moves the insertion point to the next cell; pressing [Enter] moves the insertion point to the next line in the same cell.

4. **Enter the rest of the table information shown in** FIGURE C-13
 The table would look better if it were formatted differently.

5. **Click the** More button ▾ **in the Table Styles group, scroll to the bottom of the gallery, then click** Dark Style 1 – Accent 3
 The background and text color change to reflect the table style you applied.

6. **Click the** Classic cell **in the table, click the** TABLE TOOLS LAYOUT tab **on the Ribbon, click the** Select button **in the Table group, click** Select Row, **then click the** Center button ▤ **in the Alignment group**
 The text in the top row is centered horizontally in each cell.

7. **Click the** Select button **in the Table group, click** Select Table, **then click the** Align Bottom button ▭ **in the Alignment group**
 The text in the entire table is aligned at the bottom within each cell.

8. **Click the** TABLE TOOLS DESIGN tab, **click the** Effects button **in the Table Styles group, point to** Cell Bevel, **then click** Convex (2nd row)
 The 3D effect makes the cells of the table stand out. The table would look better in a different place on the slide.

9. **Place the pointer** ⬚ **over the top edge of the table, drag the table straight down as shown in** FIGURE C-14, **click a blank area of the slide, then save the presentation**
 The slide looks better with more space between the table and the slide title.

FIGURE C-13: Inserted table with data

FIGURE C-14: Formatted table

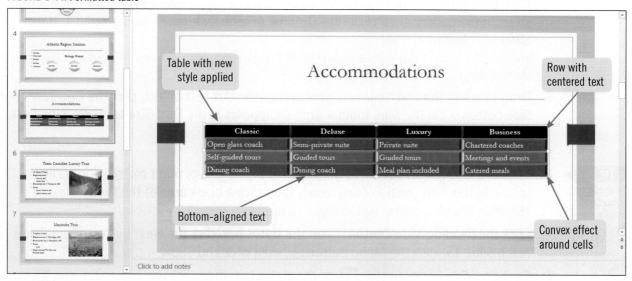

Drawing tables

Choose the slide where you want the table, click the Table button in the Tables group on the Insert tab, then click Draw Table. The pointer changes to ✐. Drag to define the boundaries of the table in the area of the slide where you want the table. A dotted outline appears as you draw . Next, you draw to create the rows and columns of your table. Click the TABLE TOOLS DESIGN tab on the Ribbon, click the Draw Table button in the Draw Borders group, then draw lines for columns and rows. Be sure to draw within the boundary line of the table. You can also create a table by clicking the Table button in the Tables group on the Insert tab, then dragging ⬚ over the table grid to create a table.

Insert and Format WordArt

As you work to create an interesting presentation, your goal should include making your slides visually appealing. Sometimes plain text can come across as dull and unexciting in a presentation. **WordArt** is a set of decorative text styles, or text effects, you can apply to any text object to help direct the attention of your audience to a certain piece of information. You can use WordArt in two different ways: you can apply a WordArt text style to an existing text object that converts the text into WordArt, or you can create a new WordArt object. The WordArt text styles and effects include text shadows, reflections, glows, bevels, 3D rotations, and transformations. **CASE** ▶ *Use WordArt to create a new WordArt text object on Slide 8.*

STEPS

1. **Click the Slide 8 thumbnail in the Thumbnails pane, click the INSERT tab on the Ribbon, then click the WordArt button in the Text group**
 The WordArt gallery appears displaying 20 WordArt text styles.

2. **Click Gradient Fill – Orange, Accent 1, Reflection (second row)**
 A text object appears in the middle of the slide displaying sample text with the WordArt style you just selected. Notice the DRAWING TOOLS FORMAT tab is open on the Ribbon.

3. **Click the edge of the WordArt text object, then when the pointer changes to ⬥, drag the text object to the blank area of the slide**

4. **Click the More button ⬥ in the WordArt Styles group, move ⬥ over all of the WordArt styles in the gallery, then click Fill – Orange, Accent 1, Outline – Background 1, Hard Shadow – Accent 1**
 The WordArt Styles change the sample text in the WordArt text object. The new WordArt style is applied to the text object.

5. **Drag to select the text Your text here in the WordArt text object, click the Decrease Font Size button A˅ in the Mini toolbar until 44 appears in the Font Size text box, type Best Value, press [Enter], then type Of the Summer**
 The text is smaller and appears on two lines.

6. **Click the Text Effects button in the WordArt Styles group, point to Transform, click Inflate in the Warp section (sixth row), then click a blank area of the slide**
 The inflate effect is applied to the text object. Compare your screen to **FIGURE C-15**.

7. **Click the Reading View button ⬥ on the status bar, click the Next button ⬥ until you reach Slide 13, click the Menu button ⬥, then click End Show**

8. **Click the Slide Sorter button ⬥ on the status bar, then click the Zoom Out icon ⬥ on the status bar until all 13 slides are visible**
 Compare your screen with **FIGURE C-16**.

9. **Click the Normal button ⬥ on the status bar, add your name and the date as a footer to the slides, save your changes, submit your presentation to your instructor, then exit PowerPoint**

FIGURE C-15: WordArt inserted on slide

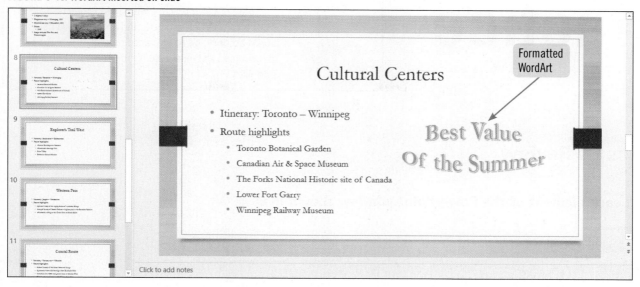

FIGURE C-16: Completed presentation in Slide Sorter view

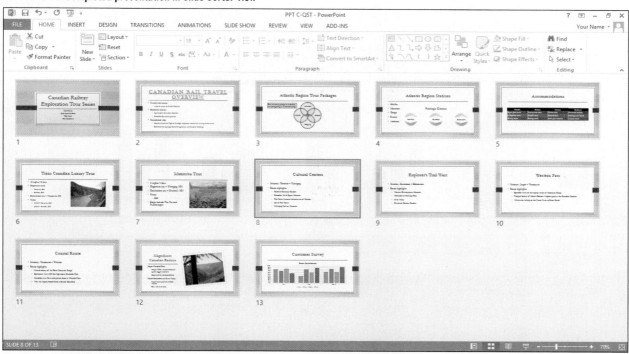

Saving a presentation as a video

You can save your PowerPoint presentation as a full-fidelity video, which incorporates all slide timings, transitions, animations, and narrations. The video can be distributed using a disc, the Web, or email. Depending on how you want to display your video, you have three resolution settings from which to choose: Computer & HD Displays, Internet & DVD, and Portable Devices. The Large setting, Computer & HD Displays (1280 X 720), is used for viewing on a computer monitor, projector, or other high-definition displays. The Medium setting, Internet & DVD (852 X 480), is used for uploading to the Web or copying to a standard DVD. The Small setting, Portable Devices (424 X 240), is used on portable devices including portable media players such as Microsoft Zune. To save your presentation as a video, click the FILE tab, click Export, click Create a Video, choose your settings, then click the Create Video button.

Practice

Concepts Review

Label each element of the PowerPoint window shown in FIGURE C-17.

FIGURE C-17

Match each term with the statement that best describes it.

9. Picture

10. Worksheet

11. Data series marker

12. Table

13. Data series

a. Each column or row of data in a worksheet

b. A digital photo or clip art

c. The graphical representation of numerical data in chart

d. Contains the numerical data displayed in a chart

e. PowerPoint object that organizes data in columns and rows

Select the best answer from the list of choices.

14. When you _____ a document into a presentation, PowerPoint creates slides from the outline based on the styles in the document.

 a. link **c.** import

 b. create **d.** package

15. According to this unit, a picture is:

 a. Created in another program. **c.** Created using the Picture Tools Format tab.

 b. Defined as an embedded painting. **d.** Only used to enhance a slide in Slide Show view.

16. A text label is best used for:

 a. WordArt. **c.** A content placeholder.

 b. A long paragraph. **d.** A small text phrase.

17. When you insert slides using the Reuse Slides pane, the current open presentation is also called the _____ presentation.

 a. reused **c.** destination

 b. source **d.** first

18. An object that has its own data source and becomes a part of your presentation after you insert it best describes which of the following?

 a. A Word outline **c.** A WordArt object

 b. An embedded object **d.** A table

19. Use _____ to apply a set of decorative text styles or text effects to text.

 a. a picture **c.** a hyperlink

 b. rich text format **d.** WordArt

20. A simple way to insert slides from another presentation is to use the _____ pane.

 a. Insert Slides **c.** Slides Group

 b. Reuse Slides **d.** Browse

Skills Review

1. Insert text from Microsoft Word.

 a. Open the file PPT C-5.pptx from the location where you store your Data Files, then save it as **PPT C-Colcom**. You will work to create the completed presentation as shown in **FIGURE C-18**.

 b. Click Slide 3 in the Thumbnails pane, then use the Slides from Outline command to insert the file PPT C-6.docx from the location where you store your Data Files.

 c. In the Thumbnails pane, drag Slide 6 above Slide 5 then delete Slide 7, "Expansion Potential".

 d. Select Slides 4, 5, and 6 in the Slides tab, reset the slides to the default theme settings, then save your work.

FIGURE C-18

Skills Review (continued)

2. Insert and style a picture.

 a. Select Slide 2 in the Thumbnails pane, then insert the picture PPT C-7.jpg from the location where you store your Data Files.

 b. Crop the top portion of the picture down to the piano keys, then crop the left side of the picture about 1/4 inch.

 c. Drag the picture up so it is in the center of the blank area of the slide.

 d. Click the Color button, then change the picture color to Tan, Accent color 3 Dark.

 e. Save your changes.

3. Insert a text box.

 a. On Slide 2, insert a text box below the picture.

 b. Type **Public submissions for music up 9%**.

 c. Delete the word **for**, then drag the word **music** after the word **Public**.

 d. Select the text object, then click the More button in the Shape Styles group on the DRAWING TOOLS FORMAT tab.

 e. Click Moderate Effect – Tan, Accent 3, then fit the text box to the text by dragging its sizing handles.

 f. Center the text object under the picture using Smart Guides.

4. Insert a chart.

 a. Go to Slide 3, Sales by Quarter, click the Chart button in the Illustrations group on the INSERT tab, click Bar in the left column, then insert a Clustered Bar chart.

 b. Close the worksheet, drag the top-middle sizing handle of the chart down under the slide title, then apply the Layout 1 quick layout to the chart.

5. Enter and edit chart data.

 a. Show the worksheet, then enter the data shown in TABLE C-2 into the worksheet.

 b. Click the Switch Row/Column button in the Data group, then close the worksheet window.

 c. Type **Top Selling Categories** in the chart title text object.

 d. Click the Chart Styles button next to the chart then change the chart style to Style 7.

 e. Click COLOR in the Charts Styles gallery, then change the color to Color 9 in the Monochromatic section.

 f. Close the Charts Styles gallery, then save your changes.

TABLE C-2

	Hip hop	Reggae	Country
1st Qtr	290,957	208,902	530,457
2nd Qtr	229,840	425,854	490,823
3rd Qtr	485,063	535,927	356,978
4th Qtr	565,113	303,750	637,902

6. Insert slides from other presentations.

 a. Make sure Slide 3 is selected, then open the Reuse Slides pane.

 b. Open the file PPT C-8.pptx from the location where you store your Data Files.

 c. Insert the second slide thumbnail, then insert the first slide thumbnail and the third thumbnail.

 d. Close the Reuse Slides pane, then using [Shift] select Slide 4 in the Thumbnails pane.

 e. Click the Reset button in the Slides group, then save your work.

7. Insert a table.

 a. Add a new slide after Slide 6 with the Title and Content layout.

 b. Add the slide title **Revised Subscription Plans**.

 c. Insert a table with three columns and four rows.

 d. Enter the information shown in TABLE C-3, then change the table style to Medium Style 2 – Accent 2.

 e. In the TABLE TOOLS LAYOUT tab, center the text in the top row.

 f. Select the whole table, open the TABLE TOOLS DESIGN tab, click the Effects button, point to Cell Bevel, then apply the Art Deco effect.

 g. Move the table to the center of the blank area of the slide, then save your changes.

TABLE C-3

Basic	Standard	Premium
$.99 per download	$11.99 per month	$34.99 per year
Unlimited downloads	Max. 100 downloads	Unlimited downloads
Limited access	Limited access	Unlimited access

Skills Review (continued)

8. Insert and format WordArt.

a. Go to Slide 10, then, insert a WordArt text object using the style Fill – White, Text 1, Outline – Background 1, Hard Shadow – Background 1.

b. Type **ColCom Productions Inc.**, then apply the WordArt style Fill – Gold, Accent 1, Outline – Background 1, Hard Shadow – Accent 1.

c. Apply the Deflate Top Transform effect (seventh row) to the text object, then move the text object to the middle of the blank area of the slide.

d. View the presentation in Slide Show view, add your name as a footer to all the slides, then save your changes.

e. Submit your presentation to your instructor, close your presentation, and exit PowerPoint.

Independent Challenge 1

You are a financial management consultant for Chapman & Rowley Investments LLP, located in Nyack, New York. One of your responsibilities is to create standardized presentations on different financial investments for use on the company Web site. As part of the presentation for this meeting, you insert a chart, add a WordArt object, and insert slides from another presentation.

a. Open the file PPT C-9.pptx from the location where you store your Data Files, then save it as **PPT C-C&R**.

b. Add your name as the footer on all of the slides, then apply the Ion Design Theme.

c. Insert a clustered column chart on Slide 2, then enter the data in TABLE C-4 into the worksheet.

d. Close the worksheet, format the chart using Style 11, then move the chart below the slide title text object.

e. Type **Annualized Return** in the chart title text object.

f. Open the Reuse Slides pane, open the file PPT C-10.pptx from the location where you store your Data Files, then insert slides 2, 3, and 4.

g. Close the Reuse Slides pane, move Slide 5 above Slide 4, then select Slide 3.

h. Insert a WordArt object with the Fill – Dark Red, Accent 1, Shadow style, type **Never too early**, press [Enter], type **To**, press [Enter], then type **Start saving**.

i. Click the Text Effects button, point to Transform, then apply the Button text effect from the Follow Path section.

j. Move the WordArt object to a blank area of the slide, click the Text Effects button, point to Shadow, then apply the shadow Offset Top.

k. View the presentation slide show, make any necessary changes, then save your work. See FIGURE C-19.

l. Submit the presentation to your instructor, then close the presentation, and exit PowerPoint.

TABLE C-4

	Stocks	Bonds	Mutual funds
1 Year	1.9%	1.2%	2.8%
3 Year	4.3%	3.4%	4.7%
5 Year	3.9%	2.8%	7.3%
7 Year	2.6%	3.0%	6.2%

FIGURE C-19

Independent Challenge 2

You work for Prince Rupert Harbor Group, a company in Prince Rupert, British Columbia, that oversees all of the commercial business at the Prince Rupert port. You have been asked to enhance a marketing presentation that is going to promote the port facilities. You work on completing a presentation by inserting two pictures, a text box, and a table.

a. Start PowerPoint, open the file PPT C-11.pptx from the location where you store your Data Files, and save it as **PPT C-PRHG**.

b. Add your name and today's date to Slide 1 in the Subtitle text box.

c. Apply the Wisp theme to the presentation.

d. On Slide 5, click the Pictures icon in the content placeholder, then insert the file PPT C-12.jpg from the location where you store your Data Files.

e. Apply the Double Frame, Black picture style to the picture, click the Color button, then change the color to Temperature: 8800 K (Color Tone section).

f. Insert a text box on the slide below the picture, type **2nd largest fishing fleet in Canada**, then format the text and text box with three formatting commands.

g. Go to Slide 2, select the picture, click the Picture Effects button, point to Soft Edges, then click 10 Point.

h. Open the Artistic Effects gallery, then apply the Blur effect to the picture.

i. Go to Slide 4, create a new table, then enter the data in TABLE C-5. Format the table using at least two formatting commands. Be able to identify which formatting commands you applied to the table.

j. View the final presentation in slide show view. Make any necessary changes (refer to FIGURE C-20).

k. Save the presentation, submit the presentation to your instructor, close the file, and exit PowerPoint.

TABLE C-5

Total	Aug 2016	Aug 2015	Variance
Total containers	47,524.0	43,418.0	9.5%
Loaded containers	35,283.0	34,016.5	3.7%
Empty containers	12,241.0	9,401.5	30.2%
Total tons	475,240.0	434,180.0	9.5%

FIGURE C-20

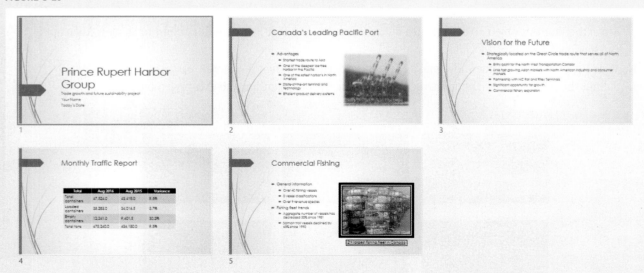

Independent Challenge 3

You work for OneGlobal Inc., a company that produces instructional software to help people learn foreign languages. Once a year, OneGlobal holds a meeting with their biggest client, the United States Department of State, to brief the government on new products and to receive feedback on existing products. Your supervisor has started a presentation and has asked you to look it over and add other elements to make it look better.

 a. Start PowerPoint, open the file PPT C-13.pptx from the location where you store your Data Files, and save it as **PPT C-OneGlobal**.

 b. Add an appropriate design theme to the presentation.

 c. Insert the Word outline PPT C-14.docx after the Product Revisions slide.

 d. Insert and format a text object and a WordArt object.

 e. Insert an appropriate table on a slide of your choice. Use your own information, or use text from a bulleted list on one of the slides.

 f. Insert and format at least two appropriate shapes that emphasize slide content. If appropriate, use the Align, Distribute, and Group commands to organize your shapes.

 g. Add your name as footer text on the slides and the notes and handouts, then save the presentation.

 h. Submit your presentation to your instructor, close the file, then exit PowerPoint.

Independent Challenge 4: Explore

You are in the Foreign Exchange Club at your college, and one of your assignments is to present information on past foreign student exchanges to different businesses and other organizations off campus. You need to create a pictorial presentation that highlights a trip to a different country. Create a presentation using your own pictures. If you don't have access to any appropriate pictures, use the three pictures provided in the Data Files for this unit: PPT C-15.jpg, PPT C-16.jpg, and PPT C-17.jpg. *(NOTE: To complete steps below, your computer must be connected to the Internet.)*

 a. Start PowerPoint, create a new blank presentation, and save it as **PPT C-Club** to the location where you store your Data Files.

 b. Locate and insert the pictures you want to use. Place one picture on each slide using the Content with Caption slide layout.

 c. Click the Crop list arrow, and use one of the other cropping options to crop a picture.

 d. Add information about each picture in the text placeholder, and enter a slide title. If you use the pictures provided, research Truro, England, using the Internet for relevant information to place on the slides.

FIGURE C-21

 e. Apply an appropriate design theme, then apply an appropriate title and your name to the title slide.

 f. View the final presentation slide show (refer to FIGURE C-21).

 g. Add a slide number and your class name as footer text to all of the slides, save your work, then submit your presentation to your instructor.

 h. Close the file, and exit PowerPoint.

Visual Workshop

Create a one-slide presentation that looks like FIGURE C-22. The slide layout shown in FIGURE C-22 is a specific layout designed for pictures. Insert the picture file PPT C-18.jpg to complete this presentation. Add your name as footer text to the slide, save the presentation as **PPT C-Alaska** to the location where you store your Data Files, then submit your presentation to your instructor.

FIGURE C-22

Finishing a Presentation

CASE You have reviewed your work and are pleased with the slides you created for the Quest Specialty Travel presentation. Now you are ready to add some final touches and effects to the slides to make the PowerPoint presentation interesting to watch.

Unit Objectives

After completing this unit, you will be able to:

- Modify masters
- Customize the background and theme
- Use slide show commands
- Set slide transitions and timings

- Animate objects
- Use proofing and language tools
- Inspect a presentation
- Evaluate a presentation

Files You Will Need

PPT D-1.pptx	PPT D-6.pptx
PPT D-2.jpg	PPT D-7.jpg
PPT D-3.jpg	PPT D-8.pptx
PPT D-4.pptx	PPT D-9.pptx
PPT D-5.jpg	

Modify Masters

Learning Outcomes
• Navigate Slide Master view
• Add and modify a picture

Each presentation in PowerPoint has a set of **masters** that store information about the theme and slide layouts. Masters determine the position and size of text and content placeholders, fonts, slide background, color, and effects. There are three Master views: Slide Master view, Notes Master view, and Handout Master view. Changes made in Slide Master view are reflected on the slides in Normal view; changes made in Notes Master view are reflected in Notes Page view, and changes made in Handout Master view appear when you print your presentation using a handout printing option. The primary benefit to modifying a master is that you can make universal changes to your whole presentation instead of making individual repetitive changes to each of your slides. **CASE** ▶ *You want to add the QST company logo to every slide in your presentation, so you open your presentation and insert the logo to the slide master.*

STEPS

1. **Start PowerPoint, open the presentation PPT D-1.pptx from the location where you store your Data Files, save the presentation as PPT D-QST, then click the VIEW tab on the Ribbon**

 The title slide for the presentation appears.

QUICK TIP
You can press and hold [Shift] and click the Normal button on the status bar to display the slide master.

2. **Click the Slide Master button in the Master Views group, scroll to the top of the Master Thumbnails pane, then click the Organic Slide Master thumbnail (first thumbnail)**

 The Slide Master view appears with the slide master displayed in the Slide pane as shown in **FIGURE D-1**. A new tab, the SLIDE MASTER tab, appears next to the HOME tab on the Ribbon. The slide master is the Organic theme slide master. Each theme comes with its own slide master. Each master text placeholder on the slide master identifies the font size, style, color, and position of text placeholders on the slides in Normal view. For example, for the Organic theme, the Master title placeholder positioned at the top of the slide uses a black, 44 pt, Garamond font. Slide titles use this font style and formatting. Each slide master comes with associated slide layouts located below the slide master in the Master Thumbnails pane. Slide layouts follow the information on the slide master, and changes you make are reflected in all of the slide layouts.

QUICK TIP
When working with slide layouts, you can right-click the thumbnail to open a shortcut menu of commands.

3. **Point to each of the slide layouts in the Master Thumbnails pane, then click the Title and Content Layout thumbnail**

 As you point to each slide layout, a ScreenTip appears identifying each slide layout by name and lists if any slides in the presentation are using the layout. Slides 2–6, and 13 are using the Title and Content Layout.

4. **Click the Organic Slide Master thumbnail, click the INSERT tab on the Ribbon, then click the Pictures button in the Images group**

 The Insert Picture dialog box opens.

5. **Select the picture file PPT D-2.jpg from the location where you store your Data Files, then click Insert**

 The QST logo picture is placed on the slide master and will now appear on all slides in the presentation. The picture is too large and needs to be repositioned on the slide.

6. **Click 1.61" in the Shape Width text box in the Size group, type .50, press [Enter], drag the QST logo to the upper-left corner of the slide, then click a blank area of the slide**

 The picture snaps into the corner of the slide.

7. **Click the SLIDE MASTER tab on the Ribbon, then click the Preserve button in the Edit Master group**

 Preserving the selected master ensures the Organic slide master remains with this presentation even if you eventually select another master. Compare your screen to **FIGURE D-2**.

8. **Click the Normal button 🖳 on the status bar, then save your changes**

FIGURE D-1: Slide Master view

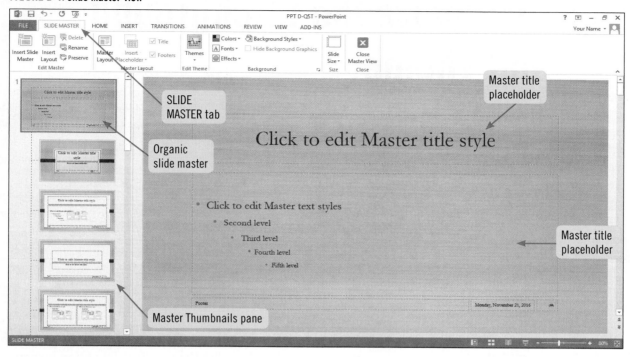

FIGURE D-2: Picture added to slide master

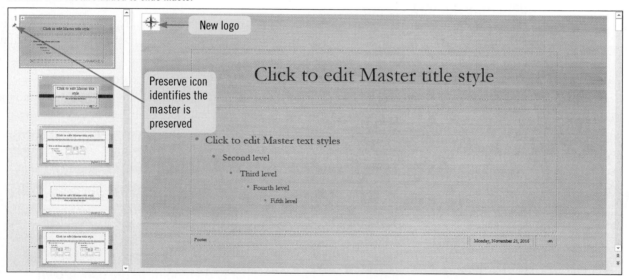

Create custom slide layouts

As you work with PowerPoint, you may find that you need to develop a customized slide layout. For example, you may need to create presentations for a client that has slides that display four pictures with a caption underneath each picture. To make everyone's job easier, you can create a custom slide layout that includes only the placeholders you need. To create a custom slide layout, open Slide Master view, and then click the Insert Layout button in the Edit Master group. A new slide layout appears below the last layout for the selected master in the slide thumbnails pane.

You can choose to add several different placeholders including Content, Text, Picture, Chart, Table, SmartArt, Media, and Picture. Click the Insert Placeholder list arrow in the Master Layout group, click the placeholder you want to add, drag � to create the placeholder, then position the placeholder on the slide. In Slide Master view, you can add or delete placeholders in any of the slide layouts. You can rename a custom slide layout by clicking the Rename button in the Edit Master group and entering a descriptive name to better identify the layout.

Customize the Background and Theme

Learning Outcomes
• Apply a slide background and change the style
• Modify presentation theme

Every slide in a PowerPoint presentation has a **background**, the area behind the text and graphics. You modify the background to enhance the slides using images and color. A **background graphic** is an object placed on the slide master. You can quickly change the background appearance by applying a background style, which is a set of color variations derived from the theme colors. Theme colors determine the colors for all slide elements in your presentation, including slide background, text and lines, shadows, fills, accents, and hyperlinks. Every PowerPoint theme has its own set of theme colors. See **TABLE D-1** for a description of the theme colors. **CASE** ▶ *The QST presentation can be improved with some design enhancements. You decide to modify the background of the slides by changing the theme colors and fonts.*

STEPS

1. **Click the DESIGN tab on the Ribbon, then click the Format Background button in the Customize group**

 The Format Background pane opens displaying the Fill options. The Picture or texture fill option button is selected indicating the slide has a texture background.

2. **Click the Solid fill option button, review the slide, click the Gradient fill option button, review the slide, click the Pattern fill option button, then click the Diagonal brick pattern (sixth row)**

 FIGURE D-3 shows the new background on Slide 1 of the presentation. The new background style does not appear over the whole slide because there are background items on the slide master preventing you from seeing the entire slide background.

3. **Click the Hide Background Graphics check box in the Format Background pane**

 All of the background items, which include the QST logo, the white box behind the text objects, and the colored shapes, are hidden from view, and only the text objects and slide number remain visible.

4. **Click the Hide Background Graphics check box, then click the Reset Background button at the bottom of the Format Background pane**

 All of the background items and the texture slide background appear again as specified by the theme.

5. **Click the File button under Insert picture from section in the Format Background pane, select the picture file PPT D-3.jpg from the location where you store your Data Files, then click Insert**

 The new picture fills the slide background behind the background items.

6. **Click the Slide 3 thumbnail in the Thumbnails pane, then point to the dark brown theme variant in the Variants group**

 Notice how the new theme variant changes the color of the shapes on the slide and the background texture. A **variant** is a custom variation of the applied theme, in this case the Organic theme. Theme variants are similar to the original theme, but they are made up of different complementary colors, slide backgrounds, such as textures and patterns, and background elements, such as shapes and pictures.

7. **Point to the other variants in the Variants group, click the third variant from the left, click the Format Background pane Close button ⊠, then save your work**

 The new variant is applied to the slide master and to all the slides in the presentation, except Slide 1. The slide background on Slide 1 did not change because you have already applied a picture to the slide background. Compare your screen to **FIGURE D-4**.

FIGURE D-3: New background style applied

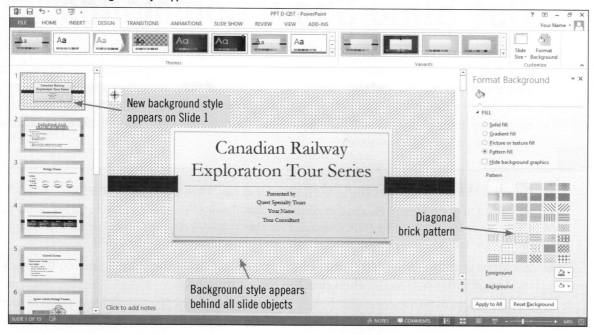

FIGURE D-4: New theme variant

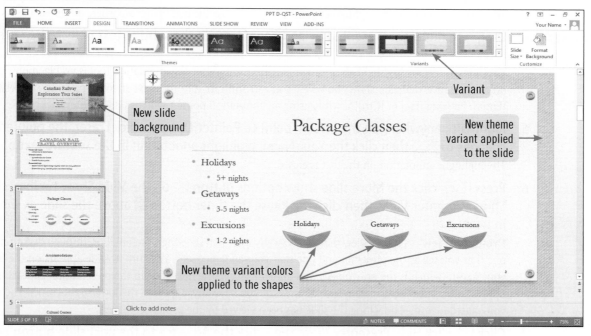

TABLE D-1: Theme colors

color element	description
Text/Background colors	Contrasting colors for typed characters and the slide background
Accent colors	There are six accent colors used for shapes, drawn lines, and text; the shadow color for text and objects and the fill and outline color for shapes are all accent colors; all of these colors contrast appropriately with background and text colors
Hyperlink color	Colors used for hyperlinks you insert
Followed Hyperlink color	Color used for hyperlinks after they have been clicked

Use Slide Show Commands

Learning Outcomes
• Preview a slide show
• Navigate a slide show
• Use slide show tools

With PowerPoint, Slide Show view is used primarily to deliver a presentation to an audience, either over the Internet using your computer or through a projector connected to your computer. As you've seen, Slide Show view fills your computer screen with the slides of the presentation, showing them one at a time. Once the presentation is in Slide Show view, you can draw, or **annotate**, on the slides or jump to other slides in the presentation. **CASE** ▶ *You run the slide show of the presentation and practice using some of the custom slide show options.*

STEPS

1. **Click the Slide Show button ▦ on the status bar, then press [Spacebar]**

 Slide 3 filled the screen first, and then Slide 4 appears. Pressing [Spacebar] or clicking the left mouse button is the easiest way to move through a slide show. See **TABLE D-2** for other basic slide show keyboard commands. You can easily navigate to other slides in the presentation during the slide show.

 TROUBLE
 The Slide Show toolbar buttons are semitransparent and blend in with the background color on the slide.

2. **Move ▷ to the lower-left corner of the screen to display the Slide Show toolbar, click the See all slides button ⊞, then click the Slide 1 thumbnail**

 Slide 1 appears on the screen with the Slide Show toolbar displayed. You can emphasize points in your presentation by annotating the slide during a slide show.

3. **Click the Pen and laser pointer tools button ⊘, on the Slide Show toolbar, then click Highlighter**

 The pointer changes to the highlighter pointer ▮. You can use the highlighter anywhere on the slide.

 QUICK TIP
 You can also use the Pen annotation tool to draw lines on a slide.

4. **Drag ▮, to highlight Presented by and Your Name in the subtitle text object, then press [Esc]**

 Two lines of text are highlighted as shown in **FIGURE D-5**. While the annotation tool is visible, mouse clicks do not advance the slide show; however, you can still move to the next slide by pressing [Spacebar] or [Enter]. Pressing [Esc] or [Ctrl][A] while using an annotation pointer switches the pointer back to ▷.

5. **Right-click anywhere on the screen, point to Pointer Options, click Eraser, the pointer changes to ⬦, then click the Your Name highlight annotation in the subtitle text object**

 The highlight annotation on the text is erased.

6. **Press [Esc], click the More slide show options button ⊙ on the Slide Show toolbar, click Show Presenter View, then click the Pause the timer button ❚❚ above the slide as shown in FIGURE D-6**

 Presenter view is a special view that you typically use when showing a presentation through two monitors; one that you see as the presenter and one that your audience sees. The current slide appears on the left of your screen (which is the only object your audience sees), the next slide in the presentation appears in the upper-right corner of the screen. Speaker notes, if you have any, appear in the lower-right corner. The timer you paused identifies how long the slide has been viewed by the audience.

7. **Click ⊙, click Hide Presenter View, then click the Advance to the next slide button ⊙ on the Slide Show toolbar**

 The next slide appears.

 QUICK TIP
 To temporarily hide your slide during a slide show, right-click the screen, point to Screen, then click Black Screen or White Screen.

8. **Press [Enter] to advance through the entire slide show until you see a black slide, then press [Spacebar]**

 If there are annotations on your slides, you have the option of saving them when you quit the slide show. Saved annotations appear as drawn objects in Normal view.

9. **Click Discard, then save the presentation**

 The highlight annotation is deleted on Slide 1, and Slide 3 appears in Normal view.

FIGURE D-5: Slide 1 in Slide Show view with annotations

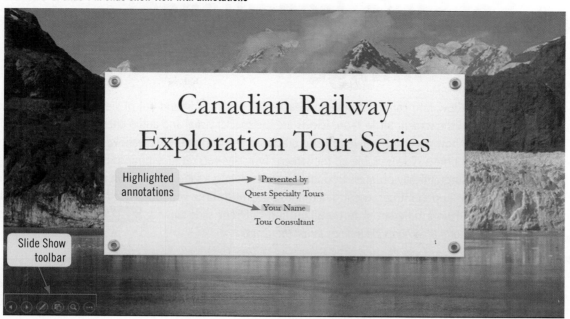

FIGURE D-6: Slide 1 in Presenter view

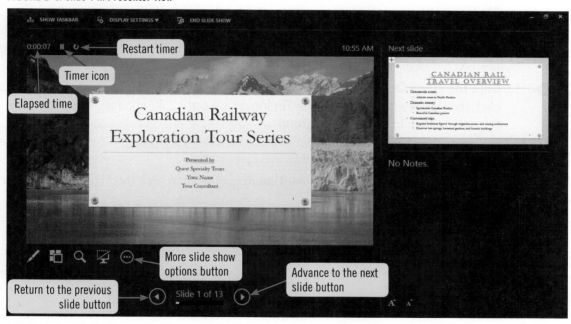

TABLE D-2: Basic Slide Show view keyboard commands

keyboard commands	description
[Enter], [Spacebar], [PgDn], [N], [down arrow], or [right arrow]	Advances to the next slide
[E]	Erases the annotation drawing
[Home], [End]	Moves to the first or last slide in the slide show
[up arrow], [PgUp], or [left arrow]	Returns to the previous slide
[S]	Pauses the slide show when using automatic timings; press again to continue
[B]	Changes the screen to black; press again to return
[Esc]	Stops the slide show

Set Slide Transitions and Timings

Learning
Outcomes
• Apply and modify
 a transition
• Modify slide
 timings

In a slide show, you can determine how each slide advances in and out of view and how long each slide appears on the screen. **Slide transitions** are the special visual and audio effects you apply to a slide that determine how each slide moves on and off the screen during the slide show. **Slide timing** refers to the amount of time a slide is visible on the screen. Typically, you set slide timings only if you want the presentation to automatically progress through the slides during a slide show. Setting the correct slide timing, in this case, is important because it determines how much time your audience has to view each slide. Each slide can have a different slide transition and different slide timing. **CASE** *You decide to set slide transitions and 8-second slide timings for all the slides.*

STEPS

1. **Click the** Slide 1 thumbnail **in the Thumbnails pane, then click the** TRANSITIONS tab **on the Ribbon**

 Transitions are organized by type into three groups.

2. **Click the** More button ⬇ **in the Transition to This Slide group, then click** Blinds **in the Exciting section**

 The new slide transition plays on the slide, and a transition icon ⭐ appears next to the slide thumbnail in the Thumbnails pane as shown in FIGURE D-7. You can customize the slide transition by changing its direction and speed.

3. **Click the** Effect Options button **in the Transition to This Slide group, click** Horizontal, **click the** Duration up arrow **in the Timing group until** 2.00 **appears, then click the** Preview button **in the Preview group**

 The Blinds slide transition now plays horizontal on the slide for 2.00 seconds. You can apply this transition with the custom settings to all of the slides in the presentation.

4. **Click the** Apply To All button **in the Timing group, then click the** Slide Sorter button ⊞ **on the status bar**

 All of the slides now have the customized Blinds transition applied to them as identified by the transition icons located below each slide. You also have the ability to determine how slides progress during a slide show—either manually by mouse click or automatically by slide timing.

5. **Click the** On Mouse Click check box **under Advance Slide in the Timing group to clear the check mark**

 When this option is selected, you have to click to manually advance slides during a slide show. Now, with this option disabled, you can set the slides to advance automatically after a specified amount of time.

6. **Click the** After up arrow **in the Timing group, until** 00:08.00 **appears in the text box, then click the** Apply To All button

 The timing between slides is 8 seconds as indicated by the time under each slide in Slide Sorter view. See FIGURE D-8. When you run the slide show, each slide will remain on the screen for 8 seconds. You can override a slide's timing and speed up the slide show by clicking the left mouse button.

7. **Click the** Slide Show button 🖳 **on the status bar**

 The slide show advances automatically. A new slide appears every 8 seconds using the Blinds transition.

8. **When you see the black slide, press [Spacebar], then save your changes**

 The slide show ends and returns to Slide Sorter view with Slide 1 selected.

FIGURE D-7: Applied slide transition

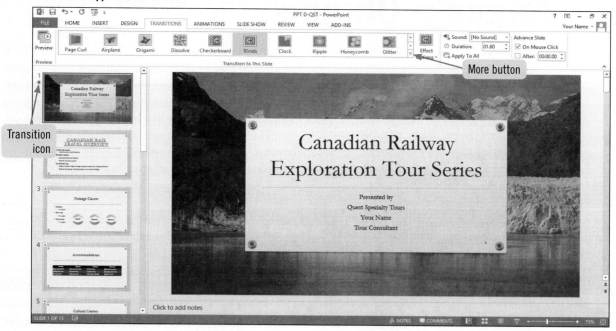

Transition icon

More button

FIGURE D-8: Slide sorter view showing applied transition and timing

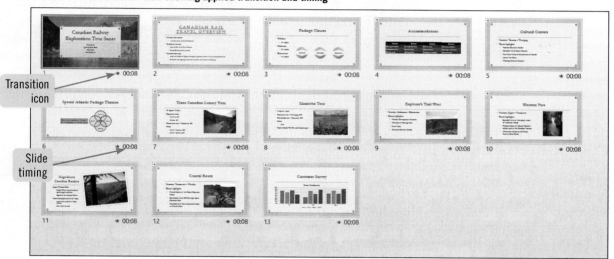

Transition icon

Slide timing

Rehearsing slide show timings

You can set different slide timings for each slide; for example, the title slide can appear for 20 seconds and the second slide for 1 minute. To set timings click the Rehearse Timings button in the Set Up group on the SLIDE SHOW tab. Slide Show view opens and the Recording toolbar shown in **FIGURE D-9** opens. It contains buttons to pause between slides and to advance to the next slide. After opening the Recording toolbar, you can practice giving your presentation by manually advancing each slide in the presentation. When you are finished, PowerPoint displays the total recorded time for the presentation and you have the option to save the recorded timings. The next time you run the slide show, you can use the timings you rehearsed.

FIGURE D-9: Recording toolbar

Click to move to the next slide

Click to pause

Time elapsed while viewing current slide

Total elapsed time for all slides

Click to reset the clock to zero for the current slide

Animate Objects

Learning Outcomes
• Animate objects
• Modify animation effects

Animations let you control how objects and text appear and move on the screen during a slide show and allow you to manage the flow of information and emphasize specific facts. You can animate text, pictures, sounds, hyperlinks, SmartArt diagrams, charts, and individual chart elements. For example, you can apply a Fade animation to bulleted text so each paragraph enters the slide separately from the others. Animations are organized into four categories, Entrance, Emphasis, Exit, and Motion Paths. The Entrance and Exit animations cause an object to enter or exit the slide with an effect. An Emphasis animation causes an object visible on the slide to have an effect and a Motion Path animation causes an object to move on a specified path on the slide. **CASE** ▸ *You animate the text and graphics of several slides in the presentation.*

STEPS

1. **Double-click the Slide 3 thumbnail to return to Normal view, click the ANIMATIONS tab on the Ribbon, then click the circle shapes object**
 Text as well as other objects, like a picture, can be animated during a slide show.

 > **QUICK TIP**
 > There are additional animation options for each animation category located at the bottom of the animations gallery.

2. **Click the More button ⤓ in the Animation group, then click Spin in the Emphasis section**
 Animations can be serious and business-like, or humorous, so be sure to choose appropriate effects for your presentation. A small numeral 1, called an animation tag ⬚, appears at the top corner of the object. **Animation tags** identify the order in which objects are animated during slide show.

3. **Click the Effect Options button in the Animation group, click Two Spins, then click the Duration up arrow in the Timing group until 03.00 appears**
 Effect options are different for every animation, and some animations don't have effect options. Changing the animation timing increases the duration of the animation and gives it a more dramatic effect. Compare your screen to **FIGURE D-10**.

4. **Click the Slide Show button 🖵 on the status bar until you see Slide 4, then press [Esc]**
 After the slide transition finishes, the shapes object spins twice for a total of three seconds.

5. **Click the Slide 2 thumbnail in the Thumbnails pane, click the bulleted list text object, then click Float In in the Animation group**
 The text object is animated with the Float In animation. Each line of text has an animation tag with each paragraph displaying a different number. Accordingly, each paragraph is animated separately.

6. **Click the Effect Options button in the Animation group, click All at Once, click the Duration up arrow in the Timing group until 02.50 appears, then click the Preview button in the Preview group**
 Notice the animation tags for each line of text in the text object now have the same numeral (1), indicating that each line of text animates at the same time.

 > **QUICK TIP**
 > If you want to individually animate the parts of a grouped object, then you must ungroup the objects before you animate them.

7. **Click Canadian in the title text object, click ⤓ in the Animation group, scroll down, then click Loops in the Motion Paths section**
 A motion path object appears over the shapes object and identifies the direction and shape, or path, of the animation. When needed, you can move, resize, and change the direction of the motion path. Notice the numeral 2 animation tag next to the title text object indicating it is animated *after* the bulleted list text object. Compare your screen to **FIGURE D-11**.

8. **Click the Move Earlier button in the Timing group, click the SLIDE SHOW tab on the Ribbon, then click the From Beginning button in the Start Slide Show group**
 The slide show begins from Slide 1. The animations make the presentation more interesting to view.

9. **When you see the black slide, press [Enter], then save your changes**

FIGURE D-10: Animation applied to shape object

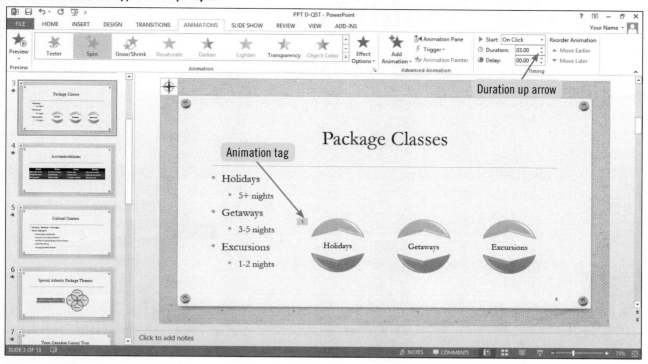

FIGURE D-11: Motion path applied to text object

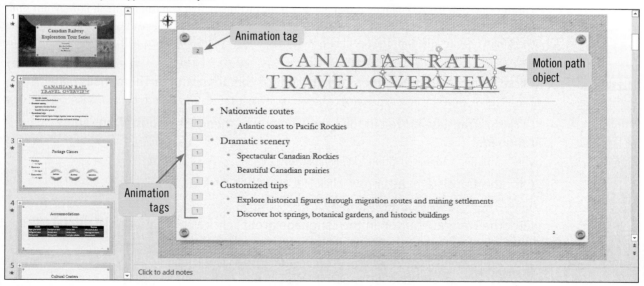

Attaching a sound to an animation

Text or objects that have animation applied can be customized further by attaching a sound for extra emphasis. First, select the animated object, then on the ANIMATIONS tab click the Animation Pane button in the Advanced Animation group. In the Animation Pane, click the animation you want to apply the sound to, click the Animation list arrow, then click Effect Options to open the animation effect's dialog box. In the Enhancements section, click the Sound list arrow, then choose a sound. Click OK when you are finished. Now, when you run the slide show, the sound you applied will play with the animation.

Finishing a Presentation

Use Proofing and Language Tools

Learning Outcomes
• Spell check a presentation
• Translate slide text

As your work on the presentation file nears completion, you need to review and proofread your slides thoroughly for errors. You can use the Spell Checker feature in PowerPoint to check for and correct spelling errors. This feature compares the spelling of all the words in your presentation against the words contained in the dictionary. You still must proofread your presentation for punctuation, grammar, and word-usage errors because the Spell Checker recognizes only misspelled and unknown words, not misused words. For example, the spell checker would not identify the word "last" as an error, even if you had intended to type the word "cast." PowerPoint also includes language tools that translate words or phrases from your default language into another language using the Microsoft Translator. **CASE** *You're finished working on the presentation for now, so it's a good time to check spelling. You then experiment with language translation because the final presentation will be translated into French.*

STEPS

1. **Click the REVIEW tab on the Ribbon, then click the Spelling button in the Proofing group**

 PowerPoint begins to check the spelling in your presentation. When PowerPoint finds a misspelled word or a word that is not in its dictionary, the Spelling pane opens, as shown in **FIGURE D-12**. In this case, PowerPoint identifies the misspelled word in the table on Slide 4 and suggests you replace it with the correctly spelled word "Business."

2. **Click Change in the Spelling pane**

 PowerPoint changes the misspelled word and then continues to check the rest of the presentation for errors. This presentation has several names that are not in the dictionary that you can ignore. If PowerPoint finds any other words it does not recognize, either change or ignore them. When the Spell Checker finishes checking your presentation, the Spelling pane closes, and an alert box opens with a message stating the spelling check is complete.

3. **Click OK in the Alert box, then click the Slide 1 thumbnail in the Thumbnails pane**

 The alert box closes. Now you need to see how the language translation feature works.

4. **Click the Translate button in the Language group, then click Choose Translation Language**

 The Translation Language Options dialog box opens.

5. **Click the Translate to list arrow, click Hebrew, then click OK**

 The Translation Language Options dialog box closes.

6. **Click the Translate button in the Language group, click Mini Translator [Hebrew], click anywhere in the subtitle text object, then select all of the text**

 The Microsoft Translator begins to analyze the selected text, and a semitransparent Microsoft Translator box appears below the text. The Mini toolbar may also appear.

7. **Move the pointer over the Microsoft Translator box**

 A Hebrew translation of the text appears as shown in **FIGURE D-13**. The translation language setting remains in effect until you reset it.

8. **Click the Translate button in the Language group, click Choose Translation Language, click the Translate to list arrow, click Arabic, click OK, click the Translate button again, then click Mini Translator [Arabic]**

 The Mini Translator is turned off, and the translation language is restored to the default setting.

FIGURE D-12: Spelling pane

FIGURE D-13: Translated text in the Microsoft Translator box

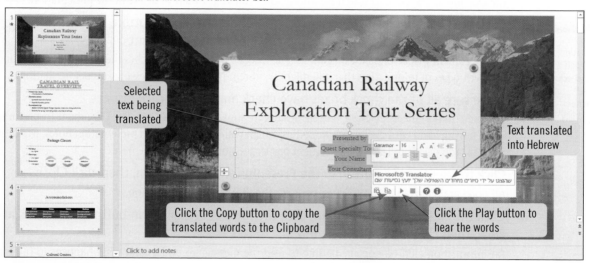

Checking spelling as you type

By default, PowerPoint checks your spelling as you type. If you type a word that is not in the dictionary, a wavy red line appears under it. To correct an error, right-click the misspelled word, then review the suggestions, which appear in the shortcut menu. You can select a suggestion, add the word you typed to your custom dictionary, or ignore it. To turn off automatic spell checking, click the FILE tab, then click Options to open the PowerPoint Options dialog box. Click Proofing in the left column, then click the Check spelling as you type check box to deselect it. To temporarily hide the wavy red lines, click the Hide spelling errors check box to select it. Contextual spelling in PowerPoint identifies common grammatically misused words, for example, if you type the word "their" and the correct word is "there," PowerPoint will identify the mistake and place a wavy red line under the word. To turn contextual spelling on or off, click Proofing in the PowerPoint Options dialog box, then click the Check grammar with spelling check box.

Inspect a Presentation

Learning Outcomes
- Modify document properties
- Inspect and remove unwanted data

Reviewing your presentation can be an important step. You should not only find and fix errors, but also locate and delete confidential company or personal information and document properties you do not want to share with others. If you share presentations with others, especially over the Internet, it is a good idea to inspect the presentation file using the Document Inspector. The **Document Inspector** looks for hidden data and personal information that is stored in the file itself or in the document properties. Document properties, also known as **metadata**, includes specific data about the presentation, such as the author's name, subject matter, title, who saved the file last, and when the file was created. Other types of information the Document Inspector can locate and remove include presentation notes, comments, ink annotations, invisible on-slide content, off-slide content, and custom XML data. **CASE** ▶ *You decide to view and add some document properties, inspect your presentation file, and learn about the Mark as Final command.*

STEPS

1. **Click the FILE tab on the Ribbon, click the Properties button, then click Show Document Panel**

 The Document Properties panel opens showing the file location and the title of the presentation. Now enter some descriptive data for this presentation file.

2. **Enter the data shown in FIGURE D-14, then click the Document Properties panel Close button** ☒

 This data provides detailed information about the presentation file that you can use to identify and organize your file. You can also use this information as search criteria to locate the file at a later time. You now use the Document Inspector to search for information you might want to delete in the presentation.

3. **Click the FILE tab on the Ribbon, click the Check for Issues button, click Inspect Document, then click Yes to save the changes to the document**

 The Document Inspector dialog box opens. The Document Inspector searches the presentation file for seven different types of information that you might want removed from the presentation before sharing it.

4. **Make sure all of the check boxes have check marks, then click Inspect**

 The presentation file is reviewed, and the results are shown in FIGURE D-15. The Document Inspector found items having to do with document properties, which you just entered, and presentation notes, which are on Slide 13. You decide to leave the document properties alone but delete the notes.

5. **Click the Remove All button in the Presentation Notes section, then click Close**

 All notes are removed from the Notes pane for the slides in the presentation.

6. **Click the FILE tab on the Ribbon, click the Protect Presentation button, click Mark as Final, then click OK in the alert box**

 An information alert box opens. Be sure to read the message to understand what happens to the file and how to recognize a marked-as-final presentation. You decide to complete this procedure.

7. **Click OK, click the HOME tab on the Ribbon, then click anywhere in the title text object**

 When you select the title text object, the Ribbon closes automatically and an information alert box at the top of the window notes that the presentation is marked as final, making it a read-only file. Compare your screen to FIGURE D-16. A **read-only** file is one that can't be edited or modified in any way. Anyone who has received a read-only presentation can only edit the presentation by changing its marked-as-final status. You still want to work on the presentation, so you remove the marked-as-final status.

8. **Click the Edit Anyway button in the information alert box, then save your changes**

 The Ribbon and all commands are active again, and the file can now be modified.

FIGURE D-14: Document Properties Panel

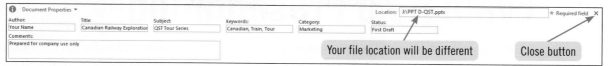

FIGURE D-15: Document Inspector dialog box

FIGURE D-16: Marked As Final presentation

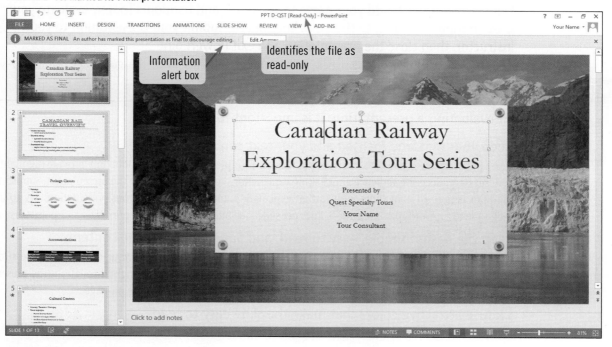

Digitally sign a presentation

What is a digital signature, and why would you want to use one in PowerPoint? A **digital signature** is similar to a handwritten signature in that it authenticates your document; however, a digital signature, unlike a handwritten signature, is created using computer cryptography and is not visible within the presentation itself. There are three primary reasons you would add a digital signature

to a presentation: one, to authenticate the signer of the document; two, to ensure that the content of the presentation has not been changed since it was signed; and three, to assure the reader of the origin of the signed document. To add a digital signature, click the FILE tab on the Ribbon, click the Protect Presentation button, click Add a Digital Signature, then follow the dialog boxes.

Evaluate a Presentation

Learning Outcomes
• Navigate Reading view
• Add section to Slides tab

A well-designed and organized presentation requires thought and preparation. An effective presentation is focused and visually appealing—easy for the speaker to present, and simple for the audience to understand. Visual elements can strongly influence the audience's attention and can influence the success of your presentation. **CASE** ▸ *You know your boss and other colleagues will critique your presentation, so you take the time to evaluate your presentation's organization and effectiveness.*

STEPS

1. Click the Reading View button 📖 on the status bar, then press [Spacebar] when the slide show finishes

QUICK TIP
You can also move, delete, collapse, and expand a section in the Thumbnails tab or in Slide Sorter view.

2. Click the Slide 5 thumbnail in the Thumbnails pane, click the Section button in the Slides group, then click Add Section

 The presentation is divided into two sections, which appear in the Thumbnails pane. The section you created is the Untitled Section, and the section for all the slides before the new section is the Default Section. Sections help you organize your slides into logical groups.

3. Right-click Untitled Section in the Thumbnails pane, click Rename Section, type Tour Packages, then click Rename

4. Click the Slide Sorter view button ⊞ on the status bar, save your work, then compare your screen to FIGURE D-17

5. Double-click Slide 1, add your name to the notes and handouts footer, evaluate your presentation according to the guidelines below, submit your presentation to your instructor, then close the presentation and exit PowerPoint

 FIGURE D-18 shows a poorly designed slide. Contrast this slide with the guidelines below and your presentation.

DETAILS

When evaluating a presentation, it is important to:

• **Keep your message focused and your text concise**

 Don't put every word you plan to say on your slides. Your presentation text should only provide highlights of your message. Keep the audience anticipating explanations to the key points in the presentation. Supplement the information on your slides with further explanation and details during your presentation. Try to limit each slide to six words per line and six lines per slide. Use bulleted lists to help prioritize your points visually.

• **Keep the design simple, easy to read, and appropriate for the content**

 A design theme makes the presentation visually consistent. If you design your own layout, use similar design elements and limit the number of design elements, using them sparingly throughout the presentation; otherwise, your audience may get overwhelmed and not understand the message.

• **Choose attractive colors that make the slide easy to read**

 Use contrasting complementary colors for slide background and text to make the text readable.

• **Choose fonts and styles that are easy to read and emphasize important text**

 As a general rule, use no more than two fonts in a presentation and vary the font size. If you are giving an on-screen presentation, use nothing smaller than 24 points. Use bold and italic attributes selectively.

• **Use visuals to help communicate the message of your presentation**

 Commonly used visuals include clip art, photographs, charts, worksheets, tables, and videos. Whenever possible, replace text with a visual, but be careful not to overcrowd your slides. White space on your slides enhances the presentation.

FIGURE D-17: Final presentation in Slide Sorter view

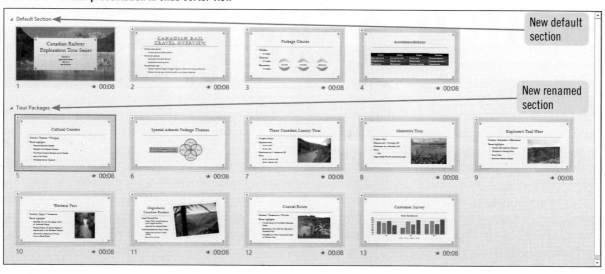

FIGURE D-18: A poorly designed slide

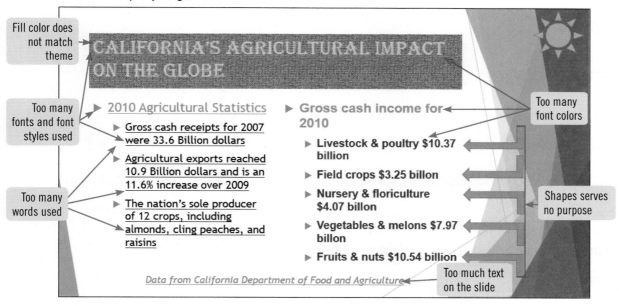

Setting permissions

In PowerPoint, you can set specific access permissions for people who review or edit your work so you have better control over your content. For example, you may want to give a user permission to edit or change your presentation but not allow them to print it. You can also restrict a user by permitting them to view the presentation without the ability to edit or print the presentation, or you can give the user full access or control of the presentation. To use this feature, you first must have access to an information rights management service from Microsoft or another rights management company. Then, to set user access permissions, click the FILE tab, click the Protect Presentation button, point to Restrict Access, then click an appropriate option.

Practice

Concepts Review

Label each element of the PowerPoint window shown in FIGURE D-19.

FIGURE D-19

Match each term with the statement that best describes it.

10. Transitions
11. Exception
12. Background graphic
13. Annotate
14. Masters
15. Animations

a. An object placed on the slide master
b. Slides that store theme and placeholder information
c. Visual effects that determine how objects appears on the slide
d. Visual effects that determine how a slide moves in and out of view during a slide show
e. A change you make to a slide that does not follow the theme
f. To draw on a slide during a slide show

Select the best answer from the list of choices.

16. The Document Inspector looks for _____ and personal information that is stored in the presentation file.
 a. Themes
 b. Hidden data
 c. Animation tags
 d. Video settings

17. Apply a(n) _____ to your presentation to quickly modify the applied theme.
 a. Variant
 b. Exception
 c. Theme
 d. Animation

18. Which PowerPoint file *can't* be edited or modified?
 a. Inspected file
 b. File saved in another file format
 c. Read-only file
 d. Template file

19. Use _____ view to show your presentation through two monitors.
 a. Reading
 b. Presenter
 c. Slide Show
 d. Projector

20. Set slide _____ to make your presentation automatically progress through the slides during a slide show.
 a. Animations
 b. Autoplay effects
 c. Variants
 d. Timings

21. According to the book, which guidelines should you follow when you create a presentation?
 a. Slides should include most of the information you wish to present.
 b. Use many different design elements to keep your audience from getting bored.
 c. Slides should outline the message in a concise way.
 d. Use text rather than visuals as often as possible.

22. Which of the following statements about masters is *not* true?
 a. Changes made to the slide master are reflected in the handout and notes masters as well.
 b. Masters store information.
 c. Each slide layout in the presentation has a corresponding slide layout in Slide Master view.
 d. The design theme is placed on the slide master.

Skills Review

1. **Modify masters.**
 a. Open the presentation PPT D-4.pptx from the location where you store your Data Files, then save the presentation as **PPT D-DataSource**.
 b. Open Slide Master view using the VIEW tab, then click the Integral Slide Master thumbnail.
 c. Insert the picture PPT D-5.jpg, then resize the picture so it is 1.0" wide.
 d. Drag the picture to the upper-right corner of the slide within the design frame of the slide, then deselect the picture.
 e. Preserve the Integral master, switch to Normal view, then save your changes.

2. **Customize the background and theme.**
 a. Click the DESIGN tab, click the More button in the Variants group, then click the first variant in the second row.
 b. Go to Slide 4, then open the Format Background pane.
 c. Click the Color button, then click Tan, Accent 2 in the top row.
 d. Set the Transparency to 50%, close the Format Background pane then save your changes.

Skills Review (continued)

3. Use slide show commands.

 a. Open Slide Show view, then go to Slide 1 using the See all slides button on the Slide Show toolbar.

 b. Use the Pen annotation tool to circle the slide title.

 c. Go to Slide 2, then use the Highlighter to highlight four points in the bulleted text on the slide.

 d. Erase two highlight annotations on the bulleted text, then press [Esc].

 e. Open Presenter view, then stop the timer.

 f. Advance the slides to Slide 5, then click the Zoom into the slide button (now called the Zoom out button) on the Slide Show toolbar, then click in the center of the graph.

 g. Click the Zoom into the slide button, then return to Slide 1.

 h. Hide Presenter view, advance through the slide show, don't save any ink annotations, then save your work.

4. Set slide transitions and timings.

 a. Go to Slide Sorter view, click the Slide 1 thumbnail, then apply the Ripple transition to the slide.

 b. Change the effect option to From Bottom-Right, change the duration speed to 2.50, then apply to all the slides.

 c. Change the slide timing to 5 seconds, then apply to all of the slides.

 d. Switch to Normal view, view the slide show, then save your work.

5. Animate objects.

 a. Go to Slide 3, click the ANIMATIONS tab, then select the double-headed arrow on the slide.

 b. Apply the Split effect to the object, click the Pricing shape, apply the Shape effect, then preview the animations.

 c. Click the COG shape, apply the Shape effect, then preview the animations.

 d. Select the Pricing shape and the COG shape, click the Effect Options button, then click Box.

 e. Click the double-headed arrow, click the Effect Options button, click Horizontal Out, then preview the animations.

6. Use proofing and language tools.

 a. Check the spelling of the document, and change any misspelled words. Ignore any words that are correctly spelled but that the spell checker doesn't recognize. There is one misspelled word in the presentation.

 b. Go to Slide 3, then set the Mini Translator language to Ukrainian.

 c. View the Ukrainian translation of text on Slide 3.

 d. Choose one other language (or as many as you want), translate words or phrases on the slide, reset the default language to Arabic, turn off the Mini Translator, then save your changes.

7. Inspect a presentation.

 a. Open the Document Properties pane, type your name in the Author text box, type **Internet Product** in the Subject text box, then type **Review** in the Status text box.

 b. Close the Document Properties pane, then open the Document Inspector dialog box.

 c. Make sure the Off-Slide Content check box is selected, then inspect the presentation.

 d. Delete the off-slide content, then close the dialog box. Save your changes.

8. Evaluate a presentation.

 a. Go to Slide 4, add a section, then rename it **Pricing and Sales**.

 b. Select the Default section at the top of the Thumbnails pane, then rename it **Intro**.

 c. Go to Slide 1, then run a slide show.

 d. Evaluate the presentation using the points described in the lesson as criteria, then submit a written evaluation to your instructor.

 e. Add the slide number and your name to the slide footer on all the slides, then save your changes.

Skills Review (continued)

f. Switch to Slide Sorter view, then compare your presentation to FIGURE D-20.

g. Submit your presentation to your instructor, then close the presentation.

FIGURE D-20

Independent Challenge 1

You are a travel consultant for Pacific Tour Enterprises, located in Houston, Texas. You have been working on a sales presentation that is going to be accessed by customers on the company Web site. You need to finish up what you have been working on by adding transitions, timings, and animation effects to the sales presentation.

a. Open the file PPT D-6.pptx from the location where you store your Data Files, and save the presentation as **PPT D-Pacific**.

b. Add the slide number and your name as the footer on all slides, except the title slide.

c. Open Slide Master View, click the Facet Slide Master thumbnail, insert the picture PPT D-7.jpg, then resize the picture so it is 1.0" wide.

d. Right-click a blank area of the master slide, point to Grid and Guides, click Add Vertical Guide, then make sure the guide is in the center of the master slide.

e. Move the picture to the top of the slide centered over the vertical guide, remove the vertical guide, then close Slide Master view.

f. Apply the Wipe animation to the title text on each slide.

g. Apply the Underline animation to the bulleted text objects on each slide.

h. Apply the Shape animation to the table on Slide 5, then change the effect option to Box.

i. Apply the Comb slide transition, apply a 7-second slide timing, then apply to all of the slides.

j. Check the spelling of the presentation, then save your changes.

k. View the slide show, and evaluate your presentation. Make changes if necessary.

l. Submit your presentation to your instructor, close the presentation, then exit PowerPoint.

Independent Challenge 2

You are a development engineer at Advanced Performance Sports, Inc., an international sports product design company located in Phoenix, Arizona. Advanced Performance designs and manufactures items such as bike helmets, bike racks, and kayak paddles, and markets these items primarily to countries in North America and Western Europe. You need to finish the work on a quarterly presentation that outlines the progress of the company's newest technologies by adding animations, customizing the background, and using the Document Inspector.

a. Open the file PPT D-8.pptx from the location where you store your Data Files, and save the presentation as **PPT D-Sports**.

Independent Challenge 2 (continued)

b. Apply an appropriate design theme, then apply a gradient fill slide background to the title slide using the Format Background pane.

c. Apply the Glitter slide transition to all slides, then animate the following objects: the bulleted text on Slide 2 and the table on Slide 4. View the slide show to evaluate the effects you added and make adjustments as necessary.

d. Use the Microsoft Translator to translate the bulleted text on Slide 2 using two different languages.

e. Run the Document Inspector with all options selected, identify what items the Document Inspector finds, close the Document Inspector dialog box, then review the slides to find the items.

f. Add a slide at the end of the presentation that identifies the items the Document Inspector found.

g. Run the Document Inspector again, and remove all items except the document properties.

h. View the slide show, and make annotations to the slides. Save the annotations at the end of the slide show.

i. Add your name as a footer to all slides, run the spell checker, save your work, then run the slide show to evaluate your presentation.

j. Submit your presentation to your instructor, then close the presentation and exit PowerPoint.

Independent Challenge 3

You work for Thomas Lincoln & Associates, a full-service investment and pension firm. Your manager wants you to create a presentation on small business pension plan options. You have completed adding the information to the presentation, now you need to add a design theme, format information to highlight certain facts, add animation effects, and add slide timings.

a. Open the file PPT D-9.pptx from the location where you store your Data Files, and save the presentation as **PPT D-Thomas**.

b. Apply an appropriate design theme, then apply a theme variant.

c. Apply animation effects to the following objects: the shapes on Slide 3 and the bulleted text on Slide 5. View the slide show to evaluate the effects you added, and make adjustments as necessary.

d. Convert the text on Slide 4 to a Radial Cycle SmartArt graphic (found in the Cycle category).

e. Apply the Polished Effect style to the SmartArt graphic.

f. Go to Slide 3, align the Sector and Quality arrow shapes to their bottoms, then align the Allocation and Maturity arrow shapes to their right edges.

g. On Slides 6 and 7 change the table style format to Light Style2 - Accent 4, and adjust the position of the tables on the slides, if necessary.

h. Apply a 10-second timing to Slides 3–7 and a 5-second timing to Slides 1 and 2.

i. Add a section between Slide 5 and Slide 6, then rename the section **Plans**.

j. Rename the Default section in the Slides tab to **Intro**.

k. Add your name as a footer to the slides, run the Spell Checker, save your work, then run the slide show to evaluate your presentation. An example of a finished presentation is shown in FIGURE D-21.

l. Submit your presentation to your instructor, then close the presentation and exit PowerPoint.

FIGURE D-21

Independent Challenge 4: Explore

You work for the operations supervisor at the Southern Alabama State University student union. Create a presentation that you can eventually publish to the college Web site that describes all of the services offered at the student union. (*Note: To complete this Independent Challenge, you may need to be connected to the Internet.*)

a. Plan and create the slide presentation that describes the services and events offered at the student union. To help create content, use the student union at your school or use the Internet to locate information on college student unions. The presentation should contain at least six slides.

b. Use an appropriate design theme.

c. Add at least one photograph to the presentation, then style and customize one photo.

d. Save the presentation as **PPT D-SASU** to the location where you store your Data Files. View the slide show, and evaluate the contents of your presentation. Make any necessary adjustments.

e. Add slide transitions and animation effects to the presentation. View the slide show again to evaluate the effects you added.

f. To help you to complete this step, use the information on rehearsing slide timings found in the Set Slide Transition and Timings lesson in this unit. Click the Slide Show tab, click the Rehearse Timings button in the Set Up group, then click the Next button on the Recording toolbar to advance each slide in the presentation.

g. Click Yes to save slides timings at the end of the slide show.

h. Go to Slide 2, translate the bottom text box into Korean, then click the Copy button on the Microsoft Translator box.

i. Insert a new text box on Slide 2, paste the Korean text into the text box, then move the Korean text box below the translated English text box.

j. Change the language in the Microsoft translator back to Arabic, then turn off the Microsoft Translator.

k. Add the slide number and your name as a footer to the slides, check the spelling, inspect, then save the presentation.

l. Submit your presentation to your instructor, then exit PowerPoint. An example of a finished presentation is shown in FIGURE D-22.

FIGURE D-22

Visual Workshop

Create a one-slide presentation that looks like FIGURE D-23, which shows a slide with a specific slide layout, slide background, theme, and theme variant. Add your name as footer text to the slide, save the presentation as **PPT D-Glacier** to the location where you store your Data Files, then submit your presentation to your instructor.

FIGURE D-23

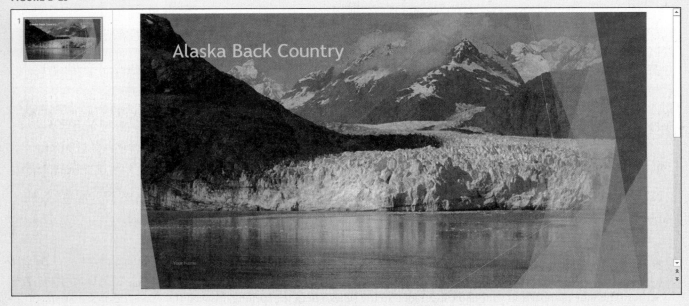

Getting Started with Excel 2013

CASE You have been hired as an assistant at Quest Specialty Travel (QST), a company offering tours that immerse travelers in regional culture. You report to Grace Wong, the vice president of finance. As Grace's assistant, you create worksheets to analyze data from various divisions of the company, so you can help her make sound decisions on company expansion and investments.

Unit Objectives

After completing this unit, you will be able to:

- Understand spreadsheet software
- Identify Excel 2013 window components
- Understand formulas
- Enter labels and values and use the AutoSum button
- Edit cell entries
- Enter and edit a simple formula
- Switch worksheet views
- Choose print options

Files You Will Need

EX A-1.xlsx
EX A-2.xlsx
EX A-3.xlsx
EX A-4.xlsx
EX A-5.xlsx

Understand Spreadsheet Software

Learning Outcomes
• Describe the uses of Excel
• Define key spreadsheet terms

Microsoft Excel is the electronic spreadsheet program within the Microsoft Office suite. An **electronic spreadsheet** is an application you use to perform numeric calculations and to analyze and present numeric data. One advantage of a spreadsheet program over pencil and paper is that your calculations are updated automatically, so you can change entries without having to manually recalculate. TABLE A-1 shows some of the common business tasks people accomplish using Excel. In Excel, the electronic spreadsheet you work in is called a **worksheet**, and it is contained in a file called a **workbook**, which has the file extension .xlsx. **CASE** ▸ *At Quest Specialty Travel, you use Excel extensively to track finances and manage corporate data.*

DETAILS

When you use Excel, you have the ability to:

- **Enter data quickly and accurately**

 With Excel, you can enter information faster and more accurately than with pencil and paper. FIGURE A-1 shows a payroll worksheet created using pencil and paper. FIGURE A-2 shows the same worksheet created using Excel. Equations were added to calculate the hours and pay. You can use Excel to recreate this information for each week by copying the worksheet's structure and the information that doesn't change from week to week, then entering unique data and formulas for each week.

- **Recalculate data easily**

 Fixing typing errors or updating data is easy in Excel. In the payroll example, if you receive updated hours for an employee, you just enter the new hours and Excel recalculates the pay.

- **Perform what-if analysis**

 The ability to change data and quickly view the recalculated results gives you the power to make informed business decisions. For instance, if you're considering raising the hourly rate for an entry-level tour guide from $12.50 to $15.00, you can enter the new value in the worksheet and immediately see the impact on the overall payroll as well as on the individual employee. Any time you use a worksheet to ask the question "What if?" you are performing **what-if analysis**. Excel also includes a Scenario Manager where you can name and save different what-if versions of your worksheet.

- **Change the appearance of information**

 Excel provides powerful features, such as the Quick Analysis tool, for making information visually appealing and easier to understand. Format text and numbers in different fonts, colors, and styles to make it stand out.

- **Create charts**

 Excel makes it easy to create charts based on worksheet information. Charts are updated automatically in Excel whenever data changes. The worksheet in FIGURE A-2 includes a 3-D pie chart.

- **Share information**

 It's easy for everyone at QST to collaborate in Excel using the company intranet, the Internet, or a network storage device. For example, you can complete the weekly payroll that your boss, Grace Wong, started creating. You can also take advantage of collaboration tools such as shared workbooks, so that multiple people can edit a workbook simultaneously.

- **Build on previous work**

 Instead of creating a new worksheet for every project, it's easy to modify an existing Excel worksheet. When you are ready to create next week's payroll, you can open the file for last week's payroll, save it with a new filename, and modify the information as necessary. You can also use predesigned, formatted files called **templates** to create new worksheets quickly. Excel comes with many templates that you can customize.

FIGURE A-1: Traditional paper worksheet

Quest Specialty Travel
Trip Advisor Division Payroll Calculator

Name	Hours	O/T Hrs	Hrly Rate	Reg Pay	O/T Pay	Gross Pay
Brueghel, Pieter	40	4	16.50	660–	132–	792–
Cortona, Livia	35	0	11–	385–	0–	385–
Klimt, Gustave	40	2	13–	520–	52–	572–
Le Pen, Jean-Marie	29	0	15–	435–	0–	435–
Martinez, Juan	37	0	13–	481–	0–	461–
Mioshi, Keiko	39	0	20.50	799.50	0–	799.50
Sherwood, Burton	40	0	16.50	660–	0–	660–
Strano, Riccardo	40	8	16–	640–	256–	896–
Wadsworth, Alicia	40	5	13–	520–	130–	650–
Yamamoto, Johji	38	0	15–	570–	0–	570–

FIGURE A-2: Excel worksheet

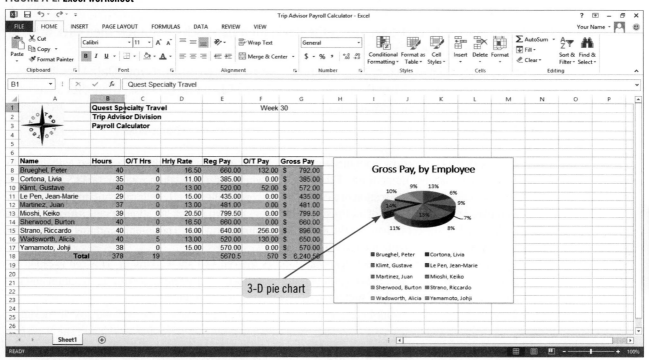

3-D pie chart

TABLE A-1: Business tasks you can accomplish using Excel

you can use spreadsheets to	by
Perform calculations	Adding formulas and functions to worksheet data; for example, adding a list of sales results or calculating a car payment
Represent values graphically	Creating charts based on worksheet data; for example, creating a chart that displays expenses
Generate reports	Creating workbooks that combine information from multiple worksheets, such as summarized sales information from multiple stores
Organize data	Sorting data in ascending or descending order; for example, alphabetizing a list of products or customer names, or prioritizing orders by date
Analyze data	Creating data summaries and short lists using PivotTables or AutoFilters; for example, making a list of the top 10 customers based on spending habits
Create what-if data scenarios	Using variable values to investigate and sample different outcomes, such as changing the interest rate or payment schedule on a loan

© 2014 Cengage Learning

Excel 2013

Identify Excel 2013 Window Components

Learning
Outcomes
• Open and save an
 Excel file
• Identify Excel
 window elements

To start Excel, Microsoft Windows must be running. Similar to starting any program in Office, you can use the Start screen thumbnail on the Windows taskbar, the Start button on your keyboard, or you may have a shortcut on your desktop you prefer to use. If you need additional assistance, ask your instructor or technical support person. **CASE** *You decide to start Excel and familiarize yourself with the worksheet window.*

STEPS

QUICK TIP
For more information on starting a program or opening and saving a file, see the unit "Getting Started with Microsoft Office 2013."

1. **Start Excel, click** Open Other Workbooks **on the navigation bar, click** Computer, **then click** Browse **to open the Open dialog box**

2. **In the Open dialog box, navigate to the location where you store your Data Files, click** EX A-1.xlsx, **click** Open

 The file opens in the Excel window.

3. **Click the** FILE **tab, click** Save As **on the navigation bar, click** Computer, **then click** Browse **to open the Save As dialog box**

TROUBLE
If you don't see the extension .xlsx on the filenames in the Save As dialog box, don't worry; Windows can be set up to display or not to display the file extensions.

4. **In the Save As dialog box, navigate to the location where you store your Data Files if necessary, type** EX A-Trip Advisor Payroll Calculator **in the File name text box, then click** Save

 Using FIGURE A-3 as a guide, identify the following items:

 • The **Name box** displays the active cell address. "A1" appears in the Name box.
 • The **formula bar** allows you to enter or edit data in the worksheet.
 • The **worksheet window** contains a grid of columns and rows. Columns are labeled alphabetically and rows are labeled numerically. The worksheet window can contain a total of 1,048,576 rows and 16,384 columns. The intersection of a column and a row is called a **cell**. Cells can contain text, numbers, formulas, or a combination of all three. Every cell has its own unique location or **cell address**, which is identified by the coordinates of the intersecting column and row. The column and row indicators are shaded to make identifying the cell address easy.
 • The **cell pointer** is a dark rectangle that outlines the cell you are working in. This cell is called the **active cell**. In FIGURE A-3, the cell pointer outlines cell A1, so A1 is the active cell. The column and row headings for the active cell are highlighted, making it easier to locate.
 • **Sheet tabs** below the worksheet grid let you switch from sheet to sheet in a workbook. By default, a workbook file contains one worksheet—but you can have as many as 255, in a workbook. The New sheet button to the right of Sheet 1 allows you to add worksheets to a workbook. **Sheet tab scrolling buttons** let you navigate to additional sheet tabs when available.
 • You can use the **scroll bars** to move around in a worksheet that is too large to fit on the screen at once.
 • The **status bar** is located at the bottom of the Excel window. It provides a brief description of the active command or task in progress. **The mode indicator** in the lower-left corner of the status bar provides additional information about certain tasks.

5. **Click cell** A4

 Cell A4 becomes the active cell. To activate a different cell, you can click the cell or press the arrow keys on your keyboard to move to it.

QUICK TIP
The button that displays in the bottom-right corner of a range is the Quick Analysis tool.

6. **Click cell** B5, **press and hold the mouse button, drag** ⌖ **to cell** B14, **then release the mouse button**

 You selected a group of cells and they are highlighted, as shown in FIGURE A-4. A selection of two or more cells such as B5:B14 is called a **range**; you select a range when you want to perform an action on a group of cells at once, such as moving them or formatting them. When you select a range, the status bar displays the average, count (or number of items selected), and sum of the selected cells as a quick reference.

FIGURE A-3: Open workbook

FIGURE A-4: Selected range

Using SkyDrive and Web Apps

If you have a free Microsoft account, you can save your Excel files to SkyDrive, a free cloud-based service from Microsoft. When you save files to SkyDrive, you can access them on other devices–such as a tablet or smart phone. SkyDrive is available as an app on smart phones, which makes access very easy. You can open files to view them on any device and you can even make edits to them using **Office Web Apps**, which are simplified versions of the apps found in the Office 2013 suite. Because the Web Apps are online, they take up no computer disk space, and you can use them on any Internet-connected device. You can find more information in the "Working in the Cloud" appendix.

Understand Formulas

Learning
Outcomes
• Explain how a
 formula works
• Identify Excel arith-
 metic operators

Excel is a truly powerful program because users at every level of mathematical expertise can make calculations with accuracy. To do so, you use formulas. A **formula** is an equation in a worksheet. You use formulas to make calculations as simple as adding a column of numbers, or as complex as creating profit-and-loss projections for a global corporation. To tap into the power of Excel, you should understand how formulas work. **CASE** *Managers at QST use the Trip Advisor Payroll Calculator workbook to keep track of employee hours prior to submitting them to the Payroll Department. You'll be using this workbook regularly, so you need to understand the formulas it contains and how Excel calculates the results.*

STEPS

1. Click cell E5

The active cell contains a formula, which appears on the formula bar. All Excel formulas begin with the equal sign (=). If you want a cell to show the result of adding 4 plus 2, the formula in the cell would look like this: =4+2. If you want a cell to show the result of multiplying two values in your worksheet, such as the values in cells B5 and D5, the formula would look like this: =B5*D5, as shown in **FIGURE A-5**. While you're entering a formula in a cell, the cell references and arithmetic operators appear on the formula bar. See **TABLE A-2** for a list of commonly used arithmetic operators. When you're finished entering the formula, you can either click the Enter button on the formula bar or press [Enter].

2. Click cell F5

An example of a more complex formula is the calculation of overtime pay. At QST, overtime pay is calculated at twice the regular hourly rate times the number of overtime hours. The formula used to calculate overtime pay for the employee in row 5 is:

O/T Hrs times (2 times Hrly Rate)

In the worksheet cell, you would enter: =C5*(2*D5), as shown in **FIGURE A-6**. The use of parentheses creates groups within the formula and indicates which calculations to complete first—an important consideration in complex formulas. In this formula, first the hourly rate is multiplied by 2, because that calculation is within the parentheses. Next, that value is multiplied by the number of overtime hours. Because overtime is calculated at twice the hourly rate, managers are aware that they need to closely watch this expense.

DETAILS

In creating calculations in Excel, it is important to:

• **Know where the formulas should be**

An Excel formula is created in the cell where the formula's results should appear. This means that the formula calculating Gross Pay for the employee in row 5 will be entered in cell G5.

• **Know exactly what cells and arithmetic operations are needed**

Don't guess; make sure you know exactly what cells are involved before creating a formula.

• **Create formulas with care**

Make sure you know exactly what you want a formula to accomplish before it is created. An inaccurate formula may have far-reaching effects if the formula or its results are referenced by other formulas, as shown in the payroll example in **FIGURE A-6**.

• **Use cell references rather than values**

The beauty of Excel is that whenever you change a value in a cell, any formula containing a reference to that cell is automatically updated. For this reason, it's important that you use cell references in formulas, rather than actual values, whenever possible.

• **Determine what calculations will be needed**

Sometimes it's difficult to predict what data will be needed within a worksheet, but you should try to anticipate what statistical information may be required. For example, if there are columns of numbers, chances are good that both column and row totals should be present.

FIGURE A-5: Viewing a formula

FIGURE A-6: Formula with multiple operators

TABLE A-2: Excel arithmetic operators

operator	purpose	example
+	Addition	=A5+A7
-	Subtraction or negation	=A5-10
*	Multiplication	=A5*A7
/	Division	=A5/A7
%	Percent	=35%
^ (caret)	Exponent	=6^2 (same as 6^2)

Enter Labels and Values and Use the AutoSum Button

To enter content in a cell, you can type in the formula bar or directly in the cell itself. When entering content in a worksheet, you should start by entering all the labels first. **Labels** are entries that contain text and numerical information not used in calculations, such as "2012 Sales" or "Travel Expenses". Labels help you identify data in worksheet rows and columns, making your worksheet easier to understand. **Values** are numbers, formulas, and functions that can be used in calculations. To enter a calculation, you type an equal sign (=) plus the formula for the calculation; some examples of an Excel calculation are "=2+2" and "=C5+C6". Functions are Excel's built-in formulas; you learn more about them in the next unit. **CASE** *You want to enter some information in the Trip Advisor Payroll Calculator workbook, and use a very simple function to total a range of cells.*

STEPS

1. **Click cell A15, then click in the formula bar**

 Notice that the **mode indicator** on the status bar now reads "Edit," indicating you are in Edit mode. You are in Edit mode any time you are entering or changing the contents of a cell.

2. **Type Totals, then click the Enter button ✓ on the formula bar**

 Clicking the Enter button accepts the entry. The new text is left-aligned in the cell. Labels are left-aligned by default, and values are right-aligned by default. Excel recognizes an entry as a value if it is a number or it begins with one of these symbols: +, -, =, @, #, or $. When a cell contains both text and numbers, Excel recognizes it as a label.

3. **Click cell B15**

 You want this cell to total the hours worked by all the trip advisors. You might think you need to create a formula that looks like this: =B5+B6+B7+B8+B9+B10+B11+B12+B13+B14. However, there's an easier way to achieve this result.

4. **Click the AutoSum button Σ in the Editing group on the HOME tab on the Ribbon**

 The SUM function is inserted in the cell, and a suggested range appears in parentheses, as shown in **FIGURE A-7**. A **function** is a built-in formula; it includes the **arguments** (the information necessary to calculate an answer) as well as cell references and other unique information. Clicking the AutoSum button sums the adjacent range (that is, the cells next to the active cell) above or to the left, although you can adjust the range if necessary by selecting a different range before accepting the cell entry. Using the SUM function is quicker than entering a formula, and using the range B5:B14 is more efficient than entering individual cell references.

5. **Click ✓ on the formula bar**

 Excel calculates the total contained in cells B5:B14 and displays the result, 378, in cell B15. The cell actually contains the formula =SUM(B5:B14), and the result is displayed.

6. **Click cell C13, type 6, then press [Enter]**

 The number 6 replaces the cell's contents, the cell pointer moves to cell C14, and the value in cell F13 changes.

7. **Click cell C18, type Average Gross Pay, then press [Enter]**

 The new label is entered in cell C18. The contents appear to spill into the empty cells to the right.

8. **Click cell B15, position the pointer on the lower-right corner of the cell (the fill handle) so that the pointer changes to ➕, drag the ➕ to cell G15, then release the mouse button**

 Dragging the fill handle across a range of cells copies the contents of the first cell into the other cells in the range. In the range B15:G15, each filled cell now contains a function that sums the range of cells above, as shown in **FIGURE A-8**.

9. **Save your work**

FIGURE A-7: Creating a formula using the AutoSum button

FIGURE A-8: Results of copied SUM functions

Navigating a worksheet

With over a million cells available in a worksheet, it is important to know how to move around in, or **navigate**, a worksheet. You can use the arrow keys on the keyboard ↑, ↓, → or ← to move one cell at a time, or press [Page Up] or [Page Down] to move one screen at a time. To move one screen to the left press [Alt][Page Up]; to move one screen to the right press

[Alt][Page Down]. You can also use the mouse pointer to click the desired cell. If the desired cell is not visible in the worksheet window, use the scroll bars or use the Go To command by clicking the Find & Select button in the Editing group on the HOME tab on the Ribbon. To quickly jump to the first cell in a worksheet press [Ctrl][Home]; to jump to the last cell, press [Ctrl][End].

Edit Cell Entries

Learning
Outcomes
• Edit cell entries in
the formula bar
• Edit cell entries in
the cell

You can change, or **edit**, the contents of an active cell at any time. To do so, double-click the cell, click in the formula bar, or just start typing. Excel switches to Edit mode when you are making cell entries. Different pointers, shown in TABLE A-3, guide you through the editing process. **CASE** ▸ *You noticed some errors in the worksheet and want to make corrections. The first error is in cell A5, which contains a misspelled name.*

STEPS

1. **Click cell A5, then click to the right of P in the formula bar**

 As soon as you click in the formula bar, a blinking vertical line called the **insertion point** appears on the formula bar at the location where new text will be inserted. See FIGURE A-9. The mouse pointer changes to I when you point anywhere in the formula bar.

2. **Press [Delete], then click the Enter button ✓ on the formula bar**

 Clicking the Enter button accepts the edit, and the spelling of the employee's first name is corrected. You can also press [Enter] or [Tab] to accept an edit. Pressing [Enter] to accept an edit moves the cell pointer down one cell, and pressing [Tab] to accept an edit moves the cell pointer one cell to the right.

 > **QUICK TIP**
 > On some keyboards, you might need to press an [F Lock] key to enable the function keys.

3. **Click cell B6, then press [F2]**

 Excel switches to Edit mode, and the insertion point blinks in the cell. Pressing [F2] activates the cell for editing directly in the cell instead of the formula bar. Whether you edit in the cell or the formula bar is simply a matter of preference; the results in the worksheet are the same.

 > **QUICK TIP**
 > The Undo button allows you to reverse up to 100 previous actions, one at a time.

4. **Press [Backspace], type 8, then press [Enter]**

 The value in the cell changes from 35 to 38, and cell B7 becomes the active cell. Did you notice that the calculations in cells B15 and E15 also changed? That's because those cells contain formulas that include cell B6 in their calculations. If you make a mistake when editing, you can click the Cancel button ✕ on the formula bar *before* pressing [Enter] to confirm the cell entry. The Enter and Cancel buttons appear only when you're in Edit mode. If you notice the mistake *after* you have confirmed the cell entry, click the Undo button ↰ on the Quick Access toolbar.

 > **QUICK TIP**
 > You can use the keyboard to select all cell contents by clicking to the right of the cell contents in the cell or formula bar, pressing and holding [Shift], then pressing [Home].

5. **Click cell A9, then double-click the word Juan in the formula bar**

 Double-clicking a word in a cell selects it. When you selected the word, the Mini toolbar automatically displayed.

6. **Type Javier, then press [Enter]**

 When text is selected, typing deletes it and replaces it with the new text.

7. **Double-click cell C12, press [Delete], type 4, then click ✓**

 Double-clicking a cell activates it for editing directly in the cell. Compare your screen to FIGURE A-10.

8. **Save your work**

 Your changes to the workbook are saved.

Recovering unsaved changes to a workbook file

You can use Excel's AutoRecover feature to automatically save (Autosave) your work as often as you want. This means that if you suddenly lose power or if Excel closes unexpectedly while you're working, you can recover all or some of the changes you made since you saved it last. (Of course, this is no substitute for regularly saving your work: this is just added insurance.) To customize the AutoRecover settings, click the FILE tab, click Options, then click Save. AutoRecover lets you decide how often and into which location it should Autosave files. When you restart Excel after losing power, a Document Recovery pane opens and provides access to the saved and Autosaved versions of the files that were open when Excel closed. You can also click the FILE tab, click Open on the navigation bar, then click any file in the Recent Workbooks list to open Autosaved workbooks.

FIGURE A-9: Worksheet in Edit mode

FIGURE A-10: Edited worksheet

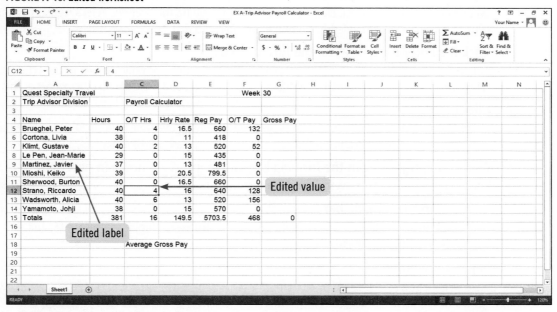

TABLE A-3: Common pointers in Excel

name	pointer	use to	visible over the
Normal		Select a cell or range; indicates Ready mode	Active worksheet
Fill handle	+	Copy cell contents to adjacent cells	Lower-right corner of the active cell or range
I-beam	I	Edit cell contents in active cell or formula bar	Active cell in Edit mode or over the formula bar
Move		Change the location of the selected cell(s)	Perimeter of the active cell(s)
Copy		Create a duplicate of the selected cell(s)	Perimeter of the active cell(s) when [Ctrl] is pressed
Column resize		Change the width of a column	Border between column heading indicators

Enter and Edit a Simple Formula

Learning Outcomes
• Enter a formula
• Use cell references to create a formula

You use formulas in Excel to perform calculations such as adding, multiplying, and averaging. Formulas in an Excel worksheet start with the equal sign (=), also called the **formula prefix**, followed by cell addresses, range names, values, and **calculation operators**. Calculation operators indicate what type of calculation you want to perform on the cells, ranges, or values. They can include **arithmetic operators**, which perform mathematical calculations (see TABLE A-2 in the "Understand Formulas" lesson); **comparison operators**, which compare values for the purpose of true/false results; **text concatenation operators**, which join strings of text in different cells; and **reference operators**, which enable you to use ranges in calculations. **CASE** *You want to create a formula in the worksheet that calculates gross pay for each employee.*

STEPS

1. **Click cell G5**

 This is the first cell where you want to insert the formula. To calculate gross pay, you need to add regular pay and overtime pay. For employee Peter Brueghel, regular pay appears in cell E5 and overtime pay appears in cell F5.

QUICK TIP
You can reference a cell in a formula either by typing the cell reference or clicking the cell in the worksheet; when you click a cell to add a reference, the Mode indicator changes to "Point."

2. **Type =, click cell E5, type +, then click cell F5**

 Compare your formula bar to FIGURE A-11. The blue and red cell references in cell G5 correspond to the colored cell outlines. When entering a formula, it's a good idea to use cell references instead of values whenever you can. That way, if you later change a value in a cell (if, for example, Peter's regular pay changes to 690), any formula that includes this information reflects accurate, up-to-date results.

3. **Click the Enter button ☑ on the formula bar**

 The result of the formula =E5+F5, 792, appears in cell G5. This same value appears in cell G15 because cell G15 contains a formula that totals the values in cells G5:G14, and there are no other values at this time.

4. **Click cell F5**

 The formula in this cell calculates overtime pay by multiplying overtime hours (C5) times twice the regular hourly rate (2*D5). You want to edit this formula to reflect a new overtime pay rate.

5. **Click to the right of 2 in the formula bar, then type .5 as shown in FIGURE A-12**

 The formula that calculates overtime pay has been edited.

6. **Click ☑ on the formula bar**

 Compare your screen to FIGURE A-13. Notice that the calculated values in cells G5, F15, and G15 have all changed to reflect your edits to cell F5.

7. **Save your work**

Understanding named ranges

It can be difficult to remember the cell locations of critical information in a worksheet, but using cell names can make this task much easier. You can name a single cell or range of contiguous, or touching, cells. For example, you might name a cell that contains data on average gross pay "AVG_GP" instead of trying to remember the cell address C18. A named range must begin with a letter or an underscore. It cannot contain any spaces or be the same as a built-in name, such as a function or another object (such as a different named range) in the workbook. To name a range, select the cell(s) you want to name, click the Name box in the formula bar, type the name you want to use, then press

[Enter]. You can also name a range by clicking the FORMULAS tab, then clicking the Define Name button in the Defined Names group. Type the new range name in the Name text box in the New Name dialog box, verify the selected range, then click OK. When you use a named range in a formula, the named range appears instead of the cell address. You can also create a named range using the contents of a cell already in the range. Select the range containing the text you want to use as a name, then click the Create from Selection button in the Defined Names group. The Create Names from Selection dialog box opens. Choose the location of the name you want to use, then click OK.

FIGURE A-11: Simple formula in a worksheet

FIGURE A-12: Edited formula in a worksheet

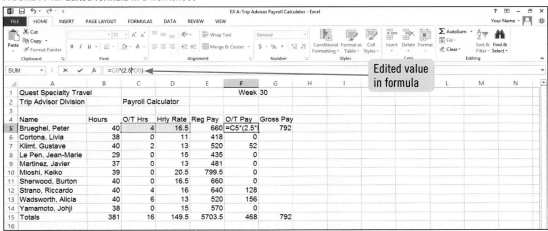

FIGURE A-13: Edited formula with changes

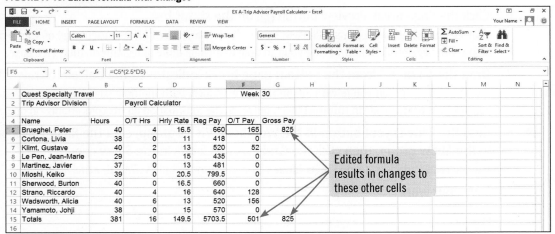

Switch Worksheet Views

Learning Outcomes
- Change worksheet views
- Create a header/footer
- Select a range

You can change your view of the worksheet window at any time, using either the VIEW tab on the Ribbon or the View buttons on the status bar. Changing your view does not affect the contents of a worksheet; it just makes it easier for you to focus on different tasks, such as entering content or preparing a worksheet for printing. The VIEW tab includes a variety of viewing options, such as View buttons, zoom controls, and the ability to show or hide worksheet elements such as gridlines. The status bar offers fewer View options but can be more convenient to use. **CASE** *You want to make some final adjustments to your worksheet, including adding a header so the document looks more polished.*

STEPS

QUICK TIP
Although a worksheet can contain more than a million rows and thousands of columns, the current document contains only as many pages as necessary for the current project.

1. **Click the VIEW tab on the Ribbon, then click the Page Layout button in the Workbook Views group**

 The view switches from the default view, Normal, to Page Layout view. **Normal view** shows the worksheet without including certain details like headers and footers, or tools like rulers and a page number indicator; it's great for creating and editing a worksheet, but may not be detailed enough when you want to put the finishing touches on a document. **Page Layout view** provides a more accurate view of how a worksheet will look when printed, as shown in **FIGURE A-14**. The margins of the page are displayed, along with a text box for the header. A footer text box appears at the bottom of the page, but your screen may not be large enough to view it without scrolling. Above and to the left of the page are rulers. Part of an additional page appears to the right of this page, but it is dimmed, indicating that it does not contain any data. A page number indicator on the status bar tells you the current page and the total number of pages in this worksheet.

2. **Move the pointer ⇖ over the header *without clicking***

 The header is made up of three text boxes: left, center, and right. Each text box is outlined in green as you pass over it with the pointer.

QUICK TIP
You can change header and footer information using the Header & Footer Tools Design tab that opens on the Ribbon when a header or footer is active. For example, you can insert the date by clicking the Current Date button in the Header & Footer Elements group, or insert the time by clicking the Current Time button.

3. **Click the left header text box, type Quest Specialty Travel, click the center header text box, type Trip Advisor Payroll Calculator, click the right header text box, then type Week 30**

 The new text appears in the text boxes, as shown in **FIGURE A-15**. You can also press the [Tab] key to advance from one header box to the next.

4. **Select the range A1:G2, then press [Delete]**

 The duplicate information you just entered in the header is deleted from cells in the worksheet.

5. **Click the VIEW tab if necessary, click the Ruler check box in the Show group, then click the Gridlines check box in the Show group**

 The rulers and the gridlines are hidden. By default, gridlines in a worksheet do not print, so hiding them gives you a more accurate image of your final document.

6. **Click the Page Break Preview button ⊞ on the status bar**

 Your view changes to Page Break Preview, which displays a reduced view of each page of your worksheet, along with page break indicators that you can drag to include more or less information on a page.

7. **Drag the pointer ⇕ from the bottom page break indicator to the bottom of row 20**

 See **FIGURE A-16**. When you're working on a large worksheet with multiple pages, sometimes you need to adjust where pages break; in this worksheet, however, the information all fits comfortably on one page.

QUICK TIP
Once you view a worksheet in Page Break Preview, the page break indicators appear as dotted lines after you switch back to Normal view or Page Layout view.

8. **Click the Page Layout button in the Workbook Views group, click the Ruler check box in the Show group, then click the Gridlines check box in the Show group**

 The rulers and gridlines are no longer hidden. You can show or hide VIEW tab items in any view.

9. **Save your work**

FIGURE A-14: Page Layout view

Turns ruler on/off

Workbook Views group

Turns gridlines on/off

Vertical ruler

Horizontal ruler

Header text box

Additional dimmed page

Current page and total number of pages

FIGURE A-15: Header text entered

HEADER & FOOTER TOOLS tab

Header text boxes

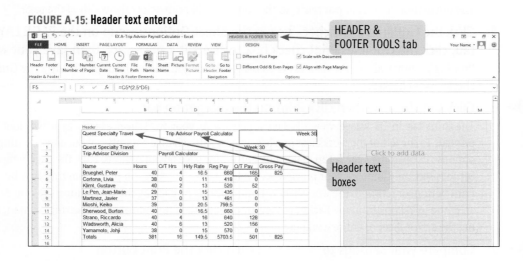

FIGURE A-16: Page Break Preview

Blue outline indicates print area

Choose Print Options

Before printing a document, you may want to review it using the PAGE LAYOUT tab to fine-tune your printed output. You can use tools on the PAGE LAYOUT tab to adjust print orientation (the direction in which the content prints across the page), paper size, and location of page breaks. You can also use the Scale to Fit options on the PAGE LAYOUT tab to fit a large amount of data on a single page without making changes to individual margins, and to turn gridlines and column/row headings on and off. When you are ready to print, you can set print options such as the number of copies to print and the correct printer, and you can preview your document in Backstage view using the FILE tab. You can also adjust page layout settings from within Backstage view and immediately see the results in the document preview. **CASE** ▶ *You are ready to prepare your worksheet for printing.*

STEPS

1. **Click cell A20, type your name, then click** ☑

2. **Click the PAGE LAYOUT tab on the Ribbon**

 Compare your screen to FIGURE A-17. The solid outline indicates the default **print area**, the area to be printed.

3. **Click the Orientation button in the Page Setup group, then click Landscape**

 The paper orientation changes to **landscape**, so the contents will print across the length of the page instead of across the width.

4. **Click the Orientation button in the Page Setup group, then click Portrait**

 The orientation returns to **portrait**, so the contents will print across the width of the page.

5. **Click the Gridlines View check box in the Sheet Options group on the PAGE LAYOUT tab, click the Gridlines Print check box to select it if necessary, then save your work**

 Printing gridlines makes the data easier to read, but the gridlines will not print unless the Gridlines Print check box is checked.

6. **Click the FILE tab, then click Print on the navigation bar**

 The Print tab in Backstage view displays a preview of your worksheet exactly as it will look when it is printed. To the left of the worksheet preview, you can also change a number of document settings and print options. To open the Page Setup dialog box and adjust page layout options, click the Page Setup link in the Settings section. Compare your preview screen to FIGURE A-18. You can print from this view by clicking the Print button, or return to the worksheet without printing by clicking the Back button ⬅. You can also print an entire workbook from the Backstage view by clicking the Print button in the Settings section, then selecting the active sheet or entire workbook.

7. **Compare your settings to FIGURE A-18, then click the Print button**

 One copy of the worksheet prints.

8. **Submit your work to your instructor as directed, then exit Excel**

Printing worksheet formulas

Sometimes you need to keep a record of all the formulas in a worksheet. You might want to do this to see exactly how you came up with a complex calculation, so you can explain it to others. To prepare a worksheet to show formulas rather than results when printed, open the workbook containing the formulas you want to

print. Click the FORMULAS tab, then click the Show Formulas button in the Formula Auditing group to select it. When the Show Formulas button is selected, formulas rather than resulting values are displayed in the worksheet on screen and when printed. (The Show Formulas button is a *toggle*: click it again to hide the formulas.)

FIGURE A-17: Worksheet with Portrait orientation

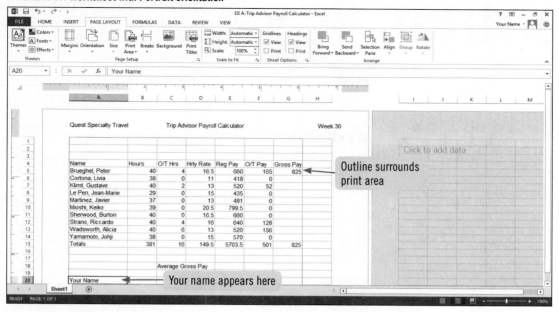

Outline surrounds print area

Your name appears here

FIGURE A-18: Worksheet in Backstage view

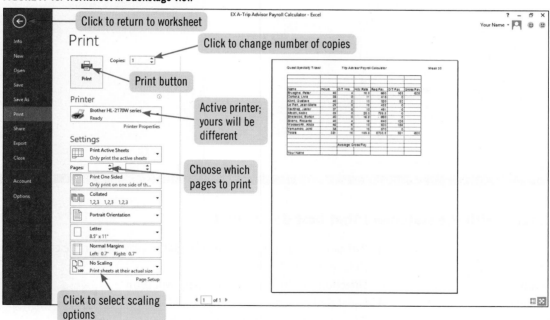

Click to return to worksheet

Click to change number of copies

Print button

Active printer; yours will be different

Choose which pages to print

Click to select scaling options

Scaling to fit

If you have a large amount of data that you want to fit to a single sheet of paper, but you don't want to spend a lot of time trying to adjust the margins and other settings, you have several options. You can easily print your work on a single sheet by clicking the No Scaling list arrow in the Settings section on the Print button in Backstage view, then clicking Fit Sheet on One Page. Another method for fitting worksheet content onto one page is to click the PAGE LAYOUT tab, then change the Width and Height settings in the Scale to Fit group each to 1 Page. You can also use the Fit to option in the Page Setup dialog box to fit a worksheet on one page. To open the Page Setup dialog box, click the dialog box launcher in the Scale to Fit group on the PAGE LAYOUT tab, or click the Page Setup link on the Print tab in Backstage view. Make sure the Page tab is selected in the Page Setup dialog box, then click the Fit to option button.

Practice

Concepts Review

Label the elements of the Excel worksheet window shown in FIGURE A-19.

FIGURE A-19

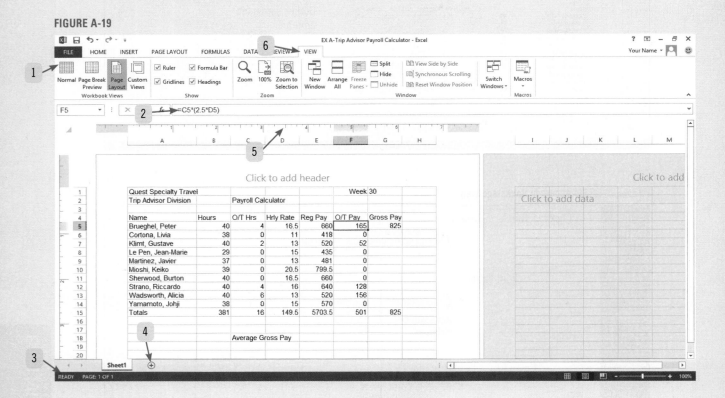

Match each term with the statement that best describes it.

7. Cell

8. Orientation

9. Normal view

10. Formula prefix

11. Workbook

12. Name box

a. Part of the Excel program window that displays the active cell address

b. Default view in Excel

c. Direction in which contents of page will print

d. Equal sign preceding a formula

e. File consisting of one or more worksheets

f. Intersection of a column and a row

Select the best answer from the list of choices.

13. The maximum number of worksheets you can include in a workbook is:
 a. 3.
 b. 250.
 c. 255.
 d. Unlimited.

14. Which feature could be used to print a very long worksheet on a single sheet of paper?
 a. Show Formulas
 b. Scale to fit
 c. Page Break Preview
 d. Named Ranges

15. Using a cell address in a formula is known as:
 a. Formularizing.
 b. Prefixing.
 c. Cell referencing.
 d. Cell mathematics.

16. A selection of multiple cells is called a:
 a. Group.
 b. Range.
 c. Reference.
 d. Package.

17. In which area can you see a preview of your worksheet?
 a. Page Setup
 b. Backstage view
 c. Printer Setup
 d. VIEW tab

18. Which worksheet view shows how your worksheet will look when printed?
 a. Page Layout
 b. Data
 c. Review
 d. View

19. Which key can you press to switch to Edit mode?
 a. [F1]
 b. [F2]
 c. [F4]
 d. [F6]

20. In which view can you see the header and footer areas of a worksheet?
 a. Normal view
 b. Page Layout view
 c. Page Break Preview
 d. Header/Footer view

21. Which view shows you a reduced view of each page of your worksheet?
 a. Normal
 b. Page Layout
 c. Thumbnail
 d. Page Break Preview

Skills Review

1. **Understand spreadsheet software.**
 a. What is the difference between a workbook and a worksheet?
 b. Identify five common business uses for electronic spreadsheets.
 c. What is what-if analysis?

2. **Identify Excel 2013 window components.**
 a. Start Excel.
 b. Open the file EX A-2.xlsx from the location where you store your Data Files, then save it as **EX A-Weather Statistics**.
 c. Locate the formula bar, the Sheet tabs, the mode indicator, and the cell pointer.

3. **Understand formulas.**
 a. What is the average high temperature of the listed cities? (*Hint*: Select the range B5:G5 and use the status bar.)
 b. What formula would you create to calculate the difference in altitude between Atlanta and Phoenix? Enter your answer (as an equation) in cell D13.

Skills Review (continued)

4. Enter labels and values and use the AutoSum button.

 a. Click cell H8, then use the AutoSum button to calculate the total snowfall.

 b. Click cell H7, then use the AutoSum button to calculate the total rainfall.

 c. Save your changes to the file.

5. Edit cell entries.

 a. Use [F2] to correct the spelling of SanteFe in cell G3 (the correct spelling is Santa Fe).

 b. Click cell A17, then type your name.

 c. Save your changes.

6. Enter and edit a simple formula.

 a. Change the value 41 in cell C8 to **52**.

 b. Change the value 37 in cell D6 to **35.4**.

 c. Select cell J4, then use the fill handle to copy the formula in cell J4 to cells J5:J8.

 d. Save your changes.

7. Switch worksheet views.

 a. Click the VIEW tab on the Ribbon, then switch to Page Layout view.

 b. Add the header **Average Annual Weather Statistics** to the center header text box.

 c. Add your name to the right header box.

 d. Delete the contents of cell A17.

 e. Delete the contents of cell A1.

 f. Save your changes.

8. Choose print options.

 a. Use the PAGE LAYOUT tab to change the orientation to Portrait.

 b. Turn off gridlines by deselecting both the Gridlines View and Gridlines Print check boxes (if necessary) in the Sheet Options group.

 c. Scale the worksheet so all the information fits on one page. If necessary, scale the worksheet so all the information fits on one page. (*Hint*: Click the Width list arrow in the Scale to Fit group, click 1 page, click the Height list arrow in the Scale to Fit group, then click 1 page.) Compare your screen to FIGURE A-20.

 d. Preview the worksheet in Backstage view, then print the worksheet.

 e. Save your changes, submit your work to your instructor as directed, then close the workbook and exit Excel.

FIGURE A-20

Independent Challenge 1

A local executive relocation company has hired you to help them make the transition to using Excel in their office. They would like to list their properties in a workbook. You've started a worksheet for this project that contains labels but no data.

a. Open the file EX A-3.xlsx from the location where you store your Data Files, then save it as **EX A-Property Listings**.

b. Enter the data shown in TABLE A-4 in columns A, C, D, and E (the property address information should spill into column B).

TABLE A-4

Property Address	Price	Bedrooms	Bathrooms
1507 Pinon Lane	525000	4	2.5
32 Zanzibar Way	325000	3	4
60 Pottery Lane	475500	2	2
902 Excelsior Drive	310000	4	3

© 2014 Cengage Learning

c. Use Page Layout view to create a header with the following components: the title **Property Listings** in the center and your name on the right.

d. Create formulas for totals in cells C6:E6.

e. Save your changes, then compare your worksheet to FIGURE A-21.

f. Submit your work to your instructor as directed.

g. Close the worksheet and exit Excel.

FIGURE A-21

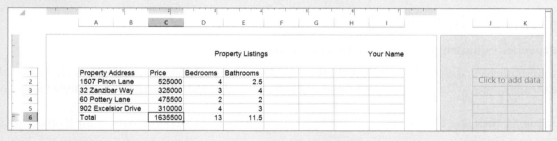

Independent Challenge 2

You are the General Manager for Prestige Import Motors, a small auto parts supplier. Although the company is just five years old, it is expanding rapidly, and you are continually looking for ways to save time. You recently began using Excel to manage and maintain data on inventory and sales, which has greatly helped you to track information accurately and efficiently.

a. Start Excel.

b. Save a new workbook as **EX A-Prestige Import Motors** in the location where you store your Data Files.

c. Switch to an appropriate view, then add a header that contains your name in the left header text box and the title **Prestige Import Motors** in the center header text box.

Independent Challenge 2 (continued)

d. Using FIGURE A-22 as a guide, create labels for at least seven car manufacturers and sales for three months. Include other labels as appropriate. The car make should be in column A and the months should be in columns B, C, and D. A Total row should be beneath the data, and a Total column should be in column E.

FIGURE A-22

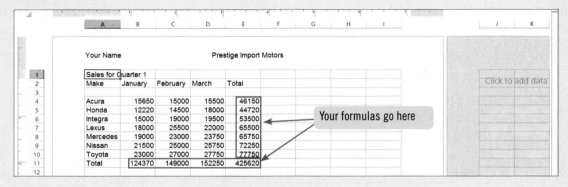

e. Enter values of your choice for the monthly sales for each make.

f. Add formulas in the Total column to calculate total quarterly sales for each make. Add formulas at the bottom of each column of values to calculate the total for that column. Remember that you can use the AutoSum button and the fill handle to save time.

g. Save your changes, preview the worksheet in Backstage view, then submit your work to your instructor as directed.

h. Close the workbook and exit Excel.

Independent Challenge 3

This Independent Challenge requires an Internet connection.

Your office is starting a branch in Paris, and you think it would be helpful to create a worksheet that can be used to convert Fahrenheit temperatures to Celsius, to help employees who are unfamiliar with this type of temperature measurement.

a. Start Excel, then save a blank workbook as **EX A-Temperature Conversions** in the location where you store your Data Files.

b. Create column headings using FIGURE A-23 as a guide. (*Hint*: You can widen column B by clicking cell B1, clicking the Format button in the Cells group on the HOME tab, then clicking AutoFit Column Width.)

c. Create row labels for each of the seasons.

d. In the appropriate cells, enter what you determine to be a reasonable indoor temperature for each season.

e. Use your Web browser to find out the conversion rate for Fahrenheit to Celsius. (*Hint*: Use your favorite search engine to search on a term such as **temperature conversion formula**.)

f. In the appropriate cells, create a formula that calculates the conversion of the Fahrenheit temperature you entered into a Celsius temperature.

g. In Page Layout View, add your name and the title **Temperature Conversions** to the header.

h. Save your work, then submit your work to your instructor as directed.

i. Close the file, then exit Excel.

Independent Challenge 3 (continued)

FIGURE A-23

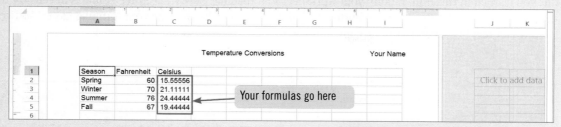

Independent Challenge 4: Explore

You've been asked to take over a project started by a co-worker whose Excel skills are not as good as your own. The assignment was to create a sample invoice for a prospective client. The invoice will include personnel, supplies, and sales tax. Your predecessor started the project, including layout and initial calculations, but she has not made good use of Excel features and has made errors in her calculations. Complete the worksheet by correcting the errors and improving the design. Be prepared to discuss what is wrong with all the items in the worksheet that you change.

a. Start Excel, open the file EX A-4.xlsx from the location where you store your Data Files, then save it as **EX A-Sample Invoice**.

b. There is an error in cell E5: please use the Help feature to find out what is wrong. If you need additional assistance, search Help on *overview of formulas*.

c. Correct the error in the formula in cell E5, then copy the corrected formula into cells E6:E7.

d. Correct the error in the formula in cell E11: then copy the corrected formula into cells E12 and E13.

e. Cells E8 and E14 each contain incorrect formulas. Cell E8 should contain a formula that calculates the total personnel expense and cell E14 should calculate the total supplies used.

f. Cell F17 should contain a formula that adds the Invoice subtotal (total personnel and total supplies).

g. Cell F18 should calculate the sales tax by multiplying the Subtotal (F17) and the sales tax (cell B18).

h. The Invoice Total (cell F19) should contain a formula that adds the Invoice subtotal (cell F17) and Sales tax (cell F18).

i. Switch to the Page Layout view and make the following changes to the Header: Sample Invoice for Week 22 (in the left header box), Client ABC (in the center header box), and your name (in the right header box).

j. Delete the contents of A1:A2, switch to the Normal view, then compare your worksheet to FIGURE A-24.

k. Save your work.

FIGURE A-24

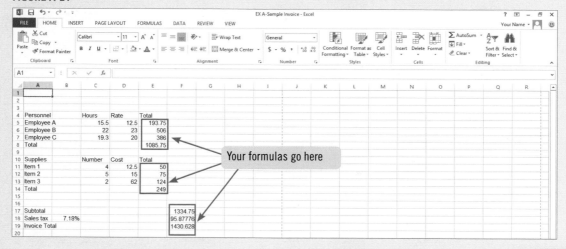

Visual Workshop

Open the file EX A-5.xlsx from the location where you store your Data Files, then save it as **EX A-Inventory Items**. Using the skills you learned in this unit, modify your worksheet so it matches FIGURE A-25. Enter formulas in cells D4 through D13 and in cells B14 and C14. Use the AutoSum button and fill handle to make entering your formulas easier. Add your name in the left header text box, then print one copy of the worksheet with the formulas displayed.

FIGURE A-25

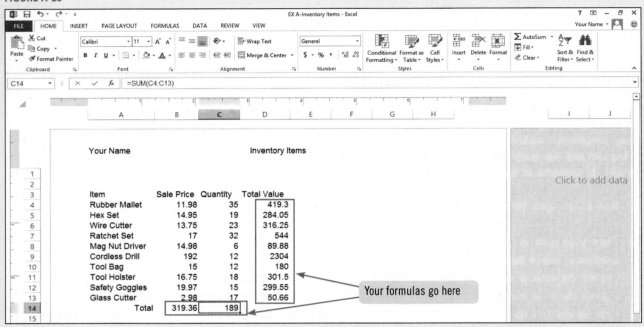

Working with Formulas and Functions

CASE ▶ Grace Wong, vice president of finance at Quest Specialty Travel, needs to analyze tour expenses for the current year. She has asked you to prepare a worksheet that summarizes this expense data and includes some statistical analysis. She would also like you to perform some what-if analysis, to see what quarterly expenses would look like with various projected increases.

Unit Objectives

After completing this unit, you will be able to:

- Create a complex formula
- Insert a function
- Type a function
- Copy and move cell entries
- Understand relative and absolute cell references
- Copy formulas with relative cell references
- Copy formulas with absolute cell references
- Round a value with a function

Files You Will Need

EX B-1.xlsx
EX B-2.xlsx
EX B-3.xlsx
EX B-4.xlsx

©Katerina Havelkova/Shutterstock

Create a Complex Formula

Learning Outcomes
- Create a complex formula by pointing
- Use the fill handle and Auto Fill

A **complex formula** is one that uses more than one arithmetic operator. You might, for example, need to create a formula that uses addition and multiplication. In formulas containing more than one arithmetic operator, Excel uses the standard **order of precedence** rules to determine which operation to perform first. You can change the order of precedence in a formula by using parentheses around the part you want to calculate first. For example, the formula =4+2*5 equals 14, because the order of precedence dictates that multiplication is performed before addition. However, the formula =(4+2)*5 equals 30, because the parentheses cause 4+2 to be calculated first. **CASE** ▶ *You want to create a formula that calculates a 20% increase in tour expenses.*

STEPS

1. **Start Excel, open the file EX B-1.xlsx from the location where you store your Data Files, then save it as EX B-Tour Expense Analysis**

2. **Select the range B4:B11, click the Quick Analysis tool 🖩, then click the Totals tab**

 The Totals tab in the Quick Analysis tool displays commonly used functions, as seen in **FIGURE B-1**.

3. **Click the AutoSum button 🖩 in the Quick Analysis tool**

 The newly calculated value displays in cell B12 and has a darker appearance than the figures in the selected range.

4. **Click cell B12, then drag the fill handle to cell E12**

 The formula in cell B12 is copied to cells C12:E12. The copied cells have the same dark appearance as that of cell B12.

5. **Click cell B14, type =, click cell B12, then type +**

 In this first part of the formula, you are using a reference to the total expenses for Quarter 1.

6. **Click cell B12, then type *.2**

 The second part of this formula adds a 20% increase (B12*.2) to the original value of the cell (the total expenses for Quarter 1).

7. **Click the Enter button ✓ on the formula bar**

 The result, 41789.556, appears in cell B14.

8. **Press [Tab], type =, click cell C12, type +, click cell C12, type *.2, then click ✓**

 The result, 41352.912, appears in cell C14.

9. **Drag the fill handle from cell C14 to cell E14**

 The calculated values appear in the selected range, as shown in **FIGURE B-2**. Dragging the fill handle on a cell copies the cell's contents or continues a series of data (such as Quarter 1, Quarter 2, etc.) into adjacent cells. This option is called **Auto Fill**.

10. **Save your work**

Using Apps for Office to improve worksheet functionality

Excel has more functionality than simple and complex math computations. Using the Apps for Office feature (found in the Apps group in the INSERT tab), you can insert an app into your worksheet that accesses the web and adds functionality to your work. Many of the available apps are free and can be used to create an email, appointment, meeting, contact, or task, or be a reference source, such as the Mini Calendar and Date Picker. When you click the Apps for Office button, you'll see any Recently Used Apps. Click See All to display the featured apps and to go to the Office store to view available apps. When you find an app you want, make sure you're logged in to Office.com (you may need to log in again), click the app, click Add, then follow the prompts to download the app. Click the Apps for Office button, click See All, click the app you just added, then click Insert. The app will display as an embedded object in your worksheet and will also appear in the Recently Used Apps palette when you click the Apps for Office button.

FIGURE B-1: Totals tab in the Quick Analysis tool

FIGURE B-2: Complex formulas in worksheet

Reviewing the order of precedence

When you work with formulas that contain more than one operator, the order of precedence is very important because it affects the final value. If a formula contains two or more operators, such as 4+.55/4000*25, Excel performs the calculations in a particular sequence based on the following rules: Operations inside parentheses are calculated before any other operations. Reference operators (such as ranges) are calculated first. Exponents are calculated next, then any multiplication and division—progressing from left to right. Finally, addition and subtraction are calculated from left to right. In the example 4+.55/4000*25, Excel performs the arithmetic operations by first dividing .55 by 4000, then multiplying the result by 25, then adding 4. You can change the order of calculations by using parentheses. For example, in the formula (4+.55)/4000*25, Excel would first add 4 and .55, then divide that amount by 4000, then finally multiply by 25.

Excel 2013

Insert a Function

Learning
Outcomes
• Use the Insert
Function button
• Select a range for
use in a function
• Select a function
from the AutoSum
list arrow

Functions are predefined worksheet formulas that enable you to perform complex calculations easily. You can use the Insert Function button on the formula bar to choose a function from a dialog box. You can quickly insert the SUM function using the AutoSum button on the Ribbon, or you can click the AutoSum list arrow to enter other frequently used functions, such as AVERAGE. You can also use the Quick Analysis tool to calculate commonly used functions. Functions are organized into categories, such as Financial, Date & Time, and Statistical, based on their purposes. You can insert a function on its own or as part of another formula. For example, you have used the SUM function on its own to add a range of cells. You could also use the SUM function within a formula that adds a range of cells and then multiplies the total by a decimal. If you use a function alone, it always begins with an equal sign (=) as the formula prefix. **CASE** *You need to calculate the average expenses for the first quarter of the year, and decide to use a function to do so.*

STEPS

1. **Click cell B15**

 This is the cell where you want to enter the calculation that averages expenses per country for the first quarter. You want to use the Insert Function dialog box to enter this function.

2. **Click the Insert Function button f_x on the formula bar**

 An equal sign (=) is inserted in the active cell and in the formula bar, and the Insert Function dialog box opens, as shown in **FIGURE B-3**. In this dialog box, you specify the function you want to use by clicking it in the Select a function list. The Select a function list initially displays recently used functions. If you don't see the function you want, you can click the Or select a category list arrow to choose the desired category. If you're not sure which category to choose, you can type the function name or a description in the Search for a function field. The AVERAGE function is a statistical function, but you don't need to open the Statistical category because this function already appears in the Most Recently Used category.

3. **Click AVERAGE in the Select a function list if necessary, read the information that appears under the list, then click OK**

 The Function Arguments dialog box opens, in which you define the range of cells you want to average.

4. **Click the Collapse button [icon] in the Number1 field of the Function Arguments dialog box, select the range B4:B11 in the worksheet, then click the Expand button [icon] in the Function Arguments dialog box**

 Clicking the Collapse button minimizes the dialog box so you can select cells in the worksheet. When you click the Expand button, the dialog box is restored, as shown in **FIGURE B-4**. You can also begin dragging in the worksheet to automatically minimize the dialog box; after you select the desired range, the dialog box is restored.

5. **Click OK**

 The Function Arguments dialog box closes, and the calculated value is displayed in cell B15. The average expenses per country for Quarter 1 is 4353.0788.

6. **Click cell C15, click the AutoSum list arrow Σ in the Editing group on the HOME tab, then click Average**

 A ScreenTip beneath cell C15 displays the arguments needed to complete the function. The text "number1" is shown in boldface type, telling you that the next step is to supply the first cell in the group you want to average. You want to average a range of cells.

7. **Select the range C4:C11 in the worksheet, then click the Enter button [icon] on the formula bar**

 The average expenses per country for the second quarter appears in cell C15.

8. **Drag the fill handle from cell C15 to cell E15**

 The formula in cell C15 is copied to the rest of the selected range, as shown in **FIGURE B-5**.

9. **Save your work**

FIGURE B-3: Insert Function dialog box

Search for a function field →

Your list of recently used functions may differ →

Or select a category list arrow

Description of selected function

FIGURE B-4: Expanded Function Arguments dialog box

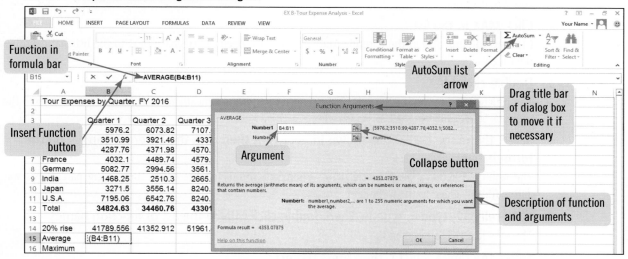

Function in formula bar

Insert Function button

Argument

Collapse button

AutoSum list arrow

Drag title bar of dialog box to move it if necessary

Description of function and arguments

FIGURE B-5: Average functions used in worksheet

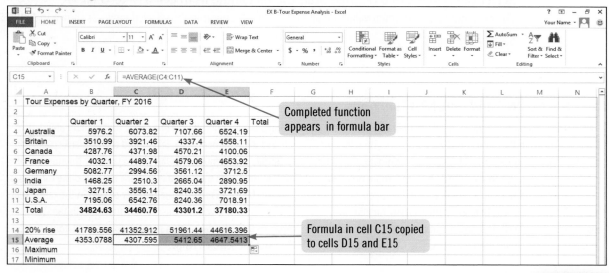

Completed function appears in formula bar

Formula in cell C15 copied to cells D15 and E15

Type a Function

Learning Outcomes
- Select a function by typing
- Use AutoComplete to copy formulas

In addition to using the Insert Function dialog box, the AutoSum button, or the AutoSum list arrow on the Ribbon to enter a function, you can manually type the function into a cell and then complete the arguments needed. This method requires that you know the name and initial characters of the function, but it can be faster than opening several dialog boxes. Experienced Excel users often prefer this method, but it is only an alternative, not better or more correct than any other method. Excel's Formula AutoComplete feature makes it easier to enter function names by typing, because it suggests functions depending on the first letters you type. **CASE** ➤ *You want to calculate the maximum and minimum quarterly expenses in your worksheet, and you decide to manually enter these statistical functions.*

STEPS

1. **Click cell B16, type =, then type m**

 Because you are manually typing this function, it is necessary to begin with the equal sign (=). The Formula AutoComplete feature displays a list of function names beginning with "M" beneath cell B16. Once you type an equal sign in a cell, each letter you type acts as a trigger to activate the Formula AutoComplete feature. This feature minimizes the amount of typing you need to do to enter a function and reduces typing and syntax errors.

2. **Click MAX in the list**

 Clicking any function in the Formula AutoComplete list opens a ScreenTip next to the list that describes the function.

3. **Double-click MAX**

 The function is inserted in the cell, and a ScreenTip appears beneath the cell to help you complete the formula. See **FIGURE B-6**.

4. **Select the range B4:B11, as shown in FIGURE B-7, then click the Enter button ✔ on the formula bar**

 The result, 7195.06, appears in cell B16. When you completed the entry, the closing parenthesis was automatically added to the formula.

5. **Click cell B17, type =, type m, then double-click MIN in the list of function names**

 The MIN function appears in the cell.

6. **Select the range B4:B11, then press [Enter]**

 The result, 1468.25, appears in cell B17.

7. **Select the range B16:B17, then drag the fill handle from cell B17 to cell E17**

 The maximum and minimum values for all of the quarters appear in the selected range, as shown in **FIGURE B-8**.

8. **Save your work**

Using the COUNT and COUNTA functions

When you select a range, a count of cells in the range that are not blank appears in the status bar. For example, if you select the range A1:A5 and only cells A1, A4 and A5 contain data, the status bar displays "Count: 3." To count nonblank cells more precisely, or to incorporate these calculations in a worksheet, you can use the COUNT and COUNTA functions. The COUNT function returns the number of cells in a range that contain numeric data, including numbers, dates, and formulas. The COUNTA function returns the number of cells in a range that contain any data at all, including numeric data, labels, and even a blank space. For example, the formula =COUNT(A1:A5) returns the number of cells in the range that contain numeric data, and the formula =COUNTA(A1:A5) returns the number of cells in the range that are not empty. If you use the COUNT functions in the Quick Analysis tool, the calculation is entered in the cell immediately beneath the selected range.

FIGURE B-6: MAX function in progress

13					
14	20% rise	41789.556	41352.912	51961.44	44616.396
15	Average	4353.0788	4307.595	5412.65	4647.5413
16	Maximum	=MAX(
17	Minimum	MAX(**number1**, [number2], ...)			

FIGURE B-7: Completing the MAX function

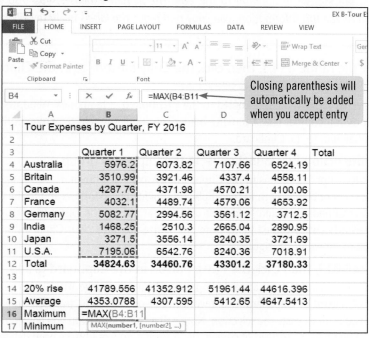

FIGURE B-8: Completed MAX and MIN functions

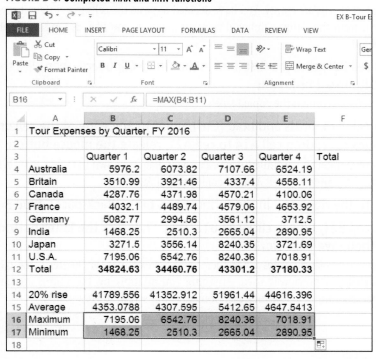

Copy and Move Cell Entries

Learning
Outcomes
• Copy a range to
 the Clipboard
• Paste a Clipboard
 entry
• Empty cell contents
• Copy cell contents

There are three ways you can copy or move cells and ranges (or the contents within them) from one location to another: the Cut, Copy, and Paste buttons on the HOME tab on the Ribbon; the fill handle in the lower-right corner of the active cell or range; or the drag-and-drop feature. When you copy cells, the original data remains in the original location; when you cut or move cells, the original data is deleted from its original location. You can also cut, copy, and paste cells or ranges from one worksheet to another. **CASE** *In addition to the 20% rise in tour expenses, you also want to show a 30% rise. Rather than retype this information, you copy and move the labels in these cells.*

STEPS

1. **Select the range B3:E3, then click the Copy button [icon] in the Clipboard group on the HOME tab**

 The selected range (B3:E3) is copied to the **Clipboard**, a temporary Windows storage area that holds the selections you copy or cut. A moving border surrounds the selected range until you press [Esc] or copy an additional item to the Clipboard.

2. **Click the dialog box launcher [icon] in the Clipboard group**

 The Office Clipboard opens in the Clipboard task pane, as shown in FIGURE B-9. When you copy or cut an item, it is cut or copied both to the Clipboard provided by Windows and to the Office Clipboard. Unlike the Windows Clipboard, which holds just one item at a time, the Office Clipboard contains up to 24 of the most recently cut or copied items from any Office program. Your Clipboard task pane may contain more items than shown in the figure.

3. **Click cell B19, then click the Paste button in the Clipboard group**

 A copy of the contents of range B3:E3 is pasted into the range B19:E19. When pasting an item from the Office Clipboard or Clipboard into a worksheet, you only need to specify the upper-left cell of the range where you want to paste the selection. Notice that the information you copied remains in the original range B3:E3; if you had cut instead of copied, the information would have been deleted from its original location once it was pasted.

4. **Press [Delete]**

 The selected cells are empty. You have decided to paste the cells in a different row. You can repeatedly paste an item from the Office Clipboard as many times as you like, as long as the item remains in the Office Clipboard.

5. **Click cell B20, click the first item in the Office Clipboard, then click the Close button [X] on the Clipboard task pane**

 Cells B20:E20 contain the copied labels.

6. **Click cell A14, press and hold [Ctrl], point to any edge of the cell until the pointer changes to [icon], drag cell A14 to cell A21, release the mouse button, then release [Ctrl]**

 The copy pointer [icon] continues to appear as you drag, as shown in FIGURE B-10. When you release the mouse button, the contents of cell A14 are copied to cell A21.

7. **Click to the right of 2 in the formula bar, press [Backspace], type 3, then press [Enter]**

8. **Click cell B21, type =, click cell B12, type *1.3, click the Enter button [✓] on the formula bar, then save your work**

 This new formula calculates a 30% increase of the expenses for Quarter 1, though using a different method from what you previously used. Anything you multiply by 1.3 returns an amount that is 130% of the original amount, or a 30% increase. Compare your screen to FIGURE B-11.

FIGURE B-9: Copied data in Office Clipboard

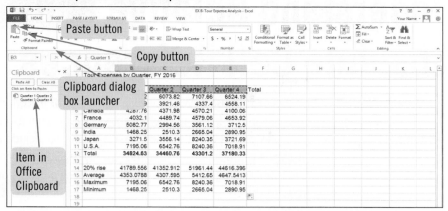

FIGURE B-10: Copying cell contents with drag-and-drop

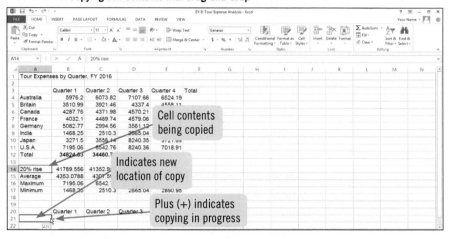

FIGURE B-11: Formula entered to calculate a 30% increase

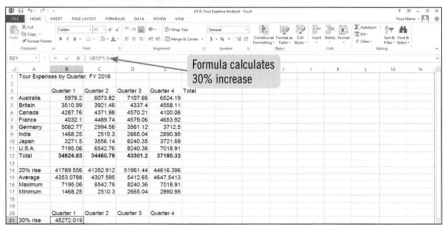

Inserting and deleting selected cells

As you add formulas to your workbook, you may need to insert or delete cells. When you do this, Excel automatically adjusts cell references to reflect their new locations. To insert cells, click the Insert list arrow in the Cells group on the HOME tab, then click Insert Cells. The Insert dialog box opens, asking if you want to insert a cell and move the current active cell down or to the right of the new one. To delete one or more selected cells, click the Delete list arrow in the Cells group, click Delete Cells, and in the Delete dialog box, indicate which way you want to move the adjacent cells. When using this option, be careful not to disturb row or column alignment that may be necessary to maintain the accuracy of cell references in the worksheet. Click the Insert button or Delete button in the Cells group to insert or delete a single cell.

Understand Relative and Absolute Cell References

Learning
Outcomes
• Identify cell refer-
 encing
• Identify when to
 use absolute or rel-
 ative cell references

As you work in Excel, you may want to reuse formulas in different parts of a worksheet to reduce the amount of data you have to retype. For example, you might want to include a what-if analysis in one part of a worksheet showing a set of sales projections if sales increase by 10%. To include another analysis in another part of the worksheet showing projections if sales increase by 50%, you can copy the formulas from one section to another and simply change the "1" to a "5". But when you copy formulas, it is impor-tant to make sure that they refer to the correct cells. To do this, you need to understand the difference between relative and absolute cell references. **CASE** *You plan to reuse formulas in different parts of your worksheets, so you want to understand relative and absolute cell references.*

DETAILS

Consider the following when using relative and absolute cell references:

• **Use relative references when you want to preserve the relationship to the formula location**

When you create a formula that references another cell, Excel normally does not "record" the exact cell address for the cell being referenced in the formula. Instead, it looks at the relationship that cell has to the cell containing the formula. For example, in **FIGURE B-12**, cell F5 contains the formula: =SUM(B5:E5). When Excel retrieves values to calculate the formula in cell F5, it actually looks for "the four cells to the left of the formula," which in this case is cells B5:E5. This way, if you copy the cell to a new location, such as cell F6, the results will reflect the new formula location, and will automatically retrieve the values in cells B6, C6, D6, and E6. These are **relative cell references**, because Excel is recording the input cells *in relation to* or *relative to* the formula cell.

In most cases, you want to use relative cell references when copying or moving, so this is the Excel default. In **FIGURE B-12**, the formulas in F5:F12 and in B13:F13 contain relative cell references. They total the "four cells to the left of" or the "eight cells above" the formulas.

• **Use absolute cell references when you want to preserve the exact cell address in a formula**

There are times when you want Excel to retrieve formula information from a specific cell, and you don't want the cell address in the formula to change when you copy it to a new location. For example, you might have a price in a specific cell that you want to use in all formulas, regardless of their location. If you use relative cell referencing, the formula results would be incorrect, because Excel would use a different cell every time you copy the formula. Therefore you need to use an **absolute cell reference**, which is a refer-ence that does not change when you copy the formula.

You create an absolute cell reference by placing a $ (dollar sign) in front of both the column letter and the row number of the cell address. You can either type the dollar sign when typing the cell address in a formula (for example, "=C12*B16"), or you can select a cell address on the formula bar and then press [F4] and the dollar signs are added automatically. **FIGURE B-13** shows formulas containing both absolute and relative references. The formulas in cells B19 to E26 use absolute cell references to refer to a potential sales increase of 50%, shown in cell B16.

FIGURE B-12: Formulas containing relative references

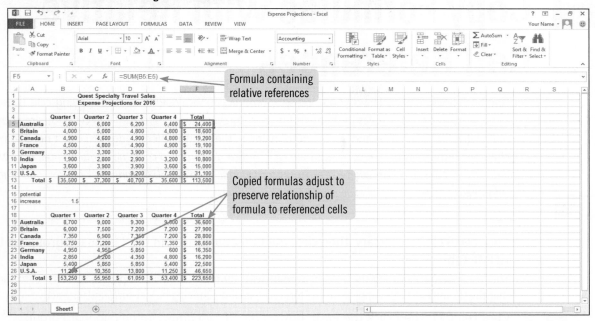

FIGURE B-13: Formulas containing absolute and relative references

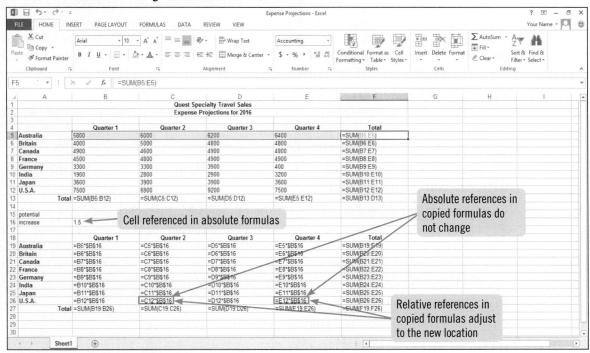

Using a mixed reference

Sometimes when you copy a formula, you want to change the row reference, but keep the column reference the same. This type of cell referencing combines elements of both absolute and relative referencing and is called a **mixed reference**. For example, when copied, a formula containing the mixed reference C$14 would change the column letter relative to its new location, but not the row number. In the mixed reference $C14, the column letter would not change, but the row number would be updated relative to its location. Like an absolute reference, a mixed reference can be created by pressing the [F4] function key with the cell reference selected. With each press of the [F4] key, you cycle through all the possible combinations of relative, absolute, and mixed references (C14, C14, C$14, and $C14).

Copy Formulas with Relative Cell References

Learning Outcomes
- Copy and Paste formulas with relative cell references
- Examine Auto Fill and Paste Options
- Use the Fill button

Copying and moving a cell allows you to reuse a formula you've already created. Copying cells is usually faster than retyping the formulas in them and helps to prevent typing errors. If the cells you are copying contain relative cell references and you want to maintain the relative referencing, you don't need to make any changes to the cells before copying them. **CASE** *You want to copy the formula in cell B21, which calculates the 30% increase in quarterly expenses for Quarter 1, to cells C21 through E21. You also want to create formulas to calculate total expenses for each tour country.*

STEPS

1. **Click cell B21, if necessary, then click the Copy button in the Clipboard group on the HOME tab**

 The formula for calculating the 30% expense increase during Quarter 1 is copied to the Clipboard. Notice that the formula =B12*1.3 appears in the formula bar, and a moving border surrounds the active cell.

QUICK TIP
To paste only specific components of a copied cell or range, click the Paste list arrow in the Clipboard group, then click Paste Special. You can selectively copy formats, formulas, values, comments, validation rules, transpose columns and rows, paste a link, or add, subtract, multiply, or divide using the Paste Special dialog box.

2. **Click cell C21, then click the Paste button *(not the list arrow)* in the Clipboard group**

 The formula from cell B21 is copied into cell C21, where the new result of 44798.988 appears. Notice in the formula bar that the cell references have changed, so that cell C12 is referenced in the formula. This formula contains a relative cell reference, which tells Excel to substitute new cell references within the copied formulas as necessary. This maintains the same relationship between the new cell containing the formula and the cell references within the formula. In this case, Excel adjusted the formula so that cell C12—the cell reference nine rows above C21—replaced cell B12, the cell reference nine rows above B21.

3. **Drag the fill handle from cell C21 to cell E21**

 A formula similar to the one in cell C21 now appears in cells D21 and E21. After you use the fill handle to copy cell contents, the **Auto Fill Options button** appears, as seen in FIGURE B-14. You can use the Auto Fill Options button to fill the cells with only specific elements of the copied cell if you wish.

4. **Click cell F4, click the AutoSum button Σ in the Editing group, then click the Enter button ✓ on the formula bar**

5. **Click in the Clipboard group, select the range F5:F6, then click the Paste button**

 See FIGURE B-15. After you click the Paste button, the **Paste Options button** appears, which you can use to paste only specific elements of the copied selection if you wish. The formula for calculating total expenses for tours in Britain appears in the formula bar. You would like totals to appear in cells F7:F11. The Fill button in the Editing group can be used to copy the formula into the remaining cells.

6. **Select the range F6:F11**

7. **Click the Fill button ⬇ in the Editing group, then click Down**

 The formulas containing relative references are copied to each cell. Compare your worksheet to FIGURE B-16.

8. **Save your work**

FIGURE B-14: Formula copied using the fill handle

FIGURE B-15: Formulas pasted in the range F5:F6

FIGURE B-16: Formula copied using Fill Down

Using Paste Preview

You can selectively copy formulas, values, or other choices using the Paste list arrow, and you can see how the pasted contents will look using the Paste Preview feature. When you click the Paste list arrow, a gallery of paste option icons opens. When you point to an icon, a preview of how the content will be pasted using that option is shown in the worksheet. Options include pasting values only, pasting values with number formatting, pasting formulas only, pasting formatting only, pasting transposed data so that column data appears in rows and row data appears in columns, and pasting with no borders (to remove any borders around pasted cells).

Using Auto Fill options

When you use the fill handle to copy cells, the Auto Fill Options button appears. Auto Fill options differ depending on what you are copying. If you had selected cells containing a series (such as "Monday" and "Tuesday") and then used the fill handle, you would see options for continuing the series (such as "Wednesday" and "Thursday") or for simply pasting the copied cells. Clicking the Auto Fill Options button opens a list that lets you choose from the following options: Copy Cells, Fill Series (if applicable), Fill Formatting Only, Fill Without Formatting, or Flash Fill. Choosing Copy Cells means that the cell's contents and its formatting will be copied. The Fill Formatting Only option copies only the formatting attributes, but not cell contents. The Fill Without Formatting option copies the cell contents, but no formatting attributes. Copy Cells is the default option when using the fill handle to copy a cell, so if you want to copy the cell's contents and its formatting, you can ignore the Auto Fill Options button. The Flash Fill option allows you to create customized fill ranges on the fly, such as 2, 4, 6, 8, 10 by entering at least two values in a pattern: Excel automatically senses the pattern.

Copy Formulas with Absolute Cell References

Learning Outcomes
• Create an absolute cell reference
• Use the fill handle to copy absolute cell references

When copying formulas, you might want one or more cell references in the formula to remain unchanged in relation to the formula. In such an instance, you need to apply an absolute cell reference before copying the formula to preserve the specific cell address when the formula is copied. You create an absolute reference by placing a dollar sign ($) before the column letter and row number of the address (for example, A1). **CASE** ▶ *You need to do some what-if analysis to see how various percentage increases might affect total expenses. You decide to add a column that calculates a possible increase in the total tour expenses, and then change the percentage to see various potential results.*

STEPS

1. **Click cell G1, type Change, then press [Enter]**

2. **Type 1.1, then press [Enter]**

 You store the increase factor that will be used in the what-if analysis in this cell (G2). The value 1.1 can be used to calculate a 10% increase: anything you multiply by 1.1 returns an amount that is 110% of the original amount.

3. **Click cell H3, type What if?, then press [Enter]**

4. **In cell H4, type =, click cell F4, type *, click cell G2, then click the Enter button ✓ on the formula bar**

 The result, 28250.1, appears in cell H4. This value represents the total annual expenses for Australia if there is a 10% increase. You want to perform a what-if analysis for all the tour countries.

> **QUICK TIP**
>
> Before you copy or move a formula, always check to see if you need to use an absolute cell reference.

5. **Drag the fill handle from cell H4 to cell H11**

 The resulting values in the range H5:H11 are all zeros, which is not the result you wanted. Because you used relative cell addressing in cell H4, the copied formula adjusted so that the formula in cell H5 is =F5*G3. Because there is no value in cell G3, the result is 0, an error. You need to use an absolute reference in the formula to keep the formula from adjusting itself. That way, it will always reference cell G2.

> **QUICK TIP**
>
> When changing a cell reference to an absolute reference, make sure the reference is selected or the insertion point is next to it in the cell before pressing [F4].

6. **Click cell H4, press [F2] to change to Edit mode, then press [F4]**

 When you press [F2], the range finder outlines the arguments of the equation in blue and red. The insertion point appears next to the G2 cell reference in cell H4. When you press [F4], dollar signs are inserted in the G2 cell reference, making it an absolute reference. See **FIGURE B-17**.

7. **Click ✓, then drag the fill handle from cell H4 to cell H11**

 Because the formula correctly contains an absolute cell reference, the correct values for a 10% increase appear in cells H4:H11. You now want to see what a 20% increase in expenses looks like.

8. **Click cell G2, type 1.2, then click ✓**

 The values in the range H4:H11 change to reflect the 20% increase. Compare your worksheet to **FIGURE B-18**.

9. **Save your work**

FIGURE B-17: Absolute reference created in formula

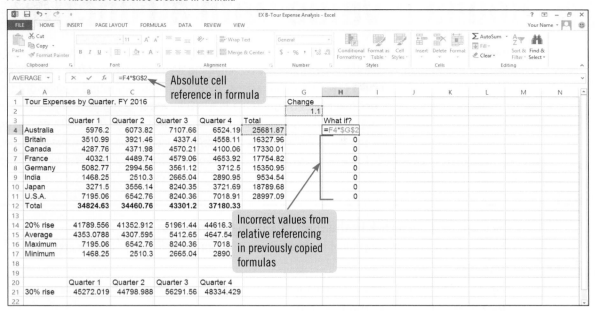

FIGURE B-18: What-if analysis with modified change factor

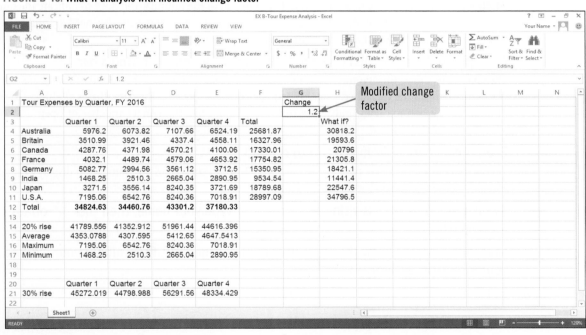

Using the fill handle for sequential text or values

Often, you need to fill cells with sequential text: months of the year, days of the week, years, or text plus a number (Quarter 1, Quarter 2,...). For example, you might want to create a worksheet that calculates data for every month of the year. Using the fill handle, you can quickly and easily create labels for the months of the year just by typing "January" in a cell. Drag the fill handle from the cell containing "January" until you have all the monthly labels you need. You can also easily fill cells with a date sequence by dragging the fill handle on a single cell containing a date. You can

fill cells with a number sequence (such as 1, 2, 3,...) by dragging the fill handle on a selection of two or more cells that contain the sequence. To create a number sequence using the value in a single cell, press and hold [Ctrl] as you drag the fill handle of the cell. As you drag the fill handle, Excel automatically extends the existing sequence into the additional cells. (The content of the last filled cell appears in the ScreenTip.) To examine all the fill series options for the current selection, click the Fill button in the Editing group on the HOME tab, then click Series to open the Series dialog box.

Round a Value with a Function

Learning Outcomes
- Use Formula AutoComplete to insert a function
- Copy an edited formula

The more you explore features and tools in Excel, the more ways you'll find to simplify your work and convey information more efficiently. For example, cells containing financial data are often easier to read if they contain fewer decimal places than those that appear by default. You can round a value or formula result to a specific number of decimal places by using the ROUND function. **CASE** ▶ *In your worksheet, you'd like to round the cells showing the 20% rise in expenses to show fewer digits; after all, it's not important to show cents in the projections, only whole dollars. You want Excel to round the calculated value to the nearest integer. You decide to edit cell B14 so it includes the ROUND function, and then copy the edited formula into the other formulas in this row.*

STEPS

1. **Click cell B14, then click to the right of = in the formula bar**

 You want to position the function at the beginning of the formula, before any values or arguments.

QUICK TIP
In the Insert Function dialog box, the ROUND function is in the Math & Trig category.

2. **Type RO**

 Formula AutoComplete displays a list of functions beginning with RO beneath the formula bar.

3. **Double-click ROUND in the functions list**

 The new function and an opening parenthesis are added to the formula, as shown in **FIGURE B-19**. A few additional modifications are needed to complete your edit of the formula. You need to indicate the number of decimal places to which the function should round numbers and you also need to add a closing parenthesis around the set of arguments that comes after the ROUND function.

TROUBLE
If you have too many or too few parentheses, the extraneous paren-thesis is displayed in red, or a warning dialog box opens with a suggested solution to the error.

4. **Press [END], type ,0), then click the Enter button ✓ on the formula bar**

 The comma separates the arguments within the formula, and 0 indicates that you don't want any decimal places to appear in the calculated value. When you complete the edit, the parentheses at either end of the formula briefly become bold, indicating that the formula has the correct number of open and closed parentheses and is balanced.

5. **Drag the fill handle from cell B14 to cell E14**

 The formula in cell B14 is copied to the range C14:E14. All the values are rounded to display no decimal places. Compare your worksheet to **FIGURE B-20**.

6. **Scroll down so row 25 is visible, click cell A25, type your name, then click ✓ on the formula bar**

7. **Save your work, preview the worksheet in Backstage view, then submit your work to your Instructor as directed**

8. **Exit Excel**

FIGURE B-19: ROUND function added to an existing formula

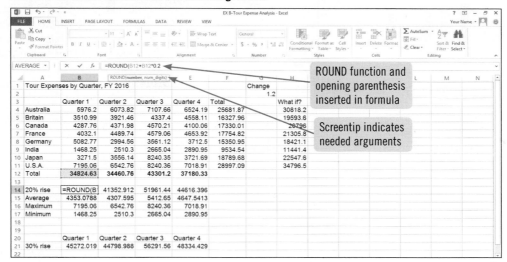

ROUND function and opening parenthesis inserted in formula

Screentip indicates needed arguments

FIGURE B-20: Completed worksheet

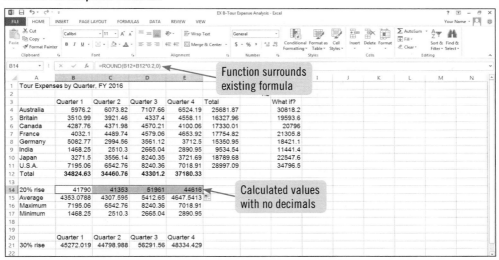

Function surrounds existing formula

Calculated values with no decimals

Creating a new workbook using a template

Excel **templates** are predesigned workbook files intended to save time when you create common documents such as balance sheets, budgets, or time cards. Templates contain labels, values, formulas, and formatting, so all you have to do is customize them with your own information. Excel comes with many templates, and you can also create your own or find additional templates on the Web. Unlike a typical workbook, which has the file extension .xlsx, a template has the extension .xltx. To create a workbook using a template, click the FILE tab, then click New on the navigation bar. The New pane in Backstage view lists templates available through Office.com. The Blank workbook template is selected by default and is used to create a blank workbook with no content or special formatting. A preview of the selected template appears in a separate window on top of the New pane. To select a template, click one of the selections in the New pane, then click Create. **FIGURE B-21** shows an Office.com template. (Your list of templates may differ.) When you click Create, a new

workbook is created based on the template; when you save the new file in the default format, it has the regular .xlsx extension. To save a workbook of your own as a template, open the Save As dialog box, click the Save as type list arrow, then change the file type to Excel Template.

FIGURE B-21: EXPENSE TRENDS template selected in Backstage view

Practice

Concepts Review

Label each element of the Excel worksheet window shown in FIGURE B-22.

FIGURE B-22

Match each term or button with the statement that best describes it.

8. **Fill handle**

9. **[Delete]**

10. **Dialog box launcher**

11. **Formula AutoComplete**

12. **Drag-and-drop method**

a. Clears the contents of selected cells

b. Item on the Ribbon that opens a dialog box or task pane

c. Lets you move or copy data from one cell to another without using the Clipboard

d. Displays an alphabetical list of functions from which you can choose

e. Lets you copy cell contents or continue a series of data into a range of selected cells

Select the best answer from the list of choices.

13. What type of cell reference changes when it is copied?
 a. Circular
 b. Absolute
 c. Relative
 d. Specified

14. What type of cell reference is C$19?
 a. Relative
 b. Absolute
 c. Mixed
 d. Certain

15. Which key do you press to copy while dragging and dropping selected cells?
 a. [Alt]
 b. [Ctrl]
 c. [F2]
 d. [Tab]

16. You can use any of the following features to enter a function *except*:
 a. Insert Function button.
 b. Formula AutoComplete.
 c. AutoSum list arrow.
 d. Clipboard.

17. Which key do you press to convert a relative cell reference to an absolute cell reference?
 a. [F2]
 b. [F4]
 c. [F5]
 d. [F6]

Skills Review

1. Create a complex formula.
 a. Open the file EX B-2.xlsx from the location where you store your Data Files, then save it as **EX B-Baking Supply Company Inventory**.
 b. Select the range B4:B8, click the Totals tab in the Quick Analysis tool, then click the AutoSum button.
 c. Use the fill handle to copy the formula in cell B9 to cells C9:E9
 d. In cell B11, create a complex formula that calculates a 30% decrease in the total number of cases of cake pans.
 e. Use the fill handle to copy this formula into cell C11 through cell E11.
 f. Save your work.

2. Insert a function.
 a. Use the AutoSum list arrow to create a formula in cell B13 that averages the number of cases of cake pans in each storage area.
 b. Use the Insert Function button to create a formula in cell B14 that calculates the maximum number of cases of cake pans in a storage area.
 c. Use the AutoSum list arrow to create a formula in cell B15 that calculates the minimum number of cases of cake pans in a storage area.
 d. Save your work.

3. Type a function.
 a. In cell C13, type a formula that includes a function to average the number of cases of pie pans in each storage area. (*Hint*: Use Formula AutoComplete to enter the function.)
 b. In cell C14, type a formula that includes a function to calculate the maximum number of cases of pie pans in a storage area.
 c. In cell C15, type a formula that includes a function to calculate the minimum number of cases of pie pans in a storage area.
 d. Save your work.

Skills Review (continued)

4. Copy and move cell entries.

 a. Select the range B3:F3.

 b. Copy the selection to the Clipboard.

 c. Open the Clipboard task pane, then paste the selection into cell B17.

 d. Close the Clipboard task pane, then select the range A4:A9.

 e. Use the drag-and-drop method to copy the selection to cell A18. (*Hint*: The results should fill the range A18:A23.)

 f. Save your work.

5. Understand relative and absolute cell references.

 a. Write a brief description of the difference between relative and absolute references.

 b. List at least three situations in which you think a business might use an absolute reference in its calculations. Examples can include calculations for different types of worksheets, such as time cards, invoices, and budgets.

6. Copy formulas with relative cell references.

 a. Calculate the total in cell F4.

 b. Use the Fill button to copy the formula in cell F4 down to cells F5:F8.

 c. Select the range C13:C15.

 d. Use the fill handle to copy these cells to the range D13:F15.

 e. Save your work.

7. Copy formulas with absolute cell references.

 a. In cell H1, enter the value **1.575**.

 b. In cell H4, create a formula that multiplies F4 and an absolute reference to cell H1.

 c. Use the fill handle to copy the formula in cell H4 to cells H5 and H6.

 d. Use the Copy and Paste buttons to copy the formula in cell H4 to cells H7 and H8.

 e. Change the amount in cell H1 to **2.5**.

 f. Save your work.

8. Round a value with a function.

 a. Click cell H4.

 b. Edit this formula to include the ROUND function showing zero decimal places.

 c. Use the fill handle to copy the formula in cell H4 to the range H5:H8.

 d. Enter your name in cell A25, then compare your work to FIGURE B-23.

 e. Save your work, preview the worksheet in Backstage view, then submit your work to your instructor as directed.

 f. Close the workbook, then exit Excel.

FIGURE B-23

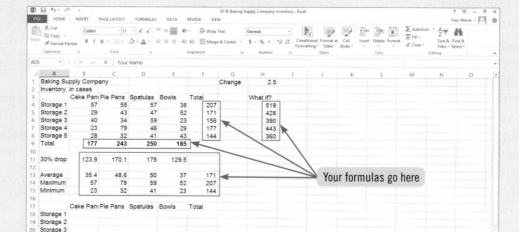

Independent Challenge 1

You are thinking of starting a small express oil change service center. Before you begin, you need to evaluate what you think your monthly expenses will be. You've started a workbook, but need to complete the entries and add formulas.

a. Open the file EX B-3.xlsx from the location where you store your Data Files, then save it as **EX B-Express Oil Change Expenses**.

b. Make up your own expense data, and enter it in cells B4:B10. (Monthly sales are already included in the worksheet.)

c. Create a formula in cell C4 that calculates the annual rent.

d. Copy the formula in cell C4 to the range C5:C10.

e. Move the label in cell A15 to cell A14.

f. Create formulas in cells B11 and C11 that total the monthly and annual expenses.

g. Create a formula in cell C13 that calculates annual sales.

h. Create a formula in cell B14 that determines whether you will make a profit or loss, then copy the formula into cell C14.

i. Copy the labels in cells B3:C3 to cells E3:F3.

j. Type **Projected Increase** in cell G1, then type **.2** in cell H2.

k. Create a formula in cell E4 that calculates an increase in the monthly rent by the amount in cell H2. You will be copying this formula to other cells, so you'll need to use an absolute reference.

l. Create a formula in cell F4 that calculates the increased annual rent expense based on the calculation in cell E4.

m. Copy the formulas in cells E4:F4 into cells E5:F10 to calculate the remaining monthly and annual expenses.

n. Create a formula in cell E11 that calculates the total monthly expenses, then copy that formula to cell F11.

o. Copy the contents of cells B13:C13 into cells E13:F13.

p. Create formulas in cells E14 and F14 that calculate profit/loss based on the projected increase in monthly and annual expenses.

q. Change the projected increase to **.17**, then compare your work to the sample in FIGURE B-24.

r. Enter your name in a cell in the worksheet.

s. Save your work, preview the worksheet in Backstage view, submit your work to your instructor as directed, close the workbook, and exit Excel.

FIGURE B-24

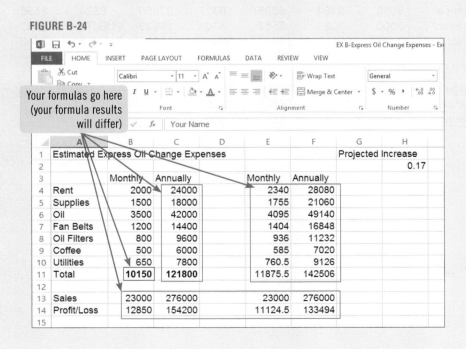

Independent Challenge 2

The Dog Days Daycare Center is a small, growing pet care center that has hired you to organize its accounting records using Excel. The owners want you to track the company's expenses. Before you were hired, one of the bookkeepers began entering last year's expenses in a workbook, but the analysis was never completed.

a. Start Excel, open the file EX B-4.xlsx from the location where you store your Data Files, then save it as **EX B-Dog Days Daycare Center Finances**. The worksheet includes labels for functions such as the average, maximum, and minimum amounts of each of the expenses in the worksheet.

b. Think about what information would be important for the bookkeeping staff to know.

c. Using the Quick Analysis tool, create a formula in the Quarter 1 column that uses the SUM function, then copy that formula into the Total row for the remaining Quarters.

d. Use the SUM function to create formulas for each expense in the Total column.

e. Create formulas for each expense and each quarter in the Average, Maximum, and Minimum columns and rows using the method of your choice.

f. Compare your worksheet to the sample shown in FIGURE B-25.

g. Enter your name in cell A25, then save your work.

h. Preview the worksheet, then submit your work to your instructor as directed.

i. Close the workbook and exit Excel.

FIGURE B-25

	A	B	C	D	E	F	G	H	I
1	Dog Days Daycare Center								
2									
3	Operating Expenses for 2016								
4									
5	Expense	Quarter 1	Quarter 2	Quarter 3	Quarter 4	Total	Average	Maximum	Minimum
6	Rent	9240	9240	9240	9240	36960	9240	9240	9240
7	Utilities	9000	7982	7229	8096	32307	8076.75	9000	7229
8	Payroll	23456	26922	25876	29415	105669	26417.3	29415	23456
9	Insurance	8550	8194	8225	8327	33296	8324	8550	8194
10	Education	3000	3081	6552	4006	16639	4159.75	6552	3000
11	Inventory	29986	27115	25641	32465	115207	28801.8	32465	25641
12	Total	83232	82534	82763	91549				
13									
14	Average	13872	13755.7	13793.8	15258.2			Your formulas go here	
15	Maximum	29986	27115	25876	32465				
16	Minimum	3000	3081	6552	4006				

Independent Challenge 3

As the accounting manager of a locally owned business, it is your responsibility to calculate accrued sales tax payments on a monthly basis and then submit the payments to the state government. You've decided to use an Excel workbook to make these calculations.

a. Start Excel, then save a new, blank workbook to the drive and folder where you store your Data Files as
EX B-Sales Tax Calculations.

b. Decide on the layout for all columns and rows. The worksheet will contain data for six stores, which you can name by store number, neighborhood, or another method of your choice. For each store, you will calculate total sales tax based on the local sales tax rate. You'll also calculate total tax owed for all six stores.

c. Make up sales data for all six stores.

d. Enter the rate to be used to calculate the sales tax, using your own local rate.

e. Create formulas to calculate the sales tax owed for each store. If you don't know the local tax rate, use **6.5%**.

f. Create a formula to total all the accrued sales tax.

g. Use the ROUND function to eliminate any decimal places in the sales tax figures for each store and the total due.

h. Add your name to the header, then compare your work to the sample shown in FIGURE B-26.

i. Save your work, preview the worksheet, and submit your work to your instructor as directed.

j. Close the workbook and exit Excel.

FIGURE B-26

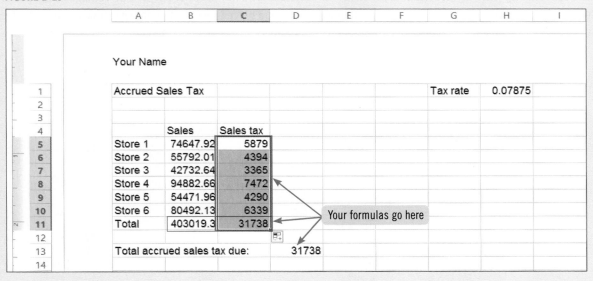

Independent Challenge 4: Explore

Since your recent promotion at work, you have started thinking about purchasing a home. As you begin the round of open houses and realtors' listings, you notice that there are many fees associated with buying a home. Some fees are based on a percentage of the purchase price, and others are a flat fee; overall, they seem to represent a substantial amount above the purchase prices you see listed. You've seen five houses so far that interest you; one is easily affordable, and the remaining four are all nice, but increasingly more expensive. Although you will be financing the home, the bottom line is still important to you, so you decide to create an Excel workbook to figure out the real cost of buying each one.

a. Find out the typical cost or percentage rate of at least three fees that are usually charged when buying a home and taking out a mortgage. (*Hint*: If you have access to the Internet you can research the topic of home buying on the Web, or you can ask friends about standard rates or percentages for items such as title insurance, credit reports, and inspection fees.)

b. Start Excel, then save a new, blank workbook to the location where you store your Data Files as **EX B-Home Purchase Costs**.

c. Create labels and enter data for at least three homes. If you enter this information across the columns in your worksheet, you should have one column for each house, with the purchase price in the cell below each label. Be sure to enter a different purchase price for each house.

d. Create labels for the Fees column and for an Amount or Rate column. Enter the information for each of the fees you have researched.

e. In each house column, enter formulas that calculate the fee for each item. The formulas (and use of absolute or relative referencing) will vary depending on whether the charges are a flat fee or based on a percentage of the purchase price. Make sure that the formulas for items that are based on a percentage of the purchase price (such as the fees for the Title Insurance Policy, Loan Origination, and Underwriter) contain absolute references.

Independent Challenge 4: Explore (continued)

f. Total the fees for each house, then create formulas that add the total fees to the purchase price. A sample of what your workbook might look like is shown in FIGURE B-27.

g. Enter a title for the worksheet in the header.

h. Enter your name in the header, save your work, preview the worksheet, then submit your work to your instructor as directed.

i. Close the file and exit Excel.

FIGURE B-27

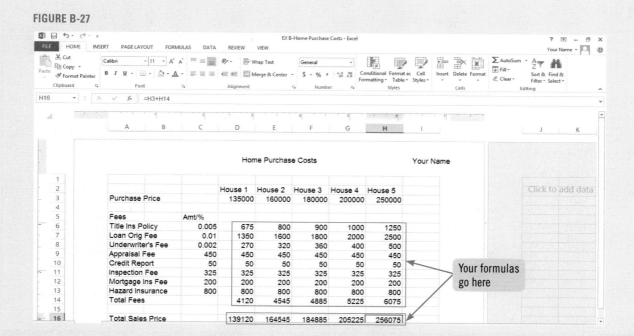

Visual Workshop

Create the worksheet shown in FIGURE B-28 using the skills you learned in this unit. Save the workbook as **EX B-Expense Analysis** to the location where you store your Data Files. Enter your name and worksheet title in the header as shown, hide the gridlines, preview the worksheet, and then submit your work to your instructor as directed. (*Hint:* Change the Zoom factor to 100% by clicking the Zoom out button twice.)

FIGURE B-28

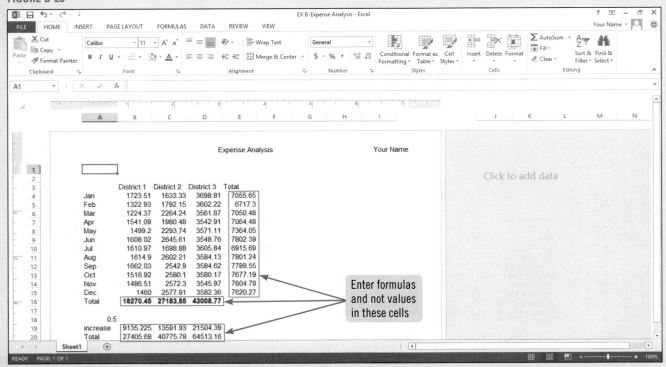

Formatting a Worksheet

CASE ▶ The corporate marketing managers at QST have requested data from all QST locations for advertising expenses incurred during the first quarter of this year. Grace Wong has created a worksheet listing this information. She asks you to format the worksheet to make it easier to read and to call attention to important data.

Unit Objectives

After completing this unit, you will be able to:

- Format values
- Change font and font size
- Change font styles and alignment
- Adjust the column width
- Insert and delete rows and columns

- Apply colors, patterns, and borders
- Apply conditional formatting
- Rename and move a worksheet
- Check spelling

Files You Will Need

EX C-1.xlsx
EX C-2.xlsx
EX C-3.xlsx
EX C-4.xlsx
EX C-5.xlsx

Format Values

Learning
Outcomes
• Format a number
• Format a date
• Increase/decrease
 decimals

The **format** of a cell determines how the labels and values look—for example, whether the contents appear boldfaced, italicized, or with dollar signs and commas. Formatting changes only the appearance of a value or label; it does not alter the actual data in any way. To format a cell or range, first you select it, then you apply the formatting using the Ribbon, Mini toolbar, or a keyboard shortcut. You can apply formatting before or after you enter data in a cell or range. **CASE** *Grace has provided you with a worksheet that details advertising expenses, and you're ready to improve its appearance and readability. You start by formatting some of the values so they are displayed as currency, percentages, and dates.*

STEPS

1. **Start Excel, open the file EX C-1.xlsx from the location where you store your Data Files, then save it as EX C-QST Advertising Expenses**

 This worksheet is difficult to interpret because all the information is crowded and looks the same. In some columns, the contents appear cut off because there is too much data to fit given the current column width. You decide not to widen the columns yet, because the other changes you plan to make might affect column width and row height. The first thing you want to do is format the data showing the cost of each ad.

2. **Select the range D4:D32, then click the Accounting Number Format button $ in the Number group on the HOME tab**

 The default Accounting **number format** adds dollar signs and two decimal places to the data, as shown in **FIGURE C-1**. Formatting this data in Accounting format makes it clear that its values are monetary values. Excel automatically resizes the column to display the new formatting. The Accounting and Currency number formats are both used for monetary values, but the Accounting format aligns currency symbols and decimal points of numbers in a column.

3. **Select the range F4:H32, then click the Comma Style button ⁹ in the Number group**

 The values in columns F, G, and H display the Comma Style format, which does not include a dollar sign but can be useful for some types of accounting data.

4. **Select the range J4:J32, click the Number Format list arrow, click Percentage, then click the Increase Decimal button ⁺⁰·⁰⁰ in the Number group**

 The data in the % of Total column is now formatted with a percent sign (%) and three decimal places. The Number Format list arrow lets you choose from popular number formats and shows an example of what the selected cell or cells would look like in each format (when multiple cells are selected, the example is based on the first cell in the range). Each time you click the Increase Decimal button, you add one decimal place; clicking the button twice would add two decimal places.

5. **Click the Decrease Decimal button ·⁰⁰→·⁰ in the Number group twice**

 Two decimal places are removed from the percentage values in column J.

6. **Select the range B4:B31, then click the dialog box launcher ⌐ in the Number group**

 The Format Cells dialog box opens with the Date category already selected on the Number tab.

7. **Select the first 14-Mar-12 format in the Type list box as shown in FIGURE C-2, then click OK**

 The dates in column B appear in the 14-Mar-12 format. The second 14-Mar-12 format in the list (visible if you scroll down the list) displays all days in two digits (it adds a leading zero if the day is only a single-digit number), while the one you chose displays single-digit days without a leading zero.

8. **Select the range C4:C31, right-click the range, click Format Cells on the shortcut menu, click 14-Mar in the Type list box in the Format Cells dialog box, then click OK**

 Compare your worksheet to **FIGURE C-3**.

9. **Press [Ctrl][Home], then save your work**

FIGURE C-1: Accounting number format applied to range

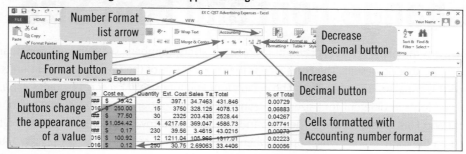

FIGURE C-2: Format Cells dialog box

FIGURE C-3: Worksheet with formatted values

Formatting as a table

Excel includes 60 predefined **table styles** to make it easy to format selected worksheet cells as a table. You can apply table styles to any range of cells that you want to format quickly, or even to an entire worksheet, but they're especially useful for those ranges with labels in the left column and top row, and totals in the bottom row or right column. To apply a table style, select the data to be formatted or click anywhere within the intended range (Excel can automatically detect a range of cells filled with data), click the Format as Table button in the Styles group on the HOME tab, then click a style in the gallery, as shown in **FIGURE C-4**. Table styles are organized in three categories: Light, Medium, and Dark. Once you click a style, Excel asks you to confirm the range selection, then applies the style. Once you have formatted a range as a table, you can use Live Preview to preview the table in other styles by pointing to any style in the Table Styles gallery.

FIGURE C-4: Table Styles gallery

Change Font and Font Size

Learning
Outcomes
• Change a font
• Change a font size
• Use the Mini
 toolbar

A **font** is the name for a collection of characters (letters, numbers, symbols, and punctuation marks) with a similar, specific design. The **font size** is the physical size of the text, measured in units called points. A **point** is equal to 1/72 of an inch. The default font and font size in Excel is 11-point Calibri. TABLE C-1 shows several fonts in different font sizes. You can change the font and font size of any cell or range using the Font and Font Size list arrows. The Font and Font Size list arrows appear on the HOME tab on the Ribbon and on the Mini toolbar, which opens when you right-click a cell or range. **CASE** ▶ *You want to change the font and font size of the labels and the worksheet title so that they stand out more from the data.*

STEPS

1. **Click the Font list arrow in the Font group on the HOME tab, scroll down in the Font list to see an alphabetical listing of the fonts available on your computer, then click Times New Roman, as shown in** FIGURE C-5

 The font in cell A1 changes to Times New Roman. Notice that the font names on the list are displayed in the font they represent.

2. **Click the Font Size list arrow in the Font group, then click 20**

 The worksheet title appears in 20-point Times New Roman, and the Font and Font Size list boxes on the HOME tab display the new font and font size information.

3. **Click the Increase Font Size button** A˄ **in the Font group twice**

 The font size of the title increases to 24 point.

4. **Select the range A3:J3, right-click, then click the Font list arrow on the Mini toolbar**

 The Mini toolbar includes the most commonly used formatting tools, so it's great for making quick formatting changes.

5. **Scroll down in the Font list and click Times New Roman, click the Font Size list arrow on the Mini toolbar, then click 14**

 The Mini toolbar closes when you move the pointer away from the selection. Compare your worksheet to FIGURE C-6. Notice that some of the column labels are now too wide to appear fully in the column. Excel does not automatically adjust column widths to accommodate cell formatting; you have to adjust column widths manually. You'll learn to do this in a later lesson.

6. **Save your work**

TABLE C-1: Examples of fonts and font sizes

font	12 point	24 point
Calibri	Excel	Excel
Playbill	Excel	Excel
Comic Sans MS	Excel	Excel
Times New Roman	Excel	Excel

FIGURE C-5: Font list

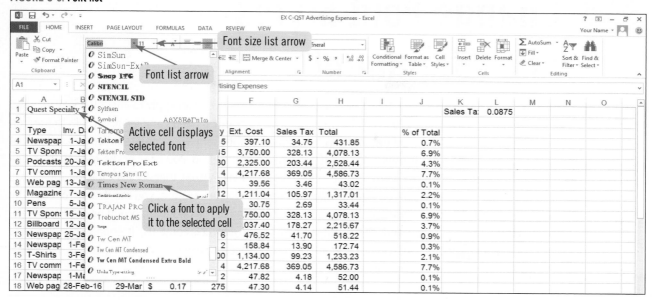

FIGURE C-6: Worksheet with formatted title and column labels

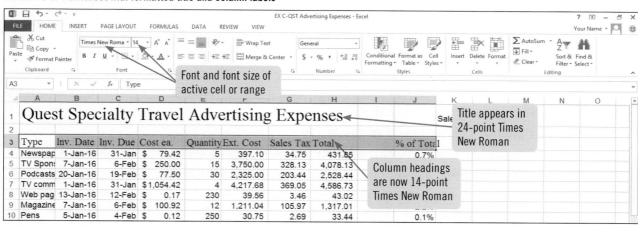

Inserting and adjusting online pictures and other images

You can illustrate your worksheets using online pictures and other images. Office.com makes many photos and animations available for your use. To add a picture to a worksheet, click the Online Pictures button in the Illustrations group on the INSERT tab. The Insert Pictures window opens. Here you can search for online pictures (or Clip Art) in Office.com, through the Bing search engine, or on your SkyDrive by typing one or more **keywords** (words related to your subject) in the appropriate Search text box, then click [Enter]. For example, pictures that relate to the keyword house in a search of Office.com appear in the Office.com window, as shown in **FIGURE C-7**. When you double-click the image you want in the window, the image is inserted at the location of the active cell. To add images on your computer (or computers on your network) to a worksheet, click the INSERT tab on the Ribbon, then click the Pictures button in the Illustrations group. Navigate to the file you want, then click Insert. To resize an

image, drag any corner sizing handle. To move an image, point inside the clip until the pointer changes to the move pointer, then drag it to a new location.

FIGURE C-7: Results of Online Picture search

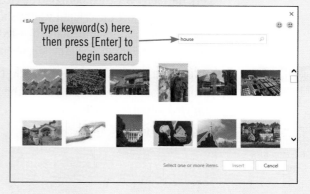

Change Font Styles and Alignment

Font styles are formats such as bold, italic, and underlining that you can apply to affect the way text and numbers look in a worksheet. You can also change the **alignment** of labels and values in cells to position them in relation to the cells' edges—such as left-aligned, right-aligned, or centered. You can apply font styles and alignment options using the HOME tab, the Format Cells dialog box, or the Mini toolbar. See TABLE C-2 for a description of common font style and alignment buttons that are available on the HOME tab and the Mini toolbar. Once you have formatted a cell the way you want it, you can "paint" or copy the cell's formats into other cells by using the Format Painter button in the Clipboard group on the HOME tab. This is similar to using copy and paste, but instead of copying cell contents, it copies only the cell's formatting. **CASE** ▶ *You want to further enhance the worksheet's appearance by adding bold and underline formatting and centering some of the labels.*

STEPS

1. **Press [Ctrl][Home], then click the Bold button B in the Font group on the HOME tab**
 The title in cell A1 appears in bold.

2. **Click cell A3, then click the Underline button U in the Font group**
 The column label is now underlined, though this may be difficult to see with the cell selected.

3. **Click the Italic button I in the Font group, then click B**
 The heading now appears in boldface, underlined, italic type. Notice that the Bold, Italic, and Underline buttons in the Font group are all selected.

4. **Click the Italic button I to deselect it**
 The italic font style is removed from cell A3, but the bold and underline font styles remain.

5. **Click the Format Painter button ❧ in the Clipboard group, then select the range B3:J3**
 The formatting in cell A3 is copied to the rest of the column labels. To paint the formats on more than one selection, double-click the Format Painter button to keep it activated until you turn it off. You can turn off the Format Painter by pressing [Esc] or by clicking ❧. You decide the title would look better if it were centered over the data columns.

6. **Select the range A1:H1, then click the Merge & Center button 🗐 in the Alignment group**
 The Merge & Center button creates one cell out of the eight cells across the row, then centers the text in that newly created, merged cell. The title "Quest Specialty Travel Advertising Expenses" is centered across the eight columns you selected. To split a merged cell into its original components, select the merged cell, then click the Merge & Center button to deselect it. The merged and centered text might look awkward now, but you'll be changing the column widths shortly. Occasionally, you may find that you want cell contents to wrap within a cell. You can do this by selecting the cells containing the text you want to wrap, then clicking the Wrap Text button 🗐 in the Alignment group on the HOME tab on the Ribbon.

7. **Select the range A3:J3, right-click, then click the Center button ☰ on the Mini toolbar**
 Compare your screen to FIGURE C-8. Although they may be difficult to read, notice that all the headings are centered within their cells.

8. **Save your work**

FIGURE C-8: Worksheet with font styles and alignment applied

FIGURE C-8: Worksheet with font styles and alignment applied

TABLE C-2: Common font style and alignment buttons

button	description
B	Bolds text
I	Italicizes text
U	Underlines text
▦	Centers text across columns, and combines two or more selected, adjacent cells into one cell
▤	Aligns text at the left edge of the cell
▤	Centers text horizontally within the cell
▤	Aligns text at the right edge of the cell
▤	Wraps long text into multiple lines

Rotating and indenting cell entries

In addition to applying fonts and font styles, you can rotate or indent data within a cell to further change its appearance. You can rotate text within a cell by altering its alignment. To change alignment, select the cells you want to modify, then click the dialog box launcher ⬚ in the Alignment group to open the Alignment tab of the Format Cells dialog box. Click a position in the Orientation box or type a number in the Degrees text box to rotate text from its default horizontal orientation, then click OK. You can indent cell contents using the Increase Indent button ⬚ in the Alignment group, which moves cell contents to the right one space, or the Decrease Indent button ⬚, which moves cell contents to the left one space.

Adjust the Column Width

Learning Outcomes
- Change a column width by dragging
- Resize a column with AutoFit
- Change the width of multiple columns

As you format a worksheet, you might need to adjust the width of one or more columns to accommodate changes in the amount of text, the font size, or font style. The default column width is 8.43 characters, a little less than 1". With Excel, you can adjust the width of one or more columns by using the mouse, the Format button in the Cells group on the HOME tab, or the shortcut menu. Using the mouse, you can drag or double-click the right edge of a column heading. The Format button and shortcut menu include commands for making more precise width adjustments. TABLE C-3 describes common column formatting commands. **CASE** *You have noticed that some of the labels in columns A through J don't fit in the cells. You want to adjust the widths of the columns so that the labels appear in their entirety.*

STEPS

1. **Position the mouse pointer on the line between the column A and column B headings until it changes to ↔**

 See FIGURE C-9. The **column heading** is the box at the top of each column containing a letter. Before you can adjust column width using the mouse, you need to position the pointer on the right edge of the column heading for the column you want to adjust. The cell entry "TV commercials" is the widest in the column.

 QUICK TIP

 If "#######" appears after you adjust a column of values, the column is too narrow to display the values completely; increase the column width until the values appear.

2. **Click and drag the ↔ to the right until the column displays the "TV commercials" cell entries fully (approximately 15.29 characters, 1.23", or 112 pixels)**

 As you change the column width, a ScreenTip is displayed listing the column width. In Normal view, the ScreenTip lists the width in characters and pixels; in Page Layout view, the ScreenTip lists the width in inches and pixels.

3. **Position the pointer on the line between columns B and C until it changes to ↔, then double-click**

 Double-clicking the right edge of a column heading activates the **AutoFit** feature, which automatically resizes the column to accommodate the widest entry in the column. Column B automatically widens to fit the widest entry, which is the column label "Inv. Date".

4. **Use AutoFit to resize columns C, D, and J**

5. **Select the range E5:H5**

 You can change the width of multiple columns at once, by first selecting either the column headings or at least one cell in each column.

 QUICK TIP

 If an entire column rather than a column cell is selected, you can change the width of the column by right-clicking the column heading, then clicking Column Width on the shortcut menu.

6. **Click the Format button in the Cells group, then click Column Width**

 The Column Width dialog box opens. Column width measurement is based on the number of characters that will fit in the column when formatted in the Normal font and font size (in this case, 11 pt Calibri).

7. **Drag the dialog box by its title bar if its placement obscures your view of the worksheet, type 11 in the Column width text box, then click OK**

 The widths of columns E, F, G, and H change to reflect the new setting. See FIGURE C-10.

8. **Save your work**

FIGURE C-9: Preparing to change the column width

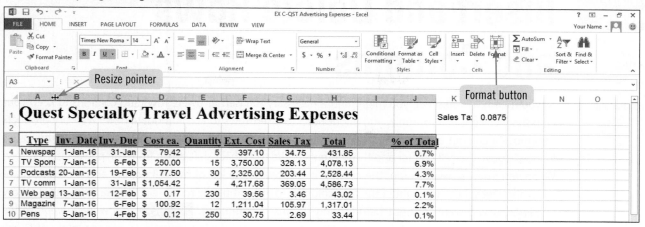

FIGURE C-10: Worksheet with column widths adjusted

TABLE C-3: Common column formatting commands

command	description	available using
Column Width	Sets the width to a specific number of characters	Format button; shortcut menu
AutoFit Column Width	Fits to the widest entry in a column	Format button; mouse
Hide & Unhide	Hides or displays hidden column(s)	Format button; shortcut menu
Default Width	Resets column to worksheet's default column width	Format button

Changing row height

Changing row height is as easy as changing column width. Row height is calculated in points, the same units of measure used for fonts. The row height must exceed the size of the font you are using. Normally, you don't need to adjust row heights manually, because row heights adjust automatically to accommodate font size changes. If you format something in a row to be a larger point size, Excel adjusts the row to fit the largest point size in the row. However, you have just as many options for changing row height as you do column width. Using the mouse, you can place the ╬ pointer on the line dividing a row heading from the heading below, and then drag to the desired height; double-clicking the line AutoFits the row height where necessary. You can also select one or more rows, then use the Row Height command on the shortcut menu, or click the Format button on the HOME tab and click the Row Height or AutoFit Row Height command.

Learning
Outcomes
• Use the Insert
 dialog box
• Use column and
 row heading
 buttons to insert
 and delete

Insert and Delete Rows and Columns

As you modify a worksheet, you might find it necessary to insert or delete rows and columns to keep your worksheet current. For example, you might need to insert rows to accommodate new inventory products or remove a column of yearly totals that are no longer necessary. When you insert a new row, the row is inserted above the cell pointer and the contents of the worksheet shift down from the newly inserted row. When you insert a new column, the column is inserted to the left of the cell pointer and the contents of the worksheet shift to the right of the new column. To insert multiple rows, select the same number of row headings as you want to insert before using the Insert command. **CASE** ▶ *You want to improve the overall appearance of the worksheet by inserting a row between the last row of data and the totals. Also, you have learned that row 27 and column J need to be deleted from the worksheet.*

STEPS

1. Right-click cell A32, then click Insert on the shortcut menu

The Insert dialog box opens. See **FIGURE C-11**. You can choose to insert a column or a row; insert a single cell and shift the cells in the active column to the right; or insert a single cell and shift the cells in the active row down. An additional row between the last row of data and the totals will visually separate the totals.

> **QUICK TIP**
> To insert a single row or column, right-click the row heading immediately below where you want the new row, or right-click the column heading to the right of where you want the new column, then click Insert on the shortcut menu.

2. Click the Entire row option button, then click OK

A blank row appears between the Billboard data and the totals, and the formula result in cell E33 has not changed. The Insert Options button 🖎▾ appears beside cell A33. Pointing to the button displays a list arrow, which you can click and then choose from the following options: Format Same As Above (the default setting, already selected), Format Same As Below, or Clear Formatting.

3. Click the row 27 heading

All of row 27 is selected, as shown in **FIGURE C-12**.

> **QUICK TIP**
> If you inadvertently click the Delete list arrow instead of the button itself, click Delete Sheet Rows in the menu that opens.

4. Click the Delete button in the Cells group; *do not click the list arrow*

Excel deletes row 27, and all rows below it shift up one row. You must use the Delete button or the Delete command on the shortcut menu to delete a row or column; pressing [Delete] on the keyboard removes only the *contents* of a selected row or column.

5. Click the column J heading

The percentage information is calculated elsewhere and is no longer necessary in this worksheet.

> **QUICK TIP**
> After inserting or deleting rows or columns in a worksheet, be sure to proof formulas that contain relative cell references.

6. Click the Delete button in the Cells group

Excel deletes column J. The remaining columns to the right shift left one column.

7. Use AutoFit to resize columns F and H, then save your work

FIGURE C-11: Insert dialog box

Entire row option button →

Insert

Insert
- ● Shift cells right
- ○ Shift cells down
- ○ Entire row
- ○ Entire column

[OK] [Cancel]

FIGURE C-12: Worksheet with row 27 selected

EX C-QST Advertising Expenses - Excel

Delete button

A27 — Hats

	A	B	C	D	E	F	G	H	I	J	K	L	M	N
15	T-Shirts	3-Feb-16	4-Mar	$ 5.67	200	1,134.00	99.23	1,233.23		2.1%				
16	TV commercials	1-Feb-16	2-Mar	$1,054.42	4	4,217.68	369.05	4,586.73		7.7%				
17	Newspaper	1-Mar-16	31-Mar	$ 23.91	2	47.82	4.18	52.00		0.1%				
18	Web page ads	28-Feb-16	29-Mar	$ 0.17	275	47.30	4.14	51.44		0.1%				
19	Magazine	27-Feb-16	28-Mar	$ 100.92	12	1,211.04	105.97	1,317.01		2.2%				
20	Podacsts	22-Feb-16	23-Mar	$ 77.50	30	2,325.00	203.44	2,528.44		4.3%				
21	TV Sponsor	1-Feb-16	2-Mar	$ 250.00	30	7,500.00	656.25	8,156.25		13.8%				
22	Newspaper	25-Feb-16	26-Mar	$ 79.42	6	476.52	41.70	518.22		0.9%				
23	W	Mar-16	9-Apr	$ 0.17	275	47.30	4.14	51.44		0.1%				
24	T	eb-16	16-Mar	$ 250.00	25	6,250.00	546.88	6,796.88		11.5%				
25	Pens	15-Mar-16	14-Apr	$ 0.12	250	30.75	2.69	33.44		0.1%				
26	TV commercials	1-Mar-16	31-Mar	$1,054.44	4	4,217.76	369.05	4,586.81		7.7%				
27	Hats	20-Mar-16	19-Apr	$ 7.20	250	1,800.00	157.50	1,957.50		3.3%				
28	Podcasts	20-Mar-16	19-Apr	$ 75.50	30	2,265.00	198.19	2,463.19		4.2%				
29	Newspaper	2	Apr	$ 79.42	2	158.84	13.90	172.74		0.3%				
30	Podcasts	2	Apr	$ 77.50	30	2,325.00	203.44	2,528.44		4.3%				
31	Billboard	28-Mar-16	27-Apr	$ 101.87	20	2,037.40	178.27	2,215.67		3.7%				
32														
33					2034	########	4,767.46	########		100.0%				

Row 27 heading

Inserted row

Insert Options button

Hiding and unhiding columns and rows

When you don't want data in a column or row to be visible, but you don't want to delete it, you can hide the column or row. To hide a selected column, click the Format button in the Cells group on the HOME tab, point to Hide & Unhide, then click Hide Columns. A hidden column is indicated by a dark green vertical line in its original position. This green line disappears when you click elsewhere in the worksheet. You can display a hidden column by selecting the columns on either side of the hidden column, clicking the Format button in the Cells group, pointing to Hide & Unhide, and then clicking Unhide Columns. (To hide or unhide one or more rows, substitute Hide Rows and Unhide Rows for the Hide Columns and Unhide Columns commands.)

Adding and editing comments

Much of your work in Excel may be in collaboration with teammates with whom you share worksheets. You can share ideas with other worksheet users by adding comments within selected cells. To include a comment in a worksheet, click the cell where you want to place the comment, click the REVIEW tab on the Ribbon, then click the New Comment button in the Comments group. You can type your comments in the resizable text box that opens containing the computer user's name. A small, red triangle appears in the upper-right corner of a cell containing a comment. If comments are not already displayed in a workbook, other users can point to the triangle to display the comment. To see all worksheet comments, as shown in FIGURE C-13, click the Show All Comments button in the Comments group. To edit a comment, click the cell containing the comment, then click the Edit Comment button in the Comments group. To delete a comment, click the cell containing the comment, then click the Delete button in the Comments group.

FIGURE C-13: Comments displayed in a worksheet

20	Podcasts	22-Feb-16	23-Mar	iPodAds	$ 75.50
21	TV Sponsor	1-Feb-16	2-Mar	Food Network	
22	Newspaper	25-Feb-16	26-Mar	Village Read	
23	Web page ads	10-Mar-16	9-Apr	Advertising C	
24	TV Sponsor	15-Feb-16	16-Mar	Food Networ	
25	Pens	15-Mar-16	14-Apr	Mass Appeal, Inc.	$ 0.12
26	TV commercial	1-Mar-16	31-Mar	Discovery Channel	$1,054.44
27	Podcasts	20-Mar-16	19-Apr	iPodAds	
28	Newspaper	1-Apr-16	1-May	University V	
29	Podcasts	10-Apr-16	10-May	iPodAds	
30	Billboard	28-Mar-16	27-Apr	Advertising Concepts	$ 101.87
31					
32					$5,166.04
33					
34					

Grace Wong: Should we continue with this market, or expand to other publications?

Grace Wong: I think this will turn out to be a very good decision.

Apply Colors, Patterns, and Borders

You can use colors, patterns, and borders to enhance the overall appearance of a worksheet and make it easier to read. You can add these enhancements by using the Borders, Font Color, and Fill Color buttons in the Font group on the HOME tab of the Ribbon and on the Mini toolbar, or by using the Fill tab and the Border tab in the Format Cells dialog box. You can open the Format Cells dialog box by clicking the dialog box launcher in the Font, Alignment, or Number group on the HOME tab, or by right-clicking a selection, then clicking Format Cells on the shortcut menu. You can apply a color to the background of a cell or a range or to cell contents (such as letters and numbers), and you can apply a pattern to a cell or range. You can apply borders to all the cells in a worksheet or only to selected cells to call attention to selected information. To save time, you can also apply **cell styles**, predesigned combinations of formats. **CASE** ▶ *You want to add a pattern, a border, and color to the title of the worksheet to give the worksheet a more professional appearance.*

STEPS

1. **Select cell A1, click the Fill Color list arrow ⬛ ˅ in the Font group, then hover the pointer over the Turquoise, Accent 2 color (first row, sixth column from the left)**
 See FIGURE C-14. Live Preview shows you how the color will look *before* you apply it. (Remember that cell A1 spans columns A through H because the Merge & Center command was applied.)

2. **Click the Turquoise, Accent 2 color**
 The color is applied to the background (or fill) of this cell. When you change fill or font color, the color on the Fill Color or Font Color button changes to the last color you selected.

3. **Right-click cell A1, then click Format Cells on the shortcut menu**
 The Format Cells dialog box opens.

4. ▶ **Click the Fill tab, click the Pattern Style list arrow, click the 6.25% Gray style (first row, sixth column from the left), then click OK**

5. ▶ **Click the Borders list arrow ⬛ ˅ in the Font group, then click Thick Bottom Border**
 Unlike underlining, which is a text-formatting tool, borders extend to the width of the cell, and can appear at the bottom of the cell, at the top, on either side, or on any combination of the four sides. It can be difficult to see a border when the cell is selected.

6. **Select the range A3:H3, click the Font Color list arrow ⬛ ˅ in the Font group, then click the Blue, Accent 1 color (first Theme color row, fifth column from the left) on the palette**
 The new color is applied to the labels in the selected range.

7. **Select the range J1:K1, click the Cell Styles button in the Styles group, click the Neutral cell style (first row, fourth column from the left) in the gallery, then AutoFit column J**
 The font and color change in the range is shown in FIGURE C-15.

8. **Save your work**

FIGURE C-14: Live Preview of fill color

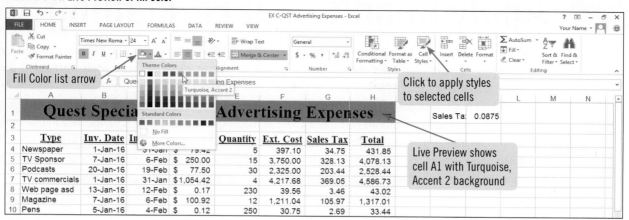

Fill Color list arrow

Click to apply styles to selected cells

Live Preview shows cell A1 with Turquoise, Accent 2 background

FIGURE C-15: Worksheet with color, patterns, border, and cell style applied

Type	Inv. Date	Inv. Due	Cost ea.	Quantity	Ext. Cost	Sales Tax	Total
Newspaper	1-Jan-16	31-Jan	$ 79.42	5	397.10	34.75	431.85
TV Sponsor	7-Jan-16	6-Feb	$ 250.00	15	3,750.00	328.13	4,078.13
Podcasts	20-Jan-16	19-Feb	$ 77.50	30	2,325.00	203.44	2,528.44
TV commercials	1-Jan-16	31-Jan	$1,054.42	4	4,217.68	369.05	4,586.73
Web page asd	13-Jan-16	12-Feb	$ 0.17	230	39.56	3.46	43.02
Magazine	7-Jan-16	6-Feb	$ 100.92	12	1,211.04	105.97	1,317.01
Pens	5-Jan-16	4-Feb	$ 0.12	250	30.75	2.69	33.44
TV Sponsor	15-Jan-16	14-Feb	$ 250.00	15	3,750.00	328.13	4,078.13
Billboard	12-Jan-16	11-Feb	$ 101.87	20	2,037.40	178.27	2,215.67
Newspaper	25-Jan-16	24-Feb	$ 79.42	6	476.52	41.70	518.22
Newspaper	1-Feb-16	2-Mar	$ 79.42	2	158.84	13.90	172.74
T-Shirts	3-Feb-16	4-Mar	$ 5.67	200	1,134.00	99.23	1,233.23
TV commercials	1-Feb-16	2-Mar	$1,054.42	4	4,217.68	369.05	4,586.73

Sales Tax 0.0875

Working with themes and cell styles

Using themes and cell styles makes it easier to ensure that your worksheets are consistent. A **theme** is a predefined set of formats that gives your Excel worksheet a professional look. Formatting choices included in a theme are colors, fonts, and line and fill effects. To apply a theme, click the Themes button in the Themes group on the PAGE LAYOUT tab to open the Themes gallery, as shown in **FIGURE C-16**, then click a theme in the gallery. **Cell styles** are sets of cell formats based on themes, so they are automatically updated if you change a theme. For example, if you apply the 20% - Accent1 cell style to cell A1 in a worksheet that has no theme applied, the fill color changes to light blue with no pattern, and the font changes to Constantia. If you change the theme of the worksheet to Ion Boardroom, cell A1's fill color changes to red and the font changes to Century Gothic, because these are the new theme's associated formats.

FIGURE C-16: Themes gallery

Formatting a Worksheet

Apply Conditional Formatting

So far, you've used formatting to change the appearance of different types of data, but you can also use formatting to highlight important aspects of the data itself. For example, you can apply formatting that changes the font color to red for any cells where ad costs exceed $100 and to green where ad costs are below $50. This is called **conditional formatting** because Excel automatically applies different formats to data if the data meets conditions you specify. The formatting is updated if you change data in the worksheet. You can also copy conditional formats the same way you copy other formats. **CASE** ▶ *Grace is concerned about advertising costs exceeding the yearly budget. You decide to use conditional formatting to highlight certain trends and patterns in the data so that it's easy to spot the most expensive advertising.*

STEPS

1. **Select the range H4:H30, click the Conditional Formatting button in the Styles group on the HOME tab, point to Data Bars, then point to the Light Blue Data Bar (second row, second from left)**

 Data bars are colored horizontal bars that visually illustrate differences between values in a range of cells. Live Preview shows how this formatting will appear in the worksheet, as shown in FIGURE C-17.

2. **Point to the Green Data Bar (first row, second from left), then click it**

3. **Select the range F4:F30, click the Conditional Formatting button in the Styles group, then point to Highlight Cells Rules**

 The Highlight Cells Rules submenu displays choices for creating different formatting conditions. For example, you can create a rule for values that are greater than or less than a certain amount, or between two amounts.

4. **Click Between on the submenu**

 The Between dialog box opens, displaying input boxes you can use to define the condition and a default format (Light Red Fill with Dark Red Text) selected for cells that meet that condition. Depending on the condition you select in the Highlight Cells Rules submenu (such as "Greater Than" or "Less Than"), this dialog box displays different input boxes. You define the condition using the input boxes and then assign the formatting you want to use for cells that meet that condition. Values used in input boxes for a condition can be constants, formulas, cell references, or dates.

5. **Type 2000 in the first text box, type 4000 in the second text box, click the with list arrow, click Light Red Fill, compare your settings to FIGURE C-18, then click OK**

 All cells with values between 2000 and 4000 in column F appear with a light red fill.

6. **Click cell F7, type 3975.55, then press [Enter]**

 When the value in cell F7 changes, the formatting also changes because the new value meets the condition you set. Compare your results to FIGURE C-19.

7. **Press [Ctrl][Home] to select cell A1, then save your work**

FIGURE C-17: Previewing data bars in a range

Data bars displayed in selected range

FIGURE C-18: Between dialog box

Format for cells meeting the condition

Input boxes

FIGURE C-19: Worksheet with conditional formatting

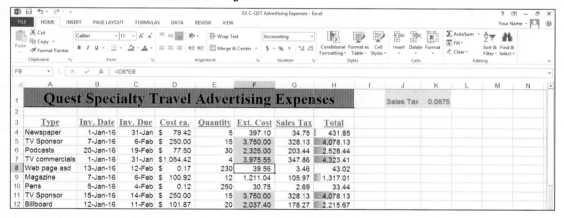

Managing conditional formatting rules

If you create a conditional formatting rule and then want to change the condition to reflect a different value or format, you don't need to create a new rule; instead, you can modify the rule using the Rules Manager. Select the cell(s) containing conditional formatting, click the Conditional Formatting button in the Styles group, then click Manage Rules. The Conditional Formatting Rules Manager dialog box opens. Select the rule you want to edit, click Edit Rule, and then modify the settings in the Edit the Rule Description area in the Edit Formatting Rule dialog box. To change

the formatting for a rule, click the Format button in the Edit the Rule Description area, select the formatting styles you want the text to have, then click OK three times to close the Format Cells dialog box, the Edit Formatting Rule dialog box, and then the Conditional Formatting Rules Manager dialog box. The rule is modified, and the new conditional formatting is applied to the selected cells. To delete a rule, select the rule in the Conditional Formatting Rules Manager dialog box, then click the Delete Rule button.

Rename and Move a Worksheet

Learning Outcomes
• Rename a sheet
• Apply color to a sheet tab
• Reorder sheets in a workbook

By default, an Excel workbook initially contains one worksheet named Sheet1, although you can add sheets at any time. Each sheet name appears on a sheet tab at the bottom of the worksheet. When you open a new workbook, the first worksheet, Sheet1, is the active sheet. To move from sheet to sheet, you can click any sheet tab at the bottom of the worksheet window. The sheet tab scrolling buttons, located to the left of the sheet tabs, are useful when a workbook contains too many sheet tabs to display at once. To make it easier to identify the sheets in a workbook, you can rename each sheet and add color to the tabs. You can also organize them in a logical way. For instance, to better track performance goals, you could name each workbook sheet for an individual salesperson, and you could move the sheets so they appear in alphabetical order. **CASE** ▶ *In the current worksheet, Sheet1 contains information about actual advertising expenses. Sheet2 contains an advertising budget, and Sheet3 contains no data. You want to rename the two sheets in the workbook to reflect their contents, add color to a sheet tab to easily distinguish one from the other, and change their order.*

STEPS

QUICK TIP
You can also rename a sheet by right-clicking the tab, clicking Rename on the shortcut menu, typing the new name, then pressing [Enter].

1. **Click the Sheet2 tab**

 Sheet2 becomes active, appearing in front of the Sheet1 tab; this is the worksheet that contains the budgeted advertising expenses. See **FIGURE C-20**.

2. **Click the Sheet1 tab**

 Sheet1, which contains the actual advertising expenses, becomes active again.

3. **Double-click the Sheet2 tab, type Budget, then press [Enter]**

 The new name for Sheet2 automatically replaces the default name on the tab. Worksheet names can have up to 31 characters, including spaces and punctuation.

QUICK TIP
To delete a sheet, click its tab, click the Delete list arrow in the Cells group, then click Delete Sheet. To insert a worksheet, click the New sheet button ⊕ to the right of the sheet tabs.

4. **Right-click the Budget tab, point to Tab Color on the shortcut menu, then click the Bright Green, Accent 4, Lighter 40% color (fourth row, third column from the right) as shown in FIGURE C-21**

5. **Double-click the Sheet1 tab, type Actual, then press [Enter]**

 Notice that the color of the Budget tab changes depending on whether it is the active tab; when the Actual tab is active, the color of the Budget tab changes to the green tab color you selected. You decide to rearrange the order of the sheets, so that the Budget tab is to the left of the Actual tab.

QUICK TIP
If you have more sheet tabs than are visible, you can move between sheets by using the tab scrolling buttons to the left of the sheet tabs: the Previous Worksheet button ◀ and the Next Worksheet button ▶.

6. **Click the Budget tab, hold down the mouse button, drag it to the left of the Actual tab, as shown in FIGURE C-22, then release the mouse button**

 As you drag, the pointer changes to ▯, the sheet relocation pointer, and a small, black triangle just above the tabs shows the position the moved sheet will be in when you release the mouse button. The first sheet in the workbook is now the Budget sheet. See **FIGURE C-23**. You can move multiple sheets by pressing and holding [Shift] while clicking the sheets you want to move, then dragging the sheets to their new location.

7. **Click the Actual sheet tab, click the Page Layout button ▣ on the status bar to open Page Layout view, enter your name in the left header text box, then click anywhere in the worksheet to deselect the header**

8. **Click the PAGE LAYOUT tab on the Ribbon, click the Orientation button in the Page Setup group, then click Landscape**

9. **Right-click the Sheet3 tab, click Delete on the shortcut menu, press [Ctrl][Home], then save your work**

FIGURE C-20: Sheet tabs in workbook

Sheet1 tab Sheet2 tab

FIGURE C-21: Tab Color palette

Sheet2 renamed

FIGURE C-22: Moving the Budget sheet

Sheet relocation pointer

FIGURE C-23: Reordered sheets

Budget sheet comes
before Actual sheet

Copying, Adding, and Deleting worksheets

There are times when you may want to copy a worksheet. For example, a workbook might contain a sheet with Quarter 1 expenses, and you want to use that sheet as the basis for a sheet containing Quarter 2 expenses. To copy a sheet within the same workbook, press and hold [Ctrl], drag the sheet tab to the desired tab location, release the mouse button, then release [Ctrl]. A duplicate sheet appears with the same name as the copied sheet followed by "(2)" indicating it is a copy. You can then rename the sheet to a more meaningful name. To copy a sheet to a different workbook, both the source and destination workbooks must be open. Select the sheet to copy or move, right-click the sheet tab, then click Move or Copy in the shortcut menu. Complete the information in the Move or Copy dialog box. Be sure to click the Create a copy check box if you are copying rather than moving the worksheet. Carefully check your calculation results whenever you move or copy a worksheet. You can add multiple worksheets to a workbook by clicking the HOME tab on the Ribbon, pressing and holding [Shift], then clicking the number of existing worksheet tabs that correspond with the number of sheets you want to add, clicking the Insert list arrow in the Cells group on the HOME tab, then clicking Insert Sheet. You can delete multiple worksheets from a workbook by clicking the HOME tab on the Ribbon, pressing and holding [Shift], clicking the sheet tabs of the worksheets you want to delete, clicking the Delete list arrow in the Cells group on the HOME tab, then clicking Delete Sheet.

Check Spelling

Learning
Outcomes
• Describe how spell
 checking works
• Change the
 spelling using
 a suggestion
• Replace a word
 using Find & Select

Excel includes a spell checker to help you ensure that the words in your worksheet are spelled correctly. The spell checker scans your worksheet, displays words it doesn't find in its built-in dictionary, and suggests replacements when they are available. To check all of the sheets in a multiple-sheet workbook, you need to display each sheet individually and run the spell checker for each one. Because the built-in dictionary cannot possibly include all the words that anyone needs, you can add words to the dictionary, such as your company name, an acronym, or an unusual technical term. Once you add a word or term, the spell checker no longer considers that word misspelled. Any words you've added to the dictionary using Word, Access, or PowerPoint are also available in Excel. **CASE** ▶ *Before you distribute this workbook to Grace and the marketing managers, you check its spelling.*

STEPS

QUICK TIP
The Spelling dialog box lists the name of the language currently being used in its title bar.

1. **Click the REVIEW tab on the Ribbon, then click the Spelling button in the Proofing group**

 The Spelling: English (U.S.) dialog box opens, as shown in FIGURE C-24, with "asd" selected as the first misspelled word in the worksheet, and with "ads" selected in the Suggestions list as a possible replacement. For any word, you have the option to Ignore this case of the flagged word, Ignore All cases of the flagged word, Change the word to the selected suggestion, Change All instances of the flagged word to the selected suggestion, or add the flagged word to the dictionary using Add to Dictionary.

2. **Click Change**

 Next, the spell checker finds the word "Podacsts" and suggests "Podcasts" as an alternative.

3. **Verify that the word Podcasts is selected in the Suggestions list, then click Change**

 When no more incorrect words are found, Excel displays a message indicating that the spell check is complete.

4. **Click OK**

5. **Click the HOME tab, click Find & Select in the Editing group, then click Replace**

 The Find and Replace dialog box opens. You can use this dialog box to replace a word or phrase. It might be a misspelling of a proper name that the spell checker didn't recognize as misspelled, or it could simply be a term that you want to change throughout the worksheet. Grace has just told you that each instance of "Billboard" in the worksheet should be changed to "Sign."

6. **Type Billboard in the Find what text box, press [Tab], then type Sign in the Replace with text box**

 Compare your dialog box to FIGURE C-25.

7. **Click Replace All, click OK to close the Microsoft Excel dialog box, then click Close to close the Find and Replace dialog box**

 Excel has made two replacements.

8. **Click the FILE tab, click Print on the navigation bar, click the No Scaling setting in the Settings section on the Print tab, then click Fit Sheet on One Page**

9. **Click the Return button to return to your worksheet, save your work, submit it to your instructor as directed, close the workbook, then exit Excel**

 The completed worksheet is shown in FIGURE C-26.

Emailing a workbook

You can send an entire workbook from within Excel using your installed email program, such as Microsoft Outlook. To send a workbook as an email message attachment, open the workbook, click the FILE tab, then click Share on the navigation bar. With the Email option selected in the Share section in Backstage view, click Send as Attachment in the right pane. An email message opens in your default email program with the workbook automatically attached; the filename appears in the Attached field. Complete the To and optional Cc fields, include a message if you wish, then click Send.

FIGURE C-24: Spelling: English (U.S.) dialog box

Misspelled word

Click to ignore all occurrences of misspelled word

Click to add word to dictionary

Suggested replacements for misspelled word

FIGURE C-25: Find and Replace dialog box

Find and Replace	?	×

Find | Replace

Find what: Billboard

Replace with: Sign

Options >>

Replace All | Replace | Find All | Find Next | Close

FIGURE C-26: Completed worksheet

Your Name

Quest Specialty Travel Advertising Expenses

Sales Tax

Type	Inv. Date	Inv. Due	Cost ea.	Quantity	Ext. Cost	Sales Tax	Total
Newspaper	1-Jan-16	31-Jan	$ 79.42	5	397.10	34.75	431.85
TV Sponsor	7-Jan-16	6-Feb	$ 250.00	15	3,750.00	328.13	4,078.13
Podcasts	20-Jan-16	19-Feb	$ 77.50	30	2,325.00	203.44	2,528.44
TV commercials	1-Jan-16	31-Jan	$ 1,054.42	4	3,975.55	347.86	4,323.41
Web page ads	13-Jan-16	12-Feb	$ 0.17	230	39.56	3.46	43.02
Magazine	7-Jan-16	6-Feb	$ 100.92	12	1,211.04	105.97	1,317.01
Pens	5-Jan-16	4-Feb	$ 0.12	250	30.75	2.69	33.44
TV Sponsor	15-Jan-16	14-Feb	$ 250.00	15	3,750.00	328.13	4,078.13
Sign	12-Jan-16	11-Feb	$ 101.87	20	2,037.40	178.27	2,215.67
Newspaper	25-Jan-16	24-Feb	$ 79.42	6	476.52	41.70	518.22
Newspaper	1-Feb-16	2-Mar	$ 79.42	2	158.84	13.90	172.74
T-Shirts	3-Feb-16	4-Mar	$ 5.67	200	1,134.00	99.23	1,233.23
TV commercials	1-Feb-16	2-Mar	$ 1,054.42	4	4,217.68	369.05	4,586.73
Newspaper	1-Mar-16	31-Mar	$ 23.91	2	47.82	4.18	52.00
Web page ads	28-Feb-16	29-Mar	$ 0.17	275	47.30	4.14	51.44
Magazine	27-Feb-16	28-Mar	$ 100.92	12	1,211.04	105.97	1,317.01
Podcasts	22-Feb-16	23-Mar	$ 77.50	30	2,325.00	203.44	2,528.44
TV Sponsor	1-Feb-16	2-Mar	$ 250.00	30	7,500.00	656.25	8,156.25
Newspaper	25-Feb-16	26-Mar	$ 79.42	6	476.52	41.70	518.22
Web page ads	10-Mar-16	9-Apr	$ 0.17	275	47.30	4.14	51.44
TV Sponsor	15-Feb-16	16-Mar	$ 250.00	25	6,250.00	546.88	6,796.88
Pens	15-Mar-16	14-Apr	$ 0.12	250	30.75	2.69	33.44
TV commercials	1-Mar-16	31-Mar	$ 1,054.44	4	4,217.76	369.05	4,586.81
Podcasts	20-Mar-16	19-Apr	$ 75.50	30	2,265.00	198.19	2,463.19
Newspaper	21-Mar-16	20-Apr	$ 79.42	2	158.84	13.90	172.74
Podcasts	23-Mar-16	22-Apr	$ 77.50	30	2,325.00	203.44	2,528.44
Sign	28-Mar-16	27-Apr	$ 101.87	20	2,037.40	178.27	2,215.67
			$ 5,304.30	1784	52,443.17	4,588.78	57,031.95

Formatting a Worksheet

Excel 69

Excel 2013

Practice

Concepts Review

Label each element of the Excel worksheet window shown in FIGURE C-27.

FIGURE C-27

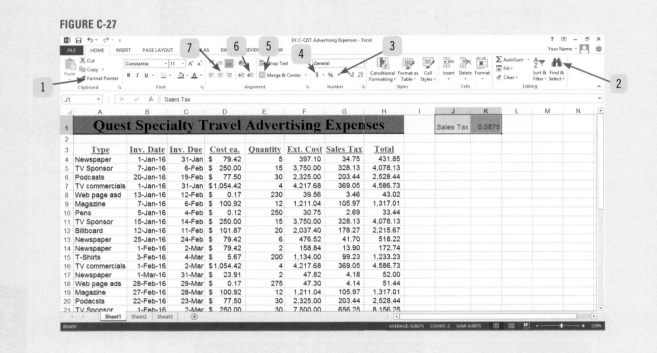

Match each command or button with the statement that best describes it.

8. **Conditional formatting**

9. $

10. **Spelling button**

11. **[Ctrl][Home]**

12. ▦

13. ▣ ▾

a. Checks for apparent misspellings in a worksheet

b. Adds dollar signs and two decimal places to selected data

c. Centers cell contents over multiple cells

d. Changes formatting of a cell that meets a certain rule

e. Moves cell pointer to cell A1

f. Displays background color options for a cell

Select the best answer from the list of choices.

14. Which button increases the number of decimal places in selected cells?

 a. [icon] **c.** [icon]

 b. [icon] **d.** [icon]

15. What feature is used to delete a conditional formatting rule?

 a. Rules Reminder **c.** Condition Manager

 b. Conditional Formatting Rules Manager **d.** Format Manager

16. Which button removes the italic font style from selected cells?

 a. [I icon] **c.** [I icon]

 b. [B icon] **d.** [U icon]

17. Which button copies multiple formats from selected cells to other cells?

 a. [icon] **c.** [A icon]

 b. [icon] **d.** [icon]

18. What is the name of the feature used to resize a column to accommodate its widest entry?

 a. AutoFormat **c.** AutoResize

 b. AutoFit **d.** AutoRefit

19. Which of the following is an example of Accounting number format?

 a. 5555 **c.** 55.55%

 b. $5,555.55 **d.** 5,555.55

Skills Review

1. Format values.

 a. Start Excel, open the file EX C-2.xlsx from the location where you store your Data Files, then save it as **EX C-Life Insurance Premiums**.

 b. Use the Sum function to enter a formula in cell B10 that totals the number of employees.

 c. Create a formula in cell C5 that calculates the monthly insurance premium for the accounting department. (*Hint*: Make sure you use the correct type of cell reference in the formula. To calculate the department's monthly premium, multiply the number of employees by the monthly premium in cell B14.)

 d. Copy the formula in cell C5 to the range C6:C10.

 e. Format the range C5:C10 using Accounting number format.

 f. Change the format of the range C6:C9 to the Comma Style.

 g. Reduce the number of decimals in cell B14 to 0 using a button in the Number group on the HOME tab.

 h. Save your work.

2. Change font and font sizes.

 a. Select the range of cells containing the column labels (in row 4).

 b. Change the font of the selection to Times New Roman.

 c. Increase the font size of the selection to 12 points.

 d. Increase the font size of the label in cell A1 to 14 points.

 e. Save your changes.

3. Change font styles and alignment.

 a. Apply the bold and italic font styles to the worksheet title in cell A1.

 b. Use the Merge & Center button to center the Life Insurance Premiums label over columns A through C.

 c. Apply the italic font style to the Life Insurance Premiums label.

 d. Add the bold font style to the labels in row 4.

 e. Use the Format Painter to copy the format in cell A4 to the range A5:A10.

 f. Apply the format in cell C10 to cell B14.

 g. Change the alignment of cell A10 to Align Right using a button in the Alignment group.

Skills Review (continued)

 h. Select the range of cells containing the column labels, then center them.

 i. Remove the italic font style from the Life Insurance Premiums label, then increase the font size to 14.

 j. Move the Life Insurance Premiums label to cell A3, then add the bold and underline font styles.

 k. Save your changes.

4. Adjust the column width.

 a. Resize column C to a width of 10.71 characters.

 b. Use the AutoFit feature to resize columns A and B.

 c. Clear the contents of cell A13 (do not delete the cell).

 d. Change the text in cell A14 to **Monthly Premium**, then change the width of the column to 25 characters.

 e. Save your changes.

5. Insert and delete rows and columns.

 a. Insert a new row between rows 5 and 6.

 b. Add a new department, **Charity**, in the newly inserted row. Enter **6** as the number of employees in the department.

 c. Copy the formula in cell C7 to C6.

 d. Add the following comment to cell A6: **New department**. Display the comment, then drag to move it out of the way, if necessary.

 e. Add a new column between the Department and Employees columns with the title **Family Coverage**, then resize the column using AutoFit.

 f. Delete the Legal row from the worksheet.

 g. Move the value in cell C14 to cell B14.

 h. Save your changes.

6. Apply colors, patterns, and borders.

 a. Add Outside Borders around the range A4:D10.

 b. Add a Bottom Double Border to cells C9 and D9 (above the calculated employee and premium totals).

 c. Apply the Aqua, Accent 5, Lighter 80% fill color to the labels in the Department column (do not include the Total label).

 d. Apply the Orange, Accent 6, Lighter 60% fill color to the range A4:D4.

 e. Change the color of the font in the range A4:D4 to Red, Accent 2, Darker 25%.

 f. Add a 12.5% Gray pattern style to cell A1.

 g. Format the range A14:B14 with a fill color of Dark Blue, Text 2, Lighter 40%, change the font color to White, Background 1, then apply the bold font style.

 h. Save your changes.

7. Apply conditional formatting.

 a. Select the range D5:D9, then create a conditional format that changes cell contents to green fill with dark green text if the value is between 150 and 275.

 b. Select the range C5:C9, then create a conditional format that changes cell contents to red text if the number of employees exceeds 10.

 c. Apply a purple gradient-filled data bar to the range C5:C9. (*Hint*: Click Purple Data Bar in the Gradient Fill section.)

 d. Use the Rules Manager to modify the conditional format in cells C5:C9 to display values greater than 10 in bold dark red text.

 e. Merge and center the title (cell A1) over columns A through D.

 f. Save your changes.

8. Rename and move a worksheet.

 a. Name the Sheet1 tab **Insurance Data**.

 b. Add a sheet to the workbook, then name the new sheet **Employee Data**.

 c. Change the Insurance Data tab color to Red, Accent 2, Lighter 40%.

Skills Review (continued)

d. Change the Employee Data tab color to Aqua, Accent 5, Lighter 40%.

e. Move the Employee Data sheet so it comes before (to the left of) the Insurance Data sheet.

f. Make the Insurance Data sheet active, enter your name in cell A20, then save your work.

9. Check spelling.

a. Move the cell pointer to cell A1.

b. Use the Find & Select feature to replace the Accounting label in cell A5 with Accounting/Legal.

c. Check the spelling in the worksheet using the spell checker, and correct any spelling errors if necessary.

d. Save your changes, then compare your Insurance Data sheet to FIGURE C-28.

e. Preview the Insurance Data sheet in Backstage view, submit your work to your instructor as directed, then close the workbook and exit Excel.

FIGURE C-28

Independent Challenge 1

You run a freelance accounting business, and one of your newest clients is Pen & Paper, a small office supply store. Now that you've converted the store's accounting records to Excel, the manager would like you to work on an analysis of the inventory. Although more items will be added later, the worksheet has enough items for you to begin your modifications.

a. Start Excel, open the file EX C-3.xlsx from the location where you store your Data Files, then save it as **EX C-Pen & Paper Office Supply Inventory**.

b. Create a formula in cell E4 that calculates the value of the items in stock based on the price paid per item in cell B4. Format the cell in the Comma Style.

c. In cell F4, calculate the sale price of the items in stock using an absolute reference to the markup value shown in cell H1.

d. Copy the formulas created above into the range E5:F14; first convert any necessary cell references to absolute so that the formulas work correctly.

e. Apply bold to the column labels, and italicize the inventory items in column A.

f. Make sure all columns are wide enough to display the data and labels.

g. Format the values in the Sale Price column as Accounting number format with two decimal places.

h. Format the values in the Price Paid column as Comma Style with two decimal places.

Independent Challenge 1 (continued)

i. Add a row under #2 Pencils for **Digital cordless telephones**, price paid **53.45**, sold individually (**each**), with **23** on hand. Copy the appropriate formulas to cells E7:F7.

j. Verify that all the data in the worksheet is visible and formulas are correct. Adjust any items as needed, and check the spelling of the entire worksheet.

k. Use conditional formatting to apply yellow fill with dark yellow text to items with a quantity of less than 25 on hand.

l. Use an icon set of your choosing in the range D4:D15 to illustrate the relative differences between values in the range.

m. Add an outside border around the data in the Item column (*do not* include the Item column label).

n. Delete the row containing the Thumb tacks entry.

o. Enter your name in an empty cell below the data, then save the file. Compare your worksheet to the sample in FIGURE C-29.

p. Preview the worksheet in Backstage view, submit your work to your instructor as directed, close the workbook, then exit Excel.

FIGURE C-29

Independent Challenge 2

You volunteer several hours each week with the Assistance League of San Antonio, and you are in charge of maintaining the membership list. You're currently planning a mailing campaign to members in certain regions of the city. You also want to create renewal letters for members whose membership expires soon. You decide to format the list to enhance the appearance of the worksheet and make your upcoming tasks easier to plan.

a. Start Excel, open the file EX C-4.xlsx from the location where you store your Data Files, then save it as **EX C-San Antonio Assistance League**.

b. Remove any blank columns.

c. Create a conditional format in the Zip Code column so that entries greater than 78249 appear in light red fill with dark red text.

d. Make all columns wide enough to fit their data and labels. (*Hint*: You can use any method to size the columns.)

e. Use formatting enhancements, such as fonts, font sizes, font styles, and fill colors, to make the worksheet more attractive.

Independent Challenge 2 (continued)

f. Center the column labels.

g. Use conditional formatting so that entries for Year of Membership Expiration that are between 2017 and 2019 appear in green fill with bold black text. (*Hint*: Create a custom format for cells that meet the condition.)

h. Adjust any items as necessary, then check the spelling.

i. Change the name of the Sheet1 tab to one that reflects the sheet's contents, then add a tab color of your choice.

j. Enter your name in an empty cell, then save your work.

k. Preview the worksheet in Backstage view, make any final changes you think necessary, then submit your work to your instructor as directed. Compare your work to the sample shown in FIGURE C-30.

l. Close the workbook, then exit Excel.

FIGURE C-30

FIGURE C-30

Member	Zip Code	Number of Employees	Year of Membership Expiration	Code	Year 2016
Candy's Candy Shop	78256	23	2020	3	
Chip Technology	78251	175	2021	3	
Computer Attic	78263	14	**2018**	2	
Deluxe Auto Shop	78245	17	**2017**	1	
Dental Associates	78287	15	**2018**	5	
Dr. Mary Terese	78263	12	2021	2	
Dunkin' Donuts	78278	10	**2018**	4	
Earl's Restaurant	78235	45	**2019**	3	
First Federal Bank	78267	36	2021	3	
Friendly Chevy	78286	17	2023	3	
From Office	78211	25	2022	5	
General Hospital	78225	538	2020	4	
Grande Table	78246	31	**2019**	4	
Holiday Inn	78221	75	**2018**	4	
Ken's Florist Shop	78241	10	**2017**	2	
Lisa's Photo Studio	78202	5	2020	4	
Meineke Muffler	78256	24	**2019**	1	
Midas Muffler	78221	22	2023	3	
Mill Shoppe	78205	165	2020	2	

Independent Challenge 3

Prestige Press is a Boston-based publisher that manufactures children's books. As the finance manager for the company, one of your responsibilities is to analyze the monthly reports from the five district sales offices. Your boss, Joanne Bennington, has just asked you to prepare a quarterly sales report for an upcoming meeting. Because several top executives will be attending this meeting, Joanne reminds you that the report must look professional. In particular, she asks you to emphasize the company's surge in profits during the last month and to highlight the fact that the Northeastern district continues to outpace the other districts.

a. Plan a worksheet that shows the company's sales during the first quarter. Assume that all books are the same price. Make sure you include the following:
 • The number of books sold (units sold) and the associated revenues (total sales) for each of the five district sales offices. The five sales districts are Northeastern, Midwestern, Southeastern, Southern, and Western.
 • Calculations that show month-by-month totals for January, February, and March, and a 3-month cumulative total.
 • Calculations that show each district's share of sales (percent of Total Sales).
 • Labels that reflect the month-by-month data as well as the cumulative data.
 • Formatting enhancements such as data bars that emphasize the recent month's sales surge and the Northeastern district's sales leadership.

b. Ask yourself the following questions about the organization and formatting of the worksheet: What worksheet title and labels do you need, and where should they appear? How can you calculate the totals? What formulas can you copy to save time and keystrokes? Do any of these formulas need to use an absolute reference? How do you show dollar amounts? What information should be shown in bold? Do you need to use more than one font? Should you use more than one point size?

c. Start Excel, then save a new, blank workbook as **EX C-Prestige Press** to the location where you store your Data Files.

Independent Challenge 3 (continued)

d. Build the worksheet with your own price and sales data. Enter the titles and labels first, then enter the numbers and formulas. You can use the information in TABLE C-4 to get started.

TABLE C-4

Prestige Press											
1st Quarter Sales Report											
		January		February		March		Total			
Office	Price	Units Sold	Sales	Units Sold	Sales	Units Sold	Sales	Units Sold	Sales	Total % of Sales	
Northeastern											
Midwestern											
Southeastern											
Southern											
Western											

e. Add a row beneath the data containing the totals for each column.

f. Adjust the column widths as necessary.

g. Change the height of row 1 to 33 points.

h. Format labels and values to enhance the look of the worksheet, and change the font styles and alignment if necessary.

i. Resize columns and adjust the formatting as necessary.

j. Add data bars for the monthly Units Sold columns.

k. Add a column that calculates a 25% increase in total sales dollars. Use an absolute cell reference in this calculation. (*Hint*: Make sure the current formatting is applied to the new information.)

l. Delete the contents of cells J4:K4 if necessary, then merge and center cell I4 over column I:K.

m. Add a bottom double border to cells I10:L10.

n. Enter your name in an empty cell.

o. Check the spelling in the workbook, change to a landscape orientation, save your work, then compare your work to FIGURE C-31.

p. Preview the worksheet in Backstage view, then submit your work to your instructor as directed.

q. Close the workbook file, then exit Excel.

FIGURE C-31

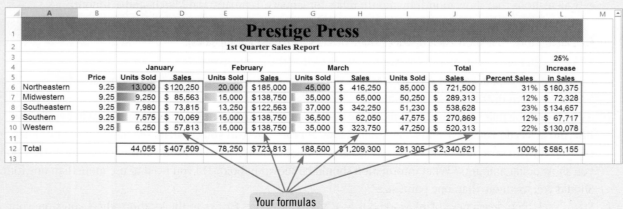

Independent Challenge 4: Explore

This Independent Challenge requires an Internet connection.

You are saving money to take the international trip you have always dreamed about. You plan to visit seven different countries over the course of 2 months, and you have budgeted an identical spending allowance in each country. You want to create a worksheet that calculates the amount of native currency you will have in each country based on the budgeted amount. You want the workbook to reflect the currency information for each country.

a. Start Excel, then save a new, blank workbook as **EX C-World Tour Budget** to the location where you store your Data Files.

b. Add a title at the top of the worksheet.

c. Think of seven countries you would like to visit, then enter column and row labels for your worksheet. (*Hint*: You may wish to include row labels for each country, plus column labels for the country, the $1 equivalent in native currency, the total amount of native currency you'll have in each country, and the name of each country's monetary unit.)

d. Decide how much money you want to bring to each country (for example, $1,000), and enter that in the worksheet.

e. Use your favorite search engine to find your own information sources on currency conversions for the countries you plan to visit.

f. Enter the cash equivalent to $1 in U.S. dollars for each country in your list.

g. Create an equation that calculates the amount of native currency you will have in each country, using an absolute cell reference in the formula.

h. Format the entries in the column containing the native currency $1 equivalent as Number number format with three decimal places, and format the column containing the total native currency budget with two decimal places, using the correct currency number format for each country. (*Hint*: Use the Number tab in the Format cells dialog box; choose the appropriate currency number format from the Symbol list.)

i. Create a conditional format that changes the font style and color of the calculated amount in the $1,000 US column to light red fill with dark red text if the amount exceeds **1000** units of the local currency.

j. Merge and center the worksheet title over the column headings.

k. Add any formatting you want to the column headings, and resize the columns as necessary.

l. Add a background color to the title and change the font color if you choose.

m. Enter your name in the header of the worksheet.

n. Spell check the worksheet, save your changes, compare your work to FIGURE C-32, then preview the worksheet in Backstage view, and submit your work to your instructor as directed.

o. Close the workbook and exit Excel.

FIGURE C-32

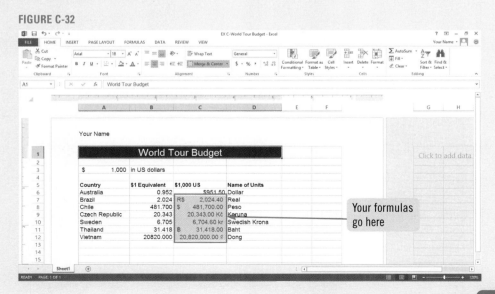

Visual Workshop

Open the file EX C-5.xlsx from the location where you store your Data Files, then save it as **EX C-Tip-Top Temps**. Use the skills you learned in this unit to format the worksheet so it looks like the one shown in FIGURE C-33. Create a conditional format in the Level column so that entries greater than 3 appear in light red fill with dark red text. Create an additional conditional format in the Review Cycle column so that any value equal to 3 appears in black fill with white bold text.

Replace the Accounting department label with **Legal**. (*Hint*: The only additional font used in this exercise is 18-point Times New Roman in row 1.) Enter your name in the upper-right part of the header, check the spelling in the worksheet, save your changes, then submit your work to your instructor as directed. (*Hint*: Zoom out until the Zoom level is 100%.)

FIGURE C-33

Working with Charts

CASE At the upcoming annual meeting, Grace Wong wants to emphasize spending patterns at Quest Specialty Travel. She asks you to create a chart showing the trends in company expenses over the past four quarters.

Unit Objectives

After completing this unit, you will be able to:

- Plan a chart
- Create a chart
- Move and resize a chart
- Change the chart design
- Change the chart format
- Format a chart
- Annotate and draw on a chart
- Create a pie chart

Files You Will Need

EX D-1.xlsx	EX D-4.xlsx
EX D-2.xlsx	EX D-5.xlsx
EX D-3.xlsx	EX D-6.xlsx

©Katerina Havelkova/Shutterstock

Plan a Chart

Learning
Outcomes
• Prepare to create
 a chart
• Identify chart
 elements
• Explore common
 chart types

Before creating a chart, you need to plan the information you want your chart to show and how you want it to look. Planning ahead helps you decide what type of chart to create and how to organize the data. Understanding the parts of a chart makes it easier to format and to change specific elements so that the chart best illustrates your data. **CASE** ▶ *In preparation for creating the chart for Grace's presentation, you identify your goals for the chart and plan its layout.*

DETAILS

Use the following guidelines to plan the chart:

• **Determine the purpose of the chart, and identify the data relationships you want to communicate graphically**

 You want to create a chart that shows quarterly tour expenses for each country where Quest Specialty Travel provides tours. This worksheet data is shown in FIGURE D-1. You also want the chart to illustrate whether the quarterly expenses for each country increased or decreased from quarter to quarter.

• **Determine the results you want to see, and decide which chart type is most appropriate**

 Different chart types display data in distinctive ways. For example, a pie chart compares parts to the whole, so it's useful for showing what proportion of a budget amount was spent on tours in one country relative to what was spent on tours in other countries. A line chart, in contrast, is best for showing trends over time. To choose the best chart type for your data, you should first decide how you want your data displayed and interpreted. TABLE D-1 describes several different types of charts you can create in Excel and their corresponding buttons on the INSERT tab on the Ribbon. Because you want to compare QST tour expenses in multiple countries over a period of four quarters, you decide to use a column chart.

• **Identify the worksheet data you want the chart to illustrate**

 Sometimes you use all the data in a worksheet to create a chart, while at other times you may need to select a range within the sheet. The worksheet from which you are creating your chart contains expense data for each of the past four quarters and the totals for the past year. You will need to use all the quarterly data contained in the worksheet except the quarterly totals.

• **Understand the elements of a chart**

 The chart shown in FIGURE D-2 contains basic elements of a chart. In the figure, QST tour countries are on the horizontal axis (also called the **x-axis**) and expense dollar amounts are on the vertical axis (also called the **y-axis**). The horizontal axis is also called the **category axis** because it often contains the names of data groups, such as locations, months, or years. The vertical axis is also called the **value axis** because it often contains numerical values that help you interpret the size of chart elements. (3-D charts also contain a **z-axis**, for comparing data across both categories and values.) The area inside the horizontal and vertical axes is the **plot area**. The **tick marks**, on the vertical axis, and **gridlines** (extending across the plot area) create a scale of measure for each value. Each value in a cell you select for your chart is a **data point**. In any chart, a **data marker** visually represents each data point, which in this case is a column. A collection of related data points is a **data series**. In this chart, there are four data series (Quarter 1, Quarter 2, Quarter 3, and Quarter 4). Each is made up of column data markers of a different color, so a **legend** is included to make it easy to identify them.

FIGURE D-1: Worksheet containing expense data

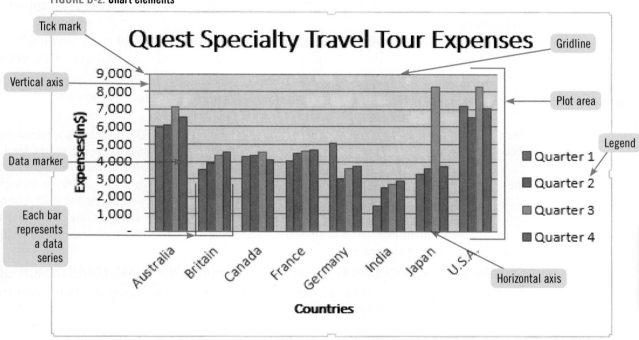

FIGURE D-2: Chart elements

Tick mark

Gridline

Quest Specialty Travel Tour Expenses

Vertical axis

Plot area

Data marker

Legend

Each bar represents a data series

Horizontal axis

Countries

Legend:
- Quarter 1
- Quarter 2
- Quarter 3
- Quarter 4

Vertical axis labels: 9,000 / 8,000 / 7,000 / 6,000 / 5,000 / 4,000 / 3,000 / 2,000 / 1,000

Expenses(in$)

Horizontal axis labels: Australia, Britain, Canada, France, Germany, India, Japan, U.S.A.

TABLE D-1: Common chart types

type	button	description
Column		Compares data using columns; the Excel default; sometimes referred to as a bar chart in other spreadsheet programs
Line		Compares trends over even time intervals; looks similar to an area chart, but does not emphasize total
Pie		Compares sizes of pieces as part of a whole; used for a single series of numbers
Bar		Compares data using horizontal bars; sometimes referred to as a horizontal bar chart in other spreadsheet programs
Area		Shows how individual volume changes over time in relation to total volume
Scatter		Compares trends over uneven time or measurement intervals; used in scientific and engineering disciplines for trend spotting and extrapolation

Create a Chart

Learning
Outcomes
• Create a chart
• Switch a chart's
 columns/rows
• Add a chart title

To create a chart in Excel, you first select the range in a worksheet containing the data you want to chart. Once you've selected a range, you can use buttons on the INSERT tab on the Ribbon to create a chart based on the data in the range. **CASE** ▶ *Using the worksheet containing the quarterly expense data, you create a chart that shows how the expenses in each country varied across the quarters.*

STEPS

QUICK TIP
When charting data for a particular time period, make sure all series are for the same time period.

1. **Start Excel, open the file** EX D-1.xlsx **from the location where you store your Data Files, then save it as** EX D-Quarterly Tour Expenses

 You want the chart to include the quarterly tour expenses values, as well as quarter and country labels. You don't include the Total column and row because the figures in these cells would skew the chart.

2. **Select the range** A4:E12, **then click the** Quick Analysis tool 📧 **in the lower-right corner of the range**

 The Quick Analysis tool contains a tab that lets you quickly insert commonly used charts. The CHARTS tab includes buttons for each major chart type, plus a More Charts button for additional chart types, such as stock charts for charting stock market data.

QUICK TIP
To base a chart on data in nonadjacent ranges, press and hold [Ctrl] while selecting each range, then use the INSERT tab to create the chart.

3. **Click the** CHARTS tab, **verify that the** Clustered Column **is selected, as shown in** FIGURE D-3, **then click** Clustered Column

 The chart is inserted in the center of the worksheet, and two contextual CHART TOOLS tabs appear on the Ribbon: DESIGN, and FORMAT. On the DESIGN tab, which is currently in front, you can quickly change the chart type, chart layout, and chart style, and you can swap how the columns and rows of data in the worksheet are represented in the chart. When seen in the Normal view, three tools display to the right of the chart: these enable you to add, remove, or change chart elements ➕, set a style and color scheme 🖌, and filter the results shown in a chart ▼. Currently, the countries are charted along the horizontal x-axis, with the quarterly expense dollar amounts charted along the y-axis. This lets you easily compare the quarterly expenses for each country.

4. **Click the** Switch Row/Column button **in the Data group on the CHART TOOLS DESIGN tab**

 The quarters are now charted along the x-axis. The expense amounts per country are charted along the y-axis, as indicated by the updated legend. See FIGURE D-4.

5. **Click the** Undo button ↺ **on the Quick Access toolbar**

 The chart returns to its original design.

QUICK TIP
You can also triple-click to select the chart title text.

6. **Click the** Chart Title placeholder **to show the text box, click anywhere in the** Chart Title text box, **press [Ctrl][A] to select the text, type** Quarterly Tour Expenses, **then click anywhere in the chart to deselect the title**

 Adding a title helps identify the chart. The border around the chart and the chart's **sizing handles**, the small series of dots at the corners and sides of the chart's border, indicate that the chart is selected. See FIGURE D-5. Your chart might be in a different location on the worksheet and may look slightly different; you will move and resize it in the next lesson. Any time a chart is selected, as it is now, a blue border surrounds the worksheet data range on which the chart is based, a purple border surrounds the cells containing the category axis labels, and a red border surrounds the cells containing the data series labels. This chart is known as an **embedded chart** because it is inserted directly in the current worksheet and doesn't exist in a separate file. Embedding a chart in the current sheet is the default selection when creating a chart, but you can also embed a chart on a different sheet in the workbook, or on a newly created chart sheet. A **chart sheet** is a sheet in a workbook that contains only a chart that is linked to the workbook data.

7. **Save your work**

FIGURE D-3: CHARTS tab in Quick Analysis tool

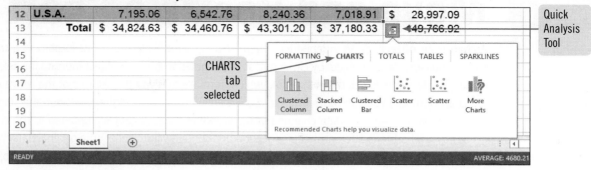

FIGURE D-4: Clustered Column chart with different presentation of data

FIGURE D-5: Chart with rows and columns restored and title added

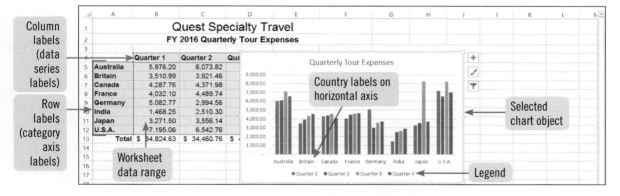

Creating sparklines

You can quickly create a miniature chart called a **sparkline** that serves as a visual indicator of data trends. You can create a sparkline by selecting a range of data, clicking the Quick Analysis tool, clicking the SPARKLINES tab, then clicking the type of sparkline you want. (The sparkline appears in the cell immediately adjacent to the selected range.) You can also select a range, click the INSERT tab, then click the Line, Column, or Win/Loss button in the Sparklines group. In the Create Sparklines dialog box that opens, enter the cell in which you want the sparkline to appear, then click OK.

FIGURE D-6 shows a sparkline created in a cell. Any changes to data in the range are reflected in the sparkline. To delete a selected sparkline from a cell, click the Clear button in the Group group on the SPARKLINE TOOLS DESIGN tab.

FIGURE D-6: Sparkline in a cell

Move and Resize a Chart

A chart is an **object**, or an independent element on a worksheet, and is not located in a specific cell or range. You can select an object by clicking it; sizing handles around the object indicate it is selected. (When a chart is selected in Excel, the Name box, which normally tells you the address of the active cell, tells you the chart number.) You can move a selected chart anywhere on a worksheet without affecting formulas or data in the worksheet. Any data changed in the worksheet is automatically updated in the chart. You can even move a chart to a different sheet in the workbook and it will still reflect the original data. You can resize a chart to improve its appearance by dragging its sizing handles. You can reposition chart objects (such as a title or legend) to predefined locations using commands using the Chart Elements button or the Add Chart Element button on the CHART TOOLS DESIGN tab, or you can freely move any chart object by dragging it or by cutting and pasting it to a new location. When you point to a chart object, the name of the object appears as a ScreenTip. **CASE** ▸ *You want to resize the chart, position it below the worksheet data, and move the legend.*

STEPS

QUICK TIP
To delete a selected chart, press [Delete].

1. **Make sure the chart is still selected, then position the pointer over the chart**

 The pointer shape ⁺ℝ indicates that you can move the chart. For a table of commonly used object pointers, refer to TABLE D-2.

TROUBLE
If you do not drag a blank area on the chart, you might inadvertently move a chart element instead of the whole chart; if this happens, undo the action and try again.

2. **Position ⁺ℝ on a blank area near the upper-left edge of the chart, press and hold the left mouse button, drag the chart until its upper-left corner is at the upper-left corner of cell A16, then release the mouse button**

 As you drag the chart, you can see the chart being dragged. When you release the mouse button, the chart appears in the new location.

3. **Scroll down so you can see the whole chart, position the pointer on the right-middle sizing handle until it changes to ↔, then drag the right border of the chart to the right edge of column G**

 The chart is widened. See FIGURE D-7.

QUICK TIP
To resize a selected chart to an exact specification, click the CHART TOOLS FORMAT tab, then enter the desired height and width in the Size group.

4. **Position the pointer over the upper-middle sizing handle until it changes to ↕, then drag the top border of the chart to the top edge of row 15**

5. **Position the pointer over the lower-middle sizing handle until it changes to ↕, then drag the bottom border of the chart to the bottom border of row 26**

 You can move any object on a chart. You want to align the top of the legend with the top of the plot area.

QUICK TIP
You can move a legend to the right, top, left, or bottom of a chart by clicking Legend in the Add Chart Element button in the Chart Layouts group on the CHART TOOLS DESIGN tab, then clicking a location option.

6. **Click the Quick Layout button in the Chart Layouts group of the CHART TOOLS DESIGN tab, click Layout 1 (in the upper-left corner of the palette), click the legend to select it, press and hold [Shift], drag the legend up using ⁺ℝ so the dotted outline is approximately 1/4″ above the top of the plot area, then release [Shift]**

 When you click the legend, sizing handles appear around it and "Legend" appears as a ScreenTip when the pointer hovers over the object. As you drag, a dotted outline of the legend border appears. Pressing and holding the [Shift] key holds the horizontal position of the legend as you move it vertically. Although the sizing handles on objects within a chart look different from the sizing handles that surround a chart, they function the same way.

7. **Click cell A12, type United States, click the Enter button ✓ on the formula bar, use AutoFit to resize column A, then save your work**

 The axis label changes to reflect the updated cell contents, as shown in FIGURE D-8. Changing any data in the worksheet modifies corresponding text or values in the chart. Because the chart is no longer selected, the CHART TOOLS tabs no longer appear on the Ribbon.

FIGURE D-7: Moved and resized chart

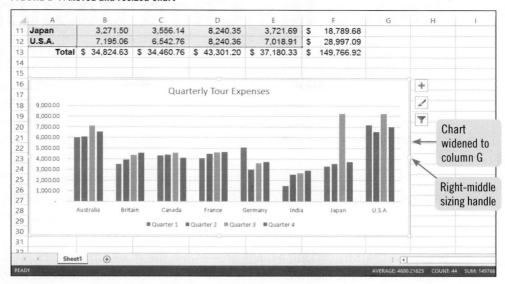

FIGURE D-8: Worksheet with modified legend and label

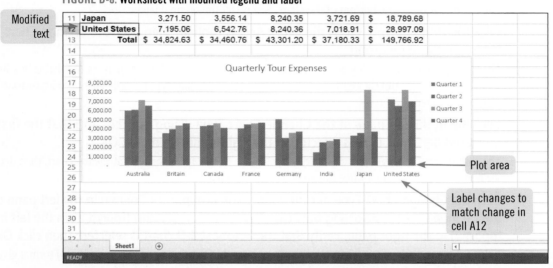

TABLE D-2: Common object pointers

name	pointer	use	name	pointer	use
Diagonal resizing	⤢ or ⤡	Change chart shape from corners	I-beam	I	Edit object text
Draw	✚	Draw an object	Move	✛	Move object
Horizontal resizing	⟷	Change object width	Vertical resizing	↕	Change object height

Moving an embedded chart to a sheet

Suppose you have created an embedded chart that you decide would look better on a chart sheet or in a different worksheet. You can make this change without recreating the entire chart. To do so, first select the chart, click the CHART TOOLS DESIGN tab, then click the Move Chart button in the Location group. The Move Chart dialog box opens. To move the chart to its own chart sheet, click the New sheet option button, type a name for the new sheet if desired, then click OK. If the chart is already on its own sheet, click the Object in option button, select the worksheet to where you want to move it, then click OK.

Excel 2013

Change the Chart Design

Once you've created a chart, you can change the chart type, modify the data range and column/row configuration, apply a different chart style, and change the layout of objects in the chart. The layouts in the Chart Layouts group on the CHART TOOLS DESIGN tab offer arrangements of objects in your chart, such as its legend, title, or gridlines; choosing one of these layouts is an alternative to manually changing how objects are arranged in a chart. **CASE** *You discovered the data for Japan and the United States in Quarter 3 is incorrect. After the correction, you want to see how the data looks using different chart layouts and types.*

STEPS

1. **Click cell D11, type 4568.92, press [Enter], type 6107.09, then press [Enter]**
 In the chart, the Quarter 3 data markers for Japan and the United States reflect the adjusted expense figures. See **FIGURE D-9**.

2. **Select the chart by clicking a blank area within the chart border, click the CHART TOOLS DESIGN tab on the Ribbon, click the Quick Layout button in the Chart Layouts group, then click Layout 3**
 The legend moves to the bottom of the chart. You prefer the original layout.

3. **Click the Undo button ↶ on the Quick Access toolbar, then click the Change Chart Type button in the Type group**
 The Change Chart Type dialog box opens, as shown in **FIGURE D-10**. The left pane of the dialog box lists the available categories, and the right pane shows the individual chart types. A pale green border surrounds the currently selected chart type.

4. **Click Bar in the left pane of the Change Chart Type dialog box, confirm that the first Clustered Bar chart type is selected in the right pane, then click OK**
 The column chart changes to a clustered bar chart. See **FIGURE D-11**. You look at the bar chart, then decide to see how the data looks in a three-dimensional column chart.

5. **Click the Change Chart Type button in the Type group, click Column in the left pane of the Change Chart Type dialog box, click 3-D Clustered Column (fourth from the left in the top row) in the right pane, verify that the left-most 3-D chart is selected, then click OK**
 A three-dimensional column chart appears. You notice that the three-dimensional column format gives you a sense of volume, but it is more crowded than the two-dimensional column format.

6. **Click the Change Chart Type button in the Type group, click Clustered Column (first from the left in the top row) in the right pane of the Change Chart Type dialog box, then click OK**

7. **Click the Style 3 chart style in the Chart Styles group**
 The columns change to lighter shades of color. You prefer the previous chart style's color scheme.

8. **Click ↶ on the Quick Access toolbar, then save your work**

Creating a combination chart

A **combination chart** is two charts in one; a column chart with a line chart, for example. This type of chart is helpful when charting dissimilar but related data. For example, you can create a combination chart based on home price and home size data, showing home prices in a column chart, and related home sizes in a line chart. Here a **secondary axis** (such as a vertical axis on the right side of the chart) would supply the scale for the home sizes. To create a combination chart, select all the data you want to plot, click Recommended Charts in the Charts group in the INSERT tab, click the All Charts tab, select Combo, supply the series information that conforms to the chart you want to create, then click OK. To change an existing chart to a combination chart, select the chart , then click Change Chart Type in the Type group on the CHART TOOLS DESIGN tab. Click Combo in the Change Chart Type dialog box, select the Secondary Axis box for each data series you want to plot, change the chart type to Line, then click OK.

FIGURE D-9: Worksheet with modified data

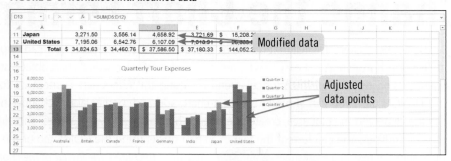

Modified data

Adjusted data points

FIGURE D-10: Change Chart Type dialog box

Chart type categories

Bar chart type category

Currently selected chart type

FIGURE D-11: Column chart changed to bar chart

Click More button to see additional chart styles

Change Chart Type button

Chart Elements button

Working with a 3-D chart

Excel includes two kinds of 3-D chart types. In a true 3-D chart, a third axis, called the **z-axis**, lets you compare data points across both categories and values. The z-axis runs along the depth of the chart, so it appears to advance from the back of the chart. To create a true 3-D chart, look for chart types that begin with "3-D," such as 3-D Column. In a 3-D chart, data series can sometimes obscure other columns or bars in the same chart, but you can rotate the chart to obtain a better view. Right-click the chart, then click 3-D Rotation. The Format Chart Area pane opens with the 3-D Rotation category active. The 3-D Rotation options let you change the orientation and perspective of the chart area, plot area, walls, and floor. The 3-D Format category lets you apply three-dimensional effects to selected chart objects. (Not all 3-D Rotation and 3-D Format options are available on all charts.)

Change the Chart Format

Learning Outcomes
- Change the gridlines display
- Add axis titles
- Change the border color
- Add a shadow to an object

While the CHART TOOLS DESIGN tab contains preconfigured chart layouts you can apply to a chart, the Chart Elements button makes it easy to add, remove, and modify individual chart objects such as a chart title or legend. Using options on this shortcut menu (or using the Add Chart Element button on the CHART TOOLS DESIGN tab), you can also add text to a chart, add and modify labels, change the display of axes, modify the fill behind the plot area, create titles for the horizontal and vertical axes, and eliminate or change the look of gridlines. You can format the text in a chart object using the HOME tab or the Mini toolbar, just as you would the text in a worksheet. **CASE** *You want to change the layout of the chart by creating titles for the horizontal and vertical axes. To improve the chart's appearance, you'll add a drop shadow to the chart title.*

STEPS

1. **With the chart still selected, click the Add Chart Element button in the Chart Layouts group on the CHART TOOLS DESIGN tab, point to Gridlines, then click Primary Major Horizontal to deselect it**

 The gridlines that extend from the value axis tick marks across the chart's plot area are removed from the chart, as shown in FIGURE D-12.

2. **Click the Chart Elements button ⊞ in the upper-right corner *outside* the chart border, click the Gridlines arrow, click Primary Major Horizontal, click Primary Minor Horizontal, then click ◼ to close the Chart Elements fly-out menu**

 Both major and minor gridlines now appear in the chart. **Major gridlines** represent the values at the value axis tick marks, and **minor gridlines** represent the values between the tick marks.

3. **Click ⊞, click the Axis Titles checkbox to select all the axis titles options, triple-click the vertical axis title on the chart, then type Expenses (in $)**

 Descriptive text on the category axis helps readers understand the chart.

4. **Triple-click the horizontal axis title on the chart, then type Tour Countries**

 The text "Tour Countries" appears on the horizontal axis, as shown in FIGURE D-13.

5. **Right-click the horizontal axis labels ("Australia", "Britain", etc.), click Font on the short-cut menu, click the Latin text font list arrow in the Font dialog box, click Times New Roman, click the Size down arrow, click until 8 is displayed, then click OK**

 The font of the horizontal axis labels changes to Times New Roman, and the font size decreases, making more of the plot area visible.

6. **With the horizontal axis labels still selected, click the HOME tab, click the Format Painter button ✦ in the Clipboard group, then click the area within the vertical axis labels**

7. **Right-click the Chart Title ("Quarterly Tour Expenses"), click Format Chart Title on the shortcut menu, click the BORDER arrow ▷ in the Format Chart Title pane to display the options if necessary, then click the Solid line option button in the Format Chart Title pane**

 A solid border will appear around the chart title with the default blue color.

8. **Click the Effects button ◻ in the Format Chart Title pane, click Shadow, click the Presets list arrow, click Offset Diagonal Bottom Right in the Outer group (first row, first from the left), click the Format Chart Title pane Close button ✖, then save your work**

 A blue border with a drop shadow surrounds the title. Compare your work to FIGURE D-14.

FIGURE D-12: Gridlines removed from chart

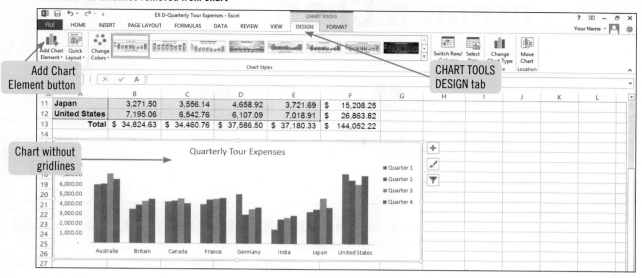

Add Chart Element button

CHART TOOLS DESIGN tab

Chart without gridlines

FIGURE D-13: Axis titles added to chart

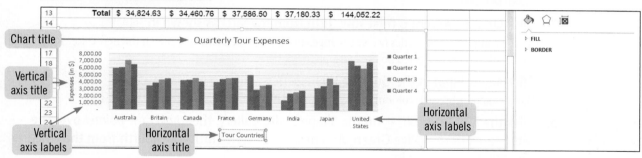

Chart title

Vertical axis title

Vertical axis labels

Horizontal axis title

Horizontal axis labels

FIGURE D-14: Enhanced chart

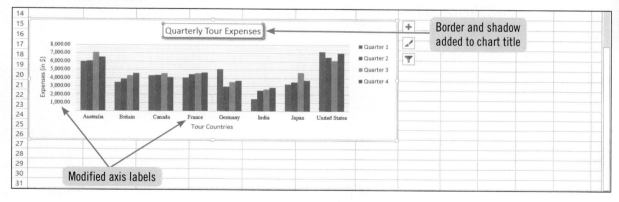

Border and shadow added to chart title

Modified axis labels

Adding data labels to a chart

There are times when your audience might benefit by seeing data labels on a chart. These labels appear next to the data markers in the chart and can indicate the series name, category name, and/or the value of one or more data points. Once your chart is selected, you can add this information to your chart by clicking the Chart Elements button in the upper-right corner outside the selected chart, clicking the Data Labels arrow, and then clicking a display option for the data labels. Once you have added the data labels, you can format them or delete individual data labels. To delete a data label, select it and then press [Delete].

Format a Chart

Formatting a chart can make it easier to read and understand. Many formatting enhancements can be made using the CHART TOOLS FORMAT tab. You can change the fill color for a specific data series, or you can apply a shape style to a title or a data series using the Shape Styles group. Shape styles make it possible to apply multiple formats, such as an outline, fill color, and text color, all with a single click. You can also apply different fill colors, outlines, and effects to chart objects using arrows and buttons in the Shape Styles group. **CASE** ▶ *You want to use a different color for one data series in the chart and apply a shape style to another to enhance the look of the chart.*

STEPS

1. **With the chart selected, click the CHART TOOLS FORMAT tab on the Ribbon, then click any column in the Quarter 4 data series**

 The CHART TOOLS FORMAT tab opens, and handles appear on each column in the Quarter 4 data series, indicating that the entire series is selected.

2. **Click the Shape Fill list arrow in the Shape Styles group on the CHART TOOLS FORMAT tab**

3. **Click Orange, Accent 6 (first row, 10th from the left) as shown in FIGURE D-15**

 All the columns for the series become orange, and the legend changes to match the new color. You can also change the color of selected objects by applying a shape style.

4. **Click any column in the Quarter 3 data series**

 Handles appear on each column in the Quarter 3 data series.

5. **Click the More button ⏷ on the Shape Styles gallery, then *hover the pointer* over the Moderate Effect – Olive Green, Accent 3 shape style (fifth row, fourth from the left) in the gallery, as shown in FIGURE D-16**

 Live Preview shows the data series in the chart with the shape style applied.

6. **Click the Subtle Effect – Olive Green, Accent 3 shape style (fourth row, fourth from the left) in the gallery**

 The style for the data series changes, as shown in FIGURE D-17.

7. **Save your work**

Previewing a chart

To print or preview just a chart, select the chart (or make the chart sheet active), click the FILE tab, then click Print on the navigation bar. To reposition a chart by changing the page's margins, click the Show Margins button ▦ in the lower-right corner of the Print tab to display the margins in the preview. You can drag the margin lines to the exact settings you want; as the margins change, the size and placement of the chart on the page changes too.

FIGURE D-15: New shape fill applied to data series

FIGURE D-16: Live Preview of new style applied to data series

FIGURE D-17: Style of data series changed

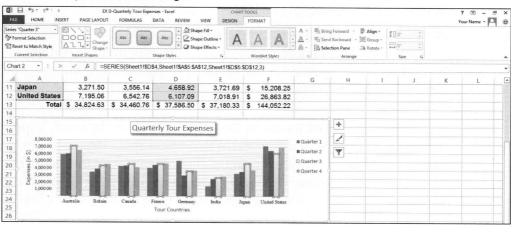

Changing alignment and angle in axis labels and titles

The buttons on the CHART TOOLS DESIGN tab provide a few options for positioning axis labels and titles, but you can customize their position and rotation to exact specifications using the Format Axis pane or Format Axis Title pane. With a chart selected, right-click the axis text you want to modify, then click Format Axis or Format Axis Title on the shortcut menu. In the pane that is displayed, click the Size & Properties button, then select the appropriate Text layout option. You can also create a custom angle by clicking the Custom angle up and down arrows. When you have made the desired changes, close the pane.

Annotate and Draw on a Chart

Learning Outcomes
- Type text in a text box
- Draw an arrow on a chart
- Modify a drawn object

You can use text annotations and graphics to point out critical information in a chart. **Text annotations** are labels that further describe your data. You can also draw lines and arrows that point to the exact locations you want to emphasize. Shapes such as arrows and boxes can be added from the Illustrations group on the INSERT tab or from the Insert Shapes group on the CHART TOOLS FORMAT tab on the Ribbon. The INSERT group is also used to insert pictures into worksheets and charts. **CASE** ▶ *You want to call attention to the Germany tour expense decrease, so you decide to add a text annotation and an arrow to this information in the chart.*

STEPS

1. **Make sure the chart is selected with the CHART TOOLS FORMAT tab selected, click the Text Box button** ▣ **in the Insert Shapes group, then move the pointer over the worksheet**

 The pointer changes to ↓, indicating that you will insert a text box where you next click.

QUICK TIP
You can also insert a text box by clicking the Text Box button in the Text group in the INSERT tab, then clicking in the worksheet.

2. **Click to the right of the chart (anywhere *outside* the chart boundary)**

 A text box is added to the worksheet, and the DRAWING TOOLS FORMAT tab appears on the Ribbon so that you can format the new object. First you need to type the text.

3. **Type Great Improvement**

 The text appears in a selected text box on the worksheet, and the chart is no longer selected, as shown in **FIGURE D-18**. Your text box may be in a different location; this is not important, because you'll move the annotation in the next step.

4. **Point to an edge of the text box so that the pointer changes to** ⬩, **drag the text box into the chart to the left of the chart title, as shown in FIGURE D-19, then release the mouse button**

 The text box is a text annotation for the chart. You also want to add a simple arrow shape in the chart.

QUICK TIP
To annotate a chart using a callout, click the Shapes button in the Illustrations group on the INSERT tab or the More button on the Insert Shapes group on the CHART TOOLS FORMAT tab, then click a shape in the Callouts category of the Shapes gallery.

5. **Click the chart to select it, click the CHART TOOLS FORMAT tab, click the Arrow button** ◻ **in the Insert Shapes group, then move the pointer over the text box on the chart**

 The pointer changes to ✚, and the status bar displays "Click and drag to insert an AutoShape." When ✚ is over the text box, black handles appear around the text in the text box. A black handle can act as an anchor for the arrow.

6. **Position ✚ on the black handle to the right of the "t" in the word "improvement" (in the text box), press and hold the left mouse button, drag the line to the Quarter 2 column for the Germany category in the chart, then release the mouse button**

 An arrow points to the Quarter 2 expense for Germany, and the DRAWING TOOLS FORMAT tab displays options for working with the new arrow object. You can resize, format, or delete it just like any other object in a chart.

7. **Click the Shape Outline list arrow in the Shape Styles group, click the Automatic color, click the Shape Outline list arrow again, point to Weight, then click 1½ pt**

 Compare your finished chart to **FIGURE D-20**.

8. **Save your work**

DRAWING
TOOLS
FORMAT tab

Text annotation

FIGURE D-19: **Text annotation on the chart**

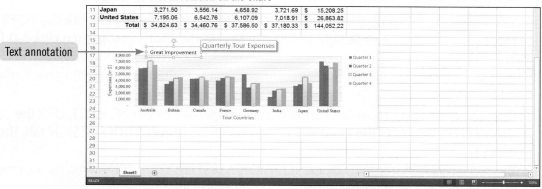

Text annotation

FIGURE D-20: **Arrow shape added to chart**

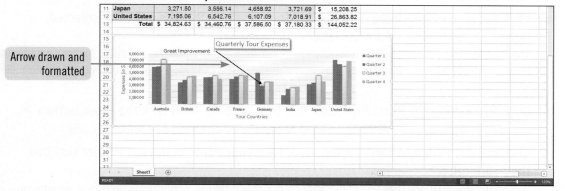

Arrow drawn and
formatted

Adding SmartArt graphics

In addition to charts, annotations, and drawn objects, you can create a variety of diagrams using SmartArt graphics. **SmartArt graphics** are available in List, Process, Cycle, Hierarchy, Relationship, Matrix, and Pyramid categories. To insert SmartArt, click the Insert a SmartArt Graphic button in the Illustrations group on the INSERT tab to open the Choose a SmartArt Graphic dialog box. Click a SmartArt category in the left pane, then click the layout for the graphic in the right pane. The right pane shows a sample of the selected SmartArt layout, as shown in **FIGURE D-21**. The SmartArt graphic appears in the worksheet as an embedded object with sizing handles. Click the Text Pane button on the SmartArt Tools Design tab to open a text pane next to the graphic; you can

enter text into the graphic using the text pane or by typing directly in the shapes in the diagram.

FIGURE D-21: **Choose a SmartArt Graphic dialog box**

Excel 2013

Create a Pie Chart

You can create multiple charts based on the same worksheet data. While a column chart may illustrate certain important aspects of your worksheet data, you may find you want to create an additional chart to emphasize a different point. Depending on the type of chart you create, you have additional options for calling attention to trends and patterns. For example, if you create a pie chart, you can emphasize one data point by **exploding**, or pulling that slice away from, the pie chart. When you're ready to print a chart, you can preview it just as you do a worksheet to check the output before committing it to paper. You can print a chart by itself or as part of the worksheet. **CASE** *At an upcoming meeting, Grace plans to discuss the total tour expenses and which countries need improvement. You want to create a pie chart she can use to illustrate total expenses. Finally, you want to fit the worksheet and the charts onto one worksheet page.*

STEPS

1. **Select the range A5:A12, press and hold [Ctrl], select the range F5:F12, click the INSERT tab, click the Insert Pie or Doughnut Chart button in the Charts group, then click 3-D Pie in the chart gallery**

 The new chart appears in the center of the worksheet. You can move the chart and quickly format it using a chart layout.

2. **Drag the chart so its upper-left corner is at the upper-left corner of cell G1, click the Quick Layout button in the Chart Layouts group of the CHART TOOLS DESIGN tab, then click Layout 2**

 The chart is repositioned on the page, and its layout changes so that a chart title is added, the percentages display on each slice, and the legend appears just below the chart title.

3. **Select the Chart Title text, then type Total Expenses, by Country**

4. **Click the slice for the India data point, click it again so it is the only slice selected, right-click it, then click Format Data Point**

 The Format Data Point pane opens, as shown in **FIGURE D-22**. You can use the Point Explosion slider to control the distance a pie slice moves away from the pie, or you can type a value in the Point Explosion text box.

5. **Double-click 0 in the Point Explosion text box, type 40, then click the Close button ☒**

 Compare your chart to **FIGURE D-23**. You decide to preview the chart and data before you print.

6. **Click cell A1, switch to Page Layout view, type your name in the left header text box, then click cell A1**

 You decide the chart and data would fit better on the page if they were printed in landscape orientation.

7. **Click the PAGE LAYOUT tab, click the Orientation button in the Page Setup group, then click Landscape**

8. **Click the FILE tab, click Print on the navigation bar, click the No Scaling setting in the Settings section on the Print tab, then click Fit Sheet on One Page**

 The data and chart are positioned horizontally on a single page, as shown in **FIGURE D-24**. The printer you have selected may affect the appearance of your preview screen.

9. **Save and close the workbook, submit your work to your instructor as directed, then exit Excel**

FIGURE D-22: Format Data Point pane

Point Explosion slider

Point Explosion text box

FIGURE D-23: Exploded pie slice

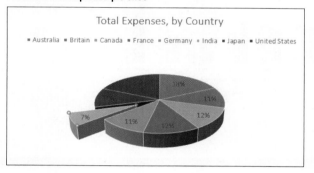

FIGURE D-24: Preview of worksheet with charts in Backstage view

Fit Sheet on One Page setting

Show Margins button

Practice

Concepts Review

Label each element of the Excel chart shown in FIGURE D-25.

FIGURE D-25

Match each chart type with the statement that best describes it.

7. **Area** **a.** Displays a column and line chart using different scales of measurement
8. **Line** **b.** Compares trends over even time intervals
9. **Column** **c.** Compares data using columns
10. **Combination** **d.** Compares data as parts of a whole
11. **Pie** **e.** Shows how volume changes over time

Select the best answer from the list of choices.

12. **Which tab appears only when a chart is selected?**
 a. INSERT
 b. CHART TOOLS FORMAT
 c. REVIEW
 d. PAGE LAYOUT

13. **Which is *not* an example of a SmartArt graphic?**
 a. Sparkline
 b. Basic Matrix
 c. Organization Chart
 d. Basic Pyramid

14. **How do you move an embedded chart to a chart sheet?**
 a. Click a button on the CHART TOOLS DESIGN tab.
 b. Drag the chart to the sheet tab.
 c. Delete the chart, switch to a different sheet, then create a new chart.
 d. Use the Copy and Paste buttons on the Ribbon.

15. **The object in a chart that identifies the colors used for each data series is a(n):**
 a. Data marker.
 b. Data point.
 c. Organizer.
 d. Legend.

16. **A collection of related data points in a chart is called a:**
 a. Data series.
 b. Data tick.
 c. Cell address.
 d. Value title.

17. **Which tab on the Ribbon do you use to create a chart?**
 a. DESIGN
 b. INSERT
 c. PAGE LAYOUT
 d. FORMAT

Skills Review

1. **Plan a chart.**
 a. Start Excel, open the Data File EX D-2.xlsx from the location where you store your Data Files, then save it as **EX D-Departmental Software Usage**.
 b. Describe the type of chart you would use to plot this data.
 c. What chart type would you use to compare the number of Excel users in each department?

2. **Create a chart.**
 a. In the worksheet, select the range containing all the data and headings.
 b. Click the Quick Analysis tool.
 c. Create a Clustered Column chart, then add the chart title **Software Usage, by Department** above the chart.
 d. If necessary, click the Switch Row/Column button so the Department appears as the x-axis.
 e. Save your work.

Skills Review (continued)

3. **Move and resize a chart.**

 a. Make sure the chart is still selected, and close any open panes if necessary.

 b. Move the chart beneath the worksheet data.

 c. Widen the chart so it extends to the right edge of column H.

 d. Use the Quick Layout button in the CHART TOOLS DESIGN tab to move the legend to the right of the charted data. (*Hint*: Use Layout 1.)

 e. Resize the chart so its bottom edge is at the top of row 25.

 f. Save your work.

4. **Change the chart design.**

 a. Change the value in cell B3 to **15**. Observe the change in the chart.

 b. Select the chart.

 c. Use the Quick Layout button in the Chart Layouts group on the CHART TOOLS DESIGN tab to apply the Layout 10 layout to the chart, then undo the change.

 d. Use the Change Chart Type button on the CHART TOOLS DESIGN tab to change the chart to a Clustered Bar chart.

 e. Change the chart to a 3-D Clustered Column chart, then change it back to a Clustered Column chart.

 f. Save your work.

5. **Change the chart layout.**

 a. Use the CHART ELEMENTS button to turn off the primary major horizontal gridlines in the chart.

 b. Change the font used in the horizontal and vertical axes labels to Times New Roman.

 c. Turn on the primary major gridlines for both the horizontal and vertical axes.

 d. Change the chart title's font to Times New Roman if necessary, with a font size of 20.

 e. Insert **Departments** as the primary horizontal axis title.

 f. Insert **Number of Users** as the primary vertical axis title.

 g. Change the font size of the horizontal and vertical axis titles to 10 and the font to Times New Roman, if necessary.

 h. Change "Personnel" in the worksheet column heading to **Human Resources**, then AutoFit column E.

 i. Change the font size of the legend to 14.

 j. Add a solid line border in the default color and a (preset) Offset Diagonal Bottom Right shadow to the chart title.

 k. Save your work.

6. **Format a chart.**

 a. Make sure the chart is selected, then select the CHART TOOLS FORMAT tab, if necessary.

 b. Change the shape fill of the Excel data series to Dark Blue, Text 2.

 c. Change the shape style of the Excel data series to Subtle Effect – Orange, Accent 6.

 d. Save your work.

7. **Annotate and draw on a chart.**

 a. Make sure the chart is selected, then create the text annotation **Needs more users**.

 b. Position the text annotation so the word "Needs" is just below the word "Software" in the chart title.

 c. Select the chart, then use the CHART TOOLS FORMAT tab to create a 1½ pt weight dark blue arrow that points from the bottom center of the text box to the Excel users in the Design department.

 d. Deselect the chart.

 e. Save your work.

Skills Review (continued)

8. Create a pie chart.

- **a.** Select the range A1:F2, then create a 3-D Pie chart.
- **b.** Drag the 3-D pie chart beneath the existing chart.
- **c.** Change the chart title to **Excel Users**.
- **d.** Apply the Style 7 chart style to the chart, then apply Layout 6 using the Quick Layout button.
- **e.** Explode the Human Resources slice from the pie chart at **25%**.
- **f.** In Page Layout view, enter your name in the left section of the worksheet header.
- **g.** Preview the worksheet and charts in Backstage view, make sure all the contents fit on one page, then submit your work to your instructor as directed. When printed, the worksheet should look like FIGURE D-26.
- **h.** Save your work, close the workbook, then exit Excel.

FIGURE D-26

Your Name

	Accounting	Marketing	Design	Human Resources	Purchasing
Excel	37	16	5	11	38
Word	15	35	17	15	10
PowerPoint	17	5	12	5	3
Access	20	25	8	10	15
Publisher	2	15	22	15	25

Independent Challenge 1

You are the operations manager for the Tulsa Arts Alliance in Oklahoma. Each year the group applies to various state and federal agencies for matching funds. For this year's funding proposal, you need to create charts to document the number of productions in previous years.

a. Start Excel, open the file EX D-3.xlsx from the location where you store your Data Files, then save it as **EX D-Tulsa Arts Alliance**.

b. Take some time to plan your charts. Which type of chart or charts might best illustrate the information you need to display? What kind of chart enhancements do you want to use? Will a 3-D effect make your chart easier to understand?

c. Create a Clustered Column chart for the data.

d. Change at least one of the colors used in a data series.

e. Make the appropriate modifications to the chart to make it visually attractive and easier to read and understand. Include a legend to the right of the chart, and add chart titles and horizontal and vertical axis titles using the text shown in TABLE D-3.

TABLE D-3

title	text
Chart title	Tulsa Arts Alliance Events
Vertical axis title	Number of Events
Horizontal axis title	Types of Events

© 2014 Cengage Learning

f. Create at least two additional charts for the same data to show how different chart types display the same data. Reposition each new chart so that all charts are visible in the worksheet. One of the additional charts should be a pie chart; the other is up to you.

g. Modify each new chart as necessary to improve its appearance and effectiveness. A sample worksheet containing three charts based on the worksheet data is shown in FIGURE D-27.

h. Enter your name in the worksheet header.

i. Save your work. Before printing, preview the worksheet in Backstage view, then adjust any settings as necessary so that all the worksheet data and charts print on a single page.

j. Submit your work to your instructor as directed.

k. Close the workbook, then exit Excel.

FIGURE D-27

Independent Challenge 2

You work at Bark Bark Bark, a locally owned day spa for dogs. One of your responsibilities at the day spa is to manage the company's sales and expenses using Excel. Another is to convince the current staff that Excel can help them make daily operating decisions more easily and efficiently. To do this, you've decided to create charts using the previous year's operating expenses including rent, utilities, and payroll. The manager will use these charts at the next monthly meeting.

a. Start Excel, open the Data File EX D-4.xlsx from the location where you store your Data Files, then save it as **EX D-Bark Bark Bark Doggie Day Spa Analysis**.

b. Decide which data in the worksheet should be charted. What chart types are best suited for the information you need to show? What kinds of chart enhancements are necessary?

c. Create a 3-D Clustered Column chart in the worksheet showing the expense data for all four quarters. (*Hint*: The expense categories should appear on the x-axis. Do not include the totals.)

d. Change the vertical axis labels (Expenses data) so that no decimals are displayed. (*Hint*: Right-click the axis labels you want to modify, click Format Axis, click the Number category in the Format Axis pane, change the number of decimal places, then close the Format Axis pane.)

e. Using the sales data, create two charts on this worksheet that compare the sales amounts. (*Hint*: Move each chart to a new location on the worksheet, then deselect it before creating the next one.)

f. In one chart of the sales data, add data labels, then add chart titles as you see fit.

g. Make any necessary formatting changes to make the charts look more attractive, then enter your name in a worksheet cell.

h. Save your work.

i. Preview each chart in Backstage view, and adjust any items as needed. Fit the worksheet to a single page, then submit your work to your instructor as directed. A sample of a printed worksheet is shown in FIGURE D-28.

j. Close the workbook, then exit Excel.

FIGURE D-28

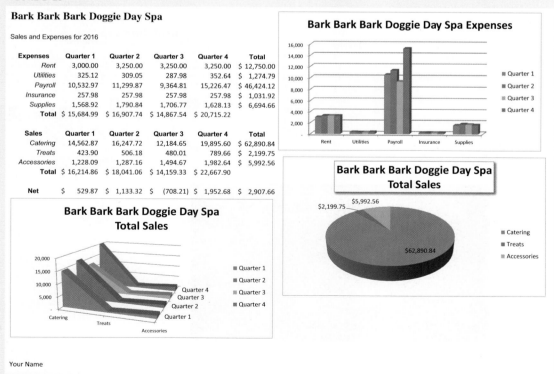

Independent Challenge 3

You are working as an account representative at a magazine called *Creativity*. You have been examining the expenses incurred recently. The CEO wants to examine expenses designed to increase circulation and has asked you to prepare charts that can be used in this evaluation. In particular, you want to see how dollar amounts compare among the different expenses, and you also want to see how expenses compare with each other proportional to the total budget.

 a. Start Excel, open the Data File EX D-5.xlsx from the location where you store your Data Files, then save it as **EX D-Creativity Magazine**.

 b. Identify three types of charts that seem best suited to illustrate the data in the range A16:B24. What kinds of chart enhancements are necessary?

 c. Create at least two different types of charts that show the distribution of circulation expenses. (*Hint*: Move each chart to a new location on the same worksheet.) One of the charts should be a 3-D pie chart.

 d. In at least one of the charts, add annotated text and arrows highlighting important data, such as the largest expense.

 e. Change the color of at least one data series in at least one of the charts.

 f. Add chart titles and category and value axis titles where appropriate. Format the titles with a font of your choice. Apply a shadow to the chart title in at least one chart.

 g. Add your name to a section of the header, then save your work.

 h. Explode a slice from the 3-D pie chart.

 i. Add a data label to the exploded pie slice.

 j. Preview the worksheet in Backstage view. Adjust any items as needed. Be sure the charts are all visible on one page. Compare your work to the sample in FIGURE D-29.

 k. Submit your work to your instructor as directed, close the workbook, then exit Excel.

FIGURE D-29

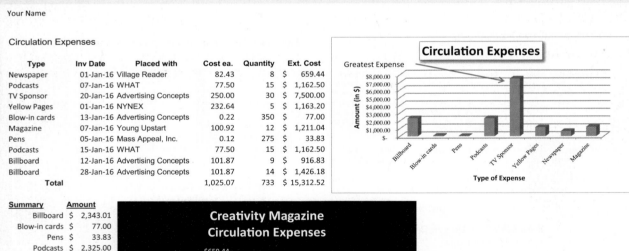

Independent Challenge 4: Explore

This Independent Challenge requires an Internet connection.

A cash inheritance from a distant relative has finally been deposited in your bank account, and you have decided to purchase a home. You have a good idea where you'd like to live, and you decide to use the web to find out more about houses that are currently available.

a. Start Excel, then save a new, blank workbook as **EX D-My Dream House** to the location where you save your Data Files.

b. Decide on where you would like to live, and use your favorite search engine to find information sources on homes for sale in that area. (*Hint*: Try using realtor.com or other realtor-sponsored sites.)

c. Determine a price range and features within the home. Find data for at least five homes that meet your location and price requirements, and enter them in the worksheet. See **TABLE D-4** for a suggested data layout.

d. Format the data so it looks attractive and professional.

e. Create any type of column chart using only the House and Asking Price data. Place it on the same worksheet as the data. Include a descriptive title.

TABLE D-4

suggested data layout					
Location					
Price range					
	House 1	House 2	House 3	House 4	House 5
Asking price					
Bedrooms					
Bathrooms					
Year built					
Size (in sq. ft.)					

© 2014 Cengage Learning

f. Change the colors in the chart using the chart style of your choice.

g. Enter your name in a section of the header.

h. Create an additional chart: a combo chart that plots the asking price on one axis and the size of the home on the other axis. (*Hint*: Use Help to get tips on how to chart with a secondary axis.)

i. Save the workbook. Preview the worksheet in Backstage view and make adjustments if necessary to fit all of the information on one page. See **FIGURE D-30** for an example of what your worksheet might look like.

j. Submit your work to your instructor as directed.

k. Close the workbook, then exit Excel.

FIGURE D-30

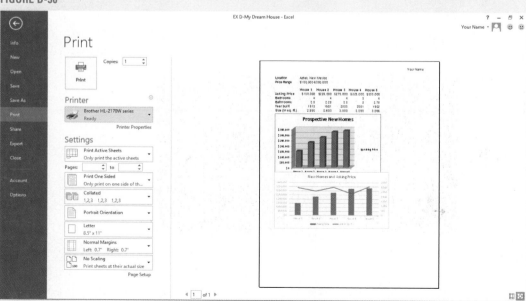

Visual Workshop

Open the Data File EX D-6.xlsx from the location where you store your Data Files, then save it as **EX D-Projected Project Expenses**. Format the worksheet data so it looks like FIGURE D-31, then create and modify two charts to match the ones shown in the figure. You will need to make formatting, layout, and design changes once you create the charts. (*Hint*: The shadow used in the 3-D pie chart title is made using the Outer Offset Diagonal Top Right shadow.) Enter your name in the left text box of the header, then save and preview the worksheet. Submit your work to your instructor as directed, then close the workbook and exit Excel.

FIGURE D-31

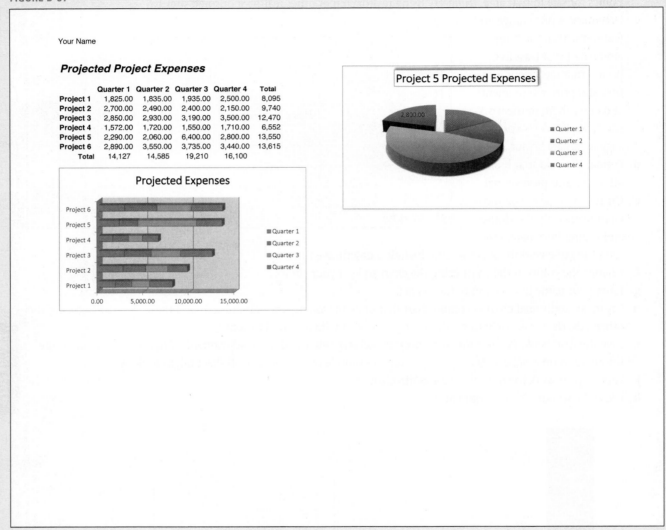

Managing Data Using Tables

CASE ▸ Quest uses tables to analyze tour data. The vice president of sales, Kate Morgan, asks you to help her build and manage a table of **2016** tour information. You will help by planning and creating a table; adding, changing, finding, and deleting table information; sorting table data, and performing calculations with table data.

Unit Objectives

After completing this unit, you will be able to:

- Plan a table
- Create and format a table
- Add table data
- Find and replace table data
- Delete table data
- Sort table data
- Use formulas in a table
- Print a table

Files You Will Need

EX G-1.xlsx EX G-4.xlsx
EX G-2.xlsx EX G-5.xlsx
EX G-3.xlsx EX G-6.xlsx

Plan a Table

Learning
Outcomes
• Plan the data
organization for
a table
• Plan the data
elements for
a table

In addition to using Excel spreadsheet features, you can analyze and manipulate data in a table structure. An Excel **table** is an organized collection of rows and columns of similarly structured worksheet data. Tables are a convenient way to understand and manage large amounts of information. When planning a table, consider what information you want your table to contain and how you want to work with the data, now and in the future. As you plan a table, you should understand its most important components. A table is organized into rows called records. A **record** is a table row that contains data about an object, person, or other item. Records are composed of fields. **Fields** are columns in the table; each field describes a characteristic of the record, such as a customer's last name or street address. Each field has a **field name**, which is a column label, such as "Address," that describes its contents. Tables usually have a **header row** as the first row, which contains the field names. To plan your table, use the guidelines below. **CASE** *Kate asks you to compile a table of the 2016 tours. Before entering the tour data into an Excel worksheet, you plan the table contents.*

DETAILS

As you plan your table, use the following guidelines:

- **Identify the purpose of the table**

 The purpose of the table determines the kind of information the table should contain. You want to use the tours table to find all departure dates for a particular tour and to display the tours in order of departure date. You also want to quickly calculate the number of available seats for a tour.

- **Plan the structure of the table**

 In designing your table's structure, determine the fields (the table columns) you need to achieve the table's purpose. You have worked with the sales department to learn the type of information they need for each tour. FIGURE G-1 shows a layout sketch for the table. Each row will contain one tour record. The columns represent fields that contain pieces of descriptive information you will enter for each tour, such as the name, departure date, and duration.

- **Plan your row and column structure**

 You can create a table from any contiguous range of cells on your worksheet. Plan and design your table so that all rows have similar types of information in the same column. A table should not have any blank rows or columns. Instead of using blank rows to separate table headings from data, use a table style, which will use formatting to make column labels stand out from your table data. FIGURE G-2 shows a table, populated with data that has been formatted using a table style.

- **Document the table design**

 In addition to your table sketch, you should make a list of the field names to document the type of data and any special number formatting required for each field. Field names should be as short as possible while still accurately describing the column information. When naming fields it is important to use text rather than numbers because Excel could interpret numbers as parts of formulas. Your field names should be unique and not easily confused with cell addresses, such as the name D2. You want your tours table to contain eight field names, each one corresponding to the major characteristics of the 2016 tours. TABLE G-1 shows the documentation of the field names in your table.

FIGURE G-1: **Table layout sketch**

Tour	Depart Date	Number of Days	Seat Capacity	Price	Air Included	Insurance Included

Each tour will be placed in a table row

Header row will contain field names

© 2014 Cengage Learning

FIGURE G-2: **Formatted table with data**

Header row contains field names

Records for each tour, organized by field name

	A	B	C	D	E	F	G	H
1	Tour	Depart Date	Number of Days	Seat Capacity	Seats Reserved	Price	Air Included	Insurance Included
2	Pacific Odyssey	1/12/2016	14	50	50	$ 2,255	Yes	No
3	Old Japan	1/13/2016	21	47	42	$ 1,984	Yes	No
4	Costa Rica	1/19/2016	10	31	28	$ 1,966	Yes	Yes
5	Yellowstone	1/21/2016	18	51	40	$ 1,850	Yes	Yes
6	Amazing Amazon	2/22/2016	14	43	39	$ 2,134	No	No
7	Hiking Patagonia	2/28/2016	7	20	15	$ 2,812	Yes	No
8	Pearls of the Orient	3/13/2016	14	45	15	$ 2,350	Yes	No
9	Silk Road Travels	3/19/2016	18	23	19	$ 2,110	Yes	Yes
10	Photographing France	3/20/2016	7	20	20	$ 1,755	Yes	Yes
11	Green Adventures in Ecuador	3/23/2016	18	25	22	$ 2,450	No	No
12	African National Parks	4/8/2016	30	12	10	$ 3,115	Yes	Yes
13	Experience Cambodia	4/11/2016	12	35	21	$ 2,441	Yes	No
14	Old Japan	4/15/2016	21	47	30	$ 1,900	Yes	No
15	Costa Rica	4/18/2016	10	30	20	$ 2,800	Yes	Yes
16	Yellowstone	4/20/2016	18	51	31	$ 1,652	Yes	Yes

TABLE G-1: **Table documentation**

field name	type of data	description of data
Tour	Text	Name of tour
Depart Date	Date	Date tour departs
Number of Days	Number with 0 decimal places	Duration of the tour
Seat Capacity	Number with 0 decimal places	Maximum number of people the tour can accommodate
Seats Reserved	Number with 0 decimal places	Number of reservations for the tour
Price	Accounting with 0 decimal places and $ symbol	Tour price (This price is not guaranteed until a 30% deposit is received)
Air Included	Text	Yes: Airfare is included in the price No: Airfare is not included in the price
Insurance Included	Text	Yes: Insurance is included in the price No: Insurance is not included in the price

© 2014 Cengage Learning

Excel 2013

Create and Format a Table

Learning
Outcomes
• Create a table
• Format a table

Once you have planned the table structure, the sequence of fields, and appropriate data types, you are ready to create the table in Excel. After you create a table, a TABLE TOOLS DESIGN tab appears, containing a gallery of table styles. **Table styles** allow you to easily add formatting to your table by using preset formatting combinations of fill color, borders, type style, and type color. **CASE** Kate asks you to build a table with the 2016 tour data. You begin by entering the field names. Then you enter the tour data that corresponds to each field name, create the table, and format the data using a table style.

STEPS

1. **Start Excel, open the file EX G-1.xlsx from the location where you store your Data Files, then save it as EX G-2016 Tours**

2. **Beginning in cell A1 of the Practice sheet, enter each field name in a separate column, as shown in** FIGURE G-3
 Field names are usually in the first row of the table.

3. **Enter the information from** FIGURE G-4 **in the rows immediately below the field names, leaving no blank rows**
 The data appears in columns organized by field name.

4. **Select the range A1:H4, click the Format button in the Cells group, click AutoFit Column Width, then click cell A1**
 Resizing the column widths this way is faster than double-clicking the column divider lines.

5. **With cell A1 selected, click the INSERT tab, click the Table button in the Tables group, in the Create Table dialog box verify that your table data is in the range A1:H4, and make sure My table has headers is checked as shown in** FIGURE G-5, **then click OK**
 The data range is now defined as a table. **Filter list arrows**, which let you display portions of your data, now appear next to each column header. When you create a table, Excel automatically applies a table style. The default table style has a dark blue header row and alternating gray and blue data rows. The TABLE TOOLS DESIGN tab appears, and the Table Styles group displays a gallery of table formatting options. You decide to choose a different table style from the gallery.

6. **Click the Table Styles More button ⊽, scroll to view all of the table styles, then move the mouse pointer over several styles without clicking**
 The Table Styles gallery on the TABLE TOOLS DESIGN tab has three style categories: Light, Medium, and Dark. Each category has numerous design types; for example, in some of the designs, the header row and total row are darker and the rows alternate colors. The available table designs use the current workbook theme colors so the table coordinates with your existing workbook content. If you select a different workbook theme and color scheme in the Themes group on the PAGE LAYOUT tab, the Table Styles gallery uses those colors. As you point to each table style, Live Preview shows you what your table will look like with the style applied. However, you only see a preview of each style; you need to click a style to apply it.

7. **Click Table Style Medium 24 to apply it to your table, then click cell A1**
 Compare your table to FIGURE G-6.

Managing Data Using Tables

	A	B	C	D	E	F	G	H
1	Tour	Depart Date	Number of Days	Seat Capacity	Seats Reserved	Price	Air Included	Insurance Included

FIGURE G-4: **Three records entered in the worksheet**

	A	B	C	D	E	F	G	H
1	Tour	Depart Date	Number of Days	Seat Capacity	Seats Reserved	Price	Air Included	Insurance Included
2	Pacific Odyssey	1/12/2016	14	50	40	2255	Yes	No
3	Old Japan	1/13/2016	21	47	42	1964	Yes	No
4	Costa Rica	1/19/2016	10	31	28	1833	Yes	Yes
5								

FIGURE G-5: **Create Table dialog box**

Table range

Verify that this box is checked

FIGURE G-6: **Formatted table with three records**

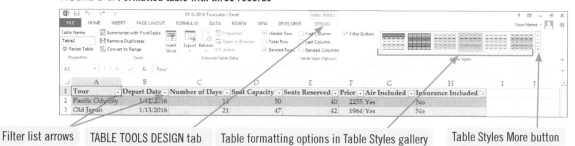

Filter list arrows TABLE TOOLS DESIGN tab Table formatting options in Table Styles gallery Table Styles More button

Changing table style options

You can change a table's appearance by using the check boxes in the Table Styles Options group on the TABLE TOOLS DESIGN tab, shown in FIGURE G-7. For example, you can turn on or turn off the following options: Header Row, which displays or hides the header row; Total Row, which calculates totals for each column; **banding**, which creates different formatting for adjacent rows and columns; and special formatting for first and last columns. Use these options to modify a table's appearance either before or after applying a table style. For example, if your table has banded rows, you can select the Banded Columns check box to change the table to be displayed with banded columns as well. Also, you may want to deselect the Header Row check box to hide a table's header row if a table will be included in a presentation where the header row repeats slide labels.

You can also create your own table style by clicking the Table Styles More button, then at the bottom of the Table Styles Gallery, clicking New Table Style. In the New Table Style dialog box, name the style in the Name text box, click a table element, then format selected table elements by clicking Format. You can also set a custom style as the default style for your tables by checking the Set as default table quick style for this document check box. You can click Clear at the bottom of the Table Styles gallery if you want to delete a table style from the currently selected table.

FIGURE G-7: **Table Styles Options**

Add Table Data

Learning Outcomes
• Add fields to a table
• Add records to a table

You can add records to a table by typing data directly below the last row of the table. After you press [Enter], the new row becomes part of the table and the table formatting extends to the new data. When the active cell is the last cell of a table, you can add a new row by pressing [Tab]. You can also insert rows in any table location. If you decide you need additional data fields, you can add new columns to a table. You can also expand a table by dragging the sizing handle in a table's lower-right corner; drag down to add rows and drag to the right to add columns. **CASE** *After entering all of the 2016 tour data, Kate decides to offer two additional tours. She also wants the table to display the number of available seats for each tour and whether visas are required for the destination.*

STEPS

1. **Click the 2016 Tours sheet tab**

 The 2016 sheet containing the 2016 tour data becomes active.

2. **Scroll down to the last table row, click cell A65, enter the data for the new Pearls of the Orient tour, as shown below, then press [Enter]**

Pearls of the Orient	7/25/2016	14	50	0	$ 2,400	Yes	No

 As you scroll down, the table headers are visible at the top of the table as long as the active cell is inside the table. The new Pearls of the Orient tour is now part of the table. You want to enter a record about a new January tour above row 6.

3. **Scroll up to and click the inside left edge of cell A6 to select the table row data as shown in FIGURE G-8, click the Insert list arrow in the Cells group, then click Insert Table Rows Above**

 Clicking the left edge of the first cell in a table row selects the entire table row, rather than the entire worksheet row. A new blank row 6 is available for the new record.

4. **Click cell A6, then enter the Yellowstone record shown below**

Yellowstone	1/28/2016	18	51	0	$ 1,850	Yes	Yes

 The new Yellowstone tour is part of the table. You want to add a new field that displays the number of available seats for each tour.

5. **Click cell I1, enter the field name Seats Available, then press [Enter]**

 The new field becomes part of the table, and the header formatting extends to the new field as shown in FIGURE G-9. The AutoCorrect menu allows you to undo or stop the automatic table expansion, but in this case you decide to leave this feature on. You want to add another new field to the table to display tours that require visas, but this time you will add the new field by resizing the table.

QUICK TIP

You can also resize a table by clicking the TABLE TOOLS DESIGN tab, clicking the Resize Table button in the Properties group, selecting the new data range for the table, then clicking OK.

6. **Scroll down until cell I66 is visible, drag the sizing handle in the table's lower-right corner one column to the right to add column J to the table, as shown in FIGURE G-10**

 The table range is now A1:J66, and the new field name is Column1.

7. **Scroll up to and click cell J1, enter Visa Required, then press [Enter]**

8. **Click the INSERT tab, click the Header & Footer button in the Text group, enter your name in the center header text box, click cell A1, click the Normal button ⊞ in the status bar, then save the workbook**

	Tour	Depart Date	Number of Days	Seat Capacity	Seats Reserved	Price	Air Included	Insurance Included
1								
2	Pacific Odyssey	1/12/2016	14	50	50	$ 2,255	Yes	No
3	Old Japan	1/13/2016	21	47	42	$ 1,984	Yes	No
4	Costa Rica	1/19/2016	10	31	28	$ 1,966	Yes	Yes
5	Yellowstone	1/21/2016	18	51	40	$ 1,850	Yes	Yes
6	Amazing Amazon	2/22/2016	14	43	39	$ 2,134	No	No
7	Hiking Patagonia	2/28/2016	7	20	15	$ 2,812	Yes	No
8	Pearls of the Orient	3/13/2016	14	45	15	$ 2,350	Yes	No
9	Silk Road Travels	3/19/2016	18	23	19	$ 2,110	Yes	Yes
10	Photographing France	3/20/2016	7	20	20	$ 1,755	Yes	Yes
11	Green Adventures in Ecuador	3/23/2016	18	25	22	$ 2,450	No	No
12	African National Parks	4/8/2016	30	12	10	$ 3,115	Yes	Yes

Row 6 selected

Place the pointer over the inside left edge of cell to select only the table row

FIGURE G-9: **New table column**

	A	B	C	D	E	F	G	H	I
1	Tour	Depart Date	Number of Days	Seat Capacity	Seats Reserved	Price	Air Included	Insurance Included	Seats Available
2	Pacific Odyssey	1/12/2016	14	50	50	$ 2,255	Yes	No	
3	Old Japan	1/13/2016	21	47	42	$ 1,984	Yes	No	
4	Costa Rica	1/19/2016	10	31	28	$ 1,966	Yes	Yes	
5	Yellowstone	1/21/2016	18	51	40	$ 1,850	Yes	Yes	
6	Yellowstone	1/28/2016	18	51	0	$ 1,850	Yes	Yes	
7	Amazing Amazon	2/22/2016	14	43	39	$ 2,134	No	No	
8	Hiking Patagonia	2/28/2016	7	20	15	$ 2,812	Yes	No	

New table column will show available seats for each tour

New record in row 6

FIGURE G-10: **Resizing a table using the resizing handle**

	Depart Date	Number of	Seat Capacity	Seats Reserved	Price	Air Included	Insurance In	Seats Avail	J	K
55	10/29/2016	14	18	8	$ 4,200	Yes	Yes			
56	10/31/2016	7	38	15	$ 1,900	Yes	No			
57	10/31/2016	12	40	2	$ 2,908	Yes	No			
58	11/18/2016	10	41	12	$ 2,200	Yes	Yes			
59	12/18/2016	10	50	21	$ 2,204	Yes	Yes			
60	12/18/2016	10	50	21	$ 2,204	Yes	Yes			
61	12/20/2016	14	15	1	$ 2,100	Yes	Yes			
62	12/20/2016	14	15	1	$ 2,100	Yes	Yes			
63	12/21/2016	14	50	10	$ 2,105	Yes	No			
64	12/30/2016	18	51	15	$ 2,922	Yes	Yes			
65	12/31/2016	21	47	4	$ 2,100	Yes	No			
66	7/25/2016	14	50	0	$ 2,400	Yes	No			

Drag sizing handle to add column J to table

Excel 2013

Selecting table elements

When working with tables you often need to select rows, columns, and even the entire table. Clicking to the right of a row number, inside column A, selects the entire table row. You can select a table column by clicking the top edge of the header. Be careful not to click a column letter or row number, however, because this selects the entire worksheet row or column. You can select the table data by clicking the upper-left corner of the first table cell. When selecting a column or a table, the first click selects only the data in the column or table. If you click a second time, you add the headers to the selection.

Find and Replace Table Data

Learning Outcomes
- Find data in a table
- Replace data in a table

From time to time, you need to locate specific records in your table. You can use the Excel Find feature to search your table for the information you need. You can also use the Replace feature to locate and replace existing entries or portions of entries with information you specify. If you don't know the exact spelling of the text you are searching for, you can use wildcards to help locate the records. **Wildcards** are special symbols that substitute for unknown characters. **CASE** ▶ *In response to a change in the bike trip from Ireland to Scotland, Kate needs to replace "Ireland" with "Scotland" in all of the tour names. She also wants to know how many Pacific Odyssey tours are scheduled for the year. You begin by searching for records with the text "Pacific Odyssey".*

STEPS

1. **Click cell A1 if necessary, click the HOME tab, click the Find & Select button in the Editing group, then click Find**

 The Find and Replace dialog box opens, as shown in FIGURE G-11. In the Find what text box, you enter criteria that specify the records you want to find. You want to search for records whose Tour field contains the label "Old Japan".

2. **Type Old Japan in the Find what text box, then click Find Next**

 A3 is the active cell because it is the first instance of Old Japan in the table.

3. **Click Find Next and examine the record for each Old Japan tour found until no more matching cells are found in the table and the active cell is A3 again, then click Close**

 There are four Old Japan tours.

4. **Return to cell A1, click the Find & Select button in the Editing group, then click Replace**

 The Find and Replace dialog box opens with the Replace tab selected and "Old Japan" in the Find what text box, as shown in FIGURE G-12. You will search for entries containing "Ireland" and replace them with "Scotland". To save time, you will use the asterisk (*) wildcard to help you locate the records containing Ireland.

5. **Delete the text in the Find what text box, type Ir* in the Find what text box, click the Replace with text box, then type Scotland**

 The asterisk (*) wildcard stands for one or more characters, meaning that the search text "Ir*" will find words such as "iron", "hair", and "bird". Because you notice that there are other table entries containing the text "ir" with a lowercase "i" (in the Air Included column heading), you need to make sure that only capitalized instances of the letter "I" are replaced.

6. **Click Options >>, click the Match case check box to select it, click Options <<, then click Find Next**

 Excel moves the cell pointer to the cell containing the first occurrence of "Ireland".

7. **Click Replace All, click OK, then click Close**

 The dialog box closes. Excel made three replacements, in cells A27, A36, and A40. The Air Included field heading remains unchanged because the "ir" in "Air" is lowercase.

8. **Save the workbook**

FIGURE G-12: **The Replace tab in the Find and Replace dialog box**

	A	B	C	D	E	F	G	H	I	J
	Tour	Depart Date	Number of Days	Seat Capacity	Seats Reserved	Price	Air Included	Insurance Included	Seats Available	Visa Require
2	Pacific Odyssey	1/12/2016	14	50	50	$ 2,255	Yes	No		
3	Old Japan	1/13/2016	21	47	42	$ 1,984	Yes	No		
4	Costa Rica					$ 1,966	Yes	Yes		
5	Yellowstone					$ 1,850	Yes	Yes		
6	Yellowstone					$ 1,850	Yes	Yes		
7	Amazing Amazon					$ 2,134	No	No		
8	Hiking Patagonia					$ 2,812	Yes	No		
9	Pearls of the Orient					$ 2,350	Yes	No		
10	Silk Road Travels					$ 2,110	Yes	Yes		
11	Photographing France	3/20/2016	7	20	20	$ 1,755	Yes	Yes		
12	Green Adventures in Ecuador	3/23/2016	18	25	22	$ 2,450	No	No		
13	African National Parks	4/8/2016	30	12	10	$ 3,115	Yes	Yes		
14	Experience Cambodia	4/11/2016	12	35	21	$ 2,441	Yes	No		
15	Old Japan	4/15/2016	21	47	30	$ 1,900	Yes	No		
16	Costa Rica	4/18/2016	10	30	20	$ 2,800	Yes	Yes		

Step 5

Find and Replace

Find · Replace

Find what: Old Japan

Replace with:

Options >>

Replace All · Replace · Find All · Find Next · Close

Step 6

Step 7

Click to replace current item that matches the Find what text box

Using Find and Select features

You can also use the Find feature to navigate to a specific place in a workbook by clicking the Find & Select button in the Editing group, clicking Go To, typing a cell address, then clicking OK. Clicking the Find & Select button also allows you to find comments and conditional formatting in a worksheet. You can use the Go to Special dialog box to select cells that contain different types of formulas or objects. Some Go to Special commands also appear on the Find & Select menu. Using this menu, you can also change the mouse pointer shape to the Select Objects pointer so you can quickly select drawing objects when necessary. To return to the standard Excel pointer, press [Esc].

Excel 2013

Delete Table Data

To keep a table up to date, you need to be able to periodically remove records. You may even need to remove fields if the information stored in a field becomes unnecessary. You can delete table data using the Delete button in the Cells group or by dragging the sizing handle at the table's lower-right corner. You can also easily delete duplicate records from a table. **CASE** *Kate is canceling the Old Japan tour that departs on 1/13/2016 and asks you to delete the record from the table. You will also remove any duplicate records from the table. Because the visa requirements are difficult to keep up with, Kate asks you to delete the field with visa information.*

STEPS

1. **Click the left edge of cell A3 to select the table row data, click the Delete list arrow in the Cells group, then click Delete Table Rows**

 The Old Japan tour is deleted, and the Costa Rica tour moves up to row 3, as shown in FIGURE G-13. You can also delete a table row or a column using the Resize Table button in the Properties group of the TABLE TOOLS DESGIN tab, or by right-clicking the row or column, pointing to Delete on the shortcut menu, then clicking Table Columns or Table Rows. You decide to check the table for duplicate records.

2. **Click the TABLE TOOLS DESIGN tab, then click the Remove Duplicates button in the Tools group**

 The Remove Duplicates dialog box opens, as shown in FIGURE G-14. You need to select the columns that will be used to evaluate duplicates. Because you don't want to delete tours with the same destination but different departure dates, you will look for duplicate data in all of the columns.

3. **Make sure that "My data has headers" is checked and that all the Columns check boxes (column headers) are checked, then click OK**

 Two duplicate records are found and removed, leaving 62 records of data and a total of 63 rows in the table, including the header row. You want to remove the last column, which contains space for visa information.

4. **Click OK, scroll down until cell J63 is visible, drag the sizing handle of the table's lower-right corner one column to the left to remove column J from the table**

 The table range is now A1:I63, and the Visa Required field no longer appears in the table.

5. **Delete the contents of cell J1, return to cell A1, then save the workbook**

	Tour	Depart Date	Number of Days	Seat Capacity	Seats Reserved	Price	Air Included	Insurance Included	Seats Available	Visa Require
2	Pacific Odyssey	1/12/2016	14	50	50	$ 2,255	Yes	No		
3	Costa Rica	1/19/2016	10	31	28	$ 1,966	Yes	Yes		
4	Yellowstone	1/21/2016	18	51	40	$ 1,850	Yes	Yes		
5	Yellowstone	1/28/2016	18	51	0	$ 1,850	Yes	Yes		
6	Amazing Amazon	2/22/2016	14	43	39	$ 2,134	No	No		
7	Hiking Patagonia	2/28/2016	7	20	15	$ 2,812	Yes	No		
8	Pearls of the Orient	3/13/2016	14	45	15	$ 2,350	Yes	No		
9	Silk Road Travels	3/19/2016	18	23	19	$ 2,110	Yes	Yes		
10	Photographing France	3/20/2016	7	20	20	$ 1,755	Yes	Yes		
11	Green Adventures in Ecuador	3/23/2016	18	25	22	$ 2,450	No	No		
12	African National Parks	4/8/2016	30	12	10	$ 3,115	Yes	Yes		
13	Experience Cambodia	4/11/2016	12	35	21	$ 2,441	Yes	No		
14	Old Japan	4/15/2016	21	47	30	$ 1,900	Yes	No		
15	Costa Rica	4/18/2016	10	30	20	$ 2,800	Yes	Yes		
16	Yellowstone	4/20/2016	18	51	31	$ 1,652	Yes	Yes		

Row is deleted and
tours move up one row

FIGURE G-14: **Remove Duplicates dialog box**

Selected columns
will be checked
for duplicate data

Sort Table Data

Usually, you enter table records in the order in which you receive information, rather than in alphabetical or numerical order. When you add records to a table, you usually enter them at the end of the table. You can change the order of the records any time using the Excel **sort** feature. Because the data is structured as a table, Excel changes the order of the records while keeping each record, or row of information, together. You can sort a table in ascending or descending order on one field using the filter list arrows next to the field name. In **ascending order**, the lowest value (the beginning of the alphabet or the earliest date) appears at the top of the table. In a field containing labels and numbers, numbers appear first in the sorted list. In **descending order**, the highest value (the end of the alphabet or the latest date) appears at the top of the table. In a field containing labels and numbers, labels appear first. TABLE G-2 provides examples of ascending and descending sorts. **CASE** ▶ *Kate wants the tour data sorted by departure date, displaying tours that depart the soonest at the top of the table.*

STEPS

1. **Click the** Depart Date filter list arrow, **then click** Sort Oldest to Newest

 Excel rearranges the records in ascending order by departure date, as shown in FIGURE G-15. The Depart Date filter list arrow has an upward pointing arrow indicating the ascending sort in the field. You can also sort the table on one field using the Sort & Filter button.

2. **Click the** HOME tab, **click any cell in the** Price column, **click the** Sort & Filter button **in the Editing group, then click** Sort Largest to Smallest

 Excel sorts the table, placing those records with the higher price at the top. The Price filter list arrow now has a downward pointing arrow next to the filter list arrow, indicating the descending sort order. You can also rearrange the table data using a **multilevel sort**. This type of sort rearranges the table data using more than one field, where each field is a different level, based on its importance in the sort. If you use two sort levels, the data is sorted by the first field, and the second field is sorted within each grouping of the first field. Since you have many groups of tours with different departure dates, you want to use a multilevel sort to arrange the table data by tours and then by departure dates within each tour.

3. **Click the** Sort & Filter button **in the Editing group, then click** Custom Sort

 The Sort dialog box opens, as shown in FIGURE G-16.

4. **Click the** Sort by list arrow, **click** Tour, **click the** Order list arrow, **click** A to Z, **click** Add Level, **click the** Then by list arrow, **click** Depart Date, **click the second** Order list arrow, **click** Oldest to Newest **if necessary, then click** OK

 FIGURE G-17 shows the table sorted alphabetically in ascending order (A–Z) by Tour and, within each tour grouping, in ascending order by the Depart Date.

5. **Save the workbook**

Sorting conditionally formatted data

If conditional formats have been applied to a table, you can sort the table using conditional formatting to arrange the rows. For example, if cells are conditionally formatted with color, you can sort a field on Cell Color, using the color with the order of On Top or On Bottom in the Sort dialog box. If the data is not in a table, you can select a cell in the column of conditionally formatted data you want to sort by, or select the range of cells to be sorted, right-click the selection, point to Sort, then select the font color, highlighted color, or icon that you want to appear on top.

	A	B	C	D	E	F	G	H	I
1	Tour	Depart Date	Number of Days	Seat Capacity	Seats Reserved	Price	Air Included	Insurance Included	Seats Available
2	Pacific Odyssey	1/12/2016	14	50		,255	Yes	No	
3	Costa Rica	1/19/2016	10	31		966	Yes	Yes	
4	Yellowstone	1/21/2016	18	51		350	Yes	Yes	
5	Yellowstone	1/28/2016	18	51		350	Yes	Yes	
6	Amazing Amazon	2/22/2016	14	43		,134	No	No	
	ing Patagonia	2/28/2016	7	20	15	$ 2,812	Yes	No	
	ls of the Orient	3/13/2016	14	45	15	$ 2,350	Yes	No	
	Road Travels	3/19/2016	18	23	19	$ 2,110	Yes	Yes	
	ographing France	3/20/2016	7	20	20	$ 1,755	Yes	Yes	
	en Adventures in Ecuador	3/23/2016	18	25	22	$ 2,450	No	No	
12	African National Parks	4/8/2016	30	12	10	$ 3,115	Yes	Yes	
13	Experience Cambodia	4/11/2016	12	35	21	$ 2,441	Yes	No	
14	Old Japan	4/15/2016	21	47	30	$ 1,900	Yes	No	
15	Costa Rica	4/18/2016	10	30	20	$ 2,800	Yes	Yes	
16	Yellowstone	4/20/2016	18	51	31	$ 1,652	Yes	Yes	

Up arrow indicates ascending sort in the field

Records are sorted by departure date in ascending order

FIGURE G-16: Sort dialog box

Click to add additional sort levels

Click to delete sort levels

Click to display fields

FIGURE G-17: Table sorted using two levels

	A	B	C	D	E	F	G	H	I
1	Tour	Depart Date	Number of Days	Seat Capacity	Seats Reserved	Price	Air Included	Insurance Included	Seats Available
2	African National Parks	4/8/2016	30	12	10	$ 3,115	Yes	Yes	
3	African National Parks	10/27/2016	30	12	8	$ 4,870	Yes	Yes	
4	Amazing Amazon	2/22/2016	14	43	39	$ 2,134	No	No	
5	Amazing Amazon	4/23/2016	14	43	30	$ 2,133	No	No	
6	Amazing Amazon	8/23/2016	14	43	18	$ 2,877	No	No	
7	Biking in France	5/23/2016	7	12	10	$ 1,635	No	No	
8	Biking in France	9/23/2016	7	12	7	$ 2,110	No	No	
9	Biking in Scotland	6/11/2016	10	15	10	$ 2,600	Yes	No	
10	Biking in Scotland	7/11/2			9	$ 2,600	Yes	No	
11	Biking in Scotland	8/11/2			6	$ 2,600	Yes	No	
12	Catalonia Adventure	5/9/2			30	$ 2,587	Yes	No	
13	Catalonia Adventure	6/9/2		15	$ 2,100	Yes	No		
14	Catalonia Adventure	10/9/2016	14	51	11	$ 2,100	Yes	No	
15	Corfu	10/2016	21	12	10	$ 2,190	Yes	No	
16	Corfu	9/2016	21	12	1	$ 2,190	Yes	No	

Second-level sort arranges records by departure date within each tour grouping

Top-level sort on Tour arranges records by tour name

TABLE G-2: Sort order options and examples

option	alphabetic	numeric	date	alphanumeric
Ascending	A, B, C	7, 8, 9	1/1, 2/1, 3/1	12A, 99B, DX8, QT7
Descending	C, B, A	9, 8, 7	3/1, 2/1, 1/1	QT7, DX8, 99B, 12A

© 2014 Cengage Learning

Specifying a custom sort order

You can identify a custom sort order for the field selected in the Sort by box. Click the Order list arrow in the Sort dialog box, click Custom List, then click the desired custom order. Commonly used custom sort orders are days of the week (Sun, Mon, Tues, Wed, etc.) and months (Jan, Feb, Mar, etc.); alphabetic sorts do not sort these items properly.

Excel 2013

Use Formulas in a Table

Many tables are large, making it difficult to know from viewing them the "story" the table tells. The Excel table calculation features help you summarize table data so you can see important trends. After you enter a single formula into a table cell, the **calculated columns** feature fills in the remaining cells with the formula's results. The column continues to fill with the formula results as you enter rows in the table. This makes it easy to update your formulas because you only need to edit the formula once, and the change will fill in to the other column cells. The **structured reference** feature allows your formulas to refer to table columns by names that are automatically generated when you create the table. These names adjust as you add or delete table fields. An example of a table reference is =[Sales]–[Costs], where Sales and Costs are field names in the table. Tables also have a specific area at the bottom called the **table total row** for calculations using the data in the table columns. The cells in this row contain a dropdown list of functions that can be used for the column calculation. The table total row adapts to any changes in the table size. **CASE** *Kate wants you to use a formula to calculate the number of available seats for each tour. You will also add summary information to the end of the table.*

STEPS

1. **Click cell I2, then type =[**
 A list of the table field names appears, as shown in FIGURE G-18. Structured referencing allows you to use the names that Excel created when you defined your table to reference fields in a formula. You can choose a field by clicking it and pressing [Tab] or by double-clicking the field name.

2. **Click [Seat Capacity], press [Tab], then type]**
 Excel begins the formula, placing [Seat Capacity] in the cell in blue and framing the Seat Capacity data in a blue border.

3. **Type -[, double-click [Seats Reserved], then type]**
 Excel places [Seats Reserved] in the cell in red and outlines the Seats Reserved data in a red border.

4. **Press [Enter]**
 The formula result, 2, is displayed in cell I2. The table column also fills with the formula displaying the number of available seats for each tour.

5. **Click the AutoCorrect Options list arrow 🔳 ▾ to view options for the column**
 Because the calculated columns option saves time, you decide to leave the feature on. You want to display the total number of available seats on all of the tours.

6. **Click any cell inside the table to close the menu, click the TABLE TOOLS DESIGN tab, then click the Total Row check box in the Table Style Options group to select it**
 A total row appears at the bottom of the table, and the sum of the available seats, 1088, is displayed in cell I64. You can select other formulas in the total row.

7. **Click cell C64, then click the cell list arrow on the right side of the cell**
 The list of available functions appears, as shown in FIGURE G-19. You want to find the average tour length.

8. **Click Average, then save your workbook**
 The average tour length, 13 days, appears in cell C64.

	A	B	C	D	E	F	G	H	I	J
1	Tour	Depart Date	Number of Days	Seat Capacity	Seats Reserved	Price	Air Included	Insurance Included	Seats Available	
2	African National Parks	4/8/2016	30	12	10	$ 3,115	Yes	Yes	=[
3	African National Parks	10/27/2016	30	12	8	$ 4,870	Yes	Yes		
4	Amazing Amazon	2/22/2016	14	43	39	$ 2,134	No	No		
5	Amazing Amazon	4/23/2016	14	43	30	$ 2,133	No	No		
6	Amazing Amazon	8/23/2016	14	43	18	$ 2,877	No	No		
7	Biking in France	5/23/2016	7	12	10	$ 1,635	No	No		
8	Biking in France	9/23/2016	7	12	7	$ 2,110	No	No		
9	Biking in Scotland	6/11/2016	10	15	10	$ 2,600	Yes	No		
10	Biking in Scotland	7/11/2016	10	15	9	$ 2,600	Yes	No		
11	Biking in Scotland	8/11/2016	10	15	6	$ 2,600	Yes	No		
12	Catalonia Adventure	5/9/2016	14	51	30	$ 2,587	Yes	No		
13	Catalonia Adventure	6/9/2016	14	51	15	$ 2,100	Yes	No		
14	Catalonia Adventure	10/9/2016	14	51	11	$ 2,100	Yes	No		
15	Corfu Sailing Voyage	6/10/2016	21	12	10	$ 2,190	Yes	No		
16	Corfu Sailing Voyage	7/9/2016	21	12	1	$ 2,190	Yes	No		
17	Costa Rica	1/19/2016	10	31	28	$ 1,966	Yes	Yes		

Field names list (Tour, Depart Date, Number of Days, Seat Capacity, Seats Reserved, Price, Air Included, Insurance Included, Seats Available)

Field names list appears

	Tour	Depart Date	Number of	Seat Capacity	Seats Reserved	Price	Air Included	Insurance In	Seats Avail
56	Wild River Escape	6/27/2016	10	21	21	$ 1,944	No	No	0
57	Wild River Escape	8/27/2016	10	21	11	$ 1,944	No	No	10
58	Yellowstone	1/21/2016	18	51	40	$ 1,850	Yes	Yes	11
59	Yellowstone	1/28/2016	18	51	0	$ 1,850	Yes	Yes	51
60	Yellowstone	4/20/2016	18	51	31	$ 1,652	Yes	Yes	20
61	Yellowstone	8/20/2016	18	51	20	$ 2,922	Yes	Yes	31
62	Yellowstone	9/11/2016	18	51	20	$ 2,922	Yes	Yes	31
63	Yellowstone	12/30/2016	18	51	15	$ 2,922	Yes	Yes	36
64	Total								1088
65									
66									
67									
68									
69									
70									
71									

Functions available in the Total Row (None, Average, Count, Count Numbers, Max, Min, Sum, StdDev, Var, More Functions...)

Using structured references

When you create a table from worksheet data, Excel creates a default table name such as Table1. This table name appears in structured references. Structured references make it easier to work with formulas that use table data. You can reference the entire table, columns in the table, or specific data. Structured references are especially helpful to use in formulas because they automatically adjust as data ranges change in a table, so you don't need to edit formulas.

Print a Table

You can determine the way a table will print using the PAGE LAYOUT tab. Because tables often have more rows than can fit on a page, you can define the first row of the table (containing the field names) as the **print title**, which prints at the top of every page. Most tables do not have any descriptive information above the field names on the worksheet, so to augment the field name information, you can use headers and footers to add identifying text, such as the table title or the report date. **CASE** *Kate asks you for a printout of the tour information. You begin by previewing the table.*

STEPS

1. **Click the FILE tab, click Print, then view the table preview**
 Below the table you see 1 of 3.

2. **In the Preview window, click the Next Page button ▶ in the Preview area to view the second page, then click ▶ again to view the third page**
 All of the field names in the table fit across the width of page 1. Because the records on pages 2 and 3 appear without column headings, you want to set up the first row of the table, which contains the field names, as a repeating print title.

3. **Return to the worksheet, click the PAGE LAYOUT tab, click the Print Titles button in the Page Setup group, click inside the Rows to repeat at top text box under Print titles, in the worksheet scroll up to row 1 if necessary, click any cell in row 1 on the table, then compare your Page Setup dialog box to FIGURE G-20**
 When you select row 1 as a print title, Excel automatically inserts an absolute reference to the row that will repeat at the top of each page.

4. **Click the Print Preview button in the Page Setup dialog box, click ▶ in the preview window to view the second page, then click ▶ again to view the third page**
 Setting up a print title to repeat row 1 causes the field names to appear at the top of each printed page. The printout would be more informative with a header to identify the table information.

5. **Return to the worksheet, click the INSERT tab, click the Header & Footer button in the Text group, click the left header section text box, then type 2016 Tours**

6. **Select the left header section information, click the HOME tab, click the Increase Font Size button A˘ in the Font group twice to change the font size to 14, click the Bold button B in the Font group, click any cell in the table, then click the Normal button ▦ in the status bar**

7. **Save the table, preview it, close the workbook, exit Excel, then submit the workbook to your instructor**
 Compare your printed table with FIGURE G-21.

FIGURE G-20: **Page Setup dialog box**

Print title is set to row 1

FIGURE G-21: **Printed table**

Setting a print area

Sometimes you will want to print only part of a worksheet. To do this, select any worksheet range, click the FILE tab, click Print, click the Print Active Sheets list arrow, then click Print Selection. If you want to print a selected area repeatedly, it's best to define a **print area**, the area of the worksheet that previews and prints when you use the Print command in Backstage view. To set a print area, select the range of data on the worksheet that you want to print, click the PAGE LAYOUT tab, click the Print Area button in the Page Setup group, then click Set Print Area. You can add to the print area by selecting a range, clicking the Print Area button, then clicking Add to Print Area. A print area can consist of one contiguous range of cells, or multiple areas in different parts of a worksheet.

Practice

Concepts Review

FIGURE G-22

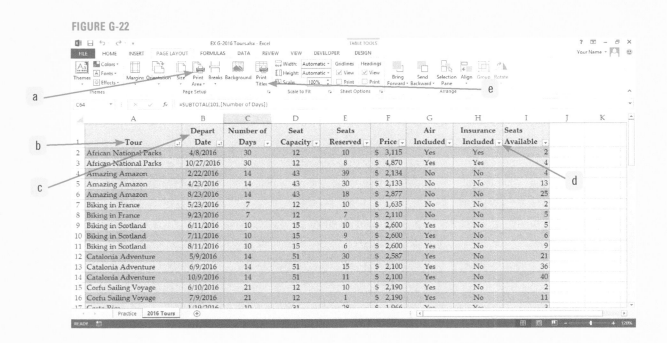

1. Which element do you click to print field names at the top of every page?
2. Which element do you click to set a range in a table that will print using the Print command?
3. Which element points to a second-level sort field?
4. Which element do you click to sort field data on a worksheet?
5. Which element points to a top-level sort field?

Match each term with the statement that best describes it.

6. **Field**
7. **Sort**
8. **Record**
9. **Table**
10. **Header row**

a. Organized collection of related information in Excel
b. Arrange records in a particular sequence
c. Column in an Excel table
d. First row of a table containing field names
e. Row in an Excel table

Select the best answer from the list of choices.

11. Which of the following Excel sorting options do you use to sort a table of employee names in order from Z to A?
 a. Ascending
 b. Absolute
 c. Alphabetic
 d. Descending

12. Which of the following series appears in descending order?

 a. 8, 6, 4, C, B, A

 b. 4, 5, 6, A, B, C

 c. 8, 7, 6, 5, 6, 7

 d. C, B, A, 6, 5, 4

13. You can easily add formatting to a table by using:

 a. Table styles.

 b. Print titles.

 c. Print areas.

 d. Calculated columns.

14. When printing a table on multiple pages, you can define a print title to:

 a. Include the sheet name in table reports.

 b. Include field names at the top of each printed page.

 c. Exclude from the printout all rows under the first row.

 d. Include gridlines in the printout.

Skills Review

1. Create and format a table.

 a. Start Excel, open the file EX G-2.xlsx from the location where you store your Data Files, then save it as **EX G-Employees**.

 b. Using the Practice sheet, enter the field names in the first row and the first two records in rows two and three, as shown in the table below, adjusting column widths as necessary to fit the text entries.

Last Name	First Name	Years Employed	Department	Full/Part Time	Training Completed
Diaz	Irina	3	Print Books	P	Y
Merril	Doreen	2	E-Books	F	N

 c. Create a table using the data you entered.

 d. On the Staff sheet, create a table with a header row. Adjust the column widths, if necessary, to display the field names. Enter your name in the center section of the worksheet footer, return to Normal view if necessary, then save the workbook.

 e. Apply a table style of Light 16 to the table.

 f. Enter your name in the center section of the worksheet footer, return to Normal view if necessary, then save the workbook.

2. Add table data.

 a. Add a new record in row seven for **Heather Walker**, a 5-year employee in the Print Books department. Heather works part time and has completed training. Adjust the height of the new row to match the other table rows.

 b. Insert a table row above Julie Kosby's record, and add a new record for **Sarah Allen**. Sarah works full time, has worked at the company for 2 years in E-Books, and has not completed training. Adjust the table formatting if necessary.

 c. Insert a new data field in cell G1 with a label **Weeks Vacation**. Adjust the column width, and wrap the label in the cell to display the field name with **Weeks** above **Vacation**. (*Hint*: Use the Wrap Text button in the Alignment group on the HOME tab.)

 d. Add a new column to the table by dragging the table's sizing handle, and give the new field a label of **Employee #**. Widen the column to fit the label.

 e. Save the file.

3. Find and replace table data.

 a. Return to cell A1.

 b. Open the Find and Replace dialog box and if necessary uncheck the Match case option. Find the first record that contains the text **Print Books**.

 c. Find the second and third records that contain the text **Print Books**.

 d. Replace all **Print Books** text in the table with **Books**, then save the file.

Skills Review (continued)

4. Delete table data.

 a. Go to cell A1.

 b. Delete the record for Irina Diaz.

 c. Use the Remove Duplicates button to confirm that the table does not have any duplicate records.

 d. Delete the Employee # table column, then delete its column header, if necessary.

 e. Save the file.

5. Sort table data.

 a. Sort the table by years employed in largest to smallest order.

 b. Sort the table by last name in A to Z order.

 c. Perform a multilevel sort: Sort the table first by Full/Part Time in A to Z order and then by last name in A to Z order.

 d. Check the table to make sure the records appear in the correct order.

 e. Save the file.

6. Use formulas in a table.

 a. In cell G2, enter the formula that calculates an employee's vacation time; base the formula on the company policy that employees working at the company less than 3 years have 2 weeks of vacation. At 3 years of employment and longer, an employee has 3 weeks of vacation time. Use the table's field names where appropriate. (*Hint*: The formula is: **=IF([Years Employed]<3,2,3).**)

 b. Check the table to make sure the formula filled into the cells in column G and that the correct vacation time is calculated for all cells in the column.

 c. Add a Total Row to display the total number of vacation weeks.

 d. Change the function in the Total Row to display the maximum number of vacation weeks. Change the entry in cell A8 from Total to **Maximum.**

 e. Compare your table to FIGURE G-23, then save the workbook.

FIGURE G-23

	A	B	C	D	E	F	G
1	Last Name	First Name	Years Employed	Department	Full/Part Time	Training Completed	Weeks Vacation
2	Allen	Sarah	2	E-Books	F	N	2
3	Green	Jane	1	Books	F	N	2
4	Kosby	Julie	4	E-Books	F	Y	3
5	Merril	Doreen	2	E-Books	F	N	2
6	Ropes	Mark	1	E-Books	P	Y	2
7	Walker	Heather	5	Books	P	Y	3
8	Maximum						3

7. Print a table.

 a. Add a header that reads **Employees** in the left section, then format the header in bold with a font size of 16.

 b. Add column A as a print title that repeats at the left of each printed page.

 c. Preview your table to check that the last names appear on both pages.

 d. Change the page orientation to landscape, preview the worksheet, then save the workbook.

 e. Submit your workbook to your instructor. Close the workbook, then exit Excel.

Independent Challenge 1

You are the marketing director for a fitness equipment sales firm. Your administrative assistant created an Excel worksheet with customer data including the results of an advertising survey. You will create a table using the customer data, and analyze the survey results to help focus the company's advertising expenses in the most successful areas.

 a. Start Excel, open the file EX G-3.xlsx from the location where you store your Data Files, then save it as **EX G-Customers**.

 b. Create a table from the worksheet data, and apply Table Style Light 18.

Independent Challenge 1 (continued)

c. Add the two records shown in the table below:

Last Name	First Name	Street Address	City	State	Zip	Area Code	Ad Source
Riley	Cate	81 Apple St.	San Francisco	CA	94177	415	Fitness Center
Jenkins	Sam	307 7th St.	Seattle	WA	98001	206	Newspaper

d. Find the record for Mike Rondo, then delete it.

e. Click cell A1 and replace all instances of **TV** with **Social Media**. Compare your table to FIGURE G-24.

FIGURE G-24

Last Name	First Name	Street Address	City	State	Zip	Area Code	Ad Source
Kahil	Kathy	14 South St.	San Francisco	CA	94177	415	Social Media
Johnson	Mel	17 Henley St.	Reading	MA	03882	413	Newspaper
Malone	Kris	1 South St.	San Francisco	CA	94177	415	Fitness Center
Worthen	Sally	2120 Central St.	San Francisco	CA	93772	415	Fitness Center
Herbert	Greg	1192 Dome St.	San Diego	CA	93303	619	Newspaper
Chavez	Jane	11 Northern St.	San Diego	CA	92208	619	Social Media
Chelly	Yvonne	900 Sola St.	San Diego	CA	92106	619	Fitness Center
Smith	Carolyn	921 Lopez St.	San Diego	CA	92104	619	Newspaper
Oren	Scott	72 Yankee St.	Brookfield	CT	06830	203	Health Website
Warner	Salvatore	100 Westside St.	Chicago	IL	60620	312	Newspaper
Roberts	Bob	56 Water St.	Chicago	IL	60618	771	Fitness Center
Miller	Hope	111 Stratton St.	Chicago	IL	60614	773	Newspaper
Duran	Maria	Galvin St.	Chicago	IL	60614	773	Health Website
Roberts	Bob	56 Water St.	Chicago	IL	60614	312	Newspaper
Graham	Shelley	989 26th St.	Chicago	IL	60611	773	Education Website
Kelly	Janie	9 First St.	San Francisco	CA	94177	415	Newspaper
Kim	Janie	9 First St.	San Francisco	CA	94177	415	Health Website
Williams	Tasha	1 Spring St.	Reading	MA	03882	413	Newspaper
Juarez	Manuel	544 Cameo St.	Belmont	MA	02483	617	Newspaper
Masters	Latrice	88 Las Puntas Rd.	Boston	MA	02205	617	Education Website
Kooper	Peter	671 Main St.	Cambridge	MA	02138	617	Social Media
Kelly	Shawn	22 Kendall St.	Cambridge	MA	02138	617	Education Website
Rodriguez	Virginia	123 Main St.	Boston	MA	02007	617	Radio
Frei	Carol	123 Elm St.	Salem	MA	01970	978	Newspaper
Stevens	Crystal	14 Waterford St.	Salem	MA	01970	508	Radio
Ichikawa	Pam	232 Shore Rd.	Boston	MA	01801	617	Newspaper
Paxton	Gail	100 Main St.	Woburn	MA	01801	508	Newspaper
Spencer	Robin	293 Serenity Dr.	Concord	MA	01742	508	Radio
Lopez	Luis	1212 City St.	Kansas City	MO	64105	816	Social Media
Nelson	Michael	229 Rally Rd.	Kansas City	MO	64105	816	Education Website

f. Remove duplicate records where all fields are identical.

g. Sort the list by Last Name in A to Z order.

h. Sort the list again by Area Code in Smallest to Largest order.

i. Sort the table first by State in A to Z order, then within the state, by Zip in Smallest to Largest order.

j. Enter your name in the center section of the worksheet footer.

k. Add a centered header that reads **Ad Survey** in bold with a font size of 16.

l. Add print titles to repeat the first row at the top of each printed page.

m. Save the workbook, preview it, then submit the workbook to your instructor.

n. Close the workbook, then exit Excel.

Independent Challenge 2

You manage Green Living, a store that sells environmentally friendly cleaning supplies in bulk online. Your customers purchase items in quantities of 10 or more. You decide to plan and build a table of sales information with eight records using the items sold.

a. Prepare a plan for a table that states your goal, outlines the data you need, and identifies the table elements.

b. Sketch a sample table on a piece of paper, indicating how the table should be built. Create a table documenting the table design including the field names, type of data, and description of the data. Some examples of items are glass cleaner, tile cleaner, carpet cleaner, stone cleaner, and paper towels.

Independent Challenge 2 (continued)

c. Start Excel, create a new workbook, then save it as **EX G-Store Items** in the location where you store your Data Files. Enter the field names shown in the table below in the designated cells:

cell	field name
A1	Customer Last
B1	Customer First
C1	Item
D1	Quantity
E1	Cost

d. Enter eight data records using your own data.
e. Create a table using the data in the range A1:E9. Adjust the column widths as necessary.
f. Apply the Table Style Light 11 to the table.
g. Add a field named **Total** in cell F1.
h. Enter a formula in cell F2 that calculates the total by multiplying the Quantity field by the Cost field. Check that the formula was filled down in the column.
i. Format the Cost and Total columns using the Accounting number format. Adjust the column widths as necessary.
j. Add a new record to your table in row 10. Add another record above row 4.
k. Sort the table in ascending order by Item.
l. Enter your name in the worksheet footer, then save the workbook.
m. Preview the worksheet, then submit your workbook to your instructor.
n. Close the workbook, then exit Excel.

Independent Challenge 3

You are a property manager at a firm that manages condominiums and apartments. You are managing your accounts using an Excel worksheet and have decided that a table will provide additional features to help you keep track of the accounts. You will use the table sorting features and table formulas to analyze your account data.

a. Start Excel, open the file EX G-4.xlsx from the location where you store your Data Files, then save it as **EX G-Accounts**.
b. Create a table with the worksheet data, and apply a table style of your choice. Adjust the column widths as necessary.
c. Sort the table on the Budget field using the Smallest to Largest order.
d. Sort the table using two fields, by Contact in A to Z order, then by Budget in Smallest to Largest order. Compare your table to FIGURE G-25. (Your table style may differ.)

FIGURE G-25

	A	B	C	D	E	F
1	Property	Type	Code	Budget	Expenses	Contact
2	South End	Apartment	SE	$ 250,000	$ 225,000	Cindy Boil
3	Northfield	Apartment	NF	$ 275,000	$ 215,000	Cindy Boil
4	Warren	Condominium	WR	$ 375,000	$ 250,000	Cindy Boil
5	Langley Place	Condominium	LP	$ 650,000	$ 550,000	Cindy Boil
6	River Place	Condominium	RP	$ 175,000	$ 150,000	Jane Smith
7	Deer Run	Condominium	DR	$ 250,000	$ 210,000	Jane Smith
8	Green Ridge	Condominium	GR	$ 350,000	$ 210,000	Jane Smith
9	Rangeley	Condominium	RG	$ 410,000	$ 320,000	Jane Smith
10	Northridge	Apartment	NR	$ 550,000	$ 525,000	Kathy Jenkins
11	West End	Apartment	WE	$ 750,000	$ 600,000	Kathy Jenkins

Independent Challenge 3 (continued)

e. Add the new field label **Balance** in cell G1, and adjust the column width as necessary.

f. Enter a formula in cell G2 that uses structured references to table fields to calculate the balance on an account as the Budget minus the Expenses.

g. Add a new record for a property named **Riverside** with a type of **Condominium**, a code of **RS**, a budget of **$350,000**, expenses of **$250,000**, and a contact of **Cindy Boil**.

h. Verify that the formula accurately calculated the balance for the new record.

i. Replace all of the Jane Smith data with **Jane Atkins**.

j. Find the record for the Green Ridge property and delete it.

k. Delete the Type field from the table.

l. Add a total row to the table and display the totals for appropriate columns. Adjust the column widths as necessary.

m. Enter your name in the center section of the worksheet footer, add a center section header of **Accounts** using formatting of your choice, change the page orientation to landscape, then save the workbook.

n. Preview your workbook, submit the workbook to your instructor, close the workbook, then exit Excel.

Independent Challenge 4: Explore

As the Vice President of Marketing at a design firm, you track the expense accounts of the associates in the department using a table in Excel. You decide to highlight accounts that are over budget for the monthly meeting.

a. Start Excel, open the file EX G-5.xlsx from the location where you store your Data Files, then save it as **EX G-Associates**.

b. Create a table with the worksheet data, and apply the table style of your choice. Adjust the column widths as necessary.

c. Sort the table on the Balance field using the Smallest to Largest order.

d. Use conditional formatting to format the cells of the table containing negative balances with a green fill with dark green text.

e. Sort the table using the Balance field with the order of no cell color on top.

f. Format the table to emphasize the Balance column, and turn off the banded rows. (*Hint*: Use the Table Style Options on the TABLE TOOLS DESIGN tab.)

g. Research how to print nonadjacent areas on a single page. (Excel prints nonadjacent areas of a worksheet on separate pages by default.) Enter the result of your research on Sheet2 of the workbook.

h. Return to Sheet1 and create a print area that prints only the Account Number, Associate, and Balance columns of the table on one page.

i. Compare your table with FIGURE G-26. Save the workbook.

j. Preview your print area to make sure it will print on a single page.

k. Enter your name in the worksheet footers, then save the workbook.

l. Submit the workbook to your instructor, close the workbook, then exit Excel.

FIGURE G-26

	A	B	F
1	Account Number ▾	Associate ▾	Balance ▾↓
2	96634	Kris Lowe	$ 5,000
3	32577	George Well	$ 10,000
4	15334	Janet Colby	$ 19,790
5	98661	Judy Makay	$ 25,000
6	84287	Joe Wood	$ 345,000
7	78441	Nancy Allen	$ 600,000
8	41557	Judy Makay	$ (15,000)
9	21889	Nancy Allen	$ (10,000)
10	57741	George Well	$ (10,000)
11	38997	Janet Colby	$ (5,000)

Visual Workshop

Start Excel, open the file EX G-6.xlsx from the location where you store your Data Files, then save it as **EX G-Products**. Create the table and sort the data as shown in FIGURE G-27. (*Hint*: The table is formatted using Table Style Medium 5.) Add a worksheet header with the sheet name in the center section that is formatted in bold with a size of 14. Enter your name in the center section of the worksheet footer. Save the workbook, preview the table, close the workbook, submit the workbook to your instructor, then exit Excel.

FIGURE G-27

	Order Number ▼	Department ▼	Amount ⬝↑	Shipping ▼	Sales Rep ⬝↑
2	1111	Shoes	$ 52.31	Air	Ellie Cranson
3	1032	Home	$ 157.22	Air	Ellie Cranson
4	2187	Home	$ 157.33	Air	Ellie Cranson
5	1251	Food	$ 255.47	Air	Ellie Cranson
6	2357	Food	$ 287.66	Ground	Ellie Cranson
7	2113	Home	$ 109.66	Ground	Gene Coburn
8	2257	Shoes	$ 179.65	Air	Gene Coburn
9	1587	Children	$ 200.52	Ground	Gene Coburn
10	2588	Shoes	$ 333.74	Ground	Gene Coburn
11	1533	Children	$ 327.88	Ground	Neil Boxer
12	2001	Children	$ 532.44	Air	Neil Boxer

Analyzing Table Data

CASE ▶ The vice president of sales, Kate Morgan, asks you to display information from a table of the 2016 scheduled tours to help the sales representatives with customer inquiries. She also asks you to prepare summaries of the tour sales for a presentation at the international sales meeting. You will prepare these using various filters, subtotals, and Excel functions.

Unit Objectives

After completing this unit, you will be able to:

- Filter a table
- Create a custom filter
- Filter a table with the Advanced Filter
- Extract table data

- Look up values in a table
- Summarize table data
- Validate table data
- Create subtotals

Files You Will Need

EX H-1.xlsx	EX H-5.xlsx
EX H-2.xlsx	EX H-6.xlsx
EX H-3.xlsx	EX H-7.xlsx
EX H-4.xlsx	

©Katerina Havelkova/Shutterstock

Filter a Table

Learning
Outcomes
• Filter records using
AutoFilter
• Filter records using
search criteria

An Excel table lets you easily manipulate large amounts of data to view only the data you want, using a feature called **AutoFilter**. When you create a table, arrows automatically appear next to each column header. These arrows are called **filter list arrows**, **AutoFilter list arrows**, or **list arrows**, and you can use them to **filter** a table to display only the records that meet criteria you specify, temporarily hiding records that do not meet those criteria. For example, you can use the filter list arrow next to the Tour field header to display only records that contain Nepal Trekking in the Tour field. Once you filter data, you can copy, chart, and print the displayed records. You can easily clear a filter to redisplay all the records. **CASE** *Kate asks you to display only the records for the Yellowstone tours. She also asks for information about the tours that sell the most seats and the tours that depart in March.*

STEPS

1. **Start Excel, open the file EX H-1.xlsx from the location where you save your Data Files, then save it as EX H-Tours**

2. **Click the Tour list arrow**

 Sort options appear at the top of the menu, advanced filtering options appear in the middle, and at the bottom is a list of the tour data from column A, as shown in FIGURE H-1. Because you want to display data for only the Yellowstone tours, your **search criterion** (the text you are searching for) is Yellowstone. You can select one of the Tour data options in the menu, which acts as your search criterion.

QUICK TIP
You can also filter
the table to display
only the Yellowstone
tour information by
clicking the Tour
list arrow, entering
"Yellowstone" in the
Search text box on
the menu options
below Text Filters,
then clicking OK.

3. **In the list of tours for the Tour field, click Select All to clear the check marks from the tours, scroll down the list of tours, click Yellowstone, then click OK**

 Only those records containing "Yellowstone" in the Tour field appear, as shown in FIGURE H-2. The row numbers for the matching records change to blue, and the list arrow for the filtered field has a filter icon. 🔽: Both indicate that there is a filter in effect and that some of the records are temporarily hidden.

4. **Move the pointer over the Tour list arrow**

 The ScreenTip Tour: Equals "Yellowstone" describes the filter for the field, meaning that only the Yellowstone records appear. You decide to remove the filter to redisplay all of the table data.

5. **Click the Tour list arrow, then click Clear Filter From "Tour"**

 You have cleared the Yellowstone filter, and all the records reappear. You want to display the most popular tours, those that are in the top five percent of seats reserved.

QUICK TIP
You can also filter
or sort a table by
the color of the
cells if conditional
formatting has been
applied.

6. **Click the Seats Reserved list arrow, point to Number Filters, click Top 10, select 10 in the middle box, type 5, click the Items list arrow, click Percent, then click OK**

 Excel displays the records for the top five percent in the number of Seats Reserved field, as shown in FIGURE H-3. You decide to clear the filter to redisplay all the records.

7. **On the HOME tab, click the Sort & Filter button in the Editing group, then click Clear**

 You have cleared the filter and all the records reappear. You can clear a filter using either the AutoFilter menu command or the Sort & Filter button on the HOME tab. The Sort & Filter button is convenient for clearing multiple filters at once. You want to find all of the tours that depart in March.

8. **Click the Depart Date list arrow, point to Date Filters, point to All Dates in the Period, then click March**

 Excel displays the records for only the tours that leave in March. You decide to clear the filter and display all of the records.

QUICK TIP
You can also clear a
filter by clicking the
Clear button in the
Sort & Filter group
on the DATA tab.

9. **Click the Sort & Filter button in the Editing group, click Clear, then save the workbook**

Tour AutoFilter list arrow

Sort Options

Advanced filtering options

List of tours

	Tour	Depart Date	Number of Days
1			
2		1/12/2016	14
3		1/13/2016	21
4		1/19/2016	10
5		1/21/2016	18
6		2/22/2016	14
7		2/28/2016	7
8		3/13/2016	14
9		3/19/2016	18
10		3/20/2016	7
11		3/23/2016	18
12		4/8/2016	30
13		4/11/2016	12
14		4/15/2016	21
15		4/18/2016	10
16		4/20/2016	18
17	Amazing Amazon	4/23/2016	14
18	Catalonia Adventure	5/9/2016	14

AutoFilter menu items: Sort A to Z, Sort Z to A, Sort by Color, Clear Filter From "Tour", Filter by Color, Text Filters, Search. Checkboxes: (Select All), African National Parks, Amazing Amazon, Biking in France, Biking in Ireland, Catalonia Adventure, Corfu Sailing Voyage, Costa Rica, Exotic Morocco, Experience Cambodia. Buttons: OK, Cancel

FIGURE H-2: Table filtered to show Yellowstone tours

	A Tour	B Depart Date	C Number of Days	D Seat Capacity	E Seats Reserved	F Price	G Air Included	H Insurance Included
5	Yellowstone	1/21/2016	18	51	40	$ 1,850	Yes	Yes
16	Yellowstone	4/20/2016	18	51	31	$ 1,652	Yes	Yes
41	Yellowstone	8/20/2016	18	51	20	$ 2,922	Yes	Yes
45	Yellowstone	9/11/2016	18	51	20	$ 2,922	Yes	Yes
63	Yellowstone	12/30/2016	18	51	15	$ 2,922	Yes	Yes
65								

List arrow changed to filter icon

Matching row numbers are blue and sequence indicates that not all rows appear

Filter displays only Yellowstone tours

FIGURE H-3: Table filtered with top 5% of Seats Reserved

	A Tour	B Depart Date	C Number of Days	D Seat Capacity	E Seats Reserved	F Price	G Air Included	H Insurance Included
2	Pacific Odyssey	1/12/2016	14	50	50	$ 2,255	Yes	No
3	Old Japan	1/13/2016	21	47	42	$ 1,984	Yes	No
5	Yellowstone	1/21/2016	18	51	40	$ 1,850	Yes	Yes
65								

Table filtered with top 5% in this field

Excel 2013

Create a Custom Filter

Learning Outcomes
• Filter records with multiple criteria
• Determine when to use AND and OR logical conditions

While AutoFilter lists can display records that are equal to certain amounts, you will often need more detailed filters. You can use more complex filters with the help of options in the Custom AutoFilter dialog box. For example, your criteria can contain comparison operators such as "greater than" or "less than" that let you display values above or below a certain amount. You can also use **logical conditions** like And and Or to narrow a search even further. You can have Excel display records that meet a criterion in a field *and* another criterion in that same field. This is often used to find records between two values. For example, by specifying an **And logical condition**, you can display records for customers with incomes between $40,000 *and* $70,000. You can also have Excel display records that meet either criterion in a field by specifying an Or condition. The **Or logical condition** is used to find records that satisfy either of two values. For example, in a table of book data you can use the Or condition to find records that contain either Beginning *or* Introduction in the title name. **CASE** ▶ *Kate wants to locate tours for customers who like active vacations. She also wants to find tours that depart between February 15, 2016, and April 15, 2016. She asks you to create custom filters to find the tours satisfying these criteria.*

STEPS

1. **Click the Tour list arrow, point to Text Filters, then click Contains**
 The Custom AutoFilter dialog box opens. You enter your criteria in the text boxes. The left text box on the first line currently displays "contains." You want to display tours that contain the word "sailing" in their names.

2. **Type sailing in the right text box on the first line**
 You want to see entries that contain either sailing or biking.

QUICK TIP
When specifying criteria in the Custom Filter dialog box, you can use the (?) wildcard to represent any single character and the (*) wildcard to represent any series of characters.

3. **Click the Or option button to select it, click the left text box list arrow on the second line, scroll to and select contains, then type biking in the right text box on the second line**
 Your completed Custom AutoFilter dialog box should match **FIGURE H-4**.

4. **Click OK**
 The dialog box closes, and only those records having "sailing" or "biking" in the Tour field appear in the worksheet. You want to find all tours that depart between February 15, 2016 and April 15, 2016.

5. **Click the Tour list arrow, click Clear Filter From "Tour", click the Depart Date list arrow, point to Date Filters, then click Custom Filter**
 The Custom AutoFilter dialog box opens. The word "equals" appears in the left text box on the first line. You want to find the departure dates that are between February 15, 2016 and April 15, 2016 (that is, after February 15 *and* before April 15).

6. **Click the left text box list arrow on the first line, click is after, then type 2/15/2016 in the right text box on the first line**
 The And condition is selected, which is correct.

7. **Click the left text box list arrow on the second line, select is before, type 4/15/2016 in the right text box on the second line, then click OK**
 The records displayed have departure dates between February 15, 2016, and April 15, 2016. Compare your records to those shown in **FIGURE H-5**.

8. **Click the Depart Date list arrow, click Clear Filter From "Depart Date", then add your name to the center section of the footer**
 You have cleared the filter, and all the tour records reappear.

FIGURE H-4: **Custom AutoFilter dialog box**

FIGURE H-5: **Results of custom filter**

	A	B	C	D	E	F	G	H
1	Tour	Depart Date	Number of Days	Seat Capacity	Seats Reserved	Price	Air Included	Insurance Included
6	Amazing Amazon	2/22/2016	14	43	39	$ 2,134	No	No
7	Hiking Patagonia	2/28/2016	7	20	15	$ 2,812	Yes	No
8	Pearls of the Orient	3/13/2016	14	45	15	$ 2,350	Yes	No
9	Silk Road Travels	3/19/2016	18	23	19	$ 2,110	Yes	Yes
10	Photographing France	3/20/2016	7	20	20	$ 1,755	Yes	Yes
11	Green Adventures in Ecuador	3/23/2016	18	25	22	$ 2,450	No	No
12	African National Parks	4/8/2016	30	12	10	$ 3,115	Yes	Yes
13	Experience Cambodia	4/11/2016	12	35	21	$ 2,441	Yes	No
65								

Departure dates are
between 2/15 and 4/15

Using more than one rule when conditionally formatting data

You can apply conditional formatting to table cells in the same way that you can format a range of worksheet data. You can add multiple rules by clicking the HOME tab, clicking the Conditional Formatting button in the Styles group, then clicking New Rule for each additional rule that you want to apply. You can also add rules using the Conditional Formatting Rules Manager, which displays all of the rules for a data range. To use the Rules Manager, click the HOME tab, click the Conditional Formatting button in the Styles group, click Manage Rules, then click New Rule for each rule that you want to apply to the data range. After you have applied conditional formatting such as color fills, icon sets, or color scales to a numeric table range, you can use AutoFilter to sort or filter based on the colors or symbols.

Filter a Table with the Advanced Filter

Learning Outcomes
• Filter records using a criteria range and the And condition
• Filter records using a criteria range and the Or condition

If you would like to see more specific information in a table, such as view date and insurance information for a specific tour or tours, then the Advanced Filter command is helpful. Using the Advanced Filter, you can specify data that you want to display from the table using And and Or conditions. Rather than entering the criteria in a dialog box, you enter the criteria in a criteria range on your worksheet. A **criteria range** is a cell range containing one row of labels (usually a copy of the column labels) and at least one additional row underneath the row of labels that contains the criteria you want to match. Placing the criteria in the same row indicates that the records you are searching for must match both criteria; that is, it specifies an **And condition**. Placing the criteria in the different rows indicates that the records you are searching for must match only one of the criterion; that is, it specifies an **Or condition**. With the criteria range on the worksheet, you can easily see the criteria by which your table is sorted. You can also use the criteria range to create a macro using the Advanced Filter feature to automate the filtering process for data that you filter frequently. Another advantage of the Advanced Filter is that you can move filtered table data to a different area of the worksheet or to a new worksheet, as you will see in the next lesson. **CASE** ▶ *Kate wants to identify tours that depart after 6/1/2016 and that cost less than $2,000. She asks you to use the Advanced Filter to retrieve these records. You begin by defining the criteria range.*

STEPS

1. **Select table rows 1 through 6, click the Insert list arrow in the Cells group, click Insert Sheet Rows; click cell A1, type Criteria Range, then click the Enter button ☑ on the Formula bar**

 Six blank rows are added above the table. Excel does not require the label "Criteria Range", but it is useful to see the column labels as you organize the worksheet and use filters.

2. **Select the range A7:H7, click the Copy button in the Clipboard group, click cell A2, click the Paste button in the Clipboard group, then press [Esc]**

 Next, you want to insert criteria that will display records for only those tours that depart after June 1, 2016 and that cost under $2,000.

3. **Click cell B3, type >6/1/2016, click cell F3, type <2000, then click ☑**

 You have entered the criteria in the cells directly beneath the Criteria Range labels, as shown in FIGURE H-6.

4. **Click any cell in the table, click the DATA tab, then click the Advanced button in the Sort & Filter group**

 The Advanced Filter dialog box opens, with the table (list) range already entered. The default setting under Action is to filter the table in its current location ("in-place") rather than copy it to another location.

5. **Click the Criteria range text box, select the range A2:H3 in the worksheet, then click OK**

 You have specified the criteria range and used the filter. The filtered table contains eight records that match both criteria—the departure date is after 6/1/2016 and the price is less than $2,000, as shown in FIGURE H-7. You'll filter this table even further in the next lesson.

	A	B	C	D	E	F	G	H
1	Criteria Range							
2	Tour	Depart Date	Number of Days	Seat Capacity	Seats Reserved	Price	Air Included	Insurance Included
3		>6/1/2016				<2000		
4								
5								
6								
7	Tour	Depart Date	Number of Days	Seat Capacity	Seats Reserved	Price	Air Included	Insurance Included
8	Pacific Odyssey	1/12/2016	14	50	50	$ 2,255	Yes	No
9	Old Japan	1/13/2016	21	47	42	$ 1,984	Yes	No
10	Costa Rica	1/19/2016	10	31	28	$ 1,966	Yes	Yes

Filtered records will match these criteria

	A	B	C	D	E	F	G	H
1	Criteria Range							
2	Tour	Depart Date	Number of Days	Seat Capacity	Seats Reserved	Price	Air Included	Insurance Included
3		>6/1/2016				<2000		
4								
5								
6								
7	Tour	Depart Date	Number of Days	Seat Capacity	Seats Reserved	Price	Air Included	Insurance Included
33	Exotic Morocco	6/12/2016	7	38	25	$ 1,900	Yes	No
34	Kayak Newfoundland	6/12/2016	7	20	15	$ 1,970	Yes	Yes
37	Wild River Escape	6/27/2016	10	21	21	$ 1,944	No	No
42	Kayak Newfoundland	7/12/2016	7	20	15	$ 1,970	Yes	Yes
44	Magnificent Montenegro	7/27/2016	10	48	0	$ 1,890	No	No
46	Kayak Newfoundland	8/12/2016	7	20	12	$ 1,970	Yes	Yes
49	Wild River Escape	8/27/2016	10	21	11	$ 1,944	No	No
61	Exotic Morocco	10/31/2016	7	38	15	$ 1,900	Yes	No
71								

Depart dates are after 6/1/2013

Prices are less than $2000

Using advanced conditional formatting options

You can emphasize top- or bottom-ranked values in a field using conditional formatting. To highlight the top or bottom values in a field, select the field data, click the Conditional Formatting button in the Styles group on the HOME tab, point to Top/Bottom Rules, select a Top or Bottom rule, if necessary enter the percentage or number of cells in the selected range that you want to format, select the format for the cells that meet the top or bottom criteria, then click OK. You can also format your worksheet or table data using icon sets and color scales based on the cell values. A **color scale** uses a set of two, three, or four fill colors to convey relative values. For example, red could fill cells to indicate they have higher values and green could signify lower values. To add a color scale, select a data range, click the HOME tab, click the Conditional Formatting button in the Styles group, then point to Color Scales. On the submenu, you can select preformatted color sets or click More Rules to create your own color sets. **Icon sets** let you visually communicate relative cell values by adding icons to cells based on the values they contain. An upward-pointing green arrow might represent the highest values, and downward-pointing red arrows could represent lower values. To add an icon set to a data range, select a data range, click the Conditional Formatting button in the Styles group, then point to Icon Sets. You can customize the values that are used as thresholds for color scales and icon sets by clicking the Conditional Formatting button in the Styles group, clicking Manage Rules, clicking the rule in the Conditional Formatting Rules Manager dialog box, then clicking Edit Rule.

Extract Table Data

Whenever you take the time to specify a complicated set of search criteria, it's a good idea to extract the matching records, rather than filtering it in place. When you **extract** data, you place a copy of a filtered table in a range that you specify in the Advanced Filter dialog box. This way, you won't accidentally clear the filter or lose track of the records you spent time compiling. To extract data, you use an Advanced Filter and enter the criteria beneath the copied field names, as you did in the previous lesson. You then specify the location where you want the extracted data to appear. **CASE** ▶ *Kate needs to filter the table one step further to reflect only the Wild River Escape or Kayak Newfoundland tours in the current filtered table. She asks you to complete this filter by specifying an Or condition, which you will do by entering two sets of criteria in two separate rows. You decide to save the filtered records by extracting them to a different location in the worksheet.*

STEPS

1. **In cell A3, enter** Wild River Escape, **then in cell A4, enter** Kayak Newfoundland

 The new sets of criteria need to appear in two separate rows, so you need to copy the previous filter criteria to the second row.

2. **Copy the criteria in B3:F3 to B4:F4**

 The criteria are shown in **FIGURE H-8**. When you use the Advanced Filter this time, you indicate that you want to copy the filtered table to a range beginning in cell A75, so that Kate can easily refer to the data, even if you use more filters later.

3. **If necessary, click the** DATA **tab, then click** Advanced **in the Sort & Filter group**

4. **Under Action, click the** Copy to another location **option button to select it, click the** Copy to **text box, then type** A75

 The last time you filtered the table, the criteria range included only rows 2 and 3, and now you have criteria in row 4.

5. **Edit the contents of the** Criteria range text box **to show the range A2:H4, click** OK, **then if necessary scroll down until row 75 is visible**

 The matching records appear in the range beginning in cell A75, as shown in **FIGURE H-9**. The original table, starting in cell A7, contains the records filtered in the previous lesson.

6. **Press [Ctrl][Home], then click the** Clear button **in the Sort & Filter group**

 The original table is displayed starting in cell A7, and the extracted table remains in A75:H80.

7. **Save the workbook**

FIGURE H-8: Criteria in separate rows

	A	B	C	D	E	F	G
1	Criteria Range						
2	Tour	Depart Date	Number of Days	Seat Capacity	Seats Reserved	Price	Air Included
3	Wild River Escape	>6/1/2016				<2000	
4	Kayak Newfoundland	>6/1/2016				<2000	
5							

Criteria on two lines indicates an OR condition

FIGURE H-9: Extracted data records

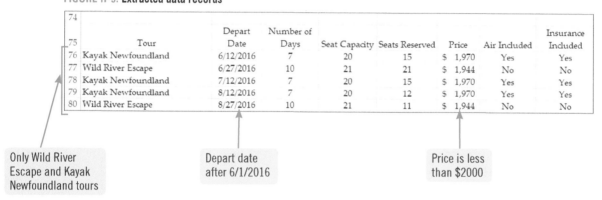

	Tour	Depart Date	Number of Days	Seat Capacity	Seats Reserved	Price	Air Included	Insurance Included
74								
75								
76	Kayak Newfoundland	6/12/2016	7	20	15	$ 1,970	Yes	Yes
77	Wild River Escape	6/27/2016	10	21	21	$ 1,944	No	No
78	Kayak Newfoundland	7/12/2016	7	20	15	$ 1,970	Yes	Yes
79	Kayak Newfoundland	8/12/2016	7	20	12	$ 1,970	Yes	Yes
80	Wild River Escape	8/27/2016	10	21	11	$ 1,944	No	No

Only Wild River Escape and Kayak Newfoundland tours

Depart date after 6/1/2016

Price is less than $2000

Understanding the criteria range and the copy-to location

When you define the criteria range and the copy-to location in the Advanced Filter dialog box, Excel automatically creates the range names Criteria and Extract for these ranges in the worksheet. The Criteria range includes the field names and any criteria rows underneath them. The Extract range includes just the field names above the extracted table. You can select these ranges by clicking the Name box list arrow, then clicking the range name. If you click the Name Manager button in the Defined Names group on the FORMULAS tab, you will see these new names and the ranges associated with each one.

Look Up Values in a Table

**Learning
Outcomes**
• Use table refer-
ences in a
VLOOKUP formula
• Find table infor-
mation using
VLOOKUP

The Excel VLOOKUP function helps you locate specific values in a table. VLOOKUP searches vertically (V) down the far left column of a table, then reads across the row to find the value in the column you specify, much as you might look up a number in a name and address list: You locate a person's name, then read across the row to find the phone number you want. **CASE** ▸ *Kate wants to be able to find a tour destination by entering the tour code. You will use the VLOOKUP function to accomplish this task. You begin by viewing the table name so you can refer to it in a lookup function.*

STEPS

QUICK TIP
You can change table
names to better rep-
resent their content
so they are easier to
use in formulas. Click
the table in the list of
names in the Name
Manager text box,
click Edit, type the
new table name in
the Name text box,
then click OK.

1. **Click the Lookup sheet tab, click the FORMULAS tab in the Ribbon, then click the Name Manager button in the Defined Names group**

 The named ranges for the workbook appear in the Name Manager dialog box, as shown in **FIGURE H-10**. The Criteria and Extract ranges appear at the top of the range name list. At the bottom of the list is information about the three tables in the workbook. Table1 refers to the table on the Tours sheet, Table2 refers to the table on the Lookup sheet, and Table3 refers to the table on the Subtotals worksheet. The Excel structured reference feature automatically created these table names when the tables were created.

2. **Click Close**

 You want to find the tour represented by the code 830L. The VLOOKUP function lets you find the tour name for any trip code. You will enter a trip code in cell M1 and a VLOOKUP function in cell M2.

3. **Click cell M1, enter 830L, click cell M2, click the Lookup & Reference button in the Function Library group, then click VLOOKUP**

 The Function Arguments dialog box opens, with boxes for each of the VLOOKUP arguments. Because the value you want to find is in cell M1, M1 is the Lookup_value. The table you want to search is the table on the Lookup sheet, so its assigned name, Table2, is the Table_array.

QUICK TIP
If you want to find
only the closest
match for a value,
enter TRUE in the
Range_lookup text
box. However, this
can give mislead-
ing results if you
are looking for an
exact match. If you
use FALSE and Excel
can't find the value,
you see an error
message.

4. **With the insertion point in the Lookup_value text box, click cell M1, click the Table_array text box, then type Table2**

 The column containing the information that you want to find and display in cell M2 is the second column from the left in the table range, so the Col_index_num is 2. Because you want to find an exact match for the value in cell M1, the Range_lookup argument is FALSE.

5. **Click the Col_index_num text box, type 2, click the Range_lookup text box, then enter FALSE**

 Your completed Function Arguments dialog box should match **FIGURE H-11**.

6. **Click OK**

 Excel searches down the far-left column of the table until it finds a trip code that matches the one in cell M1. It then looks in column 2 of the table range and finds the tour for that record, Old Japan, and displays it in cell M2. You use this function to determine the tour for one other trip code.

7. **Click cell M1, type 325B, then click the Enter button ✓ on the formula bar**

 The VLOOKUP function returns the value of Biking In France in cell M2.

8. **Press [Ctrl][Home], then save the workbook**

Finding records using the DGET function

You can also use the DGET function to find a record in a table that matches specified criteria. For example, you could use the criteria of L1:L2 in the DGET function. When using DGET, you need to include [#All] after your table name in the formula to include the column labels that are used for the criteria range. Unlike VLOOKUP, you do not have the option of using a Range_Lookup value of TRUE to find an approximate match.

FIGURE H-10: Named ranges in the workbook

Created by
Advanced Filter

Tables in the
workbook

FIGURE H-11: Completed Function Arguments dialog box for **VLOOKUP**

Location of
value you want
to search for

Range name of
table to search

Search the
second column

Finds exact
match

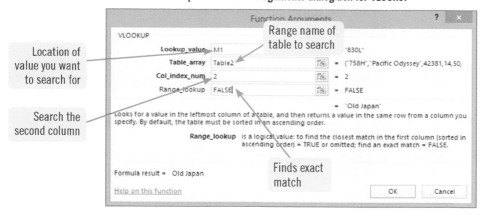

Using the HLOOKUP and MATCH functions

The VLOOKUP (Vertical Lookup) function is useful when your data is arranged vertically, in columns. When your data is arranged horizontally in rows, use the HLOOKUP (Horizontal Lookup) function. HLOOKUP searches horizontally across the upper row of a table until it finds the matching value, then looks down the number of rows you specify. The arguments for this function are identical to those for the VLOOKUP function, with one exception. Instead of a Col_index_number, HLOOKUP uses a Row_index_number, which indicates the location of the row you want to search. For example, if you want to search the fourth row from the top of the table range, the Row_index_number should be 4. You can use the MATCH function when you want the position of an item in a range. The MATCH function uses the syntax: MATCH (lookup_value,lookup_array,match_type) where the lookup_value is the value you want to match in the lookup_array range. The match_type can be 0 for an exact match, 1 for matching the largest value that is less than or equal to lookup_value, or –1 for matching the smallest value that is greater than or equal to the lookup_value.

Summarize Table Data

Learning Outcomes
- Summarize table data using DSUM
- Summarize table data using DCOUNT or DCOUNTA

Because a table acts much like a database, database functions allow you to summarize table data in a variety of ways. When working with a sales activity table, for example, you can use Excel to count the number of client contacts by sales representative or to total the amount sold to specific accounts by month. TABLE H-1 lists database functions commonly used to summarize table data. **CASE** *Kate is considering adding tours for the 2016 schedule. She needs your help in evaluating the number of seats available for scheduled tours.*

STEPS

1. **Review the criteria range for the Yellowstone tour in the range L5:L6**

 The criteria range in L5:L6 tells Excel to summarize records with the entry "Yellowstone" in the Tour column. The functions will be in cells M8 and M9. You use this criteria range in a DSUM function to sum the seats available for only the Yellowstone tours.

2. **Click cell M8, click the Insert Function button in the Function Library group, in the Search for a function text box type database, click Go, scroll to and click DSUM under Select a function, then click OK**

 The first argument of the DSUM function is the table, or database.

> **QUICK TIP**
> Because the DSUM formula uses the column headings to locate and sum the table data, the header row needs to be included in the database range.

3. **In the Function Arguments dialog box, with the insertion point in the Database text box, move the pointer over the upper-left corner of cell A1 until the pointer becomes ⬛, click once, then click again**

 The first click selects the table's data range, and the second click selects the entire table, including the header row. The second argument of the DSUM function is the label for the column that you want to sum. You want to total the number of available seats. The last argument for the DSUM function is the criteria that will be used to determine which values to total.

> **QUICK TIP**
> You can move the Function Arguments dialog box if it overlaps a cell or range that you need to click. You can also click the Collapse Dialog Box button 🔲, select the cell or range, then click the Expand Dialog Box button 🔲 to return to the Function Arguments dialog box.

4. **Click the Field text box, then click cell G1, Seats Available; click the Criteria text box and select the range L5:L6**

 Your completed Function Arguments dialog box should match FIGURE H-12.

5. **Click OK**

 The result in cell M8 is 129. Excel totaled the information in the Seats Available column for those records that meet the criterion of Tour equals Yellowstone. The DCOUNT and the DCOUNTA functions can help you determine the number of records meeting specified criteria in a database field. DCOUNTA counts the number of nonblank cells. You will use DCOUNTA to determine the number of tours scheduled.

6. **Click cell M9, click the Insert Function button 𝑓ₓ on the formula bar, in the Search for a function text box type database, click Go, select DCOUNTA from the Select a function list, then click OK**

7. **With the insertion point in the Database text box, move the pointer over the upper-left corner of cell A1 until the pointer becomes ⬛, click once, click again to include the header row, click the Field text box and click cell B1, click the Criteria text box and select the range L5:L6, then click OK**

 The result in cell M9 is 5, and it indicates that there are five Yellowstone tours scheduled for the year. You also want to display the number of seats available for the Old Japan tours.

8. **Click cell L6, type Old Japan, then click the Enter button ✓ on the formula bar**

 FIGURE H-13 shows that 67 seats are available in the four Old Japan tours, and there are four tours scheduled.

Name of table the function uses

Column containing values that are summed

Criteria range including column header and search text

FIGURE H-13: **Result generated by database functions**

	G	H	I	J	K	L	M
1	Seats Available	Price	Air Included	Insurance Included		Trip Code	325B
2	0	$ 2,255	Yes	No		Tour	Biking in France
3	5	$ 1,984	Yes	No			
4	3	$ 1,966	Yes	Yes		Tour Information	
5	11	$ 1,850	Yes	Yes		Tour	
6	4	$ 2,134	No	No		Old Japan	
7	5	$ 2,812	Yes	No			
8	30	$ 2,350	Yes	No		Seats Available	67
9	4	$ 2,110	Yes	Yes		Number of tours scheduled	4
10	0	$ 1,755	Yes	Yes			
11	3	$ 2,450	No	No			

Information for Old Japan tours

TABLE H-1: **Common database functions**

function	result
DGET	Extracts a single record from a table that matches criteria you specify
DSUM	Totals numbers in a given table column that match criteria you specify
DAVERAGE	Averages numbers in a given table column that match criteria you specify
DCOUNT	Counts the cells that contain numbers in a given table column that match criteria you specify
DCOUNTA	Counts the cells that contain nonblank data in a given table column that match criteria you specify

Validate Table Data

Learning Outcomes
- Use data validation to restrict data entry to specified values
- Insert table data using data validation

When setting up tables, you want to help ensure accuracy when you or others enter data. The Excel data validation feature allows you to do this by specifying what data users can enter in a range of cells. You can restrict data to whole numbers, decimal numbers, or text. You can also specify a list of acceptable entries. Once you've specified what data the program should consider valid for that cell, Excel displays an error message when invalid data is entered and can prevent users from entering any other data that it considers to be invalid. **CASE** *Kate wants to make sure that information in the Air Included column is entered consistently in the future. She asks you to restrict the entries in that column to two options: Yes and No. First, you select the table column you want to restrict.*

STEPS

1. **Click the top edge of the Air Included column header**

 The column data is selected.

2. **Click the DATA tab, click the Data Validation button in the Data Tools group, click the Settings tab if necessary, click the Allow list arrow, then click List**

 Selecting the List option lets you type a list of specific options.

3. **Click the Source text box, then type Yes, No**

 You have entered the list of acceptable entries, separated by commas, as shown in **FIGURE H-14**. You want the data entry person to be able to select a valid entry from a drop-down list.

4. **Click the In-cell dropdown check box to select it if necessary, then click OK**

 The dialog box closes, and you return to the worksheet.

5. **Click the HOME tab, click any cell in the last table row, click the Insert list arrow in the Cells group, click Insert Table Row Below, click the last cell in the Air Included column, then click its list arrow to display the list of valid entries**

 The drop-down list is shown in **FIGURE H-15**. You could click an item in the list to have it entered in the cell, but you want to test the data restriction by entering an invalid entry.

6. **Click the list arrow to close the list, type Maybe, then press [Enter]**

 A warning dialog box appears and prevents you from entering the invalid data, as shown in **FIGURE H-16**.

7. **Click Cancel, click the list arrow, then click Yes**

 The cell accepts the valid entry. The data restriction ensures that records contain only one of the two correct entries in the Air Included column. The table is ready for future data entry.

8. **Delete the last table row, add your name to the center section of the footer, then save the workbook**

Restricting cell values and data length

In addition to providing an in-cell drop-down list for data entry, you can use data validation to restrict the values that are entered into cells. For example, if you want to restrict cells in a selected range to values less than a certain number, date, or time, click the DATA tab, click the Data Validation button in the Data Tools group, and on the Settings tab, click the Allow list arrow, select

Whole number, Decimal, Date, or Time, click the Data list arrow, select less than, then in the bottom text box, enter the maximum value. You can also limit the length of data entered into cells by choosing Text length in the Allow list, clicking the Data list arrow and selecting less than, then entering the maximum length in the Maximum text box.

FIGURE H-14: Creating data restrictions

Restricts entries to a list of valid options

List of valid options

Displays a list of valid options during data entry

FIGURE H-15: Entering data in restricted cells

54	666B	Nepal Trekking	10/29/2016	14	18	8	10	$ 4,200	Yes	Yes
55	557N	Exotic Morocco	10/31/2016	7	38	15	23	$ 1,900	Yes	No
56	524Z	Experience Cambodia	10/31/2016	12	40	2	38	$ 2,908	Yes	No
57	509V	Treasures of Ethiopia	11/18/2016	10	41	12	29	$ 2,200	Yes	Yes
58	397S	Panama Adventure	12/18/2016	10	50	21	29	$ 2,204	Yes	Yes
59	621R	Panama Adventure	12/18/2016	10	50	21	29	$ 2,204	Yes	Yes
60	592D	Galapagos Adventure	12/20/2016	14	15	1	14	$ 2,100	Yes	Yes
61	793T	Galapagos Adventure	12/20/2016	14	15	1	14	$ 2,100	Yes	Yes
62	307R	Pacific Odyssey	12/21/2016	14	50	10	40	$ 2,105	Yes	No
63	927F	Yellowstone	12/30/2016	18	51	15	36	$ 2,922	Yes	Yes
64	448G	Old Japan	12/31/2016	21	47	4	43	$ 2,100	Yes	No
65								0		
66										

Dropdown list → Yes / No

FIGURE H-16: Invalid data warning

Microsoft Excel

The value you entered is not valid.

A user has restricted values that can be entered into this cell.

Retry Cancel Help

Adding input messages and error alerts

You can customize the way data validation works by using the two other tabs in the Data Validation dialog box: Input Message and Error Alert. The Input Message tab lets you set a message that appears when the user selects that cell. For example, the message might contain instructions about what type of data to enter. On the Input Message tab, enter a message title and message, then click OK. The Error Alert tab lets you set one of three alert levels if a user enters invalid data. The Information level displays your message with the information icon but allows the user to proceed with data entry. The Warning level displays your information with the warning icon and gives the user the option to proceed with data entry or not. The Stop level, which you used in this lesson, displays your message and only lets the user retry or cancel data entry for that cell.

Create Subtotals

In a large range of data, you will often need ways to perform calculations that summarize groups within the data. For example, you might need to subtotal the sales for several sales reps listed in a table. The Excel Subtotals feature provides a quick, easy way to group and summarize a range of data. It lets you create not only subtotals using the SUM function, but other statistics as well, including COUNT, AVERAGE, MAX, and MIN. However, subtotals cannot be used in an Excel table, nor can it rearrange data. Before you can add subtotals to table data, you must first convert the data to a range and sort it. **CASE** *Kate wants you to group data by tours, with subtotals for the number of seats available and the number of seats reserved. You begin by converting the table to a range.*

STEPS

1. **Click the** Subtotals sheet tab, **click any cell inside the table, click the** TABLE TOOLS DESIGN tab, **click the** Convert to Range button **in the Tools group, then click** Yes

 The filter list arrows and the TABLE TOOLS DESIGN tab no longer appear. Before you can add the subtotals, you must first sort the data. You decide to sort it in ascending order, first by tour and then by departure date.

2. **Click the** DATA tab, **click the** Sort button **in the Sort & Filter group, in the Sort dialog box click the** Sort by list arrow, **click** Tour, **click the** Add Level button, **click the** Then by list arrow, **click** Depart Date, **verify that the order is** Oldest to Newest, **then click** OK

 You have sorted the range in ascending order, first by tour, then by departure date within each tour grouping.

3. **Click any cell in the data range if necessary, then click the** Subtotal button **in the Outline group**

 The Subtotal dialog box opens. Here you specify the items you want subtotaled, the function you want to apply to the values, and the fields you want to summarize.

4. **Click the** At each change in list arrow, **click** Tour **if necessary, click the** Use function list arrow, **click** Sum; **in the "Add subtotal to" list, click the** Seats Reserved **and** Seats Available **check boxes to select them, if necessary, then click the** Insurance Included check box **to deselect it**

5. **If necessary, click the** Replace current subtotals **and** Summary below data check boxes **to select them**

 Your completed Subtotal dialog box should match FIGURE H-17.

6. **Click** OK, **then scroll down so you can see row 90**

 The subtotaled data appears after each tour grouping, showing the calculated subtotals and grand total in columns E and F, as shown in FIGURE H-18. Excel displays an outline to the left of the worksheet, with outline buttons to control the level of detail that appears. The button number corresponds to the detail level that is displayed. You want to show the second level of detail, the subtotals and the grand total.

7. **Click the** outline symbol ☐2

 Only the subtotals and the grand total appear.

8. **Add your name to the center section of the footer, preview the worksheet, click the** No Scaling list arrow, **click** Fit Sheet on One Page **to scale the worksheet to print on one page, then save the workbook**

9. **Close the workbook, exit Excel, then submit the workbook to your instructor**

FIGURE H-17: Completed Subtotal dialog box

Field to use in grouping data

Function to apply to groups

Subtotal these fields

FIGURE H-18: Portion of subtotaled table

Outline symbols

Subtotals

Grand total

Practice

Concepts Review

FIGURE H-19

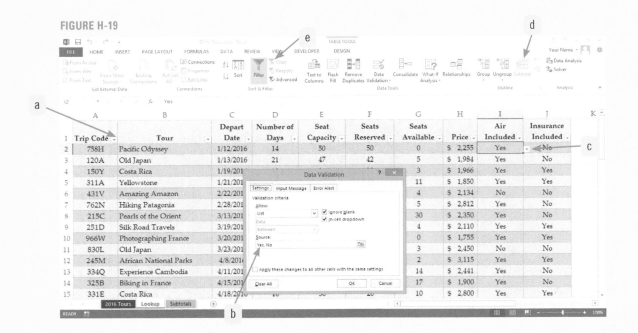

1. Which element points to an in-cell drop-down list arrow?
2. Which element would you click to remove a filter?
3. Which element points to a field's list arrow?
4. Which element do you click to group and summarize data?
5. Where do you specify acceptable data entries for a table?

Match each term with the statement that best describes it.

6. Table_array
7. Extracted table
8. Data validation
9. Criteria range
10. DSUM

a. Cell range when Advanced Filter results are copied to another location
b. Range in which search conditions are set
c. Restricts table entries to specified options
d. Name of the table searched in a VLOOKUP function
e. Function used to total table values that meet specified criteria

Select the best answer from the list of choices.

11. The _____ logical condition finds records matching both listed criteria.
 a. True
 b. Or
 c. And
 d. False
12. What does it mean when you select the Or option when creating a custom filter?
 a. Both criteria must be true to find a match.
 b. Neither criterion has to be 100% true.
 c. Either criterion can be true to find a match.
 d. A custom filter requires a criteria range.

13. What must a data range have before subtotals can be inserted?

a. Enough records to show multiple subtotals

b. Sorted data

c. Formatted cells

d. Grand totals

14. Which function finds the position of an item in a table?

a. VLOOKUP

b. MATCH

c. DGET

d. HLOOKUP

Skills Review

1. Filter a table.

a. Start Excel, open the file EX H-2.xlsx from the location where you store your Data Files, then save it as **EX H-Compensation**.

b. With the Compensation sheet active, filter the table to list only records for employees in the Boston branch.

c. Clear the filter, then add a filter that displays the records for employees in the Boston and Philadelphia branches.

d. Redisplay all employees, then use a filter to show the three employees with the highest annual salary.

e. Redisplay all the records.

2. Create a custom filter.

a. Create a custom filter showing employees hired before 1/1/2013 or after 12/31/2013.

b. Create a custom filter showing employees hired between 1/1/2013 and 12/31/2013.

c. Enter your name in the worksheet footer, then preview the filtered worksheet.

d. Redisplay all records.

e. Save the workbook.

3. Filter and extract a table with the Advanced Filter.

a. You want to retrieve a list of employees who were hired before 1/1/2014 and who have an annual salary of more than $75,000 a year. Define a criteria range by inserting six new rows above the table on the worksheet and copying the field names into the first row.

b. In cell D2, enter the criterion **<1/1/2014**, then in cell G2 enter **>75000**.

c. Click any cell in the table.

d. Open the Advanced Filter dialog box.

e. Indicate that you want to copy to another location, enter the criteria range **A1:J2**, verify that the List range is A7:J17, then indicate that you want to place the extracted list in the range starting at cell **A20**.

f. Confirm that the retrieved list meets the criteria as shown in FIGURE H-20.

g. Save the workbook, then preview the worksheet.

FIGURE H-20

	A	B	C	D	E	F	G	H	I	J
1	Employee Number	First Name	Last Name	Hire Date	Branch	Monthly Salary	Annual Salary	Annual Bonus	Benefits Dollars	Annual Compensation
2				<1/1/2014			>75000			
3										
4										
5										
6										
7	Employee Number	First Name	Last Name	Hire Date	Branch	Monthly Salary	Annual Salary	Annual Bonus	Benefits Dollars	Annual Compensation
8	1211	Mary	Lane	2/12/2013	New York	$ 4,650	$ 55,800	$ 1,370	$ 12,834	$ 70,004
9	4515	Leanne	Waters	4/1/2014	Boston	$ 5,970	$ 71,640	$ 5,725	$ 16,477	$ 93,842
10	4187	Debbie	Davie	5/6/2012	Philadelphia	$ 7,550	$ 90,600	$ 6,525	$ 20,838	$ 117,963
11	2599	Martha	Macky	12/10/2013	Boston	$ 8,450	$101,400	$ 7,550	$ 23,322	$ 132,272
12	2213	Jake	Green	2/15/2015	Boston	$ 2,950	$ 35,400	$ 680	$ 8,142	$ 44,222
13	6588	Paul	Early	3/25/2013	New York	$ 2,750	$ 33,000	$ 630	$ 7,590	$ 41,220
14	2120	Ellen	Meeb	6/23/2012	New York	$ 4,225	$ 50,700	$ 1,320	$ 11,661	$ 63,681
15	4450	Mark	Mollen	8/3/2015	Philadelphia	$ 6,750	$ 81,000	$ 5,900	$ 18,630	$ 105,530
16	9887	Hank	Randal	9/29/2014	Philadelphia	$ 8,500	$102,000	$ 7,650	$ 23,460	$ 133,110
17	3955	Jen	Richards	5/12/2013	Boston	$ 3,750	$ 45,000	$ 795	$ 10,350	$ 56,145
18										
19										
20	Employee Number	First Name	Last Name	Hire Date	Branch	Monthly Salary	Annual Salary	Annual Bonus	Benefits Dollars	Annual Compensation
21	4187	Debbie	Davie	5/6/2012	Philadelphia	$ 7,550	$ 90,600	$ 6,525	$ 20,838	$ 117,963
22	2599	Martha	Macky	12/10/2013	Boston	$ 8,450	$101,400	$ 7,550	$ 23,322	$ 132,272
23										

Skills Review (continued)

4. **Look up values in a table.**
 a. Click the Summary sheet tab. Use the Name Manager to view the table names in the workbook, then close the dialog box.
 b. You will use a lookup function to locate an employee's annual compensation; enter the Employee Number **2213** in cell A17.
 c. In cell B17, use the VLOOKUP function and enter **A17** as the Lookup_value, **Table2** as the Table_array, **10** as the Col_index_num, and **FALSE** as the Range_lookup; observe the compensation displayed for that employee number, then check it against the table to make sure it is correct.
 d. Replace the existing Employee Number in cell A17 with **4187**, and view the annual compensation for that employee.
 e. Format cell B17 with the Accounting format with the $ symbol and no decimal places.
 f. Save the workbook.

5. **Summarize table data.**
 a. You want to enter a database function to average the annual salaries by branch, using the New York branch as the initial criterion. In cell E17, use the DAVERAGE function, and click the upper-left corner of cell A1 twice to select the table and its header row as the Database, select cell G1 for the Field, and select the range D16:D17 for the Criteria. Verify that the average New York salary is 46500.
 b. Test the function further by entering the text **Philadelphia** in cell D17. When the criterion is entered, cell E17 should display 91200.
 c. Format cell E17 in Accounting format with the $ symbol and no decimal places.
 d. Save the workbook.

6. **Validate table data.**
 a. Select the data in column E of the table, and set a validation criterion specifying that you want to allow a list of valid options.
 b. Enter a list of valid options that restricts the entries to **New York**, **Boston**, and **Philadelphia**. Remember to use a comma between each item in the list.
 c. Indicate that you want the options to appear in an in-cell drop-down list, then close the dialog box.
 d. Add a row to the table. Go to cell E12, then select Boston in the drop-down list.
 e. Select the data in column F in the table, and indicate that you want to restrict the data entered to only whole numbers. In the Minimum text box, enter **1000**; in the Maximum text box, enter **10000**. Close the dialog box.
 f. Click cell F12, enter **15000**, then press [Enter]. You should get an error message.
 g. Click Cancel, then enter **7000**.
 h. Complete the new record by adding an Employee Number of **1119**, a First Name of **Cate**, a Last Name of **Smith**, a Hire Date of **2/1/2016**, and an Annual Bonus of **$5000**. Format the range F12:J12 as Accounting with no decimal places and using the $ symbol. Compare your screen to FIGURE H-21.
 i. Add your name to the center section of the footer, save the worksheet, then preview the worksheet.

FIGURE H-21

	A	B	C	D	E	F	G	H	I	J
1	Employee Number	First Name	Last Name	Hire Date	Branch	Monthly Salary	Annual Salary	Annual Bonus	Benefits Dollars	Annual Compensation
2	1211	Mary	Lane	2/12/2013	New York	$ 4,650	$ 55,800	$ 1,370	$ 12,834	$ 70,004
3	4515	Leanne	Waters	4/1/2014	Boston	$ 5,970	$ 71,640	$ 5,725	$ 16,477	$ 93,842
4	4187	Debbie	Davie	5/6/2012	Philadelphia	$ 7,550	$ 90,600	$ 6,525	$ 20,838	$ 117,963
5	2599	Martha	Macky	12/10/2013	Boston	$ 8,450	$101,400	$ 7,550	$ 23,322	$ 132,272
6	2213	Jake	Green	2/15/2015	Boston	$ 2,950	$ 35,400	$ 680	$ 8,142	$ 44,222
7	6588	Paul	Early	3/25/2013	New York	$ 2,750	$ 33,000	$ 630	$ 7,590	$ 41,220
8	2120	Ellen	Meeb	6/23/2012	New York	$ 4,225	$ 50,700	$ 1,320	$ 11,661	$ 63,681
9	4450	Mark	Mollen	8/3/2015	Philadelphia	$ 6,750	$ 81,000	$ 5,900	$ 18,630	$ 105,530
10	9887	Hank	Randal	9/29/2014	Philadelphia	$ 8,500	$102,000	$ 7,650	$ 23,460	$ 133,110
11	3955	Jen	Richards	5/12/2013	Boston	$ 3,750	$ 45,000	$ 795	$ 10,350	$ 56,145
12	1119	Cate	Smith	2/1/2016	Boston	$ 7,000	$ 84,000	$ 5,000	$ 19,320	$ 108,320
13										
14										
15										
16	Employee Number	Annual Compensation		Branch	Average Annual Salary					
17	4187	$ 117,963		Philadelphia	$ 91,200					
18										

Skills Review (continued)

7. Create subtotals.

 a. Click the Subtotals sheet tab.

 b. Use the Branch field list arrow to sort the table in ascending order by branch.

 c. Convert the table to a range.

 d. Group and create subtotals of the Annual Compensation data by branch, using the SUM function.

 e. Click the 2 outline button on the outline to display only the subtotals and the grand total. Compare your screen to FIGURE H-22.

 f. Enter your name in the worksheet footer, save the workbook, then preview the worksheet.

 g. Save the workbook, close the workbook, exit Excel, then submit your workbook to your instructor.

FIGURE H-22

	A	B	C	D	E	F	G	H	I	J
1	Employee Number	First Name	Last Name	Hire Date	Branch	Monthly Salary	Annual Salary	Annual Bonus	Benefits Dollars	Annual Compensation
6					Boston Total					$ 326,481
10					New York Total					$ 174,905
14					Philadelphia Total					$ 356,603
15					Grand Total					$ 857,989
16										

Independent Challenge 1

As the manager of Miami Dental, a dental supply company, you spend a lot of time managing your inventory. To help with this task, you have created an Excel table that you can extract information from using filters. You also need to add data validation and summary information to the table.

 a. Start Excel, open the file EX H-3.xlsx from the location where you store your Data Files, then save it as **EX H-Dental**.

 b. Using the table data on the Inventory sheet, create a filter to display information about only the product bond refill. Clear the filter.

 c. Use a Custom Filter to generate a list of products with a quantity greater than 15. Clear the filter.

 d. Copy the labels in cells A1:F1 into A16:F16. Type **Retention Pins** in cell A17, and type **Small** in cell C17. Use the Advanced Filter with a criteria range of A16:F17 to extract a table of small retention pins to the range of cells beginning in cell A20. Enter your name in the worksheet footer, save the workbook, then preview the worksheet.

 e. On the Summary sheet tab, select the table data in column B. Open the Data Validation dialog box, then indicate you want to use a validation list with the acceptable entries of **Barnes**, **Blake**, **Lyon**, **Maxwell**. Make sure the In-cell dropdown check box is selected.

 f. Test the data validation by trying to change a cell in column B of the table to **Lane**.

 g. Using FIGURE H-23 as a guide, enter a function in cell E18 that calculates the total quantity of bond refill available in your inventory. Enter your name in the worksheet footer, preview the worksheet, then save the workbook.

 h. On the Subtotals sheet, sort the table in ascending order by product. Convert the table to a range. Insert subtotals by product using the Sum function, then select Quantity in the "Add Subtotal to" box. Remove the check box for the Total field, if necessary. Use the appropriate button on the outline to display only the subtotals and grand total. Save the workbook, then preview the worksheet.

 i. Submit the workbook to your instructor. Close the workbook, then exit Excel.

FIGURE H-23

Independent Challenge 2

As the senior accountant at Cambridge Electrical Supply you are adding new features to the company's accounts receivables workbook. The business supplies both residential and commercial electricians. You have put together an invoice table to track sales for the month of June. Now that you have this table, you would like to manipulate it in several ways. First, you want to filter the table to show only invoices over a certain amount with certain order dates. You also want to subtotal the total column by residential and commercial supplies. To prevent data entry errors you will restrict entries in the Order Date column. Finally, you would like to add database and lookup functions to your worksheet to efficiently retrieve data from the table.

 a. Start Excel, open the file EX H-4.xlsx from the location where you store your Data Files, then save it as **EX H-Invoices**.

 b. Use the Advanced Filter to show invoices with amounts more than $100.00 ordered before 6/15/2016, using cells A27:B28 to enter your criteria and extracting the results to cell A33. (*Hint*: You don't need to specify an entire row as the criteria range.) Enter your name in the worksheet footer.

 c. Use the Data Validation dialog box to restrict entries to those with order dates between 6/1/2016 and 6/30/2016. Test the data restrictions by attempting to enter an invalid date in cell B25.

 d. Enter **23698** in cell G28. Enter a VLOOKUP function in cell H28 to retrieve the total based on the invoice number entered in cell G28. Make sure you have an exact match with the invoice number. Format H28 using Accounting format with two decimal places. Test the function with the invoice number 23720.

 e. Enter the date **6/1/2016** in cell J28. Use the database function, DCOUNT, in cell K28 to count the number of invoices for the date in cell J28. Save the workbook, then preview the worksheet.

 f. On the Subtotals worksheet, sort the table in ascending order by Type, then convert the table to a range. Create subtotals showing the totals for commercial and residential invoices. Display only the subtotals for the commercial and residential accounts along with the grand total.

 g. Save the workbook, preview the worksheet, close the workbook, then exit Excel. Submit the workbook to your instructor.

Independent Challenge 3

You are the manager of Nest, a paint and decorating store. You have created an Excel table that contains your order data, along with the amounts for each item ordered and the date the order was placed. You would like to manipulate this table to display product categories and ordered items meeting specific criteria. You would also like to add subtotals to the table and add database functions to total orders. Finally, you want to restrict entries in the Category column.

 a. Start Excel, open the file EX H-5.xlsx from the location where you store your Data Files, then save it as **EX H-Nest**.

 b. Create an advanced filter that extracts records with the following criteria to cell A42: orders greater than $1500 having dates either before 9/10/2016 or after 9/19/2016. (*Hint*: Recall that when you want records to meet one criterion or another, you need to place the criteria on separate lines.)

 c. Use the DSUM function in cell H2 to let worksheet users find the total order amounts for the category entered in cell G2. Format the cell containing the total order using the Accounting format with the $ symbol and no decimals. Test the DSUM function using the Paint category name. (The sum for the Paint category should be $11,558.) Preview the worksheet.

 d. Use data validation to create an in-cell drop-down list that restricts category entries to "Paint", "Wallpaper", "Hardware", and "Tile". Use the Error Alert tab of the Data Validation dialog box to set the alert level to the Warning style with the message "Data is not valid." Test the validation in the table with valid and invalid entries. Save the workbook, enter your name in the worksheet footer, then preview the worksheet.

 e. Using the Subtotals sheet, sort the table by category in ascending order. Convert the table to a range, and add Subtotals to the order amounts by category. Widen the columns, if necessary.

 f. Use the outline to display only category names with subtotals and the grand total.

 g. Save the workbook, then preview the worksheet.

 h. Close the workbook, exit Excel, then submit the workbook to your instructor.

Independent Challenge 4: Explore

You are an inventory manager at American Eyewear, an eyewear distributor. You track your inventory of eye products in an Excel worksheet. You would like to use conditional formatting in your worksheet to help track the products that need to be reordered as well as your inventory expenses. You would also like to prevent data entry errors using data validation. Finally, you would like to add an area to quickly lookup prices and quantities for customers.

a. Start Excel, open the file EX H-6.xlsx from the location where you store your Data Files, then save it as **EX H-Eyewear**.

b. Use conditional formatting to add icons to the quantity field using the following criteria: quantities greater than or equal to 300 are formatted with a green circle, quantities greater than or equal to 100 but less than 300 are formatted with a yellow circle, and quantities less than 100 are formatted with a red circle. If your icons are incorrect, select the data in the Quantity field, click the Conditional Formatting button in the Styles group of the HOME tab, click Manage Rules, click the Show formatting for list arrow, select Current Selection, then double click Icon Set and compare your formatting rule to FIGURE H-24. (*Hint:* You may need to click in the top Value text box for the correct value to display for the red circle.)

c. Conditionally format the Total data using Top/Bottom Rules to emphasize the cells containing the top 30 percent with red text.

d. Add another rule to format the bottom 20 percent in the Total column with purple text.

e. Restrict the Wholesale Price field entries to decimal values between 0 and 100. Add an input message of **Prices must be less than $100**. Add a Warning-level error message of **Please check price**. Test the validation entering a price of $105 in cell D3 and allow the new price to be entered.

f. Below the table, create a product lookup area with the following labels in adjacent cells: **Product Number**, **Wholesale Price**, **Quantity**.

g. Enter 1544 under the label Product Number in your products lookup area.

h. In the product lookup area, enter lookup functions to locate the wholesale price and quantity information for the product number that you entered in the previous step. Make sure you match the product number exactly. Format the wholesale price with the Accounting format with the $ symbol and two decimal places.

i. Enter your name in the center section of the worksheet header, save the workbook then preview the worksheet comparing it to FIGURE H-25.

j. Close the workbook, exit Excel, then submit the workbook to your instructor.

FIGURE H-24

FIGURE H-25

Your Name

American Eyewear

Product Number	Category	Vendor	Wholesale Price	Quantity	Total
1122	Reading Glasses	Berkley	$105.00	125	$13,125.00
1132	Reading Glasses	Mallory	$10.66	68	$724.88
1184	Sports Eyewear	Bromen	$18.21	187	$3,405.27
1197	Sunglasses	Lincoln	$32.22	210	$6,766.20
1225	Frames	Berkley	$33.99	87	$2,957.13
1267	Frames	Mallory	$34.19	240	$8,205.60
1298	Sports Eyewear	Berkley	$21.97	375	$8,238.75
1345	Reading Glasses	Lincoln	$21.88	105	$2,297.40
1367	Safety Goggles	Lincoln	$17.18	168	$2,886.24
1398	Sports Eyewear	Bromen	$30.39	97	$2,947.83
1422	Sunglasses	Lincoln	$25.19	157	$3,954.83
1436	Cases	Mallory	$5.12	81	$414.72
1445	Sunglasses	Rand	$45.20	150	$6,780.00
1456	Custom	Berkley	$82.33	377	$31,038.41
1498	Safety Goggles	Rand	$19.22	51	$980.22
1521	Cases	Lincoln	$7.84	87	$682.08
1531	Lenses	Lincoln	$40.34	197	$7,946.98
1544	Reading Glasses	Bromen	$23.01	472	$10,860.72
1556	Frames	Bromen	$45.06	12	$540.72
1569	Sports Eyewear	Rand	$17.36	178	$3,090.08
1578	Sunglasses	Mallory	$63.22	35	$2,212.70
1622	Reading Glasses	Mallory	$25.33	874	$22,138.42
1634	Cases	Berkley	$18.47	501	$9,253.47
1657	Sunglasses	Bromen	$34.55	10	$345.50
1688	Safety Goggles	Rand	$18.66	73	$1,362.18
1723	Reading Glasses	Rand	$8.64	534	$4,613.76
1736	Sports Eyewear	Bromen	$25.66	15	$384.90
1798	Sports Eyewear	Mallory	$32.78	640	$20,979.20
1822	Cases	Mallory	$17.44	86	$1,499.84

Product Number	Wholesale Price	Quantity
1544	$ 23.01	472

Visual Workshop

Open the file EX H-7.xlsx from the location where you save your Data Files, then save it as **EX H-Schedule**. Complete the worksheet as shown in FIGURE H-26. An in-cell drop-down list has been added to the data entered in the Room field. The range A18:G21 is extracted from the table using the criteria in cells A15:A16. Add your name to the worksheet footer, save the workbook, preview the worksheet, then submit the workbook to your instructor.

FIGURE H-26

	A	B	C	D	E	F	G
1				Spring 2016 Schedule of Yoga Classes			
2							
3	Class Code	Class	Time	Day	Room	Fee	Instructor
4	YOG100	Basics	7:30 AM	Monday	Mat Room	$15	Malloy
5	YOG101	Power	8:00 AM	Tuesday	Equipment Room	$20	Gregg
6	YOG102	Hatha	9:00 AM	Wednesday	Mat Room	$15	Malloy
7	YOG103	Kripalu	10:00 AM	Monday	Mat Room	$15	Brent
8	YOG104	Basics	11:00 AM	Friday	Mat Room	$15	Paulson
9	YOG105	Power	12:00 PM	Saturday	Equipment Room	$20	Dally
10	YOG106	Hatha	12:00 PM	Tuesday	Mat Room	$15	Rand
11	YOG107	Power	2:00 PM	Monday	Equipment Room	$20	Walton
12	YOG108	Basics	4:00 PM	Tuesday	Mat Room	15	Malloy
13					Please select Mat		
14					Room or Equipment		
15	Class				Room		
16	Basics						
17							
18	Class Code	Class	Time	Day	Room	Fee	Instructor
19	YOG100	Basics	7:30 AM	Monday	Mat Room	$15	Malloy
20	YOG104	Basics	11:00 AM	Friday	Mat Room	$15	Paulson
21	YOG108	Basics	4:00 PM	Tuesday	Mat Room	$15	Malloy
22							

Automating Worksheet Tasks

CASE ▶ Kate Morgan, the North America regional vice president of sales at Quest, wants you to automate a task in the sales workbooks by creating a macro for the sales division. Kate sees this as a timesaver for the sales group. The macro will automatically insert text that identifies the worksheet as a sales division document.

Unit Objectives

After completing this unit, you will be able to:

- Plan a macro
- Enable a macro
- Record a macro
- Run a macro
- Edit a macro
- Assign keyboard shortcuts to macros
- Use the Personal Macro Workbook
- Assign a macro to a button

Files You Will Need

EX I-1.xlsx
EX I-2.xlsm
EX I-3.xlsx

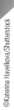
©Katerina Havelkova/Shutterstock

Plan a Macro

Learning
Outcomes
• Plan a macro
• Determine the
 storage location
 for a macro

A **macro** is a named set of instructions you can create that performs tasks automatically, in an order you specify. You create macros to automate Excel tasks that you perform frequently. For example, you can create a macro to enter and format text or to save and print a worksheet. To create a macro, you record the series of actions using the macro recorder built into Excel, or you write the instructions in a special programming language. Because the sequence of actions in a macro is important, you need to plan the macro carefully before you record it. **CASE** *Kate wants you to create a macro for the sales division that inserts the text "Quest Sales" in the upper-left corner of any worksheet. You work with her to plan the macro.*

DETAILS

To plan a macro, use the following guidelines:

- **Assign the macro a descriptive name**
 The first character of a macro name must be a letter; the remaining characters can be letters, numbers, or underscores. Letters can be uppercase or lowercase. Spaces are not allowed in macro names; use underscores in place of spaces. Press [Shift][-] to enter an underscore character. Kate wants you to name the macro "DivStamp". See **TABLE I-1** for a list of macros that could be created to automate other tasks at Quest.

- **Write out the steps the macro will perform**
 This planning helps eliminate careless errors. Kate writes a description of the macro she wants, as shown in **FIGURE I-1**.

- **Decide how you will perform the actions you want to record**
 You can use the mouse, the keyboard, or a combination of the two. Kate wants you to use both the mouse and the keyboard.

- **Practice the steps you want Excel to record, and write them down**
 Kate has written down the sequence of actions she wants you to include in the macro.

- **Decide where to store the description of the macro and the macro itself**
 Macros can be stored in an active workbook, in a new workbook, or in the **Personal Macro Workbook**, a special workbook used only for macro storage. Kate asks you to store the macro in a new workbook.

FIGURE I-1: **Handwritten description of planned macro**

Macro to create stamp with the division name

Name: DivStamp

Description: Adds a stamp to the top left of the worksheet, identifying it as a Quest sales worksheet

Steps:
1. Position the cell pointer in cell A1.
2. Type Quest Sales, then click the Enter button.
3. Click the Format button, then click Cells.
4. Click the Font tab, under Font style, click Bold; under Underline, click Single; under Color, click Blue; then click OK.

TABLE I-1: **Possible macros and their descriptive names**

description of macro	descriptive name for macro
Enter a frequently used proper name, such as "Kate Morgan"	KateMorgan
Enter a frequently used company name, such as Quest	Company_Name
Print the active worksheet on a single page, in landscape orientation	FitToLand
Add a footer to a worksheet	FooterStamp
Add totals to a worksheet	AddTotals

Enable a Macro

Learning Outcomes
- Create a macro-enabled workbook
- Enable macros by changing a workbook's security level

Because a macro may contain a **virus**—destructive software that can damage your computer files—the default security setting in Excel disables macros from running. Although a workbook containing a macro will open, if macros are disabled, they will not function. You can manually change the Excel security setting to allow macros to run if you know a macro came from a trusted source. When saving a workbook with a macro, you need to save it as a macro-enabled workbook with the extension .xlsm. **CASE** *Kate asks you to change the security level to enable all macros. You will change the security level back to the default setting after you create and run your macros.*

STEPS

1. **Start Excel, open a blank workbook, click the** Save button 🖫 **on the Quick Access toolbar, navigate to the location where you store your Data Files, in the Save As dialog box click the** Save as type list arrow, **click** Excel Macro-Enabled Workbook (*.xlsm), **in the File name text box type** EX I-Macro Workbook, **then click** Save

 The security settings that enable macros are available on the DEVELOPER tab. The DEVELOPER tab does not appear by default, but you can display it by customizing the Ribbon.

2. **Click the** FILE tab, **click** Options, **then click** Customize Ribbon **in the category list**

 The Customize the Ribbon options open in the Excel Options dialog box, as shown in FIGURE I-2.

3. **Click the** Developer check box, **if necessary, in the Main Tabs area on the right side of the screen to select it, then click** OK

 The DEVELOPER tab appears on the Ribbon. You are ready to change the security settings.

4. **Click the** DEVELOPER tab, **then click the** Macro Security button **in the Code group**

 The Trust Center dialog box opens.

5. **Click** Macro Settings **if necessary, click the** Enable all macros (not recommended; potentially dangerous code can run) option button **to select it as shown in** FIGURE I-3, **then click** OK

 The dialog box closes. Macros remain enabled until you disable them by deselecting the Enable all macros option. As you work with Excel, you should disable macros when you are not working with them.

FIGURE I-2: Excel Options dialog box

FIGURE I-3: Trust Center dialog box

Disabling macros

To prevent viruses from running on your computer, you should disable all macros when you are not working with them. To disable macros, click the DEVELOPER tab, then click the Macro Security button in the Code group. Clicking any of the first three options disables macros. The first option disables all macros without notifying you. The second option notifies you when macros are disabled, and the third option allows only digitally signed macros to run.

Record a Macro

Learning Outcomes
- Choose a macro storage location
- Create a macro by recording steps

The easiest way to create a macro is to record it using the Excel Macro Recorder. You turn the Macro Recorder on, name the macro, enter the keystrokes and select the commands you want the macro to perform, then stop the recorder. As you record the macro, Excel automatically translates each action into program code that you can later view and modify. You can take as long as you want to record the macro; a recorded macro contains only your actions, not the amount of time you took to record it. **CASE** *Kate wants you to create a macro that enters a division "stamp" in cell A1 of the active worksheet. You create this macro by recording your actions.*

STEPS

1. **Click the Record Macro button ▦ on the left side of the status bar**

 The Record Macro dialog box opens, as shown in **FIGURE I-4**. The default name Macro1 is selected. You can either assign this name or enter a new name. This dialog box also lets you assign a shortcut key for running the macro and assign a storage location for the macro.

2. **Type DivStamp in the Macro name text box**

3. **If the Store macro in list box does not display "This Workbook", click the list arrow and select This Workbook**

4. **Type your name in the Description text box, then click OK**

 The dialog box closes, and the Record Macro button on the status bar is replaced with a Stop Recording button ▢. Take your time performing the steps below. Excel records every keystroke, menu selection, and mouse action that you make.

5. **Press [Ctrl][Home]**

 When you begin an Excel session, macros record absolute cell references. By beginning the recording with a command to move to cell A1, you ensure that the macro includes the instruction to select cell A1 as the first step, in cases where A1 is not already selected.

6. **Type Quest Sales in cell A1, then click the Enter button ✓ on the formula bar**

7. **Click the HOME tab, click the Format button in the Cells group, then click Format Cells**

8. **Click the Font tab, in the Font style list box click Bold, click the Underline list arrow and click Single, click the Color list arrow and click the Blue color in the Standard Colors row, then compare your dialog box to FIGURE I-5**

9. **Click OK, click the Stop Recording button ▢ on the left side of the status bar, click cell D1 to deselect cell A1, then save the workbook**

 FIGURE I-6 shows the result of recording the macro.

FIGURE I-4: Record Macro dialog box

FIGURE I-5: Font tab of the Format Cells dialog box

FIGURE I-6: Sales Division stamp

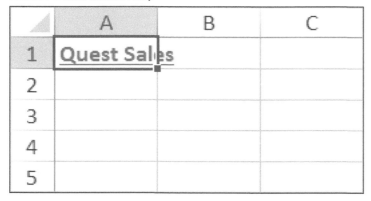

Excel 2013

Run a Macro

Learning Outcomes
• Display selected macros
• Run a macro using the Macro dialog box

Once you record a macro, you should test it to make sure that the actions it performs are correct. To test a macro, you **run** (play) it. You can run a macro using the Macros button in the Code group of the DEVELOPER tab. **CASE** *Kate asks you to clear the contents of cell A1, and then test the DivStamp macro. After you run the macro in the Macro workbook, she asks you to test the macro once more from a newly opened workbook.*

STEPS

1. **Click cell A1, click the HOME tab if necessary, click the Clear button ✐ in the Editing group, click Clear All, then click any other cell to deselect cell A1**
 When you delete only the contents of a cell, any formatting still remains in the cell. By using the Clear All option you can be sure that the cell is free of contents and formatting.

2. **Click the DEVELOPER tab, click the Macros button in the Code group, click the Macros in list arrow, then click This Workbook**
 The Macro dialog box, shown in **FIGURE I-7**, lists all the macros contained in the workbook.

3. **Click DivStamp in the Macro name list if necessary, as you watch cell A1 click Run, then deselect cell A1**
 The macro quickly plays back the steps you recorded in the previous lesson. When the macro is finished, your screen should look like **FIGURE I-8**. As long as the workbook containing the macro remains open, you can run the macro in any open workbook.

4. **Click the FILE tab, click New, then click Blank workbook**
 Because the EX I-Macro Workbook.xlsm is still open, you can use its macros.

QUICK TIP
To create a custom button on the Quick Access toolbar that will run a macro, right-click the Ribbon, click Customize Quick Access Toolbar, click the Choose commands from list arrow, select Macros, select the macro to assign to a custom button in the macro list on the left, click Add to move the macro to the list of buttons on the Quick Access Toolbar, then click OK.

5. **Deselect cell A1, click the DEVELOPER tab, click the Macros button in the Code group, click the Macros in list arrow, then click All Open Workbooks, click 'EX I-Macro Workbook. xlsm'!DivStamp, click Run, then deselect cell A1**
 When multiple workbooks are open, the macro name in the Macro dialog box includes the workbook name between single quotation marks, followed by an exclamation point which is an **external reference indicator**, indicating that the macro is outside the active workbook. Because you only used this workbook to test the macro, you don't need to save it.

6. **Close Book2 without saving changes**
 The EX I-Macro Workbook.xlsm workbook remains open.

Automating Worksheet Tasks

FIGURE I-7: Macro dialog box

Lists macros stored in the workbook

FIGURE I-8: Result of running DivStamp macro

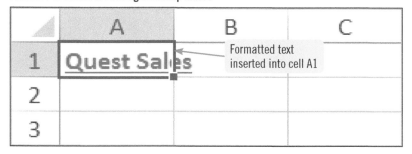

Formatted text inserted into cell A1

Running a macro automatically

You can create a macro that automatically performs certain tasks when the workbook in which it is saved is opened. This is useful for actions you want to do every time you open a workbook. For example, you may import data from an external data source into the workbook or format the worksheet data in a certain way. To create a macro that will automatically run when the workbook is opened, you need to name the macro Auto_Open and save it in that workbook.

Edit a Macro

Learning Outcomes
• Edit a macro using VBA
• Add comments to Visual Basic Code

When you use the Macro Recorder to create a macro, the program instructions, called **program code**, are recorded automatically in the **Visual Basic for Applications (VBA)** programming language. Each macro is stored as a **module**, or program code container, attached to the workbook. After you record a macro, you might need to change it. If you have a lot of changes to make, it might be best to record the macro again. But if you need to make only minor adjustments, you can edit the macro code directly using the **Visual Basic Editor**, a program that lets you display and edit your macro code. **CASE** *Kate wants you to modify the DivStamp macro to change the point size of the department stamp to 12.*

STEPS

1. **Make sure the EX I-Macro Workbook.xlsm workbook is open, click the Macros button in the Code group, make sure DivStamp is selected, click Edit, then maximize the Code window, if necessary**

 The Visual Basic Editor starts, showing three windows: the Project Explorer window, the Properties window, and the Code window, as shown in FIGURE I-9.

TROUBLE
If the Properties window does not appear in the lower-left portion of your screen, click the Properties Window button ☞ on the Visual Basic Standard toolbar, then resize it as shown in the figure if necessary.

2. **Click Module 1 in the Project Explorer window if it's not already selected, then examine the steps in the macro, comparing your screen to FIGURE I-9**

 The name of the macro and your name appear at the top of the Code window. Below this area, Excel has translated your keystrokes and commands into macro code. When you open and make selections in a dialog box during macro recording, Excel automatically stores all the dialog box settings in the macro code. For example, the line .FontStyle = "Bold" was generated when you clicked Bold in the Format Cells dialog box. You also see lines of code that you didn't generate directly while recording the DivStamp macro, for example, .Name = "Calibri".

3. **In the line .Size = 11, double-click 11 to select it, then type 12**

 Because Module1 is attached to the workbook and not stored as a separate file, any changes to the module are saved automatically when you save the workbook.

4. **Review the code in the Code window**

QUICK TIP
You can return to Excel without closing the module by clicking the View Microsoft Excel button ☒ on the Visual Basic Editor toolbar.

5. **Click File on the menu bar, then click Close and Return to Microsoft Excel**

 You want to rerun the DivStamp macro to make sure the macro reflects the change you made using the Visual Basic Editor. You begin by clearing the division name from cell A1.

6. **Click cell A1, click the HOME tab, click the Clear button 🖌 in the Editing group, then click Clear All**

QUICK TIP
Another way to start the Visual Basic Editor is to click the DEVELOPER tab, then click the Visual Basic button in the Code group.

7. **Click any other cell to deselect cell A1, click the DEVELOPER tab, click the Macros button in the Code group, make sure DivStamp is selected, click Run, then deselect cell A1**

 The department stamp is now in 12-point type, as shown in FIGURE I-10.

8. **Save the workbook**

FIGURE I-9: Visual Basic Editor showing Module1

Project Explorer window with Module1 selected

Properties window showing properties for Module1

Properties window button

Comments appear in green

Code window

FIGURE I-10: Result of running edited DivStamp macro

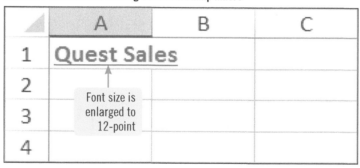

Font size is enlarged to 12-point

Adding comments to Visual Basic code

With practice, you will be able to interpret the lines of macro code. Others who use your macro, however, might want to review the code to, for example, learn the function of a particular line. You can explain the code by adding comments to the macro. **Comments** are explanatory text added to the lines of code. When you enter a comment, you must type an apostrophe (')

before the comment text. Otherwise, the program tries to interpret it as a command. On the screen, comments appear in green after you press [Enter], as shown in **FIGURE I-9**. You can also insert blank lines as comments in the macro code to make the code more readable. To do this, type an apostrophe, then press [Enter].

Learning
Outcomes
• Run a macro using
 shortcut key
 combinations

Assign Keyboard Shortcuts to Macros

For macros that you run frequently, you can run them by using shortcut key combinations instead of the Macro dialog box. You can assign a shortcut key combination to any macro. Using shortcut keys saves you time by reducing the number of actions you need to take to run a macro. You assign shortcut key combinations in the Record Macro dialog box. **CASE** ▶ *Kate also wants you to create a macro called Region to enter the company region into a worksheet. You assign a shortcut key combination to run the macro.*

STEPS

1. **Click cell B2**

 You want to record the macro in cell B2, but you want the macro to enter the region of North America anywhere in a worksheet. Therefore, you do not begin the macro with an instruction to position the cell pointer, as you did in the DivStamp macro.

2. **Click the Record Macro button 📠 on the status bar**

 The Record Macro dialog box opens. Notice the option Shortcut key: Ctrl+ followed by a blank box. You can type a letter (A–Z) in the Shortcut key text box to assign the key combination of [Ctrl] plus that letter to run the macro. Because some common Excel shortcuts use the [Ctrl][*letter*] combination, such as [Ctrl][C] for Copy, you decide to use the key combination [Ctrl][Shift] plus a letter to avoid overriding any of these shortcut key combinations.

QUICK TIP
Be careful when
choosing letters for
a keyboard shortcut.
The letters entered
in the shortcut key
text box are case
sensitive.

3. **With the default macro name selected, type Region in the Macro name text box, click the Shortcut key text box, press and hold [Shift], type C, then in the Description box type your name**

 You have assigned the shortcut key combination [Ctrl][Shift][C] to the Region macro. After you create the macro, you will use this shortcut key combination to run it. Compare your screen with FIGURE I-11. You are ready to record the Region macro.

4. **Click OK to close the dialog box**

5. **Type North America in cell B2, click the Enter button ✓ on the formula bar, press [Ctrl][I] to italicize the text, click the Stop Recording button ☐ on the status bar, then deselect cell B2**

 North America appears in italics in cell B2. You are ready to run the macro in cell A5 using the shortcut key combination.

6. **Click cell A5, press and hold [Ctrl][Shift], type C, then deselect the cell**

 The region appears in cell A5, as shown in FIGURE I-12. The macro played back in the selected cell (A5) instead of the cell where it was recorded (B2) because you did not begin recording the macro by clicking cell B2.

FIGURE I-11: **Record Macro dialog box with shortcut key assigned**

FIGURE I-12: **Result of running the Region macro**

◢	A	B	C	D	E	F	G
1	**Quest Sales**						
2		*North America* ←		Result of recording macro in cell B2			
3							
4							
5	*North America* ←		Result of running macro in cell A5				
6							
7							

Using relative referencing when creating a macro

By default, Excel records absolute cell references in macros. You can record a macro's actions based on the relative position of the active cell by clicking the Use Relative References button in the Code group prior to recording the action. For example, when you create a macro using the default setting of absolute referencing, bolding the range A1:D1 will always bold that range when the macro is run. However, if you click the Use Relative References button when recording the macro before bolding the range A1:D1, then running the macro will not necessarily result in bolding the range A1:D1. The range that will be bolded will depend on the location of the active cell when the macro is run. If the active cell is A4, then the range A4:D4 will be bolded. Selecting the Use Relative

References button highlights the button name, indicating it is active, as shown in FIGURE I-13. The button remains active until you click it again to deselect it. This is called a toggle, meaning that it acts like an off/on switch: it retains the relative reference setting until you click it again to turn it off or you exit Excel.

FIGURE I-13: **Use Relative References button selected**

Use Relative References button selected

Use the Personal Macro Workbook

Learning
Outcomes
• Determine when
when to use the
Personal Macro
Workbook
• Save a macro in
the Personal
Macro Workbook

When you create a macro, it is automatically stored in the workbook in which you created it. But if you wanted to use that macro in another workbook, you would have to copy the macro to that workbook. Instead, it's easier to store commonly used macros in the Personal Macro Workbook. The **Personal Macro Workbook** is an Excel file that is always available, unless you specify otherwise, and gives you access to all the macros it contains, regardless of which workbooks are open. The Personal Macro Workbook file is automatically created the first time you choose to store a macro in it, and is named PERSONAL.XLSB. You can add additional macros to the Personal Macro Workbook by saving them in the workbook. By default, the PERSONAL.XLSB workbook opens each time you start Excel, but you don't see it because Excel designates it as a hidden file. **CASE** *Kate often likes to print her worksheets in landscape orientation with 1" left, right, top, and bottom margins. She wants you to create a macro that automatically formats a work-sheet for printing this way. Because she wants to use this macro in future workbooks, she asks you to store the macro in the Personal Macro Workbook.*

STEPS

1. **Click the Record Macro button 📖 on the status bar**
 The Record Macro dialog box opens.

2. **Type FormatPrint in the Macro name text box, click the Shortcut key text box, press and hold [Shift], type F, then click the Store macro in list arrow**
 You have named the macro FormatPrint and assigned it the shortcut combination [Ctrl][Shift][F]. The "This Workbook" storage option is selected by default, indicating that Excel automatically stores macros in the active workbook, as shown in FIGURE I-14. You can also choose to store the macro in a new workbook or in the Personal Macro Workbook.

3. **Click Personal Macro Workbook, in the Description text box enter your name, then click OK**
 The recorder is on, and you are ready to record the macro keystrokes.

4. **Click the PAGE LAYOUT tab, click the Orientation button in the Page Setup group, click Landscape, click the Margins button in the Page Setup group, click Custom Margins, then enter 1 in the Top, Left, Bottom, and Right text boxes**
 Compare your margin settings to FIGURE I-15.

5. **Click OK, then click the Stop Recording button ☐ on the status bar**
 You want to test the macro.

6. **Add a new worksheet, in cell A1 type Macro Test, press [Enter], press and hold [Ctrl][Shift], then type F**
 The FormatPrint macro plays back the sequence of commands.

7. **Preview Sheet2 and verify in the Settings that the orientation is landscape and the Last Custom Margins are 1" on the left, right, top, and bottom**

8. **Click the Back button ⬅ then save the workbook**

FIGURE I-14: Record Macro dialog box showing macro storage options

FIGURE I-15: Margin settings for the FormatPrint macro

Working with the Personal Macro Workbook

Once you use the Personal Macro Workbook, it opens automatically each time you start Excel so you can add macros to it. By default, the Personal Macro Workbook is hidden in Excel as a precautionary measure so you don't accidentally delete anything from it. If you need to delete a macro from the Personal Macro Workbook, click the VIEW tab, click Unhide in the Window group, click PERSONAL.XLSB, then click OK. To hide the Personal Macro Workbook, make it the active workbook, click the VIEW tab, then click Hide in the Window group. If you should see a message that Excel is unable to record to your Personal Macro Workbook, check to make sure it is enabled: Click the FILE tab, click Options, click Add-ins, click the Manage list arrow, click Disabled Items, then click Go. If your Personal Macro Workbook is listed in the Disabled items dialog box, click its name, then click Enable.

Assign a Macro to a Button

When you create macros for others who will use your workbook, you might want to make the macros more visible so they're easier to use. In addition to using shortcut keys, you can run a macro by assigning it to a button on your worksheet. Then when you click the button the macro will run. **CASE** ▶ *To make it easier for people in the sales division to run the DivStamp macro, Kate asks you to assign it to a button on the workbook. You begin by creating the button.*

STEPS

1. **Add a new worksheet, click the INSERT tab, click the Shapes button in the Illustrations group, then click the first rectangle in the Rectangles group**
 The mouse pointer changes to a + symbol.

2. **Click at the top-left corner of cell A8, and drag the pointer to the lower-right corner of cell B9**
 Compare your screen to FIGURE I-16.

3. **Type Division Macro to label the button**
 Now that you have created the button, you are ready to assign the macro to it.

4. **Right-click the new button, then on the shortcut menu click Assign Macro**
 The Assign Macro dialog box opens.

5. **Click DivStamp under "Macro name", then click OK**
 You have assigned the DivStamp macro to the button.

6. **Click any cell to deselect the button, then click the button**
 The DivStamp macro plays, and the text Quest Sales appears in cell A1, as shown in FIGURE I-17.

7. **Save the workbook, preview Sheet3, close the workbook, then exit Excel, clicking Don't Save when asked to save changes to the Personal Macro Workbook**

8. **Submit the workbook to your instructor**

FIGURE I-16: **Button shape**

◢	A	B	C	D	E
1					
2					
3					
4					
5					
6					
7					
8					
9					
10					
11					
12					

Rectangle shape will become button

FIGURE I-17: **Sheet3 with the Sales Division text**

◢	A	B	C	D	E
1	Quest Sales				
2					
3					
4					
5					
6					
7					
8	Division Macro				
9					
10					

Result of running macro using the button

Creating and formatting a form control

You can add an object called a **form control** to an Excel worksheet to make it easier for users to enter or select data. Click the DEVELOPER tab on the Ribbon, click the Insert button in the Controls group, click the desired control in the Form Controls area of the Insert gallery, then draw the shape on the worksheet. After adding a control to a worksheet, you need to link it to a cell or cells in the worksheet. To do this, right-click it, select Format Control, then click the Control tab. For example, if you add a list box form control, the input range is the location of the list box selections and the cell link is the cell with the numeric value for the current position of the list control. To edit the form control's positioning properties (such as moving, sizing, and printing) right-click the form control, select Format Control and click the Properties tab. See FIGURE I-18.

FIGURE I-18: **Properties tab of the Format Control dialog box**

Practice

Concepts Review

FIGURE I-19

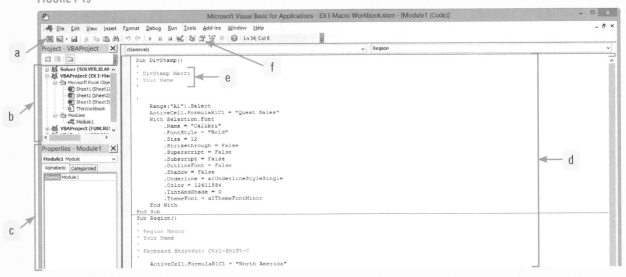

1. Which element points to comments?
2. Which element do you click to return to Excel without closing the module?
3. Which element points to the Code window?
4. Which element points to the Properties Window button?
5. Which element points to the Project Explorer window?
6. Which element points to the Properties window?

Match each term or button with the statement that best describes it.

7. Macro
8. Virus
9. Comments
10. Personal Macro Workbook
11. Visual Basic Editor

a. Set of instructions that performs a task in a specified order
b. Statements that appear in green explaining the macro
c. Destructive software that can damage computer files
d. Used to make changes to macro code
e. Used to store frequently used macros

Select the best answer from the list of choices.

12. Which of the following is the best candidate for a macro?
 a. Often-used sequences of commands or actions
 b. Nonsequential tasks
 c. Seldom-used commands or tasks
 d. One-button or one-keystroke commands

13. You can open the Visual Basic Editor by clicking the _____ button in the Macro dialog box.
 a. Edit
 b. Programs
 c. Modules
 d. Visual Basic Editor

14. A Macro named _____ will automatically run when the workbook it is saved in opens.
 a. Default
 b. Auto_Open
 c. Macro1
 d. Open_Macro

15. **Which of the following is *not* true about editing a macro?**
 a. You edit macros using the Visual Basic Editor.
 b. A macro cannot be edited and must be recorded again.
 c. You can type changes directly in the existing program code.
 d. You can make more than one editing change in a macro.

16. **Why is it important to plan a macro?**
 a. Macros can't be deleted.
 b. Planning helps prevent careless errors from being introduced into the macro.
 c. It is impossible to edit a macro.
 d. Macros won't be stored if they contain errors.

17. **Macros are recorded with relative references:**
 a. Only if the Use Relative References button is selected.
 b. In all cases.
 c. By default.
 d. Only if the Use Absolute References button is not selected.

18. **You can run macros:**
 a. From the Macro dialog box.
 b. From shortcut key combinations.
 c. From a button on the worksheet.
 d. Using all of the above.

19. **Macro security settings can be changed using the _____ tab.**
 a. Home
 b. Developer
 c. Security
 d. Review

Skills Review

1. **Plan and enable a macro.**
 a. You need to plan a macro that enters and formats your name and e-mail address in a worksheet.
 b. Write out the steps the macro will perform.
 c. Write out how the macro could be used in a workbook.
 d. Start Excel, open a new workbook, then save it as a Macro-Enabled workbook named **EX I-Macros** in the location where you store your Data Files. (*Hint*: The file will have the file extension .xlsm.)
 e. Use the Excel Options feature to display the DEVELOPER tab if it is not showing in the Ribbon.
 f. Using the Trust Center dialog box, enable all macros.

2. **Record a macro.**
 a. You want to record a macro that enters and formats your name and e-mail address in the range A1:A2 in a worksheet using the steps below.
 b. Name the macro **MyEmail**, store it in the current workbook, and make sure your name appears in the Description text box as the person who recorded the macro.
 c. Record the macro, entering your name in cell A1 and your e-mail address in cell A2. (*Hint*: You need to press [Ctrl][Home] first to ensure cell A1 will be selected when the macro runs.)
 d. Resize column A to fit the information entirely in that column.
 e. Add an outside border around the range A1:A2 and format the font using Green from the Standard Colors.
 f. Add bold formatting to the text in the range A1:A2.
 g. Stop the recorder and save the workbook.

3. **Run a macro.**
 a. Clear cell entries and formats in the range affected by the macro, resize the width of column A to 8.43, then select cell B3.
 b. Run the MyEmail macro to place your name and e-mail information in the range A1:A2.
 c. On the worksheet, clear all the cell entries and formats generated by running the MyEmail macro. Resize the width of column A to 8.43.
 d. Save the workbook.

Skills Review (continued)

4. Edit a macro.

a. Open the MyEmail macro in the Visual Basic Editor.

b. Change the line of code above the last line from Selection.Font.Bold = True to Selection.Font.Bold = False.

c. Use the Close and Return to Microsoft Excel command on the File menu to return to Excel.

d. Test the macro on Sheet1, and compare your worksheet to FIGURE I-20 verifying that the text is not bold.

e. Save the workbook.

5. Assign keyboard shortcuts to macros.

a. Create a macro named **EmailStamp** in the current workbook, assign your macro the shortcut key combination [Ctrl][Shift][Q], enter your name in the description. (*Hint*: If you get an error when trying to use [Ctrl][Shift][Q], select another key combination.)

b. Begin recording, enter your e-mail address, format it in italics with a font color of red, without underlining, in the selected cell of the current worksheet. Stop recording.

c. After you record the macro, clear the contents and formats from the cell containing your e-mail address that you used to record the macro.

d. Use the shortcut key combination to run the EmailStamp macro in a cell other than the one in which it was recorded. Compare your macro result to FIGURE I-21. Your e-mail address may appear in a different cell.

e. Save the workbook.

6. Use the Personal Macro Workbook.

a. Using Sheet1, record a new macro called **FitToLand** and store it in the Personal Macro Workbook with your name in the Description text box. If you already have a macro named FitToLand replace that macro. The macro should set the print orientation to landscape.

b. After you record the macro, Add a new worksheet, and enter **Test data for FitToLand macro** in cell A1.

c. Preview Sheet2 to verify that the orientation is set to portrait.

d. Run the FitToLand macro. (You may have to wait a few moments.)

e. Add your name to the Sheet2 footer, then preview Sheet2 and verify that it is now in Landscape orientation.

f. Save the workbook.

7. Assign a macro to a button.

a. Add a new worksheet and enter **Button Test** in cell A1.

b. Using the rectangle shape, draw a rectangle in the range A7:B8.

c. Label the button with the text **Landscape**. Compare your worksheet to FIGURE I-22.

d. Assign the macro PERSONAL.XLSB!FitToLand to the button.

e. Verify that the orientation of Sheet3 is set to portrait.

f. Run the FitToLand macro using the button.

g. Preview the worksheet, and verify that it is in landscape view.

h. Add your name to the Sheet3 footer, then save the workbook.

i. Close the workbook, exit Excel without saving the FitToLand macro in the Personal Macro Workbook, then submit your workbook to your instructor.

FIGURE I-20

	A
1	Your Name
2	yourname@yourschool.edu
3	
4	
5	

FIGURE I-21

	C	D	E
	yourname@yourschool.edu		

FIGURE I-22

	A	B	C
1	Button Test		
2			
3			
4			
5			
6			
7			
8	Landscape		
9			
10			

Independent Challenge 1

As the office manager of Ocean Point Consulting Group, you need to develop ways to help your fellow employees work more efficiently. Employees have asked for Excel macros that can do the following:

- Adjust the column widths to display all column data in a worksheet.
- Place the company name of Ocean Point Consulting Group in the header of a worksheet.

a. Plan and write the steps necessary for each macro.

b. Start Excel, open the Data File EX I-1.xlsx from the location where you store your Data Files, then save it as a macro-enabled workbook called **EX I-Consulting**.

c. Check your macro security on the DEVELOPER tab to be sure that macros are enabled.

d. Create a macro named **ColumnFit**, save it in the EX I-Consulting.xlsm workbook, assign the ColumnFit macro a shortcut key combination of [Ctrl][Shift][X], and add your name in the description area for the macro. Record the macro using the following instructions:

- Record the ColumnFit macro to adjust a worksheet's column widths to display all data. (*Hint*: Select the entire sheet, click the HOME tab, click the Format button in the Cells group, select AutoFit Column Width, then click cell A1 to deselect the worksheet.)
- End the macro recording.

e. Format the widths of columns A through G to 8.43, then test the ColumnFit macro with the shortcut key combination [Ctrl][Shift][X].

f. Create a macro named **CompanyName**, and save it in the EX I-Consulting.xlsm workbook. Assign the macro a shortcut key combination of [Ctrl][Shift][Y], and add your name in the description area for the macro.

g. Record the CompanyName macro. The macro should place the company name of Ocean Point Consulting Group in the center section of the worksheet header.

h. Enter **CompanyName test data** in cell A1 of Sheet2, and test the CompanyName macro using the shortcut key combination [Ctrl][Shift][Y]. Preview Sheet2 to view the header.

i. Edit the CompanyName macro in the Visual Basic Editor to change the company name from Ocean Point Consulting Group to **Shore Consulting Group**. Close the Visual Basic Editor and return to Excel.

j. Add a rectangle button to Sheet3 in the range A6:B7. Label the button with the text **Company Name**.

k. Assign the CompanyName macro to the button.

l. Enter **New CompanyName Test** in cell A1. Compare your screen to FIGURE I-23. Use the button to run the CompanyName macro. Preview the worksheet, checking the header to be sure it is displaying the new company name.

m. Enter your name in the footers of all three worksheets. Save the workbook, close the workbook, then submit the workbook to your instructor and exit Excel.

FIGURE I-23

New CompanyName Test

Company Name

Independent Challenge 2

You are an assistant to the VP of Sales at Twin Cities Beverage Company, a distributor of juices, water, and soda to 'supermarkets. As part of your work, you create spreadsheets with sales projections for different regions of the company. You frequently have to change the print settings so that workbooks print in landscape orientation with custom margins of 1" on the top and bottom. You also add a header with the company name on every worksheet. You have decided that it's time to create a macro to streamline this process.

a. Plan and write the steps necessary to create the macro.

b. Check your macro security settings to confirm that macros are enabled.

Independent Challenge 2 (continued)

c. Start Excel, create a new workbook, then save it as a macro-enabled file named **EX I-Sales Macro** in the location where you store your Data Files.

d. Create a macro that changes the page orientation to landscape, adds custom margins of 1" on the top and bottom of the page, adds a header of **Twin Cities Beverage Company** in the center section formatted as Bold with a font size of 14 points. Name the macro **Format**, add your name in the description, assign it the shortcut key combination [Ctrl][Shift][W], and store it in the current workbook.

e. Add a new worksheet and enter the text **Format Test** in cell A1. Test the macro using the shortcut key combination of [Ctrl][Shift][W]. Preview Sheet2 to check the page orientation, margins, and the header.

f. Add a new worksheet, enter the text **Format Test** in cell A1 add a rectangular button with the text **Format Worksheet** to run the Format macro, then test the macro using the button.

g. Preview the Visual Basic code for the macro.

h. Save the workbook, close the workbook, exit Excel, then submit the workbook to your instructor.

Independent Challenge 3

You are the Northeast regional sales manager of New England Technology, a technology consulting firm. You manage the New England operations and frequently create workbooks with data from the office locations. It's tedious to change the tab names and colors every time you open a new workbook, so you decide to create a macro that will add the office locations and colors to the three office location worksheet tabs, as shown in FIGURE I-24.

FIGURE I-24

a. Plan and write the steps to create the macro described above.

b. Start Excel and open a new workbook.

c. Create the macro using the plan you created in Step a, name it **SheetFormat**, assign it the shortcut key combination [Ctrl][Shift][Q], store it in the Personal Macro Workbook, and add your name in the description area.

d. After recording the macro, close the workbook without saving it. Save the changes to the Personal Macro workbook.

e. Open a new workbook, then save it as a macro-enabled workbook named **EX I-Office Test** in the location where you store your Data Files. Use the shortcut key combination of [Ctrl][Shift][Q] to test the macro in the new workbook.

f. Unhide the PERSONAL.XLSB workbook. (*Hint*: Click the VIEW tab, click the Unhide button in the Window group, click PERSONAL.XLSB, then click OK.)

g. Edit the SheetFormat macro using FIGURE I-25 as a guide, changing the Burlington sheet name to Portland. (*Hint*: There are three instances of Burlington that need to be changed.)

h. Open a new workbook, then save it as a macro-enabled workbook named **EX I-Office Test New** in the location where you store your Data Files. Test the edited macro using the shortcut key combination of [Ctrl][Shift][Q].

i. Add a new sheet in the workbook, and name it **Code**. Copy the SheetFormat macro code from the Personal Macro Workbook, and paste it in the Code sheet beginning in cell A1. Save the workbook, close the workbook, then submit the EX I-Office Test New workbook to your instructor.

FIGURE I-25

```
Sub SheetFormat()
'
' SheetFormat Macro
' Your Name
'
' Keyboard Shortcut: Ctrl+Shift+Q
'
    Sheets("Sheet1").Select
    Sheets("Sheet1").Name = "Boston"
    Sheets("Boston").Select
    With ActiveWorkbook.Sheets("Boston").Tab
        .Color = 12611584
        .TintAndShade = 0
    End With
    Sheets("Sheet2").Select
    Sheets("Sheet2").Name = "Concord"
    Sheets("Concord").Select
    With ActiveWorkbook.Sheets("Concord").Tab
        .Color = 65535
        .TintAndShade = 0
    End With
    Sheets("Sheet3").Select
    Sheets("Sheet3").Name = "Portland"
    Sheets("Portland").Select
    With ActiveWorkbook.Sheets("Portland").Tab
        .Color = 10498160
        .TintAndShade = 0
    End With
End Sub
```

Independent Challenge 3 (continued)

j. Hide the PERSONAL.XLSB workbook. (*Hint*: With the PERSONAL.XLSB workbook active, click the VIEW tab, then click the Hide button in the Window group.)

k. Close the workbook without saving changes to the PERSONAL.XLSB workbook, then exit Excel.

Independent Challenge 4: Explore

As the owner of a yoga studio you manage your courses using an Excel workbook. You have created a macro that will display available classes when a type of class is entered. You have been manually entering the class name and then running the macro. You have hired an assistant and would like to simplify the process of displaying class information by adding a form control to help select the data in the worksheet and then run the macro. Specifically, you will ask your assistant to use a list box which will return a numeric value for the current position of the control. That numeric value can be used with an Index function to insert the selected data in the necessary location for the macro which will use it as criteria to filter your data to return the requested course information.

a. Start Excel, open the Data File EX I-2.xlsm from the location where you store your Data Files, then save it as **EX I-Classes**.

b. Test the macro FindClass by entering **Power** in cell A20 and running the macro. Scroll down to cell A23 to see the results.

c. Insert a button form control in cells B19:C20 and assign the FindClass macro to the form control button. Label the button with the text **Find Classes**.

d. Enter **Basics** in cell A20 and test the button.

e. On the Controls sheet create a list for a List Box form control by entering **Basics** in cell A1, **Power** in cell A2, **Hatha** in cell A3, and **Kripalu** in cell A4.

f. On the Yoga Classes sheet enter **Select Class** in cell A1. Insert a list box form control in cells B1:B4. Format the control to set the Input range to A1:A4 of the Controls sheet and the Cell link to cell B1 in the Controls sheet. Compare your controls to FIGURE I-26.

g. Test the list box by clicking different classes and viewing the position in the list displayed in cell B1 of the Controls sheet, the cell link used in the previous step.

h. Replace the class in cell A20 with the index formula **=INDEX(Controls!A1:A4,Controls!B1,0)**. This will use the list position displayed in cell B1 of the Controls sheet to find the class in the range A1:A4 of the Controls sheet and display the class name in cell A20. Test the index formula by selecting different classes in the list box and verifying cell A20 matches the selection.

i. Delete the form control button in cells B19:C20.

j. Assign the FindClass macro to the list box form control.

k. Select a class from the list box and verify the macro is working properly.

l. Enter your name in the footers of both worksheets. Save the workbook, close the workbook, then submit the workbook to your instructor and exit Excel.

FIGURE I-26

Visual Workshop

Start Excel, open the Data File EX I-3.xlsx from the location where you store your Data Files, then save it as a macro-enabled workbook called **EX I-Payroll**. Create a macro with the name **TotalHours**, save the macro in the EX I-Payroll workbook that does the following:

- Totals the weekly hours for each employee by totaling the hours for the first employee and copying that formula for the other employees
- Adds a row at the top of the worksheet and inserts a label of **Hours** in a font size of 14 point, centered across all columns
- Adds your name in the worksheet footer

Test the TotalHours macro by opening the Data File EX I-3.xlsx from the location where you store your Data Files and running the macro. Compare your macro results to FIGURE I-27. Close the Data File EX I-3 without saving it, then save the EX I-Payroll workbook. Submit the EX I-Payroll workbook to your instructor.

FIGURE I-27

	A	B	C	D	E	F	G	H	I
1					Hours				
2		Monday	Tuesday	Wednesday	Thursday	Friday	Saturday	Sunday	Total
3	Mary Jacobs	7	8	6	8	5	0	1	35
4	John Malone	5	7	8	7	7	6	2	42
5	Ken Duffy	6	5	7	6	3	5	0	32
6	Sally Landry	8	7	6	5	5	1	0	32
7	Kathy Bane	8	7	5	8	7	7	0	42
8	Jacki Rand	8	7	5	5	7	8	0	40
9	Cindy Healy	7	5	2	6	8	5	3	36
10	Randy Thomas	2	7	8	6	7	2	0	32
11	Ken Yang	0	4	4	4	4	4	1	21
12	Linda Regan	7	8	2	8	8	1	0	34
13									

Analyzing Data with PivotTables

CASE ▶ Quest uses PivotTables to analyze sales data. Kate Morgan is preparing for the annual meeting for the United States region and asks you to analyze product sales in Quest's branches over the past year. You will create a PivotTable to summarize the 2016 sales data by quarter, product, and branch and illustrate the information using a PivotChart.

Unit Objectives

After completing this unit, you will be able to:

- Plan and design a PivotTable report
- Create a PivotTable report
- Change a PivotTable's summary function and design
- Filter and sort PivotTable data
- Update a PivotTable report
- Explore PivotTable Data Relationships
- Create a PivotChart report
- Use the GETPIVOTDATA function

Files You Will Need

EX L-1.xlsx EX L-5.xlsx
EX L-2.xlsx EX L-6.xlsx
EX L-3.xlsx EX L-7.xlsx
EX L-4.xlsx

Plan and Design a PivotTable Report

Learning
Outcomes
• Develop guidelines
for a PivotTable
• Develop an
understanding of
PivotTable
vocabulary

The Excel **PivotTable Report** feature lets you summarize large amounts of columnar worksheet data in a compact table format. Then you can freely rearrange, or "pivot", PivotTable rows and columns to explore the relationships within your data by category. Creating a PivotTable report (often called a PivotTable) involves only a few steps. Before you begin, however, you need to review the data and consider how a PivotTable can best summarize it. **CASE** ▶ *Kate asks you to design a PivotTable to display Quest's sales information for its branches in the United States. You begin by reviewing guidelines for creating PivotTables.*

DETAILS

Before you create a PivotTable, think about the following guidelines:

• **Review the source data**

Before you can effectively summarize data in a PivotTable, you need to understand the source data's scope and structure. The source data does not have to be defined as a table, but should be in a table-like format. That is, it should have column headings, should not have any blank rows or columns, and should have the same type of data in each column. To create a meaningful PivotTable, make sure that one or more of the fields has repeated information so that the PivotTable can effectively group it. Also be sure to include numeric data that the PivotTable can total for each group. The data columns represent categories of data, which are called **fields**, just as in a table. You are working with sales information that Kate received from Quest's U.S. branch managers, shown in **FIGURE L-1**. Information is repeated in the Product ID, Category, Branch, and Quarter columns, and numeric information is displayed in the Sales column, so you will be able to summarize this data effectively in a PivotTable.

• **Determine the purpose of the PivotTable and write the names of the fields you want to include**

The purpose of your PivotTable is to summarize sales information by quarter across various branches. You want your PivotTable to summarize the data in the Product ID, Category, Branch, Quarter, and Sales columns, so you include those fields in your PivotTable.

• **Determine which field contains the data you want to summarize and which summary function you want to use**

You want to summarize sales information by summing the Sales field for each product in a branch by quarter. You'll do this by using the Excel SUM function.

• **Decide how you want to arrange the data**

The PivotTable layout you choose is crucial to delivering the message you intend. Product ID values will appear in the PivotTable columns, Branch and Quarter numbers will appear in rows, and the PivotTable will summarize Sales figures, as shown in **FIGURE L-2**.

• **Determine the location of the PivotTable**

You can place a PivotTable in any worksheet of any workbook. Placing a PivotTable on a separate worksheet makes it easier to locate and prevents you from accidentally overwriting parts of an existing sheet. You decide to create the PivotTable as a new worksheet in the current workbook.

FIGURE L-1: Sales worksheet

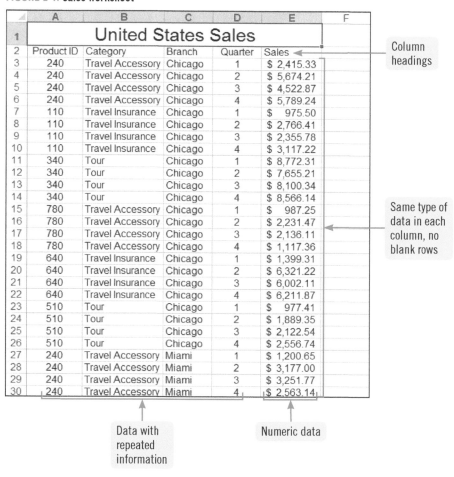

	A	B	C	D	E	F
1		United States Sales				
2	Product ID	Category	Branch	Quarter	Sales	
3	240	Travel Accessory	Chicago	1	$ 2,415.33	
4	240	Travel Accessory	Chicago	2	$ 5,674.21	
5	240	Travel Accessory	Chicago	3	$ 4,522.87	
6	240	Travel Accessory	Chicago	4	$ 5,789.24	
7	110	Travel Insurance	Chicago	1	$ 975.50	
8	110	Travel Insurance	Chicago	2	$ 2,766.41	
9	110	Travel Insurance	Chicago	3	$ 2,355.78	
10	110	Travel Insurance	Chicago	4	$ 3,117.22	
11	340	Tour	Chicago	1	$ 8,772.31	
12	340	Tour	Chicago	2	$ 7,655.21	
13	340	Tour	Chicago	3	$ 8,100.34	
14	340	Tour	Chicago	4	$ 8,566.14	
15	780	Travel Accessory	Chicago	1	$ 987.25	
16	780	Travel Accessory	Chicago	2	$ 2,231.47	
17	780	Travel Accessory	Chicago	3	$ 2,136.11	
18	780	Travel Accessory	Chicago	4	$ 1,117.36	
19	640	Travel Insurance	Chicago	1	$ 1,399.31	
20	640	Travel Insurance	Chicago	2	$ 6,321.22	
21	640	Travel Insurance	Chicago	3	$ 6,002.11	
22	640	Travel Insurance	Chicago	4	$ 6,211.87	
23	510	Tour	Chicago	1	$ 977.41	
24	510	Tour	Chicago	2	$ 1,889.35	
25	510	Tour	Chicago	3	$ 2,122.54	
26	510	Tour	Chicago	4	$ 2,556.74	
27	240	Travel Accessory	Miami	1	$ 1,200.65	
28	240	Travel Accessory	Miami	2	$ 3,177.00	
29	240	Travel Accessory	Miami	3	$ 3,251.77	
30	240	Travel Accessory	Miami	4	$ 2,563.14	

Column headings

Same type of data in each column, no blank rows

Data with repeated information

Numeric data

FIGURE L-2: PivotTable report based on Sales worksheet

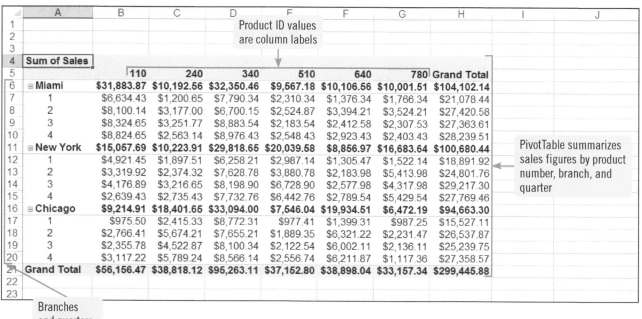

	A	B	C	D	E	F	G	H	I	J
1										
2				Product ID values						
3				are column labels						
4	Sum of Sales									
5		110	240	340	510	640	780	Grand Total		
6	⊟ Miami	$31,883.87	$10,192.56	$32,350.46	$9,567.18	$10,106.56	$10,001.51	$104,102.14		
7	1	$6,634.43	$1,200.65	$7,790.34	$2,310.34	$1,376.34	$1,766.34	$21,078.44		
8	2	$8,100.14	$3,177.00	$6,700.15	$2,524.87	$3,394.21	$3,524.21	$27,420.58		
9	3	$8,324.65	$3,251.77	$8,883.54	$2,183.54	$2,412.58	$2,307.53	$27,363.61		
10	4	$8,824.65	$2,563.14	$8,976.43	$2,548.43	$2,923.43	$2,403.43	$28,239.51		
11	⊟ New York	$15,057.69	$10,223.91	$29,818.65	$20,039.58	$8,856.97	$16,683.64	$100,680.44		
12	1	$4,921.45	$1,897.51	$6,258.21	$2,987.14	$1,305.47	$1,522.14	$18,891.92		
13	2	$3,319.92	$2,374.32	$7,628.78	$3,880.78	$2,183.98	$5,413.98	$24,801.76		
14	3	$4,176.89	$3,216.65	$8,198.90	$6,728.90	$2,577.98	$4,317.98	$29,217.30		
15	4	$2,639.43	$2,735.43	$7,732.76	$6,442.76	$2,789.54	$5,429.54	$27,769.46		
16	⊟ Chicago	$9,214.91	$18,401.65	$33,094.00	$7,546.04	$19,934.51	$6,472.19	$94,663.30		
17	1	$975.50	$2,415.33	$8,772.31	$977.41	$1,399.31	$987.25	$15,527.11		
18	2	$2,766.41	$5,674.21	$7,655.21	$1,889.35	$6,321.22	$2,231.47	$26,537.87		
19	3	$2,355.78	$4,522.87	$8,100.34	$2,122.54	$6,002.11	$2,136.11	$25,239.75		
20	4	$3,117.22	$5,789.24	$8,566.14	$2,556.74	$6,211.87	$1,117.36	$27,358.57		
21	Grand Total	$56,156.47	$38,818.12	$95,263.11	$37,152.80	$38,898.04	$33,157.34	$299,445.88		
22										
23										

PivotTable summarizes sales figures by product number, branch, and quarter

Branches and quarters are row labels

Excel 2013

Create a PivotTable Report

Learning
Outcomes
• Create a
 PivotTable
• Move PivotTable
 fields to rearrange
 data

Once you've planned and designed your PivotTable report, you can create it. After you create the PivotTable, you **populate** it by adding fields to areas in the PivotTable. A PivotTable has four areas: the Report Filter, which is the field by which you want to filter, or show selected data in, the PivotTable; the Row Labels, which contain the fields whose labels will describe the values in the rows; the Column Labels, which appear above the PivotTable values and describe the columns; and the Values, which summarize the numeric data. **CASE** ▶ *With the planning and design stage complete, you are ready to create a PivotTable that summarizes sales information.*

STEPS

1. **Start Excel if necessary, open the file EX L-1.xlsx from the location where you store your Data Files, then save it as EX L-US Sales**

 This worksheet contains the year's sales information for Quest's U.S. branches, including Product ID, Category, Branch, Quarter, and Sales. The records are sorted by branch. You decide to see what PivotTables Excel recommends for your data.

2. **Click the INSERT tab, click the Recommended PivotTables button in the Tables group, then click each of the recommended PivotTable layouts in the left side of the Recommended PivotTables dialog box, scrolling as necessary**

 The Recommended PivotTables dialog box opens, displaying recommended PivotTable layouts that summarize your data, as shown in FIGURE L-3. You decide to create your own PivotTable.

3. **Click Blank PivotTable at the bottom of the dialog box**

 A new, blank PivotTable appears on the left side of the worksheet and the PivotTable Fields List appears in a pane on the right, as shown in FIGURE L-4. You populate the PivotTable by clicking field check boxes in the PivotTable Fields List, often called the Field List. The diagram area at the bottom of the Field List represents the main PivotTable areas and helps you track field locations as you populate the PivotTable. You can also drag fields among the diagram areas to change the PivotTable layout.

4. **Click the Branch field check box in the Field List**

 Because the Branch field is a text, rather than a numeric field, Excel adds branch names to the rows area of the PivotTable, and adds the Branch field name to the ROWS area at the bottom of the Field List.

5. **Click the Product ID check box in the Field List**

 The Product ID information is automatically added to the PivotTable, and "Sum of Product ID" appears in the VALUES area in the diagram area. But because the data type of the Product ID field is numeric, the field is added to the VALUES area of the PivotTable and the Product ID values are summed, which is not meaningful. Instead, you want the Product IDs as column headers in the PivotTable.

6. **Click the Sum of Product ID list arrow in the VALUES area at the bottom of the PivotTable Fields List, then choose Move to Column Labels**

 The Product ID field becomes a column label, causing the Product ID values to appear in the PivotTable as column headers.

7. **Drag the Quarter field from the top of the PivotTable Fields List and drop it below the Branch field in the ROWS area at the bottom, select the Sales field check box in the PivotTable Fields List, then save the workbook**

 You have created a PivotTable that totals U.S. sales, with the Product IDs as column headers and Branches and Quarters as row labels. SUM is the Excel default function for data fields containing numbers, so Excel automatically calculates the sum of the sales in the PivotTable. The PivotTable tells you that Miami sales of Product #110 were twice the New York sales level and more than three times the Chicago sales level. Product #340 was the best selling product overall, as shown in the Grand Total row. See FIGURE L-5.

FIGURE L-3: Recommended PivotTables dialog box

Recommended
PivotTable layouts

Preview of
selected layout

FIGURE L-4: Empty PivotTable ready to receive field data

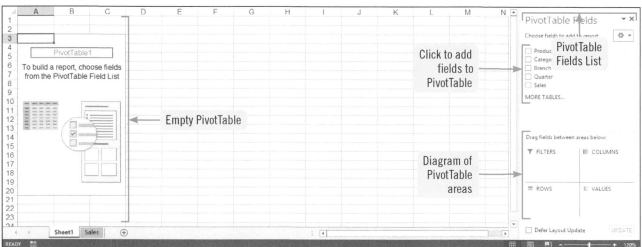

Click to add
fields to
PivotTable

PivotTable
Fields List

Empty PivotTable

Diagram of
PivotTable
areas

FIGURE L-5: New PivotTable with fields in place

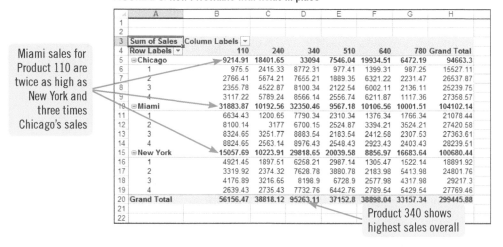

Miami sales for
Product 110 are
twice as high as
New York and
three times
Chicago's sales

Product 340 shows
highest sales overall

Changing the PivotTable layout

The default layout for PivotTables is the compact form; the row labels are displayed in a single column, and the second-level field items (such as the quarters in the U.S. Sales example) are indented for readability. You can change the layout of your PivotTable by clicking the PIVOTTABLE TOOLS DESIGN tab, clicking the Report Layout button in the Layout group, then clicking either Show in Outline Form or Show in Tabular Form. The tabular form and the outline form show each row label in its own column. The tabular and outline layouts take up more space on a worksheet than the compact layout.

Learning
Outcomes
• Change a
 PivotTable's
 summary function
• Format a PivotTable

Change a PivotTable's Summary Function and Design

A PivotTable's **summary function** controls what calculation Excel uses to summarize the table data. Unless you specify otherwise, Excel applies the SUM function to numeric data and the COUNT function to data fields containing text. However, you can easily change the default summary functions to different ones. **CASE** *Kate wants you to calculate the average sales for the U.S. branches using the AVERAGE function, and to improve the appearance of the PivotTable for her presentation.*

STEPS

QUICK TIP
You can also change the summary function by clicking the Field Settings button in the Active Field group on the PIVOTTABLE TOOLS ANALYZE tab.

1. **Right-click cell A3, then point to Summarize Values By in the shortcut menu**
 The shortcut menu shows that the Sum function is selected by default, as shown in FIGURE L-6.

2. **Click Average**
 The data area of the PivotTable shows the average sales for each product by branch and quarter, and cell A3 now contains "Average of Sales". You want to view the PivotTable data without the subtotals.

3. **Click the PIVOTTABLE TOOLS DESIGN tab, click the Subtotals button in the Layout group, then click Do Not Show Subtotals**
 After reviewing the data, you decide that it would be more useful to sum the sales information than to average it. You also want to redisplay the subtotals.

4. **Right-click cell A3, point to Summarize Values By in the shortcut menu, then click Sum**
 Excel recalculates the PivotTable—in this case, summing the sales data instead of averaging it.

QUICK TIP
You can control the display of grand totals by clicking the PIVOTTABLE TOOLS DESIGN tab, and clicking the Grand Totals button in the Layout group.

5. **Click the Subtotals button in the Layout group, then click Show all Subtotals at Top of Group**
 Just as Excel tables have styles that let you quickly format them, PivotTables have a gallery of styles to choose from. You decide to add a PivotTable style to the PivotTable to improve its appearance.

6. **Click the More button ▼ in the PivotTable Styles gallery, then click Pivot Style Light 20**
 To further improve the appearance of the PivotTable, you will remove the unnecessary headers of "Column Labels" and "Row Labels".

7. **Click the PIVOTTABLE TOOLS ANALYZE tab, then click the Field Headers button in the Show group**
 The data would be more readable if it were in currency format.

TROUBLE
If you don't see the Active Field group, click the Active Field button to display the Field Settings button.

8. **Click any sales value in the PivotTable, click the Field Settings button in the Active Field group, click Number Format in the Value Field Settings dialog box, select Currency in the Category list, make sure Decimal places is 2 and Symbol is $, click OK, click OK again, then compare your PivotTable to FIGURE L-7**
 You decide to give the PivotTable sheet a more descriptive name. When you name a PivotTable sheet, it is best to avoid using spaces in the name. If a PivotTable name contains a space, you must put single quotes around the name if you refer to it in a function.

9. **Rename Sheet1 PivotTable, add your name to the worksheet footer, save the workbook, then preview the worksheet**

FIGURE L-6: Shortcut menu showing Sum function selected

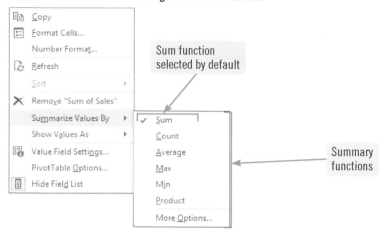

Sum function
selected by default

| Copy |
| Format Cells... |
| Number Format... |
| Refresh |
| Sort ▸ |
| ✕ Remove "Sum of Sales" |
| Summarize Values By ▸ |
| Show Values As ▸ |
| Value Field Settings... |
| PivotTable Options... |
| Hide Field List |

| ✓ Sum |
| Count |
| Average |
| Max |
| Min |
| Product |
| More Options... |

Summary
functions

FIGURE L-7: Formatted PivotTable

	A	B	C	D	E	F	G	H
1								
2								
3	**Sum of Sales**							
4		**110**	**240**	**340**	**510**	**640**	**780**	**Grand Total**
5	⊟ **Chicago**	**$9,214.91**	**$18,401.65**	**$33,094.00**	**$7,546.04**	**$19,934.51**	**$6,472.19**	**$94,663.30**
6	1	$975.50	$2,415.33	$8,772.31	$977.41	$1,399.31	$987.25	$15,527.11
7	2	$2,766.41	$5,674.21	$7,655.21	$1,889.35	$6,321.22	$2,231.47	$26,537.87
8	3	$2,355.78	$4,522.87	$8,100.34	$2,122.54	$6,002.11	$2,136.11	$25,239.75
9	4	$3,117.22	$5,789.24	$8,566.14	$2,556.74	$6,211.87	$1,117.36	$27,358.57
10	⊟ **Miami**	**$31,883.87**	**$10,192.56**	**$32,350.46**	**$9,567.18**	**$10,106.56**	**$10,001.51**	**$104,102.14**
11	1	$6,634.43	$1,200.65	$7,790.34	$2,310.34	$1,376.34	$1,766.34	$21,078.44
12	2	$8,100.14	$3,177.00	$6,700.15	$2,524.87	$3,394.21	$3,524.21	$27,420.58
13	3	$8,324.65	$3,251.77	$8,883.54	$2,183.54	$2,412.58	$2,307.53	$27,363.61
14	4	$8,824.65	$2,563.14	$8,976.43	$2,548.43	$2,923.43	$2,403.43	$28,239.51
15	⊟ **New York**	**$15,057.69**	**$10,223.91**	**$29,818.65**	**$20,039.58**	**$8,856.97**	**$16,683.64**	**$100,680.44**
16	1	$4,921.45	$1,897.51	$6,258.21	$2,987.14	$1,305.47	$1,522.14	$18,891.92
17	2	$3,319.92	$2,374.32	$7,628.78	$3,880.78	$2,183.98	$5,413.98	$24,801.76
18	3	$4,176.89	$3,216.65	$8,198.90	$6,728.90	$2,577.98	$4,317.98	$29,217.30
19	4	$2,639.43	$2,735.43	$7,732.76	$6,442.76	$2,789.54	$5,429.54	$27,769.46
20	**Grand Total**	**$56,156.47**	**$38,818.12**	**$95,263.11**	**$37,152.80**	**$38,898.04**	**$33,157.34**	**$299,445.88**
21								
22								

Using the Show buttons

To display and hide PivotTable elements, you can use the buttons in the Show group on the PIVOTTABLE TOOLS ANALYZE tab. For example, the Field List button will hide or display the PivotTable Fields List. The +/– Buttons button will hide or display the Expand and Collapse Outline buttons, and the Field Headers button will hide or display the Row and Column Label headers on the PivotTable.

Filter and Sort PivotTable Data

Learning
Outcomes
• Sort a PivotTable
 using the fields
• Filter a PivotTable
 using a slicer

Just as you used filters to hide and display table data, you can restrict the display of PivotTable data. A **slicer** is a graphic object with a set of buttons that let you easily filter PivotTable data to show only the data you need. For example, you can use slicer buttons to show only data about a specific product. You can also filter a PivotTable using a **report filter**, which lets you filter PivotTable data using a list arrow to show data for one or more field values. For example, if you add a Month field to the FILTERS area, you can filter a PivotTable so that only January sales data appears in the PivotTable. You can also sort PivotTable data in ascending or descending order. **CASE** ▶ *Kate wants to see sales data about specific products for specific branches and quarters.*

STEPS

1. **Right-click cell H5, point to** Sort **in the shortcut menu, then click** More Sort Options
 The Sort By Value dialog box opens. As you select options in the dialog box, the Summary information at the bottom of the dialog box changes to describe the sort results using your field names.

2. **Click the** Largest to Smallest option button **to select it in the Sort options section, make sure the** Top to Bottom option button **is selected in the Sort direction section, review the sort description in the Summary section of the dialog box, then click** OK
 The branches appear in the PivotTable in decreasing order of total sales from top to bottom. You want to easily display the sales for specific product IDs at certain branches.

3. **Click any cell in the PivotTable, click the** PIVOTTABLE TOOLS ANALYZE tab **if necessary, click the** Insert Slicer button **in the Filter group, click the** Product ID check box **and the** Branch check box **in the Insert Slicers dialog box to select both fields, click** OK, **then drag the slicers to the right of the PivotTable**
 Slicers appear, with buttons representing the Product ID numbers and Branch names, as shown in FIGURE L-8. You want to filter the data to show only Product IDs 110 and 510 in the New York and Chicago branches.

4. **Click the** 110 button **in the Product ID slicer, press [CTRL] then click the** 510 button **in the Product ID slicer, release [CTRL], click the** New York button **in the Branch slicer, press [CTRL], click the** Chicago button **in the Branch slicer, then release [CTRL]**
 The PivotTable displays only the data for Product IDs 110 and 510 in New York and Chicago, as shown in FIGURE L-9. In the slicers, the Filter symbol changes, indicating the PivotTable is filtered to display the selected fields. You decide to clear the filter and remove the slicers.

5. **Click the** Clear Filter button 🗐 **in the Product ID slicer, click** 🗐 **in the Branch slicer, click the top of the** Branch slicer, **press [CTRL], click the top of the** Product ID slicer, **release [CTRL], right-click the** Product ID slicer, **then click** Remove Slicers **on the shortcut menu**
 You want to display the PivotTable data by quarter using a Report Filter.

6. **In the PivotTable Fields List, click the** Quarter field list arrow **in the ROWS area, then select** Move to Report Filter
 The Quarter field moves to cell A1, and a list arrow and the word "(All)" appear in cell B1. The list arrow lets you filter the data in the PivotTable by Quarter. "(All)" indicates that the PivotTable currently shows data for all quarters. You decide to filter the data to show only data for the fourth quarter.

7. **In the PivotTable cell B1, click the** Quarter list arrow, **click** 4, **click** OK, **then save your work**
 The PivotTable filters the sales data to display the fourth quarter only, as shown in FIGURE L-10. The Quarter field list arrow changes to a filter symbol. A filter symbol also appears to the right of the Quarter field in the PivotTable Fields List, indicating that the PivotTable is filtered and summarizes only a portion of the PivotTable data.

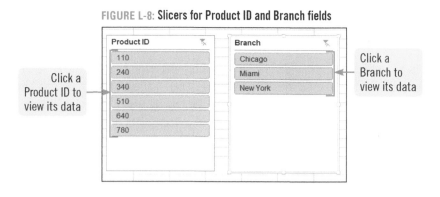

FIGURE L-8: Slicers for Product ID and Branch fields

Click a Product ID to view its data

Click a Branch to view its data

FIGURE L-9: PivotTable filtered by Product ID and Branch

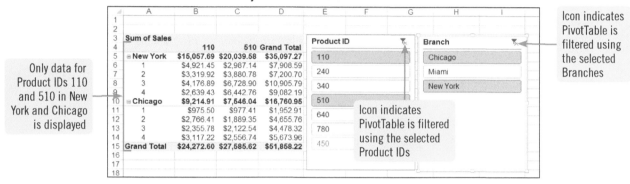

Only data for Product IDs 110 and 510 in New York and Chicago is displayed

Icon indicates PivotTable is filtered using the selected Branches

Icon indicates PivotTable is filtered using the selected Product IDs

FIGURE L-10: PivotTable filtered by fourth quarter

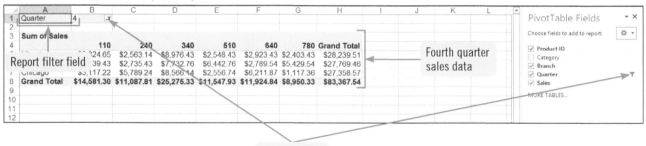

Report filter field

Fourth quarter sales data

Filter symbols

Filtering PivotTables using multiple values

You can select multiple values when filtering a PivotTable report using a report filter. After clicking a field's report filter list arrow in the top section of the PivotTable Fields List or in cell B1 on the PivotTable itself, click the Select Multiple Items check box at the bottom of the filter selections. This lets you select multiple values for the filter. For example, selecting 1 and 2 as the report filter in a PivotTable with quarters would display all of the data for the first two quarters. You can also select multiple values for the row and column labels by clicking the PIVOTTABLE TOOLS ANALYZE tab, clicking the Field Headers button in the Show group, clicking the Row Labels list arrow or the Column Labels list arrow in cells A4 and B3 on the PivotTable and selecting the data items that you want to display.

Update a PivotTable Report

The data in a PivotTable report looks like typical worksheet data. Because the PivotTable data is linked to a **data source** (the data you used to create the PivotTable), however, the values and results in the PivotTable are read-only values. That means you cannot move or modify a part of a PivotTable by inserting or deleting rows, editing results, or moving cells. To change PivotTable data, you must edit the items directly in the data source, then update, or **refresh**, the PivotTable to reflect the changes. **CASE** *Kate just learned that sales information for a custom group tour sold in New York during the fourth quarter was never entered into the Sales worksheet. Kate asks you to add information about this tour to the data source and PivotTable. You start by inserting a row for the new information in the Sales worksheet.*

STEPS

1. **Click the Sales sheet tab**

 By inserting the new row in the correct position by branch, you will not need to sort the data again.

2. **Scroll to and right-click the row 51 heading, then click Insert on the shortcut menu**

 A blank row appears as the new row 51, and the data in the old row 51, moves down to row 52. You now have room for the tour data.

3. **Enter the data for the new tour in row 51 using the following information**

Product ID	450
Category	Tour
Branch	New York
Quarter	4
Sales	3102.95

 The PivotTable does not yet reflect the additional data.

4. **Click the PivotTable sheet tab, then verify that the Quarter 4 data appears**

 The PivotTable does not currently include the new tour information, and the grand total is $83,367.54. Before you refresh the PivotTable data, you need to make sure that the cell pointer is located within the PivotTable range.

5. **Click anywhere within the PivotTable if necessary, click the PIVOTTABLE TOOLS ANALYZE tab, then click the Refresh button in the Data group**

 The PivotTable now contains a column for the new product ID, which includes the new tour information, in column H, and the grand total has increased by the amount of the tour's sales ($3,102.95) to $86,470.49, as shown in **FIGURE L-11**.

6. **Save the workbook**

Grouping PivotTable data

You can group PivotTable data to analyze specific values in a field as a unit. For example, you may want to group sales data for quarters one and two to analyze sales for the first half of the year. To group PivotTable data, first select the rows and columns that you want to group, click the PIVOTTABLE TOOLS ANALYZE tab, then click the Group Selection button in the Group group. To summarize grouped data, click the Field Settings button in the Active Field group, click the Custom option button in the Field Settings dialog box, select the function that you want to use to summarize the data, then click OK. To collapse the group and show the function results, click the Collapse Outline button ☐ next to the group name. You can click the Expand Outline button ☐ next to the group name to display the rows or columns in the group. To ungroup data, select the Group name in the PivotTable, then click the Ungroup button in the Group group.

FIGURE L-11: **Updated PivotTable report**

New data is added

	A	B	C	D	E	F	G		I
1	Quarter	4							
2									
3	**Sum of Sales**								
4		110	240	340	510	640	780	450	**Grand Total**
5	New York	$2,639.43	$2,735.43	$7,732.76	$6,442.76	$2,789.54	$5,429.54	$3,102.95	$30,872.41
6	Miami	$8,824.65	$2,563.14	$8,976.43	$2,548.43	$2,923.43	$2,403.43		$28,239.51
7	Chicago	$3,117.22	$5,789.24	$8,566.14	$2,556.74	$6,211.87	$1,117.36		$27,358.57
8	**Grand Total**	**$14,581.30**	**$11,087.81**	**$25,275.33**	**$11,547.93**	**$11,924.84**	**$8,950.33**	**$3,102.95**	**$86,470.49**
9									
10									

Totals are updated to include the new data

Adding a calculated field to a PivotTable

You can use formulas to analyze PivotTable data in a field by adding a calculated field. A calculated field appears in the Field List and can be manipulated like other PivotTable fields. To add a calculated field, click any cell in the PivotTable, click the PIVOTTABLE TOOLS ANALYZE tab, click the Fields, Items, & Sets button in the Calculations group, then click Calculated Field. The Insert Calculated Field dialog box opens. Enter the field name in the Name text box, click in the Formula text box, click a field name in the Fields list that you want to use in the formula, and click Insert Field. Use standard arithmetic operators to enter the formula you want to use. For example FIGURE L-12 shows a formula to increase Sales data by 10 percent. After entering the formula in the Insert Calculated Field dialog box, click Add, then click OK. The new field with the formula results appears in the PivotTable, and the field is added to the PivotTable Fields List as shown in FIGURE L-13.

FIGURE L-12: **Insert Calculated Field dialog box**

New field name

Formula to increase sales by 10%

Fields that can be used in the formula

FIGURE L-13: **PivotTable with calculated field**

New calculated field

	A	B	C	D	E	F	G	H
1	Quarter	4						
2								
3			110		240		340	
4		Sum of Sales	Sum of Increase Sales	Sum of Sales	Sum of Increase Sales	Sum of Sales	Sum of Increase Sales	Sum of S...
5	New York	$2,639.43	$ 2,903.37	$2,735.43	$ 3,008.97	$7,732.76	$ 8,506.04	$6,44...
6	Miami	$8,824.65	$ 9,707.12	$2,563.14	$ 2,819.45	$8,976.43	$ 9,874.07	$2,54...
7	Chicago	$3,117.22	$ 3,428.94	$5,789.24	$ 6,368.16	$8,566.14	$ 9,422.75	$2,55...
8	**Grand Total**	**$14,581.30**	**$ 16,039.43**	**$11,087.81**	**$ 12,196.59**	**$25,275.33**	**$ 27,802.86**	**$11,54...**

PivotTable Fields

Choose fields to add to report:
- ☑ Product ID
- ☐ Category
- ☑ Branch
- ☑ Quarter
- ☑ Sales
- ☑ Increase Sales

MORE TABLES...

Excel 2013

Explore PivotTable Data Relationships

Learning
Outcomes
• Change a
 PivotTable's
 organization
• Add fields to a
 PivotTable

What makes a PivotTable such a powerful analysis tool is the ability to change the way data is organized in the report. By moving fields to different positions in the report, you can explore relationships and trends that you might not see in the original report structure. **CASE** ▸ *Kate asks you to include category information in the sales report. She is also interested in viewing the PivotTable in different arrangements to find the best organization of data for her presentation.*

STEPS

QUICK TIP

You can change the amount an inner row is indented by clicking the Options button in the PivotTable group on the PIVOTTABLE TOOLS ANALYZE tab, clicking the Layout & Format tab, then changing the number for the character(s) in the Layout section.

1. **Make sure that the PivotTable sheet is active, that the active cell is located anywhere inside the PivotTable, and that the PivotTable Fields List is visible**

2. **Click the Category check box in the Field List**

 The category data is added to the ROWS area below the corresponding branch data. As you learned earlier, you can move fields within an area of a PivotTable by dragging and dropping them to the desired location.

3. **In the diagram section of the Field List, locate the ROWS area, then drag the Category field up and drop it above the Branch field**

 The category field is now the outer or upper field, and the branch field is the inner or lower field. The PivotTable is restructured to display the sales data by the category values and then the branch values within the category field. The subtotals now reflect the sum of the categories, as shown in **FIGURE L-14**. You can also move fields to new areas in the PivotTable.

QUICK TIP

As you move fields around in a PivotTable, you can control when the PivotTable structure is updated to reflect your changes. Click the Defer Layout Update check box at the bottom of the PivotTable Fields List window. When you are ready to update the PivotTable, click the Update button.

4. **In the diagram area of the Field List, drag the Category field from the ROWS area to anywhere in the COLUMNS area, then drag the Product ID field from the COLUMNS area to the ROWS area below the Branch field**

 The PivotTable now displays the sales data with the category values in the columns and then the product IDs grouped by branches in the rows. The product ID values are indented below the branches because the Product ID field is the inner row label.

5. **In the diagram area of the Field List, drag the Category field from the COLUMNS area to the FILTERS area above the Quarter field, then drag the Product ID field from the ROWS area to the COLUMNS area**

 The PivotTable now has two report filters. The upper report filter, Category, summarizes data using all of the categories. Kate asks you to display the tour sales information for all quarters.

6. **Click the Category list arrow in cell B1 of the PivotTable, click Tour, click OK, click the Quarter filter list arrow in cell B2, click All, then click OK**

 The PivotTable displays sales totals for the Tour category for all quarters. Kate asks you to provide the sales information for all categories.

QUICK TIP

You can copy each report filter field's data to a separate worksheet by selecting the report filter field on the worksheet, clicking the PIVOTTABLE TOOLS ANALYZE tab, clicking the Options list arrow in the PivotTable group, then selecting Show Report Filter Pages.

7. **Click the Category filter arrow, click All, then click OK**

 The completed PivotTable appears as shown in **FIGURE L-15**.

8. **Save the workbook, change the page orientation of the PivotTable sheet to Landscape, then preview the PivotTable**

Analyzing Data with PivotTables

FIGURE L-14: PivotTable structured by branches within categories

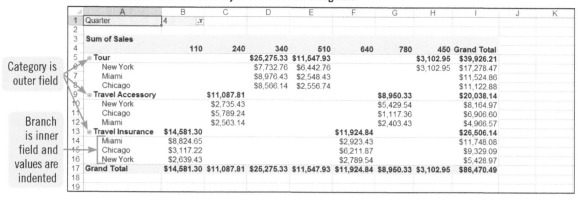

Category is outer field

Branch is inner field and values are indented

	A	B	C	D	E	F	G	H	I	J	K
1	Quarter	4									
2											
3	Sum of Sales										
4		110	240	340	510	640	780	450	Grand Total		
5	Tour			$25,275.33	$11,547.93			$3,102.95	$39,926.21		
6	New York			$7,732.76	$6,442.76			$3,102.95	$17,278.47		
7	Miami			$8,976.43	$2,548.43				$11,524.86		
8	Chicago			$8,566.14	$2,556.74				$11,122.88		
9	Travel Accessory		$11,087.81				$8,950.33		$20,038.14		
10	New York		$2,735.43				$5,429.54		$8,164.97		
11	Chicago		$5,789.24				$1,117.36		$6,906.60		
12	Miami		$2,563.14				$2,403.43		$4,966.57		
13	Travel Insurance	$14,581.30				$11,924.84			$26,506.14		
14	Miami	$8,824.65				$2,923.43			$11,748.08		
15	Chicago	$3,117.22				$6,211.87			$9,329.09		
16	New York	$2,639.43				$2,789.54			$5,428.97		
17	Grand Total	$14,581.30	$11,087.81	$25,275.33	$11,547.93	$11,924.84	$8,950.33	$3,102.95	$86,470.49		
18											
19											

FIGURE L-15: Completed PivotTable report

	A	B	C	D	E	F	G	H	I
1	Category	(All)							
2	Quarter	(All)							
3									
4	Sum of Sales								
5		110	240	340	510	640	780	450	Grand Total
6	Miami	$31,883.87	$10,192.56	$32,350.46	$9,567.18	$10,106.56	$10,001.51		$104,102.14
7	New York	$15,057.69	$10,223.91	$29,818.65	$20,039.58	$8,856.97	$16,683.64	$3,102.95	$103,783.39
8	Chicago	$9,214.91	$18,401.65	$33,094.00	$7,546.04	$19,934.51	$6,472.19		$94,663.30
9	Grand Total	$56,156.47	$38,818.12	$95,263.11	$37,152.80	$38,898.04	$33,157.34	$3,102.95	$302,548.83
10									
11									

Adding conditional formatting to a PivotTable

You can add conditional formatting to a PivotTable to make it easier to compare the data values. The conditional formatting is applied to cells in a PivotTable the same way as it is to non-PivotTable data. The conditional formatting rules follow the PivotTable cells when you move fields to different areas of the PivotTable. FIGURE L-16 shows a PivotTable that uses data bars to visually display the sales data.

FIGURE L-16: PivotTable with conditional formatting

	A	B	C	D	E	F	G	H	I	J
1	Category	(All)								
2	Quarter	(All)								
3										
4	Sum of Sales									
5		110	240	340	510	640	780	450	Grand Total	
6	Miami	$31,883.87	$10,192.56	$32,350.46	$9,567.18	$10,106.56	$10,001.51		$104,102.14	
7	New York	$15,057.69	$10,223.91	$29,818.65	$20,039.58	$8,856.97	$16,683.64	$3,102.95	$103,783.39	
8	Chicago	$9,214.91	$18,401.65	$33,094.00	$7,546.04	$19,934.51	$6,472.19		$94,663.30	
9	Grand Total	$56,156.47	$38,818.12	$95,263.11	$37,152.80	$38,898.04	$33,157.34	$3,102.95	$302,548.83	
10										
11										
12										

Create a PivotChart Report

A **PivotChart report** is a chart that you create from data or from a PivotTable report. TABLE L-1 describes how the elements in a PivotTable report correspond to the elements in a PivotChart report. When you create a PivotChart directly from data, Excel automatically creates a corresponding PivotTable report. If you change a PivotChart report by filtering or sorting the charted elements, Excel updates the corresponding PivotTable report to show the new data values. You can move the fields of a PivotChart using the PivotTable Fields List window; the new layout will be reflected in the PivotTable. **CASE** ▶ *Kate wants you to chart the fourth quarter tour sales and the yearly tour sales average for her presentation. You create the PivotChart report from the PivotTable data.*

STEPS

1. **Click the** Category list arrow **in cell B1, click** Tour, **click** OK, **click the** Quarter list arrow, **click** 4, **then click** OK

 The fourth quarter tour sales information appears in the PivotTable. You want to create the PivotChart from the PivotTable information you have displayed.

2. **Click any cell in the PivotTable, click the** PIVOTTABLE TOOLS ANALYZE tab, **then click the** PivotChart button **in the Tools group**

 The Insert Chart dialog box opens and shows a gallery of chart types.

3. **Click the** Clustered Column chart **if necessary, then click** OK

 The PivotChart appears on the worksheet as shown in FIGURE L-17. The chart has Field buttons that let you filter and sort a PivotChart in the same way you do a PivotTable. It will be easier to view the PivotChart if it is on its own sheet.

4. **Click the** PIVOTCHART TOOLS DESIGN tab, **click the** Move Chart button **in the Location group, click the** New sheet option button, **type** PivotChart **in the text box, click** OK

 The chart represents the fourth quarter tour sales. Kate asks you to change the chart to show the average sales for all quarters.

5. **Click the** Quarter field button **at the top of the PivotChart, click** All, **then click** OK

 The chart now represents the sum of tour sales for the year as shown in FIGURE L-18. You can change a PivotChart's summary function to display averages instead of totals.

6. **Click the** Sum of Sales list arrow **in the VALUES area of the PivotTable Fields List, click** Value Field Settings, **click** Average **on the Summarize Values By tab, then click** OK

 The PivotChart report recalculates to display averages. The chart would be easier to understand if it had a title.

7. **Click the** PIVOTCHART TOOLS DESIGN tab, **click the** Add Chart Element button **in the Chart Layouts group, point to** Chart Title, **click** Above Chart, **type** Average Tour Sales, **press [Enter], then drag the chart title border to center the title over the columns**

 You are finished filtering the chart data and decide to remove the field buttons.

8. **Click the** PIVOTCHART TOOLS ANALYZE tab, **then click the** Field Buttons button **in the Show/Hide group**

9. **Enter your name in the PivotChart sheet footer, save the workbook, then preview the PivotChart report**

 The final PivotChart report displaying the average tour sales for the year is shown in FIGURE L-19.

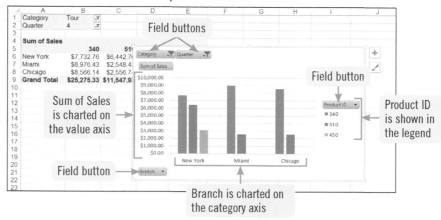

FIGURE L-17: **PivotChart with fourth quarter tour sales**

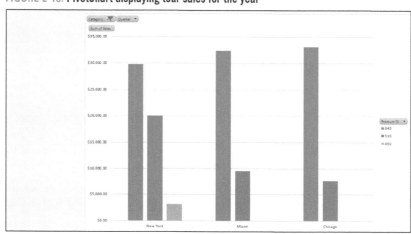

FIGURE L-18: **PivotChart displaying tour sales for the year**

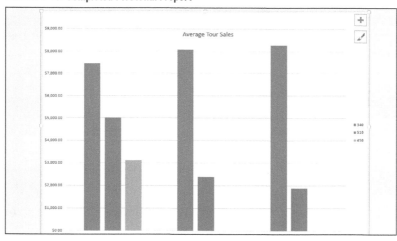

FIGURE L-19: **Completed PivotChart report**

TABLE L-1: **PivotTable and PivotChart elements**

PivotTable items	PivotChart items
Row labels	Axis fields
Column labels	Legend fields
Report filters	Report filters

Use the GETPIVOTDATA Function

Learning Outcomes
• Analyze the GETPIVOTDATA function
• Retrieve information from a PivotTable using the GETPIVOTDATA function

Because you can rearrange a PivotTable so easily, you can't use an ordinary cell reference when you want to reference a PivotTable cell in another worksheet. The reason is that if you change the way data is displayed in a PivotTable, the data moves, making an ordinary cell reference incorrect. Instead, to retrieve summary data from a PivotTable, you need to use the Excel GETPIVOTDATA function. See FIGURE L-20 for the GETPIVOTDATA function format. **CASE** ▶ *Kate wants to include the yearly sales total for the Chicago branch in the Sales sheet. She asks you to retrieve this information from the PivotTable and place it in the Sales sheet. You use the GETPIVOTDATA function to retrieve this information.*

STEPS

1. **Click the PivotTable sheet tab**

 The sales figures in the PivotTable are average values for tours. You decide to show sales information for all categories and change the summary information back to Sum.

2. **Click the Category filter arrow in cell B1, click All, then click OK**

 The PivotChart report displays sales information for all categories.

3. **Right-click cell A4 on the PivotTable, point to Summarize Values By on the shortcut menu, then click Sum**

 The PivotChart report recalculates to display sales totals. Next, you want to include the total for sales for the Chicago branch in the Sales sheet by retrieving it from the PivotTable.

4. **Click the Sales sheet tab, click cell G1, type Total Chicago Sales:, click the Enter button ✓ on the formula bar, click the HOME tab, click the Align Right button ≡ in the Alignment group, click the Bold button B in the Font group, then adjust the width of column G to display the label in cell G1**

 You want the GETPIVOTDATA function to retrieve the total Chicago sales from the PivotTable. Cell I8 on the PivotTable contains the data you want to display on the Sales sheet.

5. **Click cell G2, type =, click the PivotTable sheet tab, click cell I8 on the PivotTable, then click ✓**

 The GETPIVOTDATA function, along with its arguments, is inserted into cell G2 of the Sales sheet, as shown in FIGURE L-21. You want to format the sales total.

6. **Click the Accounting Number Format button $ in the Number group**

 The current sales total for the Chicago branch is $94,663.30. This is the same value displayed in cell I8 of the PivotTable.

7. **Enter your name in the Sales sheet footer, save the workbook, then preview the Sales worksheet**

8. **Close the file, exit Excel, then submit the workbook to your instructor**

 The Sales worksheet is shown in FIGURE L-22.

FIGURE L-20: Format of **GETPIVOTDATA** function

GETPIVOTDATA("Sales",PivotTable!A4,"Branch","Chicago")

| Field where data is extracted from | PivotTable name and cell in the report that contains the data you want to retrieve | Field and value pair that describe the data you want to retrieve |

FIGURE L-21: **GETPIVOTDATA** function in the Sales sheet

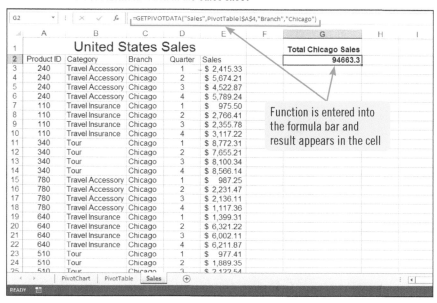

FIGURE L-22: **Completed Sales worksheet showing total Chicago sales**

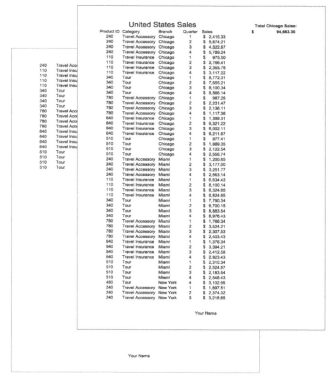

Excel 2013

Practice

Concepts Review

FIGURE L-23

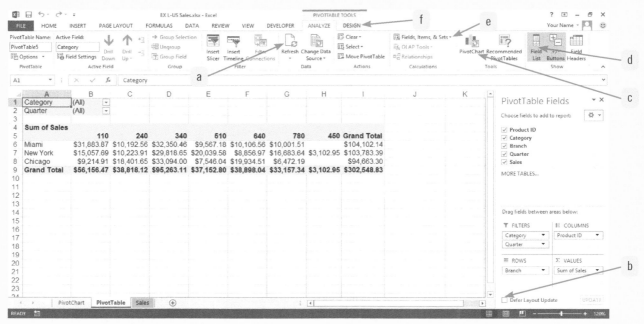

1. Which element do you click to create a calculated field in a PivotTable?
2. Which element do you click to create a chart based on the data in a PivotTable?
3. Which element do you click to display a gallery of PivotTable Styles?
4. Which element do you click to control when PivotTable changes will occur?
5. Which element do you click to display or hide the PivotTable Fields List pane?
6. Which element do you click to update a PivotTable?

Match each term with the statement that best describes it.

7. PivotTable Row Label
8. Slicer
9. Compact form
10. Summary function
11. GETPIVOTDATA function

a. Retrieves information from a PivotTable
b. Default layout for a PivotTable
c. PivotTable filtering tool
d. PivotChart axis field
e. Determines if data is summed or averaged

Select the best answer from the list of choices.

12. When a numeric field is added to a PivotTable, it is placed in the _____ area.

 a. VALUES

 b. ROWS

 c. COLUMNS

 d. FILTERS

13. Which PivotTable report area allows you to display only certain data using a list arrow?

 a. Values

 b. Column Labels

 c. Report Filter

 d. Row Labels

14. To make changes to PivotTable data, you must:

 a. Drag a column header to the column area.

 b. Create a page field.

 c. Edit cells in the PivotTable, then refresh the source list.

 d. Edit cells in the source list, then refresh the PivotTable.

15. When a nonnumeric field is added to a PivotTable, it is placed in the _____ area.

 a. VALUES

 b. Report Filter

 c. ROWS

 d. COLUMNS

Skills Review

1. Plan and design a PivotTable report.

 a. Start Excel, open the file titled EX L-2.xlsx from the location where you store your Data Files, then save it as **EX L-Product Sales**.

 b. Review the fields and data values in the worksheet.

 c. Verify that the worksheet data contains repeated values in one or more fields.

 d. Verify that there are not any blank rows or columns in the range A1:E25.

 e. Verify that the worksheet data contains a field that can be summed in a PivotTable.

2. Create a PivotTable report.

 a. Create a PivotTable report on a new worksheet using the Sales worksheet data in the range A1:E25.

 b. Add the Product ID field in the PivotTable Fields List pane to the COLUMNS area.

 c. Add the Sales field in the PivotTable Fields List pane to the VALUES Area.

 d. Add the Store field in the PivotTable Fields List pane to the ROWS area.

 e. Add the Sales Rep field in the PivotTable Fields List pane to the ROWS area below the Store field.

3. Change a PivotTable's summary function and design.

 a. Change the PivotTable summary function to Average.

 b. Rename the new sheet **Sales PivotTable**.

 c. Change the PivotTable Style to Pivot Style Light 20. Format the sales values in the PivotTable as Currency with a $ symbol and two decimal places.

 d. Enter your name in the center section of the PivotTable report footer, then save the workbook.

 e. Change the Summary function back to Sum. Remove the headers "Row Labels" and "Column Labels."

4. Filter and sort PivotTable data.

 a. Sort the stores in ascending order by total sales.

 b. Use slicers to filter the PivotTable to display sales for product IDs 100 and 200 in the DC and Seattle stores.

 c. Clear the filters and delete the slicers.

 d. Add the Region field to the FILTERS area in the PivotTable Fields List pane. Use the FILTERS list arrow to display sales for only the East region. Display sales for all regions.

 e. Save the workbook.

5. Update a PivotTable report.

 a. With the Sales PivotTable sheet active, note the NY total for Product ID 300.

 b. Activate the Sales sheet, and change K. Lyons's sales of Product ID 300 in cell D7 to **$9,000**.

 c. Refresh the PivotTable so it reflects the new sales figure.

 d. Verify the NY total for Product ID 300 decreased to $18,254. Save the workbook.

Skills Review (continued)

6. **Explore PivotTable Data Relationships.**

 a. In the PivotTable Fields List, drag the Product ID field from the COLUMNS area to the ROWS area below the Sales Rep field. Drag the Sales Rep field from the ROWS area to the COLUMNS area.

 b. Drag the Store field from the ROWS area to the FILTERS area below the Region field. Drag the Product ID field back to the COLUMNS area.

 c. Drag the Store field back to the ROWS area.

 d. Remove the Sales Rep field from the PivotTable.

 e. Compare your completed PivotTable to FIGURE L-24, save the workbook.

7. **Create a PivotChart report.**

 a. Use the existing PivotTable data to create a Clustered Column PivotChart report.

 b. Move the PivotChart to a new worksheet, and name the sheet **PivotChart**.

 c. Add the title **Total Sales** above the chart.

 d. Filter the chart to display only sales data for the east region. Display the sales data for all regions. Hide all of the Field Buttons.

 e. Add your name to the center section of the PivotChart sheet footer. Compare your PivotChart to FIGURE L-25, save the workbook.

8. **Use the GETPIVOTDATA function.**

 a. In cell D27 of the Sales sheet type =, click the Sales PivotTable sheet, click the cell that contains the grand total for LA, then press [Enter].

 b. Review the GETPIVOTDATA function that was entered in cell D27.

 c. Enter your name in the Sales sheet footer, compare your Sales sheet to FIGURE L-26, save the workbook, then preview the sales worksheet.

 d. Close the workbook and exit Excel. Submit the workbook to your instructor.

Independent Challenge 1

You are the accountant for the Service Department of an HVAC company. The Service Department employs three technicians that service heating and air conditioning. Until recently, the owner had been tracking the technicians' hours manually in a log. You have created an Excel worksheet to track the following basic information: service date, technician name, job #, job category, hours, and warranty information. The owner has asked you to analyze the billing data to provide information about the number of hours being spent on the various job categories. He also wants to find out how much of the technicians' work is covered by warranties. You will create a PivotTable that sums the hours by category and technician. Once the table is completed, you will create a column chart representing the billing information.

 a. Start Excel, open the file titled EX L-3.xlsx from the location where you store your Data Files, then save it as **EX L-Service**.

 b. Create a PivotTable on a separate worksheet that sums hours by technician and category. Use FIGURE L-27 as a guide.

 c. Name the new sheet **PivotTable**, and apply the Pivot Style Medium 14.

 d. Add slicers to filter the PivotTable using the category and technician data. Display only service data for Randal's category Level 1 jobs. Remove the filters, and remove the slicers.

FIGURE L-24

FIGURE L-25

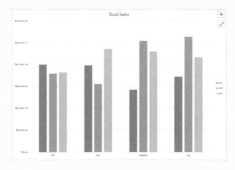

FIGURE L-26

FIGURE L-27

Independent Challenge 1 (continued)

e. Add the Warranty field to the FILTERS area of the PivotTable. Display only the PivotTable data for jobs covered by warranties.

f. Remove the headers of "Column Labels" and "Row Labels" from the PivotTable.

g. Create a clustered column PivotChart that shows the warranty hours. Move the PivotChart to a new sheet named **PivotChart**.

h. Add the title **Warranty Hours** above the chart.

i. Change the PivotChart filter to display hours where the work was not covered by a warranty. Edit the chart title to read **Nonwarranty Hours**.

j. Hide the field buttons on the chart.

k. Add your name to the center section of the PivotTable and PivotChart footers, then save the workbook. Preview the PivotTable and the PivotChart. Close the workbook and exit Excel. Submit the workbook to your instructor.

Independent Challenge 2

You are the owner of an office supply store called Buffalo Office Supplies. You sell products at the store as well as online. You also take orders by phone from your catalog customers. You have been using Excel to maintain a sales summary for the second quarter sales of the different types of products sold by the company. You want to create a PivotTable to analyze and graph the sales in each product category by month and type of order.

a. Start Excel, open the file titled EX L-4.xlsx from the location where you store your Data Files, then save it as **EX L-Office Solutions**.

b. Create a PivotTable on a new worksheet named **PivotTable** that sums the sales amount for each category across the rows and each type of sale down the columns. Add the month field as an inner row label. Use FIGURE L-28 as a guide.

c. Move the month field to the FILTERS area. Display the sum of sales data for the month of April.

d. Turn off the grand totals for the columns. (*Hint*: Use the Grand Totals button in the Layout group on the PIVOTTABLE TOOLS DESIGN tab and choose On for Rows Only.)

e. Change the summary function in the PivotTable to Average.

f. Format the sales values using the Currency format with two decimal places and the $ symbol. Widen columns C and D to display the sales data.

g. On the Sales worksheet, change the April online paper sales in cell D3 to $20,221. Update the PivotTable to reflect this increase in sales.

h. Sort the average sales of categories from smallest to largest using the grand total of sales.

i. Create a stacked column PivotChart report for the average April sales data for all three types of sales.

j. Change the PivotChart to display the June sales data.

k. Move the PivotChart to a new sheet, and name the chart sheet **PivotChart**.

l. Add the title **Average June Sales** above your chart.

m. On the PivotTable, move the Month field from the FILTERS area to the ROWS area of the PivotTable below the Category field.

n. Add a slicer to filter the PivotTable by month. Use the slicer to display the average sales in April and May.

o. Check the PivotChart to be sure that the filtered data is displayed.

p. Change the chart title to **Average Sales April and May** to describe the charted sales.

q. Add your name to the center section of the PivotTable and PivotChart worksheet footers, save the workbook, then preview the PivotTable and the PivotChart. Close the workbook and exit Excel. Submit the workbook to your instructor.

FIGURE L-28

Independent Challenge 3

You are the North American sales manager for a drug store supply company with sales offices in the United States and Canada. You use Excel to keep track of the staff in the U.S. and Canadian offices. Management asks you to provide a summary table showing information on your sales staff, including their locations, status, and titles. You will create a PivotTable and PivotChart summarizing this information.

a. Start Excel, open the file titled EX L-5.xlsx from the location where you store your Data Files, then save it as **EX L-Sales Employees**.

b. Create a PivotTable on a new worksheet that shows the number of employees in each city, with the names of the cities listed across the columns, the titles listed down the rows, and the status indented below the titles. (*Hint*: Remember that the default summary function for cells containing text is Count.) Use FIGURE L-29 as a guide. Rename the new sheet **PivotTable**.

FIGURE L-29

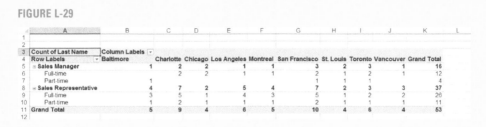

	A	B	C	D	E	F	G	H	I	J	K	L
1												
2												
3	Count of Last Name	Column Labels										
4	Row Labels	Baltimore	Charlotte	Chicago	Los Angeles	Montreal	San Francisco	St. Louis	Toronto	Vancouver	Grand Total	
5	Sales Manager	1	2	2	1	1	3	2	3	1	16	
6	Full-time		2	2	1	1	2	1	2	1	12	
7	Part-time	1					1	1	1		4	
8	Sales Representative	4	7	2	5	4	7	2	3	3	37	
9	Full-time	3	5	1	4	3	5	1	2	2	26	
10	Part-time	1	2	1	1	1	2	1	1	1	11	
11	Grand Total	5	9	4	6	5	10	4	6	4	53	
12												

c. Change the structure of the PivotTable to display the data as shown in FIGURE L-30.

d. Add a report filter using the Region field. Display only the U.S. employees.

e. Create a clustered column PivotChart from the PivotTable and move the chart to its own sheet named PivotChart. Rearrange the fields to create the PivotChart shown in FIGURE L-31.

f. Add the title **U.S. Sales Staff** above the chart.

g. Add the Pivot Style Light 18 style to the PivotTable.

h. Insert a new row in the Employees worksheet above row 7. In the new row, add information reflecting the recent hiring of Kate Conroy, a full-time sales manager at the Baltimore office. Update the PivotTable to display the new employee information.

i. Add the label **Total Chicago Staff** in cell G1 of the Employees sheet. Widen column G to fit the label.

j. Enter a function in cell H1 that retrieves the total number of employees located in Chicago from the PivotTable. Change the page orientation of the Employees sheet to landscape.

k. Use a slicer to filter the PivotTable to display only the data for the cities of Baltimore, Chicago, Los Angeles, and San Francisco.

l. Add another slicer for the Title field to display only the sales representatives.

m. Verify that the number of Chicago employees in cell H1 of the Employees sheet is now 2.

FIGURE L-30

3	Count of Last Name	Column Labels		
4	Row Labels	Full-time	Part-time	Grand Total
5	Sales Manager	12	4	16
6	Baltimore		1	1
7	Charlotte	2		2
8	Chicago	2		2
9	Los Angeles	1		1
10	Montreal	1		1
11	San Francisco	2	1	3
12	St. Louis	1	1	2
13	Toronto	2	1	3
14	Vancouver	1		1
15	Sales Representative	26	11	37
16	Baltimore	3	1	4
17	Charlotte	5	2	7
18	Chicago	1	1	2
19	Los Angeles	4	1	5
20	Montreal	3	1	4
21	San Francisco	5	2	7
22	St. Louis	1	1	2
23	Toronto	2	1	3
24	Vancouver	2	1	3
25	Grand Total	38	15	53
26				

FIGURE L-31

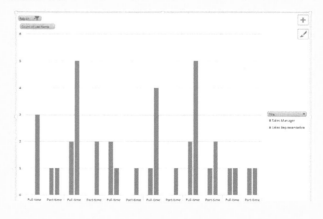

Independent Challenge 3 (continued)

n. Remove the slicers but do not remove the filters.

o. Add your name to the center section of all three worksheet footers, save the workbook, then preview the PivotTable, the first page of the Employees worksheet, and the PivotChart.

p. Close the workbook and exit Excel. Submit the workbook to your instructor.

Independent Challenge 4: Explore

You are the Regional sales manager for a Texas software support company with offices in Austin, Houston, and Dallas. You use Excel to keep track of the revenue generated by sales contracts in these offices. The CEO asks you to provide a summary table showing information on your offices' revenue over the past two years.

a. Start Excel, open the file EX L-6.xlsx, then save it as **EX L-Revenue** in the location where you save your Data Files.

b. Create a PivotTable on a separate worksheet that sums revenue by office, year, and month. Use FIGURE L-32 as a guide.

c. Name the new sheet **Summary**, and apply the Pivot Style Light 19.

d. Add slicers to filter the PivotTable using the Quarter and Office fields. Display only revenue data for Austin and Dallas for quarters 3 and 4. Remove the filters, but do not remove the slicers.

e. Format the Office slicer using the Slicer Style Light 4 in the Slicer Styles gallery on the SLICER TOOLS OPTIONS tab.

f. Change the Office slicer caption from Office to **Sales Office**. (*Hint*: Use the Slicer Caption text box in the Slicer group of the SLICER TOOLS OPTIONS tab.)

g. Change the Quarter slicer buttons to appear in two columns, with a button height of .3" and a button width of .56". (*Hint*: Use the options in the Buttons group of the SLICER TOOLS OPTIONS tab.)

h. Change the Quarter slicer shape to a height of 1.2" and width of 1.33". (*Hint*: Use the options in the Size group of the SLICER TOOLS OPTIONS tab.) Shorten the Sales Office slicer shape by dragging the lower slicer edge up to just below the bottom button.

i. Add a calculated field named **Average Sale** to the PivotTable to calculate the average sale using the formula =Revenue/Number of Contracts. Change the labels in cells C5, E5, and G5 to **Average** and format all of the Average labels as right justified.

j. Add the Quarter field to the PivotTable as a Report Filter.

k. Copy each quarter's data to a separate sheet. (*Hint*: Select the Quarter field in cell A1, click the Options list arrow in the PivotTable group of the PIVOTTABLE TOOLS ANALYZE tab, then select Show Report Filter Pages.) View the sheet for each quarter.

l. Group all of the worksheets, add your name to the center section of the footer for the worksheets, save the workbook, then preview the worksheets.

m. Close the workbook and exit Excel. Submit the workbook to your instructor.

FIGURE L-32

Excel 2013

Visual Workshop

Open the file EX L-7.xlsx from the location where you store your Data Files, then save it as **EX L-Real Estate**. Using the data in the workbook, create the PivotTable shown in FIGURE L-33 on a worksheet named PivotTable, then generate a PivotChart on a new sheet named PivotChart as shown in FIGURE L-34. (*Hint*: The PivotTable has been formatted using the Pivot Style Medium 2. Note that the PivotChart has been filtered.) Add your name to the PivotTable and the PivotChart footers, then preview the PivotTable and the PivotChart. Save the workbook, close the workbook, exit Excel, then submit the workbook to your instructor.

FIGURE L-33

	A	B	C	D	E	F
1						
2						
3	**Sum of Sales**					
4		Jan	Feb	Mar	Grand Total	
5	⊟ Commercial	$17,672,129.00	$18,851,236.00	$31,580,063.00	$68,103,428.00	
6	Boston	$10,018,009.00	$3,115,222.00	$12,025,664.00	$25,158,895.00	
7	DC	$4,711,899.00	$6,605,556.00	$9,504,845.00	$20,822,300.00	
8	Miami	$2,942,221.00	$9,130,458.00	$10,049,554.00	$22,122,233.00	
9	⊟ Land	$120,067,314.00	$165,020,142.00	$96,586,350.00	$381,673,806.00	
10	Boston	$75,518,444.00	$51,027,452.00	$41,025,444.00	$167,571,340.00	
11	DC	$18,505,645.00	$32,503,133.00	$37,515,452.00	$88,524,230.00	
12	Miami	$26,043,225.00	$81,489,557.00	$18,045,454.00	$125,578,236.00	
13	⊟ Residential	$76,578,375.00	$117,522,506.00	$182,574,063.00	$376,674,944.00	
14	Boston	$40,027,554.00	$29,011,550.00	$76,020,776.00	$145,059,880.00	
15	DC	$16,505,377.00	$68,508,511.00	$65,504,845.00	$150,518,733.00	
16	Miami	$20,045,444.00	$20,002,445.00	$41,048,442.00	$81,096,331.00	
17	**Grand Total**	$214,317,818.00	$301,393,884.00	$310,740,476.00	$826,452,178.00	
18						
19						
20						
21						
22						

FIGURE L-34

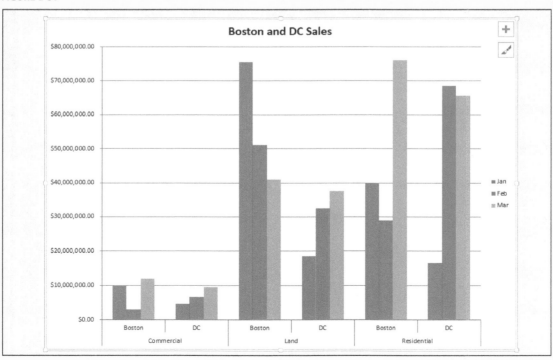

Exchanging Data with Other Programs

CASE Quest's upper management has asked Kate Morgan, the vice president of sales, to research the possible purchase of Service Adventures, a small company specializing in combining travel with volunteer work for corporate employees. Kate is reviewing the organization's files and developing a presentation on the feasibility of acquiring the company. She asks you to help set up the data exchange between Excel and other programs.

Unit Objectives

After completing this unit, you will be able to:

- Plan a data exchange
- Import a text file
- Import a database table
- Insert a graphic file in a worksheet

- Embed a workbook in a Word document
- Link a workbook to a Word document
- Link an Excel chart to a PowerPoint slide
- Import a table into Access

Files You Will Need

EX M-1.txt	EX M-13.pptx
EX M-2.accdb	EX M-14.xlsx
EX M-3.jpg	EX M-15.xlsx
EX M-4.docx	EX M-16.pptx
EX M-5.xlsx	EX M-17.txt
EX M-6.pptx	EX M-18.docx
EX M-7.xlsx	EX M-19.xlsx
EX M-8.xlsx	EX M-20.docx
EX M-9.txt	EX M-21.xlsx
EX M-10.accdb	EX M-22.xlsx
EX M-11.jpg	EX M-23.accdb
EX M-12.xlsx	

©Katerina Havelkova/Shutterstock

Plan a Data Exchange

Learning
Outcomes
• Plan a data
exchange between
Office programs
• Develop an
understanding of
data exchange
vocabulary

Because the tools available in Microsoft Office programs are designed to be compatible, exchanging data between Excel and other programs is easy. The first step involves planning what you want to accomplish with each data exchange. **CASE** ▶ *Kate asks you to use the following guidelines to plan data exchanges between Excel and other programs in order to complete the business analysis project.*

DETAILS

To plan an exchange of data:

• **Identify the data you want to exchange, its file type, and, if possible, the program used to create it**

 Whether the data you want to exchange is a graphics file, a database file, a worksheet, or consists only of text, it is important to identify the data's **source program** (the program used to create it) and the file type. Once you identify the source program, you can determine options for exchanging the data with Excel. Kate needs to analyze a text file containing the Service Adventures tour sales. Although she does not know the source program, Kate knows that the file contains unformatted text. A file that consists of text but no formatting is sometimes called an **ASCII** or **text** file. Because ASCII is a universally accepted file format, Kate can easily import an ASCII file into Excel. See TABLE M-1 for a partial list of other file formats that Excel can import.

• **Determine the program with which you want to exchange data**

 Besides knowing which program created the data you want to exchange, you must also identify which program will receive the data, called the **destination program**. This determines the procedure you use to perform the exchange. You might want to insert a graphic object into an Excel worksheet or add a spreadsheet to a Word document. Kate received a database table of Service Adventures' corporate customers created with the Access database program. After determining that Excel can import Access tables and reviewing the import procedure, she imports the database file into Excel so she can analyze it using Excel tools.

• **Determine the goal of your data exchange**

 Windows offers two ways to transfer data within and between programs that allow you to retain some connection with the source program. These data transfer methods use a Windows feature known as **object linking and embedding**, or **OLE**. The data to be exchanged, called an **object**, may consist of text, a worksheet, or any other type of data. You use **embedding** to insert a copy of the original object into the destination document and, if necessary, to then edit this data separately from the source document. This process is illustrated in FIGURE M-1. You use **linking** when you want the information you inserted to be updated automatically if the data in the source document changes. This process is illustrated in FIGURE M-2. You learn more about embedding and linking later in this unit. Kate has determined that she needs to use both object embedding and object linking for her analysis and presentation project.

• **Set up the data exchange**

 When you exchange data between two programs, it is often best to start both programs before starting the exchange. You might also want to tile the program windows on the screen either horizontally or vertically so that you can see both during the exchange. You will work with Excel, Word, Access, and PowerPoint when exchanging data for this project.

• **Execute the data exchange**

 The steps you use will vary, depending on the type of data you want to exchange. Kate is ready to have you start the data exchanges for the business analysis of Service Adventures.

FIGURE M-1: Embedded object

FIGURE M-2: Linked object

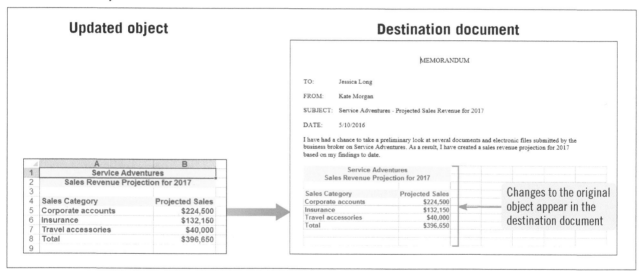

TABLE M-1: File formats Excel can import

file format	file extension(s)	file format	file extension(s)
Access	.mdb, .accdb	All Data Sources	.odc, .udl, .dsn
Text	.txt, .prn, .csv, .dif, .sylk	OpenDocument Spreadsheet	.ods
Query	.iqy, .dqy, .oqy, .rqy	XML	.xml
Web page	.htm, .html, .mht, .mhtml	dBASE	.dbf

Import a Text File

Learning
Outcomes
• Import a text file
 into an Excel
 workbook
• Format text data

You can import text data into Excel and save the imported data in Excel format. Text files use a tab or space as the **delimiter**, or column separator, to separate columns of data. When you import a text file into Excel, the Text Import Wizard automatically opens and describes how text is separated in the imported file. **CASE** ▶ *Now that Kate has planned the data exchange, she wants you to import a tab-delimited text file containing branch and profit data from Service Adventures.*

STEPS

1. **Start Excel if necessary, create a blank workbook, click the** DATA **tab, click** From Text **in the Get External Data group, then navigate to the location where you store your Data Files**

 The Import Text File dialog box shows only text files.

2. **Click** EX M-1.txt, **then click** Import

 The first Text Import Wizard dialog box opens, as shown in **FIGURE M-3**. Under Original data type, the Delimited option button is selected. In the Preview of file box, line 1 indicates that the file contains two columns of data: Branch and Profit. No changes are necessary in this dialog box.

QUICK TIP
You can select the My data has headers checkbox when importing data.

3. **Click** Next

 The second Text Import Wizard dialog box opens. Under Delimiters, Tab is selected as the delimiter, indicating that tabs separate the columns of incoming data. The Data preview box contains a line showing where the tab delimiters divide the data into columns.

4. **Click** Next

 The third Text Import Wizard dialog box opens with options for formatting the two columns of data. Under Column data format, the General option button is selected. The Data preview area shows that both columns will be formatted with the General format. This is the best formatting option for text mixed with numbers.

5. **Click** Finish, **then click** OK

 Excel imports the text file into the blank workbook starting in cell A1 of the worksheet as two columns of data: Branch and Profit.

6. **Click the** FILE **tab, click** Save, **navigate to the location where you store your Data Files, change the filename to** EX M-Branch Profit, **then click** Save

 The text file information is saved as an Excel workbook. The worksheet information would be easier to read if it were formatted and if it showed the total profit for all regions.

7. **Click cell A8, type** Total Profit, **click cell B8, click the** HOME **tab, click the** AutoSum **button in the Editing group, then click the** Enter button ✓ **on the formula bar**

8. **Rename the sheet tab** Profit, **center the column labels, apply bold formatting to them, format the data in column B using the Currency style with the $ symbol and no decimal places, then click cell** A1

 FIGURE M-4 shows the completed worksheet, which analyzes the text file data you imported into Excel.

9. **Add your name to the center section of the worksheet footer, save the workbook, preview the worksheet, close the workbook, then submit the workbook to your instructor**

FIGURE M-3: First Text Import Wizard dialog box

Original data is delimited

Two column headings

Preview of data

FIGURE M-4: Completed worksheet with imported text file

	A	B
1	**Branch**	**Profit**
2	Miami	$200,023
3	Chicago	$331,774
4	New York	$172,921
5	Los Angeles	$253,910
6	Boston	$264,512
7	Portland	$199,531
8	Total Profit	$1,422,671
9		

Columns from text file

Total profit added after importing data

Excel 2013

Importing files using other methods

Another way to open the Text Import Wizard to import a text file into Excel is to click the FILE tab, click Open, then navigate to the location where you store your Data Files. In the Open dialog box you will see only files that match the file types listed in the Files of type box—usually Microsoft Excel files. To import a text file, you need to change the file type: click All Excel Files, click Text Files (*.prn; *.txt; *.csv), click the text file name, then click Open. You can also drag the icon representing a text file on the Windows desktop into a blank worksheet window. Excel will create a worksheet from the data without using the Wizard.

Import a Database Table

Learning
Outcomes
• Import Access data
 into an Excel
 workbook
• Format imported
 data

In addition to importing text files, you can also use Excel to import data from database tables. A **database table** is a set of data organized using columns and rows that is created in a database program. A **database program** is an application, such as Microsoft Access, that lets you manage large amounts of data organized in tables. FIGURE M-5 shows an Access table. To import data from an Access table into Excel, you can copy the table in Access and paste it into an Excel worksheet. This method places a copy of the Access data into Excel; if you change the data in the Access file, the data will not change in the Excel copy. If you want the data in Excel to update when you edit the Access source file, you create a connection, or a **link**, to the database. This lets you work with current data in Excel without recopying the data from Access whenever the Access data changes. CASE ▶ *Kate received a database table containing Service Adventures' corporate customer information, which was created with Access. She asks you to import this table into an Excel workbook. She would also like you to format, sort, and total the data.*

STEPS

1. **Click the File Tab, click New, then click Blank workbook**
 A new workbook opens, displaying a blank worksheet for you to use to import the Access data.

2. **Click the DATA tab, click the From Access button in the Get External Data group, then navigate to the location where you store your Data Files**

3. **Click EX M-2.accdb, click Open, verify that the Table option button and the Existing worksheet button are selected in the Import Data dialog box, then click OK**
 Excel inserts the Access data into the worksheet as a table with the table style Medium 2 format applied, as shown in FIGURE M-6.

4. **Rename the sheet tab Customer Information, then format the data in columns F and G with the Currency format with the $ symbol and no decimal places**
 You are ready to sort the data using the values in column G.

5. **Click the cell G1 list arrow, then click Sort Smallest to Largest**
 The records are reorganized in ascending order according to the amount of the 2017 orders.

6. **Click the TABLE TOOLS DESIGN tab if necessary, click the Total Row check box in the Table Style Options group to select it, click cell F19, click the cell F19 list arrow next to cell F19, select Sum from the drop-down function list, then click cell A1**
 Your completed worksheet should match FIGURE M-7.

7. **Add your name to the center section of the worksheet footer, change the worksheet orientation to landscape, save the workbook as EX M-Customer Information, then preview the worksheet**

FIGURE M-5: **Access Table**

Table data

COMPANY NAME	CITY	STATE	CONTACT	PHONE	2016 Travel	2017 Travel
ATM Research	Jacksonville	FL	Linda Jackson	904-334-4388	6000	8050
Computer City	Chicago	IL	Mary Lindsey	872-335-9934	7350	5147
Safety Insurance	Portland	OR	Sally Wilkins	503-334-4421	3887	3287
Cornerstone Security	Naples	FL	Jack Watson	239-356-9943	1187	1475
Jones & Jones Law	New York	NY	Amy Folley	212-356-4595	1354	1211
Miami Mutual Mortgage	Miami	FL	Nancy Albert	305-332-3393	1501	1702
Symphonic Equipment	Tampa	FL	Jenny Gull	813-434-2232	2250	2641
Vista Minerals	Los Angeles	CA	Paula Gomez	323-538-7789	1878	1935
Northern Bank	Boston	MA	Alex Handy	617-733-9877	1654	1700
Recycle Paper	Jacksonville	FL	Mary Turley	904-733-9987	1322	1474
South Shore Pools	New York	NY	Corey Olsen	212-233-4432	2174	2654
First Investments	Naples	FL	Jeff Punatar	239-233-9939	2456	2474
Gulf Art	Tampa	FL	Gilbert Hahn	813-334-2203	7102	7254
Organic Foods	Orlando	FL	Lisa Sanchez	321-434-4432	8247	8364
Toddler Toys	Miami	FL	Harry Yang	305-356-9987	6324	6547
International Office	Sarasota	FL	Pam Miller	941-334-6785	5287	5471
Turners Nurseries	Tampa	FL	Willy McFee	813-538-4493	2397	3757
					0	0

FIGURE M-6: **Access table imported to Excel**

	A	B	C	D	E	F	G
1	COMPANY NAME	CITY	STATE	CONTACT	PHONE	2016 Travel	2017 Travel
2	ATM Research	Jacksonville	FL	Linda Jackson	904-334-4388	6000	8050
3	Computer City	Chicago	IL	Mary Lindsey	872-335-9934	7350	5147
4	Safety Insurance	Portland	OR	Sally Wilkins	503-334-4421	3887	3287
5	Cornerstone Security	Naples	FL	Jack Watson	239-356-9943	1187	1475
6	Jones & Jones Law	New York	NY	Amy Folley	212-356-4595	1354	1211
7	Miami Mutual Mortgage	Miami	FL	Nancy Albert	305-332-3393	1501	1702
8	Symphonic Equipment	Tampa	FL	Jenny Gull	813-434-2232	2250	2641
9	Vista Minerals	Los Angeles	CA	Paula Gomez	323-538-7789	1878	1935
10	Northern Bank	Boston	MA	Alex Handy	617-733-9877	1654	1700
11	Recycle Paper	Jacksonville	FL	Mary Turley	904-733-9987	1322	1474
12	South Shore Pools	New York	NY	Corey Olsen	212-233-4432	2174	2654
13	First Investments	Naples	FL	Jeff Punatar	239-233-9939	2456	2474
14	Gulf Art	Tampa	FL	Gilbert Hahn	813-334-2203	7102	7254
15	Organic Foods	Orlando	FL	Lisa Sanchez	321-434-4432	8247	8364
16	Toddler Toys	Miami	FL	Harry Yang	305-356-9987	6324	6547
17	International Office	Sarasota	FL	Pam Miller	941-334-6785	5287	5471
18	Turners Nurseries	Tampa	FL	Willy McFee	813-538-4493	2397	3757
19							

Sheet1

FIGURE M-7: **Completed worksheet containing imported data**

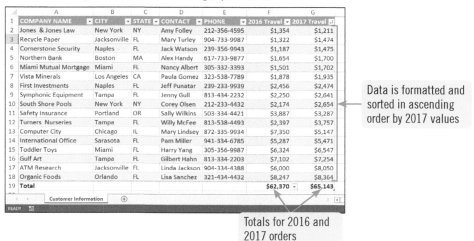

	A	B	C	D	E	F	G
1	COMPANY NAME	CITY	STATE	CONTACT	PHONE	2016 Travel	2017 Travel
2	Jones & Jones Law	New York	NY	Amy Folley	212-356-4595	$1,354	$1,211
3	Recycle Paper	Jacksonville	FL	Mary Turley	904-733-9987	$1,322	$1,474
4	Cornerstone Security	Naples	FL	Jack Watson	239-356-9943	$1,187	$1,475
5	Northern Bank	Boston	MA	Alex Handy	617-733-9877	$1,654	$1,700
6	Miami Mutual Mortgage	Miami	FL	Nancy Albert	305-332-3393	$1,501	$1,702
7	Vista Minerals	Los Angeles	CA	Paula Gomez	323-538-7789	$1,878	$1,935
8	First Investments	Naples	FL	Jeff Punatar	239-233-9939	$2,456	$2,474
9	Symphonic Equipment	Tampa	FL	Jenny Gull	813-434-2232	$2,250	$2,641
10	South Shore Pools	New York	NY	Corey Olsen	212-233-4432	$2,174	$2,654
11	Safety Insurance	Portland	OR	Sally Wilkins	503-334-4421	$3,887	$3,287
12	Turners Nurseries	Tampa	FL	Willy McFee	813-538-4493	$2,397	$3,757
13	Computer City	Chicago	IL	Mary Lindsey	872-335-9934	$7,350	$5,147
14	International Office	Sarasota	FL	Pam Miller	941-334-6785	$5,287	$5,471
15	Toddler Toys	Miami	FL	Harry Yang	305-356-9987	$6,324	$6,547
16	Gulf Art	Tampa	FL	Gilbert Hahn	813-334-2203	$7,102	$7,254
17	ATM Research	Jacksonville	FL	Linda Jackson	904-334-4388	$6,000	$8,050
18	Organic Foods	Orlando	FL	Lisa Sanchez	321-434-4432	$8,247	$8,364
19	Total					$62,370	$65,143

Data is formatted and sorted in ascending order by 2017 values

Totals for 2016 and 2017 orders

Customer Information

Learning
Outcomes
• Insert an image
 into an Excel
 worksheet
• Add a style to an
 image

Insert a Graphic File in a Worksheet

A graphic object, such as a drawing, logo, or photograph, can greatly enhance your worksheet's visual impact. You can insert a graphic image into a worksheet and then format it using the options on the Format tab. **CASE** ▶ *Kate wants you to insert the Quest logo at the top of the customer worksheet. The company's graphic designer created the image and saved it in JPG format. You insert and format the image on the worksheet. You start by creating a space for the logo on the worksheet.*

STEPS

1. **Select rows 1 through 5, click the HOME tab, then click the Insert button in the Cells group**
 Five blank rows appear above the header row, leaving space to insert the picture.

2. **Click cell A1, click the INSERT tab, then click the Pictures button in the Illustrations group**
 The Insert Picture dialog box opens. You want to insert a picture that already exists in a file. The file has a .jpg file extension, so it is called a "jay-peg" file.

3. **Navigate to the location where you store your Data Files, click EX M-3.jpg, then click Insert**
 Excel inserts the image and displays the PICTURE TOOLS FORMAT tab. The small circles around the picture's border are sizing handles. Sizing handles appear when a picture is selected; you use them to change the size of a picture.

4. **Position the pointer over the sizing handle in the logo's lower-right corner until the pointer becomes ⬉, then drag the corner up and to the left so that the logo's outline fits within rows 1 through 5**
 Compare your screen to FIGURE M-8. You decide to remove the logo's white background.

QUICK TIP
You can correct an image by selecting it, clicking the Corrections button in the Adjust group on the PICTURE TOOLS FORMAT tab, then clicking an option in the Sharpen/Soften or Brightness/Contrast section.

5. **With the image selected, click the Color button in the Adjust group of the Picture Tools Format tab, click Set Transparent Color, then use ✐ to click the white background on the logo**
 The logo is now transparent, and shows the worksheet gridlines behind it. You decide that the logo will be more visually interesting with a frame and a border color.

6. **With the image selected, click the More button ⬇ in the Picture Styles group, point to several styles and observe the effect on the graphic, click the Reflected Bevel, White style (the third from the right in the last row), click the Picture Border list arrow in the Picture Styles group, then click Blue, Accent 1, Lighter 40% in the Theme Colors group**
 You decide to add a glow to the image.

7. **Click the Picture Effects button in the Picture Styles group, point to Glow, point to More Glow Colors, click Blue, Accent 1, Lighter 80% in the Theme Colors group, resize the logo as necessary to fit it in rows 1 through 5, then drag the logo above the column D data**
 You decide to add an artistic effect to the image.

8. **Click the Artistic Effects button in the Adjust group, click Light Screen (First effect in the third row), then click cell A1**
 Compare your worksheet to FIGURE M-9.

9. **Save the workbook, preview the worksheet, close the workbook, exit Excel, then submit the workbook to your instructor**

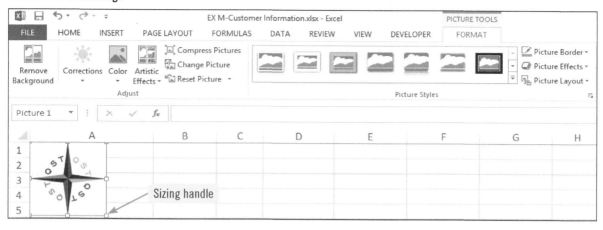

	A	B	C	D	E	F	G	H	I
1									
2					Formatted image				
3									
4									
5									
6	COMPANY NAME	CITY	STATE	CONTACT	PHONE	2016 Travel	2017 Travel		
7	Jones & Jones Law	New York	NY	Amy Folley	212-356-4595	$1,354	$1,211		
8	Recycle Paper	Jacksonville	FL	Mary Turley	904-733-9987	$1,322	$1,474		
9	Cornerstone Security	Naples	FL	Jack Watson	239-356-9943	$1,187	$1,475		

Excel 2013

Formatting SmartArt graphics

SmartArt graphics provide another way to visually communicate information on a worksheet. A **SmartArt graphic** is a professionally designed illustration with text and graphics. Each SmartArt type communicates a kind of information or relationship, such as a list, process, or hierarchy. Each type has various layouts you can choose. For example, you can choose from pyramid, process, picture, list, cycle, hierarchy, relationship and matrix layouts, allowing you to illustrate your information in many different ways. To insert a SmartArt graphic into a worksheet, click the INSERT tab, then click the SmartArt button in the Illustrations group. In the Choose a SmartArt Graphic dialog box, choose from eight SmartArt types: List, Process, Cycle, Hierarchy, Relationship, Matrix, Pyramid, and Picture. The dialog box also describes the type of information that is appropriate for each selected layout. After you choose a layout and click OK, a SmartArt object appears on your worksheet. As you enter text in the text entry areas, the font automatically resizes to fit the graphic. The SMARTART TOOLS DESIGN tab lets you choose

color schemes and styles for your SmartArt. You can add effects to SmartArt graphics using choices on the SMARTART TOOLS FORMAT tab. FIGURE M-10 shows examples of SmartArt graphics. You can create a SmartArt graphic from an existing image by clicking the image, clicking the Picture Layout button in the Picture Styles group of the PICTURE TOOLS FORMAT tab, then selecting the SmartArt type.

FIGURE M-10: **Examples of SmartArt graphics**

Embed a Workbook in a Word Document

Learning Outcomes
• Embed Excel data in a Word document
• Edit an embedded file icon caption

Microsoft Office programs work together to make it easy to copy an object (such as text, data, or a graphic) in a source program and then insert it into a document in a different program (the destination program). If you insert copied Excel data using a simple Paste command, however, you retain no connection to the source program. That's why it is often more useful to embed objects rather than simply paste them. Embedding allows you to edit an Excel workbook from within the source program using that program's commands and tools. If you send a Word document with an embedded workbook to another person, you do not need to send a separate Excel file with it. All the necessary information is embedded in the Word document. When you embed information, you can either display the data itself or an icon representing the data; users double-click the icon to view the embedded data. An icon is often used rather than the data when the worksheet data is too large to fit well on a Word document. **CASE** ▶ *Kate decides to update Jessica Long, the CEO of Quest, on the project status. She asks you to prepare a Word memo that includes the projected sales workbook embedded as an icon. You begin by starting Word and opening the memo.*

STEPS

1. **Open a File Explorer window, navigate to the location where you store your Data Files, then double-click the file EX M-4.docx to open the file in Word**

 The memo opens in Word.

2. **Click the FILE tab, click Save As, navigate to the location where you store your Data Files, change the file name to EX M-Service Adventures Memo, then click Save**

 You want to embed the workbook below the last line of the document.

3. **Press [Ctrl][End], click the INSERT tab, click the Object button in the Text group, then click the Create from File tab**

 FIGURE M-11 shows the Create from File tab in the Object dialog box. You need to indicate the file you want to embed.

QUICK TIP
To display a different icon to represent the file, click the Change Icon button in the Object dialog box, scroll down the icon list in the Change Icon dialog box, and select any icon. You can also click Browse and choose an .ico file located on your computer.

4. **Click Browse, navigate to the location where you store your Data Files, click EX M-5.xlsx, click Insert, then select the Display as icon check box**

 You will change the icon label to a more descriptive name.

5. **Click Change Icon, select the text in the Caption text box, type Projected Sales, click OK twice, then click anywhere in the Word document**

 The memo contains an embedded copy of the sales projection data, displayed as an icon, as shown in **FIGURE M-12**.

TROUBLE
If the Excel program window does not come to the front automatically, click the Excel icon in the taskbar.

6. **Double-click the Projected Sales icon on the Word memo, then maximize the Excel window and the worksheet window if necessary**

 The Excel program starts and displays the embedded worksheet, with its location displayed in the title bar, as shown in **FIGURE M-13**. Any changes you make to the embedded object using Excel tools are not reflected in the source document. Similarly, if you open the source document in the source program, changes you make are not reflected in the embedded copy.

7. **Click the FILE tab, click Close, exit Excel, click the Word FILE tab, then click Save to save the memo**

FIGURE M-11: **Object dialog box**

FIGURE M-12: **Memo with embedded worksheet displayed as an icon**

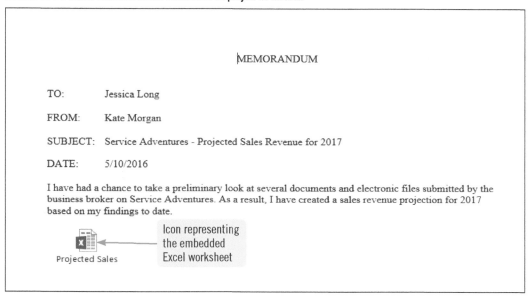

FIGURE M-13: **Embedded worksheet open in Excel**

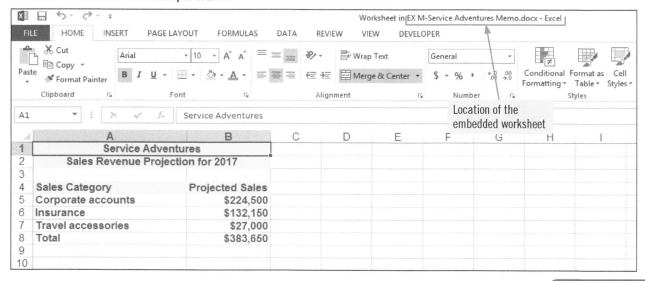

Link a Workbook to a Word Document

Learning Outcomes
• Link data from an Excel worksheet to a Word document
• Update links in a Word document

Linking a workbook to another file retains a connection with the original document as well as the original program. When you link a workbook to another program, the link contains a connection to the source document so that, when you double-click it, the source document opens for editing. In addition, any changes you make to the original workbook (the source document) are reflected in the linked object. **CASE** *Kate realizes she may need to edit the workbook she embedded in the memo to Jessica. To ensure that these changes will be reflected in the memo, she feels you should use linking instead of embedding. She asks you to delete the embedded worksheet icon and replace it with a linked version of the same workbook.*

STEPS

1. **With the Word memo still open, click the** Projected Sales Worksheet **icon to select it if necessary, then press** [Delete]

 The workbook is no longer embedded in the memo. The linking process is similar to embedding.

2. **Make sure the insertion point is below the last line of the memo, click the** INSERT **tab, click the** Object button **in the Text group, then click the** Create from File tab **in the Object dialog box**

3. **Click** Browse, **navigate to the location where you store your Data Files, click** EX M-5.xlsx, **click** Insert, **select the** Link to file check box, **then click** OK

 The memo now displays a linked copy of the sales projection data, as shown in FIGURE M-14. In the future, any changes made to the source file, EX M-5, will also be made to the linked copy in the Word memo. You verify this by making a change to the source file and viewing its effect on the memo.

4. **Click the** File tab, **click** Save, **close the Word memo, then exit Word**

5. **Start Excel, open the file** EX M-5.xlsx **from the location where you store your Data Files, click cell** B7, **type** 40000, **then press** [Enter]

 You want to verify that the same change was made automatically to the linked copy of the workbook.

6. **Start Word, open the** EX M-Service Adventures Memo.docx **file from the location where you store your Data Files, then click** Yes **if asked if you want to update the document's links**

 The memo displays the new value for Travel accessories, and the total has been updated as shown in FIGURE M-15.

7. **Click the** INSERT **tab, click the** Header button **in the Header & Footer group, click** Edit Header, **type your name in the Header area, then click the** Close Header and Footer button **in the Close group**

8. **Save the Word memo, preview it, close the file, exit Word, then submit the file to your instructor**

9. **Close the Excel worksheet without saving it, then exit Excel**

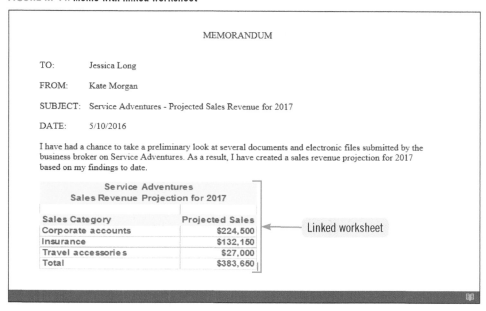

MEMORANDUM

TO: Jessica Long

FROM: Kate Morgan

SUBJECT: Service Adventures - Projected Sales Revenue for 2017

DATE: 5/10/2016

I have had a chance to take a preliminary look at several documents and electronic files submitted by the business broker on Service Adventures. As a result, I have created a sales revenue projection for 2017 based on my findings to date.

Service Adventures
Sales Revenue Projection for 2017

Sales Category	Projected Sales
Corporate accounts	$224,500
Insurance	$132,150
Travel accessories	$27,000
Total	$383,650

← Linked worksheet

FIGURE M-15: Memo with updated values

MEMORANDUM

TO: Jessica Long

FROM: Kate Morgan

SUBJECT: Service Adventures - Projected Sales Revenue for 2017

DATE: 5/10/2016

I have had a chance to take a preliminary look at several documents and electronic files submitted by the business broker on Service Adventures. As a result, I have created a sales revenue projection for 2017 based on my findings to date.

Service Adventures
Sales Revenue Projection for 2017

Sales Category	Projected Sales
Corporate accounts	$224,500
Insurance	$132,150
Travel accessories	$40,000
Total	$396,650

Values update to match those in the source document

Managing links

When you open a document containing linked data, you are asked if you want to update the linked data. You can manage the updating of links by clicking the FILE tab, and clicking Edit Links to Files in the right pane. The Links dialog box opens, allowing you to change a link's update from the default setting of automatic to manual. The Links dialog box also allows you to change the link source, permanently break a link, open the source file, and manually update a link. If you send your linked files to another user, the links will be broken because the linked file path references the local machine where you inserted the links. Because the file path will not be valid on the recipient user's machine, the links will no longer be updated when the user opens the destination document. To correct this, recipients who have both the destination and source documents can use the Links dialog box to change the link's source in the destination document to their own machines. Then the links will be automatically updated when they open the destination document in the future.

Learning
Outcomes
• Link an Excel chart
to a PowerPoint
slide
• Configure auto-
matic links in a
PowerPoint file

Link an Excel Chart to a PowerPoint Slide

Microsoft PowerPoint is a **presentation graphics** program that you can use to create slide show presentations. PowerPoint slides can include a mix of text, data, and graphics. Adding an Excel chart to a slide can help to illustrate data and give your presentation more visual appeal. **CASE** ▶ *Kate asks you to add an Excel chart to one of the PowerPoint slides, illustrating the 2017 sales projection data. She wants you to link the chart in the PowerPoint file.*

STEPS

1. **Start PowerPoint, then open the file EX M-6.pptx from the location where you store your Data Files, then save it as EX M-Management Presentation**

 The presentation appears in Normal view and contains three panes, as shown in FIGURE M-16. You need to open the Excel file and copy the chart that you will paste in the PowerPoint presentation.

TROUBLE
If you don't see Copy
on the shortcut
menu, you may have
clicked the Plot area
rather than the Chart
area. Clicking the
white area surround-
ing the pie will display
the Copy command
on the menu.

2. **Start Excel, open the file EX M-7.xlsx from the location where you store your Data Files, right-click the Chart Area on the Sales Categories sheet, click Copy on the shortcut menu, then click the PowerPoint program button on the taskbar to display the presentation**

 You need to add an Excel chart to Slide 2, "2017 Sales Projections". To add the chart, you first need to select the slide on which it will appear.

3. **Click Slide 2 in the Thumbnails pane, right-click Slide 2 in the Slide pane, then click the Use Destination Theme & Link Data button (third from the right) in the Paste Options group**

 A pie chart illustrating the 2017 sales projections appears in the slide. The chart matches the colors and fonts in the presentation, which is the destination document. You decide to edit the link so it will update automatically if the data source changes.

QUICK TIP
The default setting
for updating links in
a PowerPoint file is
Manual.

4. **Click the FILE tab, click Edit Links to Files at the bottom of the right pane, in the Links dialog box click the Automatic Update check box to select it, then click Close**

5. **Click the Back to arrow button ⊙ at the top of the pane to return to the presentation, click the Save button 🖫 on the Quick Access toolbar, then close the file**

 Kate has learned that the sales projections for the Travel accessories category has increased based on late sales for the current year.

6. **Switch to Excel, click the Sales sheet tab, change the Travel accessories value in cell B7 to 45,000, then press [Enter]**

 You decide to reopen the PowerPoint presentation to check the chart data.

QUICK TIP
To update links in an
open PowerPoint file,
click the FILE tab,
click Edit Links to
Files in the right
pane, click the link in
the Links list, click
Update now, then
click Close.

7. **Switch to PowerPoint, open the file EX M-Management Presentation.pptx, click Update Links, click Slide 2 in the Thumbnails pane, then point to the Travel accessories pie slice**

 The ScreenTip shows that the chart has updated to display the revised Travel accessories value, $45,000, you entered in the Excel workbook. Slide Show view displays the slide on the full screen the way the audience will see it.

8. **Click the Slide Show button 🖵 on the status bar**

 The finished sales projection slide is complete, as shown in FIGURE M-17.

9. **Press [Esc] to return to Normal view; with Slide 2 selected click the Insert tab, click the Header & Footer button in the Text group, select the Footer check box, type your name in the Footer text box, click Apply to All, save and close the presentation, close the Excel file without saving it, exit PowerPoint and Excel, then submit the file to your instructor**

FIGURE M-16: Presentation in Normal view

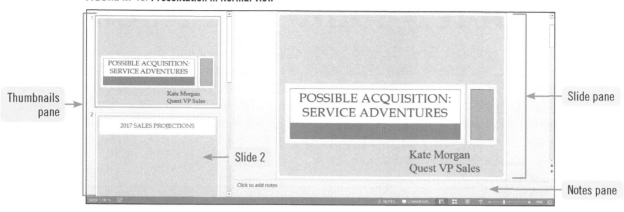

Thumbnails pane

Slide 2

Slide pane

Notes pane

FIGURE M-17: Completed Sales Projections slide in Slide Show view

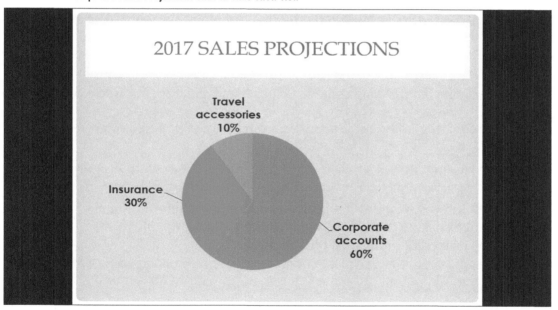

Import a Table into Access

Learning Outcomes
- Import Excel data into an Access database
- Identify a primary key for a database

If you need to analyze Excel data using the more extensive tools of a database, you can import it into Microsoft Access. When you import Excel table data into Access, the data becomes an Access table using the same field names as the Excel table. In the process of importing an Excel table, Access specifies a primary key for the new table. A **primary key** is the field that contains unique information for each record (row) of information. **CASE** ▶ *Kate has just received a workbook containing salary information for the managers at Service Adventures, organized in a table. She asks you to convert the Excel table to a Microsoft Access table.*

STEPS

1. **Start Access, click the** Blank desktop database button, **change the filename in the File Name text box to** EX M-SA Management, **click the** Browse button 🔲 **next to the filename, navigate to the location where you store your Data Files, click OK, then click** Create

 The database window for the EX M-SA Management database opens. You are ready to import the Excel table data.

2. **Click the** EXTERNAL DATA tab, **then click the** Excel button **in the Import & Link group**

 The Get External Data - Excel Spreadsheet dialog box opens, as shown in FIGURE M-18. This dialog box allows you to specify how you want the data to be stored in Access.

3. **Click the** Browse button, **navigate to the location where you store your Data Files, click** EX M-8.xlsx, **click Open, if necessary click the** Import the source data into a new table in the current database **option button, click OK, then click** Open if necessary

 The first Import Spreadsheet Wizard dialog box opens, with a sample of the sheet data in the lower section. You want to use the column headings in the Excel table as the field names in the Access database.

4. **Make sure the** First Row Contains Column Headings check box **is selected, then click** Next

 The Wizard allows you to review and change the field properties by clicking each column in the lower section of the window. You will not make any changes to the field properties.

5. **Click** Next

 The Wizard allows you to choose a primary key for the table. The table's primary key field contains unique information for each record; the ID Number field is unique for each person in the table.

QUICK TIP
Specifying a primary key allows you to retrieve data more quickly in the future.

6. **Click the** Choose my own primary key option, **make sure "ID Number" appears in the text box next to the selected option button, click** Next, **note the name assigned to the new table, click** Finish, **then click** Close

 The name of the new Access table ("Compensation") appears in the left pane, called the Navigation pane.

7. **Double-click** Compensation: in the Navigation Pane

 The data from the Excel worksheet appears in a new Access table, as shown in FIGURE M-19.

8. **Double-click the** border **between the Monthly Salary and the Click to Add column headings to widen the Monthly Salary column, then use the last row of the table to enter your name in the First Name and Last Name columns and enter 0 for an ID Number**

9. **Click the** Save button 🔲 **on the Quick Access toolbar, close the file, then exit Access**

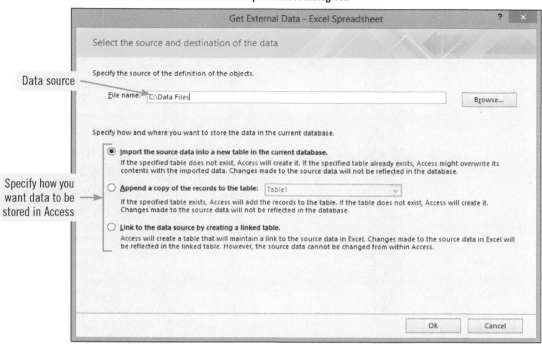

Data source

Specify how you want data to be stored in Access

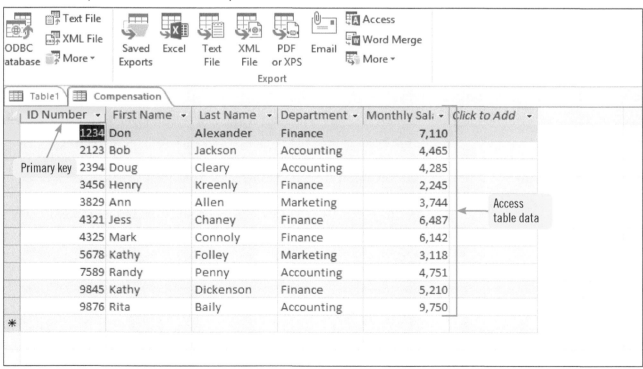

Primary key

Access table data

Practice

Concepts Review

FIGURE M-20

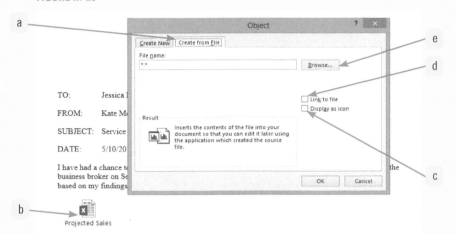

1. Which element do you click to embed information that can be viewed by double-clicking an icon?
2. Which element do you click to insert an existing object into a Word document rather than creating a new file?
3. Which element do you click to find a file to be embedded or linked?
4. Which element do you double-click to display an embedded Excel workbook?
5. Which element do you click to insert an object that maintains a connection to the source document?

Match each term with the statement that best describes it.

6. Source document
7. Embedding
8. Presentation graphics program
9. Destination document
10. OLE
11. Linking

a. File from which the object to be embedded or linked originates
b. Copies an object and retains a connection with the source program and source document
c. Document receiving the object to be embedded or linked
d. Data transfer method used in Windows programs
e. Copies an object and retains a connection with the source program only
f. Used to create slide shows

Select the best answer from the list of choices.

12. An ASCII file:
 a. Contains formatting but no text.
 b. Contains text but no formatting.
 c. Contains a PowerPoint presentation.
 d. Contains an unformatted worksheet.
13. An object consists of:
 a. Text, a worksheet, or any other type of data.
 b. A worksheet only.
 c. Text only.
 d. Database data only.
14. A column separator in a text file is called a(n):
 a. Object.
 b. Link.
 c. Primary key.
 d. Delimiter.

15. To view a workbook that has been embedded as an icon in a Word document, you need to:

a. Double-click the icon.

b. Drag the icon.

c. Click View, then click Worksheet.

d. Click File, then click Open.

16. A field that contains unique information for each record in a database table is called a(n):

a. Primary key.

b. ID Key.

c. First key.

d. Header key.

Skills Review

1. Import a text file.

a. Start Excel, open the tab-delimited text file titled EX M-9.txt from the location where you store your Data Files, then save it as a Microsoft Office Excel workbook with the name **EX M-East Campus Tea**.

b. Format the data in columns B and C using the Currency style with two decimal places.

c. Widen the columns if necessary so that all the data is visible.

d. Center the column labels and apply bold formatting, as shown in FIGURE M-21.

e. Add your name to the center section of the worksheet footer, save the workbook, preview the worksheet, close the workbook, then submit the workbook to your instructor.

FIGURE M-21

	A	B	C
1	**Item**	**Cost**	**Price**
2	Pot, small	$9.55	$18.50
3	Pot, large	$11.15	$25.00
4	Pot, decorated	$13.55	$23.70
5	Pot, china	$21.15	$30.90
6	Basket, small	$15.95	$26.80
7	Basket, large	$21.80	$32.90
8	Kettle, small	$16.75	$27.45
9	Kettle, large	$25.30	$33.75
10	Mug, large	$2.95	$4.70
11			

2. Import a database table.

a. Open a blank workbook in Excel, use the From Access button in the Get External Data group on the DATA tab to import the Access Data File EX M-10.accdb from the location where you store your Data Files, then save it as a Microsoft Excel workbook named **EX M-February Budget**.

b. Rename the sheet with the imported data **Budget**.

c. Delete the first data record in row 2.

d. Add a total row to the table to display the sum of the budgeted amounts in cell D25.

e. Apply the Medium 6 Table Style. Format range D2:D25 using the Currency style, the $ symbol, and two decimal places.

f. Save the workbook, and compare your screen to FIGURE M-22.

FIGURE M-22

	A	B	C	D
1	**Category**	**Item**	**Month**	**Amount**
2	Compensation	Bonuses	Feb	$28,147.00
3	Compensation	Commissions	Feb	$22,574.00
4	Compensation	Conferences	Feb	$74,587.00
5	Compensation	Promotions	Feb	$62,354.00
6	Compensation	Payroll Taxes	Feb	$17,887.00
7	Compensation	Salaries	Feb	$42,057.00
8	Compensation	Training	Feb	$58,741.00
9	Facility	Lease	Feb	$47,324.00
10	Facility	Maintenance	Feb	$62,478.00
11	Facility	Other	Feb	$57,148.00
12	Facility	Rent	Feb	$77,634.00
13	Facility	Telephone	Feb	$62,748.00
14	Facility	Utilities	Feb	$57,964.00
15	Supplies	Food	Feb	$61,775.00
16	Supplies	Computer	Feb	$43,217.00
17	Supplies	General Office	Feb	$47,854.00
18	Supplies	Other	Feb	$56,741.00
19	Supplies	Outside Services	Feb	$41,874.00
20	Equipment	Computer	Feb	$49,874.00
21	Equipment	Other	Feb	$43,547.00
22	Equipment	Cash Registers	Feb	$55,987.00
23	Equipment	Software	Feb	$63,147.00
24	Equipment	Telecommunications	Feb	$58,779.00
25	**Total**			**$1,194,438.00**

Budget

3. Insert a graphic file in a worksheet.

a. Add four rows above row 1 to create space for an image.

b. In rows 1 through 4, insert the picture file EX M-11.jpg from the location where you store your Data Files.

c. Resize and reposition the picture as necessary to make it fit in rows 1 through 4.

d. Apply the Beveled Matte, White Picture Style, and change the border color to Blue, Accent 5, Lighter 80%. Resize the picture to fit the image and the border in the first four rows. Move the picture to the center of the range A1:D4.

e. Compare your worksheet to FIGURE M-23, add your name to the center section of the worksheet footer, preview the workbook, save and close the workbook, then submit the workbook to your instructor.

FIGURE M-23

	A	B	C	D	E	F	G
1							
2							
3							
4							
5	**Category**	**Item**	**Month**	**Amount**			
6	Compensation	Bonuses	Feb	$28,147.00			
7	Compensation	Commissions	Feb	$22,574.00			
8	Compensation	Conferences	Feb	$74,587.00			
9	Compensation	Promotions	Feb	$62,354.00			
10	Compensation	Payroll Taxes	Feb	$17,887.00			
11	Compensation	Salaries	Feb	$42,057.00			
12	Compensation	Training	Feb	$58,741.00			
13	Facility	Lease	Feb	$47,324.00			
14	Facility	Maintenance	Feb	$62,478.00			
15	Facility	Other	Feb	$57,148.00			
16	Facility	Rent	Feb	$77,634.00			
17	Facility	Telephone	Feb	$62,748.00			
18	Facility	Utilities	Feb	$57,964.00			
19	Supplies	Food	Feb	$61,775.00			

Skills Review (continued)

4. Embed a workbook in a Word document.

 a. Start Word, create a memo with a header addressed to your instructor, enter your name in the From line, enter **February Salaries** as the subject, and enter the current date in the Date line.

 b. In the memo body, enter **The February salaries are provided in the worksheet below**:

 c. In the memo body, use the Object dialog box to embed the workbook EX M-12.xlsx from the location where you store your Data Files, displaying it as an icon with the caption **Salary Details**.

FIGURE M-24

 d. Save the document as **EX M-February Salaries** in the location where you store your Data Files, then double-click the icon to verify that the workbook opens. (*Hint*: If the workbook does not appear after you double-click it, click the Excel icon on the taskbar.)

 e. Close the workbook and return to Word.

 f. Compare your memo to FIGURE M-24.

To: Your Instructor

From: Your Name

Subject: February Sales

Date: 11/1/2016

The February salaries are provided in the worksheet below:

Salary Details

5. Link a workbook to a Word document.

 a. Delete the icon in the memo body.

 b. In the memo body, link the workbook EX M-12.xlsx, displaying the data, not an icon.

 c. Save the document, then note that Mary Glenn's salary is $7,100. Close the document.

FIGURE M-25

 d. Open the EX M-12.xlsx workbook in Excel, and change Mary Glenn's salary to **$7500**.

 e. Open the **EX M-February Salaries** document in Word, update the links, and verify that Mary Glenn's salary has changed to $7,500 and that the new total salaries amount is $48,057, as shown in FIGURE M-25. (*Hint*: If the dialog box does not open, giving you the opportunity to update the link, then right-click the worksheet object and click Update Link.)

 f. Save the **EX M-February Salaries** document, preview the memo, close the document, exit Word, then submit the document to your instructor.

 g. Close the EX M-12 workbook without saving changes, then exit Excel.

To: Your Instructor

From: Your Name

Subject: February Sales

Date: 11/1/2016

The February salaries are provided in the worksheet below:

West Street Tea Salary Summary				
First Name	Last Name	Position	Salary	
Mary	Glenn	Manager	$	7,500
Jack	Cronin	Manager	$	5,534
Mark	Donnolly	Manager	$	6,754
Karen	Walker	Sales Associate	$	7,132
Sandy	Jones	Custodian	$	6,987
Keith	Allen	Sales Associate	$	6,950
Gail	Henry	Sales Associate	$	7,200
		Total	$	48,057

6. Link an Excel chart to a PowerPoint slide.

 a. Start PowerPoint.

 b. Open the PowerPoint file EX M-13.pptx from the location where you store your Data Files, then save it as **EX M-Budget Meeting**.

 c. Display Slide 2, February Expenditures.

FIGURE M-26

 d. Link the chart, using the theme of the destination file, from the Excel file EX M-14.xlsx from the location where you store your Data Files to Slide 2. Edit the link to be updated automatically. Save and close the Ex M-Budget Meeting file.

 e. Change the Equipment amount on Sheet1 of the file EX M-14 to $207,000, open the EX M-Budget Meeting file, updating the links, and verify the Equipment percentage changed from 17% to 18% on Slide 2.

 f. View the slide in Slide Show view.

 g. Press [Esc] to return to Normal view. Resize and reposition the chart to fit on the slide if necessary. Compare your slide to FIGURE M-26.

February Expenditures

Skills Review (continued)

h. Add a footer to all of the slides with your name.

i. Save the presentation, exit PowerPoint, close EX M-14 without saving it, then submit the presentation to your instructor.

7. Import a table into Access.

a. Start Access.

b. Create a blank desktop database named **EX M-Budget** in the location where you store your Data Files.

c. Use the EXTERNAL DATA tab to import the Excel table in the file EX M-15.xlsx from the location where you store your Data Files. Store the data in a new table, use the first row as column headings, let Access add the primary key, and use the default table name February Budget.

d. Open the February Budget table in Access, and widen the columns as necessary to fully display the field names and field information.

e. Enter your name in the Budget Category column of row 25 in the table, save the database file, compare your screen to FIGURE M-27, exit Access, then submit the database file to your instructor.

FIGURE M-27

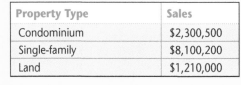

Independent Challenge 1

You are a real estate agent for the Naples office of West Coast Realty. You have been asked to give a presentation to the regional manager about your sales in the past month. To illustrate your sales data, you will add an Excel chart to one of your slides, showing the different types of property sales and the sales amounts for each type.

a. Start Excel, create a new workbook, then save it as **EX M-June Sales** in the location where you store your Data Files.

b. Enter the property types and the corresponding sales amounts shown below into the EX M-June Sales workbook. Name the sheet with the sales data **Sales**.

Property Type	Sales
Condominium	$2,300,500
Single-family	$8,100,200
Land	$1,210,000

c. Create a 3-D pie chart from the sales data. Format it using Chart Style 9.

d. Copy the chart to the Clipboard.

e. Start PowerPoint, open the Data File EX M-16.pptx from the location where you store your Data Files, then save it as **EX M-Sales Presentation**.

f. Link the Excel chart to Slide 2 using the destination theme. Use the sizing handles to change the size if necessary, and drag the edge of the chart to position it in the center of the slide if necessary.

g. View the slide in Slide Show view, then press [Esc] to end the show.

h. Add a footer to the slides with your name, then save the presentation. Slide 2 should look like FIGURE M-28.

i. Change the status of links in the PowerPoint file to update automatically.

j. Close the presentation, exit PowerPoint, then submit the PowerPoint file to your instructor.

k. Save the workbook, then close the workbook, and exit Excel.

FIGURE M-28

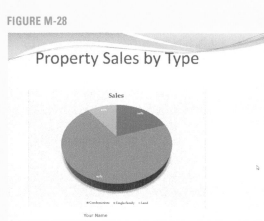

Independent Challenge 2

You are opening a new fitness center, Total Sports, in Oakland, California. The owner of a fitness center in the area is retiring and has agreed to sell you a text file containing his list of supplier information. You need to import this text file into Excel so that you can manipulate the data. Later, you will convert the Excel file to an Access table so that you can give it to your business partner who is building a supplier database.

a. Start Excel, import the file EX M-17.txt from the location where you store your Data Files, then save it as an Excel file named **EX M-Fitness Suppliers**. (*Hint*: This is a tab-delimited text file.)

b. Adjust the column widths as necessary. Rename the worksheet **Suppliers**.

c. Sort the worksheet data in ascending order by Supplier.

d. Add your name to the center section of the worksheet footer, save and close the workbook, then exit Excel.

e. Start Access, create a new blank desktop database in the location where you store your Data Files. Name the new database **EX M-Suppliers**.

f. Use the EXTERNAL DATA tab to import the Excel file EX M-Fitness Suppliers from the location where you store your Data Files. Store the data in a new table, use the column labels as the field names, let Access add the primary key, and accept the default table name.

g. Open the Suppliers table and AutoFit the columns.

h. Enter your name in the Supplier column in row 13, then compare your database file to FIGURE M-29.

i. Save and then close the table, and exit Access.

j. Submit the database file to your instructor.

FIGURE M-29

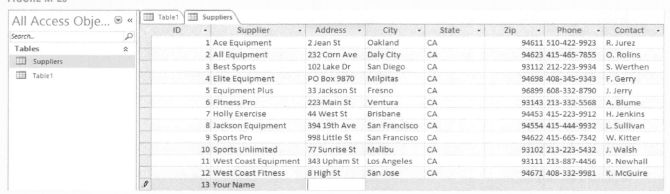

Independent Challenge 3

You are the newly hired manager at NE Financial, a mutual funds firm specializing in consumer products. An employee, Kathy Hogan, has completed a two-year training period as an assistant and you would like to promote her to an associate position with a higher salary. You have examined the salaries of the other associates in the company and will present this information to the vice president of Human Resources, requesting permission to grant Kathy a promotion and an increase in salary.

a. Start Word, open the Word file EX M-18.docx from the location where you store your Data Files, then save it as **EX M-Promotion**.

b. Add your name to the From line of the memo, and change the date to the current date.

c. At the end of the memo, embed the workbook EX M-19.xlsx as an icon from the location where you store your Data Files. Change the caption for the icon to **Salaries**. Double-click the icon to verify that the workbook opens.

d. Close the workbook, return to Word, delete the Salaries icon, and link the workbook EX M-19 to the memo, displaying the data, not an icon.

e. Save the EX M-Promotion memo, and close the file.

f. Open the EX M-19.xlsx workbook in Excel, and change Kathy Hogan's salary to $51,000.

Independent Challenge 3 (continued)

g. Open the EX M-Promotion memo, update the links, and make sure Kathy Hogan's salary is updated.

h. Save and close the memo. Exit Word and submit the memo to your instructor.

i. Close EX M-19 without saving the changes to Karen Holden's information, then exit Excel.

Independent Challenge 4: Explore

You work as a technology manager at a local town office. Each Friday afternoon you are required to submit your hours to your supervisor in a Word document. You prefer to use Excel to track your daily hours so you will link your worksheet to a Word document for your supervisor.

a. Open the file EX M-20.docx from the location where you store your Data Files, then save it as **EX M-Hours**.

b. Change "Your Name" in the FROM line with your own name.

c. Open the file EX M-21.xlsx from the location where you store your Data Files. Copy the range A1:B8 to the Clipboard.

d. Return to the EX M-Hours document, and use the Paste Special in the Paste Options to paste the copied range as a linked worksheet object with the destination style.

FIGURE M-30

(*Hint*: Using **FIGURE M-30** as a guide, right-click below the line "My hours for this week are shown below.", then click the Link & Use Destination Styles option in the Paste Options group. It is the 4th option from the left.) Save and close the memo.

e. In the EX M-21 workbook, change Sunday's hours to 5.

f. Return to Word, open the EX M-Hours memo, update links, then verify that the new hours information appears. Save and then close the memo and exit Word. Close the EX M-21 workbook without saving the file and exit Excel.

g. Using Access, create a new blank desktop database named **EX M-Week** in the location where you store your Data Files. Link the Excel data in the EX M-22.xlsx file to the EX M-Week database file using **FIGURE M-31** as a guide. View the data in the linked Hours table by double-clicking the object's name.

h. Close the database file, open the EX M-22.xlsx file, and change the hours for Sunday to 10. Save and close the Excel file.

i. Open the EX M-Week database, verify that the hours figure for Sunday was updated in the linked Hours table, then close the database and exit Access.

j. Submit the EX M-Hours Word document and the EX M-Week database file to your instructor.

FIGURE M-31

Visual Workshop

Create the worksheet shown in FIGURE M-32 by opening a blank workbook, importing the Access data in file EX M-23.accdb, sorting the data in Excel, and formatting the price data. The image is from the Microsoft ClipArt. (*Hint*: Click the Online Pictures button in the Illustrations group of the INSERT tab and search for Dog. If you don't see the image shown, select another. Notice the image's transparent background.) Add your name to the center section of the Prices worksheet. Save the workbook as **EX M-Prices**, close the workbook, then exit Excel. Submit the file to your instructor.

FIGURE M-32

	A	B	C
1			
2			
3			
4			
5			
6	**Item Code** ▼	**Product** ▼	**Price** ▾↑
7	B755	Cat Post	$18.99
8	B132	Cat Collar	$22.36
9	A135	Dog Collar	$31.19
10	A884	Dog Toy Set	$37.54
11	A252	Dog Brush Set	$39.94
12	B211	Cat Play Set	$52.99
13	A410	Dog Crate Small	$112.57
14	A408	Dog Crate Medium	$115.22
15	B111	Cat Bed	$116.99
16	A327	Dog Bed Small	$130.57
17	A407	Dog Crate Large	$141.99
18	A321	Dog Bed Large	$155.99
19			

Programming with Excel

CASE Quest's vice president of sales, Kate Morgan, has used recorded macros to insert worksheet text. Now she would like to automate some more of the division's time-consuming tasks for the sales group. She plans to create macros that she enters manually. You help Kate by creating five new Excel macros using the Visual Basic for Applications (VBA) programming language.

Unit Objectives

After completing this unit, you will be able to:

- View VBA code
- Analyze VBA code
- Write VBA code
- Add a conditional statement

- Prompt the user for data
- Debug a macro
- Create a main procedure
- Run a main procedure

Files You Will Need

EX P-1.xlsm	EX P-5.xlsm
EX P-2.xlsx	EX P-6.xlsm
EX P-3.xlsm	EX P-7.xlsm
EX P-4.xlsm	EX P-8.xlsm

©Katerina Havelkova/Shutterstock

View VBA Code

Learning Outcomes
• Identify the VBA windows
• Define VBA procedure terms

As you learned in Unit I, you can create macros using the Excel macro recorder, which automatically writes Visual Basic for Applications (VBA) instructions for you as you perform actions. For additional flexibility, you can also create entire Excel macros by typing VBA program code. To enter and edit VBA code, you work in the **Visual Basic Editor**, a tool you can start from within Excel. A common method of learning any programming language is to view existing code. In VBA macro code, a sequence of VBA statements is called a **procedure**. The first line of a procedure, called the **procedure header**, defines the procedure's type, name, and arguments. **Arguments** are variables used by other procedures that the main procedure might run. **CASE** ▶ *Each month, Kate receives text files containing tour sales information from the Quest branches. Kate has already imported the text file for the Miami January sales into a worksheet, but she still needs to format it. She asks you to work on a macro to automate the process of formatting the imported information.*

STEPS

TROUBLE
If the DEVELOPER tab does not appear on your Ribbon, click the FILE tab, click Options, click Customize Ribbon on the left side of the Excel Options dialog box, click the Developer check box to select it on the right pane, then click OK.

1. **Start Excel if necessary, open a blank workbook, click the DEVELOPER tab, then click the Macro Security button in the Code group**

 The Trust Center dialog box opens, as shown in FIGURE P-1. You know the Quest branch files are from a trusted source, so you decide to allow macros to run in the workbook.

2. **Click the Enable all macros option button if necessary, then click OK**

 You are ready to open a file and view its VBA code. A macro-enabled workbook has the extension .xlsm. Although a workbook containing a macro will open if macros are disabled, they will not function.

3. **Open the file EX P-1.xlsm from the location where you store your Data Files, save it as EX P-Monthly Sales, click the DEVELOPER tab if necessary, then click the Macros button in the Code group**

 The Macro dialog box opens with the FormatFile macro procedure in the list box. If you have any macros saved in your Personal Macro workbook, they are also listed in the Macro dialog box.

4. **If it is not already selected click the FormatFile macro, then click Edit**

 The Microsoft Visual Basic for Applications window opens, containing three windows, shown in FIGURE P-2. See TABLE P-1 to make sure your screen matches the ones shown in this unit. See also the yellow box on the next page for more information about the VBA window.

TROUBLE
To enlarge your Project Explorer window, place the mouse pointer on the right border of the window until it turns into ◀‖▶ then drag the border to the right. Your Project Explorer window may show additional VBA projects.

5. **Make sure both the Visual Basic window and the Code window are maximized to match FIGURE P-2**

 In the Code window, the different parts of the FormatFile procedure appear in various colors. **Comments** are notes explaining the code; they are displayed in green.

6. **Examine the top three lines of code, which contain comments, and the first line of code beginning with Sub FormatFile()**

 The first two comment lines give the procedure name and tell what the procedure does. The third comment line explains that the keyboard shortcut for this macro procedure is [Ctrl][Shift][F]. Items that appear in blue are **keywords**, which are words Excel recognizes as part of the VBA programming language. The keyword Sub in the procedure header indicates that this is a **Sub procedure**, or a series of Visual Basic statements that perform an action but do not return (create and display) a value. An empty set of parentheses after the procedure name means the procedure doesn't have any arguments. In the next lesson, you will analyze the procedure code to see what each line does.

FIGURE P-1: Macro settings in the Trust Center dialog box

Select to allow macros to run

FIGURE P-2: Procedure displayed in the Visual Basic Editor

Procedure header

Project Explorer window

Format module

Properties window

Comments in green

Keywords in blue

Code window

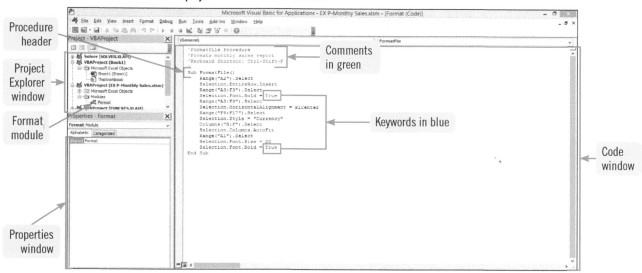

TABLE P-1: Matching your screen to the unit figures

if...	do this...
The Properties window is not displayed	Click the Properties Window button on the toolbar
The Project Explorer window is not displayed	Click the Project Explorer button on the toolbar
You see only the Code window	Click Tools on the menu bar, click Options, click the Docking tab, then make sure the Project Explorer and Properties Window options are selected
You do not see folders in the Explorer window	Click the Toggle Folders button on the Project Explorer window Project toolbar

Understanding the Visual Basic Editor

A **module** is the Visual Basic equivalent of a worksheet. In it, you store macro procedures, just as you store data in worksheets. Modules, in turn, are stored in workbooks (or projects), along with worksheets. A **project** is the collection of all procedures in a workbook. You view and edit modules in the Visual Basic Editor, which is made up of the Project Explorer window (also called the Project window), the Code window, and the Properties window. **Project Explorer** displays a list of all open

projects (or workbooks) and the worksheets and modules they contain. To view the procedures stored in a module, you must first select the module in Project Explorer (just as you would select a file in Windows Explorer). The **Code window** then displays the selected module's procedures. The **Properties window** displays a list of characteristics (or properties) associated with the module. A newly inserted module has only one property, its name.

Analyze VBA Code

Learning
Outcomes
• Examine the struc-
 ture of VBA code
• Run a procedure

You can learn a lot about the VBA language simply by analyzing the code generated by the Excel macro recorder. The more VBA code you analyze, the easier it is for you to write your own programming code. **CASE** ▸ *Before writing any new procedures, you analyze a previously written procedure that applies formatting to a worksheet. Then you open a worksheet that you want to format and run the macro.*

STEPS

1. **With the FormatFile procedure still displayed in the Code window, examine the next four lines of code, beginning with Range("A2"). Select**

 Refer to **FIGURE P-3** as you analyze the code in this lesson. Every Excel element, including a range, is considered an **object**. A **range object** represents a cell or a range of cells. The statement Range("A2").Select selects the range object cell A2. Notice that several times in the procedure, a line of code (or **statement**) selects a range, and then subsequent lines act on that selection. The next statement, Selection.EntireRow. Insert, inserts a row above the selection, which is currently cell A2. The next two lines of code select range A3:F3 and apply bold formatting to that selection. In VBA terminology, bold formatting is a value of an object's Bold property. A **property** is an attribute of an object that defines one of the object's characteristics (such as size) or an aspect of its behavior (such as whether it is enabled). To change the characteristics of an object, you change the values of its properties. For example, to apply bold formatting to a selected range, you assign the value True to the range's Bold property. To remove bold formatting, assign the value False.

2. **Examine the remaining lines of code, beginning with the second occurrence of the line Range("A3:F3"). Select**

 The next two statements select the range object A3:F3 and center its contents, then the following two statements select the F4:F17 range object and format it as currency. Column objects B through F are then selected, and their widths set to AutoFit. Finally, the range object cell A1 is selected, its font size is changed to 20, and its Bold property is set to True. The last line, End Sub, indicates the end of the Sub procedure and is also referred to as the **procedure footer**.

3. **Click the View Microsoft Excel button 🖩 on the Visual Basic Editor toolbar to return to Excel**

 Because the macro is stored in the EX P-Monthly Sales workbook, Kate can open this workbook and repeatedly use the macro stored there each month after she receives that month's sales data. She wants you to open the workbook containing data for Chicago's January sales and run the macro to format the data. You must leave the EX P-Monthly Sales workbook open to use the macro stored there.

4. **Open the file EX P-2.xlsx from the location where you store your Data Files, then save it as EX P-January Sales**

 This is the workbook containing the data you want to format.

5. **Press [Ctrl][Shift][F] to run the procedure**

 The FormatFile procedure formats the text, as shown in **FIGURE P-4**.

6. **Save the workbook**

 Now that you've successfully viewed and analyzed VBA code and run the macro, you will learn how to write your own code.

FIGURE P-3: VBA code for the FormatFile procedure

Selects range object cell A2

Formats range A3:F3 in bold

AutoFits columns B - F

Adjusts font size and bolds cell A1

Inserts a row above cell A2

Centers contents of cells A3:F3

Formats range F4:F17 as currency

```
'FormatFile Procedure
'Formats monthly sales report
'Keyboard Shortcut: Ctrl+Shift+F
'
Sub FormatFile()
    Range("A2").Select
    Selection.EntireRow.Insert
    Range("A3:F3").Select
    Selection.Font.Bold = True
    Range("A3:F3").Select
    Selection.HorizontalAlignment = xlCenter
    Range("F4:F17").Select
    Selection.Style = "Currency"
    Columns("B:F").Select
    Selection.Columns.AutoFit
    Range("A1").Select
    Selection.Font.Size = 20
    Selection.Font.Bold = True
End Sub
```

FIGURE P-4: Worksheet formatted using the FormatFile procedure

Formatted title

Row inserted

Formatted column headings

Range formatted as currency

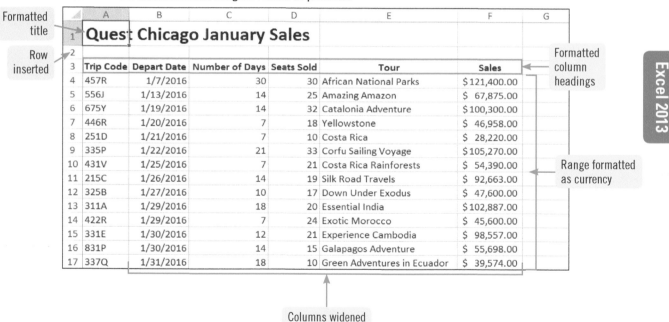

	A	B	C	D	E	F	G
1	Quest Chicago January Sales						
2							
3	Trip Code	Depart Date	Number of Days	Seats Sold	Tour	Sales	
4	457R	1/7/2016	30	30	African National Parks	$121,400.00	
5	556J	1/13/2016	14	25	Amazing Amazon	$ 67,875.00	
6	675Y	1/19/2016	14	32	Catalonia Adventure	$100,300.00	
7	446R	1/20/2016	7	18	Yellowstone	$ 46,958.00	
8	251D	1/21/2016	7	10	Costa Rica	$ 28,220.00	
9	335P	1/22/2016	21	33	Corfu Sailing Voyage	$105,270.00	
10	431V	1/25/2016	7	21	Costa Rica Rainforests	$ 54,390.00	
11	215C	1/26/2016	14	19	Silk Road Travels	$ 92,663.00	
12	325B	1/27/2016	10	17	Down Under Exodus	$ 47,600.00	
13	311A	1/29/2016	18	20	Essential India	$102,887.00	
14	422R	1/29/2016	7	24	Exotic Morocco	$ 45,600.00	
15	331E	1/30/2016	12	21	Experience Cambodia	$ 98,557.00	
16	831P	1/30/2016	14	15	Galapagos Adventure	$ 55,698.00	
17	337Q	1/31/2016	18	10	Green Adventures in Ecuador	$ 39,574.00	

Columns widened

Write VBA Code

Learning Outcomes
• Create a VBA module
• Enter VBA code

To write your own code, you first need to open the Visual Basic Editor and add a module to the workbook. You can then begin entering the procedure code. In the first few lines of a procedure, you typically include comments indicating the name of the procedure, a brief description of the procedure, and shortcut keys, if applicable. When writing Visual Basic code for Excel, you must follow the formatting rules, or **syntax**, of the VBA programming language. A misspelled keyword or variable name causes a procedure to fail. **CASE** *Kate would like to total the monthly sales. You help her by writing a procedure that automates this routine task.*

STEPS

TROUBLE
If the Code window is empty, verify that the workbook that contains your procedures (EX P-Monthly Sales) is open.

1. **With the January worksheet still displayed, click the DEVELOPER tab, then click the Visual Basic button in the Code group**
 Two projects are displayed in the Project Explorer window, EX P-Monthly Sales.xlsm (which contains the FormatFile macro) and EX P-January Sales.xlsx (which contains the monthly data). The FormatFile procedure is again displayed in the Visual Basic Editor. You may have other projects in the Project Explorer window.

2. **Click the Modules folder in the EX P-Monthly Sales.xlsm project**
 You need to store all of the procedures in the EX P-Monthly Sales.xlsm project, which is in the EX P-Monthly Sales.xlsm workbook. By clicking the Modules folder, you have activated the workbook, and the title bar changes from EX P-January Sales to EX P-Monthly Sales.

3. **Click Insert on the Visual Basic Editor menu bar, then click Module**
 A new, blank module with the default name Module1 appears in the EX P-Monthly Sales.xlsm project, under the Format module. You think the property name of the module could be more descriptive.

4. **Click (Name) in the Properties window, then type Total**
 The module name is Total. The module name should not be the same as the procedure name (which will be AddTotal). In the code shown in FIGURE P-5, comments begin with an apostrophe, and the lines of code under Sub AddTotal() have been indented using the Tab key. When you enter the code in the next step, after you type the procedure header Sub AddTotal() and press [Enter], the Visual Basic Editor automatically enters End Sub (the procedure footer) in the Code window.

TROUBLE
As you type, you may see words in drop-down lists. This optional feature is explained in the Clues to Use titled "Entering code using AutoComplete" on the next page. For now, just continue to type.

5. **Click in the Code window, then type the procedure code exactly as shown in FIGURE P-5, entering your name in the second line, pressing [Tab] to indent text and [Shift][Tab] to move the insertion point to the left**
 The lines that begin with ActiveCell.Formula insert the information enclosed in quotation marks into the active cell. For example, ActiveCell.Formula = "Monthly Total:" inserts the words "Monthly Total:" into cell E18, the active cell. As you type each line, Excel adjusts the spacing.

6. **Compare the procedure code you entered in the Code window with FIGURE P-5, make any corrections if necessary, then click the Save EX P-Monthly Sales.xlsm button 🔲 on the Visual Basic Editor toolbar**

7. **Click the View Microsoft Excel button 📰 on the toolbar, click EX P-January Sales.xlsx on the taskbar to activate the workbook if necessary, with the January worksheet displayed click the DEVELOPER tab, then click the Macros button in the Code group**
 Macro names have two parts. The first part ('EX P-Monthly Sales.xlsm'!) indicates the workbook where the macro is stored. The second part (AddTotal or FormatFile) is the name of the procedure, taken from the procedure header.

TROUBLE
If an error message appears, click Debug. Click the Reset button 🔲 on the toolbar, correct the error, then repeat Steps 6–8.

8. **Click 'EX P-MonthlySales.xlsm'!AddTotal to select it if necessary, then click Run**
 The AddTotal procedure inserts and formats the monthly total in cell F18, as shown in FIGURE P-6.

9. **Save the workbook**

FIGURE P-5: VBA code for the AddTotal procedure

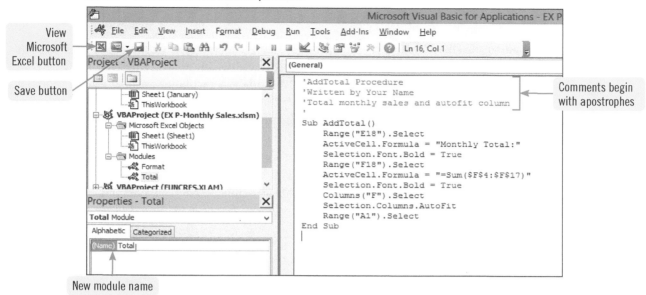

FIGURE P-6: Worksheet after running the AddTotal procedure

	A	B	C	D	E	F	G
1	Quest Chicago January Sales						
2							
3	Trip Code	Depart Date	Number of Days	Seats Sold	Tour	Sales	
4	457R	1/7/2016	30	30	African National Parks	$ 121,400.00	
5	556J	1/13/2016	14	25	Amazing Amazon	$ 67,875.00	
6	675Y	1/19/2016	14	32	Catalonia Adventure	$ 100,300.00	
7	446R	1/20/2016	7	18	Yellowstone	$ 46,958.00	
8	251D	1/21/2016	7	10	Costa Rica	$ 28,220.00	
9	335P	1/22/2016	21	33	Corfu Sailing Voyage	$ 105,270.00	
10	431V	1/25/2016	7	21	Costa Rica Rainforests	$ 54,390.00	
11	215C	1/26/2016	14	19	Silk Road Travels	$ 92,663.00	
12	325B	1/27/2016	10	17	Down Under Exodus	$ 47,600.00	
13	311A	1/29/2016	18	20	Essential India	$ 102,887.00	
14	422R	1/29/2016	7	24	Exotic Morocco	$ 45,600.00	
15	331E	1/30/2016	12	21	Experience Cambodia	$ 98,557.00	
16	831P	1/30/2016	14	15	Galapagos Adventure	$ 55,698.00	
17	337Q	1/31/2016	18	10	Green Adventures in Ecuador	$ 39,574.00	
18					Monthly Total:	$ 1,006,992.00	

Result of AddTotal procedure

Entering code using AutoComplete

To assist you in entering the VBA code, the Editor uses **AutoComplete**, a list of words that can be used in the macro statement and match what you type. The list usually appears after you press [.] (period). To include a word from the list in the macro statement, select the word in the list, then double-click it or press [Tab]. For example, to enter the Range("E12").Select instruction, type Range("E12"), then press [.] (period). Type s to bring up the words beginning with the letter "s", select the Select command in the list, then press [Tab] to enter the word "Select" in the macro statement.

Add a Conditional Statement

Learning
Outcomes
• Enter a VBA condi-
tional statement
• Run a VBA condi-
tional statement

The formatting macros you entered in the previous lesson could have been created using the macro recorder. However, there are some situations where you cannot use the recorder and must type the VBA macro code, such as when you want a procedure to take an action based on a certain condition or set of conditions. One way of adding this type of conditional statement in Visual Basic is to use an **If...Then...Else statement**. For example, *if* a salesperson's performance rating is a 5 (top rating), *then* calculate a 10% bonus; otherwise (*else*), there is no bonus. The syntax for this statement is: "If *condition* Then *statements* Else [*else statements*]." The brackets indicate that the Else part of the statement is optional. **CASE** *Kate wants the worksheet to point out if the total sales figure meets or misses the $1,000,000 monthly quota. You use Excel to add a conditional statement that indicates this information. You start by returning to the Visual Basic Editor and inserting a new module in the Monthly Sales project.*

STEPS

1. **With the January worksheet still displayed, click the** DEVELOPER **tab if necessary, then click the** Visual Basic **button in the Code group**

2. **Verify that the Total module in the Modules folder of the EX P-Monthly Sales VBAProject is selected in the Project Explorer window, click** Insert **on the Visual Basic Editor menu bar, then click** Module

 A new, blank module named Module1 is inserted in the EX P-Monthly Sales workbook.

3. **In the Properties window click** (Name), **then type** Sales

QUICK TIP
The If...Then...
Else statement is
similar to the Excel
IF function.

4. **Click in the Code window, then type the code exactly as shown in** FIGURE P-7, **entering your name in the second line**

 Notice the green comment lines in the middle of the code. These lines help explain the procedure.

5. **Compare the procedure you entered with** FIGURE P-7, **make any corrections if necessary, click the** Save EX P-Monthly Sales.xlsm **button** 🖫 **on the Visual Basic Editor toolbar, then click the** View Microsoft Excel **button** 🖾 **on the toolbar**

TROUBLE
If you get an error
message check your
code for errors, cor-
rect the errors, save
your macro, click the
Reset button ▣
on the Visual Basic
Editor toolbar, then
rerun the macro.

6. **If necessary, click** EX P-January Sales.xlsx **in the taskbar to display it, click the** Macros **button in the Code group, in the Macro dialog box click** 'EX P-Monthly Sales.xlsm'!SalesStatus, **then click** Run

 The SalesStatus procedure indicates the status "Met Quota", as shown in FIGURE P-8.

7. **Save the workbook**

FIGURE P-7: **VBA code for the SalesStatus procedure**

```
Run  Tools  Add-Ins  Window  Help

          Ln 21, Col 1

(General)

      'SalesStatus Procedure
      'Written by Your Name
      'Tests whether total sales meets the monthly quota
      '
      Sub SalesStatus()
          Range("E20").Select
          ActiveCell.Formula = "Sales Status:"
          Selection.Font.Bold = True
          'If the total is less than 1000000 then
          'insert "Missed Quota" in cell F20
          If Range("F18") <= 1000000 Then
              Range("F20").Select
              ActiveCell.Formula = "Missed Quota"
          'otherwise, insert "Met Quota" in cell F20
          Else
              Range("F20").Select
              ActiveCell.Formula = "Met Quota"
          End If
          Range("A1").Select
      End Sub
```

If ... Then ... Else statement

FIGURE P-8: **Result of running the SalesStatus procedure**

	Quest Chicago January Sales					
1	**Quest Chicago January Sales**					
2						
3	**Trip Code**	**Depart Date**	**Number of Days**	**Seats Sold**	**Tour**	**Sales**
4	457R	1/7/2016	30	30	African National Parks	$ 121,400.00
5	556J	1/13/2016	14	25	Amazing Amazon	$ 67,875.00
6	675Y	1/19/2016	14	32	Catalonia Adventure	$ 100,300.00
7	446R	1/20/2016	7	18	Yellowstone	$ 46,958.00
8	251D	1/21/2016	7	10	Costa Rica	$ 28,220.00
9	335P	1/22/2016	21	33	Corfu Sailing Voyage	$ 105,270.00
10	431V	1/25/2016	7	21	Costa Rica Rainforests	$ 54,390.00
11	215C	1/26/2016	14	19	Silk Road Travels	$ 92,663.00
12	325B	1/27/2016	10	17	Down Under Exodus	$ 47,600.00
13	311A	1/29/2016	18	20	Essential India	$ 102,887.00
14	422R	1/29/2016	7	24	Exotic Morocco	$ 45,600.00
15	331E	1/30/2016	12	21	Experience Cambodia	$ 98,557.00
16	831P	1/30/2016	14	15	Galapagos Adventure	$ 55,698.00
17	337Q	1/31/2016	18	10	Green Adventures in Ecuador	$ 39,574.00
18					**Monthly Total:**	**$ 1,006,992.00**
19						
20					**Sales Status:**	Met Quota
21						
22						

Indicates status of monthly total

Prompt the User for Data

Another situation where you must type, not record, VBA code is when you need to pause a macro to allow user input. You use the VBA InputBox function to display a dialog box that prompts the user for information. A **function** is a predefined procedure that returns (creates and displays) a value; in this case the value returned is the information the user enters. The required elements of an InputBox function are as follows: *object*.InputBox("*prompt*"), where "*prompt*" is the message that appears in the dialog box. For a detailed description of the InputBox function, use the Visual Basic Editor's Help menu. **CASE** *You decide to create a procedure that will insert the user's name in the left footer area of the worksheet. You use the InputBox function to display a dialog box in which the user can enter his or her name. You also type an intentional error into the procedure code, which you will correct in the next lesson.*

STEPS

1. **With the January worksheet displayed, click the DEVELOPER tab if necessary, click the Visual Basic button in the Code group, verify that the Sales module is selected in the EX P-Monthly Sales VBAProject Modules folder, click Insert on the Visual Basic Editor menu bar, then click Module**

 A new, blank module named Module1 is inserted in the EX P-Monthly Sales workbook.

2. **In the Properties window click (Name), then type Footer**

3. **Click in the Code window, then type the procedure code exactly as shown in FIGURE P-9 entering your name in the second line**

 Like the SalesStatus procedure, this procedure also contains comments that explain the code. The first part of the code, Dim LeftFooterText As String, **declares**, or defines, LeftFooterText as a text string variable. In Visual Basic, a **variable** is a location in memory in which you can temporarily store one item of information. Dim statements are used to declare variables and must be entered in the following format: Dim *variablename* As *datatype*. The datatype here is "string." In this case, you plan to store the information received from the input box in the temporary memory location called LeftFooterText. Then you can place this text in the left footer area. The remaining statements in the procedure are explained in the comment line directly above each statement. Notice the comment pointing out the error in the procedure code. You will correct this in the next lesson.

4. **Review your code, make any necessary changes, click the Save EX P-MonthlySales.xlsm button ◻ on the Visual Basic Editor toolbar, then click the View Microsoft Excel button ⊠ on the toolbar**

5. **With the January worksheet displayed, click the Macros button in the Code group, in the Macro dialog box click 'EX P-Monthly Sales.xlsm'!FooterInput, then click Run**

 The procedure begins, and a dialog box generated by the InputBox function opens, prompting you to enter your name, as shown in FIGURE P-10.

TROUBLE

If your macro doesn't prompt you for your name, it may contain an error. Return to the Visual Basic Editor, click the Reset button ◻ correct the error by referring to FIGURE P-9, then repeat Steps 4 and 5. You'll learn more about how to correct such macro errors in the next lesson.

6. **With the cursor in the text box, type your name, then click OK**

7. **Click the File tab, click Print, then view the worksheet preview**

 Although the customized footer with the date is inserted on the sheet, because of the error your name does *not* appear in the left section of the footer. In the next lesson, you will learn how to step through a procedure's code line by line. This will help you locate the error in the FooterInput procedure.

8. **Click the Back button ◉, then save the workbook**

 You return to the January worksheet.

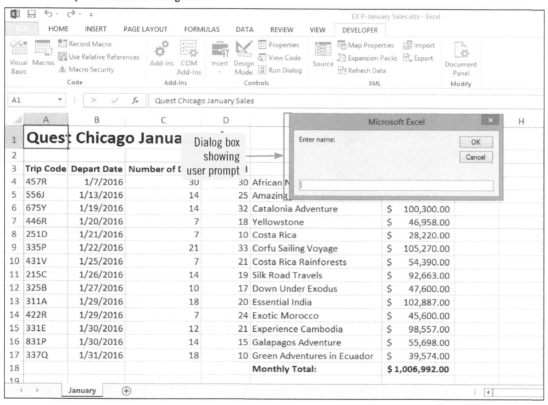

FIGURE P-10: **InputBox function's dialog box**

Naming variables

Variable names in VBA must begin with a letter. Letters can be uppercase or lowercase. Variable names cannot include periods or spaces, and they can be up to 255 characters long. Each variable name in a procedure must be unique. Examples of valid and invalid variable names are shown in TABLE P-2.

TABLE P-2: **Variable names**

valid	invalid
Sales_Department	Sales Department
SalesDepartment	Sales Department
Quarter1	1stQuarter

© 2014 Cengage Learning

Debug a Macro

Learning
Outcomes
• Locate VBA errors
• Correct VBA errors

When a macro procedure does not run properly, it can be due to an error, referred to as a **bug**, in the code. To help you find the bug(s) in a procedure, the Visual Basic Editor lets you step through the procedure's code, one line at a time. When you locate the error, you can then correct, or **debug**, it. **CASE** *You decide to debug the macro procedure to find out why it failed to insert your name in the worksheet footer.*

STEPS

1. **With the January worksheet displayed, click the DEVELOPER tab if necessary, click the Macros button in the Code group, in the Macro dialog box click 'EX P-Monthly Sales. xlsm'!FooterInput, then click Step Into**

 The Visual Basic Editor opens with the yellow statement selector positioned on the first statement of the procedure, as shown in FIGURE P-11.

2. **Press [F8] to step to the next statement**

 The statement selector skips over the comments and the line of code beginning with Dim. The Dim statement indicates that the procedure will store your name in a variable named LeftFooterText. Because Dim is a declaration of a variable and not a procedure statement, the statement selector skips it and moves to the line containing the InputBox function.

3. **Press [F8] again, with the cursor in the text box in the Microsoft Excel dialog box type your name, then click OK**

 The Visual Basic Editor opens. The statement selector is now positioned on the statement that reads Worksheets("January").PageSetup.LeftFooter = LeftFooter. This statement should insert your name (which you just typed in the text box) in the left section of the footer. This is the instruction that does not appear to be working correctly.

4. **If necessary scroll right until the end of the LeftFooter instruction is visible, then place the mouse pointer on LeftFooter**

 The value of the LeftFooter variable is displayed as shown in FIGURE P-12. Rather than containing your name, the variable LeftFooter at the end of this line is empty. This is because the InputBox function assigned your name to the LeftFooterText variable, not to the LeftFooter variable. Before you can correct this bug, you need to turn off the Step Into feature.

5. **Click the Reset button ▣ on the Visual Basic Editor toolbar to turn off the Step Into feature, click at the end of the statement containing the error, then replace the variable LeftFooter with LeftFooterText**

 The revised statement now reads Worksheets("January").PageSetup.LeftFooter = LeftFooterText.

6. **Delete the comment line pointing out the error**

7. **Click the Save EX P-Monthly Sales.xlsm button 🔲 on the Visual Basic Editor toolbar, then click the View Microsoft Excel button 🔣 on the toolbar**

8. **With the January worksheet displayed click the Macros button in the Code group, in the Macro dialog box click 'EX P-Monthly Sales.xlsm'!FooterInput, click Run to rerun the procedure, when prompted type your name, then click OK**

9. **Click the File tab, click Print, then view the worksheet preview**

 Your name now appears in the left section of the footer.

10. **Click the Back button ◉, then save the workbook**

```
Run  Tools  Add-Ins  Window  Help
■ ✔ 🔧 📋 🔨 ✳ ❓ | Ln 5, Col 1

(General)                                                    ▾   FooterInput

        'FooterInput Procedure
        'Written by Your Name
        'Customize worksheet footer
        '
   ⇨ Sub FooterInput()
            'Declares the LeftFooterText string variable
            Dim LeftFooterText As String
            'Prompts user for left footer text and stores
            'response in LeftFooter Text variable
            LeftFooterText = InputBox("Enter name:")
            'Inserts contents of LeftFooterText into left footer
            '*****THERE IS AN ERROR IN THE FOLLOWING LINE***
            Worksheets("January").PageSetup.LeftFooter = LeftFooter
            'Inserts the date in right footer
            Worksheets("January").PageSetup.RightFooter = "&D"
        End Sub
```

Statement selector →

FIGURE P-12: **Value contained in LeftFooter variable**

```
Run  Tools  Add-Ins  Window  Help
■ ✔ 🔧 📋 🔨 ✳ ❓ | Ln 13, Col 1

(General)                                                    ▾   FooterInput

        'FooterInput Procedure
        'Written by Your Name
        'Customize worksheet footer
        '
      Sub FooterInput()
            'Declares the LeftFooterText string variable
            Dim LeftFooterText As String
            'Prompts user for left footer text and stores
            'response in LeftFooter Text variable
            LeftFooterText = InputBox("Enter name:")
            'Inserts contents of LeftFooterText into left footer
            '*****THERE IS AN ERROR IN THE FOLLOWING LINE***
   ⇨ |    Worksheets("January").PageSetup.LeftFooter = LeftFooter
            'Inserts the date in right footer      ┌──────────────────┐
                                                    │ LeftFooter = Empty │
            Worksheets("January").PageSetup.RightFooter = "&D"
        End Sub
```

Indicates the LeftFooter variable is empty ←

Adding security to your macro projects

To add security to your projects, you can add a digital signature to the project. A digital signature guarantees the project hasn't been altered since it was signed. Sign macros only after you have tested them and are ready to distribute them. If the code in a digitally signed macro project is changed in any way, its digital signature is removed. To add a digital signature to a Visual Basic project, select the project that you want to sign in the Visual Basic Project Explorer window, click the Tools menu in the Visual Basic Editor, click Digital Signature, click Choose, select the certificate, then click OK twice. When you add a digital signature to a project, the macro project is automatically re-signed whenever it is saved on your computer. You can get a digital certificate from your administrator. There are also third-party certification authorities that issue certificates that are trusted by Microsoft.

Create a Main Procedure

When you routinely need to run several macros one after another, you can save time by combining them into one procedure. The resulting procedure, which processes (or runs) multiple procedures in sequence, is referred to as the **main procedure**. To create a main procedure, you type a **Call statement** for each procedure you want to run. The syntax of the Call statement is Call *procedurename*, where *procedurename* is the name of the procedure you want to run. **CASE** *To avoid having to run her macros one after another every month, Kate asks you to create a main procedure that will run (or call) each of the procedures in the EX P-Monthly Sales workbook in sequence.*

STEPS

1. **With the January worksheet displayed, click the DEVELOPER tab if necessary, then click the Visual Basic button in the Code group**

2. **Verify that EX P-Monthly Sales is the active project, click Insert on the menu bar, then click Module**

 A new, blank module named Module1 is inserted in the EX P-Monthly Sales workbook.

3. **In the Properties window click (Name), then type MainProc**

4. **In the Code window enter the procedure code exactly as shown in FIGURE P-13, entering your name in the second line**

5. **Compare your main procedure code with FIGURE P-13, correct any errors if necessary, then click the Save EX P-Monthly Sales.xlsm button 🖫 on the Visual Basic Editor toolbar**

 To test the new main procedure, you need an unformatted version of the EX P-January Sales worksheet.

6. **Click the View Microsoft Excel button 🖾 on the toolbar, then save and close the EX P-January Sales workbook**

 The EX P-Monthly Sales workbook remains open.

7. **Open the file EX P-2.xlsx from the location where you store your Data Files, then save it as EX P-January Sales 2**

 In the next lesson, you'll run the main procedure.

Copying a macro to another workbook

If you would like to use a macro in another workbook, you can copy the module to that workbook using the Visual Basic Editor. Open both the source and destination Excel workbooks, then open the Visual Basic Editor and verify that macros are enabled. In Project Explorer, drag the module that will be copied from the source workbook to the destination workbook.

FIGURE P-13: **VBA code for the MainProcedure procedure**

```
'MainProcedure Procedure
'Written by Your Name
'Calls sub procedures in sequence
'
Sub MainProcedure()
    Call FormatFile
    Call AddTotal
    Call SalesStatus
    Call FooterInput
End Sub
```

MainProcedure calls each procedure in the order shown

Writing and documenting VBA code

When you write VBA code in the Visual Basic Editor, you want to make it as readable as possible. This makes it easier for you or your coworkers to edit the code when changes need to be made. The procedure statements should be indented, leaving the procedure name and its End statement easy to spot in the code. This is helpful when a module contains many procedures. It is also good practice to add comments at the beginning of each procedure that describe its purpose and any assumptions made in the procedure, such as the quota amounts. You should also explain each code statement with a comment. You have seen comments inserted into VBA code by beginning the statement with an apostrophe. You can also add comments to the end of a line of VBA code by placing an apostrophe before the comment, as shown in FIGURE P-14.

FIGURE P-14: **VBA code with comments at the end of statements**

```
Run  Tools  Add-Ins  Window  Help
■  ⊾  ⅀  ☞  ⅍  ✳  ❷  | Ln 10, Col 8
(General)                                          ∨   MainProcedure

    'MainProcedure Procedure
    'Written by Your Name
    'Calls sub procedures in sequence
    '
    Sub MainProcedure()
        Call FormatFile 'Run FormatFile procedure
        Call AddTotal   'Run AddTotal procedure
        Call SalesStatus    'Run SalesStatus procedure
        Call FooterInput    'Run FooterInput procedure
    End Sub
```

Comments at the end of the statements in green

Run a Main Procedure

Running a main procedure allows you to run several macros in sequence. You can run a main procedure just as you would any other macro procedure. **CASE** ▶ *You have finished creating Kate's main procedure, and you are ready to run it. If the main procedure works correctly, it should format the worksheet, insert the sales total, insert a sales status message, and add your name and date to the worksheet footer.*

STEPS

1. **With the January worksheet displayed, click the DEVELOPER tab, click the Macros button in the Code group, in the Macro dialog box click 'EX P-Monthly Sales.xlsm'!MainProcedure, click Run, when prompted type your name, then click OK**

 The MainProcedure runs the FormatFile, AddTotal, SalesStatus, and FooterInput procedures in sequence. You can see the results of the FormatFile, AddTotal, and SalesStatus procedures in the worksheet window, as shown in **FIGURE P-16**. To view the results of the FooterInput procedure, you need to switch to the Preview window.

2. **Click the File tab, click Print, view the worksheet preview and verify that your name appears in the left footer area and the date appears in the right footer area, click the Back button ◉, then click the DEVELOPER tab**

3. **Click the Visual Basic button in the Code group**

 You need to add your name to the Format module.

4. **In the Project Explorer window, double-click the Format module, add a comment line after the procedure name that reads Written by [Your Name], then click the Save EX P-Monthly Sales.xlsm button ▦**

 You want to see the options for printing VBA code.

5. **Click File on the Visual Basic Editor menu bar, then click Print**

 The Print - VBAProject dialog box opens, as shown in **FIGURE P-17**. The Current Module is selected which will print each procedure separately. It is faster to print all the procedures in the workbook at one time by clicking the Current Project option button to select it. You can also create a file of the VBA code by selecting the Print to File check box. You do not want to print the modules at this time.

6. **Click Cancel in the Print - VBAProject dialog box**

7. **Click the View Microsoft Excel button ▣ on the toolbar**

8. **Save the EX P-January Sales 2 workbook, then preview the worksheet**

 Compare your formatted worksheet to **FIGURE P-18**.

9. **Close the EX P-January Sales 2 workbook, close the EX P-Monthly Sales workbook, then exit Excel**

Running a macro using a button

You can run a macro by assigning it to a button on your worksheet. Create a button by clicking the Insert tab, clicking the Shapes button in the Illustrations group, choosing a shape, then drawing the shape on the worksheet. After you create the button, right-click it, click Assign Macro, then click the macro the button will run and click OK. It is a good idea to label the button with descriptive text; select it and begin typing. You can also format macro buttons using clip art, photographs, fills, and shadows. You format a button using the buttons on the DRAWING TOOLS FORMAT tab. To add a fill to the button, click the Shape Fill list arrow and select a fill color,

picture, texture, or gradient. To add a shape effect, click the Shape Effects button and select an effect. You can also use the WordArt styles in the WordArt Styles group. **FIGURE P-15** shows a button formatted with a gradient, bevel and WordArt.

FIGURE P-15: Formatted macro button

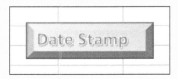

FIGURE P-16: Result of running MainProcedure procedure

Formatted title

Row inserted

	Trip Code	Depart Date	Number of Days	Seats Sold	Tour	Sales
					Quest Chicago January Sales	
3	Trip Code	Depart Date	Number of Days	Seats Sold	Tour	Sales
4	457R	1/7/2016	30	30	African National Parks	$ 121,400.00
5	556J	1/13/2016	14	25	Amazing Amazon	$ 67,875.00
6	675Y	1/19/2016	14	32	Catalonia Adventure	$ 100,300.00
7	446R	1/20/2016	7	18	Yellowstone	$ 46,958.00
8	251D	1/21/2016	7	10	Costa Rica	$ 28,220.00
9	335P	1/22/2016	21	33	Corfu Sailing Voyage	$ 105,270.00
10	431V	1/25/2016	7	21	Costa Rica Rainforests	$ 54,390.00
11	215C	1/26/2016	14	19	Silk Road Travels	$ 92,663.00
12	325B	1/27/2016	10	17	Down Under Exodus	$ 47,600.00
13	311A	1/29/2016	18	20	Essential India	$ 102,887.00
14	422R	1/29/2016	7	24	Exotic Morocco	$ 45,600.00
15	331E	1/30/2016	12	21	Experience Cambodia	$ 98,557.00
16	831P	1/30/2016	14	15	Galapagos Adventure	$ 55,698.00
17	337Q	1/31/2016	18	10	Green Adventures in Ecuador	$ 39,574.00
18					**Monthly Total:**	**$ 1,006,992.00**
19						
20					**Sales Status:**	Met Quota
21						

Total sales calculated

Sales status message inserted

FIGURE P-17: Printing options for macro procedures

Print to File check box

Current Project option button

```
Print - VBAProject                                    ×

Printer:    HP Universal Printing PS          Print to File      ┌──────┐
┌─ Range ──────────────┐  ┌─ Print What ──┐   check box          │  OK  │
│ ○ Selection          │  │ ☐ Form Image  │                      └──────┘
│ ● Current Module     │  │ ☑ Code        │                      ┌──────┐
│ ○ Current Project    │  └───────────────┘                      │Cancel│
└──────────────────────┘                                         └──────┘
                                                                 ┌──────┐
                                                                 │Setup.│
Print Quality:  High        ▾      ☐ Print to File               └──────┘
                                                                 ┌──────┐
                                                                 │ Help │
                                                                 └──────┘
```

FIGURE P-18: Formatted January worksheet

Quest Chicago January Sales

Trip Code	Depart Date	Number of Days	Seats Sold	Tour	Sales
457R	1/7/2016	30	30	African National Parks	$ 121,400.00
556J	1/13/2016	14	25	Amazing Amazon	$ 67,875.00
675Y	1/19/2016	14	32	Catalonia Adventure	$ 100,300.00
446R	1/20/2016	7	18	Yellowstone	$ 46,958.00
251D	1/21/2016	7	10	Costa Rica	$ 28,220.00
335P	1/22/2016	21	33	Corfu Sailing Voyage	$ 105,270.00
431V	1/25/2016	7	21	Costa Rica Rainforests	$ 54,390.00
215C	1/26/2016	14	19	Silk Road Travels	$ 92,663.00
325B	1/27/2016	10	17	Down Under Exodus	$ 47,600.00
311A	1/29/2016	18	20	Essential India	$ 102,887.00
422R	1/29/2016	7	24	Exotic Morocco	$ 45,600.00
331E	1/30/2016	12	21	Experience Cambodia	$ 98,557.00
831P	1/30/2016	14	15	Galapagos Adventure	$ 55,698.00
337Q	1/31/2016	18	10	Green Adventures in Ecuador	$ 39,574.00
				Monthly Total:	**$ 1,006,992.00**
				Sales Status:	Met Quota

Your Name 11/30/2016

Excel 2013

Practice

Concepts Review

1. Which element do you click to return to Excel from the Visual Basic Editor?
2. Which element points to the Project Explorer window?
3. Which element points to the Code window?
4. Which element do you click to turn off the Step Into feature?
5. Which element points to comments in the VBA code?

FIGURE P-19

Match each term with the statement that best describes it.

6. Sub procedure
7. Function
8. Keywords
9. Procedure
10. Comments

a. Another term for a macro in Visual Basic for Applications (VBA)
b. A procedure that returns a value
c. Words that are recognized as part of the programming language
d. A series of statements that perform an action but don't return a value
e. Descriptive text used to explain parts of a procedure

Select the best answer from the list of choices.

11. A location in memory where you can temporarily store information is a:
- **a.** Variable.
- **b.** Procedure.
- **c.** Sub procedure.
- **d.** Function.

12. You enter the statements of a macro in:
- **a.** The Macro dialog box.
- **b.** Any blank worksheet.
- **c.** The Properties window of the Visual Basic Editor.
- **d.** The Code window of the Visual Basic Editor.

13. If your macro doesn't run correctly, you should:
- **a.** Select the macro in the Macro dialog box, click Step Into, then debug the macro.
- **b.** Create an If...Then...Else statement.
- **c.** Click the Project Explorer button.
- **d.** Click the Properties button.

14. Comments are displayed in _____ in VBA code.
- **a.** Black
- **b.** Blue
- **c.** Red
- **d.** Green

15. Keywords are displayed in _____ in VBA code.
- **a.** Black
- **b.** Blue
- **c.** Green
- **d.** Red

Skills Review

1. View and analyze VBA code.
- **a.** Start Excel, open the file EX P-3.xlsm from the location where you store your Data Files, enable macros, then save it as **EX P-Home Products**.
- **b.** Review the unformatted December worksheet.
- **c.** Open the Visual Basic Editor.
- **d.** Select the DataFormat module, and review the Format procedure.
- **e.** Insert comments in the procedure code describing what action you think each line of code will perform. (*Hint*: One of the statements will sort the list by Store #.) Add comment lines to the top of the procedure to describe the purpose of the macro and to enter your name.
- **f.** Save the macro, return to the worksheet, then run the Format macro.
- **g.** Compare the results with the code and your comments.
- **h.** Save the workbook.

2. Write VBA code.
- **a.** Open the Visual Basic Editor, and insert a new module named **Total** in the EX P-Home Products project.
- **b.** Enter the code for the SalesTotal procedure exactly as shown in FIGURE P-20. Enter your name in the second line.
- **c.** Save the macro.
- **d.** Return to the December worksheet, then run the SalesTotal macro.
- **e.** Save the workbook.

FIGURE P-20

```
'SalesTotal Procedure
'Written by Your Name
'Totals December sales
Sub SalesTotal()
    Range("E17").Select
    ActiveCell.Formula = "=SUM($E$3:$E$16)"
    Selection.Font.Bold = True
    With Selection.Borders(xlTop)
        .LineStyle = xlSingle
    End With
    Columns("E").Select
    Selection.Columns.AutoFit
    Range("A1").Select
End Sub
```

Skills Review (continued)

3. Add a conditional statement

a. Open the Visual Basic Editor, and insert a new module named **Goal** in the EX P-Home Products project.

b. Enter the SalesGoal procedure exactly as shown in FIGURE P-21. Enter your name on the second line.

c. Save the macro.

d. Return to the December worksheet, and run the SalesGoal macro. The procedure should enter the message **Missed goal** in cell E18. Save the workbook.

4. Prompt the user for data.

a. Open the Visual Basic Editor, and insert a new module named **Header** in the EX P-Home Products project.

b. Enter the HeaderFooter procedure exactly as shown in FIGURE P-22. You are entering an error in the procedure that will be corrected in Step 5.

c. Save the macro, then return to the December worksheet, and run the HeaderFooter macro.

d. Preview the December worksheet. Your name should be missing from the left section of the footer.

e. Save the workbook.

FIGURE P-21

```
'SalesGoal Procedure
'Written by Your Name
'Tests whether sales goal was met
Sub SalesGoal()
    'If the total is >=100000, then insert "Met Goal"
    'in cell E18
    If Range("E17") >= 100000 Then
        Range("E18").Select
        ActiveCell.Formula = "Met goal"
    'otherwise, insert "Missed goal" in cell E18
    Else
        Range("E18").Select
        ActiveCell.Formula = "Missed goal"
    End If
    Range("A1").Select
End Sub
```

FIGURE P-22

```
'HeaderFooter Procedure
'Written by Your Name
'Procedure to customize the header and footer
Sub HeaderFooter()
    'Inserts the filename in the header
    Worksheets("December").PageSetup.CenterHeader = "&F"
    'Declares the variable LeftFooterText as a string
    Dim LeftFooterText As String
    'Prompts user for left footer text
    LeftFooter = InputBox("Enter your full name:")
    'Inserts response into left footer
    Worksheets("December").PageSetup.LeftFooter = LeftFooterText
    'Inserts the date into right footer
    Worksheets("December").PageSetup.RightFooter = "&D"
End Sub
```

5. Debug a macro.

a. Return to the Visual Basic Editor and use the Step Into feature to locate where the error occurred in the HeaderFooter procedure. Use the Reset button to turn off the debugger.

b. Edit the procedure in the Visual Basic Editor to correct the error. (*Hint*: The error occurs on the line: LeftFooter = InputBox("Enter your full name:"). The variable that will input the response text into the worksheet footer is LeftFooterText. The line should be: LeftFooterText = InputBox("Enter your full name:").)

c. Save the macro, then return to the December worksheet, and run the HeaderFooter macro again.

d. Verify that your name now appears in the left section of the footer, then save the file.

6. Create and run a main procedure.

a. Return to the Visual Basic Editor, insert a new module, then name it **MainProc**.

b. Begin the main procedure by entering comments in the code window that provide the procedure's name (MainProcedure) and explain that its purpose is to run the Format, SalesTotal, SalesGoal, and HeaderFooter procedures. Enter your name in a comment.

c. Enter the procedure header **Sub MainProcedure()**.

d. Enter four Call statements that will run the Format, SalesTotal, SalesGoal, and HeaderFooter procedures in sequence.

e. Save the procedure and return to Excel.

f. Open the file EX P-3.xlsm, then save it as **EX P-Home Products 2**.

g. Run the MainProcedure macro, entering your name when prompted. (*Hint*: In the Macro dialog box, the macro procedures you created will now have EX P-Home Products.xlsm! as part of their names. This is because the macros are stored in the EX P-Home Products workbook, not in the EX P-Home Products 2 workbook.)

Skills Review (continued)

h. Verify that the macro ran successfully by comparing your worksheet to FIGURE P-23.

i. Save the EX P-Home Products 2 workbook, preview the December worksheet to check the header and footer, then close the EX P-Home Products 2 workbook.

j. Save the EX P-Home Products workbook, close the workbook, exit Excel, then submit the EX P-Home Products workbook to your instructor.

FIGURE P-23

	A	B	C	D	E
1	Home Products December Sales				
2	Store #	City	State	Manager	Sales
3	11405	Juno	FL	Clifford	$ 8,645.93
4	19404	Palm Beach	FL	Cloutier	$ 8,656.83
5	29393	Tampa	FL	Nelson	$ 7,654.32
6	29396	Cape Coral	FL	Enos	$ 9,583.66
7	29399	Daytona	FL	DiBenedetto	$ 9,228.33
8	29402	Vero Beach	FL	Guapo	$ 5,534.34
9	29406	Miami	FL	Monroe	$ 4,987.36
10	39394	Naples	FL	Hamm	$ 6,715.68
11	39395	Bonita Springs	FL	Handelmann	$ 4,225.22
12	39397	Clearwater	FL	Erickson	$ 7,594.22
13	39398	Delray Beach	FL	Dever	$ 8,442.90
14	39400	Stuart	FL	Hahn	$ 8,001.34
15	39401	Neptune	FL	Pratt	$ 5,251.22
16	39403	Sanibel	FL	Lo	$ 4,643.93
17					$99,165.28
18					Missed goal
19					

Independent Challenge 1

You are the development director at a private school. The information systems manager asks you to document and test an Excel procedure that the previous director wrote for the school's accountant. You will first run the macro procedure to see what it does, then add comments to the VBA code to document it. You will also enter data to verify that the formulas in the macro work correctly.

a. Start Excel, open the file EX P-4.xlsm from the location where you store your Data Files, then save it as **EX P-First Quarter**.

b. Run the First macro, noting anything that you think should be mentioned in your documentation.

c. Review the First procedure in the Visual Basic Editor. It is stored in the FirstQtr module.

d. Document the procedure by adding comments to the code, indicating the actions the procedure performs and the objects (ranges) that are affected.

e. Enter your name in a comment line, then save the procedure.

f. Return to the Jan-Mar worksheet, and use FIGURE P-24 as a guide to enter data in cells B4:D6. The totals will appear as you enter the income data.

g. Format the range B4:D8 using the Accounting Number format with no decimals, as shown in FIGURE P-24.

h. Check the total income calculations in row 8 to verify that the macro is working correctly.

i. Enter your name in the center section of the Jan-Mar sheet footer, save the workbook, then preview the worksheet.

j. Close the workbook, exit Excel, then submit the workbook to your instructor.

FIGURE P-24

	A	B	C	D	E
1		January	February	March	
2	Income				
3					
4	Donations	$ 1,700	$ 1,700	$ 1,500	
5	Fundraisers	$ 3,000	$ 2,100	$ 2,700	
6	Grants	$ 21,000	$ 51,000	$ 92,000	
7					
8	Total Income	$ 25,700	$ 54,800	$ 96,200	
9					

Independent Challenge 2

You work in the Miami branch of Medical Resources, a medical employment recruitment agency. You have three locations where you have monthly quotas for placements. Each month you are required to produce a report stating whether placement quotas were met for the following three medical facilities: Central Hospital, Shore Clinic, and Assisted Home. The quotas for each month are as follows: Central Hospital 12, Shore Clinic 8, and Assisted Home 5. Your placement results this month were 8, 9, and 6, respectively. You decide to create a procedure to automate your monthly task of determining the placement quota status for the placement categories. You would like your assistant to take this task over when you go on vacation next month. Because he has no previous experience with Excel, you decide to create a second procedure that prompts a user with input boxes to enter the actual placement results for the month.

a. Start Excel, open the file EX P-5.xlsm from the location where you store your Data Files, then save it as **EX P-Placements**.

Independent Challenge 2 (continued)

b. Use the Visual Basic Editor to insert a new module named **Quotas** in the EX P-Placements workbook. Create a procedure in the new module named **PlacementQuota** that determines the quota status for each category and enters Yes or No in the Status column. The VBA code is shown in FIGURE P-25.

c. Add comments to the PlacementQuota procedure, including the procedure name, your name, and the purpose of the procedure, then save it.

d. Insert a new module named **MonthlyPlacement**. Create a second procedure named **Placement** that prompts a user for placement data for each placement category, enters the input data in the appropriate cells, then calls the PlacementQuota procedure. The VBA code is shown in FIGURE P-26. (*Hint*: The procedure's blank lines group the macro code in related units. These blank lines are optional and their purpose is to make the procedure easier to understand.)

e. Add a comment noting the procedure name on the first line. Add a comment with your name on the second line. Add a third comment line at the top of the procedure describing its purpose. Enter comments in the code to document the macro actions. Save the procedure.

f. Run the Placement macro, and enter **8** for hospital placement, **9** for clinic placements, and **6** for assisted placements. Correct any errors in the VBA code.

g. Add your name to the center section of the worksheet footer, save the workbook, then preview the worksheet. Close the workbook, exit Excel, then submit your workbook to your instructor.

FIGURE P-25

```
Sub PlacementQuota()

    If Range("C4") >= 12 Then
        Range("D4").Select
        ActiveCell.Formula = "Yes"
    Else
        Range("D4").Select
        ActiveCell.Formula = "No"
    End If

    If Range("C5") >= 8 Then
        Range("D5").Select
        ActiveCell.Formula = "Yes"
    Else
        Range("D5").Select
        ActiveCell.Formula = "No"
    End If

    If Range("C6") >= 5 Then
        Range("D6").Select
        ActiveCell.Formula = "Yes"
    Else
        Range("D6").Select
        ActiveCell.Formula = "No"
    End If

End Sub
```

FIGURE P-26

```
Sub Placement()

    Dim Hospital As String
    Hospital = InputBox("Enter Hospital Placements")
    Range("C4").Select
    Selection = Hospital

    Dim Clinic As String
    Clinic = InputBox("Enter Clinic Placements")
    Range("C5").Select
    Selection = Clinic

    Dim Assisted As String
    Assisted = InputBox("Enter Assisted Placements")
    Range("C6").Select
    Selection = Assisted

    Call PlacementQuota

End Sub
```

Independent Challenge 3

You are the marketing director at a car dealership business based in Cincinnati. You have started to advertise using an area magazine, billboards, TV, radio, and local newspapers. Every month you prepare a report with the advertising expenses detailed by source. You decide to create a macro that will format the monthly reports. You add the same footers on every report, so you will create another macro that will add a footer to a document. Finally, you will create a main procedure that calls the macros to format the report and adds a footer. You begin by opening a workbook with the January data. You will save the macros you create in this workbook.

a. Start Excel, open the file EX P-6.xlsm from the location where you store your Data Files, then save it as **EX P-Auto**.

b. Insert a module named **Format**, then create a procedure named **Formatting** that:
 - Selects a cell in row 3, and inserts a row in the worksheet above it.
 - Selects the cost data in column C, and formats it as currency. (*Hint*: After the row is inserted, this range is C5:C9.)
 - Selects cell A1 before ending.

c. Save the Formatting procedure.

d. Insert a module named **Foot**, then create a procedure named **Footer** that:
 - Declares a string variable for text that will be placed in the left footer.
 - Uses an input box to prompt the user for his or her name, and places the name in the left footer.
 - Places the date in the right footer.

Independent Challenge 3 (continued)

e. Save the Footer procedure.

f. Insert a module named **Main**, then create a procedure named **MainProc** that calls the Footer procedure and the Formatting procedure.

g. Save your work, then run the MainProc procedure. Debug each procedure as necessary. Your worksheet should look like FIGURE P-27.

h. Document each procedure by inserting a comment line with the procedure name, your name, and a description of the procedure.

i. Preview the January worksheet, save the workbook, close the workbook, exit Excel, then submit the workbook to your instructor.

FIGURE P-27

	A	B	C	D
1	Cincinnati Auto			
2	Ad Campaign			
3				
4	Advertising Type	Source	Cost	
5	Magazine	Ohio Magazine	$ 350.00	
6	Newspaper	Tribune	$ 150.00	
7	Billboard	Main Street	$ 450.00	
8	TV	Local Access Station	$ 170.00	
9	Radio	WAQV	$ 575.00	
10				

Independent Challenge 4: Explore

You decide to create a log of your monthly expenses in an effort to budget your income. You have received a workbook with a macro that tracks your major expenses for the first three months of the year. You want to expand this macro to track six months of expenses.

a. Start Excel, open the file EX P-7.xlsm from the location where you store your Data Files, then save it as **EX P-Expenses**.

b. Run the MonthExpenses macro and enter expense numbers to verify the macro is working properly, then clear all the expense entries in cells E2:E7.

c. Edit the MonthExpenses procedure to add the abbreviated month entries of Apr, May, and Jun. Remember to edit the selected cells, total cells and the formatting ranges in the procedure.

d. Run the macro and debug the procedure as necessary. Enter expense numbers to verify the macro is working properly. Widen columns where necessary.

e. Save your work.

f. Verify that the totals are correct for each month and each category.

g. Enter your name as a comment in the second line of the procedure, then save the procedure.

h. Change the page orientation to landscape, enter your name in the center section of the worksheet footer, then preview the worksheet.

i. Insert a module named **Preview** with a procedure named **PreviewSheetdata** that previews a worksheet. The VBA code is shown in FIGURE P-28.

j. Save the macro and return to the worksheet.

k. Assign the macro PreviewSheetdata to a button on the worksheet. (*Hint*: Use the Rectangle tool to create the button, label the button **Print Preview**, then right-click the button to assign the macro.)

l. Format the button and its label with a style of your choice.

m. Test the button, then close the Print Preview.

n. Save the workbook, close the workbook, exit Excel, then submit the workbook to your instructor.

FIGURE P-28

```
Sub PreviewSheetdata()

ActiveSheet.PrintPreview

End Sub
```

Excel 2013

Visual Workshop

Open the file EX P-8.xlsm from the location where you store your Data Files, then save it as **EX P-Florist**. Create a macro procedure named **Formatting** in a module named **FormatFile** that will format the worksheet as shown in FIGURE P-29. (*Hints*: The font size of the first two rows is 12 pt and the other rows are 11 pt. Notice that there is an added row.) Run the macro and debug it as necessary to make the worksheet match FIGURE P-29. Insert your name in a comment line under the procedure name and in the worksheet footer, then preview the worksheet. Submit the workbook to your instructor.

FIGURE P-29

	A	B	C
1	Blossoms		
2	Monthly Sales		
3			
4	Flowers	$857.89	
5	Plants	$622.87	
6	Silks	$424.58	
7	Home Décor	$469.88	
8			
9			

Getting Started with Access 2013

CASE Samantha Hooper is the tour developer for United States group travel at Quest Specialty Travel (QST), a tour company that specializes in customized group travel packages. Samantha uses Microsoft Access 2013 to store, maintain, and analyze customer and tour information.

Unit Objectives

After completing this unit, you will be able to:

- Understand relational databases
- Explore a database
- Create a database
- Create a table

- Create primary keys
- Relate two tables
- Enter data
- Edit data

Files You Will Need

QuestTravel-A.accdb
RealEstate-A.accdb
Recycle-A.accdb
BusinessContacts-A.accdb
Basketball-A.accdb

Microsoft® product screenshots used with permission from Microsoft® Corporation.

Understand Relational Databases

Learning Outcomes
• Describe relational database concepts
• Explain when to use a database

Microsoft Access 2013 is relational database software that runs on the Windows operating system. You use **relational database software** to manage data that is organized into lists, such as information about customers, products, vendors, employees, projects, or sales. Many small companies track customer, inventory, and sales information in a spreadsheet program such as Microsoft Excel. Although Excel offers some list management features and is more commonly used than Access, Access provides many more tools and advantages for managing data. The advantages are mainly due to the "relational" nature of the lists that Access manages. TABLE A-1 compares the two programs. **CASE** ▶ *You and Samantha Hooper review the advantages of database software over spreadsheets for managing lists of information.*

DETAILS

The advantages of using Access for database management include:

* **Duplicate data is minimized**

 FIGURES A-1 and A-2 compare how you might store sales data in a single Excel spreadsheet list versus three related Access tables. With Access, you do not have to reenter information such as a customer's name and address or tour name every time a sale is made, because lists can be linked, or "related," in relational database software.

* **Information is more accurate, reliable, and consistent because duplicate data is minimized**

 The relational nature of data stored in an Access database allows you to minimize duplicate data entry, which creates more accurate, reliable, and consistent information. For example, customer data in a Customers table is entered only once, not every time a customer makes a purchase.

* **Data entry is faster and easier using Access forms**

 Data entry forms (screen layouts) make data entry faster, easier, and more accurate than entering data in a spreadsheet.

* **Information can be viewed and sorted in many ways using Access queries, forms, and reports**

 In Access, you can save queries (questions about the data), data entry forms, and reports, allowing you to use them over and over without performing extra work to re-create a particular view of the data.

* **Information is more secure using Access passwords and security features**

 Access databases can be encrypted and password protected.

* **Several users can share and edit information at the same time**

 Unlike spreadsheets or word-processing documents, more than one person can enter, update, and analyze data in an Access database at the same time.

FIGURE A-1: Using a spreadsheet to organize sales data

	A	B	C	D	E	F	G	H	I
1	CustNo	FName	LName	SalesNo	SaleDate	TourName	TourStartDate	City	Price
2	1	Gracita	Mayberry	35	7/1/2014	Red Reef Scuba	7/6/2014	Islamadora	1,500.00
3	2	Jacob	Alman	34	7/1/2014	Red Reef Scuba	7/6/2014	Islamadora	1,500.00
4	3	Julia	Bouchart	33	7/1/2014	Red Reef Scuba	7/6/2014	Islamadora	1,500.00
5	3	Julia	Bouchart	7	5/1/2014	Piper-Heitman Wedding	5/30/2014	Captiva	825.00
6	4	Jane	Taylor	13	5/11/2014	Red Reef Scuba	7/6/2014	Islamadora	1,500.00
7	4	Jane	Taylor	20	6/1/2014	American Heritage Tour	8/24/2014	Philadelphia	1,200.00
8	5	Samantha	Braven	30	7/1/2014	Red Reef Scuba	7/6/2014	Islamadora	1,500.00
9	5	Samantha	Braven	52	7/11/2014	Bright Lights Expo	12/1/2014	Branson	200.00
10	6	Kristen	Collins	3	4/30/2014	Ames Ski Club	1/2/2015	Breckenridge	850.00
11	6	Kristen	Collins	21	6/1/2014	Yosemite National Park Great Cleanup	7/20/2014	Sacramento	1,100.00
12	6	Kristen	Collins	29	7/1/2014	American Heritage Tour	8/24/2014	Philadelphia	1,200.00
13	6	Kristen	Collins	40	7/7/2014	Bright Lights Expo	12/1/2014	Branson	200.00
14	7	Tom	Camel	41	7/7/2014	Bright Lights Expo	12/1/2014	Branson	200.00
15	7	Tom	Camel	36	7/1/2014	American Heritage Tour	8/24/2014	Philadelphia	1,200.00
16	7	Tom	Camel	8	5/1/2014	Ames Ski Club	1/2/2015	Breckenridge	850.00
17	7	Tom	Camel	19	6/1/2014	Yosemite National Park Great Cleanup	7/20/2014	Sacramento	1,100.00
18	8	Dick	Tracy	43	7/8/2014	Bright Lights Expo	12/1/2014	Branson	200.00
19	9	Daniel	Cabriella	45	7/9/2014	American Heritage Tour	8/24/2014	Philadelphia	1,200.00
20	9	Daniel	Cabriella	46	7/9/2014	Bright Lights Expo	12/1/2014	Branson	200.00
21	10	Brad	Eahlie	66	7/14/2014	Boy Scout Jamboree	1/13/2015	Vail	1,900.00
22	11	Nancy	Diverman	32	7/1/2014	Red Reef Scuba	7/6/2014	Islamadora	1,500.00

Customer information is duplicated when the same customer purchases multiple tours

Tour information is duplicated when the same tour is purchased by multiple customers

FIGURE A-2: Using a relational database to organize sales data

Customers table

Cust No	First	Last	Street	City	State	Zip	Phone
1	Gracita	Mayberry	52411 Oakmont Rd	Kansas City	MO	64144	(555) 444-1234
2	Jacob	Alman	2505 McGee St	Des Moines	IA	50288	(555) 111-6931
3	Julia	Bouchart	5200 Main St	Kansas City	MO	64105	(555) 111-3081

Sales table

Cust No	TourNo	Date	SalesNo
1	2	7/1/14	35
2	2	7/1/14	34
3	2	7/1/14	33

Tours table

TourNo	TourName	TourStartDate	Duration	City	Cost
1	Stanley Bay Shelling	07/06/2014	3	Captiva	$750.00
2	Red Reef Scuba	07/06/2014	3	Islamadora	$1,500.00
3	Ames Ski Club	01/02/2015	7	Breckenridge	$850.00

TABLE A-1: Comparing Excel with Access

feature	Excel	Access
Layout	Provides a natural tabular layout for easy data entry	Provides a natural tabular layout as well as the ability to create customized data entry screens called forms
Storage	Restricted to a file's limitations	Virtually unlimited when coupled with the ability to use Microsoft SQL Server to store data
Linked tables	Manages single lists of information—no relational database capabilities	Relates lists of information to reduce data redundancy and create a relational database
Reporting	Limited	Provides the ability to create an unlimited number of reports
Security	Limited to file security options such as marking the file "read-only" or protecting a range of cells	When used with SQL Server, provides extensive security down to the user and data level
Multiuser capabilities	Not allowed	Allows multiple users to simultaneously enter and update data
Data entry	Provides limited data entry screens	Provides the ability to create an unlimited number of data entry forms

Explore a Database

Learning Outcomes
- Start Access and open a database
- Identify Access components
- Open and define Access objects

You can start Access in many ways. If you double-click an existing Access *database* icon or shortcut, that specific database will open directly within Access. This is the fastest way to open an *existing* Access database. If you start Access on its own, however, you see a window that requires you to make a choice between opening a database and creating a new database. **CASE** *Samantha Hooper has developed a database called QuestTravel-A, which contains tour information. She asks you to start Access 2013 and review this database.*

STEPS

1. **Start Access**

 Access starts, as shown in **FIGURE A-3**. This window allows you to open an existing database, create a new database from a template, or create a new blank database.

TROUBLE
If a yellow Security Warning bar appears below the Ribbon, click Enable Content.

2. **Click the Open Other Files link, navigate to the location where you store your Data Files, click the QuestTravel-A.accdb database, click Open, then click the Maximize button ▭ if the Access window is not already maximized**

 The QuestTravel-A.accdb database contains five tables of data named Customers, Sales, States, TourCategories, and Tours. It also contains six queries, six forms, and four reports. Each of these items (table, query, form, and report) is a different type of **object** in an Access database and is displayed in the **Navigation Pane**. The purpose of each object is defined in **TABLE A-2**. To learn about an Access database, you explore its objects.

TROUBLE
If the Navigation Pane is not open, click the Shutter Bar Open/Close button ⯮ to open it and view the database objects.

3. **In the Navigation Pane, double-click the Tours table to open it, then double-click the Customers table to open it**

 The Tours and Customers tables open to display the data they store. A **table** is the fundamental building block of a relational database because it stores all of the data. You can enter or edit data in a table.

4. **In the Navigation Pane, double-click the TourSales query to open it, double-click any occurrence of Heritage (as in American Heritage Tour), type Legacy, then click any other row**

 A **query** selects a subset of data from one or more tables. In this case, the TourSales query selects data from the Tours, Sales, and Customers tables. Editing data in one object changes that information in every other object of the database, demonstrating the power and productivity of a relational database.

5. **Double-click the CustomerRoster form to open it, double-click Tour in "American Legacy Tour," type Rally, then click any name in the middle part of the window**

 An Access **form** is a data entry screen. Users prefer forms for data entry (rather than editing and entering data in tables and queries) because information can be presented in an easy-to-use layout.

6. **Double-click the TourSales report to open it**

 An Access **report** is a professional printout. A report is for printing purposes only, not data entry. As shown in **FIGURE A-4**, the edits made to the American Legacy Rally tour name have carried through to the report.

7. **Click the Close button ☒ in the upper-right corner of the window**

 Clicking the Close button in the upper-right corner of the window closes Access as well as the database on which you are working. Changes to data, such as the edits you made to the American Legacy Rally tour, are automatically saved as you work. Access will prompt you to save *design* changes to objects before it closes.

FIGURE A-3: Opening Microsoft Access 2013 window

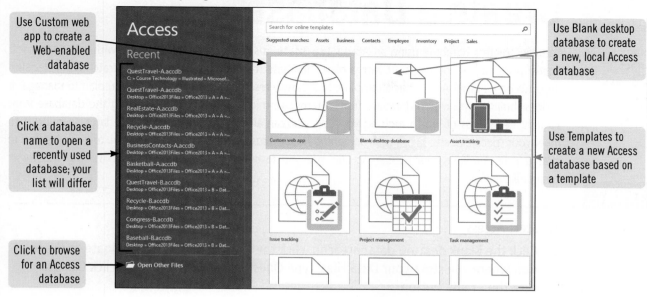

Use Custom web app to create a Web-enabled database

Click a database name to open a recently used database; your list will differ

Click to browse for an Access database

Use Blank desktop database to create a new, local Access database

Use Templates to create a new Access database based on a template

FIGURE A-4: Objects in the QuestTravel-A database

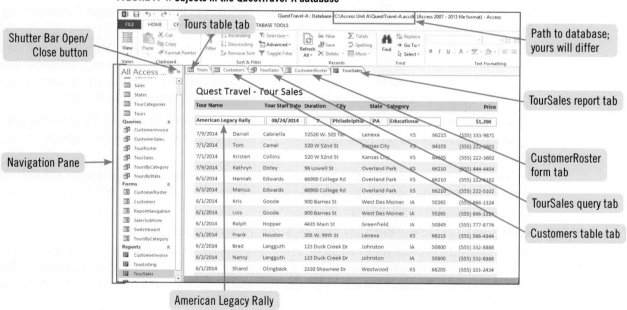

Shutter Bar Open/ Close button

Tours table tab

Navigation Pane

Path to database; yours will differ

TourSales report tab

CustomerRoster form tab

TourSales query tab

Customers table tab

American Legacy Rally

TABLE A-2: Access objects and their purpose

object	icon	purpose
Table		Contains all of the raw data within the database in a spreadsheet-like view; tables are linked with a common field to create a relational database, which minimizes redundant data
Query		Allows you to select a subset of fields or records from one or more tables; queries are created when you have a question about the data
Form		Provides an easy-to-use data entry screen
Report		Provides a professional printout of data that can contain enhancements such as headers, footers, graphics, and calculations on groups of records

Access 2013

Create a Database

Learning Outcomes
• Create a database
• Create a table
• Define key database terms

You can create a database using an Access **template**, a sample database provided within the Microsoft Access program, or you can start with a blank database to create a database from scratch. Your decision depends on whether Access has a template that closely resembles the type of data you plan to manage. If it does, building your own database from a template might be faster than creating the database from scratch. Regardless of which method you use, you can always modify the database later, tailoring it to meet your specific needs. **CASE** *Samantha Hooper reasons that the best way for you to learn Access is to start a new database from scratch, so she asks you to create a new database that will track customer communication.*

STEPS

1. **Start Access**

2. **Click the Blank desktop database icon, click the Browse button ▣, navigate to the location where you store your Data Files, type Quest in the File name box, click OK, then click the Create button**

 A new, blank database file with a single table named Table1 is created, as shown in FIGURE A-5. Although you might be tempted to start entering data into the table, a better way to build a table is to first define the columns, or **fields**, of data that the table will store. **Table Design View** provides the most options for defining fields.

3. **Click the View button ▨ on the FIELDS tab to switch to Design View, type Customers in the Save As dialog box as the new table name, then click OK**

 The table name changes from Table1 to Customers, and you are positioned in Table Design View, a window you use to name and define the fields of a table. Access created a field named ID with an AutoNumber data type. The **data type** is a significant characteristic of a field because it determines what type of data the field can store such as text, dates, or numbers. See TABLE A-3 for more information about data types.

4. **Type CustID to rename ID to CustID, press [↓] to move to the first blank Field Name cell, type FirstName, press [↓], type LastName, press [↓], type Phone, press [↓], type Birthday, then press [↓]**

 Be sure to separate the first and last names into two fields so that you can easily sort, find, and filter on either part of the name later. The Birthday field will only contain dates, so you should change its data type from Short Text (the default data type) to Date/Time.

5. **Click Short Text in the Birthday row, click the list arrow, then click Date/Time**

 With these five fields properly defined for the new Customers table, as shown in FIGURE A-6, you're ready to enter data. You switch back to Datasheet View to enter or edit data. **Datasheet View** is a spreadsheet-like view of the data in a table. A **datasheet** is a grid that displays fields as columns and records as rows. The new **field names** you just defined are listed at the top of each column.

6. **Click the View button ▦ to switch to Datasheet View, click Yes when prompted to save the table, press [Tab] to move to the FirstName field, type *your* first name, press [Tab] to move to the LastName field, type *your* last name, press [Tab] to move to the Phone field, type 111-222-3333, press [Tab], type 1/32/1980, then press [Tab]**

 Because 1/32/1980 is not a valid date, Access does not allow you to make that entry and displays an error message, as shown in FIGURE A-7. This shows that selecting the best data type for each field in Table Design View before entering data in Datasheet View helps prevent data entry errors.

7. **Press [Esc], edit the Birthday entry for the first record to 1/31/1980, press [Tab], enter two more sample records using realistic data, right-click the Customers table tab, then click Close to close the Customers table**

FIGURE A-5: Creating a database with a new table

View (Design) button

Table1 tab

Quest database

FIGURE A-6: Defining field names and data types for the Customers table in Table Design View

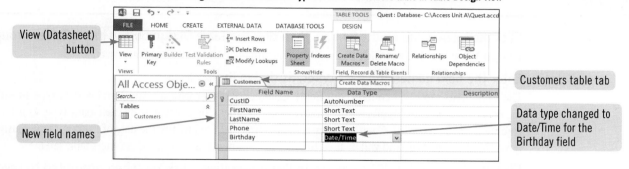

View (Datasheet) button

New field names

Customers table tab

Data type changed to Date/Time for the Birthday field

FIGURE A-7: Entering your first record in the Customers table

Field names

Invalid date creates an error message

Tab through the CustID field

Enter your first name

Enter your last name

TABLE A-3: Data types

data type	description of data
Short Text	Text or numbers not used in calculations such as a name, zip code, or phone number
Long Text	Lengthy text greater than 255 characters, such as comments or notes
Number	Numeric data that can be used in calculations, such as quantities
Date/Time	Dates and times
Currency	Monetary values
AutoNumber	Sequential integers controlled by Access
Yes/No	Only two values: Yes or No
OLE Object	OLE (Object Linking and Embedding) objects such as an Excel spreadsheet or Word document
Hyperlink	Web and e-mail addresses
Attachment	External files such as .jpg images, spreadsheets, and documents
Calculated	Result of a calculation based on other fields in the table
Lookup Wizard	The Lookup Wizard helps you set Lookup properties, which display a drop-down list of values for the field; after using the Lookup Wizard, the final data type for the field is either Short Text or Number depending on the values in the drop-down list

Create a Table

Learning Outcomes
- Create a table in Table Design View
- Set appropriate data types for fields

After creating your database and first table, you need to create new, related tables to build a relational database. Creating a table consists of these essential tasks: defining the fields in the table, selecting an appropriate data type for each field, naming the table, and determining how the table will participate in the relational database. **CASE** *Samantha Hooper asks you to create another table to store customer comments. The new table will eventually be connected to the Customers table so each customer record in the Customers table may be related to many records in the Comments table.*

STEPS

1. **Click the CREATE tab on the Ribbon, then click the Table Design button in the Tables group**

 Design View is a view in which you create and manipulate the structure of an object.

2. **Enter the field names and data types, as shown in** FIGURE A-8

 The Comments table will contain four fields. CommentID is set with an AutoNumber data type so each record is automatically numbered by Access. The Comment field has a Long Text data type so a long comment can be recorded. CommentDate is a Date/Time field to identify the date of the comment. CustID has a Number data type and will be used to link the Comments table to the Customers table later.

TROUBLE
To rename an object, close it, right-click it in the Navigation Pane, and then click Rename.

3. **Click the View button 🔲 to switch to Datasheet View, click Yes when prompted to save the table, type Comments as the table name, click OK, then click No when prompted to create a primary key**

 A **primary key field** contains unique data for each record. You'll identify a primary key field for the Comments table later. For now, you'll enter the first record in the Comments table in Datasheet View. A **record** is a row of data in a table. Refer to TABLE A-4 for a summary of important database terminology.

4. **Press [Tab] to move to the Comment field, type Interested in future tours to New Zealand, press [Tab], type 1/7/15 in the CommentDate field, press [Tab], then type 1 in the CustID field**

 You entered 1 in the CustID field to connect this comment with the customer in the Customers table that has a CustID value of 1. Knowing which CustID value to enter for each comment is difficult. After you relate the tables properly (a task you have not yet performed), Access can make it easier to link each comment to the correct customer.

TROUBLE
The CommentID field is an AutoNumber field, which will automatically increment to provide a unique value. If the number has already incremented beyond 1 for the first record, AutoNumber still works as intended.

5. **Point to the divider line between the Comment and CommentDate field names, and then drag the ✛ pointer to the right to widen the Comment field to read the entire comment, as shown in** FIGURE A-9

6. **Right-click the Comments table tab, click Close, then click Yes if prompted to save the table**

Creating a table in Datasheet View

You can also create a new table in Datasheet View using the commands on the FIELDS tab of the Ribbon. But if you use Design View to design your table before starting the data entry process, you will probably avoid some common data entry errors. Design View helps you focus on the appropriate data type for each field.

Selecting the best data type for each field before entering any data into that field helps prevent incorrect data and unintended typos. For example, if a field is given a Number, Currency, or Date/Time data type, you will not be able to enter text into that field by mistake.

FIGURE A-8: Creating the Comments table

Enter these field names →

Field Name	Data Type
CommentID	AutoNumber
Comment	Long Text
CommentDate	Date/Time
CustID	Number

← Enter these data types

FIGURE A-9: Entering the first record in the Comments table

CommentID	Comment	CommentDa	CustID
1	Interested in future tours to New Zealand	1/7/2015	1
* (New)			0

Tab through the CommentID field; AutoNumber fields automatically enter the next integer

Drag this pointer to the right to resize the Comment field

TABLE A-4: Important database terminology

term	description
Field	A specific piece or category of data such as a first name, last name, city, state, or phone number
Record	A group of related fields that describes a person, place, thing, or transaction such as a customer, location, product, or sale
Key field	A field that contains unique information for each record, such as a customer number for a customer
Table	A collection of records for a single subject such as Customers, Products, or Sales
Relational database	Multiple tables that are linked together to address a business process such as managing tours, sales, and customers at Quest Specialty Travel
Objects	The parts of an Access database that help you view, edit, manage, and analyze the data: **tables, queries, forms, reports, macros,** and **modules**

Create Primary Keys

Learning
Outcomes
• Set the primary
 key field
• Define one-to-
 many relationships

The **primary key field** of a table serves two important purposes. First, it contains data that uniquely identifies each record. No two records can have the exact same entry in the field designated as the primary key field. Second, the primary key field helps relate one table to another in a **one-to-many relationship**, where one record from one table may be related to many records in the second table. For example, one record in the Customers table may be related to many records in the Comments table. (One customer may have many comments.) The primary key field is always on the "one" side of a one-to-many relationship between two tables. **CASE** *Samantha Hooper asks you to check that a primary key field has been appropriately identified for each table in the new Quest database.*

STEPS

1. **Right-click the Comments table in the Navigation Pane, then click Design View**

 Table Design View for the Comments table opens. The field with the AutoNumber data type is generally the best candidate for the primary key field in a table because it automatically contains a unique number for each record.

TROUBLE
Make sure the
DESIGN tab is
selected on the
Ribbon.

2. **Click the CommentID field if it is not already selected, then click the Primary Key button in the Tools group on the DESIGN tab**

 The CommentID field is now set as the primary key field for the Comments table, as shown in **FIGURE A-10**.

QUICK TIP
You can also click the
Save button 💾 on
the Quick Access tool-
bar to save a table.

3. **Right-click the Comments table tab, click Close, then click Yes to save the table**

 Any time you must save design changes to an Access object such as a table, Access displays a dialog box to remind you to save the object.

4. **Right-click the Customers table in the Navigation Pane, then click Design View**

 Access has already set CustID as the primary key field for the Customers table, as shown in **FIGURE A-11**.

5. **Right-click the Customers table tab, then click Close**

 You were not prompted to save the Customers table because you did not make any design changes. Now that you're sure that each table in the Quest database has an appropriate primary key field, you're ready to link the tables. The primary key field plays a critical role in this relationship.

FIGURE A-10: Creating a primary key field for the Comments table

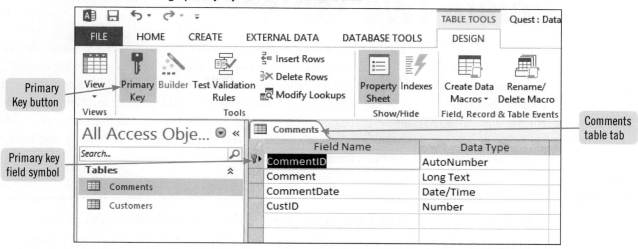

FIGURE A-11: Confirming the primary key field for the Customers table

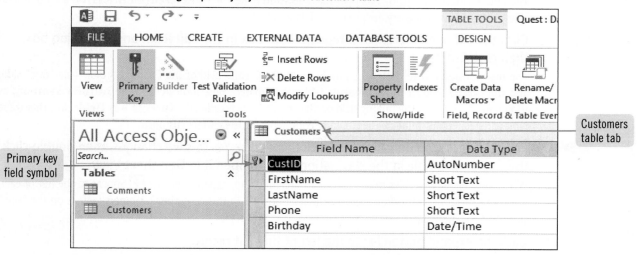

Learning about field properties

Properties are the characteristics that define the field. Two properties are required for every field: Field Name and Data Type. Many other properties, such as Field Size, Format, Caption, and Default Value, are defined in the Field Properties pane in the lower half of a table's Design View. As you add more property entries, you are generally restricting the amount or type of data that can be entered in the field, which increases data entry accuracy. For example, you might change the Field Size property for a State field to 2 to eliminate an incorrect entry such as FLL. Field properties change depending on the data type of the selected field. For example, date fields do not have a Field Size property because Access controls the size of fields with a Date/Time data type.

Relate Two Tables

Learning
Outcomes
• Define common
 field and foreign
 key field
• Create one-to-
 many relationships
• Set referential
 integrity

After you create tables and set primary key fields, you must connect the tables in one-to-many relation-ships to enjoy the benefits of a relational database. A one-to-many relationship between two tables means that one record from the first table is related to many records in the second table. You use a common field to make this connection. The common field is always the primary key field in the table on the "one" side of the relationship. **CASE** *Samantha Hooper explains that she has new comments to enter into the Quest database. To identify which customer is related to each comment, you define a one-to-many relationship between the Customers and Comments tables.*

STEPS

1. **Click the DATABASE TOOLS tab on the Ribbon, then click the Relationships button**

TROUBLE
If the Show Table dialog box doesn't appear, click the Show Table button on the DESIGN tab.

2. **In the Show Table dialog box, double-click Customers, double-click Comments, then click Close**

 Each table is represented by a small **field list** window that displays the table's field names. A key sym-bol identifies the primary key field in each table. To relate the two tables in a one-to-many relationship, you connect them using a common field, which is always the primary key field on the "one" side of the relationship.

QUICK TIP
Drag a table's title bar to move the field list.

3. **Drag CustID in the Customers field list to the CustID field in the Comments field list**

 The Edit Relationships dialog box opens, as shown in **FIGURE A-12**. **Referential integrity**, a set of Access rules that governs data entry, helps ensure data accuracy.

TROUBLE
If you need to delete an incorrect relation-ship, right-click a relationship line, then click Delete.

4. **Click the Enforce Referential Integrity check box in the Edit Relationships dialog box, then click Create**

 The **one-to-many line** shows the link between the CustID field of the Customers table (the "one" side) and the CustID field of the Comments table (the "many" side, indicated by the **infinity symbol**), as shown in **FIGURE A-13**. The linking field on the "many" side is called the **foreign key field**. Now that these tables are related, it is much easier to enter comments for the correct customer.

QUICK TIP
To print the Relationships window, click the Relationship Report button on the DESIGN tab, then click Print.

5. **Right-click the Relationships tab, click Close, click Yes to save changes, then double-click the Customers table in the Navigation Pane to open it in Datasheet View**

 When you relate two tables in a one-to-many relationship, expand buttons ⊞ appear to the left of each record in the table on the "one" side of the relationship. In this case, the Customers table is on the "one" side of the relationship.

6. **Click the expand button ⊞ to the left of the first record**

 A **subdatasheet** shows the related comment records for each customer. In other words, the subdatasheet shows the records on the "many" side of a one-to-many relationship. The expand button ⊞ also changed to the collapse button ⊟ for the first customer. Widening the Comment field allows you to see the entire entry in the Comments subdatasheet. Now the task of entering comments for the correct customer is much more straightforward.

TROUBLE
Be careful to enter complete comments for the correct customer, as shown in FIGURE A-14.

7. **Enter two more comments, as shown in FIGURE A-14**

 Interestingly, the CustID field in the Comments table (the foreign key field) is not displayed in the subdata-sheet. Behind the scenes, Access is entering the correct CustID value in the Comments table, which is the glue that ties each comment to the correct customer.

8. **Close the Customers table, then click Yes if prompted to save changes**

FIGURE A-12: Edit Relationships dialog box

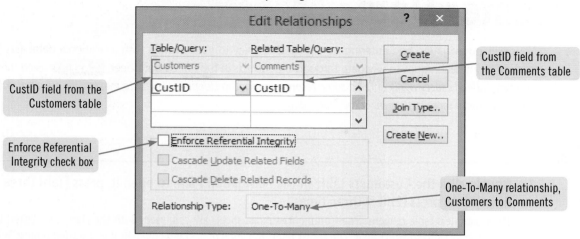

CustID field from the Customers table

Enforce Referential Integrity check box

CustID field from the Comments table

One-To-Many relationship, Customers to Comments

FIGURE A-13: Linking the Customers and Comments tables

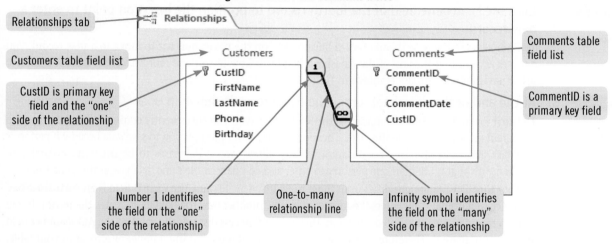

Relationships tab

Customers table field list

CustID is primary key field and the "one" side of the relationship

Comments table field list

CommentID is a primary key field

Number 1 identifies the field on the "one" side of the relationship

One-to-many relationship line

Infinity symbol identifies the field on the "many" side of the relationship

FIGURE A-14: Entering comments using the subdatasheet

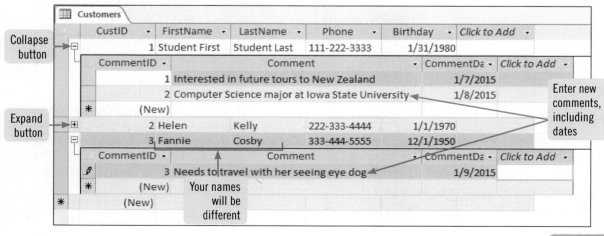

Collapse button

Expand button

Enter new comments, including dates

Your names will be different

Enter Data

Learning Outcomes
- Navigate records in a datasheet
- Enter records in a datasheet

Your skill in navigating and entering new records is a key to your success with a relational database. You can use many techniques to navigate through the records in the table's datasheet. **CASE** *Even though you have already successfully entered some records, Samantha Hooper asks you to master this essential skill by entering several more customers in the Quest database.*

STEPS

1. **Double-click the Customers table in the Navigation Pane to open it, press [Tab] three times, then press [Enter] three times**

 The Customers table reopens. The Comments subdatasheets are collapsed. Both the [Tab] and [Enter] keys move the focus to the next field. The **focus** refers to which data you would edit if you started typing. When you navigate to the last field of the record, pressing [Tab] or [Enter] advances the focus to the first field of the next record. You can also use the Next record ▶ and Previous record ◀ **navigation buttons** on the navigation bar in the lower-left corner of the datasheet to navigate through the records. The **Current record** text box on the navigation bar tells you the number of the current record as well as the total number of records in the datasheet.

 > **QUICK TIP**
 > Press [Tab] in the CustID AutoNumber field.

2. **Click the FirstName field of the fourth record to position the insertion point to enter a new record**

 You can also use the New (blank) record button ▶⁎ on the navigation bar to move to a new record. You enter new records at the end of the datasheet. You learn how to sort and reorder records later. A complete list of navigation keystrokes is shown in **TABLE A-5**.

 > **QUICK TIP**
 > Access databases are multiuser with one important limitation: two users cannot edit the same *record* at the same time. In that case, a message explains that the second user must wait until the first user moves to a different record.

3. **At the end of the datasheet, enter the three records shown in FIGURE A-15**

 The **edit record symbol** 🖉 appears to the left of the record you are currently editing. When you move to a different record, Access saves the data. Therefore, Access never prompts you to save *data* because it performs that task automatically. Saving data automatically allows Access databases to be **multiuser** databases, which means that more than one person can enter and edit data in the same database at the same time.

 Your CustID values might differ from those in **FIGURE A-15**. Because the CustID field is an **AutoNumber** field, Access automatically enters the next consecutive number into the field as it creates the record. If you delete a record or are interrupted when entering a record, Access discards the value in the AutoNumber field and does not reuse it. Therefore, AutoNumber values do not represent the number of records in your table. Instead, they provide a unique value per record, similar to check numbers.

Changing from Navigation mode to Edit mode

If you navigate to another area of the datasheet by clicking with the mouse pointer instead of pressing [Tab] or [Enter], you change from **Navigation mode** to Edit mode. In **Edit mode**, Access assumes that you are trying to make changes to the current field value, so keystrokes such as [Ctrl][End],

[Ctrl][Home], [◄], and [►] move the insertion point within the field. To return to Navigation mode, press [Tab] or [Enter] (thus moving the focus to the next field), or press [▲] or [▼] (thus moving the focus to a different record).

FIGURE A-15: New records in the Customers table

Your CustID values may vary

Edit symbol

Previous record button

First record button

Current record box

Next record button

Last record button

New (blank) record button

Your first three names will be different

Enter the last three Customer records as shown

TABLE A-5: Navigation mode keyboard shortcuts

shortcut key	moves to the
[Tab], [Enter], or [→]	Next field of the current record
[Shift][Tab] or [←]	Previous field of the current record
[Home]	First field of the current record
[End]	Last field of the current record
[Ctrl][Home] or [F5]	First field of the first record
[Ctrl][End]	Last field of the last record
[↑]	Current field of the previous record
[↓]	Current field of the next record

Cloud computing

Using SkyDrive, a free service from Microsoft, you can store files in the "cloud" and retrieve them anytime you are connected to the Internet. Saving your files to the SkyDrive is one example of cloud computing. **Cloud computing** means you are using an Internet resource to complete your work. You can find more information in the "Working in the Cloud" appendix.

Edit Data

Learning Outcomes
• Edit data in a data-sheet
• Delete records in a datasheet
• Preview and print a datasheet

Updating existing data in a database is another critical database task. To change the contents of an exist-ing record, navigate to the field you want to change and type the new information. You can delete unwanted data by clicking the field and using [Backspace] or [Delete] to delete text to the left or right of the insertion point. Other data entry keystrokes are summarized in TABLE A-6. **CASE** *Samantha Hooper asks you to correct two records in the Customers table.*

STEPS

1. **Double-click the name in the FirstName field of the second record, type Kelsey, press [Enter], type Barker, press [Enter], type 111-222-4444, press [Enter], type 2/15/84, then press [Enter]**

 You changed the name, telephone number, and birth date of the second customer. When you entered the last two digits of the year value, Access inserted the first two digits after you pressed [Enter]. You'll also change the third customer.

QUICK TIP

The ScreenTip for the Undo button ⟲ displays the action you can undo.

2. **Press [Enter] to move to the FirstName field of the third record, type Joshua, press [Enter], type Lang, press [Enter], type 222-333-4444, then press [Esc]**

 Pressing [Esc] once removes the current field's editing changes, so the Phone value changes back to the pre-vious entry. Pressing [Esc] twice removes all changes to the current record. When you move to another record, Access saves your edits, so you can no longer use [Esc] to remove editing changes to the current record. You can, however, click the Undo button ⟲ on the Quick Access toolbar to undo changes to a previous record.

3. **Retype 222-333-4444, press [Enter], type 12/1/50 in the Birthday field, press [Enter], click the 12/1/50 date you just entered, click the Calendar icon 📅, then click April 14, 1951, as shown in FIGURE A-16**

 When you are working in the Birthday field, which has a Date/Time data type, you can enter a date from the keyboard or use the **Calendar Picker**, a pop-up calendar to find and select a date.

4. **Click the record selector for the last record (Oscar Lee), click the Delete button in the Records group on the HOME tab, then click Yes**

 A message warns that you cannot undo a record deletion. The Undo button is dimmed, indicating that you cannot use it. The Customers table now has five records, as shown in FIGURE A-17. Keep in mind that your CustID values might differ from those in the figure because they are controlled by Access.

QUICK TIP

If requested to print the Customers data-sheet by your instructor, click the Print button, then click OK.

5. **Click the FILE tab, click Print, then click Print Preview to review the printout of the Customers table before printing**

6. **Click the Close Print Preview button, click the Close button in the upper-right corner of the window to close the Quest.accdb database and Access 2013, then click Yes if prompted to save design changes to the Customers table**

FIGURE A-16: Editing customer records

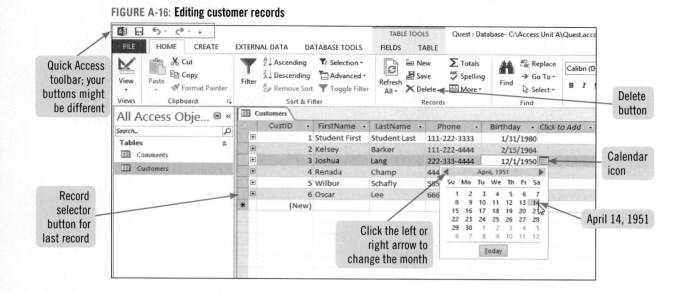

FIGURE A-17: Final Customers datasheet

	CustID	FirstName	LastName	Phone	Birthday	Click to Add
⊞	1	Student First	Student Last	111-222-3333	1/31/1980	
⊞	2	Kelsey	Barker	111-222-4444	2/15/1984	
⊞	3	Joshua	Lang	222-333-4444	4/14/1951	
⊞	4	Renada	Champ	444-555-6666	4/1/1981	
⊞	5	Wilbur	Schafly	555-666-7777	5/1/1982	
✳	(New)					

Oscar Lee record is deleted

Your name is entered in the first record

TABLE A-6: Edit mode keyboard shortcuts

editing keystroke	action
[Backspace]	Deletes one character to the left of the insertion point
[Delete]	Deletes one character to the right of the insertion point
[F2]	Switches between Edit and Navigation mode
[Esc]	Undoes the change to the current field
[Esc][Esc]	Undoes all changes to the current record
[F7]	Starts the spell-check feature
[Ctrl][']	Inserts the value from the same field in the previous record into the current field
[Ctrl][;]	Inserts the current date in a Date field

Resizing and moving datasheet columns

You can resize the width of a field in a datasheet by dragging the column separator, the thin line that separates the field names to the left or right. The pointer changes to ↔ as you make the field wider or narrower. Release the mouse button when you have resized the field. To adjust the column width to accommodate the widest entry in the field, double-click the column separator. To move a column, click the field name to select the entire column, then drag the field name left or right.

Practice

Concepts Review

Label each element of the Access window shown in FIGURE A-18.

FIGURE A-18

Match each term with the statement that best describes it.

10. Field
11. Record
12. Table
13. Datasheet
14. Query
15. Form
16. Report

a. A subset of data from one or more tables
b. A collection of records for a single subject, such as all the customer records
c. A professional printout of database information
d. A spreadsheet-like grid that displays fields as columns and records as rows
e. A group of related fields for one item, such as all of the information for one customer
f. A category of information in a table, such as a company name, city, or state
g. An easy-to-use data entry screen

Select the best answer from the list of choices.

17. **Which of the following is *not* a typical benefit of relational databases?**
 a. Minimized duplicate data entry
 b. More accurate data
 c. Faster information retrieval
 d. More common than spreadsheets

18. **Which of the following is *not* an advantage of managing data with relational database software such as Access versus spreadsheet software such as Excel?**
 a. Allows multiple users to enter data simultaneously
 b. Uses a single table to store all data
 c. Provides data entry forms
 d. Reduces duplicate data entry

19. **When you create a new database, which object is created first?**
 a. Form c. Module
 b. Query d. Table

Skills Review

1. **Understand relational databases.**
 a. Write down five advantages of managing database information in Access versus using a spreadsheet.
 b. Write a sentence to explain how the terms *field*, *record*, *table*, and *relational database* relate to one another.

2. **Explore a database.**
 a. Start Access.
 b. Open the RealEstate-A.accdb database from the location where you store your Data Files. Click Enable Content if a yellow Security Warning message appears.
 c. Open each of the four tables to study the data they contain. Complete the following table:

table name	number of records	number of fields

 d. Double-click the ListingsByRealtor query in the Navigation Pane to open it. Change any occurrence of Gordon Bono to *your* name. Move to another record to save your changes.
 e. Double-click the RealtorsMainForm in the Navigation Pane to open it. Use the navigation buttons to navigate through the 11 realtors to observe each realtor's listings.
 f. Double-click the RealtorListingReport in the Navigation Pane to open it. The records are listed in ascending order by last name. Scroll through the report to make sure your name is positioned correctly.
 g. Close the RealEstate-A database, and then close Access 2013.

3. **Create a database.**
 a. Start Access, click the Blank desktop database icon, use the Browse button to navigate to the location where you store your Data Files, type **RealEstateMarketing** as the filename, click OK, and then click Create to create a new database named RealEstateMarketing.accdb.

Skills Review (continued)

b. Switch to Table Design View, name the table **Prospects**, then enter the following fields and data types:

field name	data type
ProspectID	AutoNumber
ProspectFirst	Short Text
ProspectLast	Short Text
Phone	Short Text
Email	Hyperlink
Street	Short Text
City	Short Text
State	Short Text
Zip	Short Text

c. Save the table, switch to Datasheet View, and enter two records using *your* name in the first record and your instructor's name in the second. Tab through the ProspectID field, an AutoNumber field.

d. Enter **TX** (Texas) as the value in the State field for both records. Use school or fictitious (rather than personal) data for all other field data, and be sure to fill out each record completely.

e. Widen each column in the Prospects table so that all data is visible, then save and close the Prospects table.

4. Create a table.

a. Click the CREATE tab on the Ribbon, click the Table Design button in the Tables group, then create a new table with the following two fields and data types:

field name	data type
StateAbbrev	Short Text
StateName	Short Text

b. Save the table with the name **States**. Click No when asked if you want Access to create the primary key field.

5. Create primary keys.

a. In Table Design View of the States table, set the StateAbbrev as the primary key field.

b. Save the States table and open it in Datasheet View.

c. Enter one state record, using **TX** for the StateAbbrev value and **Texas** for the StateName value to match the State value of TX that you entered for both records in the Prospects table.

d. Close the States table.

6. Relate two tables.

a. From the DATABASE TOOLS tab, open the Relationships window.

b. Add the States, then the Prospects table to the Relationships window.

FIGURE A-19

c. Drag the bottom edge of the Prospects table to expand the field list to display all of the fields.

d. Drag the StateAbbrev field from the States table to the State field of the Prospects table.

e. In the Edit Relationships dialog box, click the Enforce Referential Integrity check box, then click Create. Your Relationships window should look similar to FIGURE A-19. If you connect the wrong fields by mistake, right-click the line connecting the two fields, click Delete, then try again.

f. Close the Relationships window, and save changes when prompted.

Skills Review (continued)

7. Enter data.

a. Open the States table and enter the following records:

StateAbbrev field	StateName field
CO	Colorado
IA	Iowa
KS	Kansas
MO	Missouri
NE	Nebraska
OK	Oklahoma
WI	Wisconsin

b. Add three more state records of your choice for a total of 11 records in the States table using the correct two-character abbreviation for the state and the correctly spelled state name.

c. Close and reopen the States table. Notice that Access automatically sorts the records by the values in the primary key field, the StateAbbrev field.

8. Edit data.

a. Click the Expand button for the TX record to see the two related records from the Prospects table.

b. Enter two more prospects in the TX subdatasheet using any fictitious but realistic data, as shown in FIGURE A-20. Notice that you are not required to enter a value for the State field, the foreign key field in the subdatasheet.

FIGURE A-20

c. If required by your instructor, print the States datasheet and the Prospects datasheet.

d. Click the Close button in the upper-right corner of the Access window to close all open objects as well as the RealEstateMarketing.accdb database and Access 2013. If prompted to save any design changes, click Yes.

Independent Challenge 1

Consider the following twelve subject areas:

- Telephone directory
- College course offerings
- Restaurant menu items
- Vehicles
- Movie listings

- Islands of the Caribbean
- Physical activities
- Shopping catalog items
- Conventions
- Party guest list

- Members of the U.S. House
- Ancient wonders of the world of Representatives

a. For each subject, build a Word table with 4–7 columns and three rows. In the first row, enter field names that you would expect to see in a table used to manage that subject.

b. In the second and third rows of each table, enter two realistic records. The first table, Telephone Directory, is completed as an example to follow.

TABLE: **Telephone Directory**

FirstName	LastName	Street	Zip	Phone
Marco	Lopez	100 Main Street	88715	555-612-3312
Christopher	Stafford	253 Maple Lane	77824	555-612-1179

Independent Challenge 2

You are working with several civic groups to coordinate a community-wide cleanup effort. You have started a database called Recycle-A, which tracks the clubs, their trash deposits, and the trash collection centers that are participating.

a. Start Access, then open the Recycle-A.accdb database from the location where you store your Data Files. Enable content if prompted.

b. Open each table's datasheet to study the number of fields and records per table. Notice that there are no expand buttons to the left of any records because relationships have not yet been established between these tables.

c. In a Word document, re-create the following table and fill in the blanks:

d. Close all table datasheets, then open the Relationships window and create the following one-to-many relationships. Drag the tables from the Navigation Pane to the Relationships window, and drag the title bars and borders of the field lists to position them as shown in **FIGURE A-21**.

table name	number of fields	number of records

field on the "one" side of the relationship	field on the "many" side of the relationship
ClubNumber in Clubs table	ClubNumber in Deposits table
CenterNumber in Centers table	CenterNumber in Deposits table

e. Be sure to enforce referential integrity on all relationships. If you create an incorrect relationship, right-click the line linking the fields, click Delete, and try again. Your final Relationships window should look like **FIGURE A-21**.

f. Click the Relationship Report button on the DESIGN tab, and if required by your instructor, click Print to print a copy of the Relationships for Recycle-A report. To close the report, right-click the Relationships for Recycle-A tab and click Close. Click Yes when prompted to save changes to the report with the name **Relationships for Recycle-A**. Save and close the Relationships window.

FIGURE A-21

g. Open the Clubs table and add a new record with fictitious but realistic data in all of the fields. Enter **8** as the ClubNumber value and *your* name in the FName (first name) and LName (last name) fields.

h. Expand the subdatasheets for each record in the Clubs table to see the related records from the Deposits table. Which club made the most deposits? Be ready to answer in class. Close the Clubs table.

i. Open the Centers table and add a new record with fictitious but realistic data in all of the fields. Enter *your* first and last names in the CenterName field and **5** as the CenterNumber.

j. Expand the subdatasheets for each record in the Centers table to see the related records from the Deposits table. Which center made the most deposits? Be ready to answer in class. Close the Centers table.

k. Close the Recycle-A.accdb database, then exit Access 2013.

Independent Challenge 3

You are working for an advertising agency that provides advertising media for small and large businesses in the midwestern United States. You have started a database called BusinessContacts-A, which tracks your company's customers. (*Note: To complete this Independent Challenge, make sure you are connected to the Internet.*)

a. Start Access and open the BusinessContacts-A.accdb database from the location where you store your Data Files. Enable content if prompted.

b. Add a new record to the Customers table, using any local business name, *your* first and last names, **$7,788.99** in the YTDSales field, and fictitious but reasonable entries for the rest of the fields.

c. Edit the Sprint Systems record (ID 1). The Company name should be changed to **MTB Mobile**, and the Street value should be changed to **4455 College St**.

d. Delete the record for St Luke's Hospital (ID 20), then close the Customers table.

e. Create a new table with two fields, **State2** and **StateName**. Assign both fields a Short Text data type. The State2 field will contain the two-letter abbreviation for state names. The StateName field will contain the full state name.

f. Set the State2 field as the primary key field, then save the table as **States**.

g. Enter at least three records into the States table, making sure that all of the states used in the Customers datasheet are entered in the States table. This includes **KS Kansas**, **MO Missouri**, and any other state you entered in Step b when you added a new record to the Customers table.

h. Close all open tables. Open the Relationships window, add both the States and Customers field lists to the window, then expand the size of the Customers field list so that all fields are visible.

i. Build a one-to-many relationship between the States and Customers tables by dragging the State2 field from the States table to the State field of the Customers table to create a one-to-many relationship between the two tables. Enforce referential integrity on the relationship. If you are unable to enforce referential integrity, it means that a value in the State field of the Customers table doesn't have a perfect match in the State2 field of the States table. Open both table datasheets, making sure every state in the State field of the Customers table is also represented in the State2 field of the States table, close all datasheets, then reestablish the one-to-many relationship between the two tables with referential integrity.

j. Click the Relationship Report button on the DESIGN tab, then if requested by your instructor, click Print to print the report.

k. Right-click the Relationships for BusinessContacts-A tab, then click Close. Click Yes when prompted to save the report with the name **Relationships for BusinessContacts-A**.

l. Close the Relationships window, saving changes as prompted.

m. Close BusinessContacts-A.accdb database, and exit Access 2013.

Independent Challenge 4: Explore

Now that you've learned about Microsoft Access and relational databases, brainstorm how you might use an Access database in your daily life or career. Start by visiting the Microsoft Web site, and explore what's new about Access 2013.

(*Note:* To complete this Independent Challenge, make sure you are connected to the Internet.)

a. Using your favorite search engine, look up the keywords *benefits of a relational database* or *benefits of Microsoft Access* to find articles that discuss the benefits of organizing data in a relational database.

b. Read several articles about the benefits of organizing data in a relational database such as Access, identifying three distinct benefits. Use a Word document to record those three benefits. Also, copy and paste the Web site address of the article you are referencing for each benefit you have identified.

c. In addition, as you read the articles that describe relational database benefits, list any terminology unfamiliar to you, identifying at least five new terms.

d. Using a search engine or a Web site that provides a computer glossary such as *www.whatis.com* or *www.webopedia. com*, look up the definition of the new terms, and enter both the term and the definition of the term in your document as well as the Web site address where your definition was found.

e. Finally, based on your research and growing understanding of Access 2013, list three ways you could use an Access database to organize, enhance, or support the activities and responsibilities of your daily life or career. Type your name at the top of the document, and submit it to your instructor as requested.

Visual Workshop

Open the Basketball-A.accdb database from the location where you store your Data Files, then enable content if prompted. Open the Offense query datasheet, which lists offensive statistics by player by game. Modify any of the Ellyse Howard records to contain *your* first and last names, then move to a different record, observing the power of a relational database to modify every occurrence of that name throughout the database. Close the Offense query, then open the Players table. Note that there are no expand buttons to the left of the records indicating that this table does not participate on the "one" side of a one-to-many relationship. Close the Players table and open the Relationships window. Drag the tables from the Navigation Pane and create the relationships with referential integrity, as shown in FIGURE A-22. Note the one-to-many relationship between the Players and Stats table. Print the Relationships report if requested by your instructor and save it with the name **Relationships for Basketball-A**. Close the report and close and save the Relationships window. Now reopen the Players table noting the expand buttons to the left of each record. Expand the subdatasheet for your name and for several other players to observe the "many" records from the Stats table that are now related to each record in the Players table.

FIGURE A-22

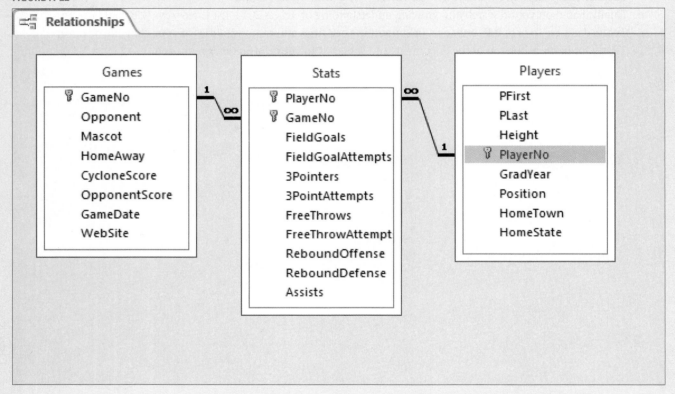

Building and Using Queries

CASE ▶ Samantha Hooper, tour developer for U.S. group travel at Quest Specialty Travel, has several questions about the customer and tour information in the Quest database. You'll develop queries to provide Samantha with up-to-date answers.

Unit Objectives

After completing this unit, you will be able to:

- Use the Query Wizard
- Work with data in a query
- Use Query Design View
- Sort and find data

- Filter data
- Apply AND criteria
- Apply OR criteria
- Format a datasheet

Files You Will Need

QuestTravel-B.accdb
Recycle-B.accdb
Membership-B.accdb
Congress-B.accdb
Vet-B.accdb
Baseball-B.accdb

Use the Query Wizard

Learning Outcomes
• Describe the purpose for a query
• Create a query with the Simple Query Wizard

A **query** answers a question about the information in the database. A query allows you to select a subset of fields and records from one or more tables and then present the selected data as a single datasheet. A major benefit of working with data through a query is that you can focus on only the specific information you need to answer a question, rather than navigating through all the fields and records from many large tables. You can enter, edit, and navigate data in a query datasheet just like a table datasheet. However, keep in mind that Access data is physically stored only in tables, even though you can select, view, and edit it through other Access objects such as queries and forms. Because a query doesn't physically store the data, a query datasheet is sometimes called a **logical view** of the data. Technically, a query is a set of **SQL (Structured Query Language)** instructions, but because you can use Access query tools such as Query Design View to create and modify the query, you are not required to know SQL to build or use Access queries. **CASE** *You use the Simple Query Wizard to create a query that displays fields from the Tours and Customers tables in one datasheet.*

STEPS

1. **Start Access, open the** QuestTravel-B.accdb database, **enable content if prompted, then maximize the window**

 Access provides several tools to create a new query. One way is to use the **Simple Query Wizard**, which prompts you for the information it needs to create a new query.

2. **Click the** CREATE **tab on the Ribbon, click the** Query Wizard button **in the Queries group, then click** OK **to start the Simple Query Wizard**

 The Simple Query Wizard dialog box opens, prompting you to select the fields you want to view in the new query. You can select fields from one or more existing tables or queries.

3. **Click the** Tables/Queries list arrow, **click** Table: Tours, **double-click** TourName, **double-click** City, **double-click** Category, **then double-click** Price

 So far, you've selected four fields from the Tours table to display basic tour information in this query. You also want to add the first and last name information from the Customers table so you know which customers purchased each tour.

TROUBLE
Click the Remove Single Field button
[<] if you need to remove a field from the Selected Fields list.

4. **Click the** Tables/Queries list arrow, **click** Table: Customers, **double-click** FName, **then double-click** LName

 You've selected four fields from the Tours table and two from the Customers table for your new query, as shown in **FIGURE B-1**.

5. **Click** Next, **click** Next **to select Detail, select** Tours Query **in the title text box, type** TourCustomerList **as the name of the query, then click** Finish

 The TourCustomerList datasheet opens, displaying four fields from the Tours table and two from the Customers table, as shown in **FIGURE B-2**. The query can show which customers have purchased which tours because of the one-to-many table relationships established in the Relationships window.

FIGURE B-1: Selecting fields using the Simple Query Wizard

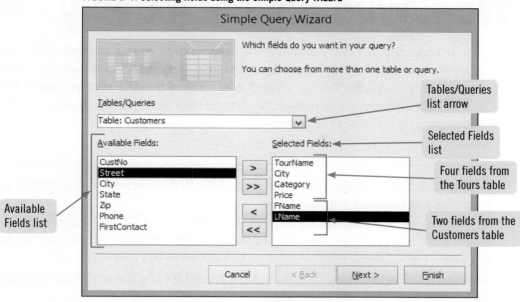

Simple Query Wizard

Which fields do you want in your query?

You can choose from more than one table or query.

Tables/Queries

Table: Customers

Tables/Queries list arrow

Available Fields:

CustNo
Street
City
State
Zip
Phone
FirstContact

Selected Fields:

TourName
City
Category
Price
FName
LName

Selected Fields list

Four fields from the Tours table

Two fields from the Customers table

Available Fields list

Cancel < Back Next > Finish

FIGURE B-2: TourCustomerList datasheet

TourCustomerList

Four fields from Tours table

TourName	City	Category	Price	FName	LName
Stanley Bay Shelling	Captiva	Adventure	$750	Ralph	Hopper
Stanley Bay Shelling	Captiva	Adventure	$750	Lisa	Wilson
Ames Ski Club	Breckenridge	Adventure	$850	Kristen	Collins
Stanley Bay Shelling	Captiva	Adventure	$750	Kris	Goode
Stanley Bay Shelling	Captiva	Adventure	$750	Lois	Goode
Stanley Bay Shelling	Captiva	Adventure	$750	Naresh	Hubert
Piper-Heitman Wedding	Captiva	Family	$550	Julia	Bouchart
Ames Ski Club	Breckenridge	Adventure	$850	Tom	Camel
Golden Footsteps	Orlando	Site Seeing	$550	Shirley	Walker
Golden Footsteps	Orlando	Site Seeing	$550	Zohra	Vogue
Golden Footsteps	Orlando	Site Seeing	$550	Kathryn	Dotey
Golden Footsteps	Orlando	Site Seeing	$550	Jose	Hammer
Red Reef Scuba	Islamadora	Adventure	$1,500	Jane	Taylor
Stanley Bay Shelling	Captiva	Adventure	$750	Kori	Yode
American Heritage Tour	Philadelphia	Educational	$1,200	Sharol	Olingback
American Heritage Tour	Philadelphia	Educational	$1,200	Lois	Goode
American Heritage Tour	Philadelphia	Educational	$1,200	Tim	Taylor
American Heritage Tour	Philadelphia	Educational	$1,200	Frank	Houston
Yosemite National Park (Sacramento	Service	$1,100	Tom	Camel
American Heritage Tour	Philadelphia	Educational	$1,200	Jane	Taylor
Yosemite National Park (Sacramento	Service	$1,100	Kristen	Collins
American Heritage Tour	Philadelphia	Educational	$1,200	Kris	Goode
American Heritage Tour	Philadelphia	Educational	$1,200	Ralph	Hopper
American Heritage Tour	Philadelphia	Educational	$1,200	Nancy	Langguth
American Heritage Tour	Philadelphia	Educational	$1,200	Brad	Langguth

Two fields from Customers table

Record: 14 ◄ 1 of 102 ► ►1 ►* No Filter Search

102 records

Work with Data in a Query

Learning Outcomes
- Edit records in a query
- Delete records in a query

You enter and edit data in a query datasheet the same way you do in a table datasheet. Because all data is stored in tables, any edits you make to data in a query datasheet are actually stored in the underlying tables and are automatically updated in all views of the data in other queries, forms, and reports. **CASE** ▶ *You want to change the name of one tour and update a customer name. You can use the TourCustomerList query datasheet to make these edits.*

STEPS

1. **Double-click Stanley in the TourName field of the first or second record, type Breeze, then click any other record**

 All occurrences of Stanley Bay Shelling automatically update to Breeze Bay Shelling because this tour name value is stored only once in the Tours table. See **FIGURE B-3**. The tour name is selected from the Tours table and displayed in the TourCustomerList query for each customer who purchased this tour.

2. **Double-click Orlando in the City field of any record for the Golden Footsteps tour, type Kissimmee, then click any other record**

 All occurrences of Orlando automatically update to Kissimmee because this value is stored only once in the City field of the Tours table for the Golden Footsteps record. The Golden Footsteps tour is displayed in the TourCustomerList query for each customer who purchased the tour.

3. **Click the record selector button to the left of the first record, click the HOME tab, click the Delete button in the Records group, then click Yes**

 You can delete records from a query datasheet the same way you delete them from a table datasheet. Notice that the navigation bar now indicates you have 101 records in the datasheet, as shown in **FIGURE B-4**.

4. **Right-click the TourCustomerList query tab, then click Close**

 Each time a query is opened, it shows a current view of the data. This means that as new tours, customers, or sales are recorded in the database, the next time you open this query, the information will include all updates.

FIGURE B-3: Working with data in a query datasheet

Record selector button for first record

Updating Stanley to Breeze in one record updates all records

TourName	City	Category	Price	FName	LName
Breeze Bay Shelling	Captiva	Adventure	$750	Ralph	Hopper
Breeze Bay Shelling	Captiva	Adventure	$750	Lisa	Wilson
Ames Ski Club	Breckenridge	Adventure	$850	Kristen	Collins
Breeze Bay Shelling	Captiva	Adventure	$750	Kris	Goode
Breeze Bay Shelling	Captiva	Adventure	$750	Lois	Goode
Breeze Bay Shelling	Captiva	Adventure	$750	Naresh	Hubert
Piper-Heitman Wedding	Captiva	Family	$550	Julia	Bouchart
Ames Ski Club	Breckenridge	Adventure	$850	Tom	Camel
Golden Footsteps	Orlando	Site Seeing	$550	Shirley	Walker
Golden Footsteps	Orlando	Site Seeing	$550	Zohra	Vogue
Golden Footsteps	Orlando	Site Seeing	$550	Kathryn	Dotey
Golden Footsteps	Orlando	Site Seeing	$550	Jose	Hammer
Red Reef Scuba	Islamadora	Adventure	$1,500	Jane	Taylor
Breeze Bay Shelling	Captiva	Adventure	$750	Kori	Yode
American Heritage Tour	Philadelphia	Educational	$1,200	Sharol	Olingback

FIGURE B-4: Final TourCustomerList datasheet

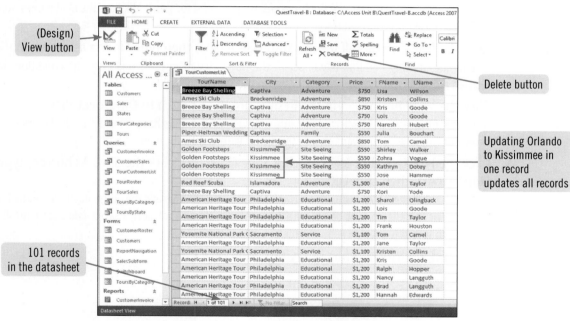

(Design) View button

Delete button

Updating Orlando to Kissimmee in one record updates all records

101 records in the datasheet

Hiding and unhiding fields in a datasheet

To hide a field in a datasheet, right-click the field name at the top of the datasheet and click the Hide Fields option on the shortcut menu. To unhide a field, right-click any field name, click Unhide Fields, and check the hidden field's check box in the Unhide Columns dialog box.

Freezing and unfreezing fields in a datasheet

In large datasheets, you may want to freeze certain fields so that they remain on the screen at all times. To freeze a field, right-click its field name in the datasheet, and then click Freeze Fields. To unfreeze a field, right-click any field name and click Unfreeze All Fields.

Access 2013

Use Query Design View

You use **Query Design View** to add, delete, or move the fields in an existing query; to specify sort orders; or to add **criteria** to limit the number of records shown in the resulting datasheet. You can also use Query Design View to create a new query from scratch. Query Design View presents the fields you can use for that query in small windows called **field lists**. If you use the fields of two or more related tables in the query, the relationship between two tables is displayed with a **join line** (also called a **link line**) identifying which fields are used to establish the relationship. **CASE** ▶ *Samantha Hooper asks you to produce a list of tours in Florida. You use Query Design View to modify the existing ToursByState query to meet her request.*

STEPS

1. **Double-click the ToursByState query in the Navigation Pane to review the datasheet**

 The ToursByState query contains the StateName field from the States table and the TourName, TourStartDate, and Price fields from the Tours table. This query contains two ascending sort orders: StateName and TourName. All records in California, for example, are further sorted by the TourName value.

 QUICK TIP

 Drag the lower edge of the field list to view more fields.

2. **Click the View button ⊠ on the HOME tab to switch to Query Design View**

 Query Design View displays the tables used in the query in the upper pane of the window. The link line shows that one record in the States table may be related to many records in the Tours table. The lower pane of the window, called the **query design grid** (or query grid for short), displays the field names, sort orders, and criteria used within the query.

 QUICK TIP

 Query criteria are not case sensitive, so Florida equals FLORIDA equals florida.

3. **Click the first Criteria cell for the StateName field, then type Florida as shown in FIGURE B-5**

 Criteria are limiting conditions you set in the query design grid. In this case, the condition limits the selected records to only those with "Florida" in the StateName field.

4. **Click the View button ▦ in the Results group to switch to Datasheet View**

 Now only nine records are selected, because only nine of the tours have "Florida" in the StateName field, as shown in FIGURE B-6. You want to save this query with a different name.

5. **Click the FILE tab, click Save As, click Save Object As, click the Save As button, type FloridaTours, then click OK**

 In Access, the **Save As command** on the FILE tab allows you to save the entire database (and all objects it contains) or just the current object with a new name. Recall that Access saves *data* automatically as you move from record to record.

6. **Right-click the FloridaTours query tab, then click Close**

Tours field list

Tours

States field list

States

* TourNo
TourName
TourStartDate
Duration
City

*
StateName
StateAbbreviation

Drag bottom edge to
expand the field list

Link line

Field names

Criteria cell for
StateName field

Field:	StateName	TourName	TourStartDate	Price
Table:	States	Tours	Tours	Tours
Sort:	Ascending	Ascending		
Show:	✓	✓	✓	✓
Criteria:	Florida			
or:				

Sort orders

FIGURE B-6: ToursByState query with Florida criterion

ToursByState

StateName ▾	TourName ▾	TourStartDate ▾	Price ▾
Florida	Breeze Bay Shelling	07/06/2014	$750
Florida	Golden Footsteps	05/23/2014	$550
Florida	Gulfside Birdwatchers	06/29/2014	$700
Florida	High Adventurers	06/05/2014	$575
Florida	Hummer Trail	05/30/2014	$725
Florida	Patriot Debate Club	06/12/2014	$605
Florida	Piper-Heitman Wedding	05/30/2014	$550
Florida	Red Reef Scuba	07/06/2014	$1,500
Florida	Tropical Sailboats	06/19/2014	$655

TourName
values are
in ascending
order

Only nine
Florida records
are selected

Access 2013

Adding or deleting a table in a query

You might want to add a table's field list to the upper pane of Query Design View to select fields from that table for the query. To add a new table to Query Design View, drag it from the Navigation Pane to Query Design View, or click the Show Table button on the Design tab, then add the desired table(s). To delete an unneeded table from Query Design View, click its title bar, then press [Delete].

Sort and Find Data

Learning Outcomes
- Apply sort orders to a query
- Find and replace data in a query
- Undo edits in a query

The Access sort and find features are handy tools that help you quickly organize and find data in a table or query datasheet. TABLE B-1 describes the Sort and Find buttons on the HOME tab. Besides using these buttons, you can also click the list arrow on the field name in a datasheet, and then click a sorting option. **CASE** ▶ *Samantha asks you to provide a list of tours sorted by TourStartDate, and then by Price. You'll modify the ToursByCategory query to answer this query.*

STEPS

1. **Double-click the ToursByCategory query in the Navigation Pane to open its datasheet**

 The ToursByCategory query currently sorts tours by Category, then by TourName. You'll add the Duration field to this query, then change the sort order for the records.

QUICK TIP

Drag a selected field selector right or left to move the column to a new position in the query grid.

2. **Click the View button ⬗ in the Views group to switch to Design View, then double-click the Duration field in the Tours field list**

 When you double-click a field in a field list, Access inserts it in the next available column in the query grid. You can also drag a field from a field list to a specific column of the query grid. To select a field in the query grid, you click its field selector. The **field selector** is the thin gray bar above each field in the query grid. If you want to delete a field from a query, click its field selector, then press [Delete]. Deleting a field from a query does not delete it from the underlying table; the field is only deleted from the query's logical view.

 Currently, the ToursByCategory query is sorted by Category and then by TourName. Access evaluates sort orders from left to right. You want to change the sort order so that the records sort first by TourStartDate then by Price.

3. **Click Ascending in the Category Sort cell, click the list arrow, click (not sorted), click Ascending in the TourName Sort cell, click the list arrow, click (not sorted), double-click the TourStartDate Sort cell to specify an Ascending sort, then double-click the Price Sort cell to specify an Ascending sort**

 The records are now set to be sorted in ascending order, first by TourStartDate, then by the values in the Price field, as shown in FIGURE B-7. Because sort orders always work from left to right, you might need to rearrange the fields before applying a sort order that uses more than one field. To move a field in the query design grid, click its field selector, then drag it left or right.

4. **Click the View button ▦ in the Results group**

 The new datasheet shows the Duration field in the fifth column. The records are now sorted in ascending order by the TourStartDate field. If two records have the same TourStartDate, they are further sorted by Price. Your next task is to replace all occurrences of "Site Seeing" with "Cultural" in the Category field.

5. **Click the Find button on the HOME tab, type Site Seeing in the Find What box, click the Replace tab, click in the Replace With box, then type Cultural**

 The Find and Replace dialog box is shown in FIGURE B-8.

TROUBLE

If your find-and-replace effort did not work correctly, click the Undo button ↺ and repeat Steps 5 and 6.

6. **Click the Replace All button in the Find and Replace dialog box, click Yes to continue, then click Cancel to close the Find and Replace dialog box**

 Access replaced all occurrences of "Site Seeing" with "Cultural" in the Category field, as shown in FIGURE B-9.

7. **Right-click the ToursByCategory query tab, click Close, then click Yes to save changes**

FIGURE B-7: Changing sort orders for the ToursByCategory query

Duration field in
Tours field list

Field selectors for Price
and Duration fields

Sort orders for Category
and TourName are removed

Ascending sort orders for
TourStartDate and Price are added

FIGURE B-8: Find and Replace dialog box

Site Seeing in the
Find What text box

Cultural in the
Replace With text box

Additional Find and
Replace options to
fine-tune the search

Replace All button

FIGURE B-9: Final ToursByCategory datasheet with new sort orders

Cultural replaces
Site Seeing in the
Category field

Find button

Records with the same
TourStartDate are further
sorted by the Price field

TABLE B-1: Sort and Find buttons

name	button	purpose
Ascending		Sorts records based on the selected field in ascending order (0 to 9, A to Z)
Descending		Sorts records based on the selected field in descending order (Z to A, 9 to 0)
Remove Sort		Removes the current sort order
Find		Opens the Find and Replace dialog box, which allows you to find data in a single field or in the entire datasheet
Replace		Opens the Find and Replace dialog box, which allows you to find and replace data
Go To		Helps you navigate to the first, previous, next, last, or new record
Select		Helps you select a single record or all records in a datasheet

Filter Data

Learning Outcomes
• Apply and remove filters in a query
• Use wildcards in criteria

Filtering a table or query datasheet *temporarily* displays only those records that match given criteria. Recall that criteria are limiting conditions you set. For example, you might want to show only tours in the state of California, or only tours with a duration of 14 days. Although filters provide a quick and easy way to display a temporary subset of records in the current datasheet, they are not as powerful or flexible as queries. Most important, a query is a saved object within the database, whereas filters are temporary because Access removes them when you close the datasheet. TABLE B-2 compares filters and queries. **CASE** ▶ *Samantha asks you to find all Adventure tours offered in the month of July. You can filter the Tours table datasheet to provide this information.*

STEPS

QUICK TIP
You can also apply a sort or filter by clicking the Sort and filter arrow to the right of the field name and choosing the sort order or filter values you want.

1. **Double-click the Tours table to open it, click any occurrence of Adventure in the Category field, click the Selection button in the Sort & Filter group on the HOME tab, then click Equals "Adventure"**

 Eighteen records are selected, some of which are shown in FIGURE B-10. A filter icon appears to the right of the Category field. Filtering by the selected field value, called **Filter By Selection**, is a fast and easy way to filter the records for an exact match. To filter for comparative data (for example, where TourStartDate is *equal to* or *greater than* 7/1/2014), you must use the **Filter By Form** feature. Filter buttons are summarized in TABLE B-3.

2. **Click the Advanced button in the Sort & Filter group, then click Filter By Form**

 The Filter by Form window opens. The previous Filter By Selection criterion, "Adventure" in the Category field, is still in the grid. Access distinguishes between text and numeric entries by placing "quotation marks" around text criteria.

QUICK TIP
To clear previous criteria, click the Advanced button, then click Clear All Filters.

3. **Click the TourStartDate cell, then type 7/*/2014 as shown in FIGURE B-11**

 Filter By Form also allows you to apply two or more criteria at the same time. An asterisk (*) in the day position of the date criterion works as a wildcard, selecting any date in the month of July (the 7th month) in the year 2014.

QUICK TIP
Be sure to remove existing filters before applying a new filter, or the new filter will apply to the current subset of records instead of the entire datasheet.

4. **Click the Toggle Filter button in the Sort & Filter group**

 The datasheet selects two records that match both filter criteria, as shown in FIGURE B-12. Note that filter icons appear next to the TourStartDate and Category field names as both fields are involved in the filter.

5. **Close the Tours datasheet, then click Yes when prompted to save the changes**

 Saving changes to the datasheet saves the last sort order and column width changes. Filters are not saved.

Using wildcard characters

To search for a pattern, you can use a **wildcard** character to represent any character in the condition entry. Use a question mark (?) to search for any single character and an asterisk (*) to search for any number of characters. Wildcard characters are often used with the **Like** operator. For example, the criterion Like "12/*/13" would find all dates in December of 2013, and the criterion Like "F*" would find all entries that start with the letter F.

FIGURE B-10: Filtering the Tours table

Selection button

Advanced button

Sort and filter buttons

Filter icon

Adventure in the Category field

Toggle Filter button is selected, indicating the records are filtered

FIGURE B-11: Filtering By Form criteria

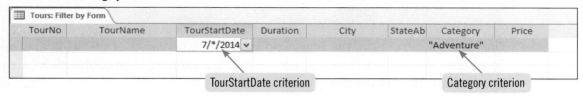

TourStartDate criterion

Category criterion

FIGURE B-12: Results of filtering by form

TourStartDate values are in July 2014

Filter icons

Category is equal to Adventure

TABLE B-2: Filters vs. queries

characteristics	filters	queries
Are saved as an object in the database		•
Can be used to select a subset of records in a datasheet	•	•
Can be used to select a subset of fields in a datasheet		•
Resulting datasheet used to enter and edit data	•	•
Resulting datasheet used to sort, filter, and find records	•	•
Commonly used as the source of data for a form or report		•
Can calculate sums, averages, counts, and other types of summary statistics across records		•
Can be used to create calculated fields		•

© 2014 Cengage Learning

TABLE B-3: Filter buttons

name	button	purpose
Filter	▼	Provides a list of values in the selected field that can be used to customize a filter
Selection	▼ᵧ	Filters records that equal, do not equal, or are otherwise compared with the current value
Advanced	▦	Provides advanced filter features such as Filter By Form, Save As Query, and Clear All Filters
Toggle Filter	▼	Applies or removes the current filter

© 2014 Cengage Learning

Access 2013

Apply AND Criteria

Learning Outcomes
- Enter AND criteria in a query
- Define criteria syntax
- Use comparison operators with criteria

You can limit the number of records that appear on a query datasheet by entering criteria in Query Design View. Criteria are tests, or limiting conditions, for which the record must be true to be selected for the query datasheet. To create **AND criteria**, which means that *all* criteria must be true to select the record, enter two or more criteria on the *same* Criteria row of the query design grid. **CASE** ▶ *Samantha Hooper asks you to provide a list of all Adventure tours in the state of Florida with a duration of 7 days or less. Use Query Design View to create the query with AND criteria to meet her request.*

STEPS

1. **Click the CREATE tab on the Ribbon, click the Query Design button, double-click Tours, then click Close in the Show Table dialog box**

 You want four fields from the Tours table in this query.

2. **Drag the bottom edge of the Tours field list down to display all of the fields, double-click TourName, double-click Duration, double-click StateAbbrev, then double-click Category to add these fields to the query grid**

 First add criteria to select only those records in Florida. Because you are using the StateAbbrev field, you need to use the two-letter state abbreviation for Florida, FL, as the Criteria entry.

3. **Click the first Criteria cell for the StateAbbrev field, type FL, then click the View button 📊 to display the results**

 Querying for only those tours in the state of Florida selects nine records. Next, you add criteria to select only the tours in Florida in the Adventure category.

4. **Click the View button 📐, click the first Criteria cell for the Category field, type Adventure, then click the View button 📊 in the Results group**

 Criteria added to the same line of the query design grid are AND criteria. When entered on the same line, each criterion must be true for the record to appear in the resulting datasheet. Querying for both FL and Adventure tours narrows the selection to five records. Every time you add AND criteria, you *narrow* the number of records that are selected because the record must be true for *all* criteria.

5. **Click the View button 📐, click the first Criteria cell for the Duration field, then type <=7, as shown in FIGURE B-13**

 Access assists you with **criteria syntax**, rules that specify how to enter criteria. Access automatically adds "quotation marks" around text criteria in Short Text and Long Text fields ("FL" and "Adventure") and pound signs (#) around date criteria in Date/Time fields. The criteria in Number, Currency, and Yes/No fields are not surrounded by any characters. See **TABLE B-4** for more information about comparison operators such as > (greater than).

TROUBLE
If your datasheet doesn't match FIGURE B-14, return to Query Design View and compare your criteria with that of FIGURE B-13.

6. **Click the View button 📊**

 The third AND criterion further narrows the number of records selected to four, as shown in **FIGURE B-14**.

7. **Click the Save button 🖫 on the Quick Access toolbar, type AdventureFL as the query name, click OK, then close the query**

 The query is saved with the new name, AdventureFL, as a new object in the QuestTravel-B database. Criteria entered in Query Design View are permanently saved with the query (as compared with filters in the previous lesson, which are temporary and not saved with the object).

FIGURE B-13: Query Design View with AND criteria

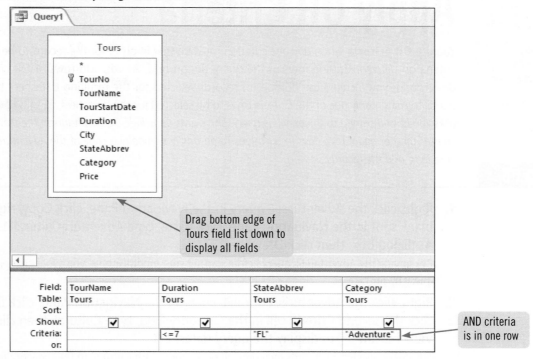

Drag bottom edge of Tours field list down to display all fields

AND criteria is in one row

FIGURE B-14: Final datasheet of AdventureFL query

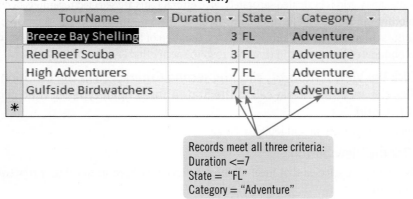

Records meet all three criteria:
Duration <=7
State = "FL"
Category = "Adventure"

TABLE B-4: Comparison operators

operator	description	expression	meaning
>	Greater than	>500	Numbers greater than 500
>=	Greater than or equal to	>=500	Numbers greater than or equal to 500
<	Less than	<"Braveheart"	Names from A to Braveheart, but not Braveheart
<=	Less than or equal to	<="Bridgewater"	Names from A through Bridgewater, inclusive
<>	Not equal to	<>"Fontanelle"	Any name except for Fontanelle

Searching for blank fields

Is Null and Is Not Null are two other types of common criteria. The **Is Null** criterion finds all records where no entry has been made in the field. **Is Not Null** finds all records where there is any entry in the field, even if the entry is 0. Primary key fields cannot have a null entry.

Learning
Outcomes
• Enter OR criteria in
 a query
• Rename a query

Apply OR Criteria

You use **OR criteria** when *any one* criterion must be true in order for the record to be selected. Enter OR criteria on *different* Criteria rows of the query design grid. As you add rows of OR criteria to the query design grid, you *increase* the number of records selected for the resulting datasheet because the record needs to match *only one* of the Criteria rows to be selected for the datasheet. **CASE** *Samantha Hooper asks you to add criteria to the previous query. She wants to include Cultural tours in the state of Florida that are shorter than or equal to 7 days in duration. To do this, you modify a copy of the AdventureFL query to use OR criteria to add the records.*

STEPS

1. **Right-click the AdventureFL query in the Navigation Pane, click Copy, right-click a blank spot in the Navigation Pane, click Paste, type AdventureCulturalFL in the Paste As dialog box, then click OK**

 By copying the AdventureFL query before starting your modifications, you avoid changing the AdventureFL query by mistake.

2. **Right-click the AdventureCulturalFL query in the Navigation Pane, click Design View, click the second Criteria cell in the Category field, type Cultural, then click the View button 📊 to display the query datasheet**

 The query selected 11 records including all of the tours with Cultural in the Category field. Note that some of the Duration values are greater than 7 and some of the StateAbbrev values are not FL. Because each row of the query grid is evaluated separately, all Cultural tours are selected regardless of criteria in any other row. In other words, the criteria in one row have no effect on the criteria of other rows. To make sure that the Cultural tours are also in Florida and have a duration of less than or equal to 7 days, you need to modify the second row of the query grid (the "or" row) to specify that criteria.

QUICK TIP
The Datasheet,
Design, and other
view buttons are also
located in the lower-
right corner of the
Access window.

3. **Click the View button 📐, click the second Criteria cell in the Duration field, type <=7, click the second Criteria cell in the StateAbbrev field, type FL, then click in any other cell of the grid**

 Query Design View should look like **FIGURE B-15**.

4. **Click the View button 📊**

 Six records are selected that meet all three criteria as entered in row one *or* row two of the query grid, as shown in **FIGURE B-16**.

5. **Right-click the AdventureCulturalFL query tab, click Close, then click Yes to save and close the query datasheet**

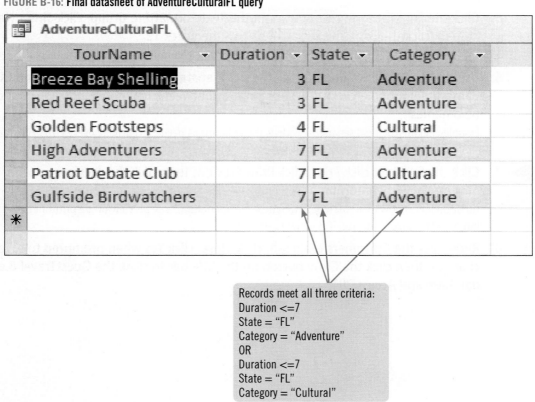

OR criteria is on
multiple rows

FIGURE B-16: Final datasheet of AdventureCulturalFL query

Records meet all three criteria:
Duration <=7
State = "FL"
Category = "Adventure"
OR
Duration <=7
State = "FL"
Category = "Cultural"

Access 2013

Format a Datasheet

**Learning
Outcomes**
• Zoom in print
 preview
• Format a datasheet
• Change page
 orientation

A report is the primary Access tool to create a professional printout, but you can print a datasheet as well. A datasheet allows you to apply some basic formatting modifications such as changing the font size, font face, colors, and gridlines. **CASE** ▸ *Samantha Hooper asks you to print a list of customers. You decide to format the Customers table datasheet before printing it for her.*

STEPS

1. **In the Navigation Pane, double-click the Customers table to open it in Datasheet View**

 Before applying new formatting enhancements, you preview the default printout.

2. **Click the FILE tab, click Print, click Print Preview, then click the header of the printout to zoom in**

 The preview window displays the layout of the printout, as shown in **FIGURE B-17**. By default, the printout of a datasheet contains the object name and current date in the header. The page number is in the footer.

3. **Click the Next Page button ▶ in the navigation bar to move to the next page of the printout**

 The last two fields print on the second page because the first is not wide enough to accommodate them. You decide to switch the report to landscape orientation so that all of the fields print on one page, and then increase the size of the font before printing to make the text easier to read.

4. **Click the Landscape button on the PRINT PREVIEW tab to switch the report to landscape orientation, then click the Close Print Preview button**

 You return to Datasheet View where you can make font face, font size, font color, gridline color, and background color choices.

5. **Click the Font list arrow** Calibri (Body) ▾ **in the Text Formatting group, click Times New Roman, click the Font Size list arrow** 11 ▾ **, then click 12**

 With the larger font size applied, you need to resize some columns to accommodate the widest entries.

6. **Use the ↔ pointer to double-click the field separator between the Street and City field names, then double-click the field separator between the Phone and FirstContact field names**

 Double-clicking the field separators widens the columns as needed to display every entry in those fields, as shown in **FIGURE B-18**.

QUICK TIP
If you need a print-
out of this datasheet,
click the Print button
on the PRINT PREVIEW
tab, then click OK.

7. **Click the FILE tab, click Print, click Print Preview, then click the preview to zoom in and out to review the information**

 All of the fields now fit across a page in landscape orientation. The preview of the printout is still two pages, but with the larger font size, it is easier to read.

8. **Right-click the Customers table tab, click Close, click Yes when prompted to save changes, then click the Close button on the title bar to close the QuestTravel-B.accdb database and Access 2013**

FIGURE B-17: Preview of Customers datasheet

Landscape button

Close Print Preview button

Table name and current date in header

FIGURE B-18: Formatting the Customers datasheet

Font list arrow

Font Size list arrow

Field separator

Drag or double-click with this pointer to resize columns

Practice

Put your skills into practice with **SAM Projects!** SAM Projects for this unit can be found online. If you have a SAM account, go to www.cengage.com/sam2013 to download the most recent Project Instruction and Start Files.

Concepts Review

Label each element of the Access window shown in FIGURE B-19.

FIGURE B-19

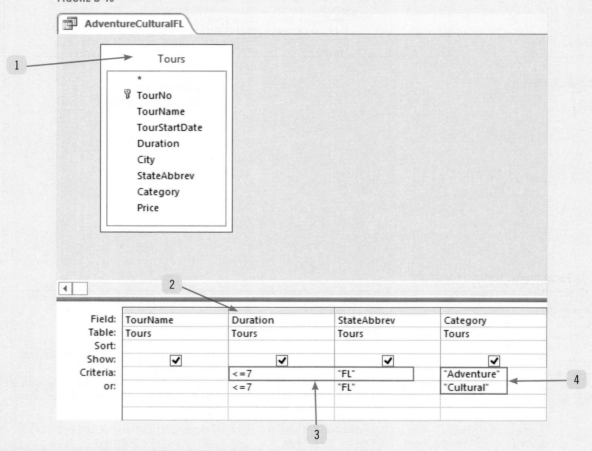

Match each term with the statement that best describes it.

5. **Query grid**
6. **Field selector**
7. **Filter**
8. **Filter By Selection**
9. **Field lists**
10. **Sorting**
11. **Join line**
12. **Is Null**
13. **Criteria**
14. **Syntax**
15. **Wildcard**

a. Putting records in ascending or descending order based on the values of a field
b. Limiting conditions used to restrict the number of records that are selected in a query
c. Creates a temporary subset of records
d. Small windows that display field names
e. Rules that determine how criteria are entered
f. Used to search for a pattern of characters
g. Criterion that finds all records where no entry has been made in the field
h. The lower pane in Query Design View
i. Identifies which fields are used to establish a relationship between two tables
j. A fast and easy way to filter the records for an exact match
k. The thin gray bar above each field in the query grid

Select the best answer from the list of choices.

16. **AND criteria:**
 a. Determine sort orders.
 b. Must all be true for the record to be selected.
 c. Determine fields selected for a query.
 d. Help set link lines between tables in a query.

17. **SQL stands for which of the following?**
 a. Structured Query Language
 b. Standard Query Language
 c. Special Query Listing
 d. Simple Query Listing

18. **A query is sometimes called a logical view of data because:**
 a. You can create queries with the Logical Query Wizard.
 b. Queries contain logical criteria.
 c. Query naming conventions are logical.
 d. Queries do not store data—they only display a view of data.

19. **Which of the following describes OR criteria?**
 a. Selecting a subset of fields and/or records to view as a datasheet from one or more tables
 b. Using two or more rows of the query grid to select only those records that meet given criteria
 c. Reorganizing the records in either ascending or descending order based on the contents of one or more fields
 d. Using multiple fields in the query design grid

20. **Which of the following is *not* true about a query?**
 a. A query is the same thing as a filter.
 b. A query can select fields from one or more tables in a relational database.
 c. A query can be created using different tools.
 d. An existing query can be modified in Query Design View.

Skills Review

1. **Use the Query Wizard.**
 a. Open the Recycle-B.accdb database from the location where you store your Data Files. Enable content if prompted.
 b. Create a new query using the Simple Query Wizard. Select the CenterName field from the Centers table, the DepositDate and Weight fields from the Deposits table, and the ClubName field from the Clubs table. Select Detail, and enter **CenterDeposits** as the name of the query.
 c. Open the query in Datasheet View, then change any record with the Barker Trash value to a center name that includes *your* last name.

2. **Work with data in a query.**
 a. Delete the first record (Hugo Trash Can with a DepositDate value of 2/4/2014).
 b. Change any occurrence of Lions of Fontanelle in the ClubName field to **Lions of Bridgewater**.
 c. Click any value in the DepositDate field, then click the Descending button on the HOME tab to sort the records in descending order on the DepositDate field.
 d. Use the Calendar Picker to choose the date of **12/16/2016** for the first record.
 e. Save and close the CenterDeposits query.

3. **Use Query Design View.**
 a. Click the CREATE tab, click the Query Design button, double-click Clubs, double-click Deposits, and then click Close to add the Clubs and Deposits tables to Query Design View.
 b. Drag the bottom edge of both field lists down to display all of the field names in both tables.
 c. Add the following fields from the Clubs table to the query design grid in the following order: FName, LName, ClubName. Add the following fields from the Deposits table in the following order: DepositDate, Weight. View the results in Datasheet View observing the number of records that are selected.
 d. In Design View, enter criteria to display only those records with a Weight value of **greater than or equal to 100**, then observe the number of records that are selected in Datasheet View.
 e. Save the query with the name **HeavyDeposits**.

4. **Sort and find data.**
 a. In Query Design View of the HeavyDeposits query, choose an ascending sort order for the ClubName field and a descending sort order for the Weight field.
 b. Display the query in Datasheet View noting how the records have been resorted.
 c. In the ClubName field, change any occurrence of Jaycees to **Dallas Jaycees**.
 d. In the FName field, change any occurrence of Tara to *your* initials.

5. **Filter data.**
 a. Filter the HeavyDeposits datasheet for only those records where the ClubName equals **Dallas Jaycees**.
 b. Apply an advanced Filter By Form and use the >= operator to further narrow the records so that only the deposits with a DepositDate value on or after 1/1/2015 are selected.
 c. Apply the filter to see the datasheet and if requested by your instructor, print the filtered HeavyDeposits datasheet.
 d. Save and close the HeavyDeposits query. Reopen the HeavyDeposits query to confirm that filters are temporary (not saved), and then close the HeavyDeposits query again.

Skills Review (continued)

6. Apply AND criteria.

 a. Right-click the HeavyDeposits query, copy it, and then paste it as **Heavy2014Deposits**.

 b. Open the Heavy2014Deposits query in Query Design View.

 c. Modify the criteria to select all of the records with a DepositDate in **2014** and a Weight value **greater than or equal to 100**.

 d. If requested by your instructor, print the Heavy2014Deposits datasheet, then save and close it.

7. Apply OR criteria.

 a. Right-click the HeavyDeposits query, copy it, then paste it as **HeavyDeposits2Clubs**.

 b. Open the HeavyDeposits2Clubs query in Design View, then add criteria to select the records with a ClubName of **Ice Kings** and a Weight value **greater than or equal to 100**.

 c. Add criteria to also include the records with a ClubName of **Junior League** with a Weight value **greater than or equal to 100**. FIGURE B-20 shows the results.

 d. If requested by your instructor, print the HeavyDeposits2Clubs datasheet, then save and close it.

8. Format a datasheet.

 a. In the Clubs table datasheet, apply an Arial Narrow font and a 14-point font size.

 b. Resize all columns so that all data and field names are visible.

 c. Display the Clubs datasheet in Print Preview, switch the orientation to landscape, click the Margins button in the Page Size group, then click Narrow to fit the printout on a single sheet of paper.

 d. If requested by your instructor, print the Clubs datasheet.

 e. Save and close the Clubs table, then close Access 2013.

FIGURE B-20

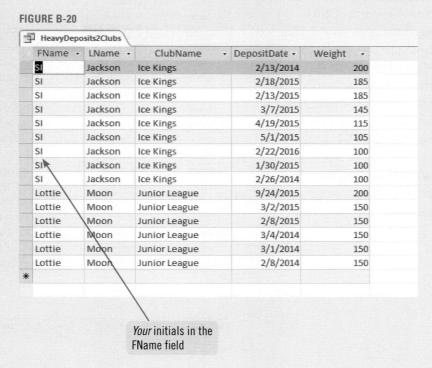

Your initials in the FName field

Independent Challenge 1

You have built an Access database to track membership in a community service club. The database tracks member names and addresses as well as their community service hours.

a. Open the Membership-B.accdb database from the location where you store your Data Files, enable content if prompted, then open the Activities, Members, and Zips tables to review their datasheets.

b. In the Zips table, click the expand button to the left of the 64131, Overland Park, KS, record to display the two members linked to that zip code. Click the expand button to the left of the Gabriel Hammer record to display the three activity records linked to Gabriel.

c. Close all three datasheets, click the DATABASE TOOLS tab, then click the Relationships button. The Relationships window also shows you that one record in the Zips table is related to many records in the Members table through the common ZipCode field, and that one record in the Members table is related to many records in the Activities table through the common MemberNo field.

d. Click the Relationship Report button, then if requested by your instructor, print the Relationship report. Close and save the report with the default name **Relationships for Membership-B**. Close the Relationships window.

e. Using Query Design View, build a query with the following fields: FirstName and LastName from the Members table and ActivityDate and HoursWorked from the Activities table.

f. View the datasheet, observe the number of records selected, then return to Query Design View.

g. Add criteria to select only those records where the ActivityDate is in March of 2014.

h. In Query Design View, apply an ascending sort order to the LastName and ActivityDate fields, then view the datasheet.

i. Change the name Quentin Garden to *your* name, widen all columns so that all data and field names are visible, and save the query with the name **March2014**, as shown in FIGURE B-21.

j. If requested by your instructor, print the March2014 datasheet, then close the March2014 query and close Access 2013.

FIGURE B-21

FirstName	LastName	ActivityDate	HoursWorked
Bart	Bouchart	3/29/2014	4
Golga	Collins	3/31/2014	8
Martha	Duman	3/27/2014	4
Allie	Eahlie	3/29/2014	4
Jana	Eckert	3/29/2014	5
Student First	Student Last	3/29/2014	4
Student First	Student Last	3/30/2014	8
Loraine	Goode	3/29/2014	5
Gabriel	Hammer	3/29/2014	5
Jeremiah	Hopper	3/27/2014	4
Helen	Hubert	3/29/2014	5
Heidi	Kalvert	3/29/2014	4
Harvey	Mackintosh	3/30/2014	4
Jon	Maxim	3/30/2014	4
Micah	Mayberry	3/29/2014	4
Patch	Mullins	3/30/2014	8
Patch	Mullins	3/31/2014	8
Young	Nelson	3/30/2014	10
Mallory	Olson	3/31/2014	8
Su	Vogue	3/30/2014	8
Sherry	Walker	3/29/2014	4
Taney	Wilson	3/30/2014	8

Record: 7 of 22 — No Filter — Search

March2014

Independent Challenge 2

You work for a nonprofit agency that tracks the voting patterns of Congress. You have developed an Access database with contact information for members of the House of Representatives. The director of the agency has asked you to create several state lists of representatives. You will use queries to extract this information.

a. Open the Congress-B.accdb database from the location where you store your Data Files, then enable content if prompted.

b. Open the Representatives and the States tables. Notice that one state is related to many representatives as evidenced by the expand buttons to the left of the records in the States tables.

c. Close both datasheets, then using Query Design View, create a query with the StateAbbrev, StateName, and Capital fields from the States table (in that order) as well as the LName field from the Representatives table.

d. Sort the records in ascending order on the StateName field, then in ascending order on the LName field.

e. Add criteria to select the representatives from Arizona or New Mexico. Use the StateAbbrev field to enter your criteria, using the two-character state abbreviations of **AZ** and **NM**.

f. Save the query with the name **ArizonaAndNewMexico** as shown in FIGURE B-22, view the results, then change the last name of Upton in the last record to *your* last name. Resize the columns as needed to view all the data and field names.

g. Print the ArizonaAndNewMexico datasheet if requested by your instructor, then close it and exit Access 2013.

FIGURE B-22

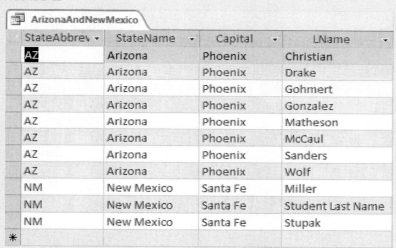

StateAbbrev	StateName	Capital	LName
AZ	Arizona	Phoenix	Christian
AZ	Arizona	Phoenix	Drake
AZ	Arizona	Phoenix	Gohmert
AZ	Arizona	Phoenix	Gonzalez
AZ	Arizona	Phoenix	Matheson
AZ	Arizona	Phoenix	McCaul
AZ	Arizona	Phoenix	Sanders
AZ	Arizona	Phoenix	Wolf
NM	New Mexico	Santa Fe	Miller
NM	New Mexico	Santa Fe	Student Last Name
NM	New Mexico	Santa Fe	Stupak

Independent Challenge 3

You have built an Access database to track the veterinarians and clinics in your area.

a. Open the Vet-B.accdb database from the location where you store your Data Files, then enable content if prompted.

b. Open the Vets table and then the Clinics table to review the data in both datasheets.

c. Click the expand button next to the Veterinary Specialists record in the Clinics table, then add *your* name as a new record to the Vets subdatasheet.

d. Close both datasheets.

e. Using the Simple Query Wizard, select the VetLast and VetFirst fields from the Vets table, and select the ClinicName and Phone fields from the Clinics table. Title the query **ClinicListing**, then view the datasheet.

f. Update any occurrence of Leawood Animal Clinic in the ClinicName field by changing Leawood to **Emergency** so the ClinicName is **Emergency Animal Clinic**.

g. In Query Design View, add criteria to select only **Emergency Animal Clinic** or **Veterinary Specialists** in the ClinicName field, then view the datasheet.

h. In Query Design View, move the ClinicName field to the first column, then add an ascending sort order on the ClinicName and VetLast fields.

i. Display the ClinicListing query in Datasheet View, resize the fields as shown in FIGURE B-23, then print the datasheet if requested by your instructor.

j. Save and close the ClinicListing datasheet, then exit Access 2013.

FIGURE B-23

Independent Challenge 4: Explore

An Access database is an excellent tool to help record and track job opportunities. For this exercise, you'll create a database from scratch that you can use to enter, edit, and query data in pursuit of a new job or career.

a. Create a new desktop database named **Jobs.accdb**.

b. Create a table named **Positions** with the following field names, data types, and descriptions:

Field name	Data type	Description
PositionID	AutoNumber	Primary key field
Title	Short Text	Title of position such as Accountant, Assistant Court Clerk, or Web Developer
CareerArea	Short Text	Area of the career field such as Accounting, Government, or Information Systems
AnnualSalary	Currency	Annual salary
Desirability	Number	Desirability rating of 1 = low to 5 = high to show how desirable the position is to you
EmployerID	Number	Foreign key field to the Employers table

c. Create a table named **Employers** with the following field names, data types, and descriptions:

Field name	Data type	Description
EmployerID	AutoNumber	Primary key field
CompanyName	Short Text	Company name of the employer
EmpStreet	Short Text	Employer's street address
EmpCity	Short Text	Employer's city
EmpState	Short Text	Employer's state
EmpZip	Short Text	Employer's zip code
EmpPhone	Short Text	Employer's phone, such as 913-555-8888

d. Be sure to set EmployerID as the primary key field in the Employers table and the PositionID as the primary key field in the Positions table.

e. Link the Employers and Positions tables together in a one-to-many relationship using the common EmployerID field. One employer record will be linked to many position records. Be sure to enforce referential integrity.

f. Using any valid source of potential employer data, enter five records into the Employers table.

g. Using any valid source of job information, enter five records into the Positions table by using the subdatasheets from within the Employers datasheet.
Because one employer may have many positions, all five of your Positions records may be linked to the same employer, you may have one position record per employer, or any other combination.

h. Build a query that selects CompanyName from the Employers table, and the Title, CareerArea, AnnualSalary, and Desirability fields from the Positions table. Sort the records in descending order based on Desirability. Save the query as **JobList**, and print it if requested by your instructor.

i. Close the JobList datasheet, then exit Access 2013.

Visual Workshop

Open the Baseball-B.accdb database from the location where you store your Data Files, and enable content if prompted. Create a query based on the Players and Teams tables, as shown in FIGURE B-24. Add criteria to select only those records where the PlayerPosition field values are equal to 1 or 2 (representing pitchers and catchers). In Query Design View, set an ascending sort order on the TeamName and PlayerPosition fields. In the results, change the name of Roy Campanella to *your* name. Save the query with the name **PitchersAndCatchers**, then compare the results with FIGURE B-24, making changes and widening columns to see all of the data. Print the datasheet if requested by your instructor. Save and close the query and the Baseball-B.accdb database, then exit Access 2013.

FIGURE B-24

TeamName	PlayerLast	PlayerFirst	Position
Brooklyn Beetles	Student Last Name	Student First Name	1
Brooklyn Beetles	Young	Cycylie	2
Mayfair Monarchs	Durocher	Luis	1
Mayfair Monarchs	Mathewson	Carl	2
Rocky's Rockets	Spalding	Andrew	1
Rocky's Rockets	Koufax	Sanford	2
Snapping Turtles	Ford	Charles	1
Snapping Turtles	Perry	Greg	2

Using Forms

CASE Samantha Hooper, a tour developer at Quest Specialty Travel, asks you to create forms to make tour information easier to access, enter, and update.

Unit Objectives

After completing this unit, you will be able to:

- Use the Form Wizard
- Create a split form
- Use Form Layout View
- Add fields to a form

- Modify form controls
- Create calculations
- Modify tab order
- Insert an image

Files You Will Need

QuestTravel-C.accdb
QuestLogo.bmp
RealEstate-C.accdb
ForSale.bmp
Dives-C.accdb

Membership-C.accdb
People.jpg
Recycle-C.accdb
Jobs-C.accdb
Baseball-C.accdb

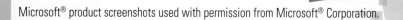

©Tumanyan/Shutterstock

Use the Form Wizard

Learning Outcomes
- Create a form with the Form Wizard
- Sort data in a form
- Describe form terminology and views

A **form** is an easy-to-use data entry and navigation screen. A form allows you to arrange the fields of a record in any layout so a **database user** can quickly and easily find, enter, edit, and analyze data. The **database designer** is the person responsible for building and maintaining tables, queries, forms, and reports for all of the database users. **CASE** ▸ *Samantha Hooper asks you to build a form to enter and maintain tour information.*

STEPS

1. **Start Access, open the QuestTravel-C.accdb database from the location where you store your Data Files, then enable content if prompted**

 You can use many methods to create a new form, but the Form Wizard is a fast and popular tool that helps you get started. The **Form Wizard** prompts you for information it needs to create a form, such as the fields, layout, and title for the form.

2. **Click the CREATE tab on the Ribbon, then click the Form Wizard button in the Forms group**

 The Form Wizard starts, prompting you to select the fields for this form. You want to create a form to enter and update data in the Tours table.

3. **Click the Tables/Queries list arrow, click Table: Tours, then click the Select All Fields button >>**

 You could now select fields from other tables, if necessary, but in this case, you have all of the fields you need.

4. **Click Next, click the Columnar option button, click Next, type Tours Entry Form as the title, then click Finish**

 The Tours Entry Form opens in **Form View**, as shown in FIGURE C-1. Access provides three different views of forms, as summarized in TABLE C-1. Each item on the form is called a **control**. A **label control** is used to *describe* the data shown in other controls such as text boxes. A label is also used for the title of the form, Tours Entry Form. A **text box** is used to *display* the data as well as enter, edit, find, sort, and also filter the data. A **combo box** is a combination of two controls: a text box and a list. The Category data is displayed in a combo box control. You click the arrow button on a combo box control to display a list of values, or you can edit data directly in the combo box itself.

5. **Click Breeze Bay Shelling in the TourName text box, click the Ascending button in the Sort & Filter group, then click the Next record button ▶ in the navigation bar to move to the second record**

 The Ames Ski Club is the second record when the records are sorted in ascending order on the TourName data. Information about the current record number and total number of records appears in the navigation bar, just as it does in a datasheet.

6. **Click the Previous record button ◀ in the navigation bar to move back to the first record, click the TourName text box, then change American Heritage Tour to Washington DC History Tour**

 Your screen should look like FIGURE C-2. Forms displayed in Form View are the primary tool for database users to enter, edit, and delete data in an Access database.

7. **Right-click the Tours Entry Form tab, then click Close**

 When a form is closed, Access automatically saves any edits made to the current record.

FIGURE C-1: Tours Entry Form in Form View

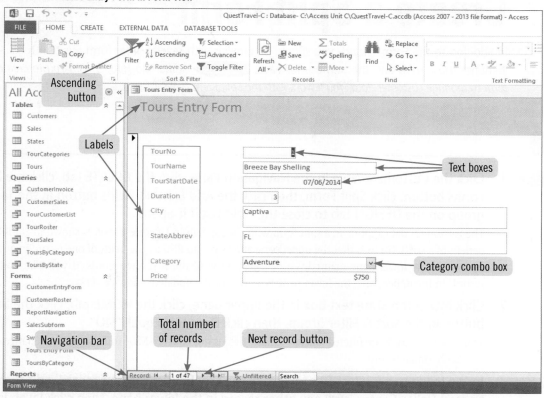

FIGURE C-2: Displaying the results of a calculation in Form View

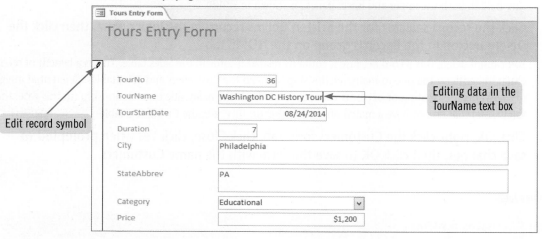

TABLE C-1: Form views

view	primary purpose
Form	To find, sort, enter, and edit data
Layout	To modify the size, position, or formatting of controls; shows data as you modify the form, making it the tool of choice when you want to change the appearance and usability of the form while viewing live data
Design	To modify the Form Header, Detail, and Footer section, or to access the complete range of controls and form properties; Design View does not display data

Create a Split Form

Learning Outcomes
- Create a split form
- Enter and edit data in a form

In addition to the Form Wizard, you should be familiar with several other form creation tools. TABLE C-2 identifies those tools and the purpose for each. **CASE** ▸ *Samantha Hooper asks you to create another form to manage customer data. You'll work with the Split Form tool for this task.*

STEPS

QUICK TIP
Layout View allows you to view and filter the data, but not edit it.

1. **Click the Customers table in the Navigation Pane, click the CREATE tab, click the More Forms button, click Split Form, then click the Add Existing Fields button in the Tools group on the DESIGN tab to close the Field List if it opens**

 The Customers data appears in a split form with the top half in **Layout View**, as shown in FIGURE C-3. The benefit of a **split form** is that the upper pane allows you to display the fields of one record in any arrangement, and the lower pane maintains a datasheet view of the first few records. If you edit, sort, or filter records in the upper pane, the lower pane is automatically updated, and vice versa.

2. **Click MO in the State text box in the upper pane, click the HOME tab, click the Selection button in the Sort & Filter group, then click Does Not Equal "MO"**

 Thirty-seven records are filtered where the State field is not equal to MO. You also need to change a value in the Jacob Alman record.

TROUBLE
Make sure you edit the record in the datasheet in the lower pane.

3. **In the lower pane, select Des Moines in the City field of the first record, edit the entry to read Dallas Center, click any other record in the lower pane, then click Jacob in the first record of the lower pane**

 Moving from record to record automatically saves data. Note that "Dallas Center" is now the entry in the City field in both the upper and lower panes, as shown in FIGURE C-4.

4. **Click the record selector for the Kristen Collins record in the lower pane, then click the Delete button in the Records group on the HOME tab**

 You cannot delete this record because it contains related records in the Sales table. This is a benefit of referential integrity on the one-to-many relationship between the Customers and Sales tables. Referential integrity prevents the creation of **orphan records**, records on the *many* side of a relationship (in this case, the Sales table) that do not have a match on the *one* side (in this case, the Customers table).

5. **Click OK, right-click the Customers form tab, click Close, click Yes when prompted to save changes, then click OK to save the form with the name Customers**

TABLE C-2: Form creation tools

tool	icon	creates a form
Form		with one click based on the selected table or query
Form Design		from scratch in Form Design View
Blank Form		from scratch in Form Layout View
Form Wizard		by answering a series of questions provided by the Form Wizard dialog boxes
Navigation		used to navigate or move between different areas of the database
More Forms		based on Multiple Items, Datasheet, Split Form, Modal Dialog, PivotChart, or PivotTable arrangements
Split Form		with two panes, the upper showing one record at a time and the lower displaying a datasheet of many records

© 2014 Cengage Learning

FIGURE C-3: Customers table in a split form

Upper pane in Layout View

Lower pane in Datasheet View

FIGURE C-4: Editing data in a split form

Selection button

Delete button

Record selector for record in upper pane

Des Moines changed to Dallas Center

Record selector for Kristen Collins record

Filtered button indicates the records are filtered

Access 2013

Use Form Layout View

Learning Outcomes
- Resize controls in Layout View
- Format controls in Layout View

Layout View lets you make some design changes to a form while you are browsing the data. For example, you can move and resize controls, add or delete a field on the form, filter and sort data, or change formatting characteristics, such as fonts and colors. **CASE** ▸ *Samantha Hooper asks you to make several design changes to the Tours Entry Form. You can make these changes in Layout View.*

STEPS

1. **Right-click Tours Entry Form in the Navigation Pane, then click Layout View**

 In Layout View, you can move through the records, but you cannot enter or edit the data as you can in Form View.

 TROUBLE
 If your third record is not Bigfoot Rafting Club, sort the records in ascending order on the TourName field.

2. **Click the Next record button in the navigation bar twice to move to the third record, Bigfoot Rafting Club**

 You often use Layout View to make minor design changes, such as editing labels and changing formatting characteristics.

3. **Click the TourNo label to select it if it is not already selected, click between the words Tour and No, then press [Spacebar]**

 You also want to edit a few more labels.

 TROUBLE
 Be sure to modify the *labels in the left column* instead of the text boxes on the right.

4. **Continue editing the labels, as shown in FIGURE C-5**

 You also want to change the text color of the first two labels, Tour No and Tour Name, to red to make them more noticeable.

5. **Click the Tour No label, click the HOME tab, click the Font Color button ☒ in the Text Formatting group, click the Tour Name label, then click ☒**

 Often, you want to apply the same formatting enhancement to multiple controls. For example, you decide to narrow the City and StateAbbrev text boxes. Select the text boxes at the same time to make the same change to both.

 TROUBLE
 Be sure to modify the *text boxes in the right column* instead of the labels on the left.

6. **Click Placerville in the City text box, press and hold [Shift], click CA in the StateAbbrev text box to select the two text boxes at the same time, release [Shift], then use the ↔ pointer to drag the right edge of the selection to the left to make the text boxes approximately half as wide**

 Layout View for the Tours Entry Form should look like **FIGURE C-6**. Mouse pointers in Form Layout and Form Design View are very important as they indicate what happens when you drag the mouse. Mouse pointers are described in **TABLE C-3**.

TABLE C-3: Mouse pointer shapes

shape	when does this shape appear?	action
▷	When you point to any unselected control on the form (the default mouse pointer)	Single-clicking with this mouse pointer *selects* a control
✛	When you point to the upper-left corner or edge of a selected control in Form Design View or the middle of the control in Form Layout View	Dragging with this mouse pointer *moves* the selected control(s)
↕ ↔ ⤡ ⤢	When you point to any sizing handle (except the larger one in the upper-left corner in Form Design View)	Dragging with one of these mouse pointers *resizes* the control

FIGURE C-5: Using Layout View to modify form labels on the Tours Entry Form

Edit these labels to include a space between the words

FIGURE C-6: Layout View for the Tours Entry Form

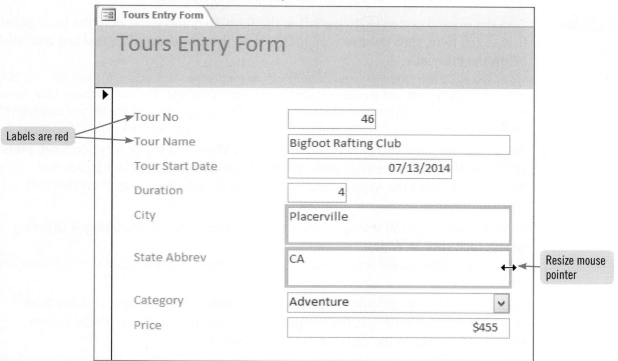

Labels are red

Resize mouse pointer

Table layouts

Layouts provide a way to group several controls together on a form or report to more quickly add, delete, rearrange, resize, or align controls. To insert a layout into a form or report, select the controls you want to group together, then choose the Stacked or Tabular button on the ARRANGE tab. Each option applies a table layout to the controls so that you can insert, delete, merge, or split the cells in the layout to quickly rearrange or edit the controls in the layout. To remove a layout, use the Remove Layout button on the ARRANGE tab in Form Design View.

Add Fields to a Form

Learning Outcomes
- Add fields to a form
- Align controls
- Resize controls

Adding and deleting fields in an existing form is a common activity. You can add or delete fields in a form in either Layout View or Design View using the Field List. The **Field List** lists the database tables and the fields they contain. To add a field to the form, drag it from the Field List to the desired location on the form. To delete a field on a form, click the field to select it, then press the [Delete] key. Deleting a field from a form does not delete it from the underlying table or have any effect on the data contained in the field. You can toggle the Field List on and off using the Add Existing Fields button on the DESIGN tab. **CASE** ▶ *Samantha Hooper asks you to add the tour description from the TourCategories table to the Tours Entry Form. You can use Layout View and the Field List to accomplish this goal.*

STEPS

1. **Click the DESIGN tab on the Ribbon, click the Add Existing Fields button in the Tools group, then click the Show all tables link in the Field List**

 The Field List opens in Layout View, as shown in FIGURE C-7. Notice that the Field List is divided into sections. The upper section shows the tables currently used by the form, the middle section shows directly related tables, and the lower section shows other tables in the database. The expand/collapse button to the left of the table names allows you to expand (show) the fields within the table or collapse (hide) them. The Description field is in the TourCategories table in the middle section.

 QUICK TIP
 If you make a mistake, click the Undo button ↰ and try again.

2. **Click the expand button ⊞ to the left of the TourCategories table, drag the Description field to the form, then use the ⳾ pointer to drag the new Description text box and label below the Price label**

 When you add a new field to a form, two controls are usually created: a label and a text box. The label contains the field name and the text box displays the data in the field. The TourCategories table moved from the middle to the top section of the Field List. You also want to align and size the new controls with others already on the form. Form Design View works well for alignment activities.

3. **Right-click the Tours Entry Form tab, click Design View, click the Description label, press and hold [Shift], click the Price label to select both labels, release [Shift], click the ARRANGE tab, click the Align button in the Sizing & Ordering group, then click Left**

 Now resize the labels.

4. **With the two labels still selected, click the Size/Space button in the Sizing & Ordering group, then click To Widest**

 With the new controls in position, you want to enter a new record. You must switch to Form View to edit, enter, or delete data.

 TROUBLE
 Don't worry if your Tour No value doesn't match FIGURE C-8. As an AutoNumber value, the value is inserted automatically and is controlled by Access.

5. **Click the HOME tab, click the View button ▦ to switch to Form View, click the New (blank) record button ▶▦ in the navigation bar, click the TourName text box, then enter a new record in the updated form, as shown in FIGURE C-8**

 Note that when you select a value in the Category combo box, the Description is automatically updated. This is due to the one-to-many relationship between the TourCategories and Tours tables in the Relationships window.

FIGURE C-7: Field List in Form Layout View

Bound versus unbound controls

Controls are either bound or unbound. **Bound controls** display values from a field such as text boxes and combo boxes. **Unbound controls** do not display data; unbound controls describe data or enhance the appearance of the form. Labels are the most common type of unbound control, but other types include lines, images, tabs, and command buttons. Another way to distinguish bound from unbound controls is to observe the form as you move from record to record. Because bound controls display data, their contents change as you move through the records, displaying the entry in the field of the current record. Unbound controls such as labels and lines do not change as you move through the records in a form.

Modify Form Controls

Learning Outcomes
• Modify control properties
• Define bound and unbound controls

You have already made many modifications to form controls, such as changing the font color of labels and the size of text boxes. Labels and text boxes are the two most popular form controls. Other common controls are listed in TABLE C-4. When you modify controls, you change their **properties** (characteristics). All of the control characteristics you can modify are stored in the control's **Property Sheet.** **CASE** ▶ *Because Quest offers more Adventure tours than any other type of tour, you decide to use the Property Sheet of the Category field to modify the default value to be "Adventure." You also use the Property Sheet to make other control modifications to better size and align the controls.*

STEPS

1. **Click the Layout View button 📊 on the HOME tab, then click the Property Sheet button in the Tools group**

 The Property Sheet opens, showing you all of the properties for the selected item.

2. **Click the Category combo box, click the Data tab in the Property Sheet (if it is not already selected), click the Default Value box, type Adventure, then press [Enter]**

 The Property Sheet should look like FIGURE C-9. Access often helps you with the **syntax** (rules) of entering property values. In this case, Access added quotation marks around "Adventure" to indicate that the default entry is text. Properties are categorized in the Property Sheet with the Format, Data, Event, and Other tabs. The All tab is a complete list of all the control's properties. You can use the Property Sheet to make all control modifications, although you'll probably find that some changes are easier to make using the Ribbon. The property values change in the Property Sheet as you modify a control using the Ribbon.

TROUBLE
Be sure to click the Tour No label on the left, not the TourNo text box on the right.

3. **Click the Format tab in the Property Sheet, click the Tour No label in the form to select it, click the HOME tab on the Ribbon, then click the Align Right button ≡ in the Text Formatting group**

 Notice that the **Text Align property** on the Format tab in the Property Sheet is automatically updated from Left to Right even though you changed the property using the Ribbon instead of within the Property Sheet.

4. **Click the Tour Name label, press and hold [Shift], then click each other label in the first column on the form**

 With all the labels selected, you can modify their Text Align property at the same time.

TROUBLE
You may need to click ≡ twice.

5. **Click ≡ in the Text Formatting group**

 Don't be overwhelmed by the number of properties available for each control on the form or the number of ways to modify each property. Over time, you will learn about most of these properties. At this point, it's only important to know the purpose of the Property Sheet and understand that properties are modified in various ways.

TROUBLE
Don't worry if your Tour No value doesn't match FIGURE C-10. It is an AutoNumber value, controlled by Access.

6. **Click the Save button 🖫 on the Quick Access toolbar, click the Form View button 📄 to switch to Form View, click the New (blank) record button ▶* in the navigation bar, then enter the record shown in FIGURE C-10**

 For new records, "Adventure" is provided as the default value for the Category combo box, but you can change it by typing a new value or selecting one from the list. With the labels right-aligned, they are much closer to the data in the text boxes that they describe.

FIGURE C-9: Using the Property Sheet

FIGURE C-10: Modified Tours Entry Form

TABLE C-4: Common form controls

name	used to	bound	unbound
Label	Provide consistent descriptive text as you navigate from record to record; the label is the most common type of unbound control and can also be used as a hyperlink to another database object, external file, or Web page		•
Text box	Display, edit, or enter data for each record from an underlying record source; the text box is the most common type of bound control	•	
List box	Display a list of possible data entries	•	
Combo box	Display a list of possible data entries for a field, and provide a text box for an entry from the keyboard; combines the list box and text box controls	•	
Tab control	Create a three-dimensional aspect on a form		•
Check box	Display "yes" or "no" answers for a field; if the box is checked, it means "yes"	•	
Toggle button	Display "yes" or "no" answers for a field; if the button is pressed, it means "yes"	•	
Option button	Display a choice for a field	•	
Option group	Display and organize choices (usually presented as option buttons) for a field	•	
Line and Rectangle	Draw lines and rectangles on the form		•
Command button	Provide an easy way to initiate a command or run a macro		•

© 2014 Cengage Learning

Create Calculations

Text boxes are generally used to display data from underlying fields. The connection between the text box and field is defined by the **Control Source property** on the Data tab of the Property Sheet for that text box. A text box control can also display a calculation. To create a calculation in a text box, you enter an expression instead of a field name in the Control Source property. An **expression** is a combination of field names, operators (such as +, –, /, and *), and functions (such as Sum, Count, or Avg) that results in a single value. Sample expressions are shown in TABLE C-5. **CASE** ▸ *Samantha Hooper asks you to add a text box to the Tours Entry Form to calculate the tour end date. You can add a text box in Form Design View to accomplish this.*

STEPS

1. **Right-click the** Tours Entry Form tab, **then click** Design View

 You want to add the tour end date calculation just below the Duration text box. First, you'll resize the City and StateAbbrev fields.

2. **Click the** City label, **press and hold** [Shift], **click the** City text box, **click the** State Abbrev label, **click the** StateAbbrev text box **to select the four controls together, release** [Shift], **click the** ARRANGE tab, **click the** Size/Space button, **then click** To Shortest

 With the City and StateAbbrev fields resized, you're ready to move them to make room for the new control to calculate the tour end date.

3. **Click a blank spot on the form to deselect the four controls, click the** StateAbbrev text box, **use the** ⬚ **pointer to move it down, click the** City text box, **then use the** ⬚ **pointer to move it down**

 To add the calculation to determine the tour end date (the tour start date plus the duration), start by adding a new text box to the form between the Duration and City text boxes.

4. **Click the** DESIGN tab, **click the** Text Box button `ab|` **in the Controls group, then click between the Duration and City text boxes to insert the new text box**

 Adding a new text box automatically adds a new label to the left of the text box.

5. **Click the new** Text20 label **on the left, double-click** Text20, **type** Tour End Date, **then press** [Enter]

 With the label updated to correctly identify the text box to the right, you're ready to enter the expression to calculate the tour end date.

6. **Click the new text box to select it, click the** Data tab **in the Property Sheet, click the** Control Source property, **type** =[TourStartDate]+[Duration], **then press** [Enter] **to update the form, as shown in** FIGURE C-11

 All expressions entered in a control start with an equal sign (=). When referencing a field name within an expression, [square brackets]—(not parentheses) and not {curly braces}—surround the field name. In an expression, you must type the field name exactly as it was created in Table Design View, but you do not need to match the capitalization.

7. **Click the** View button 🖳 **to switch to Form View, click the** value in the Tour Name text box, **click the** Ascending button, **select** 7 in the Duration text box, **type** 5, **then press** [Enter]

 Note that the tour end date, calculated by an expression, automatically changed to five days after the tour start date to reflect the new duration value. The updated Tours Entry Form with the tour date end calculation for the Ames Ski Club is shown in FIGURE C-12.

FIGURE C-11: Adding a text box to calculate a value

FIGURE C-12: Displaying the results of a calculation in Form View

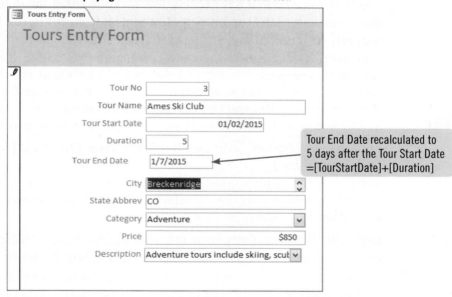

TABLE C-5: Sample expressions

sample expression	description
=Sum([Salary])	Uses the **Sum function** to add the values in the Salary field
=[Price] * 1.05	Multiplies the Price field by 1.05 (adds 5% to the Price field)
=[Subtotal] + [Shipping]	Adds the value of the Subtotal field to the value of the Shipping field
=Avg([Freight])	Uses the **Avg function** to display an average of the values in the Freight field
=Date()	Uses the **Date function** to display the current date in the form of mm-dd-yy
="Page " &[Page]	Displays the word Page, a space, and the result of the [Page] field, an Access field that contains the current page number
=[FirstName]& " " &[LastName]	Displays the value of the FirstName and LastName fields in one control, separated by a space
=Left([ProductNumber],2)	Uses the **Left function** to display the first two characters in the ProductNumber field

© 2014 Cengage Learning

Access 2013

Modify Tab Order

After positioning all of the controls on the form, you should check the tab order and tab stops. **Tab order** is the order the focus moves as you press [Tab] in Form View. A **tab stop** refers to whether a control can receive the focus in the first place. By default, the Tab Stop property for all text boxes and combo boxes is set to Yes, but some text boxes, such as those that contain expressions, will not be used for data entry. Therefore, the Tab Stop property for a text box that contains a calculation should be set to No. Unbound controls such as labels and lines do not have a Tab Stop property because they cannot be used to enter or edit data. **CASE** *You plan to check the tab order of the Tours Entry Form, then change tab stops and tab order as necessary.*

STEPS

1. **Press [Tab] enough times to move through several records, watching the focus move through the bound controls of the form**

 Because the Tour End Date text box is a calculated field, you don't want it to receive the focus. To prevent the Tour End Date text box from receiving the focus, you set its Tab Stop property to No using its Property Sheet. You can work with the Property Sheet in either Layout or Design View.

2. **Right-click the Tours Entry Form tab, click Design View, click the text box with the Tour End Date calculation if it is not selected, click the Other tab in the Property Sheet, double-click the Tab Stop property to toggle it from Yes to No, then change the Name property to TourEndDate, as shown in FIGURE C-13**

 The Other tab of the Property Sheet contains the properties you need to change the tab stop and tab order. The **Tab Stop property** determines whether the field accepts focus, and the **Tab Index property** indicates the numeric tab order for all controls on the form that have the Tab Stop property set to Yes. The **Name property** on the Other tab is also important as it identifies the name of the control, which is used in other areas of the database. To review your tab stop changes, return to Form View.

3. **Click the View button 🔳 to switch to Form View, then press [Tab] nine times to move to the next record**

 Now that the tab stop has been removed from the TourEndDate text box, the tab order flows correctly from the top to the bottom of the form, but skips the calculated field. To review the tab order for the entire form in one dialog box, you must switch to Form Design View.

4. **Right-click the Tours Entry Form tab, click Design View, then click the Tab Order button in the Tools group to open the Tab Order dialog box, as shown in FIGURE C-14**

 The Tab Order dialog box allows you to view and change the tab order by dragging fields up or down using the **field selector** to the left of the field name. Moving fields up and down in this list also renumbers the Tab Index property for the controls in their respective Property Sheets. If you want Access to create a top-to-bottom and left-to-right tab order, click **Auto Order**.

5. **Click OK to close the Tab Order dialog box, click the Property Sheet button to toggle it off, then click the Save button 🔲 on the Quick Access toolbar to save your work**

FIGURE C-13: Using the Property Sheet to set tab properties

FIGURE C-14: Tab Order dialog box

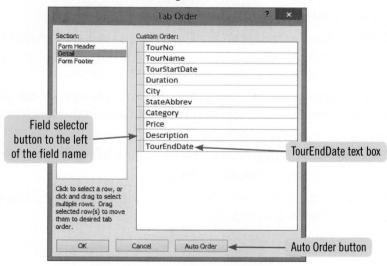

Layout positioning

If the controls on a form are organized in a layout, you can quickly modify that layout by modifying the margins, padding, and anchoring options of the layout. Each of these features is found in the Position group on the ARRANGE tab in Form Design View. **Margin** refers to the space between the outer edge of the control and the data displayed inside the control. **Padding** is the space between the controls. **Anchoring** allows you to tie controls together so you can work with them as a group.

Insert an Image

Learning Outcomes
- Insert an image on a form
- Modify form sections
- Print a selected record

Graphic images, such as pictures, logos, or clip art, can add style and professionalism to a form. The form section in which you place the images is significant. **Form sections** determine where controls are displayed and printed; they are described in TABLE C-6. For example, if you add a company logo to the Form Header section, the image appears at the top of the form in Form View as well as at the top of a printout. If you add the same image to the Detail section, it prints next to each record in the printout because the Detail section is printed for every record. **CASE** *Samantha Hooper suggests that you add the Quest logo to the top of the Tours Entry Form. You can add the control in either Layout or Design View, but if you want to place it in the Form Header section, you have to work in Design View.*

STEPS

1. **Click the Form Header section bar, click the Insert Image button in the Controls group, click Browse, then navigate to the location where you store your Data Files**

 The Insert Picture dialog box opens, prompting you for the location of the image.

2. **Double-click QuestLogo.bmp, then click in the Form Header section at about the 3" mark on the horizontal ruler**

 The QuestLogo image is added to the right side of the Form Header. You want to resize it to about 1" × 1".

 TROUBLE
 The lower-right corner of the image touches the top edge of the Detail section. To resize the Quest logo, click it to select it.

3. **With the QuestLogo image still selected, use the ⤡ pointer to drag the lower-right corner of the image up and to the left so that the image is about 1" × 1", then drag the top edge of the Detail section up using the ╬ pointer, as shown in FIGURE C-15**

 When an image or control is selected in Design View, you can use **sizing handles**, which are small squares at the corners of the selection box. Drag a handle to resize the image or control. With the form completed, you open it in Form View to observe the changes.

4. **Click the Save button 🖫 on the Quick Access toolbar, then click the View button 🖼 to switch to Form View**

 You decide to add one more record with your final Tours Entry Form.

5. **Click the New (blank) record button ▶⁕ in the navigation bar, then enter the new record shown in FIGURE C-16, using your last name in the TourName field**

 Now print only this single new record.

 TROUBLE
 If you do not click the Selected Record(s) option button, you will print *all* records, which creates a very long printout.

6. **Click the FILE tab, click Print in the navigation bar, click Print, click the Selected Record(s) option button, then click OK**

7. **Close the Tours Entry Form, click Yes if prompted to save it, close the QuestTravel-C.accdb database, then exit Access 2013**

TABLE C-6: Form sections

section	controls placed in this section print:
Form Header	Only once at the top of the first page of the printout
Detail	Once for every record
Form Footer	Only once at the end of the last page of the printout

© 2014 Cengage Learning

FIGURE C-15: Adding an image to the Form Header section

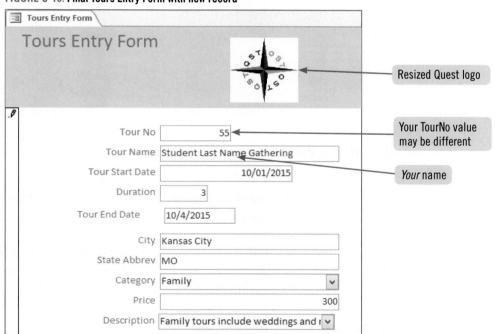

Form Header section bar

Insert Image button

3" mark on the ruler

Resize the Quest logo to be about 1" × 1"

Resize the Detail section

FIGURE C-16: Final Tours Entry Form with new record

Resized Quest logo

Your TourNo value may be different

Your name

Applying a background image

A **background image** is an image that fills the entire form or report, appearing "behind" the other controls. A background image is sometimes called a watermark image. To add a

background image, use the Picture property for the form or report to browse for the image that you want to use in the background.

Practice

Concepts Review

Label each element of Form Design View shown in FIGURE C-17.

FIGURE C-17

Match each term with the statement that best describes it.

10. **Bound control**
11. **Calculated control**
12. **Detail section**
13. **Database designer**
14. **Tab order**
15. **Form Footer section**

a. Created by entering an expression in a text box
b. Controls placed here print once for every record in the underlying record source
c. Used on a form to display data from a field
d. Controls placed here print only once at the end of the printout
e. The way the focus moves from one bound control to the next in Form View
f. Responsible for building and maintaining tables, queries, forms, and reports

Select the best answer from the list of choices.

16. **Every element on a form is called a(n):**
 a. Property.
 b. Control.
 c. Item.
 d. Tool.

17. **Which of the following is probably *not* a graphic image?**
 a. Logo
 b. Calculation
 c. Clip art
 d. Picture

18. **The most common bound control is the:**
 a. Text box.
 b. Label.
 c. Combo box.
 d. List box.

19. **The most common unbound control is the:**
 a. Combo box.
 b. Command button.
 c. Label.
 d. Text box.

20. **Which form view *cannot* be used to view data?**
 a. Datasheet
 b. Layout
 c. Preview
 d. Design

Skills Review

1. **Use the Form Wizard.**
 a. Start Access and open the RealEstate-C.accdb database from the location where you store your Data Files. Enable content if prompted.
 b. Click the CREATE tab, then use the Form Wizard to create a form based on all of the fields in the Realtors table. Use a Columnar layout and type **Realtor Entry Form** to title the form.
 c. Add a *new* record with *your* name in the RFirst and RLast text boxes. Note that the RealtorNo field is an AutoNumber field that is automatically incremented as you enter your first and last names. Enter your school's telephone number for the RPhone field value, and enter **4** as the AgencyNo field value.
 d. Save and close the Realtor Entry Form.

2. **Create a split form.**
 a. Click the Agencies table in the Navigation Pane, click the CREATE tab, click the More Forms button, then click Split Form.
 b. Switch to Form View and close the Property Sheet if it opens.
 c. Click the record selector in the lower pane for AgencyNo 3, Emerald Point Realtors, then click the Delete button in the Records group to delete this realtor. Click OK when prompted that you cannot delete this record because there are related records in the Realtors table.
 d. Navigate to the AgencyNo 4, Hollister Real Estate, record in either the upper or lower pane of the split form. Change 7744 Pokeberry Lane to **12345 Amanda Drive**.
 e. Right-click the Agencies form tab, click Close, click Yes when prompted to save changes, type **Agencies Split Form** as the name of the form, then click OK.

3. **Use Form Layout View.**
 a. Open the Realtor Entry Form in Layout View.
 b. Modify the labels on the left to read: **Realtor Number**, **Realtor First Name**, **Realtor Last Name**, **Realtor Phone**, **Agency Number**.
 c. Modify the text color of the labels to be black.
 d. Resize the RFirst, RLast, and RPhone text boxes on the right to be the same width as the RealtorNo and AgencyNo text boxes.
 e. Save the Realtor Entry Form.

4. **Add fields to a form.**
 a. Open the Field List, show all the tables, then expand the Agencies table to display its fields.
 b. Drag the AgencyName field to the form, then move the AgencyName label and combo box below the Agency Number controls.
 c. Modify the AgencyName label to read **Agency Name**.
 d. Modify the text color of the Agency Name label to black.
 e. Close the Field List and save and close the Realtor Entry Form.

Skills Review (continued)

5. Modify form controls.

 a. Reopen the Realtor Entry Form in Layout View, then use the Align Right button on the HOME tab to right-align each of the labels in the left column.

 b. Save the form, switch to Form View, then use the Agency Name combo box to change the Agency Name to **Marvin and Pam Realtors** for Realtor Number 1.

 c. If the combo box is not wide enough to display the entire entry for Marvin and Pam Realtors, switch back to Layout View and widen the combo box as much as needed to display the entire entry.

 d. In Layout View, resize and move all controls so that the labels are lined up on the left and the text boxes are lined up on the right, as shown in FIGURE C-18.

FIGURE C-18

6. Create calculations.

 a. Switch to Form Design View, then add a text box below the Realtor Entry Form label in the Form Header section. Delete the Text14 label that is created when you add a new text box. The number in your label is based on previous work done to the form, so it might vary.

 b. Widen the text box to be almost as wide as the entire form, then enter the following expression into the text box, which will add the words *Information for* to the realtor's first name, a space, and then the realtor's last name.
 ="Information for "&[RFirst]&" "&[RLast]

 c. Save the form, then view it in Form View. Be sure the new text box correctly displays spaces in the text. Return to Design View to edit the expression if #Name? appears, which indicates that the expression was entered incorrectly.

 d. In Form View, change the Realtor Last Name for Realtor Number 1 from West to **South**. Tab to the RPhone text box to observe how the expression in the Form Header automatically updates.

 e. Tab through several records, observing the expression in the Form Header section.

7. Modify tab order.

 a. Switch to Form Design View, then open the Property Sheet.

 b. Select the new text box with the expression in the Form Header section, then change the Tab Stop property from Yes to No.

 c. Select the RealtorNo text box in the Detail section, then change the Tab Stop property from Yes to No. (AutoNumber fields cannot be edited, so they do not need to have a tab stop.)

 d. Close the Property Sheet.

 e. Save the form and view it in Form View. Tab through the form to make sure that the tab order is sequential and skips the expression in the Form Header as well as the Realtor Number text box. Use the Tab Order button on the DESIGN tab in Form Design View to modify tab order, if necessary.

8. Insert an image.

 a. Switch to Design View, then click the Form Header section bar.

 b. Add the ForSale.bmp image to the right side of the Form Header, then resize the image to be about 1" × 1".

 c. Remove extra blank space in the Form Header section by dragging the top edge of the Detail section up as far as possible.

 d. Drag the right edge of the form as far as possible to the left.

 e. Save the form, then switch to Form View. Move through the records, observing the calculated field from record to record to make sure it is calculating correctly.

 f. Find the record with your name, as shown in FIGURE C-18, and if requested by your instructor, print only that record.

 g. Close the Realtor Entry Form, close the RealEstate-C.accdb database, then exit Access.

Independent Challenge 1

As the manager of the scuba divers branch of the Quest Specialty Travel tour company, you have developed a database to help manage scuba dives. In this exercise, you'll create a data entry form to manage the dive trips.

a. Start Access, then open the Dives-C.accdb database from the location where you store your Data Files. Enable content if prompted.

b. Using the Form Wizard, create a form that includes all the fields in the DiveTrips table and uses the Columnar layout, then type **Dive Trip Entry** as the title of the form.

c. Switch to Layout View, then delete the ID text box and label.

d. Using Form Design View, use the [Shift] key to select all of the text boxes except the last one for TripReport, then resize them to the shortest size using the To Shortest option on the Size/Space button on the ARRANGE tab.

e. Using Form Design View, resize the Location, City, State/Province, Country, and Lodging text boxes to be no wider than the Rating text box.

f. Using Form Design View, move and resize the controls, as shown in FIGURE C-19. Once the controls are resized, drag the top of the Form Footer section up to remove the extra blank space in the Detail section.

g. Using Form Layout View, modify the labels and alignment of the labels, as shown in FIGURE C-19. Note that there are spaces between the words in the labels, the labels are right-aligned, and the text boxes are left-aligned. Use a dark blue color for the labels and black for the text in the text boxes.

h. In Form View, find the Great Barrier Reef tour. Edit the State/Province, Certification Diving, and Trip Report fields, as shown in FIGURE C-19 for the TripReport field using *your* name.

i. Save the form, then if requested by your instructor, print only the record with your name.

j. Close the Dive Trip Entry form, close the Dives-C.accdb database, then exit Access 2013.

FIGURE C-19

Dive Master ID	1
Location	Great Barrier Reef
City	Cairns
State/Province	QLD
Country	Australia
Trip Start Date	5/14/2015
Lodging	Royal Palm
Rating	4
Certification Diving	✔
Participants	5
Trip Report	Excellent trip with friendly locals and wonderful weather. Your Name

Independent Challenge 2

You have built an Access database to track membership in a community service club. The database tracks member names and addresses as well as their status in the club, which moves from rank to rank as the members contribute increased hours of service to the community.

a. Start Access, then open the Membership-C.accdb database from the location where you store your Data Files. Enable content if prompted.

b. Using the Form Wizard, create a form based on all of the fields of the Members table and only the DuesOwed field in the Status table.

c. View the data by Members, use a Columnar layout, then enter **Member Information** as the title of the form.

d. Enter a new record with *your* name and the school name, address, and phone number of your school for the Company and address fields. Give yourself a StatusNo entry of **1**. In the DuesPaid field, enter **75**. DuesOwed automatically displays 100 because that value is pulled from the Status table and is based on the entry in the StatusNo field, which links the Members table to the Status table.

e. In Layout View, add a text box to the form and move it below the DuesOwed text box.

f. Open the Property Sheet for the new text box, display the Data tab, and in the Control Source property of the new text box, enter the expression that calculates the balance between DuesOwed and DuesPaid: **=[DuesOwed]-[DuesPaid]**.

g. Open the Property Sheet for the new label, and change the Caption property on the Format tab for the new label to **Balance**.

h. Right-align all of the labels in the first column.

i. Set the Tab Stop property for the text box that contains the calculated Balance to **No**, then close the Property Sheet.

j. In Layout or Design View, resize DuesPaid and DuesOwed text boxes to be the same width as the new Balance text box, then right-align all data within the three text boxes.

FIGURE C-20

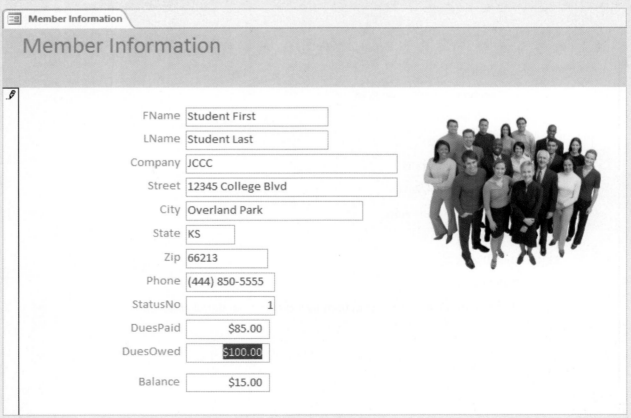

Independent Challenge 2 (continued)

k. Open the Property Sheet for the text box that contains the expression, and change the Format property on the Format tab to Currency. Close the Property Sheet.

l. Switch to Form Design View, then drag the right edge of the form to the 7" mark on the horizontal ruler. The horizontal ruler is located just above the Form Header section.

m. Click a blank spot on the right edge of the form, click the Insert Image button on the DESIGN tab, browse for the People.jpg image, then insert it on the right side of the form in the Detail section. (*Hint*: You will need to change the Web-Ready Image Files list in the Insert Picture dialog box to All Files to find .jpg images.)

n. Resize the picture to be about 2" × 2", then drag the right edge of the form to the left as far as possible. Also drag the top edge of the Form Footer up as far as possible to eliminate blank space in the Detail section.

o. Save the form, find the record with your name, change the DuesPaid value to **85**, then move and resize controls as necessary to match FIGURE C-20.

p. If requested by your instructor, print only the record with your name.

q. Save and close the Member Information form, then close the Membership-C.accdb database and exit Access 2013.

Independent Challenge 3

You have built an Access database to organize the deposits at a recycling center. Various clubs regularly deposit recyclable material, which is measured in pounds when the deposits are made.

a. Open the Recycle-C.accdb database from the location where you store your Data Files. Enable content if prompted.

b. Using the Form Wizard, create a form based on all of the fields in the CenterDeposits query. View the data by Deposits, use the Columnar layout, and title the form **Deposit Listing**.

c. Switch to Layout View, then make each label bold.

d. Modify the labels so that CenterName is **Center Name**, DepositDate is **Deposit Date**, and ClubName is **Club Name**.

e. Switch to Form Design View and resize the CenterName and ClubName text boxes so they are the same height and width as the Weight text box, as shown in FIGURE C-21.

f. Switch to Form View, find and change any entry of Dallas Jaycees in the ClubName field to *your* last name, then print one record with your name if requested by your instructor.

g. Using Form View of the Deposit Listing form, filter for all records with your last name in the ClubName field.

h. Using Form View of the Deposit Listing form, sort the filtered records in descending order on the DepositDate field.

i. Preview the first record, as shown in FIGURE C-21. If requested by your instructor, print the first record.

j. Save and close the Deposit Listing form, close the Recycle-C.accdb database, then exit Access.

FIGURE C-21

Independent Challenge 4: Explore

One way you can use an Access database on your own is to record and track your job search efforts. In this exercise, you will develop a form to help you enter data into your job-tracking database.

a. Start Access and open the Jobs-C.accdb database from the location where you store your Data Files. Enable content if prompted.

b. Click the CREATE tab, then use the Form Wizard to create a new form based on all the fields of both the Employers and Positions tables.

c. View the data by Employers, use a Datasheet layout for the subform, accept the default names for the form and subform, then open the form to view information.

d. Use Layout View and Design View to modify the form labels, text box positions, alignment, and sizes, as shown in FIGURE C-22. Note that the columns within the subform have been resized to display all of the data in the subform.

e. Change the CompanyName of IBM in the first record to *Your* **Last Name's Software**, and if instructed to create a printout, print only that record. Close the Employers form.

f. Click the Employers table in the Navigation Pane, then use the Split Form option on the More Forms button of the CREATE tab to create a split form on the Employers table. Close and save the split form with the name **Employers Split Form**.

FIGURE C-22

Independent Challenge 4: Explore (continued)

g. Open the Employers Split Form in Form View, and change the address and phone number information for EmployerID 1 to *your* school's address and phone information, as shown in FIGURE C-23.

h. Navigate through all five records, then back to EmployerID 1, observing both the upper and lower panes of the split form as you move from record to record.

i. Open the Employers form and navigate forward and backward through all five records to study the difference between the Employers form, which uses a form/subform versus the Employers Split Form. Even though both the Employers form and Employers Split Form show datasheets in the bottom halves of the forms, they are fundamentally very different. The split form is displaying the records of only the Employers table, whereas the Employers form is using a subform to display related records from the Positions table in the lower datasheet. You will learn more about forms and subforms in later units.

j. Close the Jobs-C.accdb database, then exit Access.

FIGURE C-23

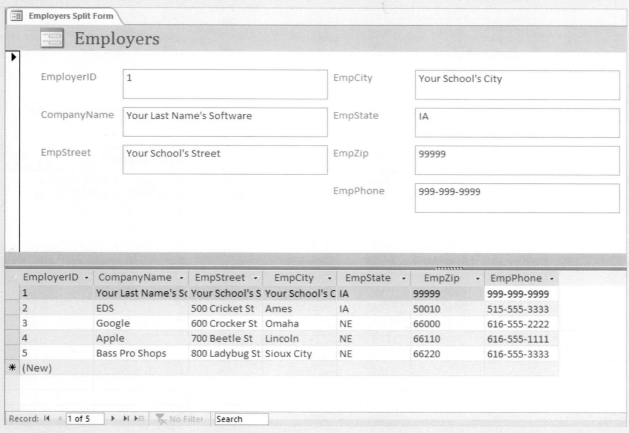

Visual Workshop

Open the Baseball-C.accdb database, enable content if prompted, then use the Split Form tool to create a form named **Players**, as shown in FIGURE C-24, based on the Players table. Resize the PlayerLast text box as shown. Modify the labels as shown. View the data in Form View, and sort the records in ascending order by last name. Change the first, last, and nickname of the Henry Aaron record in the first record to *your* name, and if instructed to create a printout, print only that record. Save and close the Players form, close the Baseball-C.accdb database, then exit Access.

FIGURE C-24

Using Reports

CASE ▶ Samantha Hooper, a tour developer at Quest Specialty Travel, asks you to produce some reports to help her share and analyze data. A report is an Access object that creates a professional looking printout.

Unit Objectives

After completing this unit, you will be able to:

- Use the Report Wizard
- Use Report Layout View
- Review report sections
- Apply group and sort orders
- Add subtotals and counts
- Resize and align controls
- Format a report
- Create mailing labels

Files You Will Need

QuestTravel-D.accdb Recycle-D.accdb
RealEstate-D.accdb JobSearch-D.accdb
Conventions-D.accdb Basketball-D.accdb
Membership-D.accdb

Use the Report Wizard

A **report** is the primary object you use to print database content because it provides the most formatting, layout, and summary options. A report may include various fonts and colors, clip art and lines, and multiple headers and footers. A report can also calculate subtotals, averages, counts, and other statistics for groups of records. You can create reports in Access by using the **Report Wizard**, a tool that asks questions to guide you through the initial development of the report. Your responses to the Report Wizard determine the record source, style, and layout of the report. The **record source** is the table or query that defines the fields and records displayed on the report. The Report Wizard also helps you sort, group, and analyze the records. **CASE** *You use the Report Wizard to create a report to display the tours within each state.*

STEPS

1. **Start Access, open the QuestTravel-D.accdb database, enable content if prompted, click the CREATE tab on the Ribbon, then click the Report Wizard button in the Reports group**

 The Report Wizard starts, prompting you to select the fields you want on the report. You can select fields from one or more tables or queries.

2. **Click the Tables/Queries list arrow, click Table: States, double-click the StateName field, click the Tables/Queries list arrow, click Table: Tours, click the Select All Fields button `>>`, click StateAbbrev in the Selected Fields list, then click the Remove Field button `<`**

 By selecting the StateName field from the States table, and all fields from the Tours table except the StateAbbrev field, you have all of the fields you need for the report, as shown in **FIGURE D-1**.

3. **Click Next, then click by States if it is not already selected**

 Choosing "by States" groups together the records for each state. In addition to record-grouping options, the Report Wizard later asks if you want to sort the records within each group. You can use the Report Wizard to specify up to four fields to sort in either ascending or descending order.

4. **Click Next, click Next again to include no additional grouping levels, click the first sort list arrow, click TourStartDate, then click Next**

 The last questions in the Report Wizard deal with report appearance and the report title.

5. **Click the Stepped option button, click the Landscape option button, click Next, type Tours by State for the report title, then click Finish**

 The Tours by State report opens in **Print Preview**, which displays the report as it appears when printed, as shown in **FIGURE D-2**. The records are grouped by state, the first state being California, and then sorted in ascending order by the TourStartDate field within each state. Reports are **read-only objects**, meaning you can use them to read and display data but not to change (write to) data. As you change data using tables, queries, or forms, reports constantly display those up-to-date edits just like all of the other Access objects.

6. **Scroll down to see the second grouping section on the report for the state of Colorado, then click the Next Page button ▶ in the navigation bar to see the second page of the report**

 Even in **landscape orientation** (11" wide by 8.5" tall as opposed to **portrait orientation**, which is 8.5" wide by 11" tall), the fields on the Tours by State report may not fit on one sheet of paper. The labels in the column headings and the data in the columns need to be resized to improve the layout. Depending on your monitor, you might need to scroll to the right to display all the fields on this page.

FIGURE D-1: Selecting fields for a report using the Report Wizard

- Tables/Queries list arrow
- Select All Fields button
- Remove Field button
- Selected fields

FIGURE D-2: Tours by State report in Print Preview

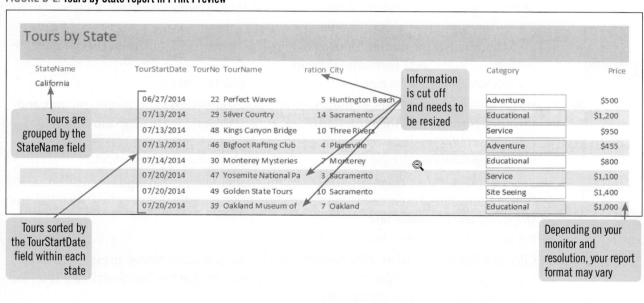

- Tours are grouped by the StateName field
- Tours sorted by the TourStartDate field within each state
- Information is cut off and needs to be resized
- Depending on your monitor and resolution, your report format may vary

Changing page orientation

To change page orientation from Portrait (8.5" wide by 11" tall) to Landscape (11" wide by 8.5" tall) and vice versa, click the Portrait or Landscape button on the PRINT PREVIEW tab when viewing the report in Print Preview. To switch to Print Preview, right-click the report in the Navigation Pane, and then choose Print Preview on the shortcut menu.

Use Report Layout View

Learning
Outcomes
• Move and resize
 controls in Layout
 View
• Modify labels

Reports have multiple views that you use for various report-building and report-viewing activities. Although some tasks can be accomplished in more than one view, each view has a primary purpose to make your work with reports as easy and efficient as possible. The different report views are summarized in **TABLE D-1**. **CASE** ▶ *Samantha Hooper asks you to modify the Tours by State report so that all of the fields fit comfortably across one sheet of paper in landscape orientation.*

STEPS

TROUBLE
If the Field List
window opens,
close it.

1. **Right-click the Tours by State report tab, then click Layout View**

 Layout View opens and applies a grid to the report that helps you resize, move, and position controls. You decide to narrow the City column to make room for the Price data.

2. **Click Huntington Beach (or any value in the City column), then use the ↔ pointer to drag the right edge of the City column to the left to narrow it to about half of its current size, as shown in FIGURE D-3**

 By narrowing the City column, you create extra space in the report.

3. **Click $500 (or any value in the Price column), use the ⸙ pointer to drag the Price values to the left of the Category column, click the Price label, then use ⸙ to move the Price label to the left of the Category label**

 All the columns are now within the boundaries of a single sheet of paper in landscape orientation. You also notice that centering some data would make it easier to read.

4. **Click 22 (or any value in the TourNo column), click the HOME tab, then click the Center button ☰ in the Text Formatting group**

 The TourName column needs more space to completely display the tour names.

QUICK TIP
Resizing with ↔
instead of moving
with ⸙ maintains
the vertical
alignment of
the controls.

5. **Use ↔ to resize both sides of the TourStartDate, TourNo, and TourName columns and their labels to the left, then use ↔ to resize the Category, Price, City, and Duration columns and their labels to the right**

 Now the report has enough room to resize the TourName column and the Duration label.

QUICK TIP
You can use the
Undo button arrow
↩ ▾ to undo
many actions in
Layout View.

6. **Resize the TourName column so that all of the data is visible, paying special attention to the longest value, Yosemite National Park Great Cleanup, then resize the Duration label to display the complete text**

 You can also rename labels in Report Layout View.

7. **Click the StateName label, click between the words State and Name, press the [Spacebar] so that the label reads State Name, then modify the TourStartDate, TourNo, and TourName labels to contain spaces as well**

8. **Continue resizing the columns so that all of the data is visible and your report looks like FIGURE D-4**

FIGURE D-3: Modifying the column width in Report Layout View

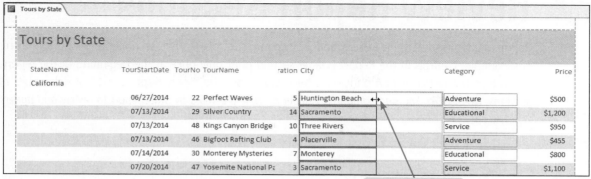

Resizing the City field to make room for other information

FIGURE D-4: Final Tours by State report in Report Layout View

Duration label is completely displayed

Labels have spaces

TourNo field values are centered

Longest tour name is clearly displayed

Price column is moved

TABLE D-1: Report views

view	primary purpose
Report View	To quickly review the report without page breaks
Print Preview	To review each page of an entire report as it will appear if printed
Layout View	To modify the size, position, or formatting of controls; shows live data as you modify the report, making it the tool of choice when you want to change the appearance and positioning of controls on a report while also reviewing live data
Design View	To work with report sections or to access the complete range of controls and report properties; Design View does not display data

Review Report Sections

Report **sections** determine where and how often controls in that section print in the final report. For example, controls in the Report Header section print only once at the beginning of the report, but controls in the Detail section print once for every record the report displays. TABLE D-2 describes report sections. **CASE** ▶ *You and Samantha Hooper preview the Tours by State report to review and understand report sections.*

STEPS

1. **Right-click the Tours by State tab, click Print Preview, then scroll up and click the light blue bar at the top of the report if you need to zoom in to display the first page of the report, as shown in FIGURE D-5**

 The first page shows four sections: Report Header, Page Header, StateAbbreviation Header, and Detail.

2. **Click the Next Page button ▶ on the navigation bar to move to the second page of the report**

 If the second page of the report does not contain data, it means that the report may be too wide to fit on a single sheet of paper. You fix that problem in Report Design View.

3. **Right-click the Tours by State tab, click Design View, scroll to the far right using the bottom horizontal scroll bar, then use the ↔ pointer to drag the right edge of the report as far as you can to the left, as shown in FIGURE D-6**

 In Report Design View, you can work with the report sections and make modifications to the report that you cannot make in other views, such as narrowing the width. Report Design View does not display any data, though. For your report to fit on one page in landscape orientation, you need to move all of the controls within the 10.5" mark on the horizontal **ruler** using the default 0.25" left and right margins. You will practice fixing this problem by moving all controls within the 10" mark on the ruler to make sure they all fit on the landscape printout.

4. **Use the ⸙ pointer to drag the page calculation about 0.5" to the left, then use ↔ to drag the right edge of the report as far as you can to the left**

 To review your modifications, show the report in Print Preview.

5. **Right-click the Tours by State tab, click Print Preview, click ▶ to navigate to the last page of the report, then click the report to zoom in and out to examine the page, as shown in FIGURE D-7**

 Previewing each page of the report helps you confirm that no blank pages are created and allows you to examine how the different report sections print on each page.

TABLE D-2: Report sections

section	where does this section print?
Report Header	At the top of the first page
Page Header	At the top of every page (but below the Report Header on the first page)
Group Header	Before every group of records
Detail	Once for every record
Group Footer	After every group of records
Page Footer	At the bottom of every page
Report Footer	At the end of the report

Tours by State

State Name	Tour Start Date	Tour No	Tour Name	Duration	City	Price	Category
California							
	06/27/2014	22	Perfect Waves	5	Huntington Beach	$500	Adventure
	07/13/2014	29	Silver Country	14	Sacramento	$1,200	Educational
	07/13/2014	48	Kings Canyon Bridge Builders	10	Three Rivers	$950	Service
	07/13/2014	46	Bigfoot Rafting Club	4	Placerville	$455	Adven
	07/14/2014	30	Monterey Mysteries	7	Monterey	$800	Educat
	07/20/2014	47	Yosemite National Park Great Cleanup	3	Sacramento	$1,100	Service
	07/20/2014	49	Golden State Tours	10	Sacramento	$1,400	Site Seeing

StateAbbreviation Header section

Detail section

Report Header section

Page Header section

Green error indicator may appear here

Report Header section

Page Header section

StateAbbreviation Header section

Detail section

Page Footer section

Report Footer section

Page calculation

10.5" mark on horizontal ruler

Resizing the right edge of the report

=Now()

="Page " & [Page] & " of " & [Pages]

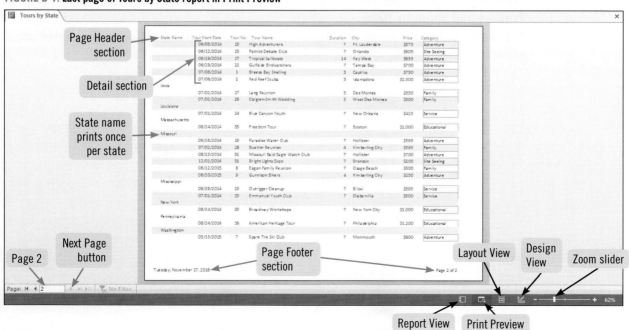

Page Header section

Detail section

State name prints once per state

Page 2

Next Page button

Page Footer section

Layout View

Design View

Zoom slider

Report View

Print Preview

Apply Group and Sort Orders

Learning Outcomes
• Group and sort records in a report
• Copy and paste controls

Grouping means to sort records by a particular field *plus* provide a header and/or footer section before or after each group of sorted records. For example, if you group records by the StateName field, the Group Header is called the StateName Header and the Group Footer is called the StateName Footer. The StateName Header section appears once for each state in the report, immediately before the records in that state. The StateName Footer section also appears once for each state in the report, immediately after the records for that state. **CASE** ▶ *The records in the Tours by State report are currently grouped by the StateAbbreviation field. Samantha Hooper asks you to further group the records by the Category field (Adventure, Educational, and Family, for example) within each state.*

STEPS

1. **Click the Close Print Preview button to return to Report Design View, then click the Group & Sort button in the Grouping & Totals group to open the Group, Sort, and Total pane**

 Currently, the records are grouped by the StateAbbreviation field and further sorted by the TourStartDate field. To add the Category field as a grouping field within each state, you work with the Group, Sort, and Total pane in Report Design View.

2. **Click the Add a group button in the Group, Sort, and Total pane, click Category, then click the Move up button [icon] on the right side of the Group, Sort, and Total pane so that Category is positioned between StateAbbreviation and TourStartDate**

 A Category Header section is added to Report Design View just below the StateAbbreviation Header section. You move the Category control from the Detail section to the Category Header section so it prints only once for each new Category instead of once for each record in the Detail section.

3. **Right-click the Category combo box in the Detail section, click Cut on the shortcut menu, right-click the Category Header section, click Paste, then use the ⁺ₖ pointer to drag the Category combo box to the right to position it as shown in FIGURE D-8**

 Now that you've moved the Category combo box to the Category Header, it will print only once per category within each state. You no longer need the Category label in the Page Header section.

4. **Click the Category label in the Page Header section, press [Delete], then switch to Print Preview and zoom to 100%**

 The Tours by State report should look like **FIGURE D-9**. Notice that the records are now grouped by category within state. Detail records are further sorted in ascending order by the tour start date.

FIGURE D-8: Group, Sort, and Total pane and new Category Header section

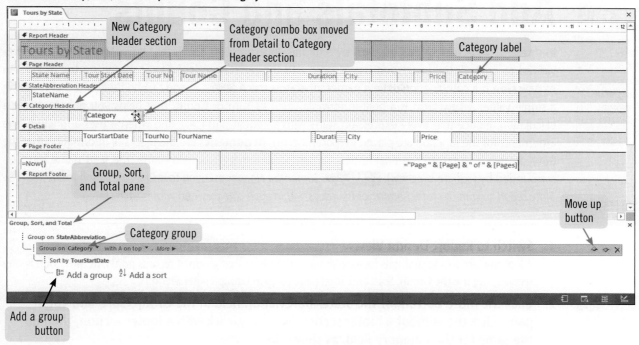

FIGURE D-9: Tours by State report grouped by category within state

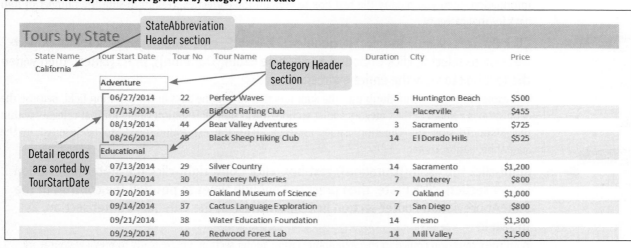

Add Subtotals and Counts

Learning Outcomes
- Create calculations to subtotal and count records
- Cut and paste controls

In a report, you create a **calculation** by entering an expression into a text box. When a report is previewed or printed, the expression is evaluated and the resulting calculation is placed on the report. An **expression** is a combination of field names, operators (such as +, −, /, and *), and functions that results in a single value. A **function** is a built-in formula, such as Sum or Count, that helps you quickly create a calculation. Notice that every expression starts with an equal sign (=), and when it uses a function, the arguments for the function are placed in (parentheses). **Arguments** are the pieces of information that the function needs to create the final answer. When an argument is a field name, the field name must be surrounded by [square brackets]. **CASE** *Samantha Hooper asks you to add a calculation to the Tours by State report to sum the total number of tour days within each category and within each state.*

STEPS

1. **Switch to Report Design View**

 A logical place to add subtotals for each group is right after that group of records prints, in the Group Footer section. You use the Group, Sort, and Total pane to open Group Footer sections.

2. **Click the More button for the StateAbbreviation field in the Group, Sort, and Total pane, click the without a footer section list arrow, click with a footer section, then do the same for the Category field, as shown in FIGURE D-10**

 With the StateAbbreviation Footer and Category Footer sections open, you're ready to add controls to calculate the total number of tour days within each category and within each state. You use a text box control with an expression to make this calculation.

3. **Click the Text Box button [ab] in the Controls group, then click just below the Duration text box in the Category Footer section**

 Adding a new text box automatically adds a new label to its left. First, you modify the label to identify the information, then you modify the text box to contain the correct expression to sum the number of tour days for that category.

4. **Click the Text19 label to select it, double-click Text19, type Total days:, click the Unbound text box to select it, click Unbound again, type =Sum([Duration]), press [Enter], then widen the text box to view the entire expression**

 The expression =Sum([Duration]) uses the Sum function to add the days in the Duration field. Because the expression is entered in the Category Footer section, it will sum all Duration values for that category within that state. To sum the Duration values for each state, the expression needs to be inserted in the StateAbbreviation Footer.

5. **Right-click the =Sum([Duration]) text box, click Copy, right-click the StateAbbreviation Footer section, click Paste, then press [→] enough times to position the controls in the StateAbbreviation Footer section just below those in the Category Footer section, as shown in FIGURE D-11**

 With the expression copied to the StateAbbreviation Footer section, you're ready to preview your work.

6. **Switch to Print Preview, navigate to the last page of the report, then click to zoom so you can see all of the Washington tours**

 As shown in FIGURE D-12, 21 tour days are totaled for the Adventure category, and 3 for the Site Seeing category, which is a total of 24 tour days for the state of Washington. The summary data would look better if it were aligned more directly under the tour Duration values. You resize and align controls in the next lesson.

FIGURE D-10: Opening group footer sections

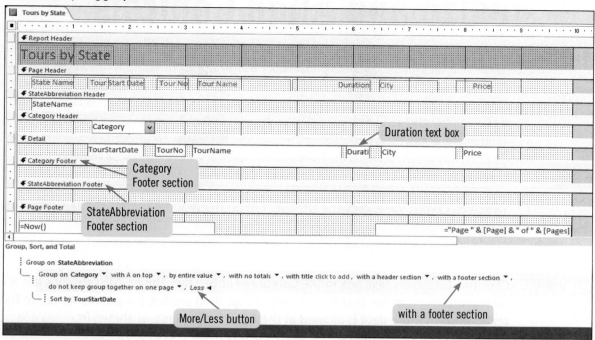

FIGURE D-11: Adding subtotals to group footer sections

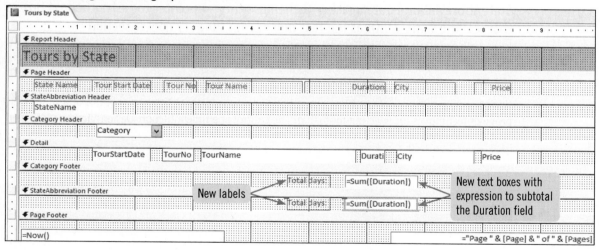

FIGURE D-12: Previewing the new group footer calculations

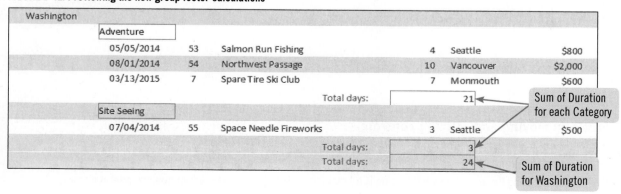

Access 2013

Resize and Align Controls

Learning Outcomes
- Align data within a control
- Align the borders of controls

After you add information to the appropriate section of a report, you might also want to align the data in precise columns and rows to make the information easier to read. To do so, you can use two different types of **alignment** commands. You can left-, right-, or center-align a control *within its own border* using the Align Left ≡, Center ≡, and Align Right ≡ buttons on the HOME tab. You can also align the edges of controls *with respect to one another* using the Left, Right, Top, and Bottom commands on the Align button of the ARRANGE tab in Report Design View. **CASE** ▶ *You decide to resize and align several controls to improve the readability of the Tours by State report. Layout View is a good choice for these tasks.*

STEPS

1. **Switch to Layout View, click the** DESIGN tab **on the Ribbon, then click the** Group & Sort **button to toggle off the Group, Sort, and Total pane**

You decide to align the expressions that subtotal the number of tour days for each category within the Duration column.

QUICK TIP
You can also use the buttons on the FORMAT tab to align and format text, including applying number formats and increasing or decreasing decimals.

2. **Click the** Total days text box **in the Category Footer, click the** HOME tab**, click the** Align Right button ≡ **in the Text Formatting group, then use the ↔ pointer to resize the text box so that the data is aligned in the Duration column, as shown in** FIGURE D-13

With the calculation formatted as desired in the Category Footer, you can quickly apply those modifications to the calculation in the StateAbbreviation Footer as well.

TROUBLE
If you make a mistake, click the Undo button ↺ on the Quick Access toolbar.

3. **Scroll down the report far enough to find and then click the** Total days text box **in the StateAbbreviation Footer, click** ≡**, then use the ↔ pointer to resize the text box so that it is the same width as the text box in the Category Footer section**

With both expressions right-aligned and resized so they line up under the Duration values in the Detail section, they are easier to read on the report.

4. **Scroll the report so you can see all of the Colorado tours, as shown in** FIGURE D-14

You can apply resize, alignment, or formatting commands to more than one control at a time. TABLE D-3 provides techniques for selecting more than one control at a time in Report Design View.

Precisely moving and resizing controls

You can move and resize controls using the mouse or other pointing device, but you can move controls more precisely using the keyboard. Pressing the arrow keys while holding [Ctrl] moves selected controls one **pixel (picture element)** at a time in the direction of the arrow. Pressing the arrow keys while holding [Shift] resizes selected controls one pixel at a time.

FIGURE D-13: Resizing controls in Layout View

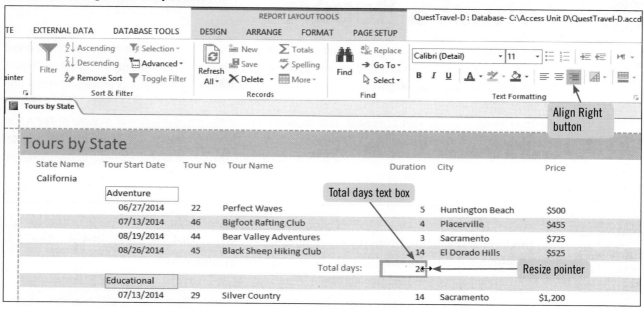

FIGURE D-14: Reviewing the aligned and resized controls

Colorado						
	Adventure					
	06/19/2014	18	Eagle Hiking Club	7	Aspen	$695
	06/29/2014	20	Team Discovery	5	Breckenridge	$550
	01/02/2015	3	Ames Ski Club	7	Breckenridge	$850
	01/13/2015	4	Boy Scout Jamboree	7	Vail	$1,900
	02/15/2015	5	Bridgewater Country	10	Aspen	$1,200
			Total days:	36		
	Family					
	03/11/2015	6	Franklin Family Reunion	3	Breckenridge	$700
			Total days:	3		
			Total days:	39		

Data is right-aligned and text boxes are resized

TABLE D-3: Selecting more than one control at a time in Report Design View

technique	description
Click, [Shift]+click	Click a control, then press and hold [Shift] while clicking other controls; each one is selected
Drag a selection box	Drag a selection box (an outline box you create by dragging the pointer in Report Design View); every control that is in or is touched by the edges of the box is selected
Click in the ruler	Click in either the horizontal or vertical ruler to select all controls that intersect the selection line
Drag in the ruler	Drag through either the horizontal or vertical ruler to select all controls that intersect the selection line as it is dragged through the ruler

© 2014 Cengage Learning

Access 2013

Format a Report

Learning
Outcomes
• Format controls
and sections of a
report
• Add labels to a
report

Formatting refers to enhancing the appearance of the information. TABLE D-4 lists several of the most popular formatting commands found on the FORMAT tab when you are working in Layout or Report Design View. Although the Report Wizard automatically applies many formatting embellishments, you often want to change the appearance of the report to fit your particular needs. **CASE** *When reviewing the Tours by State report with Samantha, you decide to change the background color of some of the report sections to make the data easier to read. Your first change will be to shade each Category Header and Footer section (rather than alternating sections, the format initially provided by the Report Wizard). To make changes to entire report sections, you work in Report Design View.*

STEPS

QUICK TIP
The quick keystroke
for Undo is [Ctrl][Z].
The quick keystroke
for Redo is [Ctrl][Y].

1. **Switch to Design View, click the Category Header section bar, click the FORMAT tab on the Ribbon, click the Alternate Row Color button arrow, click No Color, click the Shape Fill button, then click the Maroon 2 color square, as shown in** FIGURE D-15

 Make a similar modification by applying a different fill color to the Category Footer section.

2. **Click the Category Footer section bar, click the Alternate Row Color button arrow, click No Color, click the Shape Fill button, then click the Green 2 color square (just to the right of Maroon 2 in the Standard Colors section)**

 When you use the Alternate Row Color and Shape Fill buttons, you're actually modifying the **Back Color** and **Alternate Back Color** properties in the Property Sheet of the section or control you selected. Background shades can help differentiate parts of the report, but be careful with dark colors as they may print as solid black on some printers and fax machines.

3. **Switch to Layout View to review your modifications**

 The category sections are clearer, but you decide to make one more modification to emphasize the report title.

4. **Click the Tours by State label in the Report Header section, click the HOME tab, then click the Bold button** B **in the Text Formatting group**

 The report in Layout View should look like FIGURE D-16. You also want to add a label to the Report Footer section to identify yourself.

5. **Switch to Report Design View, drag the bottom edge of the Report Footer down about 0.5", click the Label button** Aa **in the Controls group, click at the 1" mark in the Report Footer, type Created by *your* name, press [Enter], click the HOME tab, then click** B **in the Text Formatting group**

6. **Save and preview the Tours by State report**

7. **If required by your instructor, print the report, and then close it**

FIGURE D-15: Formatting section backgrounds

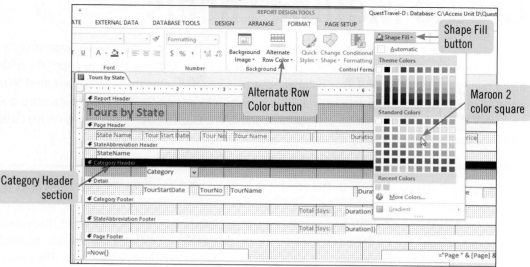

FIGURE D-16: Final formatted Tours by State report

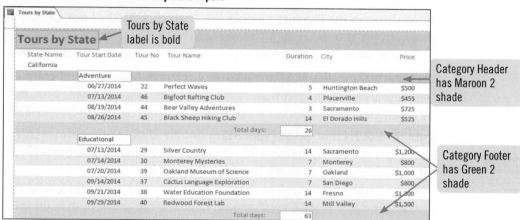

TABLE D-4: Useful formatting commands

button	button name	description
B	Bold	Toggles bold on or off for the selected control(s)
I	Italic	Toggles italic on or off for the selected control(s)
U	Underline	Toggles underline on or off for the selected control(s)
≡	Align Left	Left-aligns the selected control(s) within its own border
≡	Center	Centers the selected control(s) within its own border
≡	Align Right	Right-aligns the selected control(s) within its own border
⬧	Background Color or Shape Fill	Changes the background color of the selected control(s)
▦	Alternate Row Color	Changes the background color of alternate records in the selected section
A	Font Color	Changes the text color of the selected control(s)
✎	Shape Outline Line Thickness option Line Type option	Changes the border color of the selected control(s) Changes the border style of the selected control(s) Changes the special visual effect of the selected control(s)

Create Mailing Labels

Learning Outcomes
- Create a report of labels
- Print specific pages of a report

Mailing labels are often created to apply to envelopes, postcards, or letters when assembling a mass mailing. They have many other business purposes too, such as applying them to paper file folders or name tags. Any data in your Access database can be converted into labels using the **Label Wizard**, a special report wizard that precisely positions and sizes information for hundreds of standard business labels. **CASE** *Samantha Hooper asks you to create mailing labels for all of the addresses in the Customers table. You use the Label Wizard to handle this request.*

STEPS

1. **Click the Customers table in the Navigation Pane, click the CREATE tab, then click the Labels button in the Reports group**

 The first Label Wizard dialog box opens. The Filter by manufacturer list box provides over 30 manufacturers of labels. Because Avery is the most common, it is the default choice. With the manufacturer selected, your next task is to choose the product number of the labels you will feed through the printer. The cover on the box of labels you are using provides this information. In this case, you'll be using Avery 5160 labels, a common type of sheet labels used for mailings and other purposes.

2. **Scroll through the Product number list, then click 5160 (if not already selected), as shown in FIGURE D-17**

 Note that by selecting a product number, you also specify the dimensions of the label and number of columns.

3. **Click Next, then click Next again to accept the default font and color choices**

 The third question of the Label Wizard asks how you want to construct your label. You'll add the fields from the Customers table with spaces and line breaks to pattern a standard mailing format.

4. **Double-click FName, press [Spacebar], double-click LName, press [Enter], double-click Street, press [Enter], double-click City, type a comma (,) and press [Spacebar], double-click State, press [Spacebar], then double-click Zip**

 If your prototype label doesn't look exactly like FIGURE D-18, delete the fields in the Prototype label box and try again. Be careful to put a space between the FName and LName fields in the first row, a comma and a space between the City and State fields, and a space between the State and Zip fields.

 QUICK TIP

 In this case, all data is displayed. This message reminds you to carefully preview the data to make sure long names and addresses fully display within the constraints of the 5160 label dimensions.

5. **Click Next, double-click LName to select it as a sorting field, click Next, click Finish to accept the name Labels Customers for the new report, then click OK if prompted that some data may not be displayed**

 A portion of the new report is shown in FIGURE D-19. It is generally a good idea to print the first page of the report on standard paper to make sure everything is aligned correctly before printing on labels.

 QUICK TIP

 To include your name on the printout, change Aaron Alito's name to *your* own name in the Customers table, then close and reopen the Labels Customers report.

6. **If requested by your instructor, click the Print button on the PRINT PREVIEW tab, click the From box, type 1, click the To box, type 1, then click OK to print the first page of the report**

7. **Close the Labels Customers report, close the QuestTravel-D.accdb database, then exit Access 2013**

FIGURE D-17: Label Wizard dialog box

Product number 5160, dimensions, and number of columns

Avery is the manufacturer

FIGURE D-18: Building a prototype label

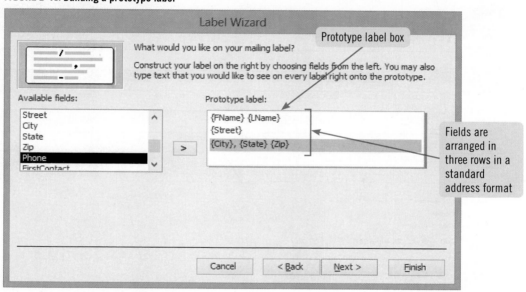

Prototype label box

Fields are arranged in three rows in a standard address format

FIGURE D-19: Labels Customers report

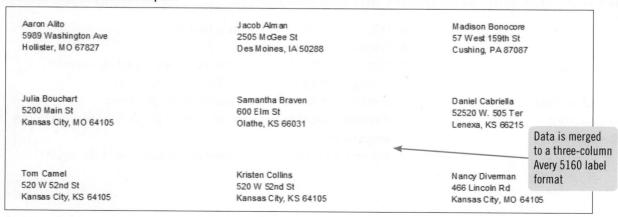

Aaron Alito
5989 Washington Ave
Hollister, MO 67827

Jacob Alman
2505 McGee St
Des Moines, IA 50288

Madison Bonocore
57 West 159th St
Cushing, PA 87087

Julia Bouchart
5200 Main St
Kansas City, MO 64105

Samantha Braven
600 Elm St
Olathe, KS 66031

Daniel Cabriella
52520 W. 505 Ter
Lenexa, KS 66215

Tom Camel
520 W 52nd St
Kansas City, KS 64105

Kristen Collins
520 W 52nd St
Kansas City, KS 64105

Nancy Diverman
466 Lincoln Rd
Kansas City, MO 64105

Data is merged to a three-column Avery 5160 label format

Practice

Concepts Review

Label each element of the Report Design View window shown in FIGURE D-20.

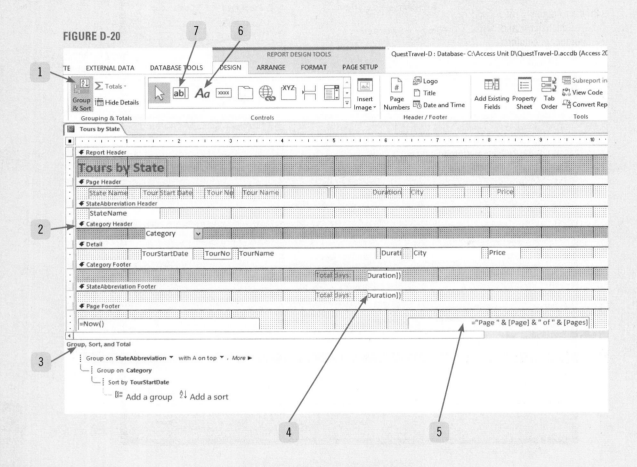

FIGURE D-20

Match each term with the statement that best describes it.

8. Alignment
9. Expression
10. Grouping
11. Section
12. Detail section
13. Formatting
14. Record source

a. Left, center, or right are common choices
b. Prints once for every record
c. Used to identify which fields and records are passed to the report
d. Sorting records *plus* providing a header or footer section
e. Determines how controls are positioned on the report
f. A combination of field names, operators, and functions that results in a single value
g. Enhancing the appearance of information displayed in the report

Select the best answer from the list of choices.

15. Which of the following is *not* a valid report view?

 a. Print Preview

 b. Section View

 c. Layout View

 d. Design View

16. Which type of control is most commonly placed in the Detail section?

 a. Image

 b. Line

 c. Text box

 d. Label

17. A title for a report would most commonly be placed in which report section?

 a. Group Footer

 b. Detail

 c. Report Header

 d. Report Footer

18. A calculated expression that presents page numbering information would probably be placed in which report section?

 a. Report Header

 b. Detail

 c. Group Footer

 d. Page Footer

19. Which of the following expressions counts the number of records using the FirstName field?

 a. =Count([FirstName])

 b. =Count[FirstName]

 c. =Count((FirstName))

 d. =Count{FirstName}

20. To align the edges of several controls with each other, you use the alignment commands on the:

 a. FORMATTING tab.

 b. DESIGN tab.

 c. PRINT PREVIEW tab.

 d. ARRANGE tab.

Skills Review

1. Use the Report Wizard.

 a. Start Access and open the RealEstate-D.accdb database from the location where you store your Data Files. Enable content if prompted.

 b. Use the Report Wizard to create a report based on the RLast and RPhone fields from the Realtors table, and the Type, SqFt, BR, Bath, and Asking fields from the Listings table.

 c. View the data by Realtors, do not add any more grouping levels, and sort the records in descending order by the Asking field. (*Hint*: Click the Ascending button to toggle it to Descending.)

 d. Use a Stepped layout and a Landscape orientation. Title the report **Realtor Listings**.

 e. Preview the first and second pages of the new report.

2. Use Report Layout View.

 a. Switch to Layout View and close the Field List and Property Sheet if they are open.

 b. Narrow the RLast, RPhone, and Bath columns enough so they are only as wide as needed to display all data.

 c. Modify the RLast label to read **Realtor**, the RPhone label to read **Phone**, the SqFt label to read **Square Feet**, the BR label to read **Bedrooms**, and the Bath label to read **Baths**.

 d. Switch to Print Preview to review your changes.

3. Review report sections.

 a. Switch to Report Design View.

 b. Drag the text box that contains the Page calculation in the lower-right corner of the Page Footer section to the left so that it is to the left of the 9" mark on the horizontal ruler.

 c. Drag the right edge of the entire report to the left so it ends within the 10" mark on the horizontal ruler. You may need to move or narrow the Baths label and Bath text box more than you did in Step 2b in order to accomplish this.

4. Apply group and sort orders.

 a. Open the Group, Sort, and Total pane.

 b. Add the Type field as a grouping field between the RealtorNo grouping field and Asking sort field. Make sure the sort order on the Asking field is in descending order (from largest to smallest).

 c. Cut and paste the Type combo box from its current position in the Detail section to the Type Header section.

 d. Move the Type combo box in the Type Header section so its left edge is at about the 1" mark on the horizontal ruler.

 e. Delete the Type label in the Page Header section.

 f. Switch to Layout View, and resize the Asking, Square Feet, Bedrooms, and Baths columns as needed so they are more evenly spaced across the page.

5. Add subtotals and counts.

 a. Switch to Report Design View, then open the RealtorNo Footer section.

 b. Add a text box control to the RealtorNo Footer section, just below the Asking text box in the Detail section. Change the label to read **Subtotal:**, and enter the expression **=Sum([Asking])** in the text box.

 c. Drag the bottom edge of the Report Footer down about 0.25" to add space to the Report Footer.

 d. Copy and paste the new expression in the RealtorNo Footer section to the Report Footer section. Position the new controls in the Report Footer section directly below the controls in the RealtorNo Footer section.

 e. Modify the Subtotal: label in the Report Footer section to read **Grand Total:**.

 f. Preview the last page of the report to view the new subtotals in the RealtorNo Footer and Report Footer sections.

6. Resize and align controls.

 a. Switch to Layout View, click the Group & Sort button on the DESIGN tab to close the Group, Sort, and Total pane if it is open, and move to the last page of the report to view the Subtotal and Grand Total calculations at the same time.

 b. Right-align the text within the Subtotal and Grand Total labels.

Skills Review (continued)

 c. Switch to Design View, click the Asking text box, press and hold [Shift], and then click the text box in the RealtorNo and also the Report Footer sections to select all three text boxes at the same time. Click the ARRANGE tab, click the Align button, then click Right to right-align the edges of the Subtotal and Grand Total text boxes.

 d. With all three text boxes still selected, click the FORMAT tab on the Ribbon, click the Apply Comma Number Format button, and click the Decrease Decimals button twice.

 e. Preview the report to view the alignment and format on the Asking data and subtotals.

7. **Format a report.**

 a. In Report Design View, change the Alternate Row Color of the Detail section to No Color.

 b. Change the Alternate Row Color of the Type Header section as well as the RealtorNo Header section to No Color.

 c. Change the Shape Fill color of the RealtorNo Header section to Green 2.

 d. Select the RLast text box in the RealtorNo Header section, and change the Shape Fill color to Green 2 to match the RealtorNo Header section. Apply the Green 2 background color to the RPhone text box as well.

FIGURE D-21

 e. Bold the title of the report, the **Realtor Listings** label in the Report Header, and resize it to make it a little wider to accommodate the bold text.

 f. Change the font color of each label in the Page Header section to black.

 g. Save and preview the report in Report View. It should look like FIGURE D-21. The report should fit on two pages and the grand total for all Asking values should be 7,771,513. If there are blank pages between printed pages, return to Report Design View and drag the right edge of the report to the left.

 h. In Report Design View, add a label to the left side of the Report Footer section with your name.

 i. Return to Print Preview, print the report if requested by your instructor, then save and close the Realtor Listings report.

8. **Create mailing labels.**

 a. Click the Agencies table in the Navigation Pane, then start the Label Wizard.

 b. Choose Avery 5160 labels and the default text appearance choices.

 c. Build a prototype label with the AgencyName on the first line, Street on the second line, and City, State, and Zip on the third line with a comma and space between City and State, and a space between State and Zip.

 d. Sort by AgencyName, and name the report **Labels Agencies**.

 e. Preview then save and close the report. Click OK if a warning dialog box appears regarding horizontal space. The data in your label report does not exceed the dimensions of the labels.

 f. If your instructor asks you to print the Labels Agencies report, open the Agencies table and change the name of Four Lakes Realtors to **_Your_ LastName Realtors**. Close the Agencies table, reopen the Labels Agencies report, then print it.

 g. Close the Labels Agencies report, close the RealEstate-D.accdb database, then exit Access 2013.

Independent Challenge 1

As the office manager of an international convention planning company, you have created a database to track convention, enrollment, and company data. Your goal is to create a report of up-to-date attendee enrollments.

a. Start Access, then open the Conventions-D.accdb database from the location where you store your Data Files. Enable content if prompted.

b. Use the Report Wizard to create a report with the AttendeeFirst and AttendeeLast fields from the Attendees table, the CompanyName field from the Companies table, and the ConventionName and CountryName from the Conventions table.

c. View your data by Conventions, do not add any more grouping levels, and sort in ascending order by CompanyName, then AttendeeLast.

d. Use the Block layout and Portrait orientation, then name the report **Convention Listing**.

e. In Layout View, change the labels in the Page Header section from ConventionName to **Convention** and AttendeeLast to **Attendee**. Delete the CountryName, CompanyName, and AttendeeFirst labels in the Page Header section.

f. In Report Design View, open the Group, Sort, and Total pane, then open the CompanyName Header and CompanyName Footer sections.

g. In Report Design View, expand the ConventionNo Header section about 0.25", then use the Cut and Paste commands to move the ConventionName text box from the Detail section to the left edge of the ConventionNo Header section.

h. Cut and paste the CountryName text box from the Detail section to the ConventionNo Header section. Move it to the right of the ConventionName text box.

i. Drag the top edge of the CompanyName Header section up to remove any extra blank space in the ConventionNo Header section.

j. Cut and paste the CompanyName text box from the Detail section to the CompanyName Header section. Move it to the right of the ConventionName text box in the ConventionNo Header section and to the left of the AttendeeLast text box in the Detail section.

k. Remove any extra blank space in the CompanyName Header section by dragging the top edge of the Detail section up as far as possible. Close the Group, Sort, and Total pane.

l. In Layout View, scroll through the entire report and resize the ConventionName, CountryName, and CompanyName text boxes as needed to show all of the data. Be careful, however, to not expand the report beyond the width of the portrait orientation of the report.

m. In Design View, expand the CompanyName Footer about 0.5", and add a new text box positioned below the AttendeeLast text box in the Detail section. Modify the new label in the Company Name Footer to read **Count:**. Enter an expression in a new text box to count the values in the AttendeeLast field, **=Count([AttendeeLast])**.

n. Format the text color of the Count: label to black and right-align the text within the label.

o. Change the color of the report title and the labels in the Page Header section to black. Preview the report. The subtotal count for the first convention should be 21.

p. Add a label with your name to the right side of the Report Header section, then print the first page if required by your instructor.

q. Save and close the Convention Listing report, close the Conventions-D.accdb database, then exit Access 2013.

Independent Challenge 2

You have built an Access database to track membership in a community service club. The database tracks member names and addresses as well as their status and rank in the club, and their hours of service to the community.

a. Start Access and open the Membership-D.accdb database from the location where you store your Data Files. Enable content if prompted.

b. Open the Members table, find and change the name of Traci Kalvert to *your* name, then close the Members table.

c. Use the Report Wizard to create a report using the Status and DuesOwed fields from the Status table, and the FName, LName, and DuesPaid fields from the Members table.

d. View the data by Status. Do not add any more grouping fields, and sort the records in ascending order by LName then FName.

e. Use a Stepped layout and Portrait orientation, title the report **Dues Report**, then preview the report.

f. Switch to Report Design View, then use the Group, Sort, and Total pane to open the StatusNo Footer section.

g. Add a text box to the StatusNo Footer section, just below the DuesPaid text box in the Detail section. Change the label to **Count:** and the expression in the text box to **=Count([DuesPaid])**.

h. Expand the StatusNo Footer section to provide more space, and add a second text box to the StatusNo Footer section, just below the first. Change the label to **Subtotal:** and the expression in the text box to **=Sum([DuesPaid])**.

i. Expand the StatusNo Footer section to provide more space, and add a third text box to the StatusNo Footer section, just below the second. Change the accompanying label to **Balance:**.

j. Change the text box expression to **=Count([DuesPaid])*[DuesOwed]–Sum([DuesPaid])**. This expression counts the number of values in the DuesPaid field, and multiplies it by the DuesOwed field. From that value, the sum of the DuesPaid field is subtracted. This calculates the balance between dues owed and dues paid.

k. Open the Property Sheet for the =Sum([DuesPaid]) text box. On the Format tab, set the Format property to **Currency** and the Decimal Places property to **2**. Repeat these property changes for the text box with the balance calculation.

l. Select the DuesPaid text box in the Detail section, press and hold [Shift], then select all three text boxes in the StatusNo Footer section. Align the right edges of all four controls using the Align button, then Right command on the ARRANGE tab of the Ribbon. Also, right-align the contents within the text boxes of the StatusNo Footer section using the Align Right button on the HOME tab of the Ribbon. Right-align the right edges of the three new labels in the StatusNo Footer section.

m. Save, then preview the Dues Report. Make sure the report does not contain blank pages and fix that in Report Design View if needed. Print the first page of the Dues Report if requested by your instructor. The StatusNo Footer section for the first status, New, is shown in FIGURE D-22.

n. Close the Dues Report, close the Membership-D.accdb database, then exit Access.

FIGURE D-22

Count:	7
Subtotal:	$375.00
Balance:	$325.00

Independent Challenge 3

You have built an Access database to organize the deposits at a recycling center. Various clubs regularly deposit recyclable material, which is measured in pounds when the deposits are made.

a. Start Access and open the Recycle-D.accdb database from the location where you store your Data Files. Enable content if prompted.

b. Open the Centers table, change **Trash Can** to *Your* **Last Name Recycling**, then close the table.

c. Use the Report Wizard to create a report with the CenterName field from the Centers table, the DepositDate and Weight fields from the Deposits table, and the ClubName field from the Clubs table.

d. View the data by Centers, do not add any more grouping levels, and sort the records in ascending order by DepositDate.

e. Use a Stepped layout and a Portrait orientation, then title the report **Deposit Listing**.

f. In Layout View, center the Weight label and Weight data within their controls. Resize the DepositDate label and data by dragging the left edge of the control farther to the left so the label text and all dates are clearly displayed.

g. Add spaces to the labels so that CenterName becomes **Center Name**, DepositDate becomes **Deposit Date**, and ClubName becomes **Club Name**.

h. In Report Design View, open the Group, Sort, and Total pane and then open the CenterNumber Footer section.

i. Add a text box to the CenterNumber Footer section just below the Weight text box with the expression **=Sum([Weight])**.

j. Rename the new label to be **Total Center Weight** and move and resize it as needed so that it doesn't overlap the text box.

k. Resize the =Sum([Weight]) text box in the CenterNumber Footer section to be the same size as the Weight text box in the Detail section. Align the right edges of the Weight text box in the Detail section with the =Sum([Weight]) text box in the CenterNumber Footer section. Center the data in the =Sum([Weight]) text box.

l. Expand the Report Footer section, then copy and paste the =Sum([Weight]) text box from the CenterNumber Footer section to the Report Footer section.

m. Move and align the controls in the Report Footer section to be positioned directly under their counterparts in the CenterNumber Footer section.

n. Change the label in the Report Footer section to **Grand Total Weight**.

o. Remove extra blank space in the report by dragging the bottom of the report as well as the section bars up, then preview a portion of the last page of the report, as shown in FIGURE D-23. The last Total Center Weight and Grand Total Weight values on your report should match the figure.

p. Save and close the Deposit Listing report, close the Recycle-D.accdb database, then exit Access.

FIGURE D-23

6/4/2013	90	Lions
6/20/2013	85	Junior League
8/31/2013	50	Girl Scouts #11
10/2/2013	90	Lions
Total Center Weight	2720	
Grand Total Weight	9365	

Independent Challenge 4: Explore

One way you can use an Access database on your own is to record and track your job search efforts. In this exercise, you create a report to help read and analyze data into your job-tracking database.

a. Start Access and open the JobSearch-D.accdb database from the location where you store your Data Files. Enable content if prompted.

b. Open the Employers table, and enter five more records to identify five more potential employers.

c. Use subdatasheets in the Employers table to enter five more potential jobs. You may enter all five jobs for one employer, one job for five different employers, or any combination thereof. Be sure to check the spelling of all data entered. For the Desirability field, enter a value from **1** to **5**, 1 being the least desirable and 5 the most desirable. Close the Employers table.

d. Use the Report Wizard to create a report that lists the CompanyName, EmpCity, and EmpState fields from the Employers table, and the Title, AnnualSalary, and Desirability fields from the Positions table.

e. View the data by Employers, do not add any more grouping levels, and sort the records in ascending order by Title.

f. Use an Outline layout and a Landscape orientation, then title the report **Job Opportunities**.

g. In Design View, revise the labels in the EmployerID Header section from CompanyName to **Company**, EmpCity to **City**, EmpState to **State**, and AnnualSalary to **Salary**.

h. In Design View, right-align the text within the Company, City, and State labels so they are closer to the text boxes they describe.

i. In Report Design View, move the Page expression in the Page Footer section and the right edge of the report to the left, within the 10.5" mark on the horizontal ruler, and then drag the right edge of the report to the left to make sure that the report fits within the margins of one sheet of paper in landscape orientation.

j. Open the EmployerID Footer section and use the Line control in the Controls group on the DESIGN tab to add a horizontal line across the width of the report in the EmployerID Footer section. (*Hint*: The Line control may be on the second row of the Controls box. Also, press and hold [Shift] while dragging the line to create a perfectly horizontal line.)

k. Click a green error indicator that appears on the labels in the EmployerID Header section, point to the warning button to read the ScreenTip, then click the drop-down arrow on the error indicator and click Ignore Error.

l. Preview and save the Job Opportunities report making sure that the report fits within one page wide, then print the first page if requested by your instructor.

m. Close the Job Opportunities report, close the JobSearch-D.accdb database, then exit Access 2013.

Visual Workshop

Open the Basketball-D.accdb database from the location where you store your Data Files and enable content if prompted. Open the Players table, enter *your* name instead of Kelsey Douglas, then close the table. Your goal is to create the report shown in FIGURE D-24. Use the Report Wizard, and select the PFirst, PLast, HomeTown, and HomeState fields from the Players table. Select the FieldGoals, 3Pointers, and FreeThrows fields from the Stats table. View the data by Players, do not add any more grouping levels, and do not add any more sorting levels. Use a Block layout and a Portrait orientation, then title the report **Scoring Report**. In Layout View, resize all of the columns so that they fit on a single piece of portrait paper, and change the labels in the Page Header section as shown. In Design View, open the PlayerNo Footer section and add text boxes with expressions to sum the FieldGoals, 3Pointers, and FreeThrow fields. Move, modify, align, and resize all controls as needed to match FIGURE D-24. Be sure to print preview the report to make sure that it fits within the width of one sheet of paper. Modify the report to narrow it in Report Design View if needed.

FIGURE D-24

Scoring Report						
Player Name		Home Town	State	Field Goals	3 Pointers	Free Throws
Student First	Student Last	Linden	IA	4	1	3
				5	2	2
				5	3	3
				6	3	5
				4	1	1
				4	2	2
				3	2	1
				4	2	3
				4	2	3
				3	2	1
			Subtotals	42	20	24

Improving Queries

CASE ▶ The Quest database has been updated to contain more customers, tours, and sales. You help Samantha Hooper, a Quest tour developer for U.S. travel, create queries to analyze this information.

Unit Objectives

After completing this unit, you will be able to:

- Create multitable queries
- Apply sorts and view SQL
- Develop AND criteria
- Develop OR criteria

- Create calculated fields
- Build summary queries
- Build crosstab queries
- Create a report on a query

Files You Will Need

QuestTravel-F.accdb
Service-F.accdb
MusicStore-F.accdb

RealEstate-F.accdb
Scholarships-F.accdb
Training-F.accdb

Create Multitable Queries

A **select query**, the most common type of query, selects fields from related tables and displays records in a datasheet where you can view, enter, edit, or delete data. You can create select queries by using the Simple Query Wizard, or you can start from scratch in Query Design View. **Query Design View** gives you more options for selecting and presenting information. When you open (or **run**) a query, the fields and records that you selected for the query are presented in **Query Datasheet View**, also called a **logical view** of the data. **CASE** *Samantha Hooper asks you to create a query to analyze customer payments. You select fields from the Customers, Tours, Sales, and Payments tables to complete this analysis.*

STEPS

1. **Start Access, open the QuestTravel-F.accdb database from the location where you store your Data Files, then enable content if prompted**

2. **Click the CREATE tab on the Ribbon, then click the Query Design button in the Queries group**

 The Show Table dialog box opens and lists all the tables in the database.

3. **Double-click Customers, double-click Sales, double-click Tours, double-click Payments, then click Close**

 Recall that the upper pane of Query Design View displays the fields for each of the selected tables in field lists. The name of the table is shown in the field list title bar. Primary key fields are identified with a small key icon. Relationships between tables are displayed with **one-to-many join lines** that connect the linking fields. You select the fields you want by adding them to the query design grid.

4. **Double-click the FName field in the Customers table field list to add this field to the first column of the query design grid, double-click LName, double-click TourName in the Tours field list, scroll then double-click Price in the Tours field list, double-click PaymentDate in the Payments field list, then double-click PaymentAmt, as shown in FIGURE F-1**

 When you *double-click* a field in a field list, it is automatically added as the next field in the query grid. When you *drag* a field to the query design grid, any existing fields move to the right to accommodate the new field.

5. **Click the View button ⊞ in the Results group to run the query and display the query datasheet**

 The resulting datasheet looks like FIGURE F-2. The datasheet shows the six fields selected in Query Design View: FName and LName from the Customers table, TourName and Price from the Tours table, and PaymentDate and PaymentAmt from the Payments table. The datasheet displays 78 records because 78 different payments have been made. Some of the payments are from the same customer. For example, Kristen Collins has made payments on multiple tours (records 2 and 20). Kristen's last name has changed to Bayes.

6. **Double-click Collins in the LName field of the second record, type Bayes, then click any other record**

 Because Kristen's data is physically stored in only one record in the Customers table (but selected multiple times in this query because Kristen has made more than one payment), changing any occurrence of her last name automatically updates all other selections of that data in this query and throughout all other queries, forms, and reports in the database, too. Note that Kristen's name has been updated to Kristen Bayes in record 20, as shown in FIGURE F-2.

Improving Queries

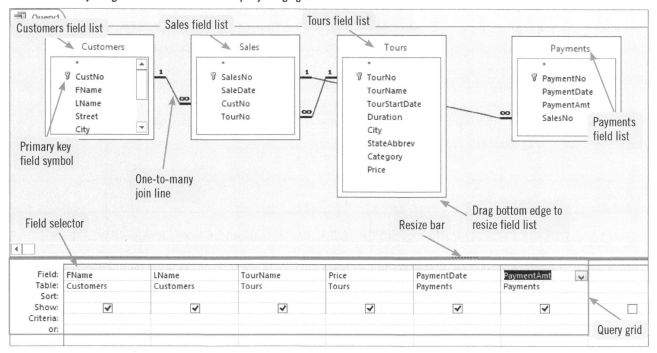

FIGURE F-2: **Query datasheet**

Access 2013

Deleting a field from the query grid

If you add the wrong field to the query design grid, you can delete it by clicking the **field selector**, the thin gray bar above each field name, then pressing [Delete]. Deleting a field from the query design grid removes it from the logical view of this query's datasheet, but does not delete the field from the database. A field is defined and the field's contents are stored in a table object only.

Apply Sorts and View SQL

Learning
Outcomes
• Apply sort orders
 in Query Design
 View
• View Structured
 Query Language
• Define SQL
 keywords

Sorting refers to reordering records in either ascending or descending order based on the values in a field. You can specify more than one sort field in Query Design View. Sort orders are evaluated from left to right, meaning that the sort field on the far left is the primary sort field. Sort orders defined in Query Design View are saved with the query object. **CASE** *You want to list the records in alphabetical order based on the customer's last name. If the customer has made more than one payment, you further sort the records by the payment date.*

STEPS

1. **Click the View button ☑ on the HOME tab to return to Query Design View**

 To sort the records by last name then by payment date, the LName field must be the primary sort field, and the PaymentDate field must be the secondary sort field.

2. **Click the LName field Sort cell in the query design grid, click the Sort list arrow, click Ascending, click the PaymentDate field Sort cell in the query design grid, click the Sort list arrow, then click Ascending**

 The resulting query design grid should look like FIGURE F-3.

3. **Click the View button ▦ in the Results group to display the query datasheet**

 The records of the datasheet are now listed in ascending order based on the values in the LName field. When the same value appears in the LName field, the records are further sorted by the secondary sort field, PaymentDate, as shown in FIGURE F-4. Jacob Alman made two payments, one on 7/26/2014 and the next on 9/1/2014. Kristen Bayes made many payments.

4. **Click the Save button 🖫 on the Quick Access toolbar, type CustomerPayments in the Save As dialog box, then click OK**

 When you save a query, you save a logical view of the data, a selection of fields and records from underlying tables. Technically, when you save a query, you are saving a set of instructions written in **Structured Query Language (SQL)**. You can view the SQL code for any query by switching to **SQL View**.

5. **Click the View button list arrow, click SQL View, then click in the lower part of the SQL window to deselect the code**

 The SQL statements shown in FIGURE F-5 start with the **SELECT** keyword. Field names follow SELECT, and how the tables are joined follow the **FROM** keyword. The **ORDER BY** keyword determines how records are sorted. Fortunately, you do not have to write or understand SQL to use Access or select data from multiple tables. The easy-to-use Query Design View gives you a way to select and sort data from underlying tables without being an SQL programmer.

6. **Close the CustomerPayments query**

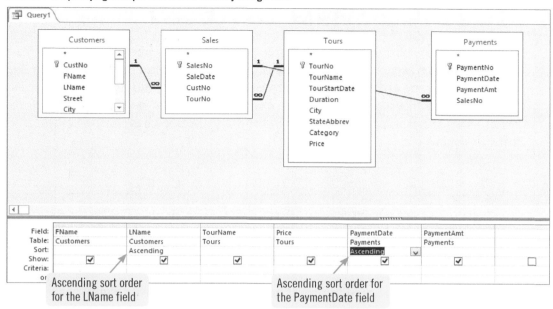

FIGURE F-4: Records sorted by LName, then by PaymentDate

Specifying a sort order different from the field order in the datasheet

If your database has several customers with the same last name, you can include a secondary sort on the first name field to distinguish the customers. If you want to display the fields in a different order from which they are sorted, you can use the solution shown in FIGURE F-6. Add a field to the query design grid twice, once to select for the datasheet, and once to use as a sort order. Use the Show check box to deselect the field used as a sort order.

FIGURE F-6: Sorting on a field that is not displayed

Field:	LName	FName	LName
Table:	Customers	Customers	Customers
Sort:	Ascending	Ascending	
Show:	☐	☑	☑
Criteria:			
or:			

Show check box is unchecked Primary sort order

Develop AND Criteria

Learning Outcomes
- Use the Like operator in query criteria
- Define advanced comparison operators

You can limit the number of records that appear on the resulting datasheet by entering criteria in Query Design View. **Criteria** are tests, or limiting conditions, that must be true for the record to be selected for a datasheet. To create **AND criteria**, which means the query selects a record only if *all* criteria are true, enter two or more criteria on the *same* Criteria row of the query design grid. **CASE** *Samantha Hooper predicts strong sales for family tours that start in or after July. She asks you to create a list of the existing tours that meet those criteria.*

STEPS

1. **Click the CREATE tab, click the Query Design button, double-click Tours, then click Close in the Show Table dialog box**

 To query for family tours, you need to add the Category field to the query grid. In addition, you want to know the tour name and start date.

2. **Drag the bottom edge of the Tours field list down to resize it to display all fields, double-click the TourName field, double-click the TourStartDate field, then double-click the Category field**

 To find tours in the Family category, you need to add a criterion for this field in the query grid.

QUICK TIP

Criteria are not case sensitive, so *family*, *Family*, and *FAMILY* are equivalent criteria entries.

3. **Click the first Criteria cell for the Category field, then type Family**

 To find all tours that start after July 1st, use the > (greater than) operator.

4. **Click the first Criteria cell for the TourStartDate field, type >7/1/2014, then press [↓]**

 As shown in **FIGURE F-7**, Access assists you with criteria syntax, rules by which criteria need to be entered. Access automatically adds quotation marks around text criteria in Short Text fields, such as "Family" in the Category field, and pound signs around date criteria in Date/Time fields, such as #7/1/2014# in the TourStartDate field. The criteria in Number, Currency, and Yes/No fields are not surrounded by any characters. See **TABLE F-1** for more information on common Access comparison operators and criteria syntax.

5. **Click the Save button 🔲 on the Quick Access toolbar, type FamilyJuly in the Save As dialog box, click OK, then click the View button 🎞 to view the query results**

 The query results are shown in **FIGURE F-8**.

6. **Close the FamilyJuly datasheet**

FIGURE F-7: Entering AND criteria on the same row

TourStartDate field criterion Category field criterion

FIGURE F-8: Datasheet for FamilyJuly records

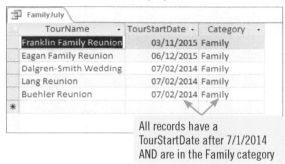

All records have a
TourStartDate after 7/1/2014
AND are in the Family category

TABLE F-1: Common comparison operators

operator	description	example	result
>	Greater than	>50	Value exceeds 50
>=	Greater than or equal to	>=50	Value is 50 or greater
<	Less than	<50	Value is less than 50
<=	Less than or equal to	<=50	Value is 50 or less
<>	Not equal to	<>50	Value is any number other than 50
Between...And	Finds values between two numbers or dates	Between #2/2/2014# And #2/2/2015#	Dates between 2/2/2014 and 2/2/2015, inclusive
In	Finds a value that is one of a list	In ("IA","KS","NE")	Value equals IA or KS or NE
Null	Finds records that have no entry in a particular field	Null	No value has been entered in a field
Is Not Null	Finds records that have any entry in a particular field	Is Not Null	Any value has been entered in a field
Like	Finds records that match the criterion, used with the * (asterisk) wildcard character	Like "A*"	Value starts with A
Not	Finds records that do not match the criterion	Not 2	Numbers other than 2

Develop OR Criteria

Learning Outcomes
• Use AND and OR criteria in the same query
• Define advanced wildcard characters

As you experienced in the previous lesson, AND criteria *narrow* the number of records in the datasheet by requiring that a record be true for multiple criteria. You also learned that AND criteria are entered on the *same* row. OR criteria work in the opposite way. **OR criteria** *expand* the number of records in the datasheet because a record needs to be true for *only one* of the criteria. You enter OR criteria in the query design grid on *different* criteria rows. **CASE** *Samantha Hooper asks you to modify the FamilyJuly query to expand the number of records to include tours in the Adventure category that start after 7/1/2014 as well.*

STEPS

1. **Right-click the FamilyJuly query in the Navigation Pane, click Copy, right-click a blank spot in the Navigation Pane, click Paste, type FamilyAdventureJuly in the Paste As dialog box, then click OK**

 By making a copy of the FamilyJuly query before modifying it, you won't change the FamilyJuly query by mistake. To add OR criteria, you have to enter criteria in the next available "or" row of the query design grid. By default, the query grid displays eight rows for additional OR criteria, but you can add even more rows using the Insert Rows button on the DESIGN tab.

2. **Right-click the FamilyAdventureJuly query, click Design View, type Adventure in the next row (the "or" row) of the Category column, then click the View button ▦ to display the datasheet**

 The datasheet expands from 5 to 26 records because 21 tours with a Category of Adventure were added to the datasheet. But notice that many of the TourStartDate values for the Adventure records are prior to 7/1/2014. To select only those Adventure tours with a TourStartDate after 7/1/2014, you need to add more criteria to Query Design View.

3. **Click the View button ▨ to return to Query Design View, click the next TourStartDate Criteria cell, type >7/1/2014, then click elsewhere in the grid, as shown in** FIGURE F-9

 Criteria in one row do not affect criteria in another row. Therefore, to select only those tours that start after 7/1/2014, you must put the same TourStartDate criterion in *both* rows of the query design grid.

4. **Click ▦ to return to Datasheet View**

 The resulting datasheet selects 18 records, as shown in FIGURE F-10. When no sort order is applied, the records are sorted by the primary key field of the first table in the query (in this case, TourNo, which is not selected for this query). All of the records have a Category of Family or Adventure and a TourStartDate value greater than 7/1/2014.

5. **Save and close the FamilyAdventureJuly query**

 The QuestTravel-F.accdb Navigation Pane displays the three queries you created plus the StateAnalysis query that was already in the database.

FIGURE F-9: Entering OR criteria on different rows

FIGURE F-10: Datasheet for FamilyAdventureJuly query

Using wildcard characters in query criteria

To search for a pattern, use a **wildcard character** to represent any character in the criteria entry. Use a **question mark (?)** to search for any single character, and an **asterisk (*)** to search for any number of characters. Wildcard characters are often used with the Like operator. For example, the criterion Like "10/*/2015" finds all dates in October of 2015, and the criterion Like "F*" finds all entries that start with the letter F.

Create Calculated Fields

Learning Outcomes
• Create calculated fields in queries
• Define functions and expressions

A **calculated field** is a field of data that can be created based on the values of other fields. For example, you can calculate the value for a Tax field by multiplying the value of the Sales field by a percentage. To create a calculated field, define it in Query Design View using an expression that describes the calculation. An **expression** is a combination of field names, operators (such as +, –, /, and *), and functions that result in a single value. A **function** is a predefined formula that returns a value such as a subtotal, count, or the current date. See TABLE F-2 for more information on arithmetic operators and TABLE F-3 for more information on functions. **CASE** *Samantha Hooper asks you to find the number of days between the sale date and the tour start date. To determine this information, you create a calculated field called LeadTime that subtracts the SaleDate from the TourStartDate. You create another calculated field to determine the commission on each tour sale.*

STEPS

1. **Click the CREATE tab on the Ribbon, click the Query Design button, double-click Tours, double-click Sales, then click Close in the Show Table dialog box**

 First, you add the fields to the grid that you want to display in the query.

QUICK TIP
Drag the bottom edge of the Tours field list down to display all fields.

2. **Double-click the TourName field, double-click the TourStartDate field, double-click the Price field, then double-click the SaleDate field**

 You create a calculated field in the Field cell of the design grid by entering a new descriptive field name followed by a colon, followed by an expression. Field names used in an expression must be surrounded by square brackets.

QUICK TIP
To display a long entry in a field cell, right-click the cell, then click Zoom.

3. **Click the blank Field cell in the fifth column, type LeadTime:[TourStartDate]-[SaleDate], then drag the ↔ pointer on the right edge of the fifth column selector to the right to display the entire entry**

 You create another calculated field to determine the commission paid on each sale, which is calculated as 11% of the Price field.

TROUBLE
Field names in expressions are surrounded by [square brackets] not {curly braces} and not (parentheses).

4. **Click the blank Field cell in the sixth column, type Commission:[Price]*0.11, then widen the column, as shown in FIGURE F-11**

 You view the datasheet to see the resulting calculated fields.

5. **Click the View button ▦, press [Tab], type 8/1/14 in the TourStartDate field for the first record, press [Tab], type 1000 in the Price field for the first record, then press [↓]**

 A portion of the resulting datasheet, with two calculated fields, is shown in FIGURE F-12. The LeadTime field is automatically recalculated, showing the number of days between the SaleDate and the TourStartDate. The Commission field is also automatically recalculated, multiplying the Price value by 11%.

6. **Click the Save button 🖫 on the Quick Access toolbar, type LeadTimesAndCommissions in the Save As dialog box, click OK, then close the datasheet**

FIGURE F-11: Creating calculated fields

Calculated field names are followed by a colon

Field:	TourName	TourStartDate	Price	SaleDate	LeadTime: [TourStartDate]-[SaleDate]	Commission: [Price]*0.11
Table:	Tours	Tours	Tours	Sales		
Sort:						
Show:	✓	✓	✓	✓	✓	✓
Criteria:						
or:						

Calculations are determined by expressions that follow the colon

Drag the column separator to widen the column

FIGURE F-12: Viewing and testing calculated fields

Query1

TourName	TourStartDate	Price	SaleDate	LeadTime	Commission
Breeze Bay Shelling	08/01/2014	$1,000	4/30/2014	93	110
Breeze Bay Shelling	**08/01/2014**	**$1,000**	**4/30/2014**	**93**	**110**
Breeze Bay Shelling	08/01/2014	$1,000	4/30/2014	93	110
Breeze Bay Shelling	08/01/2014	$1,000	4/30/2014	93	110
Breeze Bay Shelling	08/01/2014	$1,000	5/31/2014	62	110
Breeze Bay Shelling	08/01/2014	$1,000	6/30/2014	32	110
Red Reef Scuba	07/06/2014	$1,500	5/11/2014	56	165
Red Reef Scuba	07/06/2014	$1,500	7/1/2014	5	165
Red Reef Scuba	07/06/2014	$1,500	7/1/2014	5	165
Red Reef Scuba	07/06/2014	$1,500	7/1/2014	5	165
Red Reef Scuba	07/06/2014	$1,500	7/1/2014	5	165
Red Reef Scuba	07/06/2014	$1,500	7/1/2014	5	165
Red Reef Scuba	07/06/2014	$1,500	7/1/2014	5	165
Red Reef Scuba	07/06/2014	$1,500	7/2/2014	4	165
Red Reef Scuba	07/06/2014	$1,500	7/2/2014	4	165
Ames Ski Club	01/02/2015	$850	4/30/2014	247	93.5
Ames Ski Club	01/02/2015	$850	5/1/2014	246	93.5
Ames Ski Club	01/02/2015	$850	7/11/2014	175	93.5

Commission equals Price * 11%

LeadTime equals the days between the SaleDate and TourStartDate

TABLE F-2: Arithmetic operators

operator	description
+	Addition
−	Subtraction
*	Multiplication
/	Division
^	Exponentiation

TABLE F-3: Common functions

function	sample expression and description
DATE	DATE()-[BirthDate] Calculates the number of days between today and the date in the BirthDate field; Access expressions are not case sensitive, so DATE()-[BirthDate] is equivalent to date()-[birthdate] and DATE()-[BIRTHDATE]; therefore, use capitalization in expressions in any way that makes the expression easier to read
PMT	PMT([Rate],[Term],[Loan]) Calculates the monthly payment on a loan where the Rate field contains the monthly interest rate, the Term field contains the number of monthly payments, and the Loan field contains the total amount financed
LEFT	LEFT([LastName],2) Returns the first two characters of the entry in the LastName field
RIGHT	RIGHT([PartNo],3) Returns the last three characters of the entry in the PartNo field
LEN	LEN([Description]) Returns the number of characters in the Description field

Build Summary Queries

Learning Outcomes
- Create a summary query
- Define aggregate functions

A **summary query** calculates statistics for groups of records. To create a summary query, you add the **Total row** to the query design grid to specify how you want to group and calculate the records using aggregate functions. **Aggregate functions** calculate a statistic such as a subtotal, count, or average on a field in a group of records. Some aggregate functions, such as Sum or Avg (Average), only work on fields with Number or Currency data types. Other functions, such as Min (Minimum), Max (Maximum), or Count, also work on Short Text fields. TABLE F-4 provides more information on aggregate functions. A key difference between the statistics displayed by a summary query and those displayed by calculated fields is that summary queries provide calculations that describe a *group of records*, whereas calculated fields provide a new field of information for *each record*. **CASE** > *Samantha Hooper asks you to calculate total sales for each tour category. You build a summary query to provide this information.*

STEPS

QUICK TIP
In Query Design View, drag a table from the Navigation Pane to add it to the query.

1. **Click the CREATE tab on the Ribbon, click the Query Design button, double-click Sales, double-click Tours, then click Close in the Show Table dialog box**

 It doesn't matter in what order you add the field lists to Query Design View, but it's important to move and resize the field lists as necessary to clearly see all field names and relationships.

2. **Double-click the SalesNo field in the Sales field list, double-click the Category field in the Tours field list, double-click the Price field in the Tours field list, then click the View button ⊞ to view the datasheet**

 One hundred and one records are displayed, representing all 101 records in the Sales table. You can add a Total row to any datasheet to calculate grand total statistics for that datasheet.

3. **Click the Totals button in the Records group, click the Total cell below the Price field, click the Total list arrow, click Sum, then use ↔ to widen the Price column to display the entire total**

 The Total row is added to the bottom of the datasheet and displays the sum total of the Price field, $85,510. Other Total row statistics you can select include Average, Count, Maximum, Minimum, Standard Deviation, and Variance. To create subtotals per Category, you need to modify the query in Query Design View.

4. **Click the View button ⊠ to return to Query Design View, click the Totals button in the Show/Hide group, click Group By in the SalesNo column, click the list arrow, click Count, click Group By in the Price column, click the list arrow, then click Sum**

 The Total row is added to the query grid below the Table row. To calculate summary statistics for each category, the Category field is the Group By field, as shown in FIGURE F-13. With the records grouped together by Category, you will subtotal the Price field using the Sum operator to calculate a subtotal of revenue for each Category of tour sales.

5. **Click ⊞ to display the datasheet, widen each column as necessary to view all field names, click in the Total row for the SumOfPrice field, click the list arrow, click Sum, then click another row in the datasheet to remove the selection**

 The Adventure category leads all others with a count of 55 sales totaling $52,560. The total revenue for all sales is $85,510, as shown in FIGURE F-14.

TROUBLE
To delete or rename any object, close it, then right-click it in the Navigation Pane and click Delete or Rename on the shortcut menu.

6. **Click the Save button 🖫 on the Quick Access toolbar, type CategorySummary, click OK, then close the datasheet**

FIGURE F-13: **Summary query in Design View**

FIGURE F-14: **Summary query datasheet**

TABLE F-4: **Aggregate functions**

aggregate function	used to find the
Sum	Total of values in a field
Avg	Average of values in a field
Min	Minimum value in a field
Max	Maximum value in a field
Count	Number of values in a field (not counting null values)
StDev	Standard deviation of values in a field
Var	Variance of values in a field
First	Field value from the first record in a table or query
Last	Field value from the last record in a table or query

Build Crosstab Queries

Learning Outcomes
• Create a crosstab query
• Describe the Find Duplicates and Find Unmatched Query Wizards

A **crosstab query** subtotals one field by grouping records using two other fields that are placed in the column heading and row heading positions. You can use the **Crosstab Query Wizard** to guide you through the steps of creating a crosstab query, or you can build the crosstab query from scratch using Query Design View. **CASE** ▸ *Samantha Hooper asks you to continue your analysis of prices per category by summarizing the price values for each tour within each category. A crosstab query works well for this request because you want to subtotal the Price field as summarized by two other fields, TourName and Category.*

STEPS

1. **Click the CREATE tab on the Ribbon, click the Query Design button, double-click Tours, double-click Sales, then click Close in the Show Table dialog box**

 The fields you need for your crosstab query come from the Tours table, but you also need to include the Sales table in this query to select tour information for each record (sale) in the Sales table.

2. **Double-click the TourName field, double-click the Category field, then double-click the Price field**

 The first step in creating a crosstab query is to create a select query with the three fields you want to use in the crosstabular report.

3. **Click the View button ▦ to review the unsummarized datasheet of 101 records, then click the View button ⋉ to return to Query Design View**

 To summarize these 101 records in a crosstabular report, you need to change the current select query into a crosstab query.

4. **Click the Crosstab button in the Query Type group**

 Note that two new rows are added to the query grid—the Total row and the Crosstab row. The **Total row** helps you determine which fields group or summarize the records, and the **Crosstab row** identifies which of the three positions each field takes in the crosstab report: Row Heading, Column Heading, or Value. The **Value field** is typically a numeric field, such as Price, that can be summed or averaged.

5. **Click Group By in the Total cell of the Price field, click the list arrow, click Sum, click the Crosstab cell for the TourName field, click the list arrow, click Row Heading, click the Crosstab cell for the Category field, click the list arrow, click Column Heading, click the Crosstab cell for the Price field, click the list arrow, then click Value**

 The completed Query Design View should look like **FIGURE F-15**. Note the choices made in the Total and Crosstab rows of the query grid.

6. **Click ▦ to review the crosstab datasheet**

 The final crosstab datasheet is shown in **FIGURE F-16**. The datasheet summarizes all 101 sales records by the Category field used as the column headings and by the TourName field used in the row heading position. Although you can switch the row and column heading fields without changing the numeric information on the crosstab datasheet, you should generally place the field with the most entries (in this case, TourName has more values than Category) in the row heading position so that the printout is taller than it is wide.

7. **Click the Save button ▦ on the Quick Access toolbar, type TourCrosstab as the query name, click OK, then close the datasheet**

 Crosstab queries appear with a crosstab icon to the left of the query name in the Navigation Pane.

FIGURE F-15: **Query Design View of crosstab query**

FIGURE F-15: **Query Design View of crosstab query**

Total row →

Crosstab row →

Field:	TourName	Category	Price	
Table:	Tours	Tours	Tours	Sum
Total:	Group By	Group By	Sum	
Crosstab:	Row Heading	Column Heading	Value	▼
Sort:				
Criteria:				
or:				

Row Heading Column Heading Value

FIGURE F-16: **Crosstab query datasheet**

🖼 Query1

TourName ▼	Adventure ▼	Educational ▼	Family ▼	Service ▼	Site Seeing ▼
American Heritage Tour		$18,000.00			
Ames Ski Club	$11,050.00				
Bear Valley Adventures	$1,450.00				
Bigfoot Rafting Club	$910.00				
Black Sheep Hiking Club	$1,050.00				
Boy Scout Jamboree	$3,800.00				
Breeze Bay Shelling	$6,000.00				
Bridgewater Country	$9,600.00				
Bright Lights Expo					$2,400.00
Eagan Family Reunion			$2,000.00		
Franklin Family Reunion			$5,600.00		
Golden Footsteps					$2,200.00
Gunnison Bikers	$1,000.00				
Piper-Heitman Wedding			$550.00		
Red Reef Scuba	$13,500.00				
Spare Tire Ski Club	$4,200.00				
Yosemite National Park ($2,200.00	

Category field values are column headings

TourName field values are row headings

Price field values are subtotaled

Using query wizards

Four query wizards are available to help you build queries including the Simple (which creates a select query), Crosstab, Find Duplicates, and Find Unmatched Query Wizards. Use the **Find Duplicates Query Wizard** to determine whether a table contains duplicate values in one or more fields. Use the **Find Unmatched Query Wizard** to find records in one table that do not have related records in another table. To use the query wizards, click the Query Wizard button on the CREATE tab.

Create a Report on a Query

Learning Outcomes
- Create a report on a query
- Modify a report's Record Source property

When you want a more professional printout of the information than can be provided by a query datasheet, you use a report object. By first selecting the fields and records you want in a query and then basing the report on that query, you can easily add new fields and calculations to the report by adding them to the underlying query. When you base a report on a query, the query name is identified in the **Record Source** property of the report. **CASE** ▶ Samantha Hooper asks you to create a report to subtotal the revenue for each tour.

STEPS

1. **Double-click the** StateAnalysis query **in the Navigation Pane to open its datasheet**

 The StateAnalysis query contains the customer state, tour name, and price of each tour sold. Analyzing which tours are the most popular in various states will help focus marketing expenses. Creating a query to select the fields and records needed on a report is the first step in creating a report that can be easily modified later.

2. **Close the** StateAnalysis query, **click the** CREATE **tab on the Ribbon, click the** Report Wizard button, **click the** Tables/Queries list arrow, **click** Query: StateAnalysis, **click the** Select All button >> , **then click** Next

 The Report Wizard wants to group the records by the State field. This is also how you want to analyze the data.

3. **Click** Next, **click** TourName, **then click the** Select Field button > **to add the TourName field as a second grouping level, click** Next, **click** Next **to not choose any sort orders, click** Next **to accept a Stepped layout and Portrait orientation, type** State Revenue Report **as the title for the report, then click** Finish

 The report lists each tour sold within each state as many times as it has been sold. You decide to add the name of the customers who have purchased these tours to the report. First, you will need to add them to the StateAnalysis query. Given that the State Revenue Report is based on the StateAnalysis query, you can access the StateAnalysis query from Report Design View of the State Revenue Report.

 QUICK TIP
 You can also double-click the report selector button to open the Property Sheet for the report.

4. **Right-click the** State Revenue Report tab, **click** Design View, **close the Field List if it is open, then click the** Property Sheet button **in the Tools group on the DESIGN tab**

 The Property Sheet for the State Revenue Report opens.

5. **Click the** Data tab, **click** StateAnalysis **in the Record Source property, then click the** Build button ... , **as shown in** FIGURE F-17

 The StateAnalysis query opens in Query Design View.

6. **Close the Property Sheet, double-click the** FName field, **double-click the** LName field, **click the** Close button **on the DESIGN tab, then click** Yes **when prompted to save the changes**

 Now that the FName and LName fields have been added to the StateAnalysis query, they are available to the report.

 TROUBLE
 The number in the Text13 label varies based on previous activity in the report.

7. **Click the** DESIGN tab, **click the** Text Box button ab| , **click to the** left **of the Price text box in the Detail section, click the** Text13 label, **press** [Delete], **click** Unbound **in the text box, type** =[FName] &" "&[LName], **then press** [Enter]

 You could have added the FName and LName fields directly to the report but the information looks a little more professional as the result of one expression that calculates the entire name.

8. **Switch to Layout View, resize the new text box as shown in** FIGURE F-18 **to see the entire name, save and close the State Revenue Report, close the QuestTravel-F.accdb database, then exit Access**

FIGURE F-18: Final State Revenue Report

State	TourName		Price
IA			
	American Heritage Tour		
	Ralph Hopper		$1,200
	Kris Goode		$1,200
	Brad Langguth		$1,200
	Lois Goode		$1,200
	Nancy Langguth		$1,200
	Ames Ski Club		
	Lois Goode		$850
	Toby Lang		$850
	Kris Goode		$850
	Elsie Lang		$850
	Brandon Larson		$850

State Revenue Report

Resize the text box as needed

Access 2013

Practice

Concepts Review

Identify each element of Query Design View shown in FIGURE F-19.

FIGURE F-19

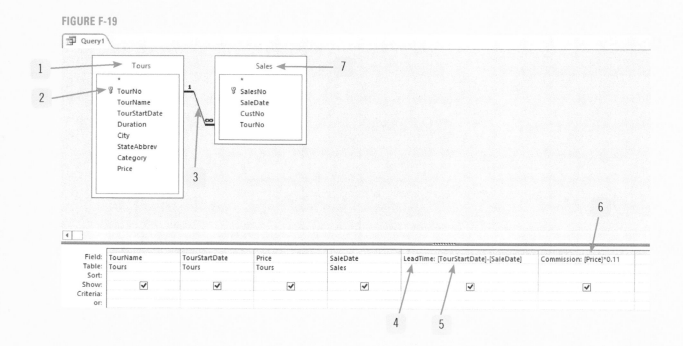

Match each term with the statement that best describes it.

8. **Record Source**
9. **Select query**
10. **Wildcard character**
11. **AND criteria**
12. **Sorting**
13. **OR criteria**

a. Placing the records of a datasheet in a certain order
b. Entered on more than one row of the query design grid
c. Report property that determines what fields and records the report will display
d. Asterisk (*) or question mark (?) used in query criteria
e. Retrieves fields from related tables and displays records in a datasheet
f. Entered on one row of the query design grid

Select the best answer from the list of choices.

14. **The query datasheet can best be described as a:**
 a. Logical view of the selected data from underlying tables.
 b. Duplication of the data in the underlying table's datasheet.
 c. Separate file of data.
 d. Second copy of the data in the underlying tables.

15. Queries may *not* be used to:

 a. Calculate new fields of data.

 b. Set the primary key field for a table.

 c. Enter or update data.

 d. Sort records.

16. When you update data in a table that is also selected in a query:

 a. You must relink the query to the table to refresh the data.

 b. The updated data is automatically displayed in the query.

 c. You must also update the data in the query datasheet.

 d. You can choose whether to update the data in the query.

17. Which of the following is *not* an aggregate function available to a summary query?

 a. Avg

 b. Subtotal

 c. Count

 d. Max

18. The order in which records in a query are sorted is determined by:

 a. The order in which the fields are defined in the underlying table.

 b. The importance of the information in the field.

 c. The alphabetic order of the field names.

 d. The left-to-right position of the fields in the query design grid that contain a sort order choice.

19. A crosstab query is generally constructed with how many fields?

 a. 1

 b. 3

 c. 2

 d. More than 5

20. In a crosstab query, which field is the most likely candidate for the Value position?

 a. FName

 b. Department

 c. Cost

 d. Country

Skills Review

1. Create multitable queries.

 a. Start Access and open the Service-F.accdb database from the location where you store your Data Files, then enable content if prompted.

 b. Create a new select query in Query Design View using the Names and Zips tables.

 c. Add the following fields to the query design grid in this order:

 • FirstName, LastName, and Street from the Names table

 • City, State, and Zip from the Zips table

 d. In Datasheet View, replace the LastName value in the Martin Chen record with *your* last name.

 e. Save the query as **AddressList**, print the datasheet if requested by your instructor, then close the query.

2. Apply sorts and view SQL.

 a. Open the AddressList query in Query Design View.

 b. Drag the FirstName field from the Names field list to the third column in the query design grid to make the first three fields in the query design grid FirstName, LastName, and FirstName.

 c. Add an ascending sort to the second and third fields in the query design grid, and uncheck the Show check box in the third column. The query is now sorted in ascending order by LastName, then by FirstName, though the order of the fields in the resulting datasheet still appears as FirstName, LastName.

 d. Click the FILE tab, click Save As, then use Save Object As to save the query as **SortedAddressList**. View the datasheet, print the datasheet if requested by your instructor, then close the SortedAddressList query.

3. Develop AND criteria.

 a. Right-click the SortedAddressList query in the Navigation Pane, click Copy, right-click a blank spot in the Navigation Pane, click Paste, then type **KansasC** as the name for the new query.

 b. Open the KansasC query in Design View, then type **C*** (the asterisk is a wildcard) in the LastName field Criteria cell to choose all people whose last name starts with *C*. Access assists you with the syntax for this type of criterion and enters Like "C*" in the cell when you click elsewhere in the query design grid.

Skills Review (continued)

 c. Enter **KS** as the AND criterion for the State field. Be sure to enter the criterion on the same line in the query design grid as the Like "C*" criterion.

 d. View the datasheet. It should select only those people from Kansas with a last name that starts with the letter C.

 e. Enter *your* hometown in the City field of the first record to uniquely identify the printout.

 f. Save the KansasC query, print the datasheet if requested by your instructor, then close the KansasC query.

4. Develop OR criteria.

 a. Right-click the KansasC query in the Navigation Pane, click Copy, right-click a blank spot in the Navigation Pane, click Paste, then type **KansasCD** as the name for the new query.

 b. Open the KansasCD query in Design View, then enter **D*** in the second Criteria row (the or row) of the LastName field.

 c. Enter **KS** as the criterion in the second Criteria row (the or row) of the State field so that those people from KS with a last name that starts with the letter D are added to this query.

 d. View the datasheet. It should select only those people from Kansas with a last name that starts with the letter C or D. Print the datasheet if requested by your instructor, then save and close the query.

5. Create calculated fields.

 a. Create a new select query in Query Design View using only the Names table.

 b. Add the following fields to the query design grid in this order: FirstName, LastName, Birthday.

 c. Create a calculated field called Age in the fourth column of the query design grid by entering the expression: **Age: Int((Now()-[Birthday])/365)** to determine the age of each person in years based on the information in the Birthday field. The Now() function returns today's date. Now()-[Birthday] determines the number of days a person has lived. Dividing that value by 365 determines the number of years a person has lived. The Int() function is used to return the integer portion of the answer. So if a person has lived 23.5 years, Int(23.5) = 23.

 d. Sort the query in descending order on the calculated Age field.

 e. Save the query with the name **AgeCalculation**, view the datasheet, print the datasheet if requested by your instructor, then close the query.

6. Build summary queries.

 a. Create a new select query in Query Design View using the Names and Activities tables.

 b. Add the following fields: FirstName and LastName from the Names table, and Hours from the Activities table.

 c. Add the Total row to the query design grid, then change the aggregate function for the Hours field from Group By to Sum.

 d. Sort in descending order by Hours.

 e. Save the query as **HoursSummary**, view the datasheet, widen all columns so that all data is clearly visible, print the datasheet if requested by your instructor, then save and close the query.

7. Build crosstab queries.

 a. Use Query Design View to create a select query with the City and State fields from the Zips table and the Dues field from the Names table. Save the query as **DuesCrosstab**, then view the datasheet.

 b. Return to Query Design View, then click the Crosstab button to add the Total and Crosstab rows to the query design grid.

Skills Review (continued)

c. Specify City as the crosstab row heading, State as the crosstab column heading, and Dues as the summed value field within the crosstab datasheet.

d. View the datasheet as shown in FIGURE F-20, print the datasheet if requested by your instructor, then save and close the DuesCrosstab query.

8. **Create a report on a query.**

a. Use the Report Wizard to create a report on all of the fields of the SortedAddressList query. View the data by Names, add State as a grouping level, add LastName then FirstName as the ascending sort orders, use a Stepped layout and Landscape orientation, then title the report **Names by State**.

b. In Design View, open the Property Sheet for the report, then open the SortedAddressList query in Design View using the Build button on the Record Source property.

c. Add the Birthday field to the SortedAddressList query then close the query.

d. To the left of the LastName field in the Detail section, add a text box bound to the Birthday field. (*Hint*: Type **Birthday** in place of Unbound or modify the text box's Control Source property to be Birthday.) Delete the label that is automatically created to the left of the text box.

e. In Layout View, resize the City and Zip columns so that all data is clearly visible, as shown in FIGURE F-21. Be sure to preview the report to make sure it fits on the paper.

f. If requested by your instructor, print the first page of the Names by State report, save and close it, close the Service-F.accdb database, then exit Access.

FIGURE F-20

City	IA	KS	MO
Blue Springs			$50.00
Bridgewater	$50.00		
Buehler		$50.00	
Des Moines	$25.00		
Dripping Spring		$25.00	
Flat Hills		$50.00	
Fontanelle	$50.00		
Greenfield	$50.00		
Kansas City		$50.00	$100.00
Langguth		$25.00	
Leawood			$50.00
Lee's Summit			$75.00
Lenexa		$25.00	
Manawatta		$25.00	
Manhattan		$25.00	
Overland Park		$100.00	
Red Bridge		$425.00	
Running Deer			$25.00
Shawnee		$200.00	
Student Home		$100.00	

FIGURE F-21

Names by State

State	LastName	FirstName	Street	City	Zip
IA					
10/6/1961	Goode	Loraine	900 Barnes Road	Greenfield	50265
7/16/1963	Martin	Benjamin	5253 Duck Creek Dr	Des Moines	52240
9/30/1960	May	Jaye	1515 Maple St	Fontanelle	50033
8/19/1980	StudentLastName	Martin	1010 Green St	Bridgewater	50022
KS					
6/4/1979	Alman	Josiah	2505 McGee St	Flat Hills	64141
10/1/1989	Bovier	Mary	110 College Blvd	Manhattan	66031
9/4/1961	Browning	Forrest	8206 Marshall Drive	Dripping Springs	66214
1/1/1954	Cabriella	Holly	52520 W. 505 Terr	Student Home Town	66215
6/19/1960	Camel	Mark	66020 King Street	Red Bridge	66210
6/12/1958	Custard	Mildred	66900 College Blvd	Red Bridge	66210

Access 2013

Independent Challenge 1

As the manager of a music store's instrument rental program, you have created a database to track rentals to schoolchildren. Now that several rentals have been made, you want to query the database for several different datasheet printouts to analyze school information.

a. Start Access and open the MusicStore-F.accdb database from the location where you store your Data Files, then enable content if prompted.

b. In Query Design View, create a query with the following fields in the following order:
- SchoolName field from the Schools table
- RentalDate field from the Rentals table
- Description field from the Instruments table

(*Hint*: Although you don't use any fields from the Customers table, you need to add the Customers table to this query to make the connection between the Schools table and the Rentals table.)

c. Sort in ascending order by SchoolName, then in ascending order by RentalDate.

d. Save the query as **SchoolRentals**, view the datasheet, replace Lincoln Elementary with *your* elementary school name, print the datasheet if requested by your instructor, then close the datasheet.

e. Copy and paste the SchoolRentals query as **SchoolCount**, then open the SchoolCount query in Query Design View.

f. Modify the SchoolCount query by deleting the Description field. Use the Totals button to group the records by SchoolName and to count the RentalDate field. Print the datasheet if requested by your instructor, then save and close the SchoolCount query.

g. Create a crosstab query named **SchoolCrosstab** based on the SchoolRentals query. (*Hint*: Select the SchoolRentals query in the Show Table dialog box.) Use Description as the column heading position and SchoolName in the row heading position. Count the RentalDate field.

h. View the SchoolCrosstab query in Datasheet View. Resize each column to best fit the data in that column, then print the datasheet if requested by your instructor. Save and close the SchoolCrosstab query.

i. Copy and paste the SchoolRentals query as **ElementaryRentals**. Modify the ElementaryRentals query in Query Design View so that only those schools with the word **Elementary** in the SchoolName field are displayed. (*Hint*: You have to use wildcard characters in the criteria.)

j. View the ElementaryRentals query in Datasheet View, print it if requested by your instructor, then save and close the datasheet.

k. Close the MusicStore-F.accdb database, then exit Access.

Independent Challenge 2

As the manager of a music store's instrument rental program, you have created a database to track rentals to schoolchildren. You can use queries to analyze customer and rental information.

a. Start Access and open the MusicStore-F.accdb database from the location where you store your Data Files, then enable content if prompted.

b. In Query Design View, create a query with the following fields in the following order:
- Description and MonthlyFee fields from the Instruments table
- LastName, Zip, and City fields from the Customers table

(*Hint*: Although you don't need any fields from the Rentals table in this query's datasheet, you need to add the Rentals table to this query to make the connection between the Customers table and the Instruments table.)

Independent Challenge 2 (continued)

c. Add the Zip field to the first column of the query grid, and specify an ascending sort order for this field. Uncheck the Show check box for the first Zip field so that it does not appear in the datasheet.

d. Add an ascending sort order to the Description field.

e. Save the query as **ZipAnalysis**.

f. View the datasheet, replace Johnson with *your* last name in the LastName field, print the datasheet if requested by your instructor, then save and close the datasheet. (*Note*: If you later view this query in Design View, note that Access changes the way the sort orders are specified but in a way that gives you the same results in the datasheet.)

g. In Query Design View, create a query with the following fields in the following order:
- Description and MonthlyFee fields from the Instruments table
- LastName, Zip, and City fields from the Customers table

(*Hint*: You'll need to add the Rentals table.)

h. Add criteria to find the records where the Description is equal to **viola**. Sort in ascending order based on the Zip then City fields. Save the query as **Violas**, view the datasheet, print it if requested by your instructor, then close the datasheet.

i. Copy and paste the Violas query as **DesMoinesViolas**, then modify the DesMoinesViolas query with AND criteria to further specify that the City must be **Des Moines**. View the datasheet, print it if requested by your instructor, then save and close the datasheet.

j. Copy and paste the DesMoinesViolas query as **DesMoinesOrViolas**, then modify the DesMoinesOrViolas query so that all records with a Description equal to Violas or a City value of **Des Moines** are selected. View the datasheet, print it if requested by your instructor, then save and close the datasheet.

k. Close the MusicStore-F.accdb database, then exit Access.

Independent Challenge 3

As a real estate agent, you use an Access database to track residential real estate listings in your area. You can use queries to answer questions about the real estate properties and to analyze home values.

a. Start Access and open the RealEstate-F.accdb database from the location where you store your Data Files, then enable content if prompted.

b. In Query Design View, create a query with the following fields in the following order:
- AgencyName from the Agencies table
- RFirst and RLast from the Realtors table
- SqFt and Asking from the Listings table

c. Sort the records in descending order by the Asking field.

d. Save the query as **AskingPrice**, view the datasheet, enter *your* last name instead of Dell for the most expensive listing, then print the datasheet if requested by your instructor.

e. In Query Design View, modify the AskingPrice query by creating a calculated field that determines price per square foot. The new calculated field's name should be **SquareFootCost**, and the expression should be the asking price divided by the square foot field, or **[Asking]/[SqFt]**.

f. Remove any former sort orders, sort the records in descending order based on the SquareFootCost calculated field, and view the datasheet. Save and close the AskingPrice query. ###### means the data is too wide to display in the column. You can make the data narrower and also align it by applying a Currency format.

g. Reopen the AskingPrice query in Query Design View, right-click the calculated SquareFootCost field, click Properties, then change the Format property to Currency. View the datasheet, print it if requested by your instructor, then save and close the AskingPrice query.

h. Copy and paste the AskingPrice query as **CostSummary**.

Independent Challenge 3 (continued)

i. In Design View of the CostSummary query, delete the RFirst, RLast, and SqFt fields.

j. View the datasheet, then change the Sun and Ski Realtors agency name to *your* last name followed by **Realtors**.

k. In Design View, add the Total row, then sum the Asking field and use the Avg (Average) aggregate function for the SquareFootCost calculated field.

l. In Datasheet View, add the Total row and display the sum of the SumOfAsking field. Widen all columns as needed, as shown in FIGURE F-22.

m. If requested by your Instructor, print the CostSummary query, then save and close it.

n. Close the RealEstate-F.accdb database, then exit Access.

FIGURE F-22

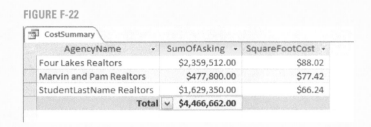

Independent Challenge 4: Explore

You're working with the local high school guidance counselor to help him with an Access database used to record college scholarship opportunities. You help him with the database by creating several queries. (*Note: To complete this Independent Challenge, make sure you are connected to the Internet.*)

a. Start Access, open the Scholarships-F.accdb database from the location where you store your Data Files, then enable content if prompted.

b. Conduct research on the Internet or at your school to find at least five new scholarships relevant to your major, and enter them into the Scholarships table.

c. Conduct research on the Internet or at your school to find at least one new scholarship relevant to a Business major as well as a Science major, and enter the two records into the Scholarships table.

d. Create a query called **Business** that displays all fields from the Scholarships table that selects all records with a Business major. If requested by your instructor, print the Business query then save and close it.

e. Copy and paste the Business query as **BusinessOrScience**. Add OR criteria to the BusinessOrScience query to select all scholarships in the Business or Science majors. If requested by your instructor, print the BusinessOrScience query then save and close it.

Independent Challenge 4: Explore (continued)

f. Create a new query that selects the ScholarshipName, DueDate, and Amount from the Scholarships table, and sorts the records in ascending order by DueDate, then descending order by Amount. Name the query **ScholarshipMasterList**. If requested by your instructor, print the ScholarshipMasterList query then save and close it.

g. Use the Report Wizard to create a report on the ScholarshipMasterList, do not add any grouping levels, sort the records in ascending order by ScholarshipName, use a Tabular layout and a Portrait orientation, and title the report **Scholarship Master List**.

h. In Design View of the Scholarship Master List report, open the Property Sheet, and use the Record Source Build button to open the ScholarshipMasterList query in Design View. Add the Major field to the query, save and close it.

i. In Report Design View, open the Group, Sort, and Total pane, add the Major field as a grouping field, then move it above the Sort by ScholarshipName sort field.

j. Add a text box to the Major Header section, and bind it to the Major field. (*Hint*: Type **Major** in place of Unbound or modify the text box's Control Source property to be Major.) Delete the label that is automatically created to the left of the text box. Preview the report, as shown in FIGURE F-23, then print it if requested by your instructor.

k. Save and close the Scholarship Master List report, close the Scholarships-F.accdb database, then exit Access.

FIGURE F-23

Scholarship Master List		

Scholarship Master List

ScholarshipName	DueDate	Amount
All Majors		
Achievement Community Scholarship	2/16/2013	$2,000.00
Alpha Kappa Alpha	3/30/2013	$1,000.00
Balanced Man Scholarship Sigma Phi	3/29/2014	$1,000.00
Delta Sigma Phi Fraternity at K-State Scholarship	3/26/2013	$500.00
Great Plains Associations of College Admissions Counseling	2/27/2013	$1,000.00
Hispanic Scholarship of Greater Kansas City	3/1/2014	$1,000.00
Kohl's Kids Who Care	3/13/2014	$1,000.00
Masonic Grand Lodge of AF & AM of Kansas	10/30/2013	$500.00

Visual Workshop

Open the Training-F.accdb database from the location where you store your Data Files, then enable content if prompted. In Query Design View, create a new select query with the DeptName field from the Departments table, the CourseCost field from the Courses table, and the Description field from the Courses table. (*Hint*: You will also have to add the Employees and Enrollments tables to Query Design View to build relationships from the Departments table to the Courses table.) Save the query with the name **DepartmentCrosstab**, then display it as a crosstab query, as shown in FIGURE F-24. Print the DepartmentCrosstab query if requested by your instructor, save and close it, then close the Training-F.accdb database.

FIGURE F-24

Description	Accounting	Engineering	Executive	Human Resc	Information	Legal	Marketing	Operations	Research	Shipping	Training	
Access Case Problems	$400.00	$200.00	$200.00			$600.00	$200.00	$200.00			$200.00	
Computer Fundamentals	$200.00	$200.00	$200.00	$400.00	$200.00	$800.00	$600.00		$400.00	$400.00	$400.00	
Dynamite Customer Service Skills			$100.00	$100.00	$100.00	$100.00	$200.00		$100.00			
Employee Benefits Made Clear		$50.00	$50.00	$100.00	$50.00	$150.00	$150.00	$50.00	$100.00	$100.00	$50.00	
Excel Case Problems	$200.00		$200.00	$200.00					$400.00	$200.00	$400.00	$200.00
Intermediate Access	$800.00	$400.00	$400.00			$1,200.00	$400.00	$400.00			$400.00	
Intermediate Excel	$400.00		$200.00	$200.00		$200.00		$400.00	$200.00	$400.00	$200.00	
Intermediate Internet Explorer	$400.00		$400.00	$400.00	$200.00	$800.00	$400.00	$200.00	$200.00	$200.00	$400.00	
Intermediate Phone Skills	$300.00		$150.00			$300.00		$300.00	$150.00		$150.00	
Intermediate PowerPoint	$400.00	$200.00	$200.00	$200.00		$600.00	$200.00	$200.00	$200.00	$200.00	$400.00	
Intermediate Tax Planning	$100.00		$100.00	$50.00	$50.00	$50.00		$50.00	$100.00	$100.00	$50.00	
Intermediate Windows			$200.00	$400.00	$200.00	$200.00	$400.00		$400.00	$400.00	$200.00	
Intermediate Word			$200.00	$200.00	$200.00	$200.00	$400.00		$200.00			
Internet Fundamentals		$200.00	$200.00	$400.00	$200.00	$600.00	$600.00		$400.00	$400.00	$400.00	
Introduction to Access	$400.00	$200.00	$200.00	$200.00		$600.00	$400.00	$200.00			$200.00	
Introduction to Excel	$400.00		$400.00	$200.00		$200.00		$400.00	$400.00	$400.00	$200.00	
Introduction to Insurance Planning	$150.00	$75.00	$75.00	$75.00		$225.00	$75.00	$75.00	$75.00	$150.00	$150.00	
Introduction to Internet Explorer	$400.00	$200.00	$400.00	$400.00	$200.00	$800.00	$600.00	$200.00	$400.00	$200.00	$400.00	
Introduction to Networking		$200.00	$200.00	$400.00	$200.00	$400.00	$600.00		$400.00	$400.00	$200.00	
Introduction to Outlook	$400.00	$200.00		$400.00		$600.00	$400.00	$400.00	$200.00	$400.00	$400.00	
Introduction to Phone Skills	$300.00	$150.00	$150.00			$450.00	$150.00	$300.00	$150.00	$150.00	$150.00	
Introduction to PowerPoint	$400.00	$200.00	$200.00	$400.00	$200.00	$800.00	$600.00	$200.00	$200.00	$200.00	$400.00	
Introduction to Project	$1,200.00	$800.00	$1,200.00	$400.00		$2,000.00	$1,600.00	$1,600.00	$1,200.00	$1,600.00	$1,200.00	
Introduction to Tax Planning	$100.00		$100.00	$50.00	$50.00	$100.00	$50.00	$50.00	$100.00	$100.00	$50.00	
Introduction to Windows		$200.00	$200.00	$400.00	$200.00	$600.00	$600.00	$200.00	$400.00	$400.00	$400.00	

Records: 1 of 31 — No Filter — Search

Improving Queries

Creating Macros

CASE Kayla Green, the network administrator at Quest Specialty Travel, has identified several Access tasks that are repeated on a regular basis. She has asked you to help her automate these processes with macros.

Unit Objectives

After completing this unit, you will be able to:

- Understand macros
- Create a macro
- Modify actions and arguments
- Assign a macro to a command button
- Use If statements
- Work with events
- Create a data macro
- Troubleshoot macros

Files You Will Need

Technology-M.accdb
Basketball-M.accdb

Patients-M.accdb
Chocolate-M.accdb

© Tumanyan/Shutterstock

Understand Macros

Learning Outcomes
• Describe the benefits of macros
• Define macro terminology
• Describe Macro Design View components

A **macro** is a database object that stores actions to complete Access tasks. Repetitive Access tasks such as printing several reports, or opening and maximizing a form, are good candidates for a macro. Automating routine tasks by using macros builds efficiency, accuracy, and flexibility into your database. **CASE** *You decide to study the major benefits of using macros, macro terminology, and the components of the Macro Design View before building your first macro.*

DETAILS

The major benefits of using macros include the following:

• Saving time by automating routine tasks
• Increasing accuracy by ensuring that tasks are executed consistently
• Improving the functionality and ease of use of forms by using macros connected to command buttons
• Ensuring data accuracy in forms by using macros to respond to data entry errors
• Automating data transfers such as collecting data from Excel
• Helping users by responding to their interactions within a form

Macro terminology:

• A **macro** is an Access object that stores a series of actions to perform one or more tasks.
• **Macro Design View** is the window in which you create a macro. FIGURE M-1 shows Macro Design View with an OpenForm action. See TABLE M-1 for a description of the Macro Design View components.
• Each task that you want the macro to perform is called an **action**. A macro may contain one or more actions.
• **Arguments** are properties of an action that provide additional information on how the action should execute.
• A **conditional expression** is an expression resulting in either a true or false answer that determines whether a macro action will execute. Conditional expressions are used in If statements.
• An **event** is something that happens to a form, window, toolbar, or control—such as the click of a command button or an entry in a field—that can be used to initiate the execution of a macro.
• A **submacro** is a collection of actions within a macro object that allows you to name and create multiple, separate macros within a single macro object.

TABLE M-1: **Macro Design View components**

component	description
Action Catalog	Lists all available macro actions organized by category. Use the Search box to narrow the number of macro actions to a particular subject.
If statement	Contains conditional expressions that are evaluated as either true or false. If true, the macro action is executed. If false, the macro action is skipped. If statements in Access 2013 may contain Else If and Else clauses.
Comment	Allows you to document the macro with explanatory text.
Arguments	Lists required and optional arguments for the selected action.
Run button	Runs the selected macro.
Expand and Collapse buttons	Allows you to expand or collapse the macro actions to show or hide their arguments.

Create a Macro

In Access, you create a macro by choosing a series of actions in Macro Design View that accomplishes the job you want to automate. Therefore, to become proficient with Access macros, you must be comfortable with macro actions. Some of the most common actions are listed in TABLE M-2. When you create a macro in other Microsoft Office products such as Word or Excel, you create Visual Basic for Applications (VBA) statements. In Access, macros do not create VBA code, though after creating a macro, you can convert it to VBA if desired. **CASE** Kayla observes that users want to open the AllEquipment report from the Employees form, so she asks you to create a macro to help automate this task.

STEPS

TROUBLE
If you do not enable content, your macros will not run.

1. **Start Access, open the Technology-M.accdb database from the location where you store your Data Files, enable content if prompted, click the CREATE tab, then click the Macro button**
 Macro Design View opens, ready for you to choose your first action.

TROUBLE
If you choose the wrong macro action, click the Delete button ☒ in the upper-right corner of the macro action block and try again.

2. **Click the Action list arrow, type op to quickly scroll to the actions that start with the letters *op*, then scroll and click OpenReport**
 The OpenReport action is now the first action in the macro, and the arguments that further define the OpenReport action appear in the action block. The **action block** organizes all of the arguments for a current action and is visually highlighted with a rectangle and gray background. You can expand or collapse the action block to view or hide details by clicking the Collapse/Expand button to the left of the action name or the Expand and Collapse buttons on the DESIGN tab in Macro Design View.

 The **OpenReport action** has three required arguments: Report Name, View, and Window Mode. View and Window Mode have default values, but the word *Required* is shown in the Report Name argument, indicating that you must select a choice. The Filter Name and Where Condition arguments are optional as indicated by their blank boxes.

QUICK TIP
Hover over any macro action or argument to see a ScreenTip of information about that item.

3. **Click the Report Name argument list arrow, then click AllEquipment**
 All of the report objects in the Technology-M.accdb database appear in the Report Name argument list, making it easy to choose the report you want.

4. **Click the View argument list arrow, then click Print Preview**
 Your screen should look like FIGURE M-2. Macros can contain one or many actions. In this case, the macro has only one action.

5. **Click the Save button 🖫 on the Quick Access toolbar, type PreviewAllEquipmentReport in the Macro Name text box, click OK, right-click the PreviewAllEquipmentReport macro tab, then click Close**
 The Navigation Pane lists the PreviewAllEquipmentReport object in the Macros group.

QUICK TIP
To print Macro Design View, click the FILE tab, click Print, click the Print button, then click OK in the Print Macro Definition dialog box.

6. **Double-click the PreviewAllEquipmentReport macro in the Navigation Pane to run the macro**
 The AllEquipment report opens in Print Preview.

7. **Close the AllEquipment report**

FIGURE M-2: Macro Design View with OpenReport action

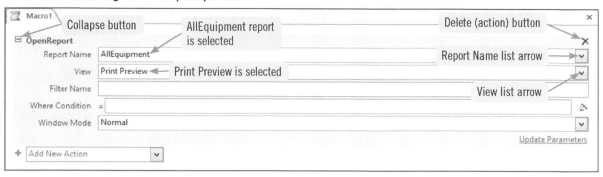

TABLE M-2: Common macro actions

subject area	macro action	description
Data Entry Operations	DeleteRecord	Deletes the current record
	SaveRecord	Saves the current record
Data Import/Export	ImportExportSpreadsheet*	Imports or exports the spreadsheet you specify
	ImportExportText*	Imports or exports the text file you specify
	EMailDatabaseObject	Sends the specified database object through Outlook with specified email settings
Database Objects	GoToControl	Moves the focus (where you are currently typing or clicking) to a specific field or control
	GoToRecord	Makes a specified record the current record
	OpenForm	Opens a form in Form View, Design View, Print Preview, or Datasheet View
	OpenReport	Opens a report in Design View or Print Preview, or prints the report
	OpenTable	Opens a table in Datasheet View, Design View, or Print Preview
	SetValue*	Sets the value of a field, control, or property
Filter/Query/Search	ApplyFilter	Restricts the number of records that appear in the resulting form or report by applying limiting criteria
	FindRecord	Finds the first record that meets the criteria
	OpenQuery	Opens a select or crosstab query; runs an action query
Macro Commands	RunCode	Runs a Visual Basic function (a series of programming statements that do a calculation or comparison and return a value)
	RunMacro	Runs a macro or attaches a macro to a custom menu command
	StopMacro	Stops the currently running macro
System Commands	Beep	Sounds a beep tone through the computer's speaker
	PrintOut*	Prints the active object, such as a datasheet, report, form, or module
	SendKeys*	Sends keystrokes directly to Microsoft Access or to an active Windows application
User Interface Commands	MessageBox	Displays a message box containing a warning or an informational message
	ShowToolbar*	Displays or hides a given toolbar
Window Management	CloseWindow	Closes a window
	MaximizeWindow	Enlarges the active window to fill the Access window

*Must click Show All Actions button on Ribbon for these actions to appear.

Modify Actions and Arguments

Macros can contain as many actions as necessary to complete the process that you want to automate. Each action is evaluated in the order in which it appears in Macro Design View, starting at the top. Whereas some macro actions open, close, preview, or export data or objects, others are used only to make the database easier to use. **MessageBox** is a useful macro action because it displays an informational message to the user. **CASE** ▶ *You add a MessageBox action to the PreviewAllEquipmentReport macro to display a descriptive message in a dialog box.*

STEPS

1. **Right-click the PreviewAllEquipmentReport macro in the Navigation Pane, then click Design View on the shortcut menu**

 The PreviewAllEquipmentReport macro opens in Macro Design View.

2. **Click the Add New Action list arrow, type me to quickly scroll to the actions that start with the letters *me*, then click MessageBox**

 Each action has its own arguments that further clarify what the action does.

3. **Click the Message argument text box in the action block, then type Click the Print button to print this report**

 The Message argument determines what text appears in the message box. By default, the Beep argument is set to "Yes" and the Type argument is set to "None."

4. **Click the Type argument list arrow in the action block, then click Information**

 The Type argument determines which icon appears in the dialog box that is created by the MessageBox action.

5. **Click the Title argument text box in the action block, then type To print this report. . .**

 Your screen should look like FIGURE M-3. The Title argument specifies what text is displayed in the title bar of the resulting dialog box. If you leave the Title argument empty, the title bar of the resulting dialog box displays "Microsoft Access."

6. **Save the macro, then click the Run button in the Tools group**

 If your speakers are turned on, you should hear a beep, then the message box appears, as shown in FIGURE M-4.

7. **Click OK in the dialog box, close the AllEquipment report, then save and close Macro Design View**

Creating Macros

Assigning a macro to a key combination

You can assign a key combination such as [Shift][Ctrl][L] to a macro by creating a macro with the name **AutoKeys**. Enter the key combination as the submacro name. Use + for Shift, % for Alt, and ^ for Ctrl. Enclose special keys such as F3 in {curly braces}. For example, to assign a macro to [Shift][Ctrl][L], use +^L as the submacro name. To assign a macro to [Shift][F3], use +{F3} as the submacro name. Any key combination assignments you make in the AutoKeys macro override those that Access has already specified. Therefore, check the Keyboard Shortcuts information in the Microsoft Access Help system to make sure that the AutoKey assignment that you are creating doesn't override an existing Access quick keystroke that may be used for another purpose.

Assign a Macro to a Command Button

Access provides many ways to run a macro: clicking the Run button in Macro Design View, assigning the macro to a command button, or assigning the macro to a ribbon or shortcut menu command. Assigning a macro to a command button on a form provides a very intuitive way for the user to access the macro's functionality. **CASE** ▶ *You decide to modify the Employees form to include a command button that runs the PreviewAllEquipmentReport macro.*

STEPS

1. **Right-click the** Employees form **in the Navigation Pane, click** Design View, **expand the** Form Footer **about 0.5", click the** Button button ⌧ **in the Controls group, then click the** left side of the Form Footer section

 The **Command Button Wizard** starts, presenting you with 28 actions on the right organized within six categories on the left. For example, if you want the command button to open a report, you choose the OpenReport action in the Report Operations category. In this case, you want to run the PreviewAllEquipmentReport macro, which not only opens a report, but also presents a message. The Miscellaneous category contains an action that allows you to run an existing macro.

2. **Click** Miscellaneous **in the Categories list, click** Run Macro **in the Actions list, as shown in** FIGURE M-5, **click** Next, **click** PreviewAllEquipmentReport, **click** Next, **click the** Text option **button, select** Run Macro, **type** All Equipment Report, **then click** Next

 The Command Button Wizard asks you to give the button a meaningful name. When assigning names, a common three-character prefix for command buttons is **cmd**.

3. **Type** cmdAllEquipment, **click** Finish, **then click the** Property Sheet button **in the Tools group to open the Property Sheet for the command button**

 The new command button that runs a macro has been added to the Employees form in Form Design View. You work with the Property Sheet to change the text color to differentiate it from the button color as well as to examine how the macro was attached to the command button.

4. **Click the** Format tab **in the Property Sheet, scroll down and click the** Fore Color list arrow, **click** Text Dark, **then click the** Event tab **in the Property Sheet, noting that the On Click property contains [Embedded Macro]**

 The PreviewAllEquipmentReport macro was attached to the **On Click property** of this command button. In other words, the macro is run when the user clicks the command button. To make sure that the new command button works as intended, you view the form in Form View and test the command button.

5. **Close the Property Sheet, click the** View button ▦ **to switch to Form View, click the** All Equipment Report command button **in the Form Footer section, click** OK **in the message box, then close the AllEquipment report**

 The Employees form with the new command button should look like FIGURE M-6. It's common to put command buttons in the Form Footer so that users have a consistent location to find them.

6. **Save and close the Employees form**

FIGURE M-5: Adding a command button to run a macro

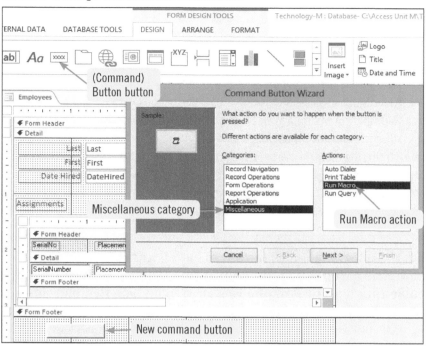

FIGURE M-6: Employees form with new command button

Using a trusted database and setting up a trusted folder

A **trusted database** allows you to run macros and VBA. By default, a database is not trusted. To trust a database, click the Enable Content button on the Security Warning bar each time you open a database. To permanently trust a database, store the database in a **trusted folder**. To create a trusted folder, open the Options dialog box from the FILE tab, click the Trust Center, click the Trust Center Settings button, click the Trusted Locations option, click the Add new location button, then browse to and choose the folder you want to trust.

Creating Macros

Use If Statements

Learning Outcomes
• Apply If statements to macros
• Enter conditional expressions

An **If statement** allows you to run macro actions based on the result of a conditional expression. A **conditional expression** is an expression such as [Price]>100 or [StateName]="MO" that results in a true or false value. If the condition evaluates true, the actions that follow the If statement are executed. If the condition evaluates false, the macro skips those actions. When building a conditional expression that refers to a value in a control on a form or report, use the following syntax: [Forms]![*formname*]![*controlname*] or [Reports]![*reportname*]![*controlname*]. Separating the object type (Forms or Reports) from the object name and from the control name by using [square brackets] and exclamation points (!) is called **bang notation.** **CASE** ▸ *At Quest Specialty Travel, everyone who has been with the company longer than five years is eligible to take their old PC equipment home as soon as it has been replaced. You use a conditional macro to help evaluate and present this information in a form.*

STEPS

1. **Click the CREATE tab, click the Macro button, click the Action Catalog button in the Show/Hide group to toggle on the Action Catalog window if it is not already visible, double-click If in the Program Flow area, then type the following in the If box:** [Forms]![Employees]![DateHired]<Date()-(5*365)

 The conditional expression shown in FIGURE M-7 says, "Check the value in the DateHired control on the Employees form and evaluate true if the value is earlier than 5 years from today. Evaluate false if the value is not earlier than 5 years ago."

TROUBLE
Be sure to click the Add New Action list arrow *in the If block.*

2. **Click the Add New Action list arrow in the If block, then scroll and click SetProperty**

 The **SetProperty** action has three arguments: Control Name, Property, and Value, which set the control, property, and value of that property.

3. **Click the Control Name argument text box in the Action Arguments pane, type LabelPCProgram, click the Property argument list arrow, click Visible, click the Value Property argument, then type True**

 Your screen should look like FIGURE M-8. The **Control Name** argument for the label is set to LabelPCProgram, which must match the **Name property** in the Property Sheet of the label that will be modified. The **Property argument** determines what property is being modified for the LabelPCProgram control. In this case, you are modifying the Visible property. The **Value argument** determines the value of the **Visible property**. For properties such as the Visible property that have only two choices in the Property Sheet, Yes or No, you enter a value of False for No and True for Yes.

4. **Save the macro with the name 5YearsPC, then close Macro Design View**

 Test the macro using the Employees form.

TROUBLE
Be sure Juan Ramirez with a hire date of 8/5/2005 is the current record.

5. **In the Navigation Pane, double-click the Employees form to open it**

 The record for Juan Ramirez, hired 8/5/2005, appears. Given that Juan has worked at Quest much longer than 5 years, you anticipate that the macro will display the label when it is run.

TROUBLE
Be sure the insertion point is in the main form when you run the 5YearsPC macro so it can find all of the controls to which it refers.

6. **Click the DATABASE TOOLS tab, click the Run Macro button, verify that 5YearsPC is in the Macro Name text box, then click OK**

 After evaluating the DateHired field of this record and determining that this employee has been working at Quest Specialty Travel longer than five years, the LabelPCProgram label's Visible property was set to Yes, as shown in FIGURE M-9. The LabelPCProgram label's **Caption property** is "Eligible for PC Program!"

7. **Navigate through several records and note that the label remains visible for each employee even though the hire date may not be longer than 5 years ago**

 Because the macro only ran once, the label's Visible property remains Yes regardless of the current data in the DateHired field. You need a way to rerun or trigger the macro to evaluate the data in the DateHired field for each employee.

8. **Close the Employees form**

FIGURE M-7: Using an If statement to set a control's Visible property

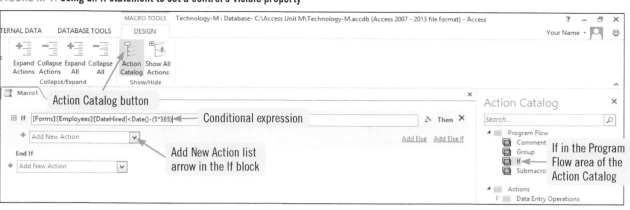

FIGURE M-8: Entering arguments for the SetProperty action

FIGURE M-9: Running the 5YearsPC macro

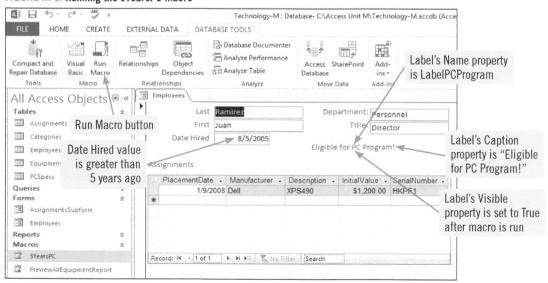

Work with Events

An **event** is a specific activity that occurs within the database, such as clicking a command button, moving from record to record, editing data, or opening or closing a form. Events can be triggered by the user or by the database itself. By assigning a macro to an appropriate event rather than running the macro from the DATABASE TOOLS tab or command button, you further automate and improve your database. **CASE** *You need to modify the 5YearsPC macro so that it evaluates the DateHired field to display or hide the label as you move from record to record.*

STEPS

1. **Right-click the 5YearsPC macro in the Navigation Pane, click Design View on the shortcut menu, click anywhere in the If block to activate it, then click the Add Else link in the lower-right corner of the If block**

 The **Else** portion of an If statement allows you to run a different set of macro actions if the conditional expression evaluates False. In this case, you want to set the Value of the Visible property to False if the conditional expression evaluates False (if the DateHired is less than five years from today's date) so that the label does not appear if the employee is not eligible for the PC program.

2. **Right-click the SetProperty action block, click Copy, right-click the Else block, click Paste, select True in the Value property, then type False, as shown in** FIGURE M-10

 With the second action edited, the macro will now turn the label's Visible property to True (Yes) *or* False (No), depending on DateHired value. To make the macro run each time you move to a new employee record, you attach the macro to the event that is triggered as you move from record to record.

3. **Save and close the 5YearsPC macro, right-click the Employees form in the Navigation Pane, click Design View, then click the Property Sheet button**

 All objects, sections, and controls have a variety of events to which macros can be attached. Most event names are self-explanatory, such as the **On Click event** (which occurs when that item is clicked).

4. **Click the Event tab in the Property Sheet, click the On Current list arrow, then click 5YearsPC**

 Your Property Sheet should look like FIGURE M-11. Because the **On Current event** occurs when focus moves from one record to another, the 5YearsPC macro will automatically run each time you move from record to record in the form. Test your new macro by moving through several records in Form View.

5. **Close the Property Sheet, click the View button ▦ to switch to Form View, then click the Next record button ▶ in the navigation bar for the main form several times while observing the Eligible for PC Program! label**

 For every DateHired value that is earlier than five years before today's date, the Eligible for PC Program! label is visible. If the DateHired is less than five years before today's date, the label is hidden.

6. **Save and close the Employees form**

Right-click SetProperty action to copy and paste it to the Else block

Else block

Change Value from True to False in Else block

Choose Form if not already selected

On Current event

5YearsPC macro attached to On Current event of form

Access 2013

Create a Data Macro

A **data macro** allows you to embed macro capabilities directly in a table to add, change, or delete data based on conditions you specify. Data macros are a new feature of Access 2013. Data macros are managed directly from within tables, and do not appear in the Macros group in the Navigation Pane. You most often run a data macro based on a table event, such as modifying data or deleting a record, but you can run a data macro separately as well, similar to how you run a regular macro. **CASE** *Quest Specialty Travel grants 10 days of regular vacation to all employees except for those in the Africa and Asia departments, who receive 15 days due to the extra travel requirements of their positions. Kayla asks you to figure out an automatic way to assign each employee the correct number of vacation days based on their department. A data macro will work well for this task.*

STEPS

1. **Double-click the** Employees table **in the Navigation Pane, then observe the Vacation field throughout the datasheet**

 Currently, the Vacation field contains the value of 10 for each record, or each employee.

2. **Right-click the** Employees table tab**, click** Design View **on the shortcut menu, click the** Create Data Macros button **in the Field, Record & Table Events group, click** After Insert**, then click the** Action Catalog button **in the Show/Hide group if the Action Catalog window is not already open**

 In this case, you chose the After Insert event, which is run after a new record is entered. See **TABLE M-3** for more information on table events. Creating a data macro is very similar to creating a regular macro. You add the logic and macro actions needed to complete the task at hand.

3. **Double-click** ForEachRecord **in the Action Catalog to add a For Each Record In block, click the** For Each Record In list arrow**, click** Employees **in the list, click the** Where Condition text box**, type** [Department]="Africa" or [Department]="Asia"**, double-click the** EditRecord data block **in the Action Catalog, double-click the** SetField data action **in the Action Catalog, click the** Name box **in the SetField block, type** Vacation**, click the** Value box **in the SetField block, then type** 15**, as shown in** FIGURE M-12

 The Default value for the Vacation field is set to 10 in Table Design View of the Employees table so all existing records should have a value of 10 in the Vacation field. Test the new data macro by adding a new record.

4. **Click the** Close button**, click** Yes **when prompted to save changes, click the** View button ▦ **to display the datasheet, click** Yes **when prompted to save changes, click the** New button **in the Records group, enter the new record, as shown in** FIGURE M-13**, except do not enter a Vacation value, then press** [Tab] **to move to a new record**

 The macro is triggered by the After Insert event of the record, and the Vacation field is automatically updated to 15 for the new record and all other records with Asia or Africa in the Department field, as shown in **FIGURE M-13**.

5. **Right-click the** Employees table tab**, then click** Close **on the shortcut menu**

 Data is automatically saved when you move from record to record or close a database object.

FIGURE M-12: Creating a data macro

FIGURE M-13: Running a data macro

TABLE M-3: Table events

table event	runs...
After Insert	...after a new record has been inserted into the table
After Update	...after an existing record has been changed
After Delete	...after an existing record has been deleted
Before Delete	...before a record is deleted, to help the user validate or cancel the deletion
Before Change	...before a record is changed, to help the user validate or cancel the edits

Access 2013

Troubleshoot Macros

Learning Outcomes
- Single step a macro
- Describe debugging techniques

When macros don't run properly, Access supplies several tools to debug them. **Debugging** means determining why the macro doesn't run correctly. It usually involves breaking down a dysfunctional macro into smaller pieces that can be individually tested. For example, you can **single step** a macro, which means to run it one action at a time to observe the effect of each specific action in the Macro Single Step dialog box. **CASE** *You use the PreviewAllEquipmentReport macro to learn debugging techniques.*

STEPS

1. **Right-click the** PreviewAllEquipmentReport macro, **click** Design View **on the shortcut menu, click the** Single Step button **in the Tools group, then click the** Run button

 The screen should look like FIGURE M-14, with the Macro Single Step dialog box open. This dialog box displays information including the macro's name, the action's name, and the action's arguments. From the Macro Single Step dialog box, you can step into the next macro action, halt execution of the macro, or continue running the macro without single stepping.

2. **Click** Step **in the Macro Single Step dialog box**

 Stepping into the second action lets the first action run and pauses the macro at the second action. The Macro Single Step dialog box now displays information about the second action.

3. **Click** Step

 The second action, the MessageBox action, is executed, which displays the message box.

4. **Click** OK, **then close the** AllEquipment report

5. **Click the** DESIGN tab, **then click the** Single Step button **to toggle it off**

 Another technique to help troubleshoot macros is to use the built-in prompts and Help system provided by Microsoft Access. For example, you may have questions about how to use the optional Filter Name argument for the OpenReport macro action.

6. **Click the** OpenReport action block, **then point to the** Filter Name argument **to view the ScreenTip that supplies information about that argument, as shown in** FIGURE M-15

 The Access 2013 Macro Design View window has been improved with interactive prompts.

7. **Save and close the** PreviewAllEquipmentReport macro, **close the** Technology-M.accdb **database, then exit Access**

Access 2013

Practice

Concepts Review

Identify each element of Macro Design View shown in FIGURE M-16.

FIGURE M-16

Match each term with the statement that best describes its function.

8. Macro
9. Action
10. Argument
11. Event
12. Debugging
13. Conditional expression

a. Specific action that occurs within the database, such as clicking a button or opening a form
b. Part of an If statement that evaluates as either true or false
c. Individual step that you want the Access macro to perform
d. Access object that stores one or more actions that perform one or more tasks
e. Provides additional information to define how an Access action will perform
f. Determines why a macro doesn't run properly

Select the best answer from the list of choices.

14. **Which of the following is *not* a major benefit of using a macro?**
 a. To make the database more flexible or easy to use
 b. To ensure consistency in executing routine or complex tasks
 c. To redesign the relationships among the tables of the database
 d. To save time by automating routine tasks

15. **Which of the following best describes the process of creating an Access macro?**
 a. Open Macro Design View and add actions, arguments, and If statements to accomplish the desired task.
 b. Use the single step recorder to record clicks and keystrokes as you complete a task.
 c. Use the macro recorder to record clicks and keystrokes as you complete a task.
 d. Use the Macro Wizard to determine which tasks are done most frequently.

16. **Which of the following would *not* be a way to run a macro?**
 a. Double-click a macro action within the Macro Design View window.
 b. Click the Run Macro button on the DATABASE TOOLS tab.
 c. Assign the macro to a command button on a form.
 d. Assign the macro to an event of a control on a form.

17. **Which of the following is *not* a reason to run a macro in single step mode?**

 a. You want to observe the effect of each macro action individually.

 b. You want to debug a macro that isn't working properly.

 c. You want to run only a few of the actions of a macro.

 d. You want to change the arguments of a macro while it runs.

18. **Which of the following is *not* true of conditional expressions in If statements in macros?**

 a. Macro If statements provide for Else and Else If clauses.

 b. Conditional expressions allow you to skip over actions when the expression evaluates as false.

 c. Conditional expressions give the macro more power and flexibility.

 d. More macro actions are available when you are also using conditional expressions.

19. **Which example illustrates the proper syntax to refer to a specific control on a form?**

 a. [Forms] ! [*formname*] ! [*controlname*] **c.** {Forms} ! {formname} ! (controlname)

 b. Forms ! formname. controlname **d.** (Forms) ! (formname) ! (controlname)

20. **Which event is executed every time you move from record to record in a form?**

 a. Next Record **c.** New Record

 b. On Current **d.** On Move

Skills Review

1. **Understand macros.**

 a. Start Access, then open the Basketball-M.accdb database from the location where you store your Data Files. Enable content if prompted.

 b. Open the PrintMacroGroup macro in Macro Design View, then record your answers to the following questions on a sheet of paper:

 • What is the name of the first submacro?

 • How many macro actions are in the first submacro?

 • What arguments does the first action in the first submacro contain?

 • What values were chosen for these arguments?

 c. Close Macro Design View for the PrintMacroGroup object.

2. **Create a macro.**

 a. Start a new macro in Macro Design View.

 b. Add the OpenQuery action.

 c. Select PlayerStats as the value for the Query Name argument.

 d. Select Datasheet for the View argument.

 e. Select Edit for the Data Mode argument.

 f. Save the macro with the name **ViewPlayerStats**.

 g. Run the macro to make sure it works, close the PlayerStats query, then close the ViewPlayerStats macro.

3. **Modify actions and arguments.**

 a. Open the ViewPlayerStats macro in Macro Design View.

 b. Add a MessageBox action as the second action of the query.

 c. Type **We had a great season!** for the Message argument.

 d. Select Yes for the Beep argument.

 e. Select Warning! for the Type argument.

 f. Type **Iowa State Cyclones** for the Title argument.

 g. Save the macro, then run it to make sure the MessageBox action works as intended.

 h. Click OK in the dialog box created by the MessageBox action, close the PlayerStats query, then close the ViewPlayerStats macro.

 i. Open the PrintMacroGroup macro object in Design View.

 j. Modify the View argument for the OpenReport object of the PlayerStatistics submacro from Print to **Print Preview**.

Skills Review (continued)

k. Modify the Message argument for the MessageBox object of the PlayerStatistics submacro to read **Click the Print button to send this report to the printer.**

l. Save and close the PrintMacroGroup macro.

4. Assign a macro to a command button.

a. In Design View of the PlayerEntryForm, use the Command Button Wizard to add a command button below the existing Print Current Record button. The new button should run the PlayerStatistics submacro in the PrintMacroGroup macro (PrintMacroGroup.PlayerStatistics).

b. The text on the button should read **View Player Statistics**.

c. The meaningful name for the button should be **cmdPlayerStatistics**.

d. Test the command button in Form View, click OK in the message box, then close the PlayerStats report.

e. Save and close the PlayerEntryForm.

5. Use If statements.

a. Start a new macro in Macro Design View, and open the Action Catalog window if it is not already open.

b. Double-click If in the Action Catalog window to add an If block to the macro.

c. Enter the following condition in the If box: **[Forms]![GameSummaryForm]![CycloneScore]> [OpponentScore]**.

d. Add the SetProperty action to the If block.

e. Type **VictoryLabel** in the Control Name box for the SetProperty action.

f. Select Visible for the Property argument for the SetProperty action.

g. Enter **True** for the Value argument for the SetProperty action to indicate Yes.

h. Click the Add Else link in the lower-right corner of the If block.

i. Copy the existing SetProperty action, then paste it under the Else clause.

j. Modify the Value property from True to **False** for the second SetProperty action.

k. Save the macro with the name **VictoryCalculator**, compare it with FIGURE M-17, make any necessary adjustments, then close Macro Design View.

6. Work with events.

a. Open the GameSummaryForm in Form Design View.

b. Open the Property Sheet for the form.

c. Assign the VictoryCalculator macro to the On Current event of the form.

d. Close the Property Sheet, save the form, then open the GameSummaryForm in Form View.

e. Navigate through the first four records. The Victory label should be visible for the first three records, but not the fourth.

f. Add your name as a label in the Form Footer section to identify your printouts, print the third and fourth records if requested by your instructor, then save and close the GameSummaryForm.

7. Create a data macro.

a. Open the Games table in Table Design View.

b. Add a field named **RoadWin** with a Yes/No data type and the following Description: **Enter Yes if the Home-Away field is Away and the CycloneScore is greater than the OpponentScore**.

c. Save the Games table and switch to Datasheet View to note that the RoadWin check box is empty (No) for every record.

d. Switch back to Table Design View, then create a data macro based on the After Insert event.

e. Insert a ForEachRecord data block, and specify **Games** for the For Each Record In argument.

f. The Where Condition should be: **[Home-Away]="A" and [CycloneScore]>[OpponentScore]**.

g. Add an EditRecord data block in the For Each Record In block, and a SetField data action. Be careful to add the EditRecord block *within* the For Each Record Block.

FIGURE M-17

Skills Review (continued)

h. Enter **RoadWin** in the Name argument and **Yes** in the Value argument, as shown in FIGURE M-18.

i. Save and close the data macro, save the Games table, switch to Datasheet View, then test the new data macro by entering a new record in the Games table as follows:
Opponent: **Tulsa**
Mascot: **Hurricanes**
Home-Away: **A**
CycloneScore: **100**
OpponentScore: **50**
GameDate: **3/1/2015**

FIGURE M-18

j. Tab to a new record. Six records where the Home-Away field is set to "A" and the CycloneScore is greater than the OpponentScore should be checked. Close the Games table.

8. Troubleshoot macros.

a. Open the PrintMacroGroup in Macro Design View.

b. Click the Single Step button, then click the Run button.

c. Click Step twice to step through the two actions of the submacro, PlayerStatistics, then click OK in the resulting message box.

d. Close the PlayerStats report.

e. Return to Macro Design View of the PrintMacroGroup macro, and click the Single Step button on the DESIGN tab to toggle off this feature.

f. Save and close the PrintMacroGroup macro, close the Basketball-M.accdb database, then exit Access.

Independent Challenge 1

As the manager of a doctor's clinic, you have created an Access database called Patients-M.accdb to track insurance claim reimbursements. You use macros to help automate the database.

a. Start Access, then open the database Patients-M.accdb from the location where you store your Data Files. Enable content if prompted.

b. Open Macro Design View of the CPT Form Open macro. (CPT stands for Current Procedural Terminology, which is a code that describes a medical procedure.) If the Single Step button is toggled on, click it to toggle it off.

c. On a separate sheet of paper, identify the macro actions, arguments for each action, and values for each argument.

d. In two or three sentences, explain in your own words what tasks this macro automates.

e. Close the CPT Form Open macro.

f. Open the Claim Entry Form in Form Design View.

g. In the Form Footer of the Claim Entry Form are several command buttons. Open the Property Sheet of the Add CPT Code button, then click the Event tab.

h. On your paper, write the event to which the CPT Form Open macro is assigned.

i. Open the Claim Entry Form in Form View, then click the Add CPT Code button in the Form Footer.

j. On your paper, write the current record number that is displayed for you.

k. Close the Patients-M.accdb database, then exit Access.

Independent Challenge 2

As the manager of a doctor's clinic, you have created an Access database called Patients-M.accdb to track insurance claim reimbursements. You use macros to help automate the database.

a. Start Access, then open the database Patients-M.accdb from the location where you store your Data Files. Enable content if prompted.

b. Start a new macro in Macro Design View, and open the Action Catalog window if it is not already open.

Independent Challenge 2 (continued)

c. Double-click the Submacro entry in the Program Flow folder to add a submacro block.

d. Type **Preview Date of Service Denied Report** as the first submacro name, then add the OpenReport macro action.

e. Select Date of Service Report - Denied for the Report Name argument, then select Print Preview for the View argument of the OpenReport action.

f. Double-click the Submacro entry in the Program Flow folder to add another submacro block.

g. Type **Preview Date of Service Fixed Report** as a new submacro name, then add the OpenReport macro action.

h. Select Date of Service Report - Fixed for the ReportName argument, then select Print Preview for the View argument of the second OpenReport action.

i. Save the macro with the name **Preview Group**, then close Macro Design View.

j. Using the Run Macro button on the DATABASE TOOLS tab, run the Preview Group.Preview Date of Service Denied Report macro to test it, then close Print Preview.

k. Using the Run Macro button on the DATABASE TOOLS tab, run the Preview Group.Preview Date of Service Fixed Report macro to test it, then close Print Preview.

FIGURE M-19

l. Open the Preview Group macro in Macro Design View, then click the Collapse buttons to the left of the Submacro statements to collapse the two submacro blocks.

m. Create two more submacros, one that previews Monthly Claims Report - Denied and the other that previews Monthly Claims Report - Fixed. Name the two macros **Preview Monthly Denied Report** and **Preview Monthly Fixed Report**, as shown in FIGURE M-19.

n. Save and close the Preview Group macro.

o. In Design View of the Claim Line Items Subform, add four separate command buttons to the Form Footer to run the four submacros in the Preview Group macro. Use the captions and meaningful names of **Date Denied** and **cmdDateDenied**, **Date Fixed** and **cmdDateFixed**, **Monthly Denied** and **cmdMonthlyDenied**, and **Monthly Fixed** and **cmdMonthlyFixed** to correspond with the four submacros in the Preview Group macro.

p. Change the font color on the new command buttons to black.

q. Select all four new command buttons and use the Size/Space and Align commands on the ARRANGE tab to precisely size, align, and space the buttons equally in the Form Footer section.

r. Save and close the Claim Line Items Subform, then open the Claim Entry Form in Form View, as shown in FIGURE M-20. Test each of the new command buttons to make sure it opens the correct report.

s. Close the Claim Entry Form, close the Patients-M.accdb database, then exit Access

FIGURE M-20

Independent Challenge 3

As the manager of a doctor's clinic, you have created an Access database called Patients-M.accdb to track insurance claim reimbursements. You use macros to help automate the database.

a. Start Access, then open the Patients-M.accdb database from the location where you store your Data Files. Enable content if prompted.

b. Start a new macro in Macro Design View, then add an If statement.

Independent Challenge 3 (continued)

c. Enter the following in the If box: **[Forms]![CPT Form]![RBRVS]=0**.

d. Select the SetProperty action for the first action in the If block.

e. Enter the following arguments for the SetProperty action: Control Name: **ResearchLabel**, Property: **Visible**, and Value: **True**.

f. Click the Add Else link.

g. Select the SetProperty action for the first action of the Else clause.

h. Enter the following arguments for the SetProperty action: Control Name: **ResearchLabel**, Property: **Visible**, and Value: **False**.

i. Save the macro with the name **Research**, as shown in FIGURE M-21, then close Macro Design View.

j. Open the CPT Form in Form Design View, then open the Property Sheet for the form.

k. Assign the Research macro to the On Current event of the form.

l. Close the Property Sheet, save the form, then open the CPT Form in Form View.

m. Use the Next record button to move quickly through all 64 records in the form. Notice that the macro displays Research! only when the RBRVS value is equal to zero.

n. Save and close the CPT Form, then close the Patients-M.accdb database.

FIGURE M-21

Independent Challenge 4: Explore

You are collecting information on international chocolate factories, museums, and stores in an Access database. You tie the forms together with macros attached to command buttons.

a. Open the Chocolate-M.accdb database from the location where you store your Data Files, enable content if prompted, then open the Countries form in Form View. The database option to show overlapping windows versus tabbed documents has been set. Overlapping windows allows you to restore and size windows.

b. Click the New (blank) record button for the main form, then type **Poland** in the Country text box.

c. In the subform for the Poland record, enter **Cadbury-Wedel Polska** in the Name field, **F** in the Type field (F for factory), **Praga** in the City field, and **Lodz** in the StateProvince field. Close the Countries form. If you want the windows of this database to be maximized when you open them, you can accomplish this with a macro attached to the On Load event of the form.

d. Open Macro Design View for a new macro, then add the MaximizeWindow action. Save the macro with the name **Maximize**, then close it. The Maximize macro helps you maximize windows if a database option is set to Overlapping Windows. To see this setting, click the FILE tab, click Options, click Current Database, and then view the settings in the Document Window Options section. When Tabbed Documents is selected, the windows are automatically maximized and tabs are provided at the top of each window to help you navigate between them. When Overlapping Windows is selected, however, windows can be any size.

e. Open the Countries form in Design View, add the Maximize macro to the On Load event of the Countries form, then open the Countries form in Form View to test it.

f. Save and close the Countries form.

g. Add the Maximize macro to the On Load event of the Places of Interest report, then open the Places of Interest report in Print Preview to test it.

h. Save and close the Places of Interest report.

i. Close the Chocolate-M.accdb database, then exit Access.

Visual Workshop

As the manager of a doctor's clinic, you have created an Access database called Patients-M.accdb to track insurance claim reimbursements. Develop a new macro called **Query Group** with the actions and argument values shown in FIGURE M-22. Run both macros to test them by using the Run Macro button on the DATABASE TOOLS tab, and debug the macros if necessary.

FIGURE M-22

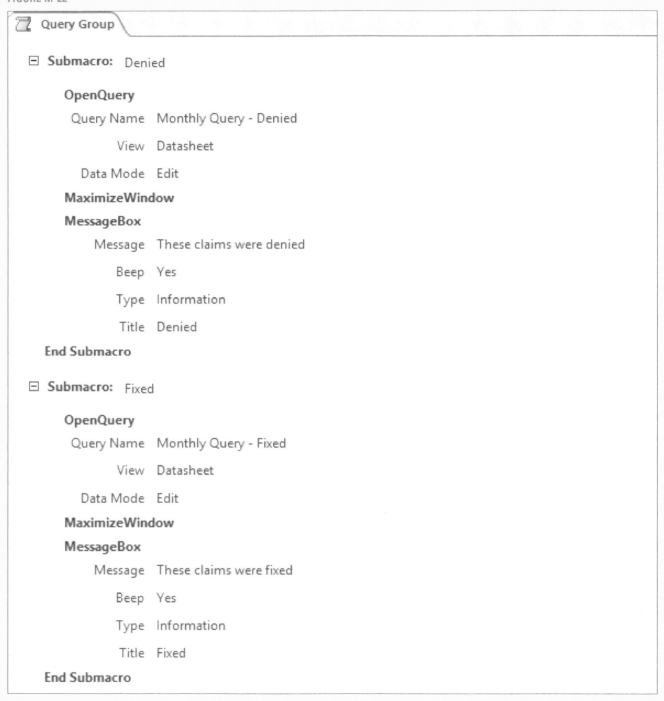

Creating Modules and VBA

CASE ▶ You want to learn about VBA and create modules to enhance the capabilities of the Technology-N database for Quest Specialty Travel.

Unit Objectives

After completing this unit, you will be able to:

- Understand modules and VBA
- Compare macros and modules
- Create functions
- Use If statements

- Document procedures
- Build class modules
- Modify sub procedures
- Troubleshoot modules

Files You Will Need

Technology-N.accdb
Baseball-N.accdb

Patients-N.accdb
Basketball-N.accdb

© Tumanyan/Shutterstock

Understand Modules and VBA

Access is a robust and easy-to-use relational database program. Access provides user-friendly tools, such as wizards and Design Views, to help users quickly create reports and forms that previously took programmers hours to build. You may, however, want to automate a task or create a new function that goes beyond the capabilities of the built-in Access tools. Within each program of the Microsoft Office suite, a programming language called **Visual Basic for Applications (VBA)** is provided to help you extend the program's capabilities. In Access, VBA is stored within modules. A **module** is an Access object that stores Visual Basic for Applications (VBA) programming code. VBA is written in the **Visual Basic Editor (VBE)**, shown in FIGURE N-1. The components and text colors of the VBE are described in TABLE N-1. An Access database has two kinds of modules. **Standard modules** contain global code that can be executed from anywhere in the database. Standard modules are displayed as module objects in the Navigation Pane. **Class modules** are stored within the form or report object itself. Class modules contain VBA code used only within that particular form or report. **CASE** ▶ *Before working with modules, you ask some questions about VBA.*

DETAILS

The following questions and answers introduce the basics of Access modules:

• **What does a module contain?**

 A module contains VBA programming code organized in procedures. A procedure contains several lines of code, each of which is called a **statement**. Modules can also contain **comments**, text that helps explain and document the code.

• **What is a procedure?**

 A **procedure** is a series of VBA statements that performs an operation or calculates an answer. VBA has two types of procedures: functions and subs. **Declaration statements** precede procedure statements and help set rules for how the statements in the module are processed.

• **What is a function?**

 A **function** is a procedure that returns a value. Access supplies many built-in functions, such as Sum, Count, Pmt, and Now, that can be used in an expression in a query, form, or report to calculate a value. You might want to create a new function, however, to help perform calculations unique to your database. For example, you might create a new function called Commission to calculate the sales commission using a formula unique to your business.

• **What is a sub?**

 A **sub** (also called **sub procedure**) performs a series of VBA statements to manipulate controls and objects. Subs are generally executed when an event occurs, such as when a command button is clicked or a form is opened.

• **What are arguments?**

 Arguments are constants, variables, or expressions passed to a procedure that the procedure needs in order to execute. For example, the full syntax for the Sum function is Sum(*expr*), where *expr* represents the argument for the Sum function, the field that is being summed. In VBA, arguments are declared in the first line of the procedure. They are specified immediately after a procedure's name and are enclosed in parentheses. Multiple arguments are separated by commas.

• **What is an object?**

 In VBA, an **object** is any item that can be identified or manipulated, including the traditional Access objects (table, query, form, report, macro, and module) as well as other items that have properties, such as controls, sections, and existing procedures.

• **What is a method?**

 A **method** is an action that an object can perform. Procedures are often written to invoke methods in response to user actions. For example, you could invoke the GoToControl method to move the focus to a specific control on a form in response to the user clicking a command button.

FIGURE N-1: Visual Basic Editor (VBE) window for a standard module

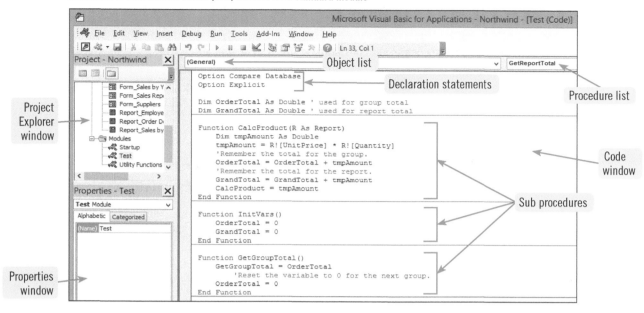

TABLE N-1: Components and text colors for the Visual Basic Editor window

component or color	description
Visual Basic Editor, VBE	Comprises the entire Microsoft Visual Basic program window that contains smaller windows, including the Code window and Project Explorer window
Code window	Contains the VBA for the project selected in the Project Explorer window
Project Explorer window	Displays a hierarchical list of the projects in the database; a **project** can be a module object or a form or report object that contains a class module
Declaration statements	Includes statements that apply to every procedure in the module, such as declarations for variables, constants, user-defined data types, and external procedures in a dynamic-link library
Object list	In a class module, lists the objects associated with the current form or report
Procedure list	In a standard module, lists the procedures in the module; in a class module, lists events (such as Click or Dblclick)
Blue	Indicates a VBA keyword; blue words are reserved by VBA and are already assigned specific meanings
Black	Indicates normal text; black words are the unique VBA code developed by the user
Red	Indicates syntax error text; a red statement indicates that it will not execute correctly because of a syntax error (perhaps a missing parenthesis or a spelling error)
Green	Indicates comment text; any text after an apostrophe is considered documentation, or a comment, and is therefore ignored in the execution of the procedure

Compare Macros and Modules

Both macros and modules help run your database more efficiently and effectively. Creating a macro or a module requires some understanding of programming concepts, an ability to follow a process through its steps, and patience. Some tasks can be accomplished by using an Access macro or by writing VBA. Guidelines can help you determine which tool is best for the task. **CASE** ▶ *You compare Access macros and modules by asking more questions.*

DETAILS

The following questions and answers provide guidelines for using macros and modules:

- **For what types of tasks are macros best suited?**

 Macros are an easy way to handle common, repetitive, and simple tasks such as opening and closing forms, positioning a form to enter a new record, and printing reports.

- **Which is easier to create, a macro or a module, and why?**

 Macros are generally easier to create because Macro Design View is more structured than the VBE. The hardest part of creating a macro is choosing the correct macro action. But once the action is selected, the arguments associated with that macro action are displayed, eliminating the need to learn any special programming syntax. To create a module, however, you must know a robust programming language, VBA, as well as the correct **syntax** (rules) for each VBA statement. In a nutshell, macros are simpler to create, but VBA is more powerful.

- **When must I use a macro?**

 You must use macros to make global, shortcut key assignments. **AutoExec** is a special macro name that automatically executes when the database first opens.

- **When must I use a module?**

 1. You must use modules to create unique functions. Macros cannot create functions. For instance, you might want to create a function called Commission that calculates the appropriate commission on a sale using your company's unique commission formula.
 2. Access error messages can be confusing to the user. But using VBA procedures, you can detect the error when it occurs and display your own message.
 3. Although Access 2013 macros have been enhanced to include more powerful If-Then logic, VBA is still more robust in the area of programming flow statements with tools such as nested If statements, Case statements, and multiple looping structures. Some of the most common VBA keywords, including If...Then, are shown in TABLE N-2. VBA keywords appear blue in the VBE code window.
 4. VBA code may declare **variables**, which are used to store data that can be used, modified, or displayed during the execution of the procedure.
 5. VBA may be used in conjunction with SQL (Structured Query Language) to select, update, append, and delete data.

 Class modules, like the one shown in FIGURE N-2, are stored as part of the form or report object in which they are created. If you develop forms and reports in one database and copy them to another, the VBA class module automatically travels with the object that stores it.

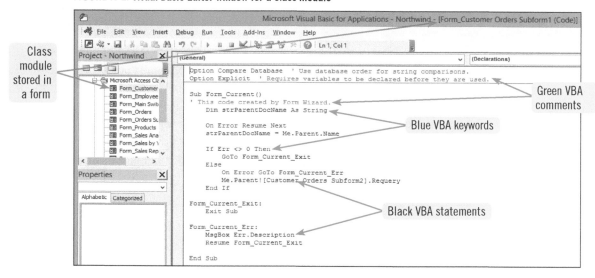

TABLE N-2: Common VBA keywords

statement	explanation
Function	Declares the name and arguments that create a new function procedure
End Function	When defining a new function, the End Function statement is required as the last statement to mark the end of the VBA code that defines the function
Sub	Declares the name for a new Sub procedure; **Private Sub** indicates that the Sub is accessible only to other procedures in the module where it is declared
End Sub	When defining a new sub, the End Sub statement is required as the last statement to mark the end of the VBA code that defines the sub
If...Then	Executes code (the code follows the Then statement) when the value of an expression is true (the expression follows the If statement)
End If	When creating an If...Then...Else clause, the End If statement is required as the last statement
Const	Declares the name and value of a **constant**, an item that retains a constant value throughout the execution of the code
Option Compare Database	A declaration statement that determines the way string values (text) will be sorted
Option Explicit	A declaration statement that specifies that you must explicitly declare all variables used in all procedures; if you attempt to use an undeclared variable name, an error occurs at **compile time**, the period during which source code is translated to executable code
Dim	Declares a **variable**, a named storage location that contains data that can be modified during program execution
On Error GoTo	Upon an error in the execution of a procedure, specifies the location (the statement) where the procedure should continue
Select Case	Executes one of several groups of statements called a **Case** depending on the value of an expression; use the Select Case statement as an alternative to using **ElseIf** in **If...Then...Else** statements when comparing one expression with several different values
End Select	When defining a new Select Case group of statements, the End Select statement is required as the last statement to mark the end of the VBA code

Access 2013

Create Functions

Learning
Outcomes
• Create a custom
 function
• Use a custom
 function

Access supplies hundreds of functions such as Sum, Count, IIf, First, Last, Date, and Hour. However, you might want to create a new function to calculate a value based on your company's unique business rules. You would create the new function in a standard module so that it can be used in any query, form, or report throughout the database. **CASE** ▶ *Quest Specialty Travel allows employees to purchase computer equipment when it is replaced. Equipment that is less than a year old will be sold to employees at 75 percent of its initial value, and equipment that is more than a year old will be sold at 50 percent of its initial value. Kayla Green, network administrator, asks you to create a new function called EmpPrice that determines the employee purchase price of replaced computer equipment.*

STEPS

TROUBLE
If you do not enable content, your VBA will not run.

1. **Start Access, open the Technology-N.accdb database from the location where you store your Data Files, enable content if prompted, click the CREATE tab, then click the Module button in the Macros & Code group**

 Access automatically inserts the Option Compare Database declaration statement in the Code window. You will create the new EmpPrice function one step at a time.

QUICK TIP
The Option Explicit statement appears if the Require Variable Declaration option is checked in the VBA Options dialog box. To view the default settings, click Options on the VBA Tools menu.

2. **Type Function EmpPrice(StartValue), then press [Enter]**

 This statement creates a new function named EmpPrice, and states that it contains one argument, StartValue. VBA automatically adds the blue **End Function** statement, a required statement to mark the end of the function. The insertion point is positioned between the statements so that you can enter more VBA statements to further define how the new EmpPrice function will calculate.

3. **Press [Tab], type EmpPrice = StartValue * 0.5, then press [Enter]**

 Your screen should look like FIGURE N-3. The EmpPrice= statement explains how the EmpPrice function will calculate. The function will return a value that is calculated by multiplying the StartValue by 0.5. It is not necessary to indent statements, but indenting code between matching Function/End Function, Sub/End Sub, or If/End If statements enhances the program's readability. When you press [Enter] at the end of a VBA statement, Access automatically adds spaces as appropriate to enhance the readability of the statement.

4. **Click the Save button on the Standard toolbar, type basFunctions in the Save As dialog box, click OK, then click the upper Close button ✕ in the upper-right corner of the VBE window to close the Visual Basic Editor**

 It is common for VBA programmers to use three-character prefixes to name objects and controls. This makes it easier to identify that object or control in expressions and modules. The prefix **bas** is short for Basic and applies to global modules. Naming conventions for other objects and controls are listed in TABLE N-3 and used throughout the Technology-N.accdb database. You can use the new function, EmpPrice, in a query, form, or report.

5. **Click the Queries bar in the Navigation Pane to expand the Queries section if it is collapsed, right-click the qryEmpPricing query in the Navigation Pane, then click Design View on the shortcut menu**

 You use the new EmpPrice function in the query to determine the employee purchase price of replaced computer equipment.

QUICK TIP
Field names used in expressions are not case sensitive, but they must exactly match the spelling of the field name as defined in Table Design View.

6. **Click the blank Field cell to the right of the InitialValue field, type Price:EmpPrice ([InitialValue]), then click the View button to switch to Datasheet View**

 Your screen should look like FIGURE N-4. In this query, you created a new field called Price that uses the EmpPrice function. The value in the InitialValue field is used for the StartValue argument of the new EmpPrice function. The InitialValue field is multiplied by 0.5 to create the new Price field.

7. **Save then close the qryEmpPricing query**

FIGURE N-3: **Creating the EmpPrice function**

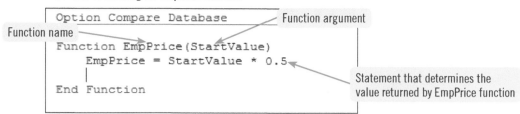

FIGURE N-4: **Using the EmpPrice function in a query**

ELast	Manufacture	Description	PlacementDat	InitialValue	Price
Joy	Micron	Transtrek4000	7/7/2014	$2,000.00	1000
Joy	Micron	Transtrek4000	7/7/2015	$2,000.00	1000
Dawson	Micron	Prosignet403	7/14/2014	$1,800.00	900
Rock	Micron	Prosignet403	7/30/2014	$1,800.00	900
McDermott	Micron	Prosignet403	7/30/2014	$1,800.00	900
Garmin	Micron	Prosignet403	7/30/2014	$1,800.00	900
Rice	Micron	Prosignet403	1/8/2014	$1,700.00	850
Boyd	Micron	Prosignet403	8/13/2014	$1,700.00	850
McDonald	Micron	Prosignet403	8/13/2015	$1,700.00	850
Long	Micron	Prosignet403	8/13/2014	$1,700.00	850
Orient	Compaq	Centuria9099	6/13/2015	$1,500.00	750
Greenfield	Compaq	Centuria9099	6/13/2015	$1,500.00	750

Calculated field, Price, uses EmpPrice custom function

TABLE N-3: **Three-character prefix naming conventions**

object or control type	prefix	example
Table	tbl	tblProducts
Query	qry	qrySalesByRegion
Form	frm	frmProducts
Report	rpt	rptSalesByCategory
Macro	mcr	mcrCloseInventory
Module	bas	basRetirement
Label	lbl	lblFullName
Text Box	txt	txtLastName
Combo box	cbo	cboStates
Command button	cmd	cmdPrint

Use If Statements

If...Then...Else logic allows you to test logical conditions and execute statements only if the conditions are true. If...Then...Else code can be composed of one or several statements, depending on how many conditions you want to test, how many possible answers you want to provide, and what you want the code to do based on the results of the tests. **CASE** *You need to add an If statement to the EmpPrice function to test the age of the equipment, and then calculate the answer based on that age. You want to modify the EmpPrice function so that if the equipment is less than one year old, the StartValue is multiplied by 75% (0.75) rather than by 50% (0.5).*

STEPS

1. **Scroll down the Navigation Pane, right-click the basFunctions module, then click Design View**

 To determine the age of the equipment, the EmpPrice function needs another argument, the purchase date of the equipment.

2. **Click just before the right parenthesis in the Function statement, type , (a comma), press [Spacebar], type DateValue, then press [↓]**

 Now that you established another argument, you can work with the argument in the definition of the function.

QUICK TIP
Indentation doesn't affect the way the function works, but does make the code easier to read.

3. **Click to the right of the right parenthesis in the Function statement, press [Enter], press [Tab], then type If (Now()–DateValue) >365 Then**

 The expression compares whether today's date, represented by the Access function **Now()**, minus the DateValue argument value is greater than 365 days (1 year). If true, this indicates that the equipment is older than one year.

4. **Indent and type the rest of the statements exactly as shown in FIGURE N-5**

 The **Else** statement is executed only if the expression is false (if the equipment is less than 365 days old). The **End If** statement is needed to mark the end of the If block of code.

TROUBLE
If a compile or syntax error appears, open the VBE window, compare your function with FIGURE N-5, then correct any errors.

5. **Click the Save button 🖫 on the Standard toolbar, close the Visual Basic window, right-click the qryEmpPricing query in the Navigation Pane, then click Design View on the shortcut menu**

 Now that you've modified the EmpPrice function to include two arguments, you need to modify the calculated Price field expression, too.

6. **Right-click the Price field in the query design grid, click Zoom on the shortcut menu, click between the right square bracket and right parenthesis, then type ,[PlacementDate]**

 Your Zoom dialog box should look like FIGURE N-6. Both of the arguments used to define the EmpPrice function in the VBA code are replaced with actual field names that contain the data to be analyzed. Field names must be typed exactly as shown and surrounded by square brackets. Commas separate multiple arguments in the function.

7. **Click OK in the Zoom dialog box, then click the View button 🏢 to display the datasheet**

TROUBLE
The new calculated Price field is based on the current date on your computer, so your results may vary.

8. **Click any entry in the PlacementDate field, then click the Ascending button in the Sort & Filter group, as shown in FIGURE N-7**

 The EmpPrice function now calculates one of two different results, depending on the age of the equipment determined by the date in the PlacementDate field.

9. **Save and then close the qryEmpPricing query**

```
Function EmpPrice(StartValue, DateValue)
    If (Now() - DateValue) > 365 Then
        EmpPrice = StartValue * 0.5
    Else
        EmpPrice = StartValue * 0.75
    End If

End Function
```

Second argument

If

Then

Else

End If

FIGURE N-6: Using the Zoom dialog box for long expressions

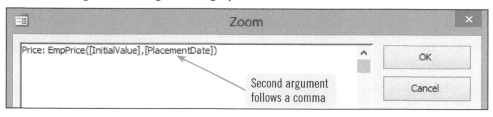

Second argument
follows a comma

FIGURE N-7: Price field is calculated at 50% or 75% based on the age of equipment

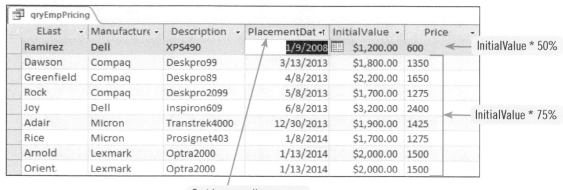

InitialValue * 50%

InitialValue * 75%

Sort in ascending
order on PlacementDate

Access 2013

Document Procedures

Learning
Outcomes
• Add VBA
 comments
• Use the VBE
 toolbar

Comment lines are statements in the code that document the code; they do not affect how the code runs. At any time, if you want to read or modify existing code, you can write the modifications much more quickly if the code is properly documented. Comment lines start with an apostrophe and are green in the VBE. **CASE** *You decide to document the EmpPrice function in the basFunctions module with descriptive comments. This will make it easier for you and others to follow the purpose and logic of the function later.*

STEPS

QUICK TIP
You can also create comments by starting the statement with the Rem statement (for remark).

TROUBLE
Be sure to use an ' (apostrophe) and not a " (quotation mark) to begin the comment line.

1. **Right-click the basFunctions module in the Navigation Pane, then click Design View**
 The VBE window for the basFunctions module opens.

2. **Click the blank line between the Option Compare Database and Function statements, press [Enter], type 'This function is called EmpPrice and has two arguments, then press [Enter]**
 As soon as you move to another line, the comment statement becomes green.

3. **Type 'Created by Your Name on Today's Date, then press [Enter]**
 You can also place comments at the end of a line by entering an apostrophe to mark that the next part of the statement is a comment.

4. **Click to the right of Then at the end of the If statement, press [Spacebar], type 'Now() returns today's date, then press [↓]**
 This comment explains that the Now() function returns today's date. All comments are green, regardless of whether they are on their own line or at the end of an existing line.

5. **Click to the right of 0.5, press [Spacebar] three times, then type 'If > 1 year, multiply by 50%**

6. **Click to the right of 0.75, press [Spacebar] twice, type 'If < 1 year, multiply by 75%, then press [↓]**
 Your screen should look like FIGURE N-8. Each comment will turn green as soon as you move to a new statement.

7. **Click the Save button 🖫 on the Standard toolbar, click File on the menu bar, click Print if requested by your instructor, then click OK**
 TABLE N-4 provides more information about the Standard toolbar buttons in the VBE window.

8. **Click File on the menu bar, then click Close and Return to Microsoft Access**

FIGURE N-8: Adding comments to a module

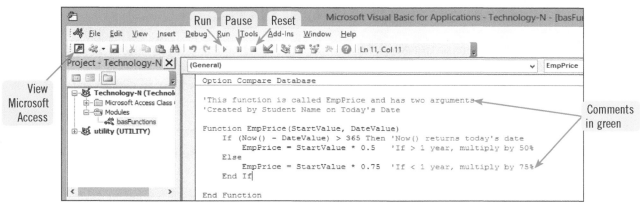

TABLE N-4: Standard toolbar buttons in the Visual Basic window

button name	button	description
View Microsoft Access		Switches from the active Visual Basic window to the Access window
Insert Module		Opens a new module or class module Code window, or inserts a new procedure in the current Code window
Run Sub/UserForm		Runs the current procedure if the insertion point is in a procedure, or runs the UserForm if it is active
Break		Stops the execution of a program while it's running and switches to Break mode, which is the temporary suspension of program execution in which you can examine, debug, reset, step through, or continue program execution
Reset		Resets the procedure
Project Explorer		Displays the Project Explorer, which displays a hierarchical list of the currently open projects (set of modules) and their contents
Object Browser		Displays the Object Browser, which lists the defined modules and procedures as well as available methods, properties, events, constants, and other items that you can use in the code

Access 2013

Build Class Modules

Class modules are contained and executed within specific forms and reports. Class modules most commonly run in response to an **event**, a specific action that occurs as the result of a user action. Common events include clicking a command button, editing data, and closing a form. **CASE** ▸ *You examine an existing class module and create sub procedures connected to events that occur on the form.*

1. **Double-click the** frmEmployees form **in the Navigation Pane to open it in Form View, then click the** Branch of Service combo box list arrow **to review the choices**

 The Branch of Service combo box provides a list of the branches of the armed services. For a choice to make sense, however, an employee would first need to be a veteran. You'll set the Visible property for the Branch of Service combo box to True if the Veteran check box is checked and False if the Veteran check box is not checked.

2. **Right-click the** Employees form tab**, click** Design View **on the shortcut menu, double-click the** edge of the Veteran check box **to open its Property Sheet, click the** Event tab **in the Property Sheet, click the** After Update property**, click the** Build button **⋯ , then click** Code Builder **and** OK **if the Choose Builder dialog box appears**

 The class module for the frmEmployees form opens. Because you opened the VBE window from within a specific event of a specific control on the form, the **stub**, the first and last lines of the sub procedure, were automatically created. The procedure's name in the first line, chkVeteran_AfterUpdate, contains *both* the name of the control, chkVeteran, as well as the name of the event, AfterUpdate, that triggers this procedure. (Recall that the **Name property** of a control is found on the Other tab in the control's property sheet. The **After Update property** is on the Event tab.) A sub procedure that is triggered by an event is often called an **event handler**.

3. **Enter the statements shown in** FIGURE N-9

 When you use three-character prefixes for all controls and objects in your database, it enhances the meaning and readability of your VBA. In this case, the name of the sub procedure shows that it runs on the AfterUpdate event of the chkVeteran control. (The sub runs when the Veteran check box is checked or unchecked.) The If structure contains VBA that makes the cboBranchOfService control either visible or not visible based on the value of the chkVeteran control. To test the sub procedure, you switch to Form View.

4. **Save the changes and close the VBE window, click the** View button **▦ to switch to Form View, click the** Veteran check box **for the first record several times to observe what happens on the After Update event, then navigate through several records**

 By clicking the Veteran check box in the first record, you triggered the procedure that responds to the After Update event of the Veteran check box. However, you also want the procedure to run every time you move from record to record. The **On Current** event of the form is triggered when you navigate through records.

5. **Right-click the** Employees form tab**, click** Design View **on the shortcut menu, click the** Form Selector button **▪, click the** Event tab **in the Property Sheet, click the** On Current event property **in the Property Sheet, click the** Build button **⋯ , click** Code Builder **and** OK **if the Choose Builder dialog box appears, then copy or retype the If structure from the** chkVeteran_AfterUpdate sub **to the** Form_Current sub**, as shown in** FIGURE N-10

 By copying the same If structure to a second sub procedure, you've created a second event handler. Now, the cboBranchOfService combo box will either be visible or not based on two different events: updating the chkVeteran check box or moving from record to record. To test the new sub procedure, you switch to Form View.

6. **Save the changes and close the VBE window, click** ▦ **to switch to Form View, then navigate to the fifth record for Gail Owen to test the new procedures**

 Now, as you move from record to record, the Branch of Service combo box should be visible for those employees with the Veteran check box selected, and not visible if the Veteran check box is not selected.

7. **Click the** Branch of Service combo box list arrow**, click** Army**, as shown in** FIGURE N-11**, then save and close the** frmEmployees form

FIGURE N-9: Creating an event handler procedure

```
Private Sub chkVeteran_AfterUpdate()
If chkVeteran.Value = True Then
    cboBranchOfService.Visible = True
Else
    cboBranchOfService.Visible = False
End If
End Sub
```

FIGURE N-10: Copying the If structure to a new event-handler procedure

Copy If structure from chkVeteran_AfterUpate sub to Form_Current sub

```
Private Sub chkVeteran_AfterUpdate()
If chkVeteran.Value = True Then
    cboBranchOfService.Visible = True
Else
    cboBranchOfService.Visible = False
End If
End Sub

Private Sub Form_Current()
If chkVeteran.Value = True Then
    cboBranchOfService.Visible = True
Else
    cboBranchOfService.Visible = False
End If
End Sub
```

FIGURE N-11: Branch of Service combo box is visible when the Veteran check box is checked

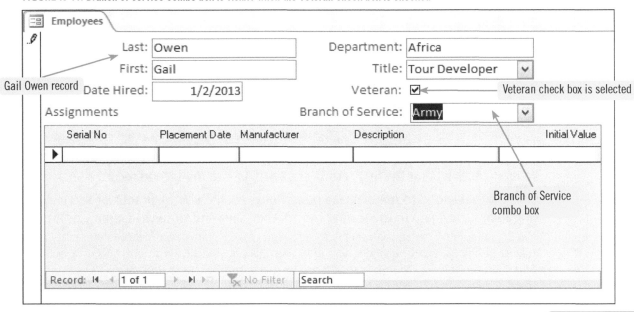

Modify Sub Procedures

Learning
Outcomes
• Attach procedures
 to events
• Use IntelliSense
 technology

Sub procedures can be triggered on any event in the Property Sheet such as **On Got Focus** (when the control gets the focus), **After Update** (after a field is updated), or **On Dbl Click** (when the control is double-clicked). Not all items have the same set of event properties. For example, a text box control has both a Before Update and After Update event property, but neither of these events exists for a label or command button because those controls are not used to update data. **CASE** ▶ *Kayla Green asks if there is a way to require a choice in the Branch of Service combo box if the Veteran check box is checked. You use VBA sub procedures to handle this request.*

STEPS

1. **Right-click the** frmEmployees **form, click** Design View **on the shortcut menu, click the** Before Update **property in the Property Sheet, click the** Build button ⸱⸱⸱ **, click** Code Builder **and** OK **if the Choose Builder dialog box appears, then enter the code in** FIGURE N-12 **into the Form_BeforeUpdate stub**

 Test the procedure.

2. **Close the VBE window, click the** View button ▦ **to switch to Form View, click the** Veteran check box **as needed to select it in the first record, then navigate to the second record**

 Given the chkVeteran control is selected but the cboBranchOfService combo box is null, the MsgBox statement produces the message shown in FIGURE N-13.

3. **Click** OK**, navigate back to the first record, then click the** Veteran check box **to uncheck it**

 The code produces the correct message, but you want the code to place the focus in the cboBranchOfService combo box to force the user to choose a branch of service when this condition occurs.

 DoCmd is a VBA object that supports many methods to run common Access commands, such as closing windows, opening forms, previewing reports, navigating records, setting focus, and setting the value of controls. As you write a VBA statement, visual aids that are part of **IntelliSense technology** help you complete it. For example, when you type the period (.) after the DoCmd object, a list of available methods appears. Watching the VBA window carefully and taking advantage of all IntelliSense clues as you complete a statement can greatly improve your accuracy and productivity in writing VBA.

4. **Right-click the** Employees form tab**, click** Design View**, click the** View Code button **in the Tools group, click after the** MsgBox **statement, press [Enter], then type** DoCmd. **(including the period)**

 Your sub procedure should look like FIGURE N-14.

5. **Type** GoToControl**, press the [Spacebar] noting the additional IntelliSense prompt, then type** "cboBranchOfService"**, as shown in** FIGURE N-15

 IntelliSense helps you fill out each statement, indicating the order of arguments needed for the method to execute. If IntelliSense displays more than one argument, the current argument is listed in bold. Optional arguments are listed in [square brackets]. Test the new procedure.

6. **Close the VBE window, click the** View button ▦ **to switch to Form View, click the** Veteran check box **for the first record, then navigate to the second record**

7. **Click** OK **to respond to the message box, choose** Navy **from the Branch of Service combo box, navigate to the second record, then save and close the Employees form**

 VBA is a robust and powerful programming language. It takes years of experience to appreciate the vast number of objects, events, methods, and properties that are available. With only modest programming skills, however, you can create basic sub procedures that greatly help users work more efficiently and effectively in forms.

```
Private Sub Form_BeforeUpdate(Cancel As Integer)
If chkVeteran.Value = True Then
    If IsNull(cboBranchOfService.Value) Then
        MsgBox "Please select a Branch of Service"
    End If
End If
End Sub
```

Form_BeforeUpdate sub

FIGURE N-13: Message produced by MsgBox statement

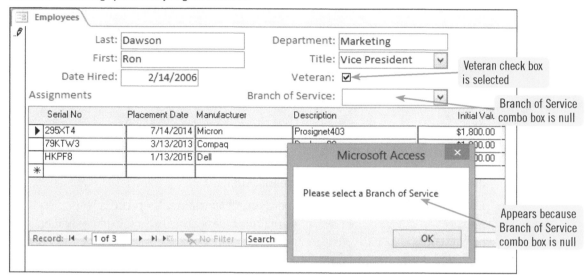

Veteran check box is selected

Branch of Service combo box is null

Appears because Branch of Service combo box is null

FIGURE N-14: IntelliSense technology prompts you as you write VBA statements

```
Private Sub Form_BeforeUpdate(Cancel As Integer)
If chkVeteran.Value = True Then
    If IsNull(cboBranchOfService.Value) Then
        MsgBox "Please select a Branch of Service"
        DoCmd.
    End If       ≡◈ AddMenu
End If            ≡◈ ApplyFilter
End Sub           ≡◈ Beep
                  ≡◈ BrowseTo
Private Sub       ≡◈ CancelEvent
If chkVetera      ≡◈ ClearMacroError
    cboBranc      ≡◈ Close
Else
```

IntelliSense list

FIGURE N-15: New DoCmd statement

```
Private Sub Form_BeforeUpdate(Cancel As Integer)
If chkVeteran.Value = True Then
    If IsNull(cboBranchOfService.Value) Then
        MsgBox "Please select a Branch of Service"
        DoCmd.GoToControl "cboBranchOfService"
    End If
End If
End Sub
```

New DoCmd statement

Troubleshoot Modules

Access provides several techniques to help you **debug** (find and resolve) different types of VBA errors. A **syntax error** occurs immediately as you are writing a VBA statement that cannot be read by the Visual Basic Editor. This is the easiest type of error to identify because your code turns red when the syntax error occurs. **Compile-time errors** occur as a result of incorrectly constructed code and are detected as soon as you run your code or select the Compile option on the Debug menu. For example, you may have forgotten to insert an End If statement to finish an If structure. **Run-time errors** occur as incorrectly constructed code runs and include attempting an illegal operation such as dividing by zero or moving focus to a control that doesn't exist. When you encounter a run-time error, VBA will stop executing your procedure at the statement in which the error occurred and highlight the line with a yellow background in the Visual Basic Editor. **Logic errors** are the most difficult to troubleshoot because they occur when the code runs without obvious problems, but the procedure still doesn't produce the desired result. **CASE** ▸ *You study debugging techniques using the basFunctions module.*

STEPS

1. **Right-click the basFunctions module in the Navigation Pane, click Design View, click to the right of the End If statement, press the [Spacebar], type *your* name, then press [↓]**
 Because the End If *your* name statement cannot be resolved by the Visual Basic Editor, the statement immediately turns red and an error message box appears.

2. **Click OK in the error message box, delete *your* name, then press [↓]**
 Another VBA debugging tool is to set a **breakpoint**, a bookmark that suspends execution of the procedure at that statement to allow you to examine what is happening.

QUICK TIP
Click the gray bar to the left of a statement to toggle a breakpoint on and off.

3. **Click the If statement line, click Debug on the menu bar, then click Toggle Breakpoint**
 Your screen should look like FIGURE N-16.

4. **Click the View Microsoft Access button 🖉 on the Standard toolbar, then double-click the qryEmpPricing query in the Navigation Pane**
 When the qryEmpPricing query opens, it immediately runs the EmpPrice function. Because you set a breakpoint at the If statement, the statement is highlighted, indicating that the code has been suspended at that point.

QUICK TIP
Pointing to an argument in the Code window displays a ScreenTip with the argument's current value.

5. **Click View on the menu bar, click Immediate Window, type ? DateValue, then press [Enter]**
 Your screen should look like FIGURE N-17. The **Immediate window** is an area where you can determine the value of any argument at the breakpoint.

6. **Click Debug on the menu bar, click Clear All Breakpoints, click the Continue button ▷ on the Standard toolbar to execute the remainder of the function, then save and close the basFunctions module**
 The qryEmpPricing query's datasheet should be visible.

7. **Close the qryEmpPricing datasheet, close the Technology-N.accdb database, then exit Access**

Breakpoint

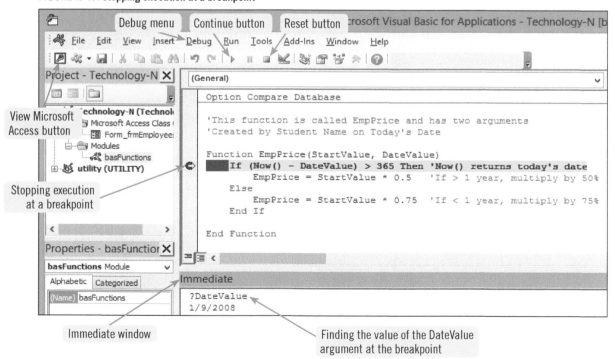

Creating Modules and VBA

Practice

Put your skills into practice with SAM! If you have a SAM account, go to www.cengage.com/sam2013 to access SAM assignments for this unit.

Concepts Review

Identify each element of the Visual Basic window shown in FIGURE N-18.

FIGURE N-18

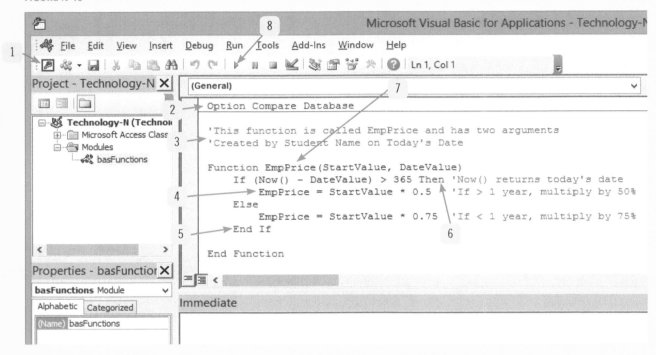

Match each term with the statement that best describes its function.

9. **Visual Basic for Applications (VBA)**

10. **Debugging**

11. **If...Then...Else statement**

12. **Class modules**

13. **Breakpoint**

14. **Function**

15. **Module**

16. **Procedure**

17. **Arguments**

a. Allows you to test a logical condition and execute commands only if the condition is true

b. The programming language used in Access modules

c. A line of code that automatically suspends execution of the procedure

d. A process to find and resolve programming errors

e. A procedure that returns a value

f. Constants, variables, or expressions passed to a procedure to further define how it should execute

g. Stored as part of the form or report object in which they are created

h. The Access object where VBA code is stored

i. A series of VBA statements that performs an operation or calculate a value

Skills Review

1. Understand modules and VBA.

a. Start Access, then open the Baseball-N.accdb (not the Basketball-N.accdb) database from the location where you store your Data Files. Enable content if prompted.

b. Open the VBE window for the basFunctions module.

Skills Review (continued)

c. Record your answers to the following questions on a sheet of paper:
- What is the name of the function defined in this module?
- What are the names of the arguments defined in this module?
- What is the purpose of the End Function statement?
- Why is the End Function statement in blue?
- Why are some of the lines indented?

2. Compare macros and modules.

a. If not already opened, open the VBE window for the basFunctions module.

b. Record your answers to the following questions on a sheet of paper:
- Why was a module rather than a macro used to create this procedure?
- Why is VBA generally more difficult to create than a macro?
- Identify each of the VBA keywords or keyword phrases, and explain the purpose for each.

3. Create functions.

a. If not already opened, open the VBE window for the basFunctions module.

b. Create a function called **TotalBases** below the End Function statement of the BattingAverage function by typing the VBA statements shown in FIGURE N-19.

FIGURE N-19

```
Function TotalBases(SingleValue, DoubleValue, TripleValue, HRValue)
    TotalBases = (SingleValue + 2 * DoubleValue + 3 * TripleValue + 4 * HRValue)
End Function
```

In baseball, total bases is a popular statistic because it accounts for the power of each hit. In the TotalBases function, each hit is multiplied by the number of bases earned (1 for single, 2 for double, 3 for triple, and 4 for home run).

c. Save the basFunctions module, then close the VBE window.

d. Use Query Design View to create a new query using the PlayerFName and PlayerLName fields from the tblPlayers table, and the AtBats field from the tblPlayerStats table.

e. Create a calculated field named **Batting** in the next available column by carefully typing the expression as follows: **Batting: BattingAverage([1Base],[2Base],[3Base],[4Base],[AtBats])**. (*Hint*: Use the Zoom dialog box to enter long expressions.)

f. Create a second calculated field named **Bases** in the next available column by carefully typing the expression as follows: **Bases: TotalBases([1Base],[2Base],[3Base],[4Base])**. (*Hint*: Use the Zoom dialog box to enter long expressions.)

g. View the datasheet, change Doug Schaller to *your* first and last name, save the query with the name **qryStats**, then close qryStats.

4. Use If statements.

a. Open the VBE window for the basFunctions module, then modify the BattingAverage function to add the If structure shown in FIGURE N-20. The If structure prevents the error caused by attempting to divide by zero. The If structure checks to see if the AtBatsValue argument is equal to 0. If so, the BattingAverage function is set to 0. Else, the BattingAverage function is calculated.

FIGURE N-20

```
Function BattingAverage(SingleValue, DoubleValue, TripleValue, HRValue, AtBatsValue)
If AtBatsValue = 0 Then
    BattingAverage = 0
Else
    BattingAverage = (SingleValue + DoubleValue + TripleValue + HRValue) / AtBatsValue
End If
End Function

Function TotalBases(SingleValue, DoubleValue, TripleValue, HRValue)
    TotalBases = (SingleValue + 2 * DoubleValue + 3 * TripleValue + 4 * HRValue)
End Function
```

Skills Review (continued)

b. Save the basFunctions module, then close the VBE window.

c. Open the qryStats datasheet, then change the AtBats value to **0** for the first record and press [Tab] to test the If statement. The Batting calculated field should equal 0.

d. Close the datasheet.

5. Document procedures.

a. Open the VBE window for the basFunctions module, and add the two statements above the End Function statement for the BattingAverage function, as shown in FIGURE N-21. The statements use the Format function to format the calculation as a number with three digits to the right of the decimal point. The comments help clarify the statement.

b. Add a comment at the end of the VBA code that identifies *your* name and today's date, as shown in FIGURE N-21.

FIGURE N-21

```
Function BattingAverage(SingleValue, DoubleValue, TripleValue, HRValue, AtBatsValue)
If AtBatsValue = 0 Then
    BattingAverage = 0
Else
    BattingAverage = (SingleValue + DoubleValue + TripleValue + HRValue) / AtBatsValue
End If
'Format as a number with three digits to the right of the decimal point
BattingAverage = Format(BattingAverage, "0.000")
End Function

Function TotalBases(SingleValue, DoubleValue, TripleValue, HRValue)
    TotalBases = (SingleValue + 2 * DoubleValue + 3 * TripleValue + 4 * HRValue)
End Function

'Created by Your Name on Today's Date
```

c. Save the changes to the basFunctions module, print the module if requested by your instructor, then close the VBE window.

d. Open the qryStats query datasheet and change the AtBats value to **3** for the first record and press [Tab] to observe how the value in the Batting calculated field changes and how it is now formatted with three digits to the right of the decimal point due to the VBA statement you added to the BattingAverage function.

e. Print the qryStats datasheet if requested by your instructor, then close it.

6. Build class modules.

a. Open frmPlayerEntry in Form View, then move through several records to observe the data.

b. Switch to Design View, and on the right side of the form, select the Print Current Record button.

c. Open the Property Sheet for the button, click the Event tab, click the On Click property, then click the Build button to open the class module.

d. Add a comment to the last line to show *your* name and the current date. Save the module, print it if requested by your instructor, then close the VBE window.

7. Modify sub procedures.

a. Open the frmPlayerEntry form in Form View, move through a couple of records to observe the txtSalary text box (currently blank), then switch to Design View.

b. The base starting salary in this league is $30,000. You will add a command button with VBA to help enter the correct salary for each player. Use the Button button to add a command button below the txtSalary text box, then cancel the Command Button Wizard if it starts.

c. Open the Property Sheet for the new command button, then change the Caption property on the Format tab to **Base Salary**. Change the Name property on the Other tab to **cmdBaseSalary**.

d. On the Event tab of the Property Sheet, click the On Click property, click the Build button, then click Code Builder if prompted. The stub for the new cmdBaseSalary_Click sub is automatically created for you.

e. Enter the following statement between the Sub and End Sub statements:
txtSalary.Value = 30000

Skills Review (continued)

f. Save the changes, then close the VBE window.

g. Close the Property Sheet, then save and open the frmPlayerEntry form in Form View.

h. Click the Base Salary command button for the first player, move to the second record, then click the Base Salary command button for the second player.

i. Save, then close the frmPlayerEntry form.

8. Troubleshoot modules.

a. Open the VBE window for the basFunctions module.

b. Click anywhere in the If AtBatsValue = 0 Then statement in the BattingAverage function.

c. Click Debug on the menu bar, then click Toggle Breakpoint to set a breakpoint at this statement.

d. Save the changes, then close the VBE window and return to Microsoft Access.

e. Open the qryStats query datasheet. This action will attempt to use the BattingAverage function to calculate the value for the Batting field, which will stop and highlight the statement in the VBE window where you set a breakpoint.

f. Click View on the menu bar, click Immediate Window (if not already visible), delete any previous entries in the Immediate window, type **?AtBatsValue**, then press [Enter]. At this point in the execution of the VBA, the AtBatsValue should be 3, the value for the first record.

g. Type **?SingleValue**, then press [Enter]. At this point in the execution of the VBA code, the SingleValue should be 1, the value for the first record. (*Hint*: You can resize the Immediate window taller by dragging the top edge.)

h. Click Debug on the menu bar, click Clear All Breakpoints, then click the Continue button on the Standard toolbar. Close the VBE window.

i. Return to the qryStats query in Datasheet View.

j. Close the qryStats query, close the Baseball-N.accdb database, then exit Access.

Independent Challenge 1

As the manager of a doctor's clinic, you have created an Access database called Patients-N.accdb to track insurance claim reimbursements and general patient health. You want to modify an existing function within this database.

a. Start Access, then open the Patients-N.accdb database from the location where you store your Data Files. Enable content if prompted.

b. Open the basBodyMassIndex module in Design View, and enter the **Option Explicit** declaration statement just below the existing Option Compare Database statement.

c. Record your answers to the following questions on a sheet of paper:
- What is the name of the function in the module?
- What are the function arguments?
- What is the purpose of the Option Explicit declaration statement?

d. Edit the BMI function by adding a comment below the last line of code with *your* name and today's date.

e. Edit the BMI function by adding a comment above the Function statement with the following information: **'A healthy BMI is in the range of 21-24**.

f. Edit the BMI function by adding an If clause that checks to make sure the height argument is not equal to 0. The final BMI function code should look like FIGURE N-22.

g. Save the module, print it if requested by your instructor, then close the VBE window.

FIGURE N-22

```
Option Compare Database
Option Explicit

'A healthy BMI is in the range of 21-24

Function BMI(weight, height)

If height = 0 Then
    BMI = 0
Else
    BMI = (weight * 0.4536) / (height * 0.0254) ^ 2
End If

End Function

'Student Name - Today's Date
```

Independent Challenge 1 (continued)

h. Create a new query that includes the following fields from the tblPatients table: **PtLastName**, **PtFirstName**, **PtHeight**, **PtWeight**.

i. Create a calculated field with the following field name and expression: **BodyMassIndex: BMI([PtWeight], [PtHeight])**. (*Hint*: Use the Zoom dialog box for long expressions.)

j. Save the query as **qryPatientBMI**, view the qryPatientBMI query datasheet, then test the If statement by entering **0** in the PtHeight field for the first record. Press [Tab] to move to the BodyMassIndex field, which should recalculate to 0.

k. Edit the first record to contain *your* last and first names, print the datasheet if requested by your instructor, then close the qryPatientBMI query.

l. Close the Patients-N.accdb database, then exit Access.

Independent Challenge 2

As the manager of a doctor's clinic, you have created an Access database called Patients-N.accdb to track insurance claim reimbursements. You want to study the existing sub procedures stored as class modules in the Claim Entry Form.

a. Start Access, then open the Patients-N.accdb database from the location where you store your Data Files. Enable content if prompted.

b. Open frmClaimEntryForm in Form View, then switch to Design View.

c. Open the VBE window to view this class module, then record your answers to the following questions on a sheet of paper:
- What are the names of the sub procedures in this class module? (*Hint*: Be sure to scroll the window to see the complete contents.)
- What Access functions are used in the PtFirstName_AfterUpdate sub?
- How many arguments do the functions in the PtFirstName_AfterUpdate sub have?
- What do the functions in the PtFirstName_AfterUpdate sub do? (*Hint*: You may have to use the Visual Basic Help system if you are not familiar with the functions.)
- What is the purpose of the On Error command? (*Hint*: Use the Visual Basic Help system if you are not familiar with this command.)

d. Use the Property Sheet of the form to create an event-handler procedure based on the On Load property. The statement will be one line using the Maximize method of the VBA DoCmd object, which will maximize the form each time it is loaded.

e. Save the changes, close the VBE window and the Claim Entry Form, then open frmClaimEntryForm in Form View to test the new sub.

f. Close frmClaimEntryForm, close the Patients-N.accdb database, then exit Access.

Independent Challenge 3

As the manager of a doctor's clinic, you have created an Access database called Patients-N.accdb to track insurance claim reimbursements that are fixed (paid at a predetermined fixed rate) or denied (not paid by the insurance company). You want to enhance the database with a class module.

a. Start Access, then open the Patients-N.accdb database from the location where you store your Data Files. Enable content if prompted.

b. Open frmCPT in Form Design View.

c. Use the Command Button Wizard to add a command button in the Form Header section. Choose the Add New Record action from the Record Operations category.

d. Accept **Add Record** as the text on the button, then name the button **cmdAddRecord**.

Independent Challenge 3 (continued)

e. Use the Command Button Wizard to add a command button in the Form Header section to the right of the existing Add Record button. (*Hint*: Move and resize controls as necessary to put two command buttons in the Form Header section.)

f. Choose the Delete Record action from the Record Operations category.

g. Accept **Delete Record** as the text on the button, and name the button **cmdDeleteRecord**.

h. Size the two buttons to be the same height and width, and align their top edges. Move them as needed so that they do not overlap.

i. Save and view frmCPT in Form View, then click the Add Record command button.

j. Add a new record (it will be record number 65) with a CPTCode value of **999** and an RBRVS value of **1.5**.

k. To make sure that the Delete Record button works, click the record selector for the new record you just entered, click the Delete Record command button, then click Yes to confirm the deletion. Close frmCPT.

l. In Design View of the frmCPT form, open the Property Sheet for the Delete Record command button, click the Event tab, then click the Build button beside [Embedded Macro]. The Command Button Wizard created the embedded macro that deletes the current record. You can convert macro objects to VBA code to learn more about VBA. To convert an embedded macro to VBA, you must first copy and paste the embedded macro actions to a new macro object. (*Hint*: You can widen the property sheet by dragging the left edge.)

m. Press [Ctrl][A] to select all macro actions, then press [Ctrl][C] to copy all macro actions to the Clipboard.

n. Close the macro window, then save and close frmCPT.

o. On the CREATE tab, open Macro Design View, then press [Ctrl][V] to paste the macro actions to the window.

p. Click the Convert Macros to Visual Basic button, click Yes when prompted to save the macro, click Convert, then click OK when a dialog box indicates the conversion is finished.

q. Save and close all open windows with default names. Open the Converted Macro-Macro1 VBE window. Add a comment as the last line of code in the Code window with *your* name and the current date, save the module, print it if requested by your instructor, then close the VBE window.

r. Close the Patients-N.accdb database, then exit Access.

Independent Challenge 4: Explore

(*Note: To complete this Independent Challenge, make sure you are connected to the Internet.*)

Learning a programming language is sometimes compared with learning a foreign language. Imagine how it would feel to learn a new programming language if English wasn't your primary language, or if you had another type of accessibility challenge. Advances in technology are helping to break down many barriers to those with vision, hearing, mobility, cognitive, and language issues. In this challenge, you explore the Microsoft Web site for resources to address these issues.

a. Go to www.microsoft.com/enable, then print that page. Explore the Web site.

b. After exploring the Web site for products, demos, tutorials, guides, and articles, write a two-page, double-spaced paper describing five types of accessibility solutions that might make a positive impact on someone you know. Refer to your acquaintances as "my friend," "my cousin," and so forth as appropriate. Do not include real names.

c. Use bold headings for the five types of accessibility solutions to make those sections of your paper easy to find and read. Be sure to spell and grammar check your paper.

Visual Workshop

As the manager of a college basketball team, you are helping the coach build meaningful statistics to compare the relative value of the players in each game. The coach has stated that one offensive rebound is worth as much to the team as two defensive rebounds, and would like you to use this rule to develop a "rebounding impact statistic" for each game. Open the Basketball-N.accdb (not the Baseball-N.accdb) database, enable content if prompted, and use FIGURE N-23 to develop a new function in a standard module. Name the new function **ReboundImpact** in a new module called **basFunctions** to calculate this statistic. Include *your* name and the current date as a comment in the last row of the function.

FIGURE N-23

```
Function ReboundImpact(OffenseValue As Integer, DefenseValue As Integer) As Integer
    ReboundImpact = (OffenseValue * 2) + DefenseValue
End Function

'Student Name - Today's Date
```

Create a query called **qryRebounds** with the fields shown in FIGURE N-24. Note that the records are sorted in ascending order on GameNo and LastName. The **ReboundPower** field is created using the following expression: **ReboundImpact([Reb-O],[Reb-D])**. Enter *your* first and last name instead of Kristen Czyenski, and print the datasheet if requested by your instructor.

FIGURE N-24

GameNo	FirstName	LastName	Reb-O	Reb-D	ReboundPower
1	Student First	Student Last	2	2	6
1	Denise	Franco	2	3	7
1	Theresa	Grant	1	3	5
1	Megan	Hile	1	2	4
1	Amy	Hodel	5	3	13
1	Ellyse	Howard	1	2	4
1	Jamie	Johnson	0	1	1
1	Lindsey	Swift	1	2	4
1	Morgan	Tyler	4	6	14
2	Student First	Student Last	3	2	8
2	Denise	Franco	5	3	13

Creating Modules and VBA

Integrating Word, Excel, Access, and PowerPoint

CASE Meg Marshall, the general manager of QST Vancouver, creates presentations for clients that often include objects from Word, Excel, and Access. She asks you to explore how to use linking and embedding in PowerPoint, and then how to insert linked objects from Word, Excel, and Access into a PowerPoint presentation.

Unit Objectives

After completing this unit, you will be able to:

- Integrate data among Word, Excel, Access, and PowerPoint
- Import a Word outline into PowerPoint
- Embed an Excel worksheet in PowerPoint

- Link Access and Excel objects to PowerPoint
- Manage links

Files You Will Need

INT C-1.docx INT C-6.accdb
INT C-2.accdb INT C-7.docx
INT C-3.docx INT C-8.accdb
INT C-4.accdb INT C-9.accdb
INT C-5.docx

Microsoft® product screenshots used with permission from Microsoft® Corporation.

©Dimec/Shutterstock

Integrate Data Among Word, Excel, Access, and PowerPoint

You can integrate information into a PowerPoint presentation using the linking and embedding techniques you learned with Word, Excel, and Access. As with those programs, you embed data created in other programs in PowerPoint when you want to be able to edit the data from within the destination file. You use linking when you want the linked data in the destination file to be updated when you change the data in the source file. In addition, you can import a Word outline into PowerPoint to automatically create slides without having to reenter information. The PowerPoint presentation in **FIGURE C-1** includes information originally created in Word, Excel, and Access. **CASE** *Before you create the presentation, you review some of the ways you can integrate information among Word, Excel, Access, and PowerPoint.*

DETAILS

You can integrate Word, Excel, Access, and PowerPoint by:

• **Importing a Word outline into PowerPoint**

In the course of your work, you may create Word documents that contain information that you also want to use in a PowerPoint presentation. Instead of retyping the information in PowerPoint, you can save time by importing it directly from Word into PowerPoint. **FIGURE C-1** shows how a Word outline appears before and after it is imported into a PowerPoint presentation. Each Level 1 heading in the outline becomes a slide, and the Level 2 headings become bullets on the slides. Before you import a Word outline, you need to make sure all the headings and subheadings are formatted with heading styles. When you import an outline from Word to PowerPoint, you cannot create a link between the two files.

• **Embedding objects**

Recall that when you embed an object, you do not create a link to the source file. However, you can use the source program tools to edit the embedded object within the destination file. An embedded object becomes a part of the PowerPoint file, which means that the file size of the PowerPoint presentation increases relative to the file size of the embedded object; a large embedded object, such as a graphic, will increase the size of the PowerPoint presentation considerably. To embed an object in a PowerPoint presentation, you use the Object command in the Text group on the INSERT tab. In **FIGURE C-1**, the table on Slide 3 is an embedded Excel worksheet object.

To edit an embedded object, you double-click it. The source program starts, and the Ribbon and tabs of the source program appear inside the PowerPoint window.

• **Linking objects**

When you link an object to a PowerPoint slide, a representation or picture of the object is placed on the slide instead of the actual object. This representation of the object is connected, or linked, to the original file. The object is still stored in the source file in the source program, unlike an embedded object, which is stored directly on the PowerPoint slide. Any change you make to a linked object's source file is reflected in the linked object. The pie chart shown on Slide 4 of the presentation in **FIGURE C-1** is linked to values entered in an Excel worksheet, which is, in turn, linked to data entered in an Access database. The differences between embedding and linking are summarized in **FIGURE C-2**.

You can open the source file and make changes to the linked object as long as all files remain on your computer. When you move files among machines or transmit files to other people, the links will not be maintained. However, recipients can open and view the linked files. After opening the workbook in Excel, they need to click No, close the workbook without saving it, then reopen the workbook and click Don't Update. In Word, they click No to update links.

FIGURE C-1: PowerPoint presentation with integrated objects

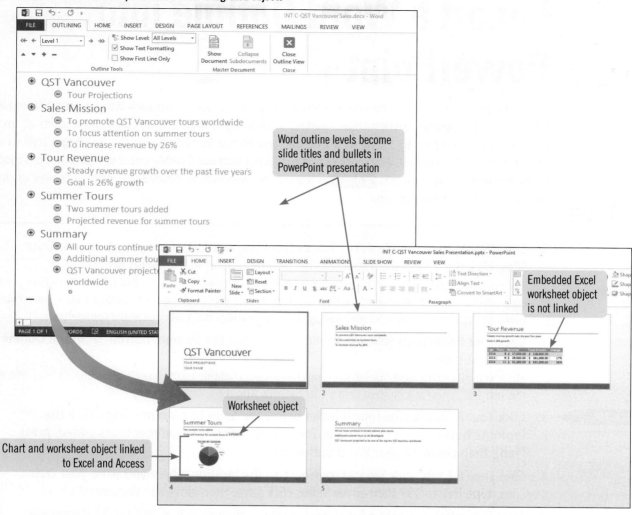

Word outline levels become slide titles and bullets in PowerPoint presentation

Embedded Excel worksheet object is not linked

Worksheet object

Chart and worksheet object linked to Excel and Access

FIGURE C-2: Embedding vs. linking

When you would embed	When you would link
• You are the only user of an object, and you want the object to be a part of your presentation	• You always want your object to include the latest information
• You want to access the object in its source program, even if the source file is not available	• The object's source file is shared on a network or where other users have access to the file and can change it
• You want to update the object manually while working in PowerPoint	• You want to keep the file size of the presentation small

Import a Word Outline into PowerPoint

Learning
Outcomes
• Prepare a Word
outline for
PowerPoint
• Import a Word
outline into
PowerPoint

Before you import a Word outline into PowerPoint, you should ensure that each Word outline heading is formatted with a heading style such as Heading 1, Heading 2, and so on. PowerPoint imports all text formatted with the Heading 1 style as a slide title and all text formatted with the Heading 2 style as a Level 1 item in a bulleted list. Any block of text that is not formatted with a heading style is not included in the PowerPoint presentation. **CASE** ▶ *You use tour information included in a Word document as the basis of a PowerPoint presentation.*

STEPS

1. **Start Word, open the file INT C-1.docx from the location where you store your Data Files, click the VIEW tab, then click the Outline button in the Views group**

 The document appears in Outline view. Each Level 1 heading will become a slide title in PowerPoint, and each Level 2 heading will become a bulleted item. Before you import a Word outline into a PowerPoint presentation, you check that all the headings and subheadings are positioned at the correct levels.

2. **Click Tour Projections (the second line), then click the Demote button ➔ in the Outline Tools group once**

 The text moves to the right one tab stop and changes from Subtitle text to a Level 2 heading. In PowerPoint, this text will appear as a bulleted item under the slide title "QST Vancouver."

QUICK TIP
You can also use [Tab] and [Shift][Tab] to demote and promote headings in Outline view.

3. **Click Tour Revenue (the fourth bullet below the Sales Mission heading), click the Promote button ⬅ in the Outline Tools group, click Two summer tours added, press [Tab], then compare your Word outline to FIGURE C-3**

4. **Click the FILE tab, click Save As, navigate to the location where you store your Data Files, type INT C-QST Vancouver Sales, click Save, then close the document**

5. **Start PowerPoint, create a blank presentation, then save it as INT C-QST Vancouver Sales Presentation in the location where you store your Data Files**

6. **Click the New Slide list arrow in the Slides group, click Slides from Outline, navigate to the location where you stored INT C-QST Vancouver Sales, then double-click INT C-QST Vancouver Sales**

 The Slides pane and the status bar indicate the presentation now contains six slides. Slide 1 is blank, and Slides 2 through 6 represent the Level 1 headings in the Word outline.

7. **Click Slide 1 in the Slides pane, press [Delete], click the Layout button in the Slides group, click Title Slide, click the VIEW tab, click the Outline View button in the Presentation Views group, click after Tour Projections on Slide 1, press [Enter], then type your name**

 You change the slide layout for the first slide so the title of the presentation and your name appear in the middle of the slide.

QUICK TIP
When you import slides into PowerPoint, you need to reset the layout of the slides to conform to the PowerPoint slide design you have applied.

8. **Click the DESIGN tab, click the More button ⬇ in the Themes group, then click the Retrospect theme**

9. **Click the VIEW tab, click the Slide Sorter button in the Presentation Views group, press [Ctrl][A] to select all the slides, click the HOME tab, click the Reset button in the Slides group, then save the presentation**

 The formatted presentation appears as shown in FIGURE C-4.

FIGURE C-3: Edited outline in Word Outline view

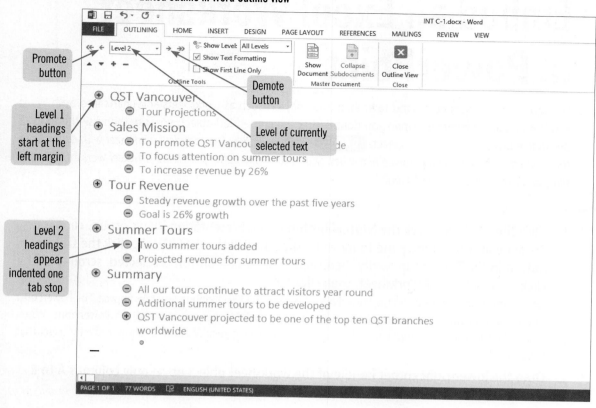

Promote button

Level 1 headings start at the left margin

Level 2 headings appear indented one tab stop

Demote button

Level of currently selected text

FIGURE C-4: Formatted presentation in Slide Sorter view

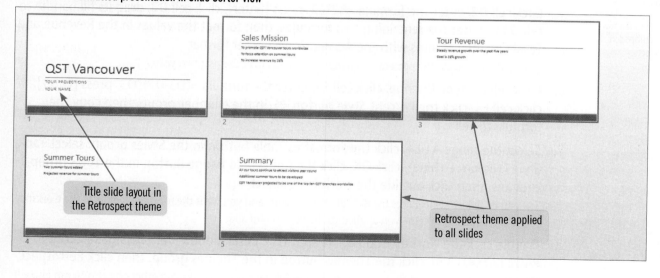

Title slide layout in the Retrospect theme

Retrospect theme applied to all slides

Integration 2013

Embed an Excel Worksheet in PowerPoint

Learning Outcomes
• Embed a Worksheet object in PowerPoint
• Edit an embedded worksheet

You can use the Object command to embed Excel objects such as worksheets and charts into both Word and PowerPoint documents. When you double-click the embedded object, you can then use the tools of the source program to edit the object. **CASE** ▶ *You want Slide 3 to include a worksheet with calculations that you can edit from within PowerPoint when you obtain new data. You create an Excel worksheet on the slide, and then edit it using Excel tools.*

STEPS

1. **Click the VIEW tab, click the Normal button in the Presentation Views group, click Tour Revenue in the Outline pane to move to Slide 3, click the INSERT tab, click the Object button in the Text group, verify the Create new option button is selected, scroll to and click Microsoft Excel Worksheet, then click OK**

 An Excel worksheet appears on the PowerPoint slide, and the Excel Ribbon and tabs appear. The PowerPoint title bar and menu bar, above the Excel tools, indicate that Excel is operating within PowerPoint. When you embed a worksheet object in a PowerPoint slide, you generally want to show only the cells that contain data.

> **TROUBLE**
> You move the mouse over the bottom-right corner of the embedded worksheet to show the resize pointer ⬉, then drag up and to the left until you see columns A to E and rows 1 to 4. You may need to adjust the view by dragging again.

2. **Drag the lower-right corner handle of the worksheet object up so only columns A to E and rows 1 to 4 are visible, as shown in FIGURE C-5**

 You want to clearly see the data you need to enter into the worksheet object.

3. **Click the Select All button ◢ in the upper-left corner of the embedded worksheet to select all the worksheet cells, change the font size to 24 point, then click cell A1**

4. **Enter the labels and values in the range A1:D4 as shown in FIGURE C-6, widening columns as needed**

> **TROUBLE**
> Press the arrow keys, use the scroll bars, or press [Ctrl][Home] to move to the top of the embedded worksheet.

5. **Click cell D2, enter the formula =B2*C2, press [Enter], click cell D2, drag its fill handle to cell D4 to enter the remaining two formulas, then format the values in the Revenue and Total Growth columns with the Accounting Number format**

 You need to calculate the percentage change in revenue over the past two years.

6. **Click cell E1, type Change, click cell E3, enter the formula =(D3-D2)/D3, press [Enter], click cell E3, click the Percent Style button ％ in the Number group, then copy the formula to cell E4**

7. **Select the range A1:E4, click the Format as Table button in the Styles group, select Table Style Medium 2 (blue), click OK, click the Convert to Range button in the Tools group, click Yes, then click outside the worksheet object**

 The embedded worksheet uses the default Office theme, and you want the fonts and colors of the worksheet to use the Retrospect theme you applied to the PowerPoint slide.

8. **Double-click the worksheet object to show the Excel Ribbon and tabs again, click the PAGE LAYOUT tab, click the Themes button in the Themes group, then click Retrospect**

 The worksheet is an object that you can move around the screen just like any other object. You can also edit the contents of the worksheet object.

9. **Change 12 in cell B4 to 11, press [Tab], click outside the worksheet object, drag the object below the text as shown in FIGURE C-7, then save the presentation**

 The percentage growth for 2016 is now 26%.

FIGURE C-5: Resizing the worksheet object

Select All button

Excel worksheet object resized to Row 4 and Column E

FIGURE C-6: Labels and values entered in the Excel worksheet object

	A	B	C	D	E
1	Year	Tours	Revenue	Total Growth	
2	2014	8	27000		
3	2015	9	29000		
4	2016	12	32000		

Double-click column dividers to widen columns

Sheet1

FIGURE C-7: Completed Excel worksheet object

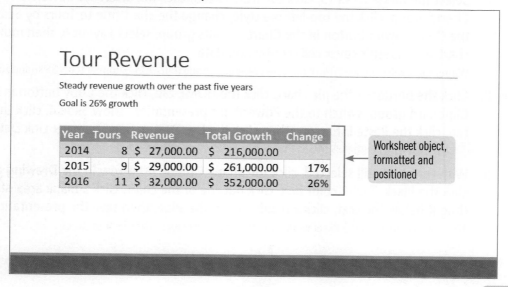

Tour Revenue

Steady revenue growth over the past five years

Goal is 26% growth

Year	Tours	Revenue	Total Growth	Change
2014	8	$ 27,000.00	$ 216,000.00	
2015	9	$ 29,000.00	$ 261,000.00	17%
2016	11	$ 32,000.00	$ 352,000.00	26%

Worksheet object, formatted and positioned

Link Access and Excel Objects to PowerPoint

Learning Outcomes
- Link an Access table to Excel
- Link an Excel chart to PowerPoint

You can copy an Access table from Access to PowerPoint; however, you cannot paste the table as a link. To link data from an Access database to a PowerPoint presentation, you first copy the data to Excel as a link and then copy the data from Excel and paste it as a link into PowerPoint. **CASE** ➤ *You already have tour data stored in an Access database that you want to include in the PowerPoint presentation. You want any changes you make to the table in Access also to appear in the PowerPoint presentation.*

STEPS

QUICK TIP

To save the database with a new name, click the FILE tab, click Save As, click the Save As button, navigate to the location where you store your Data Files, type the new filename, then click Save.

1. **Start Access, open the file** INT C-2.accdb **from the location where you store your Data Files, save the database as** INT C-QST Vancouver Tours, **click** Enable Content, **double-click the** Tours table, **then review the Season field**

 You need to sort the Tours table alphabetically by Season so you can use the data in a chart you create in Excel. You create a query to sort the data so the sorting is maintained when you copy the data to Excel.

2. **Close the Tours table, click the** CREATE **tab, click the** Query Wizard button **in the Queries group, click** OK, **click the** Select All Fields button >> **to add all the fields in the Tours table to the query, click** Next, **click** Next, **then click** Finish

3. **Click the** HOME **tab, click the** View button **in the Views group to go to Design view, click the** blank line **below "Tours" in the [Season] column, click the** Season Sort list arrow, **then select** Ascending **as shown in** FIGURE C-8

4. **Close and save the Tours query, click** Tours Query **in the Navigation Pane, then click the** Copy button **in the Clipboard group**

5. **Create a new blank workbook in Excel, click the** Paste list arrow **in the Clipboard group, click the** Paste Link button 🗐, **click cell** G1, **type** Total, **click cell** G2, **enter the formula** =E2*F2, **copy the formula to the range** G3:G11, **format the values in columns E and G with the Accounting Number format, then widen columns as necessary**

6. **Save the file as** INT C-QST Vancouver Tour Seasons **in the location where you store your Data Files, click cell** C14, **then enter the labels and formulas as shown in** FIGURE C-9

7. **Select the range** C14:F15, **click the** INSERT **tab, click the** Insert Pie button 🥧 **in the Charts group, click the** top-left pie style, **change the chart title to** Tours by Season, **click the** Quick Layout button **in the Chart Layouts group, select** Layout 6, **then move the chart so it doesn't cover cells containing data**

 Winter tours will generate 20% of projected revenue, Spring tours 10%, Summer tours 55%, and Fall tours 15%.

QUICK TIP

The chart you copied from Excel is linked by default to the source file but takes on the theme of the destination file.

8. **Click the** border **of the pie chart, click the** HOME **tab, click the** Copy button **in the Clipboard group, switch to the PowerPoint presentation, show Slide 4, click the HOME tab, click the** Paste list arrow, **then click the** Use Destination Theme & Link Data button 🗐 **as shown in** FIGURE C-10

9. **With the chart still selected, click the** Shape Outline list arrow **in the Drawing group, click the** Black, Text 1 color box, **click outside of the chart, click a blank area of the chart, drag it below the text, click a blank area of the slide, then save the presentation**

 The chart is linked to the Excel worksheet and the Tours Query datasheet in Access.

FIGURE C-8: Sorting the Season field in Query Design view

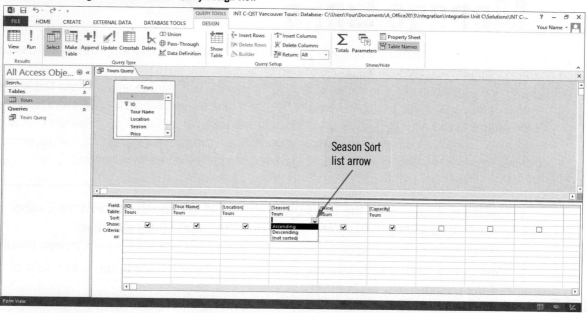

FIGURE C-9: Formulas to calculate total tours by Category

	A	B	C	D	E	F	G	H
1	ID	Tour Name	Location	Season	Price	Capacity	Total	
2	9	Cariboo Trail Ride	Kamloops	Fall	$ 4,000.00	19	$76,000.00	
3	7	Ski Whistler	Vancouver	Spring	$ 3,000.00	13	$39,000.00	
4	6	Whale Watching Adventure	Victoria	Spring	$ 1,000.00	15	$15,000.00	
5	8	Gulf Island Cruising	Victoria	Summer	$ 3,500.00	15	$52,500.00	
6	5	West Coast Kayaking	Victoria	Summer	$ 3,000.00	18	$54,000.00	
7	4	Bowron Lakes Adventure	Kamloops	Summer	$ 4,000.00	12	$48,000.00	
8	3	Ultimate Cycle Tour	Vancouver	Summer	$ 6,000.00	14	$84,000.00	
9	1	Icefields Parkway Cycling	Calgary	Summer	$ 3,500.00	15	$52,500.00	
10	10	Yukon Adventure	Whiteho					
11	2	Powder Skiing	Calgary					
12								
13								
14			Winter	Spring	Summer	Fall		
15			$ 104,500.00	$54,000.00	$ 291,000.00	$ 76,000.00		
16								
17								

Formula in cell D15 is =G3+G4

Formula in cell E15 is =SUM(G5:G9)

Formula in cell C15 is =G10+G11

Formula in cell F15 is =G2

FIGURE C-10: Linking a copied chart to PowerPoint

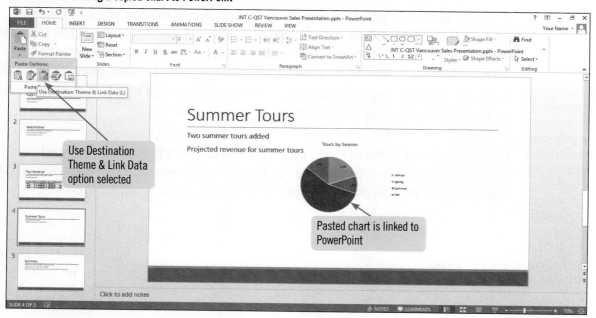

Use Destination Theme & Link Data option selected

Pasted chart is linked to PowerPoint

Manage Links

You frequently need to manage the links you create between files and programs. You may need to update links manually, find the source of a link, or even break a link. You normally break a link when you need to send a file to another user. In PowerPoint, Word, and Excel, you manage links between files in the Edit Links dialog box, which you open from the FILE tab. TABLE C-1 summarizes all the integration tasks you performed in this unit. **CASE** *You want to modify the chart on Slide 4 of the presentation to reflect changing tour prices, then update the links you've created in the database, the spreadsheet, and the presentation. Finally, you break the links so you can send the presentation to the marketing department.*

STEPS

1. **Switch to Access, open the Tours Query datasheet, change the price of the Cariboo Trail Ride tour to $5,000, press [Enter], then close the Tours Query datasheet**

 When you change data in the Tours Query datasheet, the corresponding data in the Tours table also changes.

2. **Switch to Excel, click the FILE tab, then click Edit Links to Files in the lower-right corner of the screen, as shown in** FIGURE C-11

 The Edit Links dialog box opens.

3. **Click Update Values, click Close, click ⬅ to return to the worksheet, verify that Fall tours now account for 18% of projected tour revenue, then save the workbook**

4. **Switch to PowerPoint, then verify that the Fall tours slice is now 18%**

5. **Click the pie chart, click the CHART TOOLS DESIGN tab, click the More button ⬇ in the Chart Styles group, then select Style 9**

 When you insert an Excel chart into a PowerPoint presentation, you usually need to select a new chart style so the data is easy to read on a slide.

6. **Switch to Excel, copy cell E15, switch back to PowerPoint, click after "tours" in the second bulleted item, press [Spacebar], type is, click the Paste list arrow, click Paste Special, click the Paste link option button, click OK to paste the link as a Microsoft Excel Worksheet Object, then position the worksheet object to the right of "is" and increase its size slightly**

 The copied object appears as $291,000.00.

7. **Switch to Access, open the Tours Query datasheet, change the cost of each of the five Summer tours to $5,000, close the datasheet, switch to Excel and open the Edit Links dialog box on the FILE tab, update the link in Excel, switch to PowerPoint, then verify the worksheet object in PowerPoint is now $370,000.00 and the Summer Tours pie slice is 59%**

8. **In PowerPoint, click the FILE tab, click Edit Links to Files, click the top link, click Break Link, click the remaining link, click Break Link, then click Close**

 Now when you change data in the Access file, the linked Excel chart in PowerPoint will not be updated.

9. **Click ⬅ to return to PowerPoint, click the VIEW tab, click the Slide Sorter button in the Presentation Views group, compare the completed presentation to** FIGURE C-12, **save and close all open files and programs, then submit your files to your instructor**

FIGURE C-11: Updating links using the FILE tab

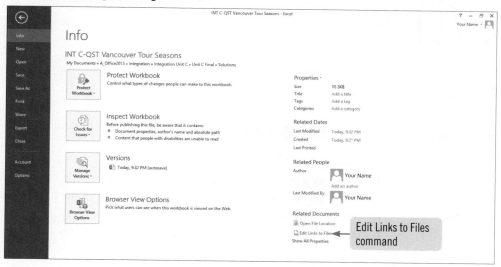

FIGURE C-12: Completed presentation in Slide Sorter view

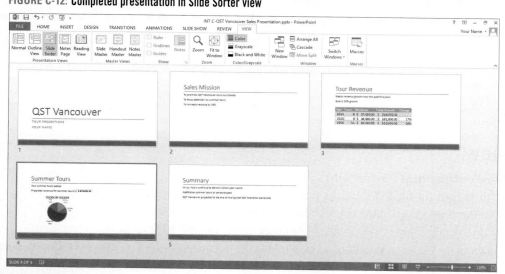

TABLE C-1: Unit C integration tasks

object	commands	source program(s)	destination program	result	connection	page no.
Word outline	In PowerPoint: New Slide/Slides from Outline	Word	PowerPoint	Word outline inserted into PowerPoint; Level 1 headings are slide titles, and Level 2 headings are text items	None	36
Excel worksheet	In PowerPoint: Insert/Object/ Create New	Excel	PowerPoint	Excel worksheet created in PowerPoint, then updated by double-clicking and using Excel tools	Embedded	38
Access query	Copy/Paste Link	Access	Excel	Access query is pasted into Excel as a link; linked data can only be formatted in Excel	Linked	40
Excel chart	Copy/Paste Link	Access/Excel	PowerPoint	Chart created from linked Access query is pasted into PowerPoint as a link; when Access data changes, Excel and PowerPoint data is updated	Linked	40

Practice

Concepts Review

Match each term with the statement that best describes it.

1. Linked object
2. Link
3. Embedded object
4. Destination program
5. Edit Links

a. Edit by making changes in the source file
b. The dialog box containing commands to manage connections between files
c. Contains embedded objects that can be edited using the tools of source programs
d. Increases the size of the destination file
e. The best way to share information when the file size should remain small

Select the best answer from the list of choices.

6. In Word, which view do you work in to prepare text to import into a PowerPoint presentation?
 a. Draft
 b. Print
 c. Full Screen Reading
 d. Outline

7. In Excel, which Paste option do you choose to paste a linked Access table?
 a. Import
 b. New Link
 c. Paste
 d. Paste Link

Skills Review

1. **Import a Word outline into PowerPoint.**
 a. Start Word, then open the file INT C-3.docx from the location where you store your Data Files.
 b. Switch to Outline view, then demote the subheading "San Diego, CA" to Level 2.
 c. Demote the three subheadings: "Townhouses," "Houses," and "Estates" to Level 3.
 d. Promote the Property Values subheading to Level 1, save the document as **INT C-Pacific Crest Realty Outline**, then close the document.
 e. Open a new presentation in PowerPoint, then save it as **INT C-Pacific Crest Realty Presentation** in the location where you store your Data Files.
 f. Import the INT C-Pacific Crest Realty Outline document as slides into PowerPoint.
 g. Delete the blank Slide 1, apply the Title Slide layout to the new Slide 1, then add your name after the subtitle on Slide 1.
 h. Apply the Facet slide design.
 i. Switch to Slide Sorter view, select all the slides, reset the layout, then save the presentation.

2. **Embed an Excel worksheet in PowerPoint.**
 a. Switch to Outline view, move to Slide 4, delete the blank text placeholder, then insert a Microsoft Excel Worksheet object.
 b. Resize the object so only columns A to D and rows 1 to 5 are visible.
 c. Change the font size of all the cells to 28 point, enter labels and values as shown in FIGURE C-13, then adjust column widths.
 d. Enter a formula in cell D2 to multiply the number of homes by the average price for the first quarter, then copy the formula to the range D3:D5.

FIGURE C-13

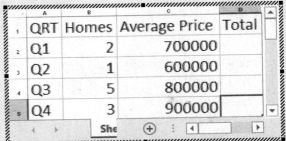

QRT	Homes	Average Price	Total
Q1	2	700000	
Q2	1	600000	
Q3	5	800000	
Q4	3	900000	

Skills Review (continued)

e. Apply the Facet theme to the embedded workbook, apply the Table Style Medium 3 style, convert the table to a range, format the dollar values in columns C and D with the Accounting Number format, then widen columns as needed. (*Hint*: To widen column D, resize the object to show column E, widen Column D, then reduce the object size again.)

f. Position the worksheet object below the slide title.

g. In the worksheet object, change the number of homes sold in the third quarter to **6**, then save the presentation.

3. Link Access and Excel objects to PowerPoint.

a. Start Access, open the file INT C-4.accdb from the location where you store your Data Files, save it as **INT C-Pacific Crest Realty Properties**, then enable the content.

b. Create a query called **Properties Query** from the Properties table, that contains all fields and that sorts the contents of the Category field in ascending order. (*Hint*: Remember to sort the Category field in Design view.)

c. Close and save the query, copy it, create a new workbook in Excel, then paste the query datasheet as a link into cell A1.

d. Format the values in column E using the Accounting Number format, then widen columns as necessary.

e. In the range B16:D17, enter labels and formulas to calculate the total value of all the houses in each of the three categories: Estate, House, and Townhouse, then save the workbook as **INT C-Pacific Crest Realty Property Values**.

f. Create a pie chart in the first 2D style from the range B16:D17, then apply Layout 1.

g. Change the chart title to **Breakdown of Property Values**, copy the chart, then paste it on Slide 5 in the PowerPoint presentation using the Use Destination Theme and Link Data option.

h. Move the worksheet object below the bullet point, then add a black outline.

4. Manage links.

a. In the Access query, change the price of the Sorrento estate to **$4,500,000**, then close the query.

b. Switch to Excel, then update the link in the Edit Links dialog box if the value in cell E3 does not automatically update to 4,500,000.

c. Switch to PowerPoint, then update the link, if necessary, and verify that the Estate wedge is now 44%.

d. Size and position the pie chart so it fills the blank area on the slide attractively, then apply Chart Style 6.

e. In Excel, copy cell B17, then paste it as a linked worksheet object on Slide 5 in PowerPoint.

f. Position the Excel object after "is" and resize it so its font size is comparable to the bullet text.

g. In the Properties Query datasheet in Access, change the price of the first Coronado Estate to **$4,200,000**, then close the datasheet.

h. Update the link in Excel, increase the width of column B so the value in cell B17 is visible, switch to PowerPoint, then, if necessary, update the links to the chart and the worksheet object. The worksheet object is now $11,100,000.00 and the Estate slice is 48%.

i. Break the links to the Excel chart and worksheet, view the presentation in Slide Sorter view, compare the presentation to FIGURE C-14, save and close all open files and programs, then submit your files to your instructor.

FIGURE C-14

Independent Challenge 1

You work at Dog Days, a boutique pet store that sells purebred puppies and dog accessories. You have collected data about recent sales in an Access database, and now you need to create a presentation in PowerPoint that contains links to the sales figures. You also need to import some of the slides needed for the presentation from a Word outline.

a. In Word, open the file INT C-5.docx from the location where you store your Data Files.

b. In Outline view, demote the Dog Breed Information subtitle to Level 2, then demote the list of the four breeds under the Promotions Level 1 heading to Level 3.

c. Save the document as **INT C-Dog Days Outline**, then close the document.

d. Start a new presentation in PowerPoint, then save it as **INT C-Dog Days Presentation** in the location where you store your Data Files.

e. Insert the Dog Days Outline document into PowerPoint, delete Slide 1, apply the Title Slide layout to the new Slide 1, then add your name after the subtitle on Slide 1.

f. In Slide Sorter view, reset the layout of all the slides, then apply the slide design of your choice.

g. On the new Slide 2 (Top Sellers), embed an Excel Worksheet object resized to column B and row 5 with a 22 pt font size and containing the information and formatted as shown in FIGURE C-15.

h. Calculate the total revenue in cell B5.

i. Apply the table style of your choice, convert the table to a range, apply the same theme as you applied to the presentation, then position the worksheet object attractively on the slide.

j. Start Access, open the file INT C-6.accdb from the location where you store your Data Files, then save the database as **INT C-Dog Days Inventory** and enable content.

FIGURE C-15

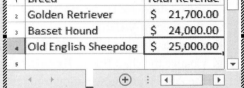

k. Add two new records to the Breeds table (records 16 and 17) as follows: a Poodle and an Irish Wolfhound. Describe each breed as Large, with sales of 5 dogs and a cost of $500.

l. Create a query called **Breeds Query** from the Breeds table, using all fields, that sorts the contents of the Size field in ascending order. Save and close the query, copy the query, paste it as a link into a new Excel workbook, then save the workbook as **INT C-Dog Days Breed Information** in the location where you save your Data Files.

m. Calculate the total revenue for each breed in column F, then starting in cell D20, enter labels and formulas to calculate the total revenue from each of the three sizes of dogs. (*Hint*: Enter **Small** in cell D20, **Medium** in cell E20, and **Large** in cell F20, then enter the required calculations in cells D21:F21.)

n. Format all dollar amounts with the Accounting Number format, then use the data in the range D20:F21 to create a 2D pie chart entitled **Sales by Dog Size** using Layout 6.

o. Move the chart to the right of the data, copy the pie chart, then paste it on the appropriate slide in the presentation using the Use Destination Theme & Link Data option.

p. In Excel, copy the total revenue from Medium dogs, then paste it as a linked worksheet object in the appropriate location on the slide containing the chart.

q. Size and position the worksheet object attractively, then apply the chart style of your choice and resize the chart so it is easy to read. Enclose the chart in a black outline.

r. In Access, change the Cocker Spaniel sale price to **$700** and the quantity sold to **10**, then update the links.

s. Break the links in PowerPoint, view the presentation in Slide Sorter view, save and close all open files and programs, then submit your files to your instructor.

Independent Challenge 2

You are the Assistant Manager at Cloud Nine, a store in Denver, Colorado, that sells camping, hiking, and mountaineering equipment. To assist your customers, you have created a database of trail information they can access online. You have also decided to create a short PowerPoint presentation from information you have stored in Word. The presentation will include data from the database, an embedded worksheet, and a linked chart.

a. Start Word, open the file INT C-7.docx from the location where you store your Data Files, demote the subtitle and the line "All skill levels are accommodated" to Level 2 and promote "Distances" to Level 1.

b. Save the document as **INT C-Cloud Nine Outline**, and close the document.

c. Start a new PowerPoint presentation, save it as **INT C-Cloud Nine Presentation**, then import the INT C-Cloud Nine Outline document into the presentation.

d. Delete the blank Slide 1, apply the Title Slide layout to the new Slide 1, add your name below the subtitle on Slide 1, then apply the Organic slide design. Select the far-right variant in the Variant group to change the background color of the slide design.

e. In Slide Sorter view, reset the layout of all the slides.

f. On Slide 2, embed an Excel Worksheet object displaying three columns and five rows, apply a larger font size so the cells are visible, then enter the information shown in FIGURE C-16 and adjust column widths.

FIGURE C-16

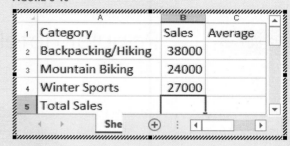

g. Calculate the total sales in cell B5, then, in cell C2, enter =B2/B5 to calculate the average percent of sales of Backpacking/Hiking products.

h. Copy the formula to the other two product categories, then format values with the Accounting Number and Percent formats, and widening columns, as necessary.

i. Apply a theme that matches the presentation, apply the table style of your choice, convert the table to a range, right-align and bold "Total Sales" and bold the total, then position the worksheet object on the slide.

j. Replace XX in the bulleted item with the appropriate value from the embedded worksheet.

k. Start Access, open the file INT C-8.accdb from the location where you store your Data Files, save the database as **INT C-Cloud Nine Trails Database**, then enable content.

l. Create a query called **Colorado Trails Query** from all the fields in the Colorado Trails table that sorts the contents of the Type field in ascending order.

m. Close and save the query, copy it, then paste it as a link into a new Excel workbook saved as **INT C-Cloud Nine Trails Information** in the location where you store your Data Files. Widen columns as needed.

n. Starting in cell C15 of the worksheet, enter labels and formulas to calculate the total miles covered in each of the three trip types: Backpacking, Hiking, and Walking.

o. Create a pie chart of the totals, apply Layout 1, and add a chart title: **Total Distances by Trail Type**.

p. Copy the chart, then paste it using the Use Destination Theme and Link Data paste option on the appropriate slide in the presentation. Resize and reposition it to fit the space attractively.

q. Apply Chart Style 4 to the chart and remove the legend. (*Hint*: Click the Add Chart Element button in the Chart Layouts group, point to Legend, then click None.)

r. Copy cell C16 in the source workbook, then paste it as a linked worksheet object so it replaces the YY placeholder. (*Hint*: Move "miles" to the right using the Spacebar, then size and position the object so it fits.)

s. In the Access query, change the distance of the Mount Sopris Summit Trail to **5** miles and the Capitol Creek trail to **18** miles, then close the query.

t. Update links in Excel and PowerPoint. Note that you will need to adjust the position of the worksheet object. Verify that the value is now 70.3.

u. In PowerPoint, break the links, view the presentation, save and close all open files and programs, then submit your files to your instructor.

Visual Workshop

For a course on tourism in Australia, you have decided to create a presentation that focuses on popular hotels in various locations. The presentation will contain one slide displaying a pie chart showing the breakdown of hotel guests by location. In Access, open the file INT C-9.accdb from the location where you store your Data Files, then save the database as **INT C-Australia Hotels**. Create a query called **Locations** that includes all fields and that sorts the Hotels table in ascending order by Location. Copy the query, and paste it as a link into Excel, then create the 3D pie chart similar to the one shown in FIGURE C-17, and save the Excel workbook as **INT C-Australia Hotels Data**. As shown in the figure, create a one-slide PowerPoint presentation called **INT C-Australia Hotels Presentation**, apply the Title Only slide layout, then copy the pie chart from Excel and paste it onto the slide. Format the slide as shown: add the slide title, apply the Wisp slide design, and format the chart with Style 2. Switch to Access, open the Locations query, change the number of guests who stayed at the Desert Oasis Resort in Alice Springs to **100**, close the query, update the links in Excel and PowerPoint, then enter your name in the slide footer. Break the link to the PowerPoint presentation, save and close all open files and programs, then submit your files to your instructor.

FIGURE C-17

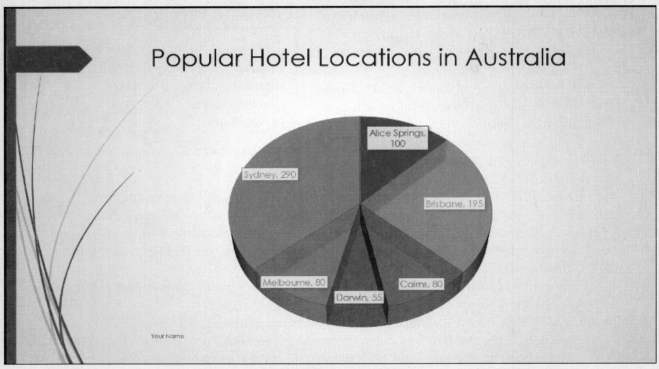

Understanding File Management

**Files You
Will Need:**

No files needed.

To work with the folders and files on your computer, you need to understand how your computer stores them. You should also know how to organize them so you can always find the information you need. These skills are called **file management** skills. When you create a document and save it as a file, it is important that you save the file in a place where you can find it later. To keep your computer files organized, you will need to copy, move, and rename them. When you have files you don't need any more, it's a good idea to move or delete them so your computer has only current files. Your supervisor, Evelyn Swazey, asks you to learn how to manage your computer files so you can begin creating and organizing documents for the upcoming Oceania tours.

OBJECTIVES

Understand folders and files

Create and save a file

Explore the files and folders on your computer

Change file and folder views

Open, edit, and save files

Copy files

Move and rename files

Search for files, folders, and programs

Delete and restore files

Understanding Folders and Files

As you work with your computer programs, you create and save files, such as letters, drawings, or budgets. When you save files, you usually save them inside folders, which are storage areas on your computer. You use folders to group related files, as with paper folders in a file cabinet. The files and folders on your computer are organized in a **file hierarchy**, a system that arranges files and folders in different levels, like the branches of a tree. Figure B-1 shows a sample file hierarchy. ▧▧▧▧ Evelyn asks you to look at some important facts about files and folders to help you store your Oceania tour files.

DETAILS

Use the following guidelines as you organize files using your computer's file hierarchy:

- **Use folders and subfolders to organize files**

 As you work with your computer, you can add folders to your hierarchy and rename them to help you organize your work. You should give folders unique names that help you easily identify them. You can also create **subfolders**, which are folders that are inside of other folders. Windows comes with several existing folders, such as My Documents, My Music, and My Pictures, that you can use as a starting point.

QUICK TIP
You can also start Windows Explorer by clicking the Windows Explorer button on the taskbar.

- **View files in windows**

 You view your computer contents by opening a **window**, like the one in Figure B-2. A window is divided into sections. The **Navigation pane** on the left side of the window shows the folder structure on your computer. When you click a folder in the Navigation pane, you see its contents in the **File list** on the right side. The **Details pane** at the bottom of the window provides information about selected files in the File list. A window actually opens in an accessory program called **Windows Explorer**, although the program name does not appear on the window. You can open this program from the Start menu, or just double-click a folder to open its window and view its contents.

- **Understand file addresses**

 A window also contains an **Address bar**, an area just below the title bar that shows the location, or address, of the files that appear in the File list. An **address** is a sequence of folder names separated by the ▸ symbol that describes a file's location in the file hierarchy. An address shows the folder with the highest hierarchy level on the left and steps through each hierarchy level toward the right, sometimes called a **path**. For example, the My Documents folder might contain a subfolder named Notes. In this case, the Address bar would show My Documents ▸ Notes. Each location between the ▸ symbols represents a level in the file hierarchy.

QUICK TIP
Remember that you single-click a folder or subfolder in the Address bar to show its contents. But in the File list, you double-click a subfolder to open it.

- **Navigate upward and downward using the Address bar and File list**

 You can use the Address bar and the File list to move up or down in the hierarchy one or more levels at a time. To **navigate upward** in your computer's hierarchy, you can click a folder or subfolder name in the Address bar. For example, in Figure B-2, you would move up in the hierarchy by clicking once on Users in the Address bar. Then the File list would show the subfolders and files inside the Users folder. To **navigate downward** in the hierarchy, double-click a subfolder in the File list. The path in the Address bar then shows the path to that subfolder.

- **Navigate upward and downward using the Navigation pane**

 You can also use the Navigation pane to navigate among folders. Move the mouse pointer over the Navigation pane, then click the small triangles or to the left of a folder name to show ▷ or hide ◢ the folder's contents under the folder name. Subfolders appear indented under the folders that contain them, showing that they are inside that folder. Figure B-2 shows a folder named Users in the Navigation pane. The subfolders Katharine, Public, and Your User Name are inside the Users folder.

FIGURE B-1: Sample folder and file hierarchy

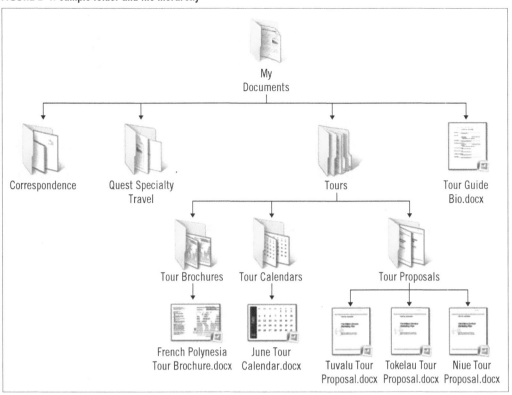

FIGURE B-2: Windows Explorer window

Address shows path to Your User Name folder in file hierarchy

Navigation pane

Users folder

Subfolders inside the Your User Name folder

Click Users to move up one level in hierarchy

Double-click any folder to move one level down in hierarchy

File list shows contents of selected Your User Name folde

Details pane

Plan your file organization

As you manage your files, you should plan how you want to organize them. First, identify the types of files you work with, such as images, music, and reports. Think about the content, such as personal, business, clients, or projects. Then think of a folder organization that will help you find them later. For example, use subfolders in the My Pictures folder to separate family photos from business photos or to group them by year. In the My Documents folder, you might group personal files in one subfolder and business files in another subfolder. Then create additional subfolders to further separate sets of files. You can always move files among folders and rename folders. You should periodically reevaluate your folder structure to make sure that it continues to meet your needs.

Creating and Saving a File

After you start a program and create a new file, the file exists only in your computer's **random access memory (RAM)**, which is a temporary storage location. RAM only contains information when your computer is on. When you turn off your computer, it automatically clears the contents of RAM. So you need to save a new file onto a storage device that permanently stores the file so that you can open, change, and use it later. One important storage device is your computer's hard disk built into your computer. Another popular option is a **USB flash drive**, a small, portable storage device. ▓▓▓▓▓ Evelyn asks you to use the WordPad accessory program to create a short summary of an Oceania tour planning meeting and save it.

1. **Start Windows if necessary, click the** Start button ⊕ **on the taskbar, point to** All Programs, **click** Accessories, **then click** WordPad

 The WordPad program opens. Near the top of the screen you see the Ribbon containing command buttons, similar to those you used in Paint in Unit A. The Home tab appears in front. A new, blank document appears in the document window. The blinking insertion point shows you where the next character you type will appear.

2. **Type** Meeting Notes, October 11, **then press** [Enter]

 WordPad inserts a new blank line and places the insertion point at the beginning of the next line.

 > **TROUBLE**
 > If you make a typing mistake, press [Backspace] to delete the character to the left of the insertion point.

3. **Type** The 2013 tour will visit:, **press** [Enter], **type** Australia, **press** [Enter], **type** Micronesia, **press** [Enter], **type** New Zealand, **press** [Enter], **then type your name; see Figure B-3**

4. **Click the** WordPad button ▦▾ **on the upper-left side of the window below the title bar, then click** Save **on the WordPad menu**

 The first time you save a file using the Save button, the Save As dialog box opens. Use this dialog box to name the document file and choose a storage location for it. The Save As dialog box has many of the same elements as a Windows Explorer window, including an Address bar, a Navigation pane, and a File list. Below the Address bar, the **toolbar** contains command buttons you can click to perform actions. In the Address bar, you can see that WordPad chose the Documents library (which includes the My Documents folder) as the storage location.

 > **TROUBLE**
 > If you don't have a USB flash drive, save the document in the My Documents folder instead.

5. **Plug your USB flash drive into a USB port ▯ on your computer, if necessary**

 On a laptop computer, the USB port is on the left or right side of your computer. On a desktop computer, the USB port is on the front panel (you may need to open a small door to see it), or on the back panel.

6. **In the Navigation pane scroll bar, click the** Down scroll arrow ▾ **as needed to see** Computer **and any storage devices listed under it**

 Under Computer, you see the storage locations available on your computer, such as Local Disk (C:) (your hard drive) and Removable Disk (H:) (your USB drive name and letter might differ). These storage locations act like folders because you can open them and store files in them.

 > **TROUBLE**
 > If your Save As dialog box or title bar does not show the .rtf file extension, open any Windows Explorer window, click Organize in the toolbar, click Folder and search options, click the View tab, then under Files and Folders, click to remove the check mark from Hide extensions for known file types.

7. **Click the name for your USB flash drive**

 The files and folders on your USB drive, if any, appear in the File list. The Address bar shows the location where the file will be saved, which is now Computer > Removable Disk (H:) (or the name of your drive). You need to give your document a meaningful name so you can find it later.

8. **Click in the** Filename text box **to select the default name** Document, **type** Oceania Meeting, **compare your screen to Figure B-4, then click** Save

 The document is saved as a file on your USB flash drive. The filename Oceania Meeting.rtf appears in the title bar at the top of the window. The ".rtf" at the end of the filename is the file extension. A **file extension** is a three- or four-letter sequence, preceded by a period, that identifies the file as a particular type of document, in this case Rich Text Format, to your computer. The WordPad program creates files using the RTF format. Windows adds the .rtf file extension automatically after you click Save.

9. **Click the** Close button ▣ **on the WordPad window**

 The WordPad program closes. Your meeting minutes are now saved on your USB flash drive.

Understanding File Management

FIGURE B-3: **Saving a document**

WordPad
button

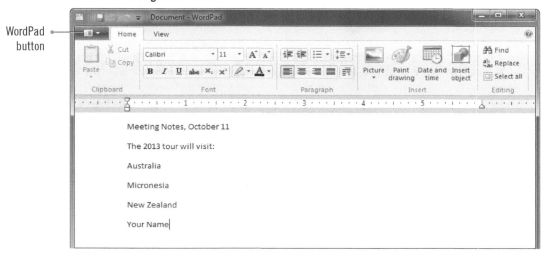

Meeting Notes, October 11

The 2013 tour will visit:

Australia

Micronesia

New Zealand

Your Name

FIGURE B-4: **Save As dialog box**

After you click Save, your
Oceania Meeting.rtf file
will be saved at this
address

Storage devices
on your computer
(yours will differ)

New filename

Toolbar

Folders on USB
flash drive (your
folders will differ)

Using Windows 7 libraries

The Navigation pane contains not only files and folders, but also Libraries. A **library** gathers files and folders from different locations on your computer and displays them in one location. For example, you might have pictures in several different folders on your storage devices. You can add these folder locations to your Pictures library. Then when you want to see all your pictures, you open your Pictures library, instead of several different folders. The picture files stay in their original locations, but their names appear in the Pictures library. A library is not a folder that stores files, but rather a way of viewing similar types of documents that you have stored in multiple locations on your computer. Figure B-5 shows the four libraries that come with Windows 7: Documents, Music, Pictures, and Videos. To help you distinguish between library locations and actual folder locations, library names differ from actual folder names. For example, the My Documents folder is on your hard drive, but the library name is Documents. To add a location to a library, click the blue locations link (at the top of the File list) in the library you want to add to, click the Add button, navigate to the folder location you want to add,

then click Include folder. If you delete a file or folder from a library, you delete them from their source locations. If you delete a library, you do not delete the files in it. The Documents Library that comes with Windows already has the My Documents folder listed as a save location. So if you save a document to the Documents library, it is automatically saved to your My Documents folder.

FIGURE B-5: **Libraries**

Exploring the Files and Folders on Your Computer

In the last lesson, you navigated to your USB flash drive as you worked in the Save As dialog box. But even if you're not saving a document, you will want to examine your computer and its existing folder and file structure. That way, you'll know where to save files as you work with Windows application programs. In a Windows Explorer window, you can navigate through your computer contents using the File list, the Address bar, and the Navigation pane. ░░░░░ As you prepare for the Oceania tours, you look at the files and folders on your computer.

STEPS

1. Click the Start button ⊕ on the taskbar, then click Computer

Your computer's storage devices appear in a window, as shown in Figure B-6, including hard drives; devices with removable storage, such as CD and DVD drives or USB flash drives; and portable devices such as personal digital assistants (PDAs). Table B-1 lists examples of different drive types. A colored bar shows you how much space has been taken up on your hard drive. You decide to move down a level in your computer's hierarchy and see what is on your USB flash drive.

2. In the File list, double-click Removable Disk (H:) (or the drive name and letter for your USB flash drive)

You see the contents of your USB flash drive, including the Oceania Meeting.rtf file you saved in the last lesson. You decide to navigate one level up in the file hierarchy.

3. In the Address bar, click Computer

You return to the Computer window showing your storage devices. You decide to look at the contents of your hard drive.

4. In the Navigation pane, click Local Disk (C:)

The contents of your hard drive appear in the File list. The Users folder contains a subfolder for each user who has a user account on this computer. Recall that you double-click items in the File list to open them. In the Address bar and in the Navigation pane, you only need to single-click.

5. In the File list, double-click the Users folder

You see folders for each user registered on your computer. You might see a folder with your user account name on it. Each user's folder contains that person's documents. User folder names are the log-in names that were entered when your computer was set up. When a user logs in, the computer allows that user access to the folder with the same user name. If you are using a computer with more than one user, you might not have permission to view other users' folders. There is also a Public folder that any user can open.

6. Double-click the folder with your user name on it

Depending on how your computer is set up, this folder might be labeled with your name; however, if you are using a computer in a lab or a public location, your folder might be called Student or Computer User or something similar. You see a list of folders, such as My Documents, My Music, and others. See Figure B-7.

7. Double-click My Documents

You see the folders and documents you can open and work with. In the Address bar, the path to the My Documents folder is Computer ▸ Local Disk (C:) ▸ Users ▸ Your User Name ▸ My Documents. You decide to return to the Computer window.

8. In the Navigation pane, click Computer

You moved up three levels in your hierarchy. You can also move one level up at a time in your file hierarchy by pressing the [Backspace] key on your keyboard. You once again see your computer's storage devices.

FIGURE B-6: Computer window showing storage devices

Colored bar indicates
the hard drive is about
one-third full

Your computer's
storage devices
might differ

FIGURE B-7: Your User Name folder

Path to your
User Name folder
contents

Your User Name
folder contents
might differ

TABLE B-1: Drive names and icons

drive type	drive icon	drive name
hard drive		C:
CD drive		Next available drive letter, such as D:
DVD drive		Next available drive letter, such as E:
USB flash drive		Next available drive letter, such as F:, G:, or H:

Sharing information with homegroups and libraries

Windows 7 lets you create a **homegroup**, a named set of computers
that can share information. If your computer is in a homegroup with
other Windows 7 computers, you can share libraries and printers
with those computers. Click Start, then click Control Panel. Under
Network and Internet, click Choose homegroup and sharing options.
Click to place a check mark next to the libraries and printers you
want to share, then click Save changes. To share libraries that you
have created on your computer with others in your homegroup,
click Start, click your user name, then in the Navigation pane, click
the library you want to share, click Share with on the toolbar, then
click the sharing option you want, as shown in Figure B-8.

FIGURE B-8: Sharing a library

Changing File and Folder Views

As you view your folders and files, you might want to see as many items as possible in a window. At other times, you might want to see details about each item. Windows 7 lets you choose from eight different **views**, which are appearance choices for your folder contents. Each view provides different information about the files and folders in different ways. You can list your folders and files by using several different-sized icons or in lists. You can also **sort** them to change the order in which the folders and files are listed. If you want to see what a file looks like, but don't want to open the file, you can see a preview of it in the window. ▀▀▀▀ As you plan the Oceania tour, you review picture files in various views.

STEPS

1. **In the Navigation pane, under Libraries, click** Pictures, **then in the File list, double-click the** Sample Pictures folder

 You opened the Sample Pictures folder, which is inside your Pictures library.

2. **In the toolbar, click the** More options list arrow **next to the Change your view icon** ▣▾

 The list of available views appears in a shortcut menu. See Figure B-9.

3. **Click** Large Icons

 In this view, the pictures appear as large-sized icons in the File list, as shown in Figure B-10. For image files, this view is very helpful. You can click any view name or you can drag a slider control to move through each of the available views.

4. **Click the** Change your view More options list arrow ▣▾ **again, point to the slider** ▣▭ , **then drag it so it's next to** Details

 As you drag, Live Preview shows you how each view looks in your folder. In Details view, you can see file-names, the date that files were created or modified, and other information. In Details view, you can also control the order in which the folders and files appear. In the Name column heading, you see a small triangle ┌─────────┐ ˄ └ Name ─────┘ . This indicates that the sample pictures are in alphabetical order (A, B, C,...).

5. **Click the** Name column heading

 The items now appear in descending (Z, Y, X,...) order. The icon in the column header changes to ┌─────────┐ ˅ └ Name ─────┘ .

6. **Click the** Show the preview pane button ▣ **in the toolbar**

 The Preview pane opens on the right side of the screen. The **Preview pane** is an area on the right side of a window that shows you what a selected file looks like without opening it. It is especially useful for document files so you can see the first few paragraphs of a large document.

7. **Click the name of your USB flash drive in the Navigation pane, then click the** Oceania Meeting.rtf **filename in the File list**

 A preview of the Oceania Meeting file you created earlier in this unit appears in the Preview pane. The Word-Pad file is not open, but you can still see its contents. The Details pane gives you information about the se-lected file. See Figure B-11.

8. **Click the** Hide the preview pane button ▣

 The Preview pane closes.

9. **Click the window's** Close button ▣

FIGURE B-9: **More options shortcut menu showing views**

Slider

FIGURE B-10: **Sample pictures library as large icons**

Your pictures might differ

FIGURE B-11: **Preview of selected Oceania Meeting.rtf file**

Selected document

USB flash drive selected

Show the preview pane button

Preview pane shows preview of selected document

Details pane

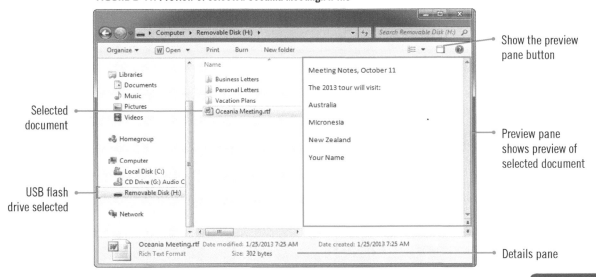

Understanding File Management

Opening, Editing, and Saving Files

Once you have created a file and saved it with a name in a folder on a storage device, you can easily open it and **edit** (make changes to) it. For example, you might want to add or delete text to a document, or change the color in a drawing. Then you save the file again so that it contains your latest changes. Usually you save a file with the same filename and in the same location as the original, which replaces the existing file with the latest, updated version. When you save a file you have changed, you use the Save command. ▨▨▨▨▨ Evelyn asks you to complete the meeting notes.

STEPS

1. **Click the Start button ⊕ on the taskbar, point to All Programs, click the Accessories folder, then click WordPad**

 If you use WordPad frequently, it's name might appear on the left side of the Start menu. If it does, you can click it there to open it.

2. **Click the WordPad button ▣▾, then click Open**

 The Open dialog box opens. It has the same sections as the Save As dialog box and the Windows Explorer windows you used earlier in this unit. You decide to navigate to the location where you saved your Oceania Meeting.rtf file so you can open it.

TROUBLE
If you are not using a USB flash drive, click an appropriate storage location in the Navigation pane.

3. **Scroll down in the Navigation pane if necessary until you see Computer, then click Removable Disk (H:) (or the drive name and letter for your USB flash drive)**

 The contents of your USB flash drive appear in the File list, as shown in Figure B-12.

QUICK TIP
You can also double-click the filename in the File list to open the file.

4. **Click Oceania Meeting.rtf in the File list, then click Open**

 The document you created earlier opens.

5. **Click to the right of the "d" in New Zealand, press [Enter], then type Evelyn Swazey closed the meeting.**

 The edited document includes the text you just typed. See Figure B-13.

QUICK TIP
Instead of using the WordPad menu and Save command to save a document, you can also click the Save button. 🖫 in the Quick Access toolbar at the top of the WordPad window.

6. **Click the WordPad button ▣▾, then click Save, as shown in Figure B-14**

 WordPad saves the document with your most recent changes, using the filename and location you specified when you saved it for the first time. When you save an existing file, the Save As dialog box does not open.

7. **Click ▣▾, then click Exit**

Comparing Save and Save As

The WordPad menu has two save command options—Save and Save As. When you first save a file, the Save As dialog box opens (whether you choose Save or Save As). Here you can select the drive and folder where you want to save the file and enter its filename. If you edit a previously saved file, you can save the file to the same location with the same filename using the Save command. The Save command updates the stored file using the same location and filename without opening the Save As dialog box. In some situations, you might want to save another copy of the existing document using a different filename or in a different storage location. To do this, open the document, use the Save As command, and then navigate to a different location, and/or edit the name of the file.

FIGURE B-12: **Navigating in the Open dialog box**

The folders on your
drive will differ

FIGURE B-13: **Edited document**

Meeting Notes, October 11

The 2013 tour will visit:

Australia

Micronesia

New Zealand

Evelyn Swazey closed the meeting.

Your Name

Added text

FIGURE B-14: **Saving a revised document**

Copying Files

As you have learned, saving a file in a location on your hard drive stores it so you can open it later. But sometimes you will want to make a copy of a file. For example, you might want to put a copy on a USB flash drive so you can open the file on another machine or share a file with a friend or colleague. Or you might want to create a copy as a **backup**, or replacement, in case something happens to your original file. You copy files and folders using the Copy command and then place the copy in another location using the Paste command. You cannot have two copies of a file with the same name in the same folder. If you attempt to do this, Windows 7 will ask you if you want to replace the first one then gives you a chance to give the second copy a different name. ▓▓▓▓▓ Evelyn asks you to create a backup copy of the meeting notes document you created and paste it in a new folder you create on your USB flash drive.

STEPS

1. **Click the** Start button ⊛ **on the taskbar, then click** Computer

2. **In the File list, double-click** Removable Disk (H:) **(or the drive name and letter for your USB flash drive)**

 First you create the new folder Evelyn needs.

3. **In the toolbar, click the** New folder button

 A new folder appears in the File list, with its name, New folder, selected. Because the folder name is selected, any text you type replaces the selected text as the folder name.

4. **Type** Meeting Notes, **then press** [Enter]

 You named the new folder Meeting Notes. Next, you copy your original Oceania Meeting.rtf file.

5. **In the File list, click the** Oceania Meeting.rtf **document you saved earlier, click the** Organize **button on the toolbar, then click** Copy, **as shown in Figure B-15**

 When you use the Copy command, Windows 7 places a duplicate copy of the file in an area of your computer's random access memory called the **clipboard**, ready to paste, or place, in a new location. Copying and pasting a file leaves the file in its original location. The copied file remains on the clipboard until you copy something else or end your Windows 7 session.

6. **In the File list, double-click the** Meeting Notes folder

 The folder opens.

7. **Click the** Organize **button on the toolbar, then click** Paste

 A copy of your Oceania Meeting.rtf file is pasted into your new Meeting Notes folder. See Figure B-16. You now have two copies of the Oceania Meeting.rtf file: one on your USB flash drive in the main folder, and a copy of the file in a folder called Meeting Notes on your USB flash drive. The file remains on the clipboard so you can paste it again to other locations if you like.

FIGURE B-15: **Copying a file**

FIGURE B-16: **Duplicate file pasted into Meeting Notes folder**

Copying files using Send to

You can also copy and paste a file to an external storage device using the Send to command. In a window, right-click the file you want to copy, point to Send to, then in the shortcut menu, click the name of the device where you want to send a copy of the file. This leaves the original file on your hard drive and creates a copy on the external device, all with just one command. See Table B-2 for a short summary of other shortcut menu commands.

TABLE B-2: **Selected Send to menu commands**

menu option	use to	menu option	use to
Compressed (zipped) folder	Create a new compressed (smaller) file with a .zip file extension	Documents	Copy the file to the Documents library
Desktop (create shortcut)	Create a shortcut (link) for the file on the desktop	DVD RW Drive (D:)	Copy the file to your computer's DVD drive
Mail recipient	Create an e-mail with the file attached to it (only if you have an e-mail program on your computer)	Removable Disk (H:)	Copy the file to your removable disk (H:)

Moving and Renaming Files

As you work with files, you might need to move files or folders to another location. You can move one or more files or folders. You might move them to a different folder on the same drive or a different drive. When you **move** a file, the file is transferred to the new location and no longer exists in its original location. You can move a file using the Cut and Paste commands. After you create a file, you might find that the original name you gave the file isn't clear anymore, so you can rename it to make it more descriptive or accurate. ████ You decide to move your original Oceania Meeting.rtf document to your Documents library. After you move it, you decide to edit the filename so it better describes the file contents.

STEPS

QUICK TIP

You can also cut a file by right-clicking the file in the File list and then clicking Cut. To use the keyboard, press and hold [Ctrl] and press [X], then release both keys.

1. **In the Address bar, click** Removable Disk (H:) **(or the drive name and letter for your USB flash drive)**

2. **Click the** Oceania Meeting.rtf **document to select it**

3. **Click the** Organize **button on the toolbar, then click** Cut

 The icon representing the cut file becomes lighter in color, indicating you have cut it, as shown in Figure B-17. You navigate to your Documents library, in preparation for pasting the cut document there.

4. **In the Navigation Pane, under Libraries, click** Documents

QUICK TIP

You can also paste a file by right-clicking an empty area in the File list and then clicking Paste. To use the keyboard, press and hold [Ctrl] and press [V], then release both keys.

5. **Click the** Organize **button on the toolbar, then click** Paste

 The Oceania Meeting.rtf document appears in your Documents library. See Figure B-18. The filename could be clearer, to help you remember that it contains notes from your meeting.

6. **With the Oceania Meeting.rtf file selected, click the** Organize **button on the toolbar, then click** Rename

 The filename is highlighted. In a window, the file extension cannot change because it identifies the file to WordPad. If you delete the file extension, the file cannot be opened. You could type a new name to replace the old one, but you decide to add the word "Notes" to the end of the filename instead.

7. **Click the** I **after the "g" in "Meeting", press [Spacebar], then type** Notes, **as shown in Figure B-19, then press [Enter]**

 You changed the name of the document copy in the Documents library. The filename now reads Oceania Meeting Notes.rtf.

8. **Close the window**

FIGURE B-17: **Cutting a file**

Icon is lighter, indicating you have cut the file

FIGURE B-18: **Pasted file in Documents library**

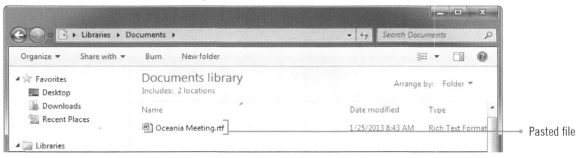

Pasted file

FIGURE B-19: **Renaming a file**

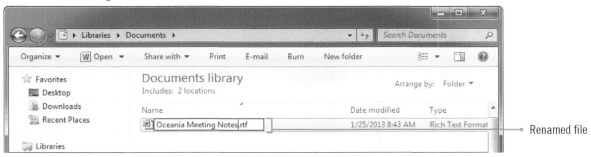

Renamed file

Using drag and drop to copy or move files to new locations

You can also use the mouse to copy a file and place the copy in a new location. **Drag and drop** is a technique in which you use your pointing device to drag a file or folder into a different folder and then drop it, or let go of the mouse button, to place it in that folder. Using drag and drop does not copy your file to the clipboard. If you drag and drop a file to a folder on another drive, Windows *copies* the file. See Figure B-20. However, if you drag and drop a file to a folder on the same drive, Windows 7 *moves* the file into that folder instead. If you want to move a file to another drive, hold down [Shift] while you drag and drop. If you want to copy a file to another folder on the same drive, hold down [Ctrl] while you drag and drop.

FIGURE B-20: **Copying a file using drag and drop**

Searching for Files, Folders, and Programs

After copying or moving folders and files, you might forget where you stored a particular folder or file, its name, or both. Or you might need help finding a program on your computer. **Windows Search** helps you quickly find any file, folder, or program. You must type one or more letter sequences or words that help Windows 7 identify the item you want. The search text you type is called your **search criteria**. Your search criteria can be a filename, part of a filename, or any other characters you choose. Windows 7 will find files with that information in its name or with that information inside the file. For example, if you type "word," Windows 7 will find the program Microsoft Word, any documents with "word" in its title, or any document with "word" inside the file. To search your entire computer, including its attached drives, you can use the Search box on the Start menu. To search within a particular folder, you can use the Search box in a Windows Explorer window. ▓▓▓▓▓ You want to locate the copy of the Oceania Meeting Notes.rtf document so you can print it for a colleague.

1. **Click the Start button ⊙ on the taskbar**

 The Search programs and files box at the bottom of the Start menu already contains the insertion point, ready for you to type search criteria. You begin your search by typing a part of a word that is in the filename.

2. **Type me**

 Even before you finish typing the word "meeting", the Start menu lists all programs, files, and Control Panel items that have the letters "me" in their title or somewhere inside the file or the file properties. See Figure B-21. Your search results will differ, depending on the programs and files on your computer. **File properties** are details that Windows stores about a file. Windows arranges the search results into categories.

3. **Type e**

 The search results narrow to only the files that contain "mee". The search results become more specific every time you add more text to your criteria finding the two versions of your meeting notes file. See Figure B-22.

4. **Point to the Oceania Meeting.rtf filename under Files**

 The ScreenTip shows the file location. This Oceania Meeting.rtf file is on the USB flash drive. The filenames are links to the document. You only need to single-click a file to open it.

5. **Under Documents, click Oceania Meeting Notes.rtf**

 The file opens in WordPad.

6. **Click the Close button ▣ in the program window's title bar**

 You can search in a folder or on a drive using the search box in any Windows Explorer window.

7. **Click ⊙, click Computer, in the Navigation pane click Removable Disk (H:) (or the drive name and letter for your USB flash drive)**

8. **Click the Search Removable Disk (H:) text box, to the right of the Address bar**

9. **Type mee to list all files and folders on your USB flash drive that contain "mee"**

 The search criterion, mee, is highlighted in the filenames. The results include the folder called Meeting Notes and the file named Oceania Meeting.rtf. Because you navigated to your USB flash drive, Windows only lists the document version that is on that drive. See Figure B-23.

10. **Double-click Oceania Meeting.rtf in the File list to open the document file in WordPad, view the file, close WordPad, then close the Windows Explorer window**

FIGURE B-21: Searching on criterion "me"

Search criterion

Search results divided
into categories (your
search results will differ)

FIGURE B-22: Searching on criterion "mee"

Search results narrow down
to fewer documents (your
search results will differ)

FIGURE B-23: Searching using the Search Computer text box in folder window

Search criterion in
Search Computer
text box

Search results

Search criterion
highlighted

Performing more advanced searches

To locate all files that have the same file extension (such as .rtf), type the file extension as your search criterion. If you want to locate files created by a certain person, use the first name, last name, or first and last name as your search criteria. If you want to locate files created on a certain date, type the date (for example, 7/9/2012) as your search criterion. If you remember the title in a document, type the title as your search criterion. If you have created e-mail contacts in your Contacts folder, you can type the person's name to find his or her e-mail address.

Deleting and Restoring Files

If you no longer need a folder or file, you can delete (or remove) it from the storage device. By regularly deleting files and folders you no longer need and emptying the Recycle Bin, you free up valuable storage space on your computer. This also keeps your computer uncluttered. Windows 7 places folders and files you delete from your hard drive in the Recycle Bin. If you delete a folder, Windows 7 removes the folder as well as all files and subfolders stored in it. If you later discover that you need a deleted file or folder, you can restore it to its original location, but only if you have not yet emptied the Recycle Bin. Emptying the Recycle Bin permanently removes the deleted folders and files from your computer. However, files and folders you delete from a removable drive, such as a USB flash drive, do not go to the Recycle Bin. They are immediately and permanently deleted and cannot be restored. **░░░░░** You delete the meeting notes copy saved in the Documents library and then restore it.

STEPS

1. **Click the Start button ⊙ on the taskbar, then click Documents**
 Your Documents library opens.

2. **Click Oceania Meeting Notes.rtf to select it, click the Organize button on the toolbar, then click Delete**
 The Delete File dialog box opens so you can confirm the deletion, as shown in Figure B-24.

3. **Click Yes**
 You deleted the file from the Documents library. Windows moved it into the Recycle Bin.

> **QUICK TIP**
> If the Recycle Bin icon does not contain crumpled paper, then it is empty.

4. **Click the Minimize button ▭ on the window's title bar and examine the Recycle Bin icon**
 The Recycle Bin icon appears to contain crumpled paper. This tells you that the Recycle Bin contains deleted folders and files.

5. **Double-click the Recycle Bin icon on the desktop**
 The Recycle Bin window opens and displays any previously deleted folders and files, including the Oceania Meeting Notes.rtf file.

> **QUICK TIP**
> To delete a file completely in one action, click the file to select it, press and hold [Shift], then press [Delete]. A message will ask if you want to permanently delete the file. If you click Yes, Windows deletes the file without sending it to the Recycle Bin. Use caution, however, because you cannot restore the file.

6. **Click the Oceania Meeting Notes.rtf file to select it, then click the Restore this item button on the Recycle Bin toolbar, as shown in Figure B-25**
 The file returns to its original location and no longer appears in the Recycle Bin window.

7. **In the Navigation pane, click the Documents library**
 The Documents library window contains the restored file. You decide to permanently delete this file.

8. **Click the Oceania Meeting Notes.rtf file, press the [Delete] key on your keyboard, then click Yes in the Delete File dialog box**
 The Oceania Meeting Notes.rtf file moves from the Documents library to the Recycle Bin. You decide to permanently delete all documents in the Recycle Bin.
 NOTE: If you are using a computer that belongs to someone else, or that is in a computer lab, make sure you have permission to empty the Recycle Bin before proceeding with the next step.

9. **Minimize the window, double-click the Recycle Bin, click the Empty the Recycle Bin button on the toolbar, click Yes in the dialog box, then close all open windows**

FIGURE B-24: **Delete File dialog box**

FIGURE B-25: **Restoring a file from the Recycle Bin**

Selecting more than one file

You might want to select a group of files or folders in order to cut, copy, or delete them all at once. To select a group of items that are next to each other in a window, click the first item in the group, press and hold [Shift], then click the last item in the group. Both items you click and all the items between them become selected. To select files that are not next to each other, click the first file, press and hold [Ctrl], then click the other items you want to select as a group. Then you can copy, cut, or delete the group of files or folders you selected.

Practice

For current SAM information, including versions and content details, visit SAM Central (http://samcentral.course.com). If you have a SAM user profile, you may have access to hands-on instruction, practice, and assessment of the skills covered in this unit. Since various versions of SAM are supported throughout the life of this text, check with your instructor for the correct instructions and URL/Web site for accessing assignments.

Concepts Review

Label the elements of the Windows 7 window shown in Figure B-26.

FIGURE B-26

Match each term with the statement that best describes it.

8. File management
9. File extension
10. Address bar
11. Path
12. Library
13. Toolbar
14. File hierarchy

a. Shows file's path
b. Structure of files and folders organized in different levels
c. Describes a file's location in the file hierarchy
d. Skills that help you organize your files and folders
e. Contains buttons in a Windows Explorer window
f. A three- or four-letter sequence, preceded by a period, that identifies the type of file
g. Gathers files and folders from different computer locations

Select the best answer from the list of choices.

15. The way your files appear in the Details window is determined by the:
 a. Path.
 b. View.
 c. Subfolder.
 d. Criterion.

16. When you move a file:
 a. It remains in its original location.
 b. It is no longer in its original location.
 c. It is copied to another location.
 d. It is no longer in your file hierarchy.

17. The text you type in the Search programs and files box on the Start menu is called:
 a. Search criteria.
 b. RAM.
 c. Sorting.
 d. Clipboard.

18. Which of the following is not a window section?

 a. Address bar **c.** Navigation pane

 b. File list **d.** Clipboard

19. Which part of a window lets you see a file's contents without opening the file?

 a. File list **c.** Navigation pane

 b. Preview pane **d.** Address bar

20. In a file hierarchy, a folder inside another folder is called a:

 a. Subfolder. **c.** Clipboard.

 b. Internal hard disk. **d.** Path.

21. After you delete a file from your hard disk, it is automatically placed in the:

 a. USB flash drive. **c.** Recycle bin.

 b. Clipboard. **d.** Search box.

22. When you copy a file, it is automatically placed on the:

 a. Preview pane. **c.** Hierarchy.

 b. My Documents folder. **d.** Clipboard.

Skills Review

1. Understand folders and files.

 a. Assume that you sell books as a home business. How would you organize your folders and files using a file hierarchy? How would you use folders and subfolders? Draw a diagram and write a short paragraph explaining your answer.

2. Create and save a file.

 a. Connect your USB flash drive to a USB port on your computer, then open WordPad from the All Programs menu.

 b. Type **Marketing Plan: Oceania Tours** as the title, then start a new line.

 c. Type your name, then press [Enter] twice.

 d. Create the following list:

 Brochures

 Direct e-mail

 Web ads

 Travel conventions

 e. Save the WordPad file with the filename **Oceania Marketing Plan.rtf** on your USB flash drive.

 f. View the filename in the WordPad title bar, then close WordPad.

3. Explore the files and folders on your computer.

 a. Open a Windows Explorer window that shows the contents of your computer.

 b. Use the File list to navigate to your USB flash drive. (If you do not have a USB flash drive, navigate to your Documents library using the Navigation pane.)

 c. Use the Address bar to navigate to Computer again.

 d. Use the Navigation pane to navigate to your hard drive.

 e. Use the File list to open the Users folder, and then open the folder that represents your user name.

 f. Open the My Documents folder. (*Hint*: The path is Local Disk (C:) ▸ Users ▸ [Your User Name] ▸ My Documents.)

 g. Use the Navigation pane to navigate back to your computer contents.

4. Change file and folder views.

 a. Navigate to your USB flash drive using the method of your choice.

 b. View its contents as large icons.

 c. Use the View slider to view the drive contents in all the other seven views.

 d. Use the Change your view button to cycle through the five available views.

 e. Open the Preview pane, then click a file and view its preview. Repeat with two more files.

 f. Close the Preview pane.

Skills Review (continued)

5. **Open, edit, and save files.**

 a. Open WordPad.

 b. Use the Open dialog box to open the Oceania Marketing Plan.rtf document you created.

 c. After the text "Travel conventions," add a line with the text **Canadian magazines**.

 d. Save the document and close WordPad.

6. **Copy files.**

 a. In the Windows Explorer window, navigate to your USB flash drive if necessary.

 b. Copy the Oceania Marketing Plan.rtf document.

 c. Create a new folder named **Marketing** on your USB flash drive, then open the folder. (If you don't have a USB flash drive, create the folder in your Documents library.)

 d. Paste the document copy in the new folder.

7. **Move and rename files.**

 a. Navigate to your USB flash drive.

 b. Select the original Oceania Marketing Plan.rtf document, then cut it.

 c. Navigate to your Documents library and paste the file there.

 d. Rename the file **Oceania Marketing Plan - Backup.rtf**.

8. **Search for files, folders, and programs.**

 a. Use the Search programs and files box on the Start menu to enter the search criterion **ma**.

 b. Change your search criterion so it reads **mar**.

 c. Open the backup copy of your Oceania Marketing Plan document from the Start menu, then close WordPad.

 d. In Windows Explorer, navigate to your Documents library, then use the criterion **mar** in the Search Documents box.

 e. Open the backup copy of the Oceania Marketing Plan document from the File list, then close WordPad.

9. **Delete and restore files.**

 a. Navigate to your Documents library if necessary.

 b. Delete the Oceania Marketing Plan - Backup.rtf file.

 c. Open the Recycle Bin, and restore the document to its original location, navigate to your Documents library, then move the Oceania Marketing Plan - Backup file to your USB flash drive.

Independent Challenge 1

To meet the needs of pet owners in your town, you have opened a pet-sitting business named PetCare. Customers hire you to care for their pets in their own homes when the pet owners go on vacation. To promote your new business, you want to develop a newspaper ad and a flyer.

 a. Connect your USB flash drive to your computer, if necessary.

 b. Create a new folder named **PetCare** on your USB flash drive.

 c. In the PetCare folder, create two subfolders named **Advertising** and **Flyers**.

 d. Use WordPad to create a short ad for your local newspaper that describes your business:

 • Use the name of the business as the title for your document.

 • Write a short paragraph about the business. Include a fictitious location, street address, and phone number.

 • After the paragraph, type your name.

 e. Save the WordPad document with the filename **Newspaper Ad** in the Advertising folder, then close the document and exit WordPad.

 f. Open a Windows Explorer window, and navigate to the Advertising folder.

 g. View the contents in at least three different views, then choose the view option that you prefer.

 h. Copy the Newspaper Ad.rtf file, and paste a copy in the Flyers folder.

 i. Rename the copy **Newspaper Ad Backup.rtf**.

 j. Close the folder.

Independent Challenge 2

As a freelance editor for several national publishers, you depend on your computer to meet critical deadlines. Whenever you encounter a computer problem, you contact a computer consultant who helps you resolve the problem. This consultant asked you to document, or keep records of, your computer's current settings.

a. Connect your USB flash drive to your computer, if necessary.

b. Open the Computer window so that you can view information on your drives and other installed hardware.

c. View the window contents using three different views, then choose the one you prefer.

d. Open WordPad and create a document with the title **My Hardware Documentation** and your name on separate lines.

e. List the names of the hard drive (or drives), devices with removable storage, and any other hardware devices, installed on the computer you are using. Also include the total size and amount of free space on your hard drive(s) and removable storage drive(s). (*Hint*: If you need to check the Computer window for this information, use the taskbar button for the Computer window to view your drives, then use the WordPad taskbar button to return to WordPad.)

Advanced Challenge Exercise

■ Navigate your computer's file hierarchy, and determine its various levels.

■ On paper, draw a diagram showing your file hierarchy, starting with Computer at the top, and going down at least four levels if available.

f. Save the WordPad document with the filename **My Hardware Documentation** on your USB flash drive.

g. Preview your document, print your WordPad document, then close WordPad.

Independent Challenge 3

You are an attorney at Lopez, Rickland, and Willgor, a large law firm. You participate in your firm's community outreach program by speaking at career days in area high schools. You teach students about career opportunities available in the field of law. You want to create a folder structure on your USB flash drive to store the files for each session.

a. Connect your USB flash drive to your computer, then open the window for your USB flash drive.

b. Create a folder named **Career Days**.

c. In the Career Days folder, create a subfolder named **Mather High**.

Advanced Challenge Exercise

■ In the Mather High folder, create subfolders named **Class Outline** and **Visual Aids**.

■ Rename the Visual Aids folder **Class Handouts**.

■ Create a new folder named **Interactive Presentations** in the Class Handouts subfolder.

d. Close the Mather High window.

e. Use WordPad to create a document with the title **Career Areas** and your name on separate lines, and the following list of items:

Current Opportunities:
Attorney
Corrections Officer
Forensic Scientist
Paralegal
Judge

f. Save the WordPad document with the filename **Careers Listing.rtf** in the Mather High folder. (*Hint:* After you switch to your USB flash drive in the Save As dialog box, open the Career Days folder, then open the Mather High folder before saving the file.)

g. Close WordPad.

Independent Challenge 3 (continued)

h. Open WordPad and the Careers Listing document again, then add **Court Reporter** to the bottom of the list, then save the file and close WordPad.

i. Using pencil and paper, draw a diagram of your new folder structure.

j. Use the Start menu to search your computer using the search criterion **car**. Locate the Careers Listing.rtf document in the list, and use the link to open the file.

k. Close the file.

Real Life Independent Challenge

Think of a hobby or volunteer activity that you do now, or one that you would like to do. You will use your computer to help you manage your plans or ideas for this activity.

a. Using paper and a pencil, sketch a folder structure using at least two subfolders that you could create on your USB flash drive to contain your documents for this activity.

b. Connect your USB flash drive to your computer, then open the window for your USB flash drive.

c. Create the folder structure for your activity, using your sketch as a reference.

d. Think of at least three tasks that you can do to further your work in your chosen activity.

e. Open WordPad and create a document with the title **Next Steps** at the top of the page and your name on the next line.

f. List the three tasks, then save the file in one of the folders you created on your USB flash drive, using the title **To Do.rtf**.

g. Close WordPad, then open a Windows Explorer window for the folder where you stored the document.

h. Create a copy of the file, give the copy a new name, then place a copy of the document in your Documents library.

i. Delete the document copy from your Documents library.

j. Open the Recycle Bin window, and restore the document to the Documents library.

Visual Workshop

You are a technical support specialist at Emergency Services. The company supplies medical staff members to hospital emergency rooms in Los Angeles. You need to respond to your company's employee questions quickly and thoroughly. You decide that it is time to evaluate and reorganize the folder structure on your computer. That way, you'll be able to respond more quickly to staff requests. Create the folder structure shown in Figure B-27 on your USB flash drive. As you work, use WordPad to prepare a simple outline of the steps you follow to create the folder structure. Add your name to the document, and store it in an appropriate location.

FIGURE B-27

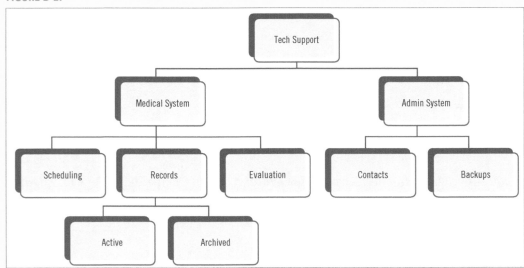

Index

Appointment Recurrence dialog box, OUT 32, OUT 33
Apps for Office, WD 37
 improving worksheet functionality, EX 26
architecture, ECC 6
area charts, EX 81
arguments, EX 8
 separating with commas, EX 40
arithmetic operators, EX 6, EX 7, EX 12
 order of precedence, EX 26, EX 27
arrow pointers, WD 5
arrow symbol (→), WD 10
artistic effects, PPT 76
Ascending button, AC 35
assistive devices, ECC 13
asterisk (*)
 multiplication operator, EX 7
 wildcard character, AC 36, AC 37
at sign (@)
 email addresses, OUT 4, OUT 5
 values, EX 8
Attach File button, OUT 14
attachment(s), email, EX 68, OUT 14–15
Attachment data type, AC 7
audience, identifying, PPT 4
Auto Fill Options button, EX 36, EX 37
Auto Order option, Tab Order dialog box, AC 66
AutoComplete feature, WD 6, WD 7
AutoCorrect feature, WD 6, WD 7
 inserting text, WD 35
 reversing adjustments, WD 6
AutoFit Column Width command, EX 59
AutoFit Row Height command, EX 59
automatic page breaks, WD 82
automatic responses, email, OUT 11
automatic spell checking, PPT 85
AutoNumber data type, AC 7
AutoNumber field, AC 8, AC 14
AutoRecover feature, EX 10
AutoSum button, EX 8, EX 9, EX 28
AutoSum list arrow, EX 28
axes, charts, PPT 58
axis labels, changing alignment and angle, EX 91
axis titles, EX 88, EX 89
 changing alignment and angle, EX 91

B

Back button, IE 5
 Save As dialog box, WD 9
Back Color property, AC 92
background, customizing, PPT 76, PPT 77
Background Color or Shape Fill button, AC 93
background graphics, PPT 76
background images, AC 69
Backspace key, correcting errors, WD 6, WIN 28
Backstage view, OFF 6, OFF 7, WD 4, WD 14, WD 15
 template list, EX 41
backup copies, WIN 36
backward compatibility, OFF 11
bar charts, EX 81

bar tabs, WD 59
basic input/output system (BIOS), ECC 8
BD-R(s), ECC 11
BD-REs, ECC 11
Between dialog box, EX 64, EX 65
bibliographies, WD 94, WD 95
binary digits. See bits
BIOS (basic input/output system), ECC 8
bits, ECC 17
bits per second (bps), ECC 19
black and white presentations, PPT 7
Black and White tab, VIEW tab, PPT 7
blank fields, searching for, AC 39
Blank Form tool, AC 56
Block Senders List, OUT 28
blocking pop-ups, IE 15
blog(s), WD 36, WIN 16
 posting documents, WD 39
 publishing directly from Word, WD 36
bloggers, WD 36
Bluetooth, ECC 18
Blu-ray, ECC 10, ECC 11
BMP (Device Independent Bitmap) format, PPT 53
Bold button, AC 93
bold text, WD 52
boot process (booting up), ECC 8
border(s)
 chart objects, EX 88
 tables, WD 88
 windows, WIN 12
 Word documents, WD 64, WD 65
Border tab, Format Cells dialog box, EX 62
Borders and Shading dialog box, WD 64, WD 65
Borders button, EX 62
bound controls, AC 61, AC 63
bps (bits per second), ECC 19
broadband connections, ECC 19
browser(s), ECC 20, IE 2–3. See also Internet
 Explorer (IE)
browser window, IE 4, IE 5
browsing
 safety, IE 12–13
 tabbed, IE 4, IE 8–9
building blocks, WD 87
built-in graphics cards. See graphics cards
bullets, WD 62, WD 63
business cards, electronic, OUT 33
buttons, WIN 6. See also specific button names
 alignment, EX 57
 command, WIN 15
 font styles, EX 57
 groups, WIN 10, WIN 11
 IE, IE 6
 Mini toolbar, WD 13
 navigation, AC 14, IE 4
 option, WIN 15
 power, WIN 2
 sheet tab scrolling, EX 4, EX 5
 tab scrolling, EX 66
 toggle, AC 63, WD 10
bytes, ECC 17

U